Calm, Clear, and Loving

Also by Mitchell D. Ginsberg

Mind and Belief:
Psychological Ascription and the Concept of Belief

The Far Shore:
Vipassanā, The Practice of Insight

The Inner Palace:
Mirrors of Psychospirituality
in Divine and Sacred Wisdom-Traditions

Forthcoming:

Peace and War and Peace

Calm, Clear, and Loving

Soothing the Distressed Mind, Healing the Wounded Heart

Mitchell D. Ginsberg, Ph.D.

Wisdom Moon Books

CALM, CLEAR, AND LOVING:
SOOTHING THE DISTRESSED MIND,
HEALING THE WOUNDED HEART

Copyright © 2010 Mitchell D. Ginsberg

Published by Wisdom Moon Publishing, San Diego, CA, USA

Wisdom Moon Books is an imprint of Wisdom Moon Publishing

Wisdom Moon™, Wisdom Moon Books™, and the Wisdom Moon logo™ are trademarks of Wisdom Moon Publishing.

Cataloging-in-Publication Data

Ginsberg, Mitchell D.
Calm, clear, and loving : soothing the distressed mind, healing the wounded heart / Mitchell D. Ginsberg.
Includes bibliographical references.
ISBN 978-0-9846090-9-3 (hardback, alk. paper)
ISBN 978-0-9846090-3-1 (paperback, alk. paper)
ISBN 978-0-9846090-2-4 (eBook – digitalized Electronic Book edition)
  1. Philosophy of Mind. 2. Trauma. 3. The Emotions. 4. Mindfulness.
5. Buddhist Psychology. 6. Insight Meditation. 7. Consciousness Studies.
8. Psychotherapy. 9. Phenomenology. 10. Nietzsche, Friedrich. 11. Janet, Pierre.
12. Psychological Integration. 13. Mentalizing. 14. Freud, Sigmund. 15. Daoism.
16. Solomon, Robert C. 17. Resilience. 18. Cyrulnik, Boris. 19. Szasz, Thomas.

Library of Congress Control Number (LCCN): 2010930048

Front cover photo by Tania Ginsberg; front cover concept and design by Tania Ginsberg and Etienne Jambou. Back cover photo by Anatole Ginsberg. Cover realizations by Paula Hendricks (Cinnabar Bridge).

Frontispiece: Computer-created image, based on The Lotus Awaiting the Sun to Open It Fully, 1974, New Haven; yìnzhāng 印章 (Chinese seal or chop) imprint, with characters hand-chiseled by Zhāng Chūnshēng 张春生, 2009, Beijing.

Printed in the United States of America
10 9 8 7 6 5 4 3 2 1

TABLE OF CONTENTS

ORIENTATIONS (AND APPLICATIONS)

APPLICATIONS (AND ORIENTATIONS)

Dedication Page

This book was inspired by my friend Bob Solomon (1942-2007).

Dedicated to my Siberian-born grandfather, Solomon (1888-1966), and his calm wisdom, to my teachers, students, and friends, near and far, to those dear to my heart, to my children, to all of the children of the world, and to all of us just trying to live life in peace and security, with some fulfillment and human warmth along the way.

In recognition of Lepidoptera such as the caterpillar/chrysalis/butterfly, as a model for human development: able to close off 🖐 when appropriate in order to allow self-transformation ୨ ➷ ♭ ☞ to occur in its due time, and then, ready to break through self-imposed limitations, to flutter by 🦋 and fly forth 🦋 in radiant beauty ✧ through the world 🦋.

Adapted from the dedication page of Mitchell Ginsberg, *The Inner Palace: Reflections of Psychospirituality in Divine and Sacred Wisdom-Traditions* (Sixth edition, 2010)

And dedicated most warmly and respectfully to those who have had the courage to reveal to me their deepest heart-felt pains, including experiences of trauma or violence, in the search for resolution, peace, and the chance to live a fuller and more satisfying life. I bow admiratively to their determination and resilience.

Calm, Clear, and Loving

Preface

This book is a guide to understanding consciousness and a tool to deal with life's struggles. It is written for students and scholars of the mind and its transformations, for clinicians, healers, and psychotherapists, for those who have experienced trauma or abuse, and for those who through meditative practices are learning about the mind and its workings, as part of a life path.

This book concerns the mind—not the intellectual mind, but the vibrant consciousness that is *the sum of our thinking, feeling, **and** emotional processes*, called the wise heart or the heart-mind. This precious heart-mind, our wise, caring, and understanding heart, is our consciousness in its most dynamic, most soulful forms. It is known as *xīn* 心 (in Chinese)[1] or *citta* (in Sanskrit and Pāli).[2]

The Table of Contents, this Preface, and the Introduction provide an overview of the scope and organization of this collection. The Forewords, written each from its own perspective and core interests, give a further sense of the book's range and breadth. The overall approach is that of a Meditative Phenomenology that is psychospiritual (concerned with personal transformation), within the field of Consciousness Studies. *More in the Introduction, below.*

The chapters all circle around a central interest in *the mind and its operations, in how we as humans deal with the world based on our perception, interpretation, focus, and understanding of what it is that we are experiencing.*

Some chapters explore our understanding of significant features of the mind in theoretical or philosophical terms. Others focus on states of consciousness such as shame or remorse, on experiential processes of the troubled mind, on ways in which the mind undergoes transformations to overcome limitations.

Further, some chapters include background information, offering an easy approach to the given topic for readers who are not specialists, and serving simply as an orienting reminder for others. In chapters that begin with preliminary remarks, these orient the reader and give a context to the discussion.

One approach is to begin with reading the body of the chapter, returning then to the preliminary remarks, which address some of the historical, theoretical, and personal background context of the paper, as in the first chapter. An addendum there presents recent theorizing in various related fields of interest.

This book is a project that came into form following two events: the death of my decades-long friend Robert (Bob) Solomon, in January 2007, and a conference in his memory held in February 2008 at the University of Texas, Austin, which I attended and which inspired me to compose this book. I write about this conference and Bob in the essay following the Introduction.

---

[1] To honor Chinese calligraphy here, let me show *xīn* in various scripts through the ages: 囪, 㥁, 心, 心, 心, 心, 心, 心, 心, 心, 心, 心, 心, 心, 心, etc.

[2] Pāli is the Indic language of Theravāda Buddhism's original texts.

After his death, I nostalgically revisited an article I had written at his request for a book on Nietzsche that he was editing (then, in the early '70s). Not totally surprisingly, that chapter ("Nietzschean Psychiatry") in his collection seemed timely to me, even after all these years (now, almost 4 decades later).

After the conference, which immersed me again in Nietzsche and in the philosophy of the emotions, which Bob was fundamentally instrumental in developing in recent decades, I decided to return to and expand on those topics. I came to see that the resultant paper on Nietzsche's perspective on the search for self-transformation (and what has come to be called psychotherapy) would form part of this endeavor, with further essays complementing that focus. I see this revision of that essay as my following up on Bob's encouraging me in those years to make further use of that article, either in the fashion found here or—an alternative idea for a book that was never realized—by publishing an edition with the full text of all relevant passages from Nietzsche's works in footnotes or on pages facing the essay's discussions and citations.

Given that conference and the focus of this book, I have included here three other early papers. One that is most relevant to the conference is a paper on love (offered to a graduate-school seminar at the University of Michigan) that may be considered to be an early venture into the philosophy of the emotions.[3]

The other two address theorizing about mind with a more psychiatric orientation. One presents a theory of action and communication, in terms of which I discuss the Double-bind Theory (a theory of schizophrenogenesis, the way in which schizophrenia develops out of a particular early-life familial structure). The second discusses individual psychotherapy and family therapy in the world of psychiatry, contrasting their distinct theoretical assumptions and practical applications. (The family is also discussed in other parts of this book.[4])

Overall, the chapters are gathered into two groups (as the Table of Contents shows), not on the basis of topics or fields of study, but in terms of the degree to which the given chapter centers on more theoretical or more practical concerns. An alternative grouping of topics that are addressed in the chapters of this book would be based on the areas or fields of study they most centrally con-

---

[3] Precedents from earlier centuries are considered in the Preliminary Remarks to the chapter on the concept of love and its logic (Chap. 1 of this book).

[4] More on this in the Introduction and elsewhere, where the influence of the family of origin (the family in which we grew up) is seen as varying, depending on whether a nuclear family or an extended family—also called an "extended kinship group," as in J.A. Silk, "Child Abandonment and Homes for Unwed Mothers in Ancient India: Buddhist Sources," *Journal of the American Oriental Society*, vol. 127, no. 3 (Jul.-Sep. 2007), p. 303—whether loving, discouraging, supportive, respectful, demeaning, cloyingly sweet, smothering, suffocating, indifferent, distancing, safe, violent, explosive, rigid, chaotic, secure, etc.

cern—in terms of the ways in which humanity has organized and subdivided human knowledge (or at least human understanding, beliefs, and pretense to knowledge)—this book wanders from area to area, from field to field.

Since the range of topics addressed in this book meanders from field to field, it will not fit neatly into any single category of human knowledge. In this way, this collection is composed in the spirit of what in academia (the world of the university) is called interdisciplinary studies.

The interest here in the human condition, or in *the nature, theory, and experience of consciousness*, does not sit neatly in the domain of one university department or another. As Rebecca W. Bushnell, the Dean of the University of Pennsylvania's College of Arts and Sciences (in Philadelphia), has written,

> One of the most thrilling transformations of the last quarter century [she wrote in 2008] is the growing value we place on faculty who display a multidisciplinary hunger and curiosity. Increasingly, the boundaries between departments and disciplines are dissolving. The world's problems are complex and multifaceted, and they can't always be contained in the traditional academic silos.[5]

Or, as Bob (Solomon) put it in a parenthetical remark long ago:

> "Interdisciplinary" studies [he wrote in 1979] are those that inconveniently refuse to fit in the standard-size cans.[6]

Perhaps this tendency to compartmentalize (or to departmentalize) is not a problem per se, especially when recognized and put into balance: after all, we are in life repeatedly facing the tension between understanding, which tends to put things in boxes, and our realization that we do not understand it all, or perhaps do not understand at all, which tends to incline us to break out of these very same boxes (or silos or cans).

The interests that inspire this collection are of precisely such an interdisciplinary or multidisciplinary scope. And yet, there is an integrity or constant focus here. *The core of all of these is a unifying interest in the understanding of the workings of the mind in its various manifestations.*

In this context, the fact that we are sometimes (if not often) experiencing our situation in ways that are unsatisfying or frustrating or painful or tormented or confusing, leads us in a rather direct way to our being concerned with improving things, with making things more harmonious and satisfying, more relaxing, secure, interesting, and inspiring. And ultimately to questions of how our society deals with such issues, in a more inclusive way.

---

[5] R.W. Bushnell, "Dean's Column: Transformations," *Penn Arts and Sciences Magazine, Spring/Summer 2008*, p. 3.

[6] R.C. Solomon, *History and Human Nature: A Philosophical Review of European Philosophy and Culture, 1750-1850*, p. xvii.

I have worked at presenting the various issues I wanted to address here so that there was clarity without becoming simplistic. This presentation was at times the outcome of an earlier process, that of looking at texts and teachings in a way that would allow a sense that they were actually understood as they were meant (a task with no guarantee of success and not always achieved on a first or even a second reading). This earlier process would sometimes take several steps to reach its completion.[7] For me personally, this would sometimes involve a first consideration in which the ideas I came across seemed confused or of little value. If I nonetheless pursued the ideas, there might be what some (Jean Piaget, for example) call assimilation—I would interpret these ideas in ways that fit with what I already understood, so that they at least became intelligible and acceptable to me, consistent with what I was already thinking about the issue.

This I came to find was sometimes a constricted resolution, a premature conclusion. If this was not allowed, I would then find myself wrestling with the ideas, trying to take them in their own light, in which some perhaps minor aspect of their presentation came to highlight some difference from how I was interpreting them. It was as if I were giving these ideas permission to disagree with what or how I was already thinking, and to offer me something new and unexpected. As may happen, this wrestling was most powerful when it would come at unpredictable moments. I have found that nighttime is a most productive time to wrestle with ideas most intensely and illuminatingly, whether through dreams or with thoughts coming to mind quite unexpectedly. (Jacob also dreamt and did night wrestling.[8]) In any case, sometimes I would even come to see that what a position or author was getting at was quite different from, if not diametrically opposed to, what I had first read into that position. While this is a somewhat challenging practice, its rewards are quite satisfying.

I invite readers to join me in applying the reflections of this book, to develop a deeper understanding of the most universal and defining features of mind. And, *for those who want also to live their philosophy*, in applying that understanding, to develop a respect for our psychological second nature (patterns to notice and to refine or redefine with wisdom), to guide ourselves in this ultimately unique life we are each variously experiencing. May it thus be as French novelist Marcel Proust remarked in 1905: Reading initiates us, its magical keys unlocking the door to our deepest, otherwise unattainable inner chambers, and yet we sense very well that our wisdom begins where that of the author ends.[9]

---

[7] This partially analyzes the process that Bob (Solomon) described as my applying the "principle of charity" in the art of being "mercifully undogmatic" (to quote his Foreword to M. Ginsberg, *The Inner Palace*, pp. iii-iv).

[8] See *Genesis* 28:10-16, 32:25-33, respectively.

[9] This rendering of Proust juxtaposes two passages from M. Proust, *Sur la lecture*, pp. 37, 32, respectively. The title in English would be *On Reading*.

Introduction

This book addresses the nature of human consciousness and, in particular, processes of mind that promote serenity, clarity, and healing. It offers a well-rounded appreciation of this domain by weaving together the wisdom of various disciplines and traditions into essays, narratives, and poems.

In reflecting on our understanding of the mind and as well as on emotionally powerful issues that may arise in life, the approach throughout is gentle, respectful, encouraging, personal. The book guides the reader in unhurried thinking and careful reflection, nurtures inner stillness, and encourages the cultivation of mental focus and emotional groundedness. It invites the liberating integration of clear open-minded thinking with intuitive full-hearted understanding.

This orientation reflects my education and experience. I have investigated contemporary philosophical issues about the nature of the mind (as discussed in philosophy of mind, philosophical psychology, and psycholinguistics). In my psychotherapy practice, I have worked with people experiencing troubled, agitated minds, in both subtle and more extreme forms. In this, I have become familiar with ways in which torture and other traumas make a powerful impact on the mind and on how we deal with life. I have also led residential meditation retreats and maintained decades of a mindfulness practice (with its ongoing attention to oneself and others), observing the human realities we have occasion to experience, of frustration, fulfillment, agitation, calm, anger, love, fear, safety, violence, peace, pain, sickness, recovery, old age, death, and survival.

The general focus throughout this book is in understanding and describing the mind and experienced consciousness, both in their basic forms and in somewhat unusual variations (not all of which are joyous) that highlight some of the more subtle processes in this fascinating, most human domain.

This focus involves a theoretical interest and a practical concern with the ways these principles and processes work themselves out in specific realities. So, this book addresses the nature of the mind (its conceptual features) and also concerns itself with how the mind is transformed (structured or influenced) by the life experiences that we individually live through.

The book's chapters are grouped into two sets. The first chapters—Orientations (and Applications)—look at the theoretical or conceptual frameworks used to understand experience (thought and emotion, for example, in Western concepts), with chapters on schizophrenia and on psychotherapy à la Nietzsche. They are in this way philosophical. These discussions include applications to make sense of theory.

The second chapters—Applications (and Orientations)—investigate self-awareness practices and transformative processes discussed in various traditions and desired by people all around the world. These include presentations of theory to orient our understanding of the various practices and experiences that are specifically being discussed. They are in this way quite practical and con-

cerned with shifting the unhappy patterns we experience into a sense of fulfillment and completeness in life. In other words, these chapters address psychospirituality and its defining issue of a personal transformation to a soulful, integrated completeness of heart-and-mind.

The distinction between these two groups is not absolute, but is a matter
of focus, perspective, and emphasis. Relatedly, many issues are addressed in
passages found in both groups here.

This book is phenomenological in its interest in the nature of experience, investigating experienced reality as a path to understanding consciousness
(as in the tradition of Edmund Husserl). Further, it is psychospiritual in its interest in personally transformative processes (as defined just above). In short, it is a
work in *psychospiritual Meditative Phenomenology*, being meditative in a Western sense, in its reflecting on important issues (as in *The Meditations* of Descartes). And in an Eastern perspective, it is meditative in its respect for deep
calm and joy, and in its vision of integrating skilful wisdom with an inclusive
compassion (as in a traditional Buddhist practice of cultivating mindfulness, insight, and lovingkindness).

This meditative, phenomenological approach is illustrated by the many
descriptions of consciousness in my book, *The Far Shore: Vipassanā, The Practice of Insight*, inspired by mindfulness practice.

This transformative practice involves establishing a foundation of equanimity on which is cultivated an open awareness of each passing moment of
consciousness. This open awareness or judgment-free attentiveness might be our
awareness of our own bodily sensations, of moments of consciousness as pleasant or not, of our moods or general states of mind, or of various perceptions that
come to us through the six senses. The six senses in Buddhist psychology are the
five bodily senses recognized in the West plus the mind as the sense allowing
awareness of particular ideas, thoughts, mental images and imagined situations,
memories, judgments, reasoning, compassion, caring, and so forth.

The ongoing investigation of mind described in this practice is said to
lead to greater understanding, a lessening of torment, an increase in compassion,
and perhaps even to some wisdom (if not to enlightened awakening).

Some of this transformative mindfulness of consciousness occurs in an
ongoing way in everyone's life (as in our evaluating and redirecting ourselves in
various ways); some, in the context of psychotherapeutic interactions and reflection; and some, in a more systematic approach to our being openly aware of our
own mind and consciousness, recognized in the East (east of the Khyber Pass) as
the meditative practice of cultivating calm, clarity, and an open, caring heart.

*This is an awakening of our deepest being, the birth of richly vibrant
living, the nourishing of our very soul, the blossoming eruption of heart-wisdom,
the gradual cultivation of our precious heart-mind.*

This transformation, varying from person to person, is a process consisting of an individual path of particular steps to this awakening. Part of this in-

volves fundamental shifts in our relationship with our past and our experience. Our seeing clearly what various difficult moments in our life involved—coming to a new clarity about them—is a first step in our becoming free of their ongoing disturbing influence on us. In a teaching found in various spiritual traditions, it is thus said that the way out is the way in. To use a Wittgensteinian image, the fly needing to leave the bottle must pass through the neck of the bottle and out the mouth—reversing its path in.[1]

We will go beyond this image to more helpful specifics in various discussions that follow throughout this book.

The chapters of this collection all contribute from various points of view to an understanding and appreciation of the mind that will encourage this transformation to be more thorough, powerful, radical, and fulfilling.

This process in part uses the unclouded mind to free our spirit, a practice known in Indic philosophical psychology as jñāna yoga, "using mind to see through mind to come to mind." The practice here, putting it differently, uses calm and clarity to appreciate our conditioned, reactive patterns of thinking and acting, in a way that cultivates a consciousness not limited by that reactivity.

The fruit of this practice is the precious mind, a radiant and vital consciousness, alluded to by some who call it the soul (ψυχή psyché, anima, Seele, âme, alma). It is in part an opening of our sensitive, caring nature that naturally and freely responds to signs of distress with an urge to be of help and aid, sometimes termed the path of the heart, in Indic contexts called bhakti yoga. Furthermore, these paths of mind or understanding (jñāna yoga) and of heart or loving-kindness (bhakti yoga) ultimately complement and intensify one another.

Overall in this book, the search for understanding does not employ controlled experiments or statistical analysis. From that model of science or theory construction, *some discussions here are not even anecdotal*, but hypothetical or imaginary descriptions of given states of mind, life situations, or experiences.

And yet there is something of value that transcends this limitation: as French author René Thom (1923-2002), one of the most respected mathematicians of the twentieth century—1958 recipient of the Fields Medal (the "Nobel Prize in Mathematics") and a principal author on catastrophe theory, a mathematical model of processes operating in various scales or domains of our world (physical, biological, psychological, interpersonal)—wrote in 1983,

> If we are to believe Karl Popper, psychoanalysis is not 'falsifiable', and hence must be placed outside science. And yet psychoanalysis offers infinitely more *interest* than many scientific theories whose truth is indisputably assured. It is in this spirit that I offer here these models, not so much as testable hypo-

---

[1] See L. Wittgenstein, *Philosophical Investigations*, Sect. 309: "What is your aim in philosophy?—To shew [show] the fly the way out of the fly-bottle."

theses or as experimentally controllable models but as a stimulus to the imagination which leads to the exercise of thought
and thus an increase in our understanding of the world and of
man.[2]

Let our theories of theory-construction here not constrict our awareness, imagination, and yearning to understand what is most defining about being human.

One tradition holds that all transmission of mind (or wisdom-heart)
takes place outside of words, and yet in this transmission, teachers often use
words in offering glimpses of the wisdom-heart, a fully clear-thinking and richly
sensitive consciousness, which is waiting to be recognized, experienced, and
nurtured. Here, more simply, I offer the various reflections and perspectives in
this book, in essay, narrative, and poetry, for your interest and consideration.

When we are struggling, when life is not easy,
The desire for love and human closeness may come upon us.
In a Poetic Image
Love pushes us to new heights.
It brings us
  to recognize the tension
  between our hopes and wishes,
  and the way it is.
We can taste the disappointment —
a bittersweet sense of connection
  not yet harmonized.
Let's not go off into cold
  indifference,
  disconnection,
  isolation.
May we have the courage,
  the inspired energy,
  to go through
  what we must
  to come to feel
  whole and safe, vibrant and alive,
  where human contact and warmth
  allow for deep
  soulful connection.

Moving stepwise in this search, we discuss the Robert C. Solomon Conference
next; others then offer their perspectives on this book, leading us into Chapter 1.

---

[2] R. Thom, *Mathematical Models of Morphogenesis*, from his Foreword to the
English translation of *Modèles mathématiques de la morphogenèse*, at p. 9.

The Passionate Robert C. Solomon Memorial Conference

The Memorial Conference was quite unusual and so very special.

First of all, since I first learned about academic philosophy (philosophy professors and philosophy departments) back in the late 1950s—when my older brother was a philosophy major at the University of Pennsylvania, talking with intensity and admiration of his professors Nelson Goodman and Chaïm Perelman (a visiting professor from Brussels), and I in turn became an undergraduate philosophy major at the same university, continuing through the doctorate at the University of Michigan, and then taught in the Philosophy Department at Yale and in various departments through these many years—I have only heard of a conference dedicated entirely to the work and contributions of one contemporary professor as a tribute, in his later years, before or at the time of retirement, with papers presented there gathered together in a then-to-be-published *Festschrift*. This conference was not for such a time nor with such a scholarly end in mind.

Second, I have never heard of an entire conference dedicated to gathering people together on the occasion of the death of a contemporary professor. (Perhaps there have been such conferences, but I have not heard of them.)

This unusual conference was dedicated to Professor Robert C. Solomon of the Philosophy *and* Business Ethics *and* Psychology Departments of the University of Texas (Austin), a friend of mine. At the time of his death, in early 2007, I learned of the conference arranged to honor Bob's work and life from Kathleen Higgins, his wife, co-author, and co-member of that Philosophy Department. The conference took place on February 15-16, 2008. People came from all over: there were colleagues of Bob's, professors who were former students of Bob's, and some old friends. (I turned out to be the person there who had known him the longest time, since his two brothers were unable at the last minute to make it to the conference.) His first wife, Elke, was there from New York City. (I had been best man at their marriage, sharing the honors with Bob's middle brother, Andy.) Several professors came from the East Coast. One scholar flew in from New Zealand (flying Wednesday and Thursday to attend the conference Friday and Saturday, then flying back Sunday and Monday), reflecting a strong connection with Bob, who had taught there with Kathy quite regularly for many years. Well, I could go on and on (as I have on other occasions).

As soon as I heard about the gathering in its early planning stage, announced shortly after his sudden death at the Zurich Airport on January 2, 2007, I made up my mind to attend. Still, I was hesitating to go to the conference. After all, I hadn't been to a philosophy convention since the mid-1980s, when one was held up in Long Beach ("up" meaning north, relatively speaking, given that I was living in San Diego at that time). And I hadn't missed attending them in any heart-felt sense. So why go to another conference with such a focus?

The reason, of course, was that this was a conference to honor Bob, the person and his work. My sense was that it would be vital for me to let the event pour over me and impact me in ways I could not exactly foresee or foretell—a chance to "dive into the void!" as I once wrote (in a book, *The Far Shore*).

The short of it is that Bob and I had been close and long-time friends. *Further recollections about Bob follow now: optional reading offered here to all those interested in his life or in the background inspiration for this book.*

Bob and I had gone to the same high school together just outside of Philadelphia (Cheltenham High School, 1957-1960, which we renamed, tongue-in-cheek, The Chelt'numm School—with "Chelt'n'm" a trochaic dissyllable), where I got to know his parents and brothers; one of my two favorite families to spend time with in those years (my own being third, perhaps). We were close friends even then; we studied together, double dated together, discussed matters of concern together. We discussed love both in practical and theoretical terms, a discussion that continued through our years together at the University of Michigan. (More on this in the chapter on the concept of love.)

We had been classmates and roommates at the University of Pennsylvania, and during the Summer of 1963, after graduating from Penn, the two of us had traveled together. After an inspired fortnight in Amsterdam, we took off for a tour of Europe with our futures well defined: Bob with the intention of beginning that autumn at the University of Amsterdam Medical School, and I, at Harvard Law School. My, but our ignorance of what time would actually bring each of us was exquisitely, sweetly naïve! First, the car we bought in Amsterdam for those travels for $220 had a literal meltdown of its engine near Chur, to the southeast of Zurich at whose airport Bob was decades later to breathe his last breath. Next, Bob renounced the idea of studying medicine in Amsterdam, and returned to the USA to start medical school there, in Ann Arbor, and I decided to forego law school for medical school that autumn, in Philadelphia. Then, just after New Year 1964—after recognizing that we were each quite immiscible with Medical School—we both shifted into Philosophy, and in 1967 completed doctorates at the University of Michigan, focusing on philosophy and folding in a good measure of psychology.

I had been best man at his first marriage with Elke (sharing honors with his younger brother Andy, who—at Bob's request to me—became a housemate of mine in a house I was renting with others, in my last year at Michigan, 1966-1967). Then, as Bob wrote, "By the mid-Sixties we had both become 'bright young men' and we precociously became enthusiastic teachers of philosophy (at Yale and Princeton, respectively)."[1] Bob and I continued our contact and friendship through the decades. At a visit to him and Elke when he was teaching at Princeton (and I in New Haven, at Yale), I was given a gift of two special kittens, Pushkin and Raskolnikoff (renamed Montgomery Clift and Humphrey Bogart). And when he was going to teach at Esalen in Spring 1981, I drove him

---

[1] At p. i of his Foreword to M. Ginsberg, *The Inner Palace*.

down from Berkeley (where he had been visiting me) to Big Sur, during which trip we had long conversations on love; at the time, he was not very impressed with a chapter on the experiencing of love that he glanced at from the then-new book that I had just given him as a gift, the first edition of *The Far Shore* (1980); I think his judgment decree, flipping the book down with panache, was the succinct "Totally wrong!" There's of course more to say about that and about so many other interactions we have had these many years, these decades. (He did sincerely apologize a couple of decades later for that curt and categorical dismissal, let me mention.) The stories go on and on.

My last email exchange from him in mid-December 2006 was when I told him of the death of my mother; in reply he welcomed me somewhat tongue-in-cheek to orphanhood, and mentioned that he did not know how much longer he could continue traveling the world. I wrote more about that email in my web page memorial to Bob. That email came two weeks before he breathed his last.

In any case, returning to the conference here, I did not know at all what it would involve, but I suspected strongly that it would be emotionally intense for me, and, presumably, for others as well. I was not wrong in that suspicion. Before the end of the conference, I came to realize what a special person Bob had been in the eyes of so many people.

Some recalled how helpful he had been to them in carefully encouraging their early steps in philosophy, or how he had worked behind the scenes to help them with fellowships or with the administrative hurdles of getting a doctorate. I knew that Bob himself had seen how difficult that could be, from his own case, when he would have to travel back from Princeton to Ann Arbor that year of 1966-1967, when he felt the need to reestablish a mutually respectful atmosphere for discussing the contents of his thesis, on the road to the acceptance of a final version of that dissertation. Details aside, this travail was something Bob seemed not to have forgotten. It presumably gave him, rather, compassion for the difficulties that others were experiencing in their own climb to the Ph.D.

Mostly, at that conference there was just the great admiration and appreciation and love that I felt from so many people directed at this very special philosopher and human being. Overall, one thing that impressed me deeply was how caring and giving and encouraging Bob had been for so many people, whether colleagues or former students or students at the time of his death.

At the conference, I myself was quite happy being quiet and not talking, but every so often there would be a comment (including one by Bob discussing himself in a film clip) that made me want to add to the discussion. At one point, I realized that the group was coming to a close and that we were at the last chance to talk to the group, that I was at the last chance there to talk for myself, to talk to Bob, about Bob, while I was still at the University of Texas (which I had last visited 35 years earlier, when Bob had me appointed as Visiting Scholar in Buddhist Studies in the Philosophy Department), after which I would be kicking myself for not having done so for the rest of my life. Or so I felt. Now, I sometimes encourage people to do what they feel is important to do, even if in doing so they might feel uncomfortable; I thought this was an excellent moment to act on that principle myself.

So when Professor Greg Reihman was talking about an idea he had, to set up an exercise that to me sounded like a way to end the discussion and the entire conference, leaving me no further time to say what I felt important to say, I stood myself up, moved myself to the front of the room, and sat down at the "Octavian" Discussion Table. Once there, I asked Greg quietly if he was planning on drawing the discussion to a close, because I wanted to say something first. I needed to speak out some of my memories. And, appreciating the context, I looked for things that would also be of some interest to others there.[2]

I found that at least some people listening to my little vignettes of my familiarity with Bob's youth and pre-philosopher life were touched and privately expressed to me their appreciation (and sweet salty tears of remembrance) at my sharing this past, giving a broader, more palpable sense of the boy who became the man Robert C. Solomon Philosopher, so to speak.

Given feedback that my stories were appreciated—I thank these individuals for their warm comments—and supposing that this information might also be of some interest to some other people,[3] *I would like to present some more of these memories in this context, letting the situations speak for themselves.*

Some of these recollections show the depth of Bob's intensity and its roots in his early years. Some go against Bob's claim in one of the videos that not only did he teach philosophy but that he was a philosopher (perhaps a poor paraphrase): when I heard that statement of his, I thought back to when philosophy was a word we held in distant respect, even if in those (high school) years we had read Spinoza and Bertrand Russell and even Huang Po (the spelling in those pre-pinyin years).

One of our very first conversations, in adolescent days when we were so innocent and candid and unsocialized, began with my simple question about why he did not take gym class and why he seemed to have a very flushed face sometimes. He gave me a private tutorial where I learned to say without hesitation and without stuttering the phrase 'interventricular septal defect' and where I swore never to tell anyone (outside of my immediate family who were already aware on their own that he had some sort of medical problem) about it, a pro-

---

[2] I want to thank everyone at the conference for patience with an old friend reminiscing about a friendship of some five decades. And for gently supporting me in that endeavor. I hope that some of the things I recalled and spoke about gave people a fuller sense of Bob than they had previously had, or for those who have known him even more intimately than I, to have occasion for a sweet memory or three to come by, to warm the heart.

[3] See above note. What follows is for readers interested in this history.

mise I kept until his death except one day in early 1967, during my last year at the University of Michigan: still under the influence of sodium pentathol ("the truth serum") I had been given as the anesthesia for some surgery I underwent, I mentioned Bob's heart condition to a friend whose stunned look made me realize that I had just revealed some private information. I immediately explained the situation and had this person likewise promise never to mention that fact to anyone else. I assume that my commitment to silence about that has now become, as they say in French, *caduc*, lapsed, no longer operant or valid.

One story to tell is how Bob dealt with the fraternity situation. Bob wanted to join a particular fraternity, Sigma Chi (ΣΧ), which at Penn at that time was strongly Catholic. Now, Bob with his blond hair and complexion (or should I say cyanotic flush?), interpreted by the casual observer simply as a robust Anglo-Saxon ruddiness, clearly passed muster visually. But invitations to join Sigma Chi required unanimity, he was told; it was hinted there was one vote against him, since his family name suggested a possibly Jewish background. I offered to have Bob invited to join the fraternity that I was going to join, Pi Lambda Phi (ΠΛΦ), which was multi-racial, non-religious, and international. But Bob did not want to join the fraternity, which may remind us of Groucho Marx's quip, "I don't want to belong to any club that will accept me as a member."

In any case, Bob's way of dealing with this rejection was to envision a fraternity of his own design, Gamma Delta Ipsilon (ΓΔΙ). He put these letters on the bottom of his car's back window. (This was the car whose automatic transmission he had replaced with a standard transmission. He writes or talks about that part of the car's history somewhere. The most interesting thing about that car's transmission that I remember was that when he shifted gears, we would never know what gear he had shifted into. He had to pull out the clutch, carefully, to make it clear what the shift had brought on—an adventure.) These fraternity letters, he explained, should be understood to abbreviate God Damn Independent. *I found this to be a defiantly inspired response to the situation.*

Earlier, when I would visit Bob's home in the late 1950s, I was regularly treated to a sparks-filled discussion, I mean one that was pleasantly and excitingly alive to me, in which all members of the family had a voice. (I knew from my own experience that dinners were not always the most exciting and mind-stimulating part of the day in some families!) There was much in the way of punning and playfulness of ideas. In the background were sounds from the parrot (traditionally, "Polly"), adopted, I was told, by Charles (Bob's father) when it was already a grown bird and cursed like a sailor, as the expression puts it. Polly would frequently imitate the voice of Vita (Bob's mother). My memory is of Vita's voice—or, rather, of Polly's version of Vita's voice—calling out (in a singsong voice, a series of high-then-low-toned dissyllables, repeated over and over again, through the years), "Charles! Bob! Andy! Jon!" At those dinners, Bob would meticulously eat one item on the plate at a time until finished and he would then start on the next item, much to the chagrin of his father.

Or again, there is my recollection of the warm connection between Bob and his two younger brothers, Andy and Jon, as they watched the Three Stooges.

Or, there was the playful interaction between his parents. I told one story at the conference about that: Bob's dad had graduated from the Law School of the University of Pennsylvania with the highest grades in the history of the school, up until then, while at the same time helping to support himself by making money playing saxophone in a club in downtown Philadelphia at night, and had then become an FBI agent into counter-espionage during World War II, stationed in Detroit (where, consequently, Bob was born). Bob at times would casually mention that as a boy he had been bounced (innocently) on the knee of J. Edgar Hoover, the Head of the FBI in those years. The point being that Bob's dad was rather a traditional, civic-minded individual, with Republican leanings (aside from being obviously quite brilliant). Relatedly, one night at dinner, Bob's father reported (in an impersonal, general-truth-making, Greek-chorus type of statement) that after voting he had learned at the city hall that there had been one single vote cast for the Socialist candidate. Vita's reply (he had not addressed her directly) was, "I can vote for whomever I want!" His eyes sparkled in fun. I saw in that brief interchange, that despite this great difference between their political views, there was a deep mutual respect and caring between them.

And of course, there were Vita's paintings of Bob and his brothers in rather large oil canvases all over the house. It was only later that I learned that she had had one of her paintings hung in the National Portrait Gallery in Washington, DC. When Bob and I went through Europe (spending much of our time in museum after museum), one small suggestion from Vita had been for us to pay special attention to the way each artist portrayed the fingers of people whose portraits we were looking at—quite a powerful key into the remarkable differences in painting technique. It was a beautiful and practical gift she gave us, so casually proposed. In brief, it was quite a special family.

Even their network of friends included people that I appreciated and admired. As one particular example, I learned that Ruth Ehrlich, a Latin teacher and my own respected and beloved eighth-grade English teacher (and mother of Stanford Professor Paul Ehrlich), the person I credited with teaching me in depth the foundations of English grammar, happened to be a good friend of Vita's.

Well! My memories abound. Let me stop here, however limited a sampling of these are compared to my many very resonant memories of Bob. (I return to specific parts of our history, where relevant, elsewhere.) In closing, let me offer an overall remaining impression of the conference, in an image:

In a dream that came to me in the days (or nights, rather) following returning from the conference, I saw an image of the entire group of people who had traveled to the gathering, some from great distances, and ultimately, from several continents of our home earth. And over them was a magnificent rainbow, presumably representing that beautiful heterogeneity.

Foreword by Kathleen M. Higgins, Ph.D.

Philosophy as many understand it these days is an ivory tower diversion in the extreme. Completely cerebral, it is seen as an effete exercise aimed at reaching conclusions that are "merely academic." This is the sense of "philosophy" that emerged when one 2008 presidential candidate rejected another's claim that they had a philosophical disagreement, saying, "Our differences are not just philosophical." Mitchell Ginsberg's book demonstrates how mistaken is this idea of philosophy as irrelevant pastime. Philosophy, the love of wisdom, is basic to living a happy human life.

Mitchell exhibits the value of philosophy in multiple ways. I especially admire his efforts to apply ideas that are usually deemed pure theory to concrete therapeutic situations. His bringing Bertrand Russell's theory of logical types to bear on the problem of double bind situations is a notable case in point. Mitchell directly challenges the view that commonly underpins the idea that philosophy is largely irrelevant, the position that thought and emotion are antithetical, when he argues that love, which essentially involves certain attitudes, depends on thoughts as well as feelings. He also points out the practical usefulness of the acumen that philosophy cultivates. When he argues that we need managerial skill with ourselves to achieve integrity, he points out that this requires a critical mind, not a mind that criticizes, but one that can make sharp distinctions. What is needed, in other words, is a philosophical mind. Mitchell illustrates the usefulness of analytical skill, for example, in examining the operations of the non-integrated personality. Most crucially, he reveals philosophy's role in bringing one to a "pivot" point, in Daoist terminology, a point at which transformation can occur because one recognizes the possibility of doing something other than repeating a dysfunctional pattern. The freshness of vision that enables one to pivot is precisely the stance of philosophical insight.

When Mitchell invited me to write a foreword for this book, he suggested that I approach it from the standpoint of a Nietzsche scholar, given the attention given to Nietzsche. From that perspective I am delighted that the book draws so much attention to Nietzsche's psychoanalytic observations and his psychotherapeutic concerns. All too often, he is categorized as the great destroyer of tradition and a diagnostician of modern decadence, with little attention given to his more pervasive interest with the restoration of health to modern society. Entirely missed is the outlook suggested when Nietzsche's Zarathustra asks, "Where is that justice that is love with open eyes?" or when Nietzsche commences his autobiography by asking, "How can I fail to be grateful to my whole life?" Mitchell recognizes this affirmative side of Nietzsche, the Nietzsche who himself advocated a point of view that is calm, clear, and loving.

The Nietzschean themes that most conspicuously involve a calm, clear, and loving stance are the linked notions of eternal recurrence and *amor fati*. Nietzsche's idea of eternal recurrence is the notion that time is repeating itself over and over endlessly. This idea can be interpreted in various ways, but the images Nietzsche associates with it resonate with Mitchell's book's idea of clear and calm appreciation of the temporal whole of which each moment is a part. Nietzsche describes his "discovery" of this idea while he was visiting Sils Maria, Switzerland. He was hiking and reached a rock from which he could look out over the Silvaplana Lake. The landscape, with mountains on either side of the lake and mist obscuring the distant point where the mountains come together, offers a spatial metaphor for the point at which one observes the whole of one's temporal trajectory in tranquility. Like Mitchell, Nietzsche suggests that the present moment is the point at which one can take the measure of what one has done and experienced (as well as what experiences of others shape one's life) and gain insights that may help one to navigate the course ahead.

Amor fati, literally "love of fate," meant for Nietzsche the attitude of affirmation toward one's life as a whole, including past distresses and traumas. It embraces the whole of one's life as constituting a single fabric, a fabric that is continuous with that of others' lives. The achievement of *amor fati* requires coming to grips with whatever is objectionable in the past. Making peace with the past and being able to alter patterns that cause suffering are the central concerns of this book, and Mitchell acknowledges the extent to which these are Nietzsche's concerns as well. *Amor fati* is one way of expressing the whole project of self-transformation and integration that this book aims to nurture, the very aspiration of Nietzsche's Zarathustra when he seeks to "create and carry together into One what is fragment and riddle and dreadful accident."[1]

Nietzsche's characterization of the goal of drawing "riddles and fragments and dreadful accident" into One is an apt account of much of psychic development. Riddles, fragments, and dreadful accidents are, to a large extent, the sources of what we call our personalities themselves, as well as of psychological problems. Mitchell emphasizes the importance of recognizing that our personalities are not set but can evolve. Psychiatry, etymologically "soul healing," is a matter of assisting such spiritual evolution.

Mitchell's term "psychospirituality" avoids the implication of "psychotherapy" that psychological distress is a disease to be cured, casting the project involved as instead a spiritual adventure. His book is heartening in the same way that some of Nietzsche's writings and the classics of Daoism are. All of these texts emphasize the on-going process and the potential for one to take matters in hand *right now*. One of the gifts this book offers to the reader is a sense of empowerment in the present, wherever in life one happens to be. As a Nietzsche

---

[1] Friedrich Nietzsche, *Thus Spoke Zarathustra*, Part II, "On Redemption"; trans. and ed. Walter Kaufmann, in *The Portable Nietzsche* (New York: Viking, 1954), p. 251.

scholar, I am reminded of Nietzsche praising theater for helping us to recognize the hero concealed inside ourselves. Mitchell's book urges us to take a calm, clear, and loving look at that hero within.

Mitchell's account of mindfulness practice also indicates a method to facilitate the recognition of the inner hero as well as of the heroes concealed in others. Empathy is in part an appreciation of another person as a protagonist whose concerns we feel as our own. Mitchell encourages a stance of universal empathy, self-directed and also emanating ever farther beyond egotistical self-concern. In this respect he again concurs with Nietzsche, who writes movingly of such empathy as the essence of being humane:

> Anyone who manages to experience the history of humanity as a whole as *his own history* will feel in an enormously generalized way all the grief of an invalid who thinks of health, of an old man who thinks of the dreams of his youth, of a lover deprived of his beloved, of the martyr whose ideal is perishing, of the hero on the evening after a battle that has decided nothing but brought him wounds and the loss of his friend. But if one endured, if one *could* endure this immense sum of grief of all kinds while yet being the hero who, as the second day of battle breaks, welcomes the dawn and his fortune, being a person whose horizon encompasses thousands of years past and future, being the heir of all the nobility of all past spirit—an heir with a sense of obligation. . . .; if one could burden one's soul with all of this—the oldest, the newest, losses, hopes, conquests, and the victories of humanity; if one could finally contain all this in one soul and crowd it into a single feeling—this would surely have to result in a happiness that humanity has not known so far; the happiness of a god full of power and love, full of tears and laughter, a happiness that, like the sun in the evening, continually bestows its inexhaustible riches, pouring them into the sea, feeling richest, as the sun does, only when even the poorest fisherman is still rowing with golden oars! This godlike feeling would then be called—humaneness.[2]

In personal terms, this book's emphasis on transformation, and the effort to accept disturbing emotions in a calm, clear, and loving way, is especially meaningful to me in the wake of the death of my husband, Mitchell's long-time friend, Bob Solomon. I am tremendously touched, as I know Bob would be, by Mitchell's reflections on the ways their lives were connected and on the confer-

---

[2] Friedrich Nietzsche, *The Gay Science*, Sect. 337, trans. Walter Kaufmann (New York: Random House, 1974), pp. 268-269.

ence held at the University of Texas at Austin in Bob's honor. These reflections draw attention to the basic truth that inspires family therapy – that human lives are interpenetrated with the lives of those who are close to them. Bob's life remains organically joined both to Mitchell's and to mine, and, as Bob put it in one of his theoretical works on emotion, we grieve because we love, and our grieving is a form of loving. But grief is not the endpoint. Our continuing to draw inspiration from Bob testifies to the possibility of carrying our relationships forward in a way that is not a form of psychological dysfunction. Instead, in fortunate circumstances, it can be cause for gratitude and celebration. To Mitchell, and to Bob, I am grateful.

> Kathleen M. Higgins, Ph.D.
> Professor of Philosophy
> The University of Texas at Austin
> Author (with Robert C. Solomon) of *What Nietzsche* Really *Said*,
>   Schocken, 2000.

Foreword by Claudio Naranjo, M.D., Ed.D.

I vaguely remember meeting Mitchell Ginsberg some time after I invited Dhiravamsa to teach vipassana meditation in the US in the early seventies, but I was only aware of him as a teaching assistant of Dhiravamsa, and I did not begin to know him properly until some years ago when he wrote me to request an endorsement for his remarkable book *The Inner Palace*. I then became aware of him as one with a rare combination of spiritual understanding and erudition, and for this I felt it had been appropriate for him to ask me, since I too am one who has both read many books in spite of being mainly interested in experience. But our affinities didn't stop there, and included a serious involvement in Sufism, a deep interest in Nietzsche, and a special regard for Robert Solomon's thinking on the emotions.

And then, when I was in San Diego weeks ago as a speaker at the Brief Therapy Conference staged by the Erickson Foundation, I received an email from him, saying that he lives in San Diego and inviting me to dinner some day during my stay there. Which I accepted with pleasure, and turned out to be an occasion to come to know him much better—in part indirectly through his beautiful house, his library, Tibetan thangkas and other precious objects that he and his then-absent wife have collected, in part through the Zen-like perfection of his cooking, serving, and table manners, and mostly through some hours of conversation. And I was interested to discover one more unusual interest that we have shared: the therapeutic approach and ideas of Hellmuth Kaiser, who never became as famous as Otto Rank or Fritz Perls, and yet seemed to belong with them in originality. I had read about Kaiser in the sixties in the only book about him, by Louis Fierman, and now I learnt that Fierman had been Mitchell's therapist.

He told me of his new book, and wished I would write a foreword for it, and I told him how unlikely I saw my having time or energy for its reading during my coming season in Berkeley, where, having come to the age of 76, I needed to rest a little after the busiest year of my life and was committed to many tasks before taking off again for my yearly teaching tour in South America. He proposed that I take with me a memory stick containing his work, however, and I agreed to look at it.

Indeed, I ended up reading *Calm, Clear, and Loving*, and I hope that the fact that I did so mostly between 5-6 AM is proof enough of my appreciation for its author. As for writing about it, however, I found it a more problematic thing, for it seems that as I read, I was more in contact with Mitchell's fine mind than with the specifics of his content; I mostly read in outer and inner silence, inasmuch as my own mind was not interested in making commentaries. I explained this to Mitchell days ago, hoping that he would let me off the hook, saying that I could well understand the reasonableness of his expectation that, given my rich and complex background I might be able to reflect on his ideas from the vantage point of my many-faceted background and experience—"as musician, psychiatrist, Gestalt therapist, university professor in several fields, expert on the psychology of meditation, as theoretician and practitioner in the field of pedagogy etc.," and yet just as theory may fail to anticipate life, I found that my response to his book refused to be channeled into a intellectual commentary.

I said: "I might explain it with an old joke of someone who buys a parrot said to speak several languages and then complains that it refuses to say a single word. The salesman insists that his multi-lingual silence is very precious, but understandably his client is dissatisfied." And I proceeded to ask his advice on the matter:

"What can I do?"—I asked him—"True as it may be that I could theoretically look at what you say from the perspective of many fields of experience, I have found to my surprise that as I read my mind refused to make comments, much as when one becomes silent in a conversation. Perhaps this is a time in my life when I am not available for what you ask of me, however willing I have been to include the reading of your manuscript in my heavy agenda. Or perhaps my wish to endorse you is not matched by the wish to dwell in the statements you make; but I have gone through enough self-squeezing to know that my body-mind says "no" to my intent and your request. Commentary is not something that I could offer you without straying into an inauthentic response. Yet if you excuse me from a Foreword of several pages—about which, by the way, I was not sure about when you asked me in San Diego, and could be satisfied with a few words—perhaps including the remarks that I already sent you on interpersonal meditation and even about the silent parrot that I seem to have become, let me know."

I feared that Mitchell might take offence, but to my delight has agreed, and his openness has stimulated me to write what I have just said with great pleasure.

Of the content of this book I'll just say that I have particularly appreciated the chapters on Nietzsche as Psychotherapist and on Interpersonal Meditation.

The former states what I have believed for long and even written and talked about implicitly when I state that Nietzsche was Freud's most important influence, and that in his critique of conventional morality we should recognize both the remote source of the super-ego concept and Freud's perception of the straight-jacketing of *eros*. But I thought Mitchell gave too much credit to Nietzsche as a philosopher of love, for it seemed to me that "the last temptation of Zarathustra" reflected Nietzsche's pessimism and cynicism vis-à-vis true compassion. I told him so, and I was happy to be proved wrong, for in his erudition, Mitchell was able to point out that the German word in Nietzsche's writing that has been translated as "compassion" ('Mitleid') is often used in discussing the phenomenon of condescending if not contemptuous pity, and while critical of manipulative pity, which strengthens people's senses of failure, Nietzsche wrote more than once about using difficult life experiences to grow stronger, and described another sort of response to people's distress, in which each is acting from power and mutual respect, each maintaining self-respect in the process (a most compassionate alternative to pity).

I was very interested in the fact that in the other chapter that I mentioned above, Mitchell addresses the subject of meditation-in-relation (or whatever one chooses to call it), for this too is something that has especially interested me over decades of ongoing practical exploration in my teaching activity, and about which I have written something in my book *The Way of Silence and the Talking Cure*.

I suppose that any meditation practitioner knows how much more difficult it is to keep a calm, clear and loving state of mind in the city than in seclusion, yet also understands how important it should be to bring the touch of meditation to the whole realm of one's experience. For me, the difficulty of extending meditation to ordinary life became a challenge that interested me some forty year ago to approach through the practice of face to face meditation with friends, which opened for me a field of experience that I later continued to explore in the context of psychotherapy training—where the complexity of the situation increases as a dyad sharing silence becomes one where one meditates while listening to another speak.

It is easy to conjecture that as children we were spontaneously able to balance self-awareness and the awareness of objects, and that we lost this as a result of training in compulsive attention, so that it seems normal for an adult person to need to choose between self-absorption and self-forgetting.

The feedback I have by now received from innumerable persons though the years leaves me with the definite impression that for most people meditation in dyads is not only a natural step after meditation with closed eyes and meditation facing a wall, but also a valuable stimulus to the challenge of pursuing the clear-calm-warm state of mental health.

Though I suspect that only a minority of readers will be interested in the full spectrum of subjects dealt with in *Calm, Clear, and Loving*, I cannot help feeling that an author who covers so much with comparable mastery is like a rare flower, and that his panoramic gaze is a beautiful thing to see; and so I hope that, beyond its subject matter, the present volume may constitute to some extent a cultural influence remedial to our overspecialized and greedy times, when wonder has gone the way of extinct species, and when the love of knowledge is now only rarely free and disinterested.

Claudio Naranjo, M.D., Ed.D.
Founder of the SAT Institute for Personal and Professional Development
and President of the CN Foundation for Educational Change

Foreword by Audrey Rachel Stevenson

Calm, Clear, and Loving by Mitchell Ginsberg offers with gentle and heartfelt compassion, very pragmatic suggestions for alleviating torment in our lives. For anyone who has experienced violence, this book shows how to shift from automatic patterns of self-blame, shame, self-attacking, and fear, to a state of calm, clarity, and lovingkindness to ourselves and to others.

This book teaches how to begin to live a full and vibrant life. For those individuals who will meet Mitchell for the first time by reading this book, let me say that you are in for a special treat.

Use of a pen name—Audrey Rachel Stevenson was chosen for this foreword—has allowed me to speak to you more freely here. Beginning at the age of five, I was subjected to torture, sexual abuse, physical abuse, and emotional abuse from people I looked to for love and support, to care for me, and whom I trusted wholeheartedly. Those moments were horrific, and no human being should ever have to experience those depths of sickening, nauseating terror.

On an intellectual level, it was evident to me that traumatic memories had remained isolated in my psyche. It was an extremely daunting task to have to deal day in and day out with this very emotionally draining process. Most of the time my mind operated in a self-criticizing mode and I was encapsulated by intense fear and shame. Deep in my heart, I desperately wanted to heal from the torment, and to learn how to live, not just exist. But I didn't know how.

I had a profound yearning to work "outside the box," especially not in psychotherapy. I define an outside the box approach to healing as being tailored specifically to the individual, because each of us, after all, is a unique person. Relatedly, my personal history is different than that of other individuals; therefore, my healing journey would require an approach specific to me.

After numerous attempts, I developed a path for healing, which involves having a deep commitment, a strong motivation to heal, to change my life circumstances and who and how I am in the world. I wanted to find myself, to understand and to accept myself, and to find inner peace. I became a successful professional; we each have our own path to a sense of self-worth: may *you* find your own path of healing in this venture.

The journey is a long and difficult one, filled with many ups and downs. However, as I continue on my quest for healing, I discover that there is hope for a better or a different today, or even tomorrow. Let me share with you what this means for me.

I have experienced the recurrence of dark and painful memories, which invade every part of your being, your heart, your soul, and every inch of your body. It is an aching inside that never lets up; it is feeling completely, absolutely overwhelmed.

At such moments, when the mind is spinning ferociously, trying to process the information and look for ways to make a shift into a more grounded, clear, calm, and loving state of mind, it may appear as though there is no hope. I can attest to the fact that there is hope, if you completely surrender yourself to the darkness, the pain, and remain as present as possible with the overflow of emotions and feelings. If you allow the cascading wave of emotions and feelings to go through the core of your being, the end result can be the beginning of the release of gut-wrenching pain, these dukkha-filled (pain-filled) memories.

For a long time, I barely existed in life. I walked around like a little girl in an adult's body, lost in a world that seemed so complex and overwhelmingly cruel. I was searching for someone to understand my world, which was dark, cold, and lonely. This is when I met Mitchell. I am happy to find many of the powerful teachings I learned in my self-awareness work with him to be presented in this book as an offering to you, the reader.

What I find refreshing and inspiring about this book is that it is *not* a quick-fix, one-size-fits-all, standardized, all-encompassing cookbook (or set of "recipes" or "skills training homework") for healing from violence, *not* another "just-do-this-and-all-your-problems-will-disappear" book.

It is, rather, a compilation of poems—rich in content and quite special, each in its own way (they take my breath away)—and writings that are insightful and thought-provoking. These invite us to have a clearer appreciation of how we actually deal with what life presents us, and then, of how we might deal with these in alternative ways. With this overview, we can implement pragmatic, practical applications (tools for change) for shifting to more calm, clarity, and groundedness.

To anyone who has ever experienced violence, I personally want to direct you to some chapters that I have found to be of great value—Chapters 1, 3, 8-11, 13-14, 16, 18-19, 21, and 27. Let me give you a taste of *some* of these.

Chapter 8, "From Psychotherapy to Psychospirituality," helped me to become clear that my quest to live a more vibrant, rich, and meaningful life through a connection with the universe can be understood as a yearning for psychospirituality. The two terms of the title mark a substantive difference.

One thing I learned in my insight meditation work with Mitchell that is touched upon in the chapter, is how each of these approaches leads us to ask further questions, or focus in on other issues.

In the first case, when hearing that we have a psychological problem, especially when it's presented to us as a diagnosis for a mental illness or "disorder" (to use the more current term), we may wonder, Will I get better, Doctor? How did I develop this illness? What's wrong with me? Is there a cure? Can you prescribe drugs to make this all go away? Are there side effects I should worry about? Will I need to take them for the rest of my life? Are you saying I should just learn to accept my debility? Will I ever be OK?

In contrast, from a psychospiritual perspective, considering our situation and how we are, feel, and act, the natural questions which arise are more like, What is specific about this way of thinking or feeling? How can I learn to take it all into account better? How have others made use of this particular reality to lead fulfilling lives? How have these patterns led to great inspiration or spiritual wisdom?

This is a path extending beyond our conditioned mind or ego-defined consciousness. It is "Our mind that is a radiant and vital consciousness," as described by Mitchell. The basic distinction discussed in this chapter has helped me to understand my frustrations with traditional psychotherapy (talk plus meds) and to refocus my own definition of what my path is: a healing journey, my soaring to new heights, a spiritual journey to my heart.

A most powerful and relevant chapter to peruse is Chapter 9, on the first step. According to John Pierrakos, a psychiatrist, "The first step in personal development toward a full and vibrant life is to recognize and to acknowledge one's negative emotions *without blaming oneself.*" (Italics added.)

This chapter emphasizes the power of two key facets in being able to take this first step: experiencing and feeling *without* self-blame *and without* self-criticism. In particular, it discusses the ramifications if this "first" step is not taken. For example, if we are spinning in self-blame and self-criticism, we are unable to make a shift to calm and clarity. Here is where making use of our insightful intelligence would help, in that it allows us to view ourselves in a non-judgmental way.

From reading this chapter, an important insight that I came to appreciate was that my self-criticism shielded *and* blocked me from being able to fully engage in self-observation, which is vital to achieving self-transformation. This distracted my attention and perpetuated grave feelings of ill-will toward myself, instead of allowing me to look at core issues related to my trauma, such as my confusion, depression, flashbacks, and anxiety. I also learned that my criticizing mind kept me spinning in this repetitive pattern that was limiting my own personal development.

Chapter 10, "The Liberating Power of Mindfulness," and Chapter 11, "Inter-Personal Mindfulness Practice (IPMP)," present valuable information on what mindfulness practice entails, how to develop it, and how to use it to bring tranquility and liberating understanding into your life. Mindfulness practice or what is known as Vipassana or Insight Meditation, advocates our paying attention at each moment to what we are experiencing, recognizing and accepting the present reality without fighting it, moving onward to the next moment of consciousness, and then discerning what direction to take.

Here, sitting meditation was instrumental in teaching me how to observe my mind, which in turn, helped to calm me when I experienced vehement agitation. I came to see that my yearning was to become more self-aware, and that for this, the help of an inspiring spiritual friend (kalyana mitta) from a self-awareness meditative practice would be most valuable. More generally, a "spiritual friend" is anyone who guides, coaches, inspires, encourages, and calls on us to reach beyond ourselves (especially as defined by the past) by looking *honestly and non-judgmentally* at who we are and what we are now experiencing.

In Chapter 11 (on IPMP), we examine our own experience and behavior, and the manner in which others are interacting with us. We may notice both intellectually and emotionally what is there to experience in a particular situation. This is the "experientially felt realization" that Mitchell alludes to. Relatedly, this practice (of IPMP) can strengthen our ability to remain open to our experience when we feel discomfort or overwhelmed by negative feelings, and can strengthen our ability as humans to empathize with others.

This practice of ongoing open mindfulness, coupled with a serene state of mind that is able to notice how we and others are feeling, can be used as a starting point to explore further what we then bring up for consideration and discussion with others we are interacting with. For example, part of our coming to appreciate what is going on for us or between us and others is describing these experiences in words. After all, writing down our thoughts, feelings, and emotions (verbalizing them) serves as our voice, a means to shift our state of consciousness and to come to clarity, understanding, and appreciation of what we are experiencing.

I appreciate that at one point this chapter addresses the phenomenon of fear, important to me given that I found myself being encapsulated in it most of the time. The chapter inspired me to dig deeper into this issue; it was such a relief to arrive at the realization that when I was spinning in fear, what I was longing for was security and acceptance, which I perceived as being threatened. I learned that the key ingredient to cultivate here is a sense of reassurance.

Chapter 13, "The Second Transformation: Our Third Nature & Recalibration," introduces the concept of our second nature: our patterns of thinking and acting that have been deeply rooted over time. When I was tortured and sexually and physically abused, I hated my body and was ashamed of it. According to Mitchell, "If we were made to feel ashamed at a part of our body, or at our way of responding to certain situations, we have here examples of what seems quite natural to us, but which have been learned, often through much anguish or pain." I came to the realization that although these matters of second nature can be very arduous to shift, it is indeed possible to make significant shifts (into self-acceptance).

Through my work with Mitchell, especially facing very dark and extremely painful memories, having experienced not being judged or criticized by him was critical in my healing work. Instead, I experienced being heard, understood, appreciated, and respected, which enabled me to make further shifts much quicker and on a consistent and permanent basis, with increased groundedness and stability. To experience these types of profound shifts and resultant life-changing moments is truly heartwarming, liberating, invigorating, and inspiring. To find someone who is such a "spiritual friend" as I described above, is truly a special gift to ourselves.

Chapter 14, "The Transmission of Mind," begins with a discussion of Chinese Buddhism (Chan or Zen) with its idea that each primary teacher in the tradition ("Patriarch") would pass on a very special state of consciousness (or "mind" or "heart-mind") to a disciple who would become the next Patriarch. This specific state of consciousness was the awakened or enlightened mind. The tradition speaks of this as a state of consciousness that is rich with respect, gentleness, compassion, and appreciation toward all humans including ourselves. This is a nonjudgmental consciousness integrating wisdom and good-will.

In coming to understand this process, the chapter goes beyond the specific Zen focus just described, and discusses our much more general human interconnectedness with others and our ability to nurture one another in a very profound way. Transmission of mind in the context of our interpersonal relationships makes use of our understanding, appreciating, and sympathizing with one another. In this realm of human interconnectedness, when we experience deep compassion, understanding, and full acceptance for who and what we are, we can then begin to come to calm, clarity, wisdom, and happiness. A nurturing and respectful human connection, feeling our sense of reality validated, can provide a foundation where we experience in a grounded and heartfelt way.

This chapter reinforced my sense about the value of human interconnectedness that is compassionate, understanding, supportive, gentle, nurturing, and respectful. This type of interpersonal relationship enriches our lives and encourages us as we continue our self-awareness work on the path toward a calm, clear, and loving state of consciousness and a secure and vibrant connection with the world.

Chapter 16, "Shame," addresses the intensity of shame where an individual feels awful inside, desires to vanish, and does not want to be seen by anyone. I have experienced shame at this level and it's heartbreaking. This chapter teaches how to bring about a sense of calm, safety, and self-worth when experiencing intense feelings of shame and panic, and how to cultivate a state of mind that replaces shame when it is controlling our awareness. The chapter laid this process out in a way that allowed me to begin this important shift.

As Mitchell writes, immense shame "is at most our second nature, a 'nature' that we have come to have because of important life experiences"—it is "conditioning that can be modified by further life experiences, of a different and more heart-filled nature." For example, on some occasions, I opted to stop my work on my healing journey because I was so ashamed of my personal history and didn't feel that I was deserving of his help. But Mitchell believed in me, even when I didn't believe in myself, and he didn't give up on me. These are examples of the "further life experiences" that he talks about here.

Chapter 18, "Forgive and Remember," is a poignant chapter that offers a treasure chest of wisdom and valuable, practical information on forgiveness when we have been harmed or betrayed by someone. Having experienced violence, it was extremely helpful at this stage in my healing journey to better understand the tug-of-war or roller-coaster of intense emotions, such as sadness, anger, rage, frustration, and hurt that kept re-surfacing repeatedly, not an uncommon occurrence, and often without warning. I sensed there were matters still unsettled for me and learned that before we try to forgive, there are some significant aspects of the core past situation it helps to come to clarity about first, with clear perception, as a start in the overall reconciliation process.

The process of uprooting the emotions is an important, powerful, and liberating experience that requires awareness of sensations from various parts of the body coupled with the memories, images, and thoughts. I embraced the gentle and encouraging guidance offered by Mitchell not to attack myself when I felt stuck, not knowing what to do to move forward, or feeling conflicted with my head and heart in wanting to forgive. Or, at times, thinking that I had forgiven someone, when in my heart I realized I had not. Relatedly, I learned to appreciate and observe all of my thoughts, but not to allow them to be the sole indicator of reality.

While I have come a long way in forgiving some of the individuals who have hurt and betrayed me, there are others whom I still have not forgiven. This part of the journey is ongoing and a work in progress. Through this long and arduous process, I have transformed some of my feelings of ill-will to good-will toward these individuals, a huge step forward that I am not sure I would have been able to take, without first reading this inspiring chapter on forgiveness.

Chapter 19, "Life, Death, and Survival," discusses death as a natural part of life. It is not uncommon for someone who has experienced violence, not to think about the possibility of dying, even at a young age, or to fear death in general. After all, to survive violence is not a small feat. From a mindfulness practice or insight meditation viewpoint, looking at life, death, and survival can be the start of an individual quest into what life and death mean to us. The power of death is one of life's gifts that brings us back to our core values and what is meaningful and precious. In this greater context, we can then view some of the most powerful and important moments of our life with calm, clarity, compassion, and groundedness, as Mitchell puts it.

As I continue to reconcile myself with the topics of death and of dying in general, and the related feelings, mostly fear, I am reminded by Mitchell to "appreciate life while it is still here." For those individuals who were close to me and are now gone, I have a great appreciation and deep gratitude for having known these remarkable human beings, and for their memories that will remain warmly and tenderly with me always.

Chapter 21, "The Yearnings of Psychospirituality," echoed my deepest inner feelings and yearnings for calm, clarity, and inner peace. The words in the poem moved me to soft tears of joy and touched my heart in a tender way.

And Chapter 27, "Options When Overwhelmed," provides priceless information and pragmatic suggestions for anyone in an agitated, anxious, confused, or even bewildered, state of mind. Examples are offered as a general guide of what to do to shift from a spinning mind to our becoming tranquil, clear, and tenderhearted. I appreciated learning that when feeling overwhelmed, it is critical to be gentle with ourselves, and to care for ourselves in kind and loving ways. *The key here is to identify what will work for us individually.* This is another example of nourishing our heart-mind; the part of us that continues on the path toward an awakened and enlightened state of consciousness.

Mitchell's tenderhearted and genuine compassion, never-ending display of good-will, encouragement, and astute ability to view a situation in a positive light is heartwarming. The world is a much better place because in it there are "spiritual teachers" such as Mitchell.

With an open heart, I gently invite you to embark on a journey of self-transformation through self-observation. I encourage you to take this first critical, necessary step. This book can change your life in profound ways; the time and energy of your courageous work can reap unlimited rewards. You are worth it. And now, I extend a sincere invitation to you, to read this book with your heart.

Audrey Rachel Stevenson

Acknowledgments

I would like to acknowledge and to thank a number of individuals whose good will, interest, expertise, and advice have all helped shape this book.

In particular, I would like to thank for their communication: Joanna Attridge, Babette E. Babich, Mei-I Chang, Catherine Combeau, Lance Cousins, Wim De Reu, Vichtr Ratna Dhiravamsa, Michael G. Essex, Christopher Fynn, Branko Gačić, Jane Geaney, Anatole Ginsberg, Françoise Ginsberg, Tania Ginsberg, Yvonne Ginsberg, Eric Gruenwald, Kathleen Higgins, Brenda L. Hood (Hú Bìlíng), Florent Hélène Houssemaine, Etienne Jambou, Mila Kandibur, Samantha Kirk, Jack Kornfield, Jerry Krakowski, Gérard Kouchner, Dan Lusthaus, Kwai Lin Majersky, Paul J. Mills, Claudio Naranjo, Uschi Nussbaumer-Benz, Dušan Pajin, Anne Parries (Pèi Lǎoshī), Elliot Rayfield, Regina Reinhardt, Naomi Rose, Henry Rosemont, Jr., Judith R. Sanders, Audrey Rachel Stevenson, Terry Stiemsma, Henry Suo (Suǒ Yǔhuán), Piya Tan, Bryan W. Van Norden, and Robert B. Zeuschner.

Let me express here my sincere appreciation to Audrey, Claudio, and Kathleen, for their forewords. I also want to thank Etienne and Tania for their ideas for the cover design, and for the creative and technical work in developing that design.

In particular, my thanks to those who read chapters of special interest to them personally or professionally, and especially to those who read through multiple drafts of the book—Eric and Yvonne for valuable substantive input and proof-reading, and Kwai Lin for many detailed, focused editorial discussions—with my sincere acknowledgment of the time and commitment that these offerings represent. My thanks to all for invaluable comments, critiques, and significant questions, thereby prodding and encouraging many of my rewrites.

The suggestions, hesitations, and even indications of strong displeasure with what I had written from these individuals, I might add, often led me to reconsider issues of style and of substance, bringing me to refocus and reformulate what I was presenting, hopefully in ways that are more accurate and informative, more clear and readable, more inspiring, encouraging, and beneficial.

I would also like to acknowledge those who have given me technical assistance in this project. Relatedly here, I would like to thank those who helped in final preparations for printing and publication, Pam Dover, Carrie Fox, and Anne Pollock (all, Lightning Source), Naomi Rose (Rose Press), and, for general technical advice and work on final design and the formatting of covers and images, carried out with creative competence, Paula Hendricks (Cinnabar Bridge).

Having listened respectfully to all suggestions made—but not having always followed them—this book is my personal offering, based on my own sense of the issues I address. I invite readers to join me in these reflections, entering into their own experiential histories to make sense of these considerations, and in this way cultivating their own insights and inspirations.

Mitchell Ginsberg

The most valuable gift of our teachers is perhaps not the answers they offer, but the respectful attention they give to the questions they address, inspiring and challenging us to grapple earnestly with those issues ourselves.

Mitchell Ginsberg, adapted from *The Inner Palace: Mirrors of Psychospirituality in Divine and Sacred Wisdom-Traditions*, 2002/2010, p. 102.

What's the point ... if you only repeat the words of others?
Give us [your] answer to these questions according to your own understanding.

Tibetan scholar Mi-pham Rinpoche, 1846-1912, *The Beacon of Certainty*, Sect. 0.1.1.2.2.1.2, following the rendering in J.W. Pettit, *Mi-pham's Beacon of Certainty: Illuminating the View of Dzogchen, the Great Perfection*, p. 194. Capitalization simplified.

Let's be candid, then,
and tell the truth about ourselves.
Let's add up our anxieties together,
recount them with one another, and with others —
the way we cannot be any more,
the way we want to be now ...
Character
          begins taking form
with the first hint of anxiety about ourselves.

Russian poet Yevgeny Yevtushenko (Евгений Евтушенко), born 1933, from his 1953 poem «Я что-то часто замечаю» ("I have often noticed something"), pp. 81-82, at p. 82, in the 1959 anthology of his poems, Стихи разных лет, *Stikhi raznykh let* (*Verses From Various Years*).

We cannot skip over confusion. It seems an important ingredient in our thinking and its development.

Hellmuth Kaiser (from Scene 5 of his play "Emergency"), in Louis B. Fierman, editor, *Effective Psychotherapy: The Contribution of Hellmuth Kaiser*, p. 190.

I find a deep poetry in the clear awareness that we can develop for ourselves. There is a power in this clarity that can lead us to a heartfelt appreciation of life and to a sense of deep peace and connectedness with the universe. My starting point for this is to invite the reader to investigate with me some of the varieties of human experience that we consider in these pages.

In doing so, we may gradually come to understand better the role that experience plays in our life, which is a phenomenon of finite length—an invitation to us to appreciate what a joy it is simply to be alive! After all, consciousness and awareness, contact between human beings, and life itself are rare gifts.

With this clarity, we can see each turn in our road, and appreciate that each step we take (the present) has greater meaning for us depending on where we have been (the past) and where we will next find ourselves (the future).

The unpredictable course of our life unfolds through time as a unique reality, a mosaic that evolves moment by moment, inviting our ongoing appreciation. This consideration may remind us of elders who remark that they treasure being alive more and more as the decades pass.

How magnificent when we take care to live fully, to be open to all of this reality—not only to what fits our model of some "proper" or "correct" or even "enlightened" life. This is fully experiencing and honoring each moment and situation in our overall journey. Here we can feel creative, alert, light, flexible, clear in our perception, and open to life's intense and rich possibilities.

Mitchell Ginsberg, rephrased from *The Far Shore: Vipassanā, The Practice of Insight*, 1980/2009, pp. 8, 76.

1. The Concept of Love and its Logic[1]
Preliminary Remarks

Why begin a book with a chapter on love?

Our interest is in understanding and appreciating human consciousness, a rich world of many processes and realities—of particular experiences, thoughts, memories, satisfactions, frustrations, hopes, fears, periods of agitation or joy (excitement), of exhaustion or calm (quiet), of loves and hates (interaction with others), and of loneliness or peaceful aloneness (solitude).

Perhaps reason enough is the importance of love in human life, experienced in the gut sense of how central love is to our feelings of well-being and vitality, rooted in human warmth and connection with others. Even proverbs and songs praise love: it makes the world go 'round, makes a house into a home, is more needed than food, and without it, life is tedious, long, lonely, and bitter.

Looking forward here, the body of this chapter, below, at pp. 8-21, presents an analysis of love. Originally a paper written in the autumn of 1964 (with the title "The Concept of Love"), it is retained here in its own light, with the freshness that it had then, the product of a philosophically-inclined 22-year-old.

Structurally, some chapters in this book, as here, have several parts. First are the preliminary remarks (front material). Then there is the body of the chapter itself. Closing is a selection of further readings, an addendum, or other material for additional consideration (back material). When all are present, these three parts complement one another and allow for a more complete discussion.

These preliminary remarks, here through page 7, offer a context to the paper—broader issues in the history of philosophy, especially in philosophy of mind and of the emotions—and also place the paper in its more personal context, providing that added dimension. The addendum, below, pp. 21-25, is an update, highlighting some developments in various related fields of interest.

The front and back material here complementing the body of this chapter take the reader into a number of theoretical issues that may be of great interest or open up new avenues of consideration and reflection.

I invite you to focus here, and throughout this book, on the body of the chapter at hand, and to consult front and back material for further orientation allowing a richer appreciation of the given topic.

~ ~ ~

In this paper, I address the conceptual structure of love (love and its central features) and question various distorting preconceptions about what love is. Some of these distortions are deeply rooted in Western culture (philosophical tradition, worldview) and in the thinking of those brought up in this culture.

---

[1] In this chapter, I italicize foreign words only as is done for English words: for emphasis, in titles, if in italics in the original text being quoted, etc.

*In particular, I am questioning in this paper from 1964 the traditional
distinction (going back to the Greeks) between thinking and the emotions.*

Back in the 1700s, including the time of Hume and his contemporaries,
emotions were named as a group and termed the passions. There is the idea here
that an emotion is essentially a passive phenomenon, something which happens
to us or that we suffer (as reflected in the etymology underlying this old name).[2]
The tension between reason and the emotions that is posited in this worldview
(or in this informal, non-formal theory of the mind) suggests that the two are opposites or different sorts of process that have no commonality.

We may distinguish between various beliefs or understandings that
people have of their situation and their judgments (or attitudes) about features of
the situation, on the one hand, and, on the other, the emotions that they are said
to be feeling. Of course even this might suggest that emotions are simply particular moments of consciousness. That, too, is questioned in this paper. Further,
there is the question of whether the emotions are illogical or without any logic,
and that is certainly put into question here, as well.

I believe that my decades-long friend (Robert Solomon) in his parallel
work in the area of the emotions was taking this basic idea from 1964 much
further. (Historically, I can mention that our discussions together on this topic go
back several years beyond that, back to the late 1950s. In those years, we did not
think of writing out our reflections and inspired thoughts,[3] so there remains noth-

---

[2] The root sense of the term 'passion' has to do with being acted upon, being
passive, being the recipient of some action rather than acting oneself. Compare
the notion of the passion of the martyrs, so named because of its referral to what
various martyrs underwent, suffered, experienced passively, or were subjected
to. In passion is the idea of enduring, living through; it is ultimately related to
patience (same root).

A patient patient is a person who is accepting of the treatment being
received, combining both derivative senses of 'patient' here (first as an adjective, then as a noun). The Latin intermediary is patior, passus, to be subjected to,
experience, undergo; to put up with; to submit to sexually; to bear with equanimity, related to Greek παθ- path- (as in πάθος páthos). From Liddell and Scott,
Greek-English Lexicon, p. 1285b; C.T. Lewis and C. Short, *A Latin Dictionary*,
pp. 1314-1315; and *Oxford Latin Dictionary*, pp. 1308-1310.

[3] Limiting himself to printed material, Bob in the first paragraph of the Preface
to a 2003 collection of his published papers (*Not Passion's Slave: Emotions and
Choice*, p. vii), writes of "my earliest publications on the subject, 'Emotions and
Choice,' in 1973, and of my first book, *The Passions*, in 1976." Clearly, he was
addressing these issues long before any publication of his came to fruition. This
is such ancient history that in his Preface to *The Passions* (1976), he refers to me
(at p. xxv) as Mitch, a name of my childhood and adolescence.

ing in print from those earlier times, to the best of my knowledge at this time. I just want to give the larger historical context its recognition here.[4])

In a way, Bob and I were both students of William Alston (who has written on many topics in his professional career, including on the topic of the emotions[5]). We both took courses from him—including the course for which this paper ("The Concept of Love") was written and read by the seminar, along with the papers by Bob (on unconscious processes such as emotions and desires, as I recall) and by the others in the seminar; Alston was on the dissertation committee of both of our doctoral theses (and the chair of Bob's). And we both studied with Frithjof Bergmann, Alvin Goldman, Abraham Kaplan, Julius Moravcsik, and J.O. Urmson.[6] Bob and I were students and young scholars together.

This shared interest in these theoretical questions concerning the emotions and love, in particular, can perhaps be seen in print back to Bob's 1977 project of "the total demolition of the age-old distinctions between emotion and reason, passion and logic" (as he put it, with his typically vibrant flair and panache),[7] which can be considered along with some of his much more recent extended analyses of the logic of emotions.[8] From his discussion on love (1976):

---

[4] I mentioned this and other related matters (mostly relevant to a fuller appreciation of his person and the extent of his philosophizing) in the informal reminiscing allowed me during the Robert C. Solomon Memorial Conference held in Austin at the University of Texas on Feb. 15-16, 2008, at the final Octavian Discussion Session, at the close of the conference, on February 16th. I would like to thank those present for allowing me that poignant and bittersweet privilege.

[5] E.g., W. Alston, "Emotion and Feeling" (1967), *The Encyclopedia of Philosophy*, P. Edwards, ed., vol. 2, pp. 479-486.

[6] See mention of Julius Moravcsik, in R.C. Solomon, "A More Severe Morality: Nietzsche's Affirmative Ethics," in Y. Yovel, ed., *Nietzsche as Affirmative Thinker: Papers Presented at the Fifth Jerusalem Philosophical Encounter, April 1983*, pp. 69-89, at p. 83. Bob mentions studies with J.O. Urmson and Alvin Goldman, in his Doctoral Dissertation, *Unconscious Motivation* (Univ. of Michigan, 1967), p. ii, with mention of his committee, William Alston (Chair), Frithjof Bergmann, and Abraham Kaplan.

[7] R.C. Solomon, "The Logic of Emotion," *Nous*, vol. 11, no. 1 (Mar. 1977), pp. 41-49, at p. 45. In *Not Passion's Slave: Emotions and Choice* (2003), Preface, pp. vii, ix, resp., he referred to some of his own earlier writings as "polemical (which is to say a bit overbold and unnuanced)" and wrote of including "two of the most rabid sections of my book" (referring to *The Passions*, 1976).

[8] See R.C. Solomon, *Love: Emotion, Myth, and Metaphor* (1981), *Not Passion's Slave: Emotions and Choice* (2003)—being a collection of essays (1973-2001), *True to Our Feelings: What Our Emotions Are Really Telling Us* (2006), and R. C. Solomon and K. Higgins, eds., *The Philosophy of (Erotic) Love* (1991).

Love is intimacy and trust; love is mutual respect and admiration; love is the insistence on mutual independence and auton-
omy, free from possessiveness but charged with desire; love is
unqualified acceptance of the other's welfare and happiness as
one's own. Nothing else deserves the name.[9]

This present paper suggests (as do many sections of my book, *The Far Shore*) an
understanding of various emotions and emotional states (love, fear, anger, resentment, etc.) that does not rely on the above-distinction between emotion and
reason that Solomon was intent on demolishing.

Of course, that we do not take the distinction between emotion and reason to be absolute or categorical, or representing two distinct and non-overlapping domains, does not mean that our experience of emotions is always the paradigm of cool rationality. As Bob wrote twelve years after the above excerpt, in
About Love: Reinventing Romance for Our Times (1988), in what is perhaps a
series of precocious over-generalizations on a basis of difficult relationships that
were in selective focus for some reason:

Instability is the mark of love—as opposed to the stability of
friendship, for example. Love may last, but it typically does so
by way of convulsions rather than mere stasis... Whatever else
it may be or become, love is not ... a stabilizing force in our
lives... [Love] seems secure, even eternal, but at any moment a
single ill-considered comment, a moment's silence, an evening's neglect...[10] but then the two lovers begin to realize how
much is already at stake, and swallowing pride, they go back to
try again. They "make up" (a remarkable psychological ritual)
and continue the dynamic of love.[11]

One alternative to attempting to fight our way free from a conceptual
mental jacket (requiring the dexterity in thought that Harry Houdini demon-
strated in the body) is to take *a different starting point, one that does not take as
axiomatic the distinction between mind and heart.* There is a hint for this project
in Nietzsche (such as at *Genealogy of Morals*, II, 16) in taking a non-Eurocentric
perspective as is available in Buddhist Abhidhamma (or Abhidharma, the theoretical psychology of Buddhism), in Daoism, and in other theoretical orientations
or worldviews. More contemporary is the comment by Marianne in the 1965
Jean-Luc Godard film, *Pierrot le fou*, "There are thoughts [pensées] inside feelings [sentiments]."[12] These and related issues are addressed elsewhere in this

---

[9] R.C. Solomon, *The Passions* (1976), p. 337.
[10] This particular ellipsis occurred in the text being quoted. Cf. next note.
[11] R.C. Solomon, *About Love: Reinventing Romance for Our Times* (1988), p.
271. Ellipses indicate text omitted (other than that mentioned in preceding note).
[12] Ca. 50 min. into the film; cf. D. Wills, ed., *Jean-Luc Godard's Pierrot le fou.*

book, following some of these various orientations. I also find myself in harmony with Bob's overriding interest in linking emotions, choice, and responsibility.[13] (This precedes our first readings of Jean-Paul Sartre.[14])

Even more ancient (to start looking back in time) are various texts from the 1800s that addressed these very same issues, arguing long before our generation that there is a logic or rational-conceptual structure to the various emotions, including love.

One discussion that reviews some of the earlier theorizing and contributes a new synthesis, by the French psychologist Théodule Ribot (the founder and editor in chief of the French scholarly journal, *La revue philosophique de la France et de l'étranger*, and mentor of the French philosopher-psychiatrist Pierre Janet[15]) is entitled *La logique des sentiments* (1905/1907).[16]

Relatedly, in a work dedicated to the memory of this same Théodule Ribot, Ludovic Dugas spoke of passion and reason (la passion et la raison) as always going together, and of passion-inspired logic (la logique passionnelle).[17] Some distinctions made there that are not always made in more recent writings

---

[13]   See esp. his essay "On the Passivity of the Passions" (2001), pp. 195-232 in *Not Passion's Slave: Emotions and Choice* (2003), where he talks of his long-term goal of focusing in on emotions and choices ("rather than in terms of visceral reactions, metaphorical or neurological 'chemistry,' or passively undergone feelings," to quote from his initial orienting comments at p. 195).

[14]   My own acquaintanceship with Sartre's philosophy began in a year-long course for Philosophy Honors Majors at the University of Pennsylvania, in 1962-1963, taught by Marvin Farber (whom I remember with great appreciation, warmth, and respect), with a thorough reading and study of key works of Sartre, Kant, C.I. Lewis, and Edmund Husserl, Farber's own teacher in Germany in the 1920s. For more on Farber (and Husserl), see R.M. Chisholm, "Marvin Farber, 1901-1980," *Proceedings and Addresses of the American Philosophical Association*, vol. 55, no. 5 (Jun. 1982), pp. 578-579.

[15]   Janet, in his introductory comments to his work, *The Major Symptoms of Hysteria: Fifteen Lectures Given in the Medical School of Harvard University*, 1907 (p. 3), speaks of the progress in France in the understanding of pathological psychology "under the influence of two of my masters, whose names I like to recall,—Charcot and Professor Ribot." These were neurologist and psychiatrist Jean-Martin Charcot and Psychology Professor Théodule Ribot.

[16]   In English, *The Logic of the Sentiments*. Ribot refers back to the work of Auguste Comte, John Stuart Mill, Bernard Bosanquet, Wilhelm Wundt, Franz Brentano, William James, and other earlier and then-contemporary theoreticians.

[17]   L. Dugas, "Les passions," in Georges Dumas *et al.*, *Traité de Psychologie* (1923), pp. 480-501, esp. pp. 487-489. Dugas also discusses Stendhal there. On 'passionnelle,' cf. *Larousse Lexis*, p. 1350. Cf. below, p. 139.

may be of interest for those who wish to go further in this area, such as the functions of rationality in the emotions: the role of emotions in discovery, in determining or defining the situation, their justificatory role, their directive role, their having us feel and think that we are correct in what we are doing, their leading us to clarity about what to do or how to act, and so forth.[18] *This would suggest that emotions are not only logical but perhaps multidimensionally logical!* Relatedly, The Hungarian-born psychoanalyst René Spitz acknowledged the French role in bringing the issue of the emotions to the center of our psychological understanding, explicitly mentioning the line from Charcot through Janet.[19] I will not pursue this century-old line of consideration further here.

Even more ancient, if we would like to take in a larger vision of the history of this topic, we can consider the writings of Robert Burton, author of *The Anatomy of Melancholy*,[20] first published at Oxford in 1621.

And if we want to go beyond the Occidental (Euro-centric) focus here, Chinese author Féng Mènglóng 馮夢龍 (1574-1646) is cited as addressing the contrasting concepts of a person rich in feeling or emotion (qíng 情), yǒuqíng rén 有情人, vs. a person who lacks emotions, wúqíng rén 無情人, in a worldview with presuppositions and logic—such as the role of qíng 情 in preferences and actions, or the relationship of qíng 情 to hé 和 (harmony)—quite distinct from what we find in the Occident.[21] Much earlier, there are the poems addressing the interweaving of thoughts and emotions, such as in works by the ninth-century CE (Tang Dynasty) poet, Sīkōng Tú 司空圖 (837-908 CE); also cited as Tú Sīkōng.[22] And even further back in time is the Buddha on the emotions.[23]

---

[18] Chap. III (Les principales formes de la logique des sentiments), pp. 65-126.

[19] R.A. Spitz, "La perte de la mère par le nourrisson. Troubles du développement psycho-somatique," *Enfance*, vol. 1, no. 5 (Nov.-Dec. 1948), p. 373.

[20] Full title, with obsolete spelling: *THE ANATOMY OF MELANCHOLY: VVHAT IT IS. VVITH ALL THE KINDES, CAVSES, SYMPTOMES, PROGNOSTICKS, AND SEVERALL CVRES OF IT. IN THREE MAINE PARTITIONS, with their feuerall SECTIONS, MEMBERS, and SVBSECTIONS. PHILOSOPHICALLY, MEDICINALLY, HISTORICALLY, opened and cut vp* (following the title page of 1624 edition). We might replace that "opened and cut up" last part by mention of analytic philosophy and analysis or "unpacking" of the conceptual features of melancholy. Whatever the style and contents of this seventeenth-century Elizabethan text, the interest in understanding the nature and characteristics of the emotions (here, esp. that of melancholy) is not new.

[21] M.W. Huang, "Sentiments of Desire: Thoughts on the Cult of *Qing* [qíng 情] in Ming-Qing [Míng 明 - Qīng 清] Literature," *Chinese Literature: Essays, Articles, Reviews,* vol. 20 (Dec. 1998), esp. pp. 154-155, 161.

[22] L. Sundararajan, "The Plot Thickens—or Not: Protonarratives of Emotions and the Chinese Principle of Savoring," *Journal of Humanistic Psychology*, vol.

To go beyond these earlier considerations, and to speak from my own experience, in my more recent work in psychotherapy (going back to early beginnings in 1968), I have had more than one occasion to put to good use this general understanding of the interconnected nature of thinking and the emotions, in helping people to appreciate their own *emotive thinking process*, to put these two into one integrated phrase. I write about this elsewhere.

In thinking about this paper and its vicissitudes, I remember that I was later told by George Schrader, Jr., the Chairman of the Philosophy Department at Yale who in late 1966 offered me a faculty position at Yale, that he appreciated the mix of my work in analytic philosophy[24] with my readiness to tackle a subject as far-afield from the core of analytic philosophy's interests in those years as the concept of love. So in a way, this paper was instrumental in my being hired back then at my first post-graduate position in academia, at Yale.

In any case, the underlying idea here is that rationality (thinking) and the emotions are actually not distinct domains of human experience. The two are, rather, interconnected in ways we will consider further in the body of this chapter. *See also the poetic chapter on love (chap. 29), below, p. 273.*

The 1964 paper will now speak for itself. I retain its punctuation, which respected writing conventions of academic philosophy of that era. E.g., sentences would have closing punctuation within the quotation and, if appropriate, after, as: John stated, 'I love Mary.'. See further, below, p. 20, note 11.

Following the paper with its supplemental bibliography, an addendum (2010) broadens the context of this topic of the concept of love and its logic, and raises more sophisticated issues that may be of interest to some readers.

48, no. 2 (Apr. 2008), pp. 243-263. This name is Ssū-K'ūng T'ú in Wade-Giles spelling; see further, below, p. 186, and the appendix at end of this book. Sikong is famous as the mountain that was home to the Third Chinese Buddhist Patriarch, Jiànzhì Sēngcàn, in Japanese, Kanchi Sōsan 鑑智僧璨; on Sēngcàn, see M. Ginsberg, *The Inner Palace: Mirrors of Psychospirituality in Divine and Sacred Wisdom-Traditions*, pp. 111, 220, 242, 245, 277, 422, 502, 534. On the use of names of locales (mountains, monasteries, etc.) as the "family name" of recluses and monks, see more on poet Hán Shān 寒山 and Buddhist monks Huáng Bò 黄檗 (known to some as Huang Po) and Bǎi Zhàng 百丈, below, at p. 241, n. 19.

[23] See esp. discussion in P. de Silva, *An Introduction to Buddhist Psychology.*

[24] Schrader had been given a copy of my then-recently published article, "Katz on Semantic Theory and 'Good,'" *The Journal of Philosophy*, vol. LXIII, no. 18 (Sep. 29, 1966), pp. 517-521, which had been submitted for publication (at the time, rather unusual in philosophy, for a graduate student) on the suggestion of Julius Moravscik, a professor of mine at the University of Michigan. A graduate student certainly appreciates such encouragement, as I did, and as I let Professor Moravscik know then. (And I thank him again, here.)

1. The Concept of Love and its Logic (1964)

In this paper we shall be discussing love. But we shall not be discussing religious fervor, nor parental respect, nor brotherly affection. We shall concentrate our attention on the love of lovers. We are not committed, however, to accepting a reduction of love to sex. Nor do we accept this reduction: love is not sex. It might be more exact to say that love is not solely sex. *Perhaps* love is not always even partly sex.

But we have not yet defined love. Do we have to *start* by defining it? Would it help? I say passionately, fervently, that I love her with all my heart. Would an academic verbal equation help you to understand what I am saying? Indeed it might, but a definition now would either be incorrect—and why propose an incorrect definition?—or it wouldn't be incorrect. But in that case the analysis is closed and little of what is thereby meant would be disclosed. I am not interested merely in giving a definition of several terms of the language of emotions. My interest is in coming to a sharper understanding of love.

What is love? It is often claimed that to be in love with someone is to have certain feelings when with that person and other feelings when without him (or her). It is, it is claimed, to feel on the top of cotton-soft clouds, or to feel crushed and beaten. Anyone who can have these kinds of feelings, who is even slightly sensitive, can, therefore, be in love. It also follows that only he can truly know whether he has these feelings. And to know that he is in love, *all* that he has to do is "look" to his own feelings. And if he "looks" and sees that he has these certain feelings, then there can be no doubt: he *is* in love.

Is love a feeling? Is it a particular feeling, or just a type of feeling? Is it continuous? Or is it pulsatingly discontinuous? What does this picture of love suggest? It suggests that love is something that affects you, which you notice (if you only bother to take notice). Love is pictured as something which comes over you; it is like being hit on the knee and noticing your foot kick forward: Love is something which happens to you. The grammatical structure of this phrase is important. It illuminates the usual view of what love is. *You* are not the subject of the sentence. You are an object. You are *completely* passive. This is the import of the expression 'to fall in love with ...'. This general view of love is usually accompanied by the opinion that love is a state. (You needn't act to *feel* love.) It is how you "stand". Thus it is that 'to be', expressing a state, is used in 'to be in love with ...'. (Still, let us not read too much into the peculiarities of English expression here, even if the grammar is suggestive in its own way.)

This paper proposes that the above-described picture of love as a feeling is faulty. This picture attempts to portray love as completely independent of the mind, as if the non-thinker, the non-intellectual were, *because* of being that, in a better position to love. As if love were hindered by thinking; indeed, that thinking about such an emotion destroyed it. In this (rejected) view, one holds that intellect and emotion are opposed as water is to fire.

Love does not just happen to you. Even Stendhal noticed this: in spite of his overly Romantic, soppy ideas concerning love, he did notice that love itself does not come into being by falling on you. If you can't think, you can't think about the one you "love". But you begin to be in love only *after* thinking about her (or him). So far Stendhal is on the right road. But for him, this thinking is an act of idealization (the act of "crystallization"[1]): here Stendhal errs.

In what way is this an error? It might be asked whether this is not what love *was* for Stendhal. How can he be wrong about that? The answer to this is: even if it *were* impossible for him to be wrong about what a given concept (that of love) meant to him (it is quite possible for one to be mistaken about such matters), that does not mean that Stendhal was not wrong. We are not asking here 'Of what did love consist for Stendhal?' but 'Of what does love consist?'.

Again we ask: In what way is this an error? First of all, this would make it reasonable to believe that after once seeing a young wench in the market place, one could return home to begin his "crystallization", and, without ever seeing her again, *later* fall in love with her. One must hold on this view that even if one were to be content to reflect on his love, without ever trying to see her, to talk to her, to kiss her, he might easily be in love with her. And *that* is love (so says Stendhal). Is love this intellectual representative contemplation? This is indeed placing much too much emphasis on the role of the mind in love. Love is not merely a contemplative state.

This criticism holds for a view expressed by Jules Laforgue in his poem "Coup de foudre" ("Love at first sight"). The tone expressed is of youthful jubilance:

> I am in love, I am in love ... If she doesn't love me, if
> she can't be wholly mine, what difference will it make? I am in
> love, that's enough ...[2]

I wish to argue: that's not enough. Indeed, if that were enough, then that would not be love. It might be a star-filled sky, a good meal, contentment, perhaps even infatuation. But there is a difference between these and love.

Two people meet. They are infatuated with one another. Sometimes they continue seeing one another, and are later in love with one another. Sometimes they discover that the other holds no appeal for them at all. They become uninterested in one another. Why?

In first meeting another, many begin "playing a role", "acting out of character", "putting on a front". The other may begin finding *this* character appealing. But first impressions are often (but: not always) misleading. What a per-

---

[1] "I call crystallization that process of the mind which discovers fresh *perfections* in its beloved at every turn of events." (M.H. Beyle, using the pen name of Stendhal, *On Love*, "The Birth of Love", p. 7, my emphasis).

[2] *An Anthology of French Poetry*, p. 224.

son is like (characteristically) is often different from what he is like (when first being introduced to people). Stendhal seems to be overlooking just this facet of human conduct. To take it into consideration is, however, to allow for an explanation of the abrupt end to many an infatuation. (Abrupt, drastic personality changes are not overly conducive to consistent attitudes on the part of others.)

One may become infatuated by a fleeting glimpse that is found appealing. But one does not love a glimpse. (Here is one difference between love and infatuation.) It is for this reason that the statement 'I only saw him once, when I was a young woman. We didn't say a word to one another. After being in the same room with him for five minutes, I had to leave. I never saw him again, yet I was from that time forward madly in love with him. It is fifty years later, yet I still love him with all my heart.' would be more likely spoken in a farce on love than earnestly by a woman in discussing part of her own life.

Is it *sufficient* to have certain feelings to be in love? No. For then one could be in love without thinking at all. Is one in love if he *never* thinks about the one he is supposed to love? And does he love her if he "feels" a certain way about her and thinks some (any) thoughts about her? Suppose that a certain young man has certain "warm" feelings when he is with Janet, yet he never thinks of her except with the desire to beat her brutally. It is (absurd) conceptually inaccurate to say that he loves her. He may be in love with her, however, without ever thinking 'I wonder how she feels.', or 'It is bad that she is so depressed.'. Perhaps he thinks 'I hope that she is able to smile tomorrow.'. Perhaps another thinks 'I am in love with her.' and is in love with the person about whom he is thinking.

Is this suggesting that thinking that one is in love is the same as being in love? No. I may think to myself 'I am in love with her.' without being in love: think now to yourself 'I am in love with Mary Prattle.'. You have thought it, but you have no emotional involvement with her (You do not even know if the name 'Mary Prattle' is anyone's name.); you are not in love with her. You may think a thought without believing it.

Is it being maintained that: if one believes that one is in love, then it must be the case that one is in love? No. This does not follow. Nor is it so. One might be terribly infatuated with someone and (mistakenly) believe himself to be in love.

It may be the case that Charles believes that he is in love with Janet. He may be saddened by seeing her cry. He may find her extremely attractive. He may think earnestly of doing things for her sake. He may, at the same time, beat her brutally every time that he sees her. If this is love, then it is a very demented love. But is demented love love?

You may believe that you are in love and yet not be in love. You may be in love and yet not believe that you are in love: it is not necessary to believe that you are in love in order to be in love. Thus, it may be that one simply begins to feel close to another, to empathize with that person, to desire to be with her (or with him), to desire her (or him), without ever considering the question 'Are you in love with her (or him)?'. It may thus happen that one "finds" himself in love. In such a case, the metaphor of 'to fall in love' makes some sense.

It is also seen from this that one needn't think about *love* in order to be in love. (This directly opposes Stendhal.) This is necessary in order to know that one is in love; *that* is another problem. But: this does not mean that being in love may come about with complete lack of thinking. For if one *never* thought about his "Love"[3] at all, then it would be odd to talk of his being in love at all.

One may note in passing that this allows for the conclusion that love is not (solely) sex (see above): although one cannot be said to love someone else if he never thinks of his "love" in a certain way (to be explicated directly below), it is sometimes (often?) the case that one copulates without any such thoughts.

A person in love (sometimes) thinks about his love. These thoughts essentially reflect his having certain attitudes about his love. A person who takes no attitudes cannot be in love, cannot love. Love is a kind of psychological commitment.

Some thoughts reflecting these attitudes are those which show interest in the loved one, concern, empathy, and sympathy with him (or her), desire to be with him (or her), desire to make love to him (or her). In the discussions that follow, talk about the attitudes which one in love has concerning his loved one shall make non-explicit reference to these kinds of thoughts. (For the sake of brevity, and because I feel that what is meant is made clear by the context, reference shall remain implicit.) Yet one need not be thinking some of these thoughts at all times. One sleeps, one listens to a Bartok string quartet, one even gets angry with the one he loves and then (sometimes) thinks thoughts which are far from those typical of one in love. One may also think of drinking a golden beer and still be in love with someone. One needn't be a monomaniac to be in love; not every thought need be about the loved one in order for one to be in love. Love is not an instantaneous concept: one is not in love one moment, thinking about a beer the next, and then back in love again.

But thinking in these ways is not sufficient as a sole criterion for being in love; one may assert 'I love her.', believing it to be so, without its being so. We here (again) face the problem of mistaken beliefs. One may believe that he believes something yet not truly believe it.

Let us take an example. John believes that he is in love with Madeleine. He thinks (earnestly) to himself 'I love Madeleine. I want only what is best for her.'. When John strolls alone down the boulevard without his Madeleine, he often thinks of her and wishes that she were with him.—Note that *this* may be explained either by his being in love with her, or, by his general loneliness in crowds.—As he sees another woman every night he says to himself 'It is

---

[3] That is, his belovèd (the person loved, not the emotion of love).

Madeleine that I love. *This* woman means nothing to me.'. We assume that he believes what he says. Further, let us assume that he knows that Madeleine wants only to be with him, and that she knows that he is with other women nightly. He also knows that this greatly saddens her and she cries. And with all this, he may believe: 'I do not want very much to be with Jeanne, or Enid, or Charlotte, or Denise, or Anne, or Marie, or ...'. Furthermore, he might explain each of these trysts as "seeing an old friend" (hardly noting that it is an old flame and not an old buddy that he is to see), or, as "giving *** a chance to go to the opera" (hardly noticing that she thus also has a chance to be his love for the evening). In short, all of these factors may be believed by him to be *irrelevant* to the question of his loving Madeleine.

And if these are all of the salient issues of this example, we might answer our question 'Is John in love with Madeleine?' by a complex response including an explanation of John's desire for company (the boulevard incident), his being at ease with Madeleine, his having convinced himself that his psychological easiness *is* love, his desiring to glorify himself by having many loves, and his *not* being in love with Madeleine.

It might be held that this reflects a conceptual claim that one cannot love two at the same time, in the sense of 'love' being analyzed here. I do not hold this. If one does hold certain attitudes, have certain interests, act taking certain feelings into consideration, etc., etc., with reference to two others, then I can see no reason for not saying that this person does in fact love two others at the same time. Yet acting out of love is sometimes refraining from certain alternative actions that would hurt the loved one if performed. In much of this society, for example, it is considered a sign of lack of love to have a love affair with another.) And if, for example, Madeleine holds this, then for John to make love to Jeanne might hurt Madeleine deeply. In *this* case, acting out of love for Madeleine would involve *not* making love to Jeanne. Certain beliefs held by one we love might indeed make it impossible to make love to another at the same time (while acting in a considerate, loving way toward this first loved one). If certain beliefs, attitudes, etc. are held by Madeleine such as the above-mentioned ones, then loving (if it includes making love) Jeanne would be *not* loving Madeleine. (It would be hurting Madeleine deliberately instead of acting out of consideration for her.) If, however, this set of beliefs, etc. is not held by any of the three in question, such a complex of love is in fact possible.)

It may be, however, that John needs his Madeleine. But there is a difference between (i) needing something, (ii) needing someone, and, (iii) loving someone.

Alissa may feel isolated without Jerome. When she is in his company, she may feel content. His kiss may excite her. She may want to be with him. Is she in love with Jerome? She may be; she may not be. That is to say, so far her feelings and wants may be explained either assuming that she *is* in love, or assuming that she is *not*.

When she sees Jerome she may melt into his arms and may say to herself 'I believe that I am in love with Jerome.'. To what extent does she empathize with him? To what extent are her feelings of "love" directly associated with Jerome, and to what extent to *her* feelings of loneliness and later contentment? (*Love of another is outer-directed*. The answers to questions such as the above will reflect whether she is in fact in love at all.)

We may sketch in this example such that it begins to resemble the above case (of John and Madeleine) in certain relevant respects.

We say, for example, that she has been lonely, that she has known Jerome and can feel relaxed in his presence. She may also be excited by him. Yet during the day while feeling isolated, she may think just that: 'I feel isolated.'. She may think of Jerome only as he who is standing next to her, holding her hand, allowing her to feel psychologically comfortable. And she might turn readily to Jim and, with him, be excited, and not feel alone, and not think about her Jerome until much later (when once again she is alone and feeling alone). And perhaps just one week ago Alissa had no thoughts of Jerome at all, but did in fact feel lonely. Suppose also that since then he has returned to her after a long absence, that Alissa saw his return as a means to eliminate her dating problem indefinitely.

We add that she also wants to see Jim very much in spite of Jeremy's return. In *this* case, it seems much more reasonable to say that Alissa has a need for affection and security than to say that she loves Jerome (or even that she has a need for Jerome: Jim will satisfy her needs as well). Yet, ex hypothesi, she might believe that she loves Jerome.

Another elaboration is as follows: Alissa is happy when being with Jerome. She believes that she could not find such happiness with anyone else. She desires very much that Jerome shower her with attention, that he idolize her. When she is with others she wishes that Jerome were by her side. Being without Jerome makes her feel depressed. At the same time, she takes only superficial interest in his interests; she often hurts him deliberately; she is only slightly bothered when seeing that he is upset, or ill. In *this* case, it seems reasonable to say that Alissa has a need for Jerome, but that she does *not* love him.

We may sketch in this example in a third way such as to lead us to say that she does in fact love Jerome.

Suppose, for example, that she takes a strong interest in his problems and his successes, becomes very anxious upon learning of a present illness of his, takes his feelings into consideration when doing something which she knows will effect him. She also, ex hypothesi, has no other romantic interests except Jerome. She considers Jerome to be unique and believes that she could not be happy with another, i.e., there is no "Jim".

It now seems reasonable to talk of Alissa's loving Jerome, i.e., *these* seem to be sufficient (although not necessary) conditions for allowing us reasonably to say that she is in love.

What do these two examples (John et al. and Alissa et al.) show? They show at least that believing that one is in love is not sufficient for concluding that one is in love.

The opposite of this is true also: one may be in love without believing that he is in love.[4] Paul may love Simone without believing that he does. He may want to see her often without realizing it: he may go to the store where she works in order to buy bon bons very often, even developing a strong desire for bon bons. Or he may want to be with her often and want her to want to be with him, and yet think of her just as a good friend of his. If he loves her, then he is interested in knowing her feelings, her pleasures, her anxieties. These too he may interpret as manifestations of platonic friendship. If he loves her then he takes her feelings into consideration when acting in ways that affect her. If he loves her, then he may want to express himself emotionally by the act of love.[5]

Paul may love Simone, and feel the way he does about her (The way he feels about her is *not* a set of sensations. It is a set of attitudes.), yet not believe that he holds these attitudes. Or he might not *interpret* his holding these attitudes as his being in love. He may be in love without believing that he holds these attitudes, or that he is in love. In the case in which he doesn't believe that he holds *any* of these, it becomes a bit odd to talk of his being in love. But *this* is due only to a belief held intuitively: that man cannot be incorrect about all of his beliefs.

This extreme was mentioned only to bring attention to the extremely important fact that one's *attitudes*, and not one's *beliefs about* one's attitudes, are the crucial factors in whether or not one is in fact in love.

This is extremely important to our understanding some common misconceptions about love. It shows, for example, why some believe that to be in love is to believe that one is in love (it being thought that such beliefs *cannot* be mistaken ones). It also explains how one can be mistaken about this (that indeed they can be mistaken beliefs). Of course one may think that love is merely physical attraction and thus believe himself to be in love when in fact he is only sexually frustrated. But this is a case of the correct application of a very mistaken conceptualization. Yet it may be the case that one believes himself to be in love, employing the concept correctly, and be mistaken. For example, being in love involves having certain attitudes toward the beloved. Peter may believe that

---

[4] This is what seems to happen to David in T. Rubin, *Lisa and David*. David becomes deeply emotionally attached to Lisa and yet claims (earnestly) that his interest in her is as "an interesting case" (esp. pp. 91-92,142,143).

[5] There are cases in which one is said to love another without desire for sexual intercourse being present (e.g., man and wife both in eighties who love each other). It seems that this is love, although of a slightly aberrant variety; it seems that there are cases in which love is not even partly sex. (See first pages.)

he has these, but in fact does not. He may believe that he would go to the ends of the earth for his Roberta but decide, when the occasion arises, that he would rather have a beer with the boys.

We have here an intertwining of attitudes and actions. Yet these two are *not* the same. To have an attitude is *not* to act in a certain way, although one's acting in a certain way may be explained (partially) by certain attitudes, which he does in fact have. One can act considerately without being a considerate person (people can act "out of character"): a nurse can be hired to treat an infant considerately, but she cannot be hired to be a considerate person. The nurse may act in a loving way while hating the infant who is under her care. (This would be nonsense if having attitudes and merely acting the way those who have these attitudes do in fact act were exactly the same: they are different.) To have a certain attitude does not *mean* to act in a certain way.

It is easily explained how one can think that he is in love and yet not be, i.e., it may be that he thinks that he has certain attitudes, but does not have them. It might be the case that no revealing decisions have been required on his part yet. And *this* explains why infatuation and early love are ofttimes (always?) inseparable. But as the relationship continues, the two individuals in question (here: Peter and Roberta) see one another and do things together; they interact socially. And as they react to one another in various contexts, they begin revealing their attitudes. It need not be the case that they thereby come to realize how they feel about one another (what attitudes they do in fact have) but it becomes continually more difficult for them to err. (Still, some manage to.) It becomes increasingly more difficult to be mistaken about the general attitudes which one oneself has, and the general effects of his "beloved" on him. In this way, one is less likely to be mistaken about his being in love after his being with her for some time.

But this is *not* the complete picture. For notice what has been happening. Peter and Roberta have been together. They have done things together. That is simple enough. But what does this consist of? They stand on the corner. She wants to see a Fernandel movie while he wants to see Terry-Thomas. And perhaps they then go to a showing of a Charlie Chaplin film. What do they do? They are two people who are doing something together, but are still two people, not all of whose wants are the same. They change their minds about what they want to do. Do they compromise? Do they decide to compromise?

They do compromise in the sense that their original wants are changed to others. But is there any self-sacrifice? In some cases one does sacrifice his own interests for those of the beloved: consider the Romantic picture of the woman running in front of a fatal bullet meant for her love.[6] Yet it seems that a

---

[6] Compare this with the Romantic lines of F. García Lorca (*Antología poética*, "Es verdad") and, then, E. Piaf (from "C'est l'amour"):

high need for continual self-sacrifice for the sake of the relationship is one of the best reasons for terminating the relationship: it is obvious that the two people in question are incompatible.

They do decide to do something more acceptable to both of them. But do they feel that they are compromising? that they are losing something by doing what they end up doing? that they have to sacrifice for the sake of the relationship? Do they think of what they are doing as a sacrifice of individual wants to allow for a "smoother" relationship? Perhaps he takes her hand and they walk toward the two movie houses. And when they pass the theater at which the Chaplin film is being shown they merely look at one another and enter. (They both forget about the other films.) Perhaps they would answer 'Why are you compromising?' with 'Who's compromising? We've just decided to do something else together.'.

And how did this situation in which love later evolved differ from another infatuation that ended abruptly? Perhaps only in his reluctance in the latter case to go to a tea (the beer party was just too appealing!).

But it is not the case that on the fifth activity together they suddenly were in love. Love does not have such *distinct* temporal boundaries. One does not say (except here, as an example): 'I have been in love with her since 9:47 P.M. of the fourth of May 1963.'. Part of love is a continual but discontinuous (in the sense of the word used in the calculus) process of doing things together. And part of *this* is deciding to do certain things; part is wanting to do certain things.

A strong emotional involvement may sometimes be reached by making many small decisions, developing many attitudes without noticing that these are being developed. It is in this sense that it is an insight to say that one may find himself in love, and, although out of context *highly* misleading, to say that love is partly a habit: one may have certain attitudes and act on the basis of them ('He ran into the flaming building in order to save his beloved.') without having to

---

(i)   ¡Ay qué trabajo me cuesta
quererte como te quiero!
      Oh how difficult it is for me
      To love you as I love you!

(ii)   Dans l'amour il faut des larmes,
dans l'amour il faut donner, ...
j'ai donné, donné mes larmes,
j'ai pleuré pour mieux t'aimer.
      In love tears are necessary,
      in love giving is necessary, ...
      I've given, given my tears,
      I've cried in order to love you better.

think carefully: He sees that the building is in flames, he sees that his love is at a second story window, and he runs into the building. (To say that he thought out the problem in order to come to a decision so that he might act is a very big extension of the concept of ratiocination.) Being in love calls for action, yet it needn't call for careful ratiocination (as, for example, in this case). It is in this sense that love is partly a habit: one needn't think through each step; 'I just felt that I had to save her life.'.

But it is also an insight to say that these two pictures (finding oneself in love and love's being a habit) are misleading. They are insights in the sense that one may look back and see the implications to be drawn from many such actions and attitudes; misleading in the sense that they did not happen *to* him — *he* took certain attitudes; *he* acted in certain ways.

In many cases, however, one does decide to act in a certain way before acting. Decisions as leading to one's acting in a certain way play a large part in being in love, although decisions not followed by the relevant act are, at best, secondary. (Actions speak in a way in which words do not.)

Yet some have overemphasized this aspect of the social interaction that is love. The stress on decisions is apparent in some views which hold love to be a completely "reflective" process (e.g., Stendhal's). (Consider the saddened youth convincing herself that she shall learn to love her husband-to-be (especially in societies in which marriages are arranged, e.g., in India).) Yet love pictured as a series of decisions is an incomplete picture of love. This is not to say that it is never a complete picture. But *that* love is an exception, and that it is should be explained.

For this, let us return to the role played by attitudes. One cannot force oneself to find a situation moving (usually). Note that a strong willed person may be able to do exactly this: and thus we hint at explaining the exception. But in most cases feeling sympathy is **not** a matter of deciding to feel sympathy. Having attitudes is not merely a matter of deciding to have attitudes.

It is in this sense that one does not control falling in love. And it is here that this metaphor is effective, although perhaps still somewhat misleading. One does not (usually) decide that one person will be found attractive, intriguing, appealing, and another unattractive or boring. One finds oneself attracted to someone more than to someone else. (It is important to note that one may decide just this. But this is an exception; it can be understood on this basis, however.) This factor in love (viz., of the non-active nature of finding some attractive, others not) is often overemphasized. The role played one is made to look like that of a completely passive agent. But that some "strike" one as attractive and others do not *should* be taken into account. And a picture of love as simply a process of decisions does *not* do this.

Love is not simply a matter of arriving at certain decisions. It is not always "arriving" at a decision at all. (Sometimes there is no time to arrive at a decision; one has to act before it is too late.)

Yet at the same time, an analysis of love that holds it to be antithetical to any thoughts is extremely misleading. For the having of attitudes is central to being in love, and in order to have certain attitudes (and to act on them), certain *realizations* are necessary: If one has no mind, has never thought, then he could not *realize*, for example, that his love was in a burning building. If a person couldn't think at all, he couldn't be in love. (Imbeciles do not fall in love.) Yet it doesn't take a mental giant to realize that a building is burning, that a girl is at a certain window, and that that girl is his loved one, although it might take good eyes. (Not all people in love are exceedingly bright.) Love is in this sense closer to feeling (i.e., having attitudes) than to knowing (i.e., realizing). (A genius does not, for being a genius, love better.)

It is often held that thinking and the emotions do not mix, that thinking destroys the emotion. (This is especially prominent in the writings of Gide.[7]) The person who thinks is viewed as calculating; the emotional person is often supposed to be, thereby, illogical.

But in love, the having of certain attitudes is central. If one were never affected either positively or adversely by the actions or conditions of another, would it make sense to say that the first loved (hated, cared at all about, etc.) the other?

The acting on the basis of these attitudes is also central. If Joe said, believing himself to be telling the truth, that he *wanted* to help Elaine when she needed his aid, *wanted* to ask her whether she felt better after a recent illness, yet *never* did *anything* to show that he did—except to *say* that he did—would it make sense to say that he loved her? So far he has given no sign of love at all.[8] Talking about loving someone is not (the same as) loving that someone; deciding to do certain things is not (the same as) doing them; saying that you are in love is not to be in love; thinking that you have certain attitudes is not having these attitudes; acting in a loving way is not acting *out of* love. (What is meant here is that one can be described as acting, in such a way that the first of each of these pairs is a correct description yet the second is not.)

Being in love is a matter of: *having* certain attitudes, *wanting* to do certain things, *doing* certain things out of love, *deciding* at times to act (or to refrain from acting) in a certain way, and, *acting* (or *refraining* from acting) on these decisions—as mentioned above, love of another is outer-directed.

Does it take a long time to fall in love? It is of course ridiculous to answer this by 'It takes three months to fall in love.', or 'One cannot be in love

---

[7] See especially A. Gide, *The Counterfeiters*.

[8] Having a certain feeling, claiming that certain attitudes are in fact held is, minimally, not all there is to love. Cf. the comment made by Helen in S. Delaney, *A Taste of Honey:* "Anybody can fall in love, do you know that? But what do you know about the rest of it?" (Act I, Scene 2, p. 41).

with someone unless he has been with that person for over a week.', or 'If you are with anyone for long enough, you have to end up loving that person.'. Each of these is a confused answer in that it has a confused concept of love as its basis. More exactly, a person in answering the above question with any of these answers seems to be making certain assumptions that are false about what it is to love. Falling in love is not falling at all. One does not fall in love at thirty-two feet per second per second. It is the obtaining of certain attitudes, desires, etc. How long does it take to obtain an attitude? (Does one ever ask 'How long does it take to step on a nail?'?) Instead of this question let us ask 'How long must you know someone before you have certain attitudes about that person?'. Sometimes you have an attitude about someone after knowing him only a few moments ('He's an immense bore!')

But how long, minimally, must you know another before you can love him? That depends partly on you. Some people are sensitive and are not overly inner-directed. They act for the benefit of others they consider to be their friends because they want to do so. They act unselfishly (or as psychologists might say, "outer-directedly"); they (sometimes) decide to do so.

Others are insensitive and self-centered. They take little interest in the activities of others. They notice little of others' needs. They will *never* have certain attitudes; they will *never* want to do certain things. These will never fall in love (although they might develop certain needs).

Some people are hypersensitive. Some of these are quite desirous of acting for others because they want friendship, love, etc. And some can fall in love overnight. (Some people are not stable.)

The length of time which passes from the meeting of another, to the holding of some attitudes about this person, having certain wants with regard to this other, etc. is sometimes a matter of hours; sometimes love never comes. In this sense, love is *not* a matter of habit.

We have given a general outline of love. (Can a fuzzy concept accurately be given a clear outline?) What of several of the above mentioned aberrant cases of "love", which we do not want simply to call love (love *tout court*)? As these have varied from the picture of what love is, so has our reluctance to call them love (love *tout court*) grown.

The Laforgue claim in "Coup de foudre", for example, is aberrant in that certain desires (attitudes, etc.), viz., to be with the beloved, to have love returned, etc. are completely absent. And for this reason we are reluctant to call this love, although "infatuation" is acceptable.

An aberration from the general outline of love in the case in which Charles continually beat Janet was called demented love. Charles *never* acted out of consideration for Janet. This consideration *is* part of love: if this case is to be love at all, *how* it is must be explained. (It seems that *this* case is not love at all.)

The other examples considered could be explicated in a similar manner, by noting certain variances between the case in question and our general picture.

In discussing individual cases, it would be necessary that one aspect of the picture play a more important role than in others: aberrations can take place in any of many ways. And that is because the phenomenon of love is not the monomorphic process[9] of one billiard ball hitting another. The picture of complexity must itself be complex in certain important respects.

This analysis has allowed us also to understand why various conceptualizations of love have been suggested. It has also shown why these are (partially) true and (partially) false: they overemphasize one aspect of love at the expense of another in an attempt to explain a complex phenomenon simply.

To draw such a simplified picture is to melt complexity into something that it is not.

Mitchell Ginsberg, Philosophy Department,[10] University of Michigan
From *Philosophy Reprints*, University of Michigan, Ann Arbor, 1964.[11]

FURTHER READINGS ON THE CONCEPT OF LOVE AND OF EMOTION
BEDFORD, Errol. "Emotions," *Aristotelian Society Proceedings*, vol. 57 (1956-57), pp. 281-304.

---

[9] Cf. "But of love I know only that mixture of desire, affection, and intelligence that binds me to this or that creature. That compound is not the same for another person." ("Don Juanism", *The Myth of Sisyphus*, p. 55, by A. Camus.)

[10] [NOTE, 2010] This essay was originally conceived of as part of a term paper for a graduate French course (Philosophy in French Literature). I was told that my analyses of the concept of love as presented in the French authors being studied (Gide, Camus, Sartre, and others) were welcome, but that I should not bother including my own positive views on the subject, given that there was no interest in them. Professor Alston, by way of contrast, was quite interested in these latter (but not especially in the former) as a term paper for his course in Philosophy of Mind, resulting in this paper: a serendipitous complementarity!

[11] [NOTE, 2010] *Cf. the poetic chapter on love (chap. 29), below, p. 273.*

Punctuation in this 1964 essay is more British than American, with a preciseness of punctuation then popular in Anglo-American analytic philosophy, as in P. Ziff, *Semantic Analysis*. Cf. above, p. 7. A key feature was the precise use of single and double quotation marks, in which punctuation marks (period, comma, etc.) are within the quotation only when being quoted. Compare this style in the next sentence, followed by the more usual (American) variation:

Let us consider the expression 'to fall in love'.

Let us consider the expression "to fall in love."

Some minor changes to the original essay (which was entitled "The Concept of Love") have been made here, including the correcting of typographical errors. Nothing has been added to, nor changed substantially from, the original paper.

CASANOVA, Giacomo (1725-1798). *Mémoires*. In 3 volumes. 1958-1960, Paris (Gallimard). Unabridged translation by Arthur MACHEN as *Memoirs*. 1959-1961, New York (Putnam).
EWING, Alfred Cyril. "The Justification of Emotions," *Aristot. Soc. Suppl. Volume* 31 (1957), pp. 59-74.
FREUD, Sigmund. "The Unconscious" (1915e) SE 14: 161/GW 10: 264/CP 4: 98.
GIDE, André. *La porte étroite*. 1917/1951, Paris (Mercure de France). Translated by Dorothy Bussy as *Strait is the Gate*. 1949, New York (A.A. Knopf).
HAWTHORNE, Charles. "Chance, Love, and Incompatibility," *Philosophical Review*, vol. 58 (1949), pp. 429-450.
HUME, David. *A Treatise of Human Nature* (1740). 1898, Oxford (Clarendon Press). [Especially II, 2, 1.]
KENNY, Anthony. *Action, Emotion, and Will*. 1963, London (Routledge & Kegan Paul) and New York (Humanities Press).
KIERKEGAARD, Søren. *Works of Love: Some Christian Reflections in the Form of Discourses*. Translated by Howard and Edna HONG. 1962, New York (Harper and Brothers, Publishers).
MACE, Cecil Alec. "Emotions and the Category of Passivity," *Aristot. Soc. Proceedings*, vol. 62 (1961-62), pp.135-142.
MANDLER, George. "Emotion," in *New Directions in Psychology*, pp. 269-343. 1962, New York (Holt, Rinehart & Winston). [Especially pp. 309, 315, 338.]
MCDOUGALL, William. "An Introduction to Social Psychology," pp.1290-1336, in Thorne SHIPLEY, editor, *Classics in Psychology*. 1961, New York (Philosophical Library). [Especially p.1313.]
MENNINGER, Karl, M.D. *Love Against Hate*. 1942, New York (Harcourt, Brace).
PETERS, Richard S. "Emotions and the Category of Passivity," *Aristot. Soc. Proceedings*, vol. 62 (1961-62), pp.117-134.
SARTRE, Jean-Paul. *L'être et le néant. Essai sur l'ontologie phénoménologique*. 1943, Paris (Gallimard). Translated by Hazel BARNES as *Being and Nothingness: An Essay on Phenomenological Ontology*. 1956, New York (Philosophical Library). [Especially "First Attitude Toward Others: Love, Language, Masochism," pp. 364-378.]
YOUNG, Paul Thomas. *Emotion in Man and Animal*. 1943, New York (J. Wiley & Sons). [Especially "Love-hate attitudes and the sexual appetite," pp. 372-382.]

ADDENDUM (2010): TO DEEPEN AND BROADEN THE TOPIC
This update is for those who would like to expand the frames of reference for considering this topic (cf. pp. 1-7) into new domains of understanding.

My own work in a purely philosophical perspective on, and interest in, the nature of mind led to my later involvement in the Soteria Project research into alternative treatments of schizophrenia with Loren Mosher, M.D. (Chief of Schizophrenia Studies at NIMH during some 16 years—although I met him earlier, when he was a ward chief in New Haven at the Connecticut Mental Health Center facility administered by the Psychiatry Department of Yale University's Medical School). Recently, I discovered a link between this and the earlier interest in the rationality of emotions this paper investigated: Luc Ciompi, a Swiss psychiatrist, in consultation with Loren Mosher, set up a Soteria-inspired project in Berne. Ciompi writes in *The Psyche and Schizophrenia* (1988),

> In my view, feeling and thinking, affect and logic, are interacting forces that together constitute the psyche and operate in conjunction; they *resonate* together. I became convinced that this perspective could lead to a new understanding of both normal and abnormal psychological phenomena. In particular I came increasingly to see the most important psychosis, schizophrenia, in a new light."[1]

So wrote Luc Ciompi of his impressions of the issues being considered here.

Now, when we look at this distinction between thought and emotions, between thinking and feeling, and question its ultimate validity, or search into its limits, one interesting application is in the field of psychopathology. There, various patterns of distress of the human are classified in various ways. One of the most central ways of classifying psychopathologies (extremes of torment put into a medical model) is in terms of a distinction between those of thinking versus those of the emotions.

To give two important examples, schizophrenia is considered to be a very clear example of a pathology of reasoning,[2] while bipolar disorder (earlier

---

[1] L. Ciompi, *The Psyche and Schizophrenia*, Preface, p. viii. This is the English translation of Ciompi's *Affektlogik. Über die Struktur der Psyche und ihre Entwinklung. Ein Beitrag zur Schizophrenieforschung* (1982; second ed., 1998). Ciompi's concept was rendered in Japanese as kanjō ronri 感情論理 (alternatively, 感情論理; cf. kanji section of Appendix), emotion-logic, as in his Special Lecture at the 93rd Annual Meeting of the Japanese Society of Psychiatry and Neurology (Tokyo, May 29-31, 1997), which was printed as "The Soteria Concept. Theoretical Bases and Practical 13-Year Experience with a Milieu-Therapeutic Approach of Acute Schizophrenia," *Psychiatria et Neurologia Japonica*, vol. 99 (1997), pp. 634-650; the phrase kanjō ronri 感情論理 is found on p. 634.

[2] In a way, I should be grateful for this conceptual confusion about "mental illnesses" in general and schizophrenia in particular (if that is what it is), because it led to a seminar (led by Loren Mosher) on Language and Thought in Schizophrenia (using as a starting point Vygotsky's *Language and Thought*), and I was invited to that because my next-door-neighbor in Yale faculty housing, Glenn Miller, M.D., at that time a psychiatry resident with Dr. Mosher, spoke of my be-

called being manic-depressive) is said to be a pathology of the emotions. If the distinction breaks down, schizophrenia might then be seen as having features of emotional problems, and manic-depression, features of thinking problems.

Synoptically speaking, we can see that that theoretical bias made it difficult for us to appreciate the emotional features of schizophrenic processes and the logical or rational or mental (thinking) features of manic-depressive ones. The distinction, that is, can make for a perspective that reflects a limited understanding, and when that is transcended, we may then draw the opposite—differently distorted—conclusion: here, that schizophrenia is an emotional problem, and manic-depression, a thinking problem. In any case, this describes my own distorting tendencies back in 1972-73, I can say, retrospectively.

In going beyond that bias, that is, we may at first have the opposite take on things, as here described. This is the way of our mind: categorizing by elimination (which puts a limit on our options). We have a general tendency, in other words, to perceive—or to understand—that which we take to be not-quite-A as being almost-A', where A' is the closest in our set of expected or recognized possibilities in the given context. For example, in language perception, when the English-trained ear hears the Japanese sound that is between the L and the R as different from either; for this reason when we hear this Japanese sound, we hear an L-like sound when we expect an R, and vice versa; for example, *lice* when we expect to hear "rice" or *rink* when we expect to hear "link" or even nonsense syllables, as in hearing *erephant* when we expect to hear "elephant."

Invitation to a journey into theorizing further: On the questioned distinction between reason and emotion, one essay to consider is "Is Schizophrenia an Affective Disease? The Hypothesis of Affect-Logic and Its Implications for Psychopathology" (by Luc Ciompi, 1998).[3] Further,[4] for Ciompi's views that go

---

ing a professor teaching the Philosophy of Language at Yale, which in turn got me invited to that seminar (that was 1967-1968). Ultimately that shifted my life work from theoretical philosophy to clinical psychotherapy. *Perhaps even confusions end up having benefits that only become obvious to us much later!*

[3]   In William F. Flack, Jr. and James D. Laird, eds., *Emotions in Psychopathology: Theory and Research*, 1998, pp. 283-297.

[4]   See H. Haken, *Synergetics: Introduction and Advanced Topics*, for synoptic overviews of synergetics and its wide applications: (i) Part I, Preface, p. v: "Synergetics deals with complex systems, i.e. systems that are composed of many individual parts that are able to spontaneously form spatial, temporal, or functional structures by means of self-organization." Plus (ii) "Some Historical Remarks and Outlook," p. 351: "The reader who has followed us through our book has been most probably amazed by the profound analogies between completely different systems when they pass through an instability. This instability is caused by a change of external parameters and leads eventually to a new macroscopic

beyond the thought-affect dichotomy in understanding human distress (which some describe as mental illness), see his work on non-linear fractal affect-logic (with mention of various of the theoretical background of this logic).[5]

For those who would like to read further here,[6] let me recommend some texts that present this background: the mathematics of Benoit Mandelbrot[7] on fractals (and chaos theory), the mathematics and physics of René Thom[8] on discontinuous bifurcations, the work of 1977 Nobel Laureate Ilya Prigogine and Isabelle Stengers[9] and others on the mathematical concept of discontinuous functions (from the calculus), known in this rather precise applied-mathematical sense as chaos theory or catastrophe theory, as well as what has recently been termed Complexity Science, and the understanding of processes that we might describe as polyholonic,[10] that is, intensely or multiply holonic (these terms based on the related word from the writings of Arthur Koestler, 'holon').[11]

*These are processes that have a number of **dimensions of scale** that make use of different conceptual schemes (sub-atomic and molecular physics,*

---

spatio-temporal pattern of the system.") Plus (iii) Part II, Introduction, p. 1: "Synergetics deals with systems composed of many systems, which may be of quite different natures, such as electrons, atoms, molecules, cells, neurons, mechanical elements, photons, organs, animals, or even humans. In this book we wish to study how the cooperation of these subsystems brings about spatial, temporal or functional structures on macroscopic scales."

[5] L. Ciompi, "Non-linear dynamics of complex systems: The chaos theoretical approach to schizophrenia," in H. Brenner, W. Böker, and R. Genner, eds., *Towards a Comprehensive Therapy of Schizophrenia*, pp. 18-31.

[6] This is to provide several pathways into the theorizing behind this perspective.

[7] B.B. Mandelbrot, *Les objets fractals: Forme, hasard et dimension* [*Form, Chance and Dimension*] (1975), *The Fractal Geometry of Nature* (1982), as well as his more recent *Fractals and Chaos* (2004).

[8] R. Thom, *Stabilité structurelle et morphogénèse: essai d'une théorie générale des modèles* (1972) [*Structural Stability and Morphogenesis: An Outline of a General Theory of Models*]; *Modèles mathématiques de la morphogenèse* (1974) [*Mathematical Models of Morphogenesis*]; *Parabole e catastrofi: intervista su matematica, scienza e filosofia* (1980) or *Paraboles et catastrophes: Entretiens sur les mathématiques, la science, et la philosophie* (1983) [*Parabolas and Catastrophes: Interviews on Mathematics, Science, and Philosophy*].

[9] I. Prigogine et al., *Chaos: The New Science* (1993); I. Prigogine and I. Stengers, *La nouvelle alliance: Métamorphose de la science* (1979), *Order out of Chaos: Man's New Dialogue with Nature* (1984).

[10] Cf. M. Ginsberg, *The Inner Palace*, Chap. XX (Polysociative Vision).

[11] See A. Koestler, *The Ghost in the Machine*, pp. 45-58. On his concept of the holon, see M. Ginsberg, *The Inner Palace*, esp. pp. 59, 299, 385-386, 504, 567.

chemistry, physiology, biology, geology, astronomy, etc.), which have subtle and perhaps not obvious interrelationships,[12] *or which influence one another in various immediate and delayed feedback loops that some people are just beginning to make sense of (steps toward a study of poly-scale processes).*[13] Thus, in contrast with the more traditional concept that nature is continuous, in Latin, natura saltum non facit, Nature does not makes leaps—let us insert here 'nonnunquam!' (sometimes!)—in considering nonlinearity, bifurcation, and chaos theory, discontinuity or nonlinearity is described in one text in these terms:

> In spite of the basic theoretical assumption of continuity in nature (natura saltum non facit),[14] the complex dynamics of self-organizing systems is able *to jump* from one to another stable state of order. These non-equilibrium phase transitions are caused by autocatalytic amplification of elementary fluctuations which enables the emergence of new macroscopic states of order in self-organizing systems. From a microscopic point of the view the systems are unpredictable. In phases of instability they are open to *minimal influences causing maximal behavioural effects.*[15]

As examples, consider small changes that lead to major shifts in mood, to an organism dying vs. barely surviving, to being almost vs. narrowly elected, etc.

This addendum (2010) has placed this chapter into a larger context of the past fifty-plus-years of theorizing composed of many fascinating branches, some of whose ramifications I discuss elsewhere in my writings.

---

[12] See M. Ginsberg, *The Inner Palace*, esp. the closing chapter, on the complementarity and interconnectedness of various theoretical understandings.

[13] E.g., mathematician David Rand, "Getting a Mathematical Hold on Life" (at www.epsrc.ac.uk), which ends with the inspiring overview, "A challenging aspect of this problem is the need *to span several scales*, to go from neurons to networks and interconnected regions of the brain and from there to the 'feedback loops' of the whole organism that connect the brain signal to the key energy-storing and energy-using organs and tissue of the body." *On integrating this poly-scale appreciation*, see extended discussion in Chap. XX (Polysociative Vision) in M. Ginsberg, *The Inner Palace*. Cf. below, p. 143, n. 74.

[14] The basic idea is that nature does not make leaps, that its transitions and transformations are always accomplished smoothly (in mathematical terms of the calculus, always exhibiting continuous functions).

[15] From an article by P. Kruse and M. Stadler (of Bremen), in a text ed. by H. Haken (of Stuttgart) and A.S. Mikhailov (of Berlin): "The Significance of Nonlinear Phenomena for the Investigation of Cognitive Systems," in H. Haken and A.S. Mikhailov, eds., *Interdisciplinary Approaches to Nonlinear Complex Systems*, pp. 138-160, at p. 138. Italics added.

2. Action and Communication & Schizophrenogenesis
Preliminary Remarks[1]

These preliminary remarks provide a broad context here. I include this paper (in its original form) for its remarks about processes of misunderstanding on a psychiatric ward at a respected facility (the first community mental health center in the USA), for its relevance to a systemic understanding of interactions, and for its discussion of the history of theorizing about schizophrenia. These are presented together, with examples intertwined with theoretical presentations.

Background on the journal and on this article

The international journal, *The Human Context*, founded by Paul A. Senft, earlier a student of Edmund Husserl at Prague's Charles University and subsequently a psychotherapist at London's Maudsley and University College Hospitals, had its debut issue in the Summer of 1968. (See Adrian Laing, *R.D. Laing: A Life*, 2nd edition, Sutton Publishing Ltd, 2006, p. 79.)

This essay was written in late summer and autumn, 1968, on invitation by Dr. Loren Mosher (thereafter Head of Center for Studies of Schizophrenia at NIMH for 16 years, and on the Editorial Staff of the London journal, *The Human Context*, from its initial to its final issues). His proposal was that I organize into a more formal structure my occasional comments to him about the (Yale University) Connecticut Mental Health Center ward where he was Ward Chief, and I was a volunteer aide. It was submitted for publication to the journal at that time. Gregory Bateson was mailed a copy and made some comments, criticisms, and suggestions, which were taken into account in the final version submitted.

The paper, not received in London, was apparently lost in the mails in transit there. I ultimately remailed that revised manuscript to the London offices of the journal in 1971. It was accepted at that time for review by Senft, and was published under the title "Action and Communication" in the Spring 1974 issue of the journal (volume VI, no. 1), pp. 81-102.

A little over a year later, Senft died from a protracted illness, on August 11, 1975. The journal's final number, its Autumn 1975 issue (volume VII, number 3), began (p. 365) with Senft's obituary, written by HJK (Hugh J. Klare, who had been on the journal's Advisory Board from its inception to its demise), below which was the announcement by the editors of the journal's termination.

This article followed the British conventions of spelling and punctuation; its notes were endnotes, not footnotes.

I have made corrections to typographical errors of the original text, reformulated one sentence for clarity's sake, and made a few paragraph reformatting changes, altering nothing substantial in any of these processes. The

---

[1] In this chapter, I italicize foreign words only as is done for English words.

original pagination is marked by page numbers inserted in bold font within square brackets before the given page's text. For example: [98], indicating the *beginning* of the page so numbered in the journal.

Some background considerations as introduction

The theorizing in this article is part of an understanding of the world, and of the human being, that we may describe as Western, meaning Euro-centric. In other words, that comes out of the worldview of the ancient Greeks and (later) Romans. There are roots to these as well, but the key point here is that this understanding takes as basic a contrast between reason and the emotions. At various times this has been described as mind versus heart, or between rational thinking and the passions (an old term for what is now referred to as the emotions), and so forth. This was discussed in the preceding chapter.

We can take this basic understanding (or grid, or framework, for trying to make sense of what we become aware of in our world) and apply it to the world of human experience and activity. We may do so, becoming interested in the various degrees of human dissatisfactions and worries, and focus in on some extremes of these features of human experience. With this perspective and focus, we see—or can see—these extremes of distress as functions of either how we are thinking ("the thinking mind") or how we are dealing emotionally ("the feeling heart") with the situation we are variously facing in our lives.

This has led to the perspective that looks at extremes of distress as "pathological" (or in less sophisticated terms, as "sick") as either pathologies (or, in a more specifically medical model of what pathology amounts to, as "diseases") of thinking or pathologies of feeling, in the sense of the term 'feeling' that is taken to be covering the emotions (mentioned in the preceding chapter).

This general structure has been used throughout the twentieth century. To give one example already presented, also in the preceding, we may consider the distinction between schizophrenia as a pathology of thinking versus manic-depression (also called bipolar disorder) as a pathology of the emotions.

Questioning this distinction rooted in the Graeco-roman worldview leads us in directions beyond the scope of the present focus, but will already allow us to appreciate features of the human condition that are obscured or not noticed because of the focus and filter created by the dichotomy being questioned here, between thinking and feeling, rational and emotional, mind and heart.

To take a step back, to get a more general perspective that we will then use to return to this postulated mind-heart duality, we can notice, in any case, an ongoing interest through the centuries, through the millennia, in fact, in recognizing, understanding, and helping those in stress and torment (in helping ourselves as a species, and as individuals, each in varying levels of contentment and clarity and loving caring about others, or in their lack). And that with each new scientific revolution, with each new scientific discovery, there is a natural tendency to want to understand these variations on human unhappiness in this new context. How much these discoveries or revolutions have actually helped is also a question that leads in directions beyond the scope of this focus.

As an example: when Newtonian theory was presented, with its articulation of such things as force and resolution of forces and the mutual attraction of physical bodies, there was an interest in seeing how to describe certain human phenomena (earlier termed "animal" or "vital" in rather precise senses, as an attempt to talk—to use cognates of these two terms here—of what makes humans act or be directed by the "anima," to be "animated," and to talk of what makes for human life, to have "vitality"). And when the invisible movement in the world was discovered that is understood now as electricity, for example, this interest took the precise form of talking of human electricity. If we take this in a literal sense, we may try to identify or measure electrical charge and the flow of electricity. *(Metaphoric descriptions are not always recognized as metaphoric.)*

In general, with new areas of discovery there were ongoing attempts to develop new vocabularies. When we look back at these from an outsider's point of view, perhaps at a distance of several generations or centuries, these earlier attempts may seem quaint, but it is important to realize the ways in which we may be misunderstanding what earlier theoreticians were attempting to say.

Another example: it was noticed that some people would be in an unusual state of mind (or state of consciousness) where they seemed not to be fully present (something we can notice in ourselves if we try to be aware of each moment of experience, as in awareness or mindfulness meditation practice), to be in a different or "altered" state of mind ("other" than what is the usual for the person judging), to be focused in a limited sense (as in our own "tunnel vision" at various times) and yet able to listen, hear, and speak.

We might describe such states of consciousness in current terms as trance states, or states of altered consciousness, perhaps with a more detailed description of how these are different from what is taken to be the "ordinary."

And here, if we shift in our thinking here in terms of what is ordinary or usual to what is normal, we are only one step from describing these altered states as abnormal. This would take us into theorizing about pathologies.

When there was an interest in coming up with a term that described this state, its similarity to sleepwalking was noted. *But this was* not *sleepwalking and was understood as* not *being sleepwalking, at the time!* We are not always appreciating this in our own reading back on this literature! It made total sense, for example, to speak of someone as being in this state of "somnambulism" (from the Latin roots for sleep + walking) who was sitting still, and might be conversing and later remembering (in a very waking-state way). *The point being that this somnambulism was realized as being distinct from sleeping.* In reading original texts, we can see that this realization is quite explicit (to the author).[2]

---

[2]   See, e.g., J.M. Charcot, *Leçons sur les maladies du système nerveux*, vol. III

Or, in terms of the model of machinery, with force, levers, and such, we had a further development in the description and thinking about the human activity. Much of the nineteenth century (in the Eurocentric context) involved thinking about human drives (as pushes and pulls in various ways). Even today, playful images of the "brain" at work still evoke interlocking gears and pulleys.

A further example: with brain anatomy developing, it became an interest to attempt to understand what our various extremes of distress (or these "diseases" or pathologies) were, with measurements of brain size, comparative studies on autopsy of the relative sizes of different parts of the brain, etc.

Again: with the chemistry to analyze substances, studies of the urine or blood samples of patients (we are now looking at the world of hospitalization of the distressed, to care for or "cure" such distressed people), discoveries were made that *have not stood the test of time.* The differences in urine chemistry that at one time were thought to be the basis of different "mental diseases" turned out to be a function of the diet in the hospitals. Some of the changes in the brain that are noticed and changes in other physiological characteristics of individuals have been determined to be a function of the treatment, including that of chemicals given to them (prescription drugs, not "street drugs").

And: even more recently, we see interest in genetics and the genome, as well as in neuroplasticity, neurobiology, and related transformational processes.

We might say that we look where our seemingly most sophisticated technical breakthroughs allow us to go, and where research grant money will be found. (We may be looking under the street lamp for the key we dropped by the unlighted front door, as the Sufi story about Nasruddin, the wise idiot, puts it.)

In a similar way: studies in the mid-twentieth century are perhaps of interest here, whatever the outcome of the currently popular interest in the genome, in the study of identical twins. Of course, identical twins (or monozygotic

---

(1887), p. 339, where it is explicitly stated that by somnambulique (the adjective related to the noun, somnambulisme) is meant only a state of cloudy consciousness, a mental torpor more or less pronounced (un état d'obnubilation, d'engourdissement mental plus ou moins accentué). Cf. pp. 450-451, where it is again clear that the topic is that of a mental state *and not anything concerning walking about.* Similarly, the French psychiatrist J.-J. Moreau de Tours, earlier wrote (1845) in a book dedicated to his late mentor Esquirol—himself the disciple of Pinel (both Moreau and François Leuret had worked under Esquirol at the Salpêtrière)—that although there was an analogy or resemblance between le délire (frenzy, or madness) and the state of dreaming, or reverie, and that, therefore, there was reason to speak of frenzy (le délire) as dreamlike, it was obvious that the two were not identical with one another. See J.-J. Moreau, *Du hachisch et de l'aliénation mentale. Etudes psychologiques,* pp. 357-360, cf. pp. 60, 95 (in translation, *Hashish and Mental Illness,* pp. 186-189, cf. pp. 32, 50).

twins, twins developing out of a single fertilized egg) have identical genetic structure from the very start of their separation from one egg. There was great interest, given that particular situation, in studying how one individual (with a given genetic or genome physical basis) has turned out to be so different from the twin in that one is hospitalized as schizophrenic and the other not. And so, these studies looked, of course, at what was going on other than the genetic story, because it was assumed that the genetic story was one and the same in the two cases. (This question of differences in monozygotic twins that cannot be accounted for simply in terms of genetic differences, there being none, is of course not limited to the issue of schizophrenia.)

This specific interest in monozygotic twins led to the work of such researchers as the group led by Ted Lidz, a psychiatrist at YPI (Yale Psychiatric Institute) in New Haven, some of whose papers came out in the late 1940s.

And then, in 1956, came the paper that is considered in this current reprinted essay (beginning below, at p. 34). The authors were Gregory Bateson, Don Jackson, John Weakland, and Jay Haley.[3] This paper of theirs proposed a conceptualization of schizophrenogenesis, of the genesis of schizophrenia. This term 'schizophrenogenic' itself (originally used in characterizing the life context that is typically present in the early years of individuals diagnosed as schizophrenic, and in particular to the characteristic personalities of the mothers of such individuals) is taken from the earlier work (1948) of the well-known psychiatrist and psychoanalyst Frieda Fromm-Reichmann,[4]. The work of Ted Lidz,

---

[3]   This was the ground-breaking essay "Toward a Theory of Schizophrenia," in *Behavioral Science*, vol. 1, no. 4 (Oct. 1956), pp. 251-264. In the theory of communication I offer in the following article, I make use of the concept of intentionality. This was further developed, *inter alia*, in a paper of mine, "How To Say It And Mean It," *Philosophical Studies*, 22: 43-48 (4/1971), which was cited in L. Danneberg and H.-H. Müller, ",Der intentionale Fehlschluß'—ein Dogma? Systematischer Forschungsbericht zur Kontroverse um eine intentionalistische Konzeption in den Textwissenschaft. Teil II," *Zeitschrift für allgemeine Wissenschaftstheorie*, vol. XIV, no. 2 (1983), at p. 394, note 264, and in its bibliography, p. 402. The note cites both this article of mine and one by Paul Ziff, who had been a professor of mine at the University of Pennsylvania in 1963-64, a welcome juxtapositioning. The note has a typo in the citation, referring to it in a standard-style abbreviated form as "Ginberg 1971" (misspelling 'Ginsberg').

[4]   F. Fromm-Reichmann, "Notes on the Development of Treatment of Schizophrenics by Psychoanalytic Psychotherapy," *Psychiatry*, vol. 11 (1948), pp. 263-273. Cf. F. Fromm-Reichmann, *Principles of Intensive Psychotherapy*, G.A. Hornstein, *To Redeem One Person Is to Redeem the World: The Life of Frieda Fromm-Reichmann*, and H. Green, *I Never Promised You A Rose Garden* (a recounting by Joanne Greenberg, using a penname, of her therapy with Frieda

mentioned just above, who had trained with Fromm-Reichmann and Harry Stack Sullivan, was an interesting and non-dogmatic questioning of and development from these earlier ideas.

On the relationship between some of the issues in this paper and the field of cybernetics—both so-called first-degree cybernetics and second-degree cybernetics—see the brief note added as an addendum (2009), below, at p. 59.

For some more of the historical context here, we may note that the name 'schizophrenia' goes back directly to the terminology (1906) of the Swiss psychiatrist, Paul Eugen Bleuler (1857-1939), who was renaming 'démence précose' (1860; Bénédict Augustin Morel, 1809-1873) and its Latinized version, *Dementia praecox* (1899; Emil Kraepelin, 1856-1926). Bleuler, incidentally, saw the phenomenon as neither a dementia nor always as a premature condition.

This idea that schizophrenia (whatever its name) is a disorder of the thinking process relied, in turn, on the Euro-centric distinction between rational and emotional (or "irrational") thinking that was mentioned above. The current understanding of this term is that it is equivalent to a split mind. The *"schizo"* part is from the Greek verb σχίζων skhízōn, to separate, divide, cut out, branch off, curdle or separate into curds and whey, etc. *But the "phren" or "phrenic" part is not from a word for mind!*

Given this, we may suspect a misunderstanding of the root meaning, if not of the actual sense in which the term was originally meant. (As with "somnambulism" above.) This part of the term is from the Greek noun φρήν phrén or φρενός phrenós, the midriff, the heart as seat of passions, fear, joy, grief, or courage, the mind as seat of faculties, perception, and thought, the will, purpose, said of persons in their senses, etc.[5] (We might note that the word 'frenzy' and the related 'frenetic' or 'phrenetic' all derive from this same Greek root, φρήν phrén.) With this rather rich, and in ways more specific, term, we might understand the attempt to point to the human situation that is called upon to deal with fear, joy, grief, courage, and a sense of purpose in life.

This literal understanding may suggest a more informative interpretation than simply thinking of the problem as a question of a split mind. If we look at the overall history of this notion, we may notice that this one term has very

---

Fromm-Reichmann, fictionalized as therapy with "Dr. Fried").
[5] Liddell and Scott, *Greek-English Lexicon*, pp. 1746a-b, 1954b, respectively. We may note that the Greek sense of a dissociating in the emotional life of the individual, was reduced and distorted when the term was interpreted to mean no more than split consciousness. E. Shorter writes (*A History of Psychiatry: From the Era of the Asylum to the Age of Prozac*, p. 108), "The term schizophrenia was probably an unfortunate choice, for subsequent generations of physicians and nonphysicians alike would associate it with some kind of splitting or divided consciousness." (Is it the term's fault that the concept was "dumbed down"?)

different definitions, making it harder to appreciate that one word is being used to express different concepts. When the term 'schizophrenia' is variously defined and used to cover a wide range of phenomena, we may have problems in keeping track of just what is being said about what.

There are questions from the philosophy of science to reflect on here in evaluating what counts as a well-constructed scientific theory. The various understandings of schizophrenia here may remind us of the requirement of well-defined concepts to avoid multiple definitions (avoiding homonyms, the principle that began Aristotle's *Categories*). And, where schizophrenia and other categories are defined as a smorgasbord of features, in the "four out of six from group A and five out of nine from group B" way of defining terms—as regularly proposed in recent decades of psychiatric diagnostics—the result is a motley set of characteristics ("psychopathological profiles"). This raises fundamental questions about the coherence and intelligibility of these categories that may be addressed in the light of the sophisticated presentations in Nelson Goodman, *Fact, Fiction, and Forecast* (1955), and in the literature this book has spawned. I leave further reflections on these questions for the philosophically-inclined reader.

Application on the ward: In the practical context of a psychiatric ward, there was an ideal followed by the psychiatric staff for the patients, and that was the preparing that person to return to the familial living situation that was present *before* hospitalization (distinct from the procedure of isolating the person from the family in a therapy context, *during* the hospitalization). I questioned this practice, suggesting independence from a noxious network, the family, as potentially beneficial *after* leaving the hospital setting for the development and health of the person in focus. The issue was not considered worth addressing.

It was only decades later, concerning this idea of helping the person arrange for a living situation independent from the family, taken by the staff there to be a rather novel and heterodox perspective, that I read a passage describing a very similar point of view, proposed by the man called the father of modern psychiatry, Philippe Pinel, 1745-1826, famous for taking off the chains of the insane in the Parisian insane asylum (asile des aliénés), the Salpêtrière, upon his becoming the director of that institution. This passage was in a work by French psychiatrist (and philosopher) Pierre Janet. Janet wrote, "It is necessary," he [Pinel] said, "to isolate the patient from his family, from his friends, to distance from him all those whose imprudent affection might bring on a condition of constant agitation or even aggravate the danger: in other words, it is necessary to change the moral atmosphere in which the insane must live."[6]

---

[6] P. Janet, *La médecine psychologique* (1923), Part I (Évolution des psychothérapies), Chap. III (Les thérapeutiques issues des pratiques religieuses), Sect. 1 (Les maisons d'isolement); p. 48; Fr. electronic edition, p. 30; 2005 Fr. reprint ed., p. 28; cmp. Eng. tr., *Principles of Psychotherapy* (1924), p. 49.

And more recently (relatively speaking)—although I was likewise not aware of it at the time of my writing this paper—the point had been researched and substantiated in England, and reported in a British journal. This was some five years before my approaching the issue. I became aware of this particular research many years later, in reading that article. *It should be noted that it was what we might call the stressful nature of the ties that was key, not simply living with relatives.* The study states in its résumé that overall the "proportion of patients who deteriorated amongst those living in lodgings and those living with relatives was similar."[7] And that there was "evidence that the risk of deterioration in clinical condition was increased when prolonged contact with close relatives in the house was unavoidable ... and *it was concluded that it might not always be best for the schizophrenic patient to return to the close emotional ties of affection or hostility often found in parental or marital homes.*"[8] And, further, that *"a significant tendency for more frequent readmission of patients who return to homes where there is a high emotional involvement with a key relative."*[9] All of this is perhaps not surprising with contemporary hindsight and a systemic vision of such things, despite the ward staff's resistance to this idea back then.[10]

Furthermore, to look at the issue of communication in a much broader, more general way, we may appreciate how difficult, indeed, is clear, non-confusing, non-manipulative, respectful, and skillful speech and communication.

In a novel by the Chinese author Xiaolu Guo about a young Chinese woman learning English in London, for example, at one point this central character feels so frustrated with trying to speak English that she shifts into writing the text in Chinese characters.[11] On the next page, the translation appears, culminating with, "Why is the process of communication so troubled and so painful?"

I was reminded of what an art communication is, and how it is not an innate human ability (like breathing or sneezing). It is rather like dancing a ballet, graceful when elegantly performed, but reflects years of fine-tuning the way one's body moves through space. Similarly, let me suggest, the art of speaking and of communicating with respect, articulateness, and skillfulness is a hard-won ability.[12] This chapter addresses only one dimension of this larger topic.

---

[7] G.W. Brown, Elizabeth M. Monck, G.M. Carstairs, and J.K. Wing, "Influence of Family Life on the Course of Schizophrenic Illness," *British Journal of Preventive and Social Medicine*, vol. 16 (1962), p. 66.

[8] G.W. Brown et al., idem (as in preceding note), p. 55. Italics added.

[9] A. Esterson, D. Cooper, and R.D. Laing, "Results of Family-oriented Therapy with Hospitalized Schizophrenics," *British Medical Journal*, vol. 2 (Dec. 18, 1965), p. 1465. Italics added.

[10] See esp. L. von Bertalanffy, *General System Theory.*

[11] X. Guo [郭小櫓], *A Concise Chinese-English Dictionary for Lovers*, p. 179.

[12] See M. Rosenberg, *Nonviolent Communication: A Language of Compassion.*

2. Action and Communication & Schizophrenogenesis*

The ideas in this paper are a product of concerns of mine related both to strictly theoretical issues and also to some problems which I noticed occurring between patients and staff in the summer of 1968, when I was a volunteer aide at the Connecticut Mental Health Center in New Haven, Connecticut. This paper evolved in my trying to understand better the miscommunication, the mistrust, the insensitivity, etc. present on the ward.

This paper concerns itself with one aspect of what psychiatrists and psychologists call meta-psychology and what philosophers call philosophy of mind or, perhaps more understandably, philosophical psychology. Since it is directed primarily to an audience of non-philosophers I will keep the strictly philosophical digressions and references to a minimum, although, of course, what I have to say is relevant to and a manifestation of certain recent (twentieth-century) developments in philosophical thought. (For those interested in more narrowly philosophical issues, see Ginsberg 1972, especially chapters 2 and 3.)

Directly below I sketch the classical formulation of the double bind hypothesis. Before directing my attention to that theory in detail, however, I present the outline of a much more general theory of communication in terms of which certain interesting kinds of interrelating can be understood (including but definitely not limited to the double bind variety). After this general theory is presented, I address the specific question of the double bind theory. After raising some questions about the adequacy of (meta-theoretic) descriptions *of the concepts* which the theory employs (suggesting that some of the descriptions *of the theory itself* are misleading), I propose an alternative way of understanding the theory in which it is viewed as addressing one particular instance which rests within the much wider range of phenomena to which my general theory is applicable.

1 *Sketch of the Double Bind Theory*
Bateson *et al.* ([1956], pp. 253f.) define a double bind situation as containing six elements:

(1 and 2) an ongoing pattern of communicating involving at least two people;

(3) a primary injunction containing a threat of punishment for non-obedience;
[82]

(4) a second injunction conflicting with the first *at a more abstract level*, also containing a threat of punishment for non-obedience;

(5) a third injunction prohibiting avoidance of the situation established by the placement of the other injunctions.

---

*NB: The title of this published journal article was "Action and Communication." The text here reproduces the original with its endnotes (not footnotes).

The sixth element need not be considered here. It seems to allow for formally incomplete situations which function as 'complete' double bind situations (that is those in which the first five elements have come about) for those who are the so-called victims.[1]

The authors explicate the notion of levels of abstractness (see element 4 above) in terms of Russell's theory of logical types. (This is presented by Russell in several works. See Whitehead and Russell [1962], especially Introduction, Chapter II, Sections B, *12 and C, *20, Russell [1966b], especially pp. 259-69, and Russell [1966a], especially p. 40.)

It seems that Bateson *et al.* (1956) have chosen Russell's theory of logical types for want of a better framework within which to describe the double bind situation. Perhaps the fit would suggest that an alternative ought to be sought. (There *are* alternatives available.) Rather than beginning a discussion about the relationship between Russell's theory of types and the double bind theory at this point by first presenting a sketch of the Russell's theory, I will postpone this until after my more general theory is introduced directly below. This is partly because use of my theory will, I believe, facilitate discussion of the double bind theory. (See Section 7 of this paper, entitled 'Closing Remarks on the Double Bind Theory'.)

2 Background Considerations

In the next few sections I will discuss certain aspects of the phenomenon of communication. With the help of certain concepts I introduce, I consider various kinds of what I call confusing communication. Having done this, I will return to a discussion of the double bind phenomenon. Calling upon certain technical concepts (to be introduced), I suggest a hopefully more adequate theoretical framework within which to discuss double bind situations as well as *other* problematic communication systems. The bulk of this paper is concerned with the presentation of such a theoretical framework.

Some take as a paradigm of communication one's uttering some sentence and thereby making some statement. This makes intelligible the emphasis on language when dealing with the question of communication. Correlatively we may note that there is a general lack of articulation of a framework in which other types of communication are characterized systematically.

As a result of this emphasis and this lack, there has been a collapsing together of the concepts of language and of communication. This is reflected in the views that linguistic (verbal) communication is identical with, rather than one type of, communication, and that communication, viewed as the uttering of declarative sentences, is the function of language. All of this overlooks a great deal.

In virtue of a person's having uttered a given utterance in a given context, an observer may correctly claim that that person has performed any number of acts. (In what follows, I intend to identify acts as behavior under a descrip-

tion.) Consequently, I will consider two different descriptions of the same behavior as designating two different acts.[2] For example, in virtue of the person's
having uttered 'hi' in a *certain* context, [83] an observer may correctly claim that
that person has performed each of the following acts: 1) uttered the word 'hi'; 2)
said hello; 3) greeted a passer-by; 4) shown recognition of a neighbor. These do
not, of course, provide us with an exhaustive list of the actions thereby performed by the person in question. They merely show that it is quite easy to do
many things at once.

There are several interesting implications of the facts that 1) in uttering
certain utterances one is performing certain actions, and 2) in virtue of one piece
of behavior one can be correctly described as performing any of a number of
acts. In this paper I will deal with only a few of these implications.

When someone observes any phenomenon taking place, and attempts to
understand what is happening, he does so by employing certain presuppositions
about how that phenomenon can be characterized.

Thus when we see two liquids poured together and then see little particles dropping to the bottom of the container, we conclude that a precipitate has
formed. In fact we assume that one of the data to be explained by a theory is the
fact that when liquid A is added to liquid B, a precipitate is formed. (It is taken
as an observable to be explained by a theory.)

It is extremely important to see, however, that this description is itself
embedded in a theory. That is, what is observed can be described in this way
only if the observer assumes that what is occurring is a chemical reaction, and
that what is occurring amounts to an example of certain processes hypothesized
as possible within a chemical theory. (An alternate description not making this
presupposition would be the following: pouring the clear refreshing drink in that
jug into the steaming one on the stove, we see some dirt that we hadn't noticed
before.) To describe what is observed in this way is to require the explanation to
employ a chemical theory if it is going to be acceptable. In this way the theory
with which we come to a given phenomenon structures what we can possibly
see.[3]

To rephrase this in another vocabulary, let me note that observing some
phenomenon will provide the observer with certain bits of information (at least)
some of which suggest that a certain theory is relevant to the explanation of the
phenomenon in question. The information which is gleaned from a given observation depends on the knowledge (or presuppositions) with which the observer
comes to the phenomenon. I will state this theoretical point more fully below.

If we apply this to the case of someone's performing a linguistic act, the
information which an observer will obtain by observing this person in this context will vary according to what suppositions the observer has concerning this
behavior (and concerning certain other theory-related facts). Note that insofar as
it is true not only of linguistic behavior but also of any behavior whatsoever that
the information content of that behavior for any observer depends on his theore-

tical presuppositions concerning that behavior, linguistic behavior is not different from non-linguistic behavior.

One kind of example of this theoretical point is that which occurs in interpersonal communication. For example, if, given presuppositions about an individual, that individual says (to refer to the above example) 'hi', then one can conclude, among other things, that that individual has noticed his neighbor walking down the street. In this case certain information concerning this individual has been gotten from the supposition that he has performed the act of saying hello. (This information is, of course, other [84] than that identical to and/or deducible from the supposition itself.) One way of viewing this gleaning of information is as part of the process of theory construction by someone in an effort to understand these actions of this individual (to have a theory in which these actions are explicable).

This may be stated in the following generalized form: one can come to certain information about an individual on the basis of certain background information and the observing of certain behavior which could not have been arrived at on the basis of the background information alone.

In what follows I would like to focus attention on the particular case in which one is more interested in what a person communicates about himself, about those addressed, and about the community they form by performing certain verbal acts than in the literal content of what is uttered in those acts. (More interested, for example, in the fact that Jane wants to appear sophisticated by her performing the act of criticizing her twin sister's supposedly 'childish' behavior than in the literal content of her utterance 'Joan is such a child'.)[4]

If we seriously consider what I have suggested above about the possibility of deriving information about the person in question by having noticed that he had performed certain verbal and/or non-verbal acts, it is possible to view everything that one does—all acts both verbal and non-verbal, conscious and unconscious, intentional and non-intentional, etc.—as communications about oneself. Thus the typical politician is telling us what a hypocrite he is, and the youth in the protest march is telling us what a concerned citizen he is. Other examples could easily be imagined. I might mention explicitly here, however, that I do not see action as *merely* communication. There is still the action even if no communication at all is involved, and even more so even if no successful communication is involved. In this sense, nothing is totally exhibitionistic.

What we should be looking for at the present time is a conceptual grid (a set of systematically interrelated concepts) according to which we might be able to categorize all sorts of communications in an interesting, theoretically heuristic, etc. way.

As mentioned above, a long-stressed distinction is that between verbal and non-verbal communication. This use of this distinction as central to an understanding of the phenomenon of communication has not tended to allow for an appreciation of all that these two modes of communication have in common.

Through both one comes to have certain bits of behavior to be explained. And this brings about the theoretical description of certain characteristics to the person involved (the one who has attempted to communicate), such as desires, beliefs, certain emotions (for example jealousy, pride, love), certain character traits (for example being proud, reserved, brave, considerate), etc.

This phenomenon of one's constructing a personal image or concept (a set of beliefs which state that someone is a given kind of person) amounts to a complex process of theory construction that would allow for a comprehensive explanation and/or understanding of the person whose behavior, verbal and non-verbal, is to be explained.

Another distinction usually called upon in discussing communication is that between kinds of subject matter. It seems initially plausible to expect that such distinctions could be based on a grammatical consideration of the sentences uttered in the communication in question (even admitting that this basis is relevant only to verbal communication).

If, however, we direct our attention to the information that is being [85] communicated, such a program loses appeal. For example, the fact that one can say that a bunch of flowers is *simply* lovely (with a certain intonation contour) and thereby tell the listener or observer that the speaker is very annoyed about something, suggests that the (major or 'real') topic of communication and the topic of the sentence uttered in that bit of communication may be quite different.[5]

3 *Introduction of Some Theoretical Concepts*
We can now turn to the problem of presenting a conceptual grid for structuring (verbal and non-verbal) communication.

Perhaps the basic concept in terms of which we can define other notions that we will use is that of information itself. Unfortunately the technical notion of information used in information theory does not seem to be adequate for our purposes here. In any case, I will not rely on that notion in what follows.

I intend to use the word 'information' as it is ordinarily used in English. It seems that what we need is *not* a new concept of information, but, rather, a framework that is more structured than that of which this concept of information is now a part.

Let us take a unit of information to be a 'point' of information (a 'point' and not a 'bit' because the word 'bit' has already been transformed into a term with a technical information-theory meaning). Provisionally we can identify a point of information in terms of the statements by which it is expressed. We can say, then, that two points of information are actually the same point if the statements of these two are identical. (We might be requested to give an analysis of statements, but one must stop somewhere. Such an analysis, not given here, may be found in Ginsberg [1970]. Hopefully stopping here will not raise any problems.)

A message is any point of information considered to be that which is or can be communicated by some actions, verbal or non-verbal.

To explicate the notion of communicating some message by an action, we should recall what was said about presuppositions. We suggested there that there is a rather specific relation between what presuppositions one makes about a given phenomenon and what information can be derived given that that phenomenon has occurred. In that example we pointed out that certain descriptions of a phenomenon can only be made by presupposing that a certain theoretical framework is relevant to the understanding of that phenomenon.

Given, however, that one assumes that some theoretical framework *is* thus relevant, that phenomenon can be described in terms of that framework. We are thus provided with a point of information, namely that the phenomenon in question, described in terms of certain concepts belonging to the given framework, has occurred. If one has presupposed certain other points of information (what we take to be background information), one can now come to new information on the basis of accepting the above-mentioned description of the phenomenon observed. Interestingly, the new information is not limited to the one point of information that that phenomenon (as described) has occurred. To make this clearer let us consider an example.

If we assume as background information that one of two liquids before us is a water solution of silver nitrate and that the other liquid is a water solution of sodium chloride, then, upon seeing these two liquids mixed together, the phenomenon which we describe [86] as the forming of a precipitate will provide us not only with the additional information that a precipitate has been formed, but also with the information that the first liquid contained silver ions in considerable concentration. (If we have certain other information about the context in which we have come to perform this little experiment, we might also conclude that the person who gave us the liquids was kind in making our task of chemical analysis so simple.)

More generally, if we refer to our background assumptions as B (which is defined as *not* containing P), and to the statement that the phenomenon under the given description has occurred as P, then there is a set of statements S which are derivable assuming B and P, but not so assuming only B.[6]

We can now apply this general formulation to the specific phenomenon of human behavior. Parallel to the above, let us take P to be the statement that the behavior in question, referred to under some description (and hence seen as some specific action), has occurred. Let us also take B to be our background assumptions, and S to be the corresponding set of derivable statements. Then, assuming these abbreviations, we can define the notion of being a message of some verbal or non-verbal action as follows: a message M is a message of some action if and only if M is a member of the set S.

For example: B includes certain theoretical statements about human behavior, such as the fact that there is a general reluctance to leave oneself defenseless ('open'), etc., and also the fact that Mr R. talks very little, if at all, in crowds. Then his explicitly requesting help in moments of uncontrollable silence - a bit of behavior now considered under this description - has as one of its messages the message that Mr R. has made an uncommon and uncommonly open request. We *might* also be inclined to hold that Mr R. is thereby conveying the message that he feels incapable of solving certain personal problems without the help of others.[7]

It is within this framework that we will discuss certain bits of both verbal and non-verbal communication. Before we get into that, however, it might be convenient to have a categorization of messages available for our use. How many different kinds (categories) of messages, then, are there? Either one or more, up to an infinity of kinds, depending on how many messages are to be grouped together.

Although some seem to hold that a certain system of categorization is 'normal', reasonable, a manifestation of the power of abstract thinking, etc., and that other ways lack these characteristics, the categorization chosen seems to be completely arbitrary except for the non-trivial consideration of its function, of what kinds of structuring and understanding of various phenomena are desired. What I want to propose here is a small set of categories of information and, cor-relatively, of messages, which may be augmented or replaced by other sets when other phenomena are being discussed.

What kinds of messages are there? I will give several kinds of *information* below. These will provide a list of kinds of *messages*. (See the definition of a message above.)

A 'subject point' is information about the explicit subject matter. What the subject matter is is determined by syntactic criteria. It seems, then, that this kind of information can be conveyed only by verbal behavior. (I will modify this below.) If one says, 'The sun is shining', the subject *matter* is the sun, and the subject *point* is that the sun is shining. We might say that the subject point is the verbal message (the statement itself) considered literally. This latter approach would circumvent problems arising [87] out of more complicated syntactic struc-tures (where it is not so obvious what the subject matter is). For more on deter-mining what the subject matter (elsewhere termed 'topic') is, see Ginsberg (1971).

One complication here is that there seem to be certain non-verbal equiv-alents of some verbal behavior. A simple example is a nod, which is (in some Western cultures) equivalent to a yes (to the utterance 'yes'). Similarly a raising of the eyebrows is equivalent (in a Turkish setting) to a no. A groan might conceivably be equivalent to 'I'm in pain', and still less simple to 'translate' are any of a number of facial expressions, such as grimacing (equivalent to 'that's horrible!' ?), winking (at times equivalent to 'Do you understand that I'm jok-ing?'?, at times to 'I like you', at times to something else?), glaring, gloating, smirking, smiling, glowing, etc. I will not dwell on this problem in length; I merely want to mention it. (I do not explicitly know how to determine *which* verbal act a given token [instance of some *kind*] of non-verbal behavior is equivalent to.) What is clear is that there will not be a unique 'equivalent' for all such tokens of any one kind.

A 'non-subject point' is any information other than a subject point. Often the 'real' message is held to be of this sort, and non-subject points are usually overlooked by those intensely interested in literalness. The difficulties involved in determining which non-subject points are the real messages of some behavior sometimes lead people to a love of literalness. It may be added that the usual importance of non-subject points has, conversely, led some (*some* psychiatrists, for example) systematically to overlook subject points. *This practice is rather questionable.*

The four categories that follow cut across the above two. That is to say, a given message-token (an instance of some message-kind) may be in one of the above categories and also in any of the categories that follow.

A 'self point' is information about the 'message-sender' himself. That is, it is information about him whose communicating behavior is in consideration. If (in *some* context) John is laughing, then a self point thereby communicated is that John is happy.

A 'you point' is information about the person or people to whom the communication is overtly addressed. Jill's glance in Al's direction may contain the you point that Al has just made a clever comment. (This of course depends on a great deal, such as the nature of the glance.)

An 'other point' is information about some person or people, other than either the message-sender himself or the person or people overtly addressed. To take the example of Jill's glance, an other point might be that Jill is annoyed with Tom. (By lauding Al she is showing [communicating] her annoyance with Tom.)

A 'meta point' is information about some message. If Sam is challenged to express how he feels about Art, and he replies, 'I *hate* Art. So there!', the 'So there!' communicates at least two meta points (two points of information about his saying 'I hate Art'), namely, that in saying this he *has* expressed how he feels and *has* met the challenge.

(These meta points tell how his *saying* 'I hate Art' is to be categorized.) Generally speaking, other meta points might be, for example, that a given message was intentional, was the main or 'real' message of a bit of behavior, etc.

Let me at this point merely provide a suggested addition to the preceding six categories. As sub-categories of the third through sixth categories we might have: [88]

1) a 'want point': information about what the person or people in question desire,

2) a 'belief point': information about what the person or people in question believe or think to be the case,

3) an 'emotion point': information about which emotion(s) the person or people in question have,

4) an 'emotional-state point': information about which emotional state(s) the person(s) in question is in,

5) a 'personality point': information about which personality or character traits the person(s) in question has,

6) an 'attitude point': information about which attitude(s) the person(s) in question has.

(These sub-categories are, of course, not exhaustive as they stand.)

The preceding six major categories do not pretend to be complete. First, the last four do not allow for any explicit categorization of information other than that about people or about some message. In this way, this set of major categories emphasizes (over-emphasizes?) certain messages while de-emphasizing other messages.

In addition, it provides only extremely large categories. It thus overlooks the fact that in each category are many different types of message which one might distinguish between by use of a large set of sub-categories. But hopefully this will not prove a problem in what follows. If need be, more categories *can* be added later, according to one's interests and needs. (The preceding list of sub-categories may be seen as one such small supplementation.)

4 *Problems in Communication*

Interpreting communication: a major problem in communication is to determine what the messages of a given bit of behavior are. Most attention seems to have been paid to verbal behavior, and much less to non-verbal behavior, where the connection between behavior and communicated message is so complex as to appear at times to be tenuous. I do not think that this problem is insurmountable,[8] but let me state explicitly that what the preceding (especially Section 3) has done is to introduce this phenomenon and to provide a provisionary framework within which to discuss it. It does not provide anything like a decision procedure by which to overcome this or other similar problems that are present.

The determination of what the messages of a given bit of behavior are seems to be part of what can be seen as (usually informal) theory construction. What one attempts to do is generate a theory by which to explain and understand a given person's behavior, states, etc.

We can take as a most general formulation of the basic problem to be discussed in this section the claim that it is possible to misinterpret what the messages of a given bit of behavior are. (It might be interesting to contrast what is said below about possible problems in this theory construction with the theoretical import of Sullivan's concept of participant observation. See Sullivan [1953], pp. 14, 367-68, and especially 379-80.)

It might at first seem then that the next step in distinguishing types of this possibility depends on which classification of messages we take to be most

important. What I want to say below, however, is independent of such choices.
[89]

One important aspect of the general problem introduced above is that of the possibility of the failure of (what seems to be) one language to serve successfully in inter-personal communication. This is sometimes introduced in a simplified way by the question of whether someone (really) means what some other individual (really) means by a given term, such as a color word.

One manifestation of this aspect is the philosophic interest in 'private' languages, which are essentially languages that can be understood by only one individual. Such writers as Carnap (1966), Wittgenstein (1963) and Rhees (1954) have individually attempted to resolve this aspect of the general problem in parts of their writing.

Another formulation of this aspect is that it is possible for others to misinterpret what one is saying or doing. If we take advantage of the conceptual grid introduced above, we can say that it is possible for others to think that someone's verbal or non-verbal behavior communicates a given set of messages that in fact it does not. Stated slightly differently *by making reality testing explicitly relative to given individuals*, it is possible that certain people may think that someone's behavior contains (communicates) a given set of messages which some given person (for example [*not* 'that is'] the message-sender himself) or persons think that it does *not* contain.

To see this let us consider a case. Bob wants to say to others that Miss Jones does not appreciate the complexity of some phenomenon. On the other hand he does not want others to take this communication to be a comment about himself, e.g. that he is condescending. He wants, that is, to communicate the subject point that Miss Jones does not appreciate the complexity of some phenomenon, but does not want to communicate *any* self point, including the self point that he is condescending. If he seriously considers the possibility of others focusing their attention on which self points he might thereby be communicating, he may feel that it is simply impossible to achieve his goal. He may feel that language makes this goal unattainable. Consider the following reasoning in support of this conclusion. If he simply says what he wants to say, how is he to ensure the listeners' *not* taking his communication to be in part, or even primarily, communication about himself, that is communication of certain self points? On the other hand if he attempts to make sure that this is not how others interpret his behavior, by saying (conveying the meta point) that the communication is *not* to be taken to be communication of self points, there is no reason for him to feel secure that others will not take it to be just that. His conveying this meta point, after all, shows that he *has* thought about the communication (at least possibly) conveying certain specific self points. In either case it is possible if not likely that a misinterpretation of the intended communication will occur.

A more theoretical consideration to make this same kind of point as suggested in the above case is the following. One might say that it is always possible to misinterpret a given bit of behavior, whether verbal or non-verbal, but that this possibility can always be eliminated by the communication of certain meta points. This, of course, presupposes the possibility of correct interpretation of these meta points. This may suggest the additional necessity of meta points to ensure the correct interpretation of meta points etc., ad infinitum. If one is skeptical about successful communication, this step, or even an indefinitely long series of such steps, will not necessarily move him from his skepticism.

This point can be made in the following way. One function of the communication [90] of meta points is to eliminate certain interpretations of given bits of behavior and to ensure that a desired interpretation is generally accepted. The assumption that this is likely to bring about the elimination of misinterpretation is based on the presupposition that differences in interpretation will become manifested in noticeable differences in some communicated meta bit. It is possible, however, that all questions about the interpretation of given behavior will concern only those aspects in which two distinctly different interpretations agree. We might compare this to two distinct theories that agree about what observable data ought to be manifest wherever the two are compared, but which nonetheless contain basic yet never compared (never realized) differences.

These lines of reasoning suggest the live possibility of miscommunication of the sort described. (This possibility is taken most seriously, some suggest cavalierly, by certain 'schizophrenics'.)

5 Misleading Communication

Another issue that I want to introduce in some detail here is that of misleading communication. This is communication that *can* be structured by theory construction. That is, it is a type of communication that can be explained and understood; one can construct a theory in terms of which the communicating behavior can be explained. But this communication differs from (other intelligible yet) *non*-misleading communication in virtue of the fact that the theory thus developed is inadequate for the basic reason that it contains false statements. (It is a 'false' theory; it cannot stand up to adequate reality testing.) Of course a certain message may be what is communicated in misleading communication without its being an *intentionally* misleading message (although some, such as the following example, *are* intentionally misleading) or an intentional message, misleading or otherwise.

As an example of misleading communication, consider the following. A student wants to impress others, including the teacher, with his knowledge and understanding of the subject matter. When the teacher asks a question of the class, the student raises his hand, thereby hoping to impress the others. But he is nonetheless certain that he has no answer to offer. Insofar as his hand-raising is his communication of the messages that (1) he has an answer, (2) he wants the teacher to call on him, and (3) he wants to answer and thereby show others that he has a knowledge and an understanding of the subject matter, he is communicating misleadingly. That is, these points of communication are examples of misleading communication. Since this misleading is intentional, the student is being dishonest. In fact there is good reason to take this communication to be a case of lying. It seems that the only reason that it would *not* be one is that lying is an intentional attempt to communicate misleadingly by *verbal* behavior. And this reflects a point of view that holds the difference between verbal and non-verbal behavior to be extremely basic. The rejection of such a view might eventually lead to a modification of the concept of lying to that of an intentional attempt to communicate misleadingly by any (either verbal or *non*-verbal) behavior.

6 *Confusing Communication*

Confusing communication is a type of communication in which it is impossible to [91] determine which messages are being sent. This type of communication is confusing in virtue of the fact that it cannot be explained and understood. One cannot, that is, construct a theory in terms of which the communicating behavior can be explained.

In this way confusing communication can be seen as being the complementary communication of intelligible communication, one type of which is misleading communication.

It should be obvious, here as elsewhere (*everywhere*), that the objective formulation ('one can', 'one cannot', 'it is the case that. . .', etc.) can be seen as an abstraction from an implicit sub-society or group of people. When all of the given group have the same opinion, no problem arises by substituting a statement in the objective formulation for a large set of individual opinions (of each member of the group). *It should be kept in mind, however*, that when individuals or groups of individuals with different views are to be taken into consideration, complications arise.

In this case, whether or not it is advisable to make explicit which group of individuals finds a given bit of communication intelligible or confusing depends on several factors, including that of whether confusion will be thereby eliminated. This will be made clearer by what follows. Let us say here simply that making the notions of confusing and intelligible communication relative to (or realizing that they *are* implicitly *relative* to) a community of 'like-minded' individuals can clarify certain phenomena.

Communication can be confusing for any number of reasons. For the purposes of this paper I would like to distinguish between two types of confusing communication. The first of the two is, to speak roughly (but see the next paragraph), due to inadequate information, for example insufficient background information. We can call this confusing communication due to isolation, or isolatedly confusing communication. The other is, again speaking roughly, due to incompatible evidence. We can call this type of communication incompatibly confusing communication.

In this first type (that is, isolatedly confusing communication), the background information and the behavior are such that no message can be determined. This may be due to either/both insufficient background information of the individual or group of people in question, or/also the 'meaninglessness' of the behavior. In general the responsibility for the confusion will be held to be a function of where there is a difference (in ways to be made explicit below) from some implicit group of people. One example of such an implicit group is the 'scientific' community. Another interesting one is that of a given family, the 'private' messages of which can be understood only by other members of the family (unless one is aided by a 'translation' by such a member).

The reason that will be given to explain the fact that a given communication is confusing will depend on where certain idiosyncrasies, relative to this implicit group, appear. Let us assume, for example, that the given bit of communicating behavior in question is that of John's digging his nails into his arm and that one of the intended messages is that John hates his nurse's attitude towards him. If Bill has only a general knowledge of psychological phenomena and knows nothing of John's situation, then Bill will see John's communicating (in part, of the fact that he hates his nurse's attitude towards him) as confusing. If the implicit group is that, say, of a scientific community unfamiliar with John, then this confusion may well be held to be due to John's manner of communicating. Note that responsibility for such confusion can be ascribed to [92] John by claiming that John is using a private, idiosyncratic system or 'language' to communicate his feelings.

Whether or not one will accept the claim that this is in fact a private, idiosyncratic communication system ('language') depends in part, it seems, on whether John is capable of giving a 'translation function' according to which one can translate into a generally intelligible (*to the implicit group in question*) mode of communication. The giving of such a translation function can serve both to make the message of the idiosyncratic communication system intelligible and also to show that the message-sender is not confused. (The function can make obvious the method in the message.)

On the other hand, if the implicit group is that of, say, sensitive or 'aware' people, extremely well acquainted with John and his situation, then this confusion may be held to be due to Bill's lack of adequate background information (which includes, quite centrally, John's understanding of what's happening). Here Bill may be held to be ignorant of what John is 'all about', to lack empathy, to be unaware of the situation, etc.

Let us now turn to the second type, to incompatibly confusing communication. Since in this type there is evidence that is conflicting (or which is *held* to be conflicting by the implicit group of people), we might best discuss this after introducing the notion of a system of communication.

A system of communication is a set of instances of communication. (The following will be what I have called the 'objective formulation': see the beginning paragraphs of this Section 6, above.) What happens in this second type is that one received (some of) the messages of a system of communication. This received set is such that certain of the messages must be rejected if a consistent theory or understanding of the system is to obtain. Or, requiring a theory to be consistent (holding that an inconsistent theory is no] some of the system's messages are not taken into consideration (rationality through blocking?).

As a sketch of an example, consider the following conversation:

A: (C1) 'You're not sarcastic, are you?' (C2) 'I'm glad.' (C3) 'I couldn't take someone like me.'

B: (C4) 'Why?' (C5) 'Are you sarcastic?'

A:(C6) 'No.'

If we consider A's comments here as a system of communication, then under one interpretation, one of the messages of that system is that A is sarcastic (cf. the utterances labelled C1 through C3). Another is that A is *not* sarcastic (cf. that labelled C6).

If this is how we interpret A's system of communication, we will see this as A's sending out confusing communications. In order to reject this interpretation, we must postulate somehow that these messages are not in fact those communicated by A's system. We might say, for example, that A is a foreigner and doesn't speak English well, or that A is absent-minded and misunderstands B's question (C5). In either of these two, we might alter the status of, say, C6, by saying, for example, that A's answer expresses that A is sarcastic. (We might have background information that gives us good reason to believe that A confuses the English words 'yes' and 'no'.) [93]

It is important to realize that whether the messages of a given system of communication will be held to be inconsistent, and the system therefore an example of incompatibly confusing communication, depends in part on certain theoretical assumptions that are generally part of the background information (although sometimes part of the messages of the system). These theoretical ('possibility') assumptions are those concerning which states of affairs are possible. In the above example it was implicitly assumed that an individual could not both have a personality trait or communication style here (namely that of being sarcastic) and not have that same trait or communication style.

As we can make explicit the individual or group of individuals in terms of which a given system is held to be confusing, we might also make explicit the (theoretical) possibility assumptions in virtue of which the given system is held to be confusing. Thus we might get an individual to hold a system to be *non*-confusing by first altering his possibility assumptions.

An example will clarify this.

Consider the following exchange of communication between a mother (M) and her child (C):

M: (C1) Smiles tenderly at C.

C: (C2) Walks over to M. (C3) Kisses M's cheek.

M: (C4) Pushes C away while (C5) saying to C, 'Leave me alone! Can't you see Mommy's busy?'

C may interpret M's system as communicating, among others, the following messages. First of all, that M loves C (Cl). Secondly, that M is rejecting C (C4), and, thirdly, that M hates C (C4 and C5). This might be rather difficult for C to understand, and he might conclude that he has misinterpreted something. (Drawing such a conclusion is of course one course of action to take when faced with what one takes to be incompatibly confusing communication.)

If we make explicit the possibility assumptions operant in C's concluding tentatively that M's system is incompatibly confusing communication, most central may well be the assumptions (1) than an individual could not have both a certain emotion towards a given individual and also the 'opposite' emotion towards that same individual (at the same time), and (2) that love and hate are opposite emotions. Note that by rejecting (1) and replacing it by the assumption that one *could* have both of two 'opposite' emotions towards a given individual at a given time, that is, that ambivalence is possible, we could make M's system *quite* understandable. Correlatively, by getting C to make this replacement of theoretical possibility assumptions (to 'see' the possibility of ambivalence), we might reorient him, that is have him understand otherwise unintelligible behavior (an otherwise confusing system of communication).

A special case of the phenomenon of incompatibly confusing communication is when one of the messages of the confusing system is a possibility message. This message may be such that it allows one to determine which of the messages of this system is to be rejected (if an understanding of the system is to obtain). Or it may simply be such that it ensures that the system will have to be interpreted as exemplifying incompatibly confusing communication. An example of the communicating of a possibility message would be a mother's answering a hesitating 'Doesn't Mommy love me any more?' with the following: 'Of course Mommy loves you.' At this point the child interrupts with 'Do you?' and the mother continues: 'Shouldn't she know whether she loves you [94] or not?': This mother's answer communicates, *inter alia*, the possibility assumption point that it is not possible for one not to have a certain emotion (not love) yet think that he *does* have that emotion. Fortunately for most and perhaps unfortunately for some is the fact that such possibility points may be rejected. One *can*, that is, assume in a given context that a person is conveying a given false (!) possibility point.

7 Closing Remarks on the Double Bind Theory

It is now appropriate to apply the preceding theory of communication to the particular phenomenon of the double bind situation (see Section 1).

After discussing the application of Russell's theory of types to the double bind theory, I hope to show that putative examples of the double bind situation can individually be formulated as instances of one or another kind of what we have called incompatibly confusing communication, although not always of the same kind. Hopefully this will allow for a theoretical formulation (using my theory) of certain phenomena not describable within the theoretical apparatus introduced by discussions about the double bind. Let us first look at Russell's theory of types and then at the adequacy of the application of this theory to the double bind theory.

Very sketchily, the concept of logical types was introduced by Russell in order (among other things) to resolve certain logical paradoxes.[10] It is perhaps a manifestation of the fecundity and wide applicability of the theory of types that there are several distinct ways in which it has been formulated. Thus one can read of types of entities (e.g. Russell [1966a] especially p. 40), types of prepositional functions (e.g. Whitehead and Russell [1962], Introduction, Chapter II, especially p. 51 of Section V, and Reichenbach [1963], especially p. 38), types of classes (e.g. this last Reichenbach citation, Russell [1966b], especially p. 264, and Whitehead and Russell [1962], especially p. 81), types of concepts (e.g. Carnap [1966], especially p. 140), and types of propositions (e.g. Russell [1966b], especially pp. 263f., and Whitehead and Russell [1962], especially p. 51).

Since it is inappropriate here to attempt a unified reconstruction of all of the formulations of the theory of types, the choice of which formulation to consider will be made on the basis of the context of discussion in which it is to appear. Were we mostly interested in those formulations which would allow for an obvious exposition of the role of the theory of types in the solution or dissolution of certain antinomies, we might consider the references immediately above to the formulations in terms of types of prepositional functions and of classes.

That formulation, however, which seems to allow best for a discussion of the theory's application to the double bind theory is that in Russell (1966b). As the theory appears there, it is part of a program suggesting the reformulation of certain statements or propositions. The kind of reformulation proposed is that which will supposedly allow for the replacement of misleading ways of formulating statements by non-misleading ways.

According to the theory, these replacements provide an accurate representation or mirroring of the universe, and it is precisely in virtue of such an accurate mirroring that these replacements are held to be non-misleading. (What such a mirroring amounts to is not a problem I will consider here, since to do so would take us too far afield.)

Several kinds of reformulation are suggested. Russell's position is that each of these [95] reformulations has as a major advantage the fact that it provides the most accurate way of describing reality.[11]

The theory of types itself, considered in this context, calls for a division of statements or propositions into different types. A proposition is of the first type if it makes no reference to any set of propositions. A proposition of the second type is one that makes reference to a set of propositions of the first type.

In general, an nth type of proposition is one that makes reference to a set of propositions of the $n-1^{st}$ type.

In this context of his consideration of propositions which make reference to different sets of propositions of various types, Russell suggests both that no totality of any sort can be a member of itself and (more importantly in *this* context) that a proposition which explicitly refers to a class or set is in need of reformulation. The reformulation if correct will eliminate explicit reference to any class or set at all.

All of this suggests that, at least in one formulation, propositions of the second or higher type are inadequate and are in need of replacement, because of the fact that they make (explicit) reference to sets. If we allow for the replacements of propositions of a given type to be of that same type (although this is perhaps a questionable allowance in virtue of the definition of a logical type), we might conclude that a major function of the theory of types is to insist that one make explicit what type of proposition is being referred to by a given proposition P. This type of insistence might allow for a determination of the subject matter of the ascription in question, and consequently for a determination of whether the given proposition P is true.[12]

This is one intelligible account I can give of the theory of types which both accurately (although sketchily) represents at least some of Russell's expositions of the theory and also can illuminate its use in the double bind theory. I intend here to avoid a serious questioning of several of the more problematic aspects of this theory and must also avoid any specific discussion of other formulations of the theory and their inter-relations with the formulation presented in this context.

If we now consider the preceding formulation of the theory of types, we are in a position to evaluate the Bateson *et al.* (1956) presentation of the related aspects of their double bind theory.

Roughly speaking, Bateson *et al.* make use of only the first two types of propositions. These two are 1) propositions that do not refer to any sets of propositions at all; and 2) propositions that refer to sets of propositions of the first type. Of course that part of the motivation of Russell's for the introduction of the theory of types based on the intention to eliminate these statements which are not accurate mirrorings of reality seems to be irrelevant to the Bateson et al. application of the theory. (It doesn't follow from the fact that their motivation is different from Russell's that their application involves any illegitimate or confused use of the theory of types.)

Consider the programmatic insistence of Russell's that one determine the level of any given proposition (cf. note 12). This would allow one to be able to tell what type of proposition is being referred to in the proposition in question and, possibly, what specific propositions are therein being referred to.

This suggests that Bateson *et al.* might consider the basic confusion to involve either a misinterpretation of the type of a given proposition, or an

ignorance of which propositions are being referred to by the given proposition.
[96]

One might suppose that the problem involving communication on the two levels in consideration would amount to taking some given message of one logical type to be of another logical type. It seems, however, that this is *not* what is in focus in the discussions about the double bind phenomenon in the literature, including the Bateson *et al.* article. The focus is not on the misinterpretation of the logical level of some communication. It is, rather, the misinterpretation of the *import* (the most important messages communicated in the context in question) of some given bit of communication, whatever its logical type.

Before coming to a conclusion about the adequacy of the application of the theory of types to the double bind theory, it might be relevant to add that the concepts in terms of which Bateson *et al.* explicate their notion of levels of abstraction are not quite the Russellian concepts of first and second 'types', but rather concepts of an extension[13] of the theory of types to a theory of levels of language usually attributed to Carnap and Tarski. This theory holds that one must distinguish functionally, that is in terms of the functions served, between an 'object language' about which one speaks, and a 'meta language' with which one speaks about an object language.[14]

If we apply these concepts to questions of communication, we can introduce the concepts of object communication and meta communication on the model of the concepts of object language and meta language. Thus object communication is communication about the "object" (or the subject) about which one communicates. Meta communication is communication about some given communication. (Note that we need not limit communication to verbal communication nor to intentional communication.)

With these concepts, we might state that a double bind situation is basically one in which there is communication on both the meta and non-meta (object) levels such that the 'victim'[15] cannot intelligibly and correctly interpret, and, consequently, cannot successfully respond to.

This first formulation of some of the central aspects of the double bind phenomenon not in terms of logical types but in terms of meta and non-meta or object communication amounts to an introductory sketch of the Bateson *et al.* theoretical description of the structure of a double bind situation. I do not think that it would be worthwhile to present such a complete reformulation because, unfortunately, I think that there are still questions to be raised about even these essentials of such a reformulation.

First, some of the putative examples of a double bind situation do not seem to illustrate even this revised formulation of the model being proposed. For example, in stressing the centrality of inconsistency between messages on different 'logical levels' (reformulated to: between non-meta and meta communication), Bateson *et al.* give the example of the mother who is, it seems, manifesting ambivalence towards her child, the 'victim'. First she acts hostilely and then lovingly towards the child. The theoretical comment they make is that the 'important point is that her loving behavior is then a comment on (since it is compensatory for) her hostile behavior and consequently it is of a different *order* of message than the hostile behavior - it is a message about a sequence of messages' (p. 257, their emphasis).

The most obvious problem with this example is that it does not seem to be an example involving messages of different logical types (reformulated to: involving both meta and non-meta messages) which conflict with one another, in spite of the suggestion [97] by the authors that it is such an example. A message does not become a comment on a bit of behavior (nor on the messages therein communicated) simply in virtue of its being compensatory for that bit of behavior.

Unless the distinction between an inconsistency involving only one logical level and an inconsistency involving statements of different logical levels (reformulated to: involving both non-meta and meta communication) is to be obliterated, it seems that this example is not one involving two bits of communication on different levels, but rather two which contradict one another (but do they?) on *one* level. And what this suggests is that we might look for a framework allowing discussions of the double bind situation and allowing discussions of examples such as the above one (in which the mother acts hostilely and then lovingly towards the child), as well. What this also suggests that the double bind framework is neither as inclusive as it at first seems nor as inclusive as we might want.

Below I will suggest how such pseudo-examples of the double bind situation might be adequately described. At this point let me say that at least some of those examples which *do* most clearly seem to involve points of both meta and non-meta communication might be understood as involving inconsistent points of communication on the level of meta communication or on the level of non-meta communication or on both. Thus, one's seriously stating that he didn't like a movie and adding (for example, in response to the comment 'You didn't? I thought it was great!') that he *wasn't* serious can be seen as communicating the inconsistent messages that he is and is not serious in making the comment that he didn't like the movie (the meta level) and that he did and did not like the movie (the non-meta or object level).

This is not to say that there are no examples which should be seen as inconsistency in which both meta and non-meta communication are essentially involved, but simply that not all putative examples of this kind of inconsistency need be so seen. (I leave the former question open.)

Communication which involves inconsistencies between points of different types (meta and non-meta) of communication are just one kind of incompatibly confusing communication. To see that there are types of incompatibly confusing communication which are not also examples of the double bind phenomenon, we need only consider communication which is self-contradictory on a single level.[16] One might, that is, communicate a set of messages the only confusing portion of which involves only two object (non-meta) messages such as (1) she is angry, and (2) she is not angry. We can easily view all such pseudo-examples of the double bind situation similar to the above one of the mother as instances of this simple type of incompatibly confusing communication. (We might add that by holding ambivalence to be possible, we would hold the system of communication in the example of the mother to be a *pseudo*-example of incompatibly confusing communication, and actually to be non-confusing or intelligible communication.)

Furthermore, to state the perhaps too obvious, all systems of confusing communication which do not contain injunctions of all three types which are logically or conceptually necessary for there to be a double bind situation (cf. the beginning of Section 1), are not examples of the double bind phenomenon. Since the double bind phenomenon was defined in terms of all these types of injunction being present, it should be [98] obvious that many cases of incompatibly confusing systems will simply not be cases of the double bind situation.

8 *Brief Overview*

In the preceding portions of this paper I have tried to show both that some of the examples introduced in the original discussion of the double bind phenomenon have actually illustrated points different from what they were meant to, and also that some instances of confusing (baffling, mystifying etc.) communication could not fit into this double bind framework proper at all.

There has been proposed here an alternative manner of conceptualizing and thereby understanding people's relating to one another. To extend this alternative framework, in order to bring out some other differences between it and the classical double bind theory, let me add the following. This will actually be partly explication and clarification and partly extension.

The concept of the double bind, as suggested above, was originally introduced in order to structure a system of communication between members of a small set of individuals, one of whom was considered as the basically passive recipient of a stricture-producing barrage of communication, the consequence of which was held to be this recipient's development into a 'schizophrenic', because of which he or she was termed the victim (see note 1.)

I have tried here to introduce a larger overview of what might be called communing, to adapt a word to a new use (communing being taken here as what conversing would be if it included not only verbal but also non-verbal communication).

This framework in which to structure communing, furthermore, is not limited to what have been called schizophrenogenic situations, but is applicable to any bit of communing whatsoever. I think that the characteristics of communing first brought to articulate light in the Bateson *et al.* article obtain in almost all communing (perhaps in all but the briefest, and possibly even in these).

That is, I hold the following. In all cases of communing, any given bit of behavior amounts to communicating very many information points, about many topics. Many of these messages must be left unresponded to, and it is very often the case that prior communications have made it clear which of the relevant (considering only the immediately preceding communication behavior) steps are possible, which is to say, allowable. Bateson, in written communication dated June 1969, held the pattern of what I've called communing to be quite like a dance in which each bit of communicating (dancing) structures subsequent steps. I think on this matter that limitations on further communing are established not only in double bind situations, but in all (or perhaps merely practically all) communing. To a large degree this suggesting (or demanding or pleading or . . .) that such limitations be accepted as operant or in force is accomplished nonverbally, for example by looks or sighs of boredom, signs of irritation or anxiety, clearings of the throat, mumbled asides that only some of the group can hear clearly, questioning or hostile glances, etc. The, or at least one, important point is that such usually non-verbal messages about what is or is not a possible step are not peculiar to double bind situations. Communing very quickly establishes boundaries of the unquestionable, that is of what cannot be questioned *if* the commun[99]ing is to continue. I think that one of the major steps taken in the classical double bind theory is the articulation of the fact that part of communication amounts to the establishment of restrictions on subsequent communications. Part of what *this* paper has tried to do is to make it explicit that the set of what was referred to as one or another type of double bind injunction can be seen as a proper sub-set (in the set-theoretic sense) of a more inclusive, general and basic class of phenomena occurring in almost all communing.

As an aside, I see as a means to the goal of totally free communing (that is, in which anything at all can be questioned without bringing about the termination of the 'community' or 'commune') the diligent attempt at constant awareness of such tendencies to boundary establishment, whether this boundary is seen as excluding comments which are impolite, insensitive, prying into the private, etc. Relatedly, consider Ginsberg (1973) and especially the issue of mutual respect therein discussed.

Secondly, what has been presented here does not require the acceptance of the presupposition that the individual is the most heuristic basic unit in terms of which to understand such communing groups. I agree with more recent comments made by Bateson *et al.* that there is no need to, and reason not to, reify the person, and in particular, that 'individual' behavior can only be understood as it develops within a larger system. (Cf. more recent work of Bateson, Beavin, Haley, Jackson, Watzlawick and others, as well as Ginsberg [1973] pp. 314f.)

Incidentally this has, I take it, important implications for those who take there to be such a thing as schizophrenia, and especially for those who take there to be such individuals who are thereby in a state of torment and who should and can be helped. And that is that if an 'individual' is to be understood as being 'restricted' and 'victimized' only within a certain type of nexus of communing, then a *prima facie* manner of eliminating this restriction and victimization is to remove that individual from that nexus and to keep him or her out of that nexus. And assuming that this primary goal is held to be unattainable by those in practical power, the second goal would seem to be to introduce this 'individual' into as many new nexus as possible, in order to diminish the strength and influence over the so-called victim of this double bind nexus as much as possible. Oddly enough, from this point of view some if not many ward philosophies hold that the goal of a stay on the ward - for a 'patient' - is to prepare that individual as quickly and efficiently as possible for placement back into the nexus responsible for that individual's originally becoming a patient. 'Schizophrenics', that is, are often deliberately related to by staff in an organized attempt at returning them, in the staff's viewpoint, to the strength and psychological capacity to be placed back into society. As a practical matter, this means back into the original 'schizophrenogenic' nexus, which in almost all cases is the family. Suggestions about bringing up the possibility of other alternatives to the 'patient' are, somewhat paradoxically, dismissed on grounds of being 'unrealistic'. This I take to be either a manifestation of the fact that many wards amount to guardians of the on-going social organization, and thus to a societal force for the *status quo ante*, or of mere lip service to a theory whose implications are otherwise claimed to be importantly correct, or both.

Finally, the communing which can be brought into consideration using the framework above is not limited to messages between one or more individuals and another. [100] Bits of communication may be *directed at* the nexus in question in general, suggesting or demanding that it have a certain pattern or characteristic in general, that is, without regard to which of various 'individuals' therein contribute most centrally to the realization of that pattern. If this were not possible, phenomena manifesting what Jay Haley (in lecture, West Haven VA Hospital, June 1968) called family homeostasis would be somewhat if not totally unintelligible. Family homeostasis is illustrated by such facts as that if one child in a family is 'cured' of 'schizophrenia', a second child inexplicably (at least *superficially* inexplicably) has a sudden 'break'.

Furthermore, bits of communication need not *originate* in the behavior of one individual in the nexus. A pattern of behavior can convey information, and patterns of behavior may involve a plurality of people. Basically and imagistically, several people can hold up one sign; several people by a complex of acts involving all of them can as a unit be communicating to others (as well as to themselves). Some people sharing driving to a distant city to visit other people, for example, may well be telling these friends that they are loved and liked.

All of this suggests that the double bind phenomenon can be structured within the framework presented above in a way that shows that it is one form (out of a plurality of forms) which a certain type of communication confusion can take. Hopefully this structuring will allow for a more complete understanding of more communications confusion than is allowed for within the isolated theory of the double bind and will at the same time allow for a general theoretical context in which to place discussions of the double bind phenomenon. In addition, the double bind can now be seen as a particular instance of a more general phenomenon obtaining in communications networks ('communes' might be another way of describing these), networks that have been discussed here in a more abstract (inclusive) manner.[17]

MITCHELL GINSBERG, PH.D., *Post-Doctoral Fellow, Department of Philosophy, Yale University, New Haven, Connecticut. Contributor to* Nietzsche, *edited by Robert Solomon (Doubleday & Co., Anchor Books 1973). Author of* Mind and Belief *(New York: Humanities Press and London: Allen and Unwin 1972).*

Manuscript received February 1971.

[1] This is part of the terminology of the classical formulation. It seems quite reasonable for this loaded (non-neutral and possibly question-begging) term to have been dropped in later formulations.

[2] In this I follow such recent works as Goldman (1965), in which one may find reasons for opting for this alternative. (Other conventions of jargon *are* available.)

[3] This might be the import of 'The limit of the empirical — is *concept-formation*' (Wittgenstein [1956] III; 29, his emphasis).

[4] As an aside which I will not elaborate on in this context, we might be able to understand what some individ[101]ual's idiosyncratic language (e.g. 'schizophrenese') means by determining how that person uses certain instances of that language in an effort to communicate something about himself.

(This suggests that adequate [linguistic] translation theory should include certain psychological considerations. Cf. e.g. Wittgenstein [1963], Paragraph 206, and Schlesinger [1967].)

[5] The same kind of fact makes it possible to learn a great deal about an individual without having him talk about himself. It thus makes intelligible how such tests as the Rorschach are plausible means of determining something about the person being tested.

[6] The notion of derivability used here can be explicated as follows: X is derivable assuming Y if and only if Y provides reasonable grounds for assuming X. There is some question as to whether the notion of providing reasonable grounds for an assumption is preferable to some stronger one, such as that of entailing it (i.e. if and only if one can validly deduce X from Y), or to some weaker one, such as that of providing some (not necessarily conclusive) evidence for it. It can be argued that the weakest notion here is most preferable, as it most clearly mirrors what we take to be shown by some phenomenon. We will return to this low (see note 7).

[7] Note that such a position would require us to assume that X is derivable from Y if and only if Y provides some (not necessarily conclusive) evidence for X.

Note that this is the weakest of the three interpretations of derivability offered (see discussion above and also note 6).
[8] Some suggest that 'schizophrenics' are those who differ from 'normal' people in assuming that such a problem is insurmountable. Although interesting, it seems to involve an over-simplification and unwarranted generalization.
[9] An extremely clear example of this is Hamlet's explanation (iv. iii) of why he calls Claudius (his step-father) his mother.
[10] Tarski (1956) comments that 'the theory of types was thought of chiefly as a kind of prophylactic to guard the deductive sciences against possible antinomies' (p. 215).
[11] Consider in this context Russell's passages concerned with the topics of definite descriptions, general and particular existence claims, classes and the theory of types.
[12] Thus, if we consider 'the person who says "I am lying", ... he will have to say what type of liar he is ... [If] he said he was asserting a false proposition of the 30,000th type, that would be a statement of the 30,001st type.' (Russell [1966b] p. 264.)
[13] See, for example, the discussion about this extension in Reichenbach (1963), especially p. 39.
[14] See, for example, Tarski (1956), p. 167.
[15] See note 1.
[16] See the modifications to the double bind theory suggested in Sluzki et al. (1967), for example, in their discussion of the 'redundant question' on p. 499. The conclusions in this paper were reached before I became acquainted with this Sluzki et al. article.
[17] I have enjoyed and appreciated conversations and/or personal (written) communication on a slightly earlier version of this paper with Gregory Bateson, Yvonne Ginsberg, Allen Hazen, Ray Holland, Loren Mosher, M.D., and Roland Pfaff.

Bibliography
G. Bateson, D. Jackson, J. Haley and J. Weakland, 'Toward a Theory of Schizophrenia', *Behavioral Science*, 1, 4 (October 1956), pp. 251-64.
R. Carnap, 'The Old and the New Logic', in *Logical Positivism*, ed. A. J. Ayer (New York: The Free Press 1966), pp. 133-46.
R. Carnap, 'Psychology in Physical Language', in *Logical Positivism*, ed. A. J. Ayer (New York: The Free Press 1966), pp. 165-98.
M. Ginsberg, 'Concern and Topic', *Nous*, 5, 2 (May 1971), pp. 107-38.
M. Ginsberg, *Mind and Belief* (New York: Humanities Press and London: Allen and Unwin, 1972).
M. Ginsberg, 'Nietzschean Psychiatry' in *Nietzsche*, ed. Rbt. C. Solomon (New York: Doubleday 1973), pp. 293-315.

M. Ginsberg, 'Towards Statement Identity', *Crítica (Revista hispano-americana de Filosofía*, México, D.F.) [**102**] 4 11-12 (May-September 1970), pp. 13-41.

A. Goldman, 'Action' (Doctoral thesis. Department of Philosophy, Princeton University 1965).

H. Reichenbach, 'Bertrand Russell's Logic', in *The Philosophy of Bertrand Russell*, vol. 1, ed. P. A. Schilpp (New York: Harper and Row 1963), pp. 21-54.

R. Rhees, 'Can There Be a Private Language?', *Supplementary Volume of the Aristotelian Society*, 28 (1954), pp. 77-94.

B. Russell, 'Logical Atomism', in *Logical Positivism*, ed. A. J. Ayer (New York: The Free Press 1966a), pp. 31-50.

B. Russell, 'The Philosophy of Logical Atomism', in *Logic and Knowledge*, ed. R. C. Marsh (London: Allen and Unwin 1966b), pp. 175-281.

I. M. Schlesinger, 'A Note on the Relationship between Psychological and Linguistic Theories', *Foundations of Language*, 3, 4 (November 1967), pp. 397-402.

C. Sluzki, J. Beavin, A. Tarnopolsky and E. Veron, 'Transactional Disqualification', *Archives of General Psychiatry*, 16 (April 1967), pp. 494-504.

H. S. Sullivan, *The Interpersonal Theory of Psychiatry* (New York: W. W. Norton & Co. 1953).

A. Tarski, *Logic, Semantics, Metamathematics*, trans. J. H. Woodger (Oxford: Oxford University Press 1956).

A. N. Whitehead and B. Russell, *Principia Mathematica To *56* (New York: Cambridge University Press 1962).

L. Wittgenstein, *Philosophical Investigations*, trans. G. E. M. Anscombe (Oxford: Blackwell 1963).

L. Wittgenstein, *Remarks on the Foundations of Mathematics*, trans. G. E. M. Anscombe (London: Macmillan 1956).

BRIEF NOTE ADDED AS AN ADDENDUM (2010)

If a study of the system of interactions within a group (e.g., a couple, a family), of their feedback loops of mutual influence, is part of cybernetics, or first-degree cybernetics, then the analysis of interactions of an outside party (esp. a therapist) with that group would be the cybernetics of cybernetics, or second-degree cybernetics. See H. von Foerster, ed., *Cybernetics* (1952) and *Cybernetics of Cybernetics* (1995). On the history of cybernetic theorizing in therapy, see B. Cyrulnik and M. Elkaïm, *Entre résilience et résonance* (2009), p. 41.

The journal article from 1968/1974 reprinted here, *"Action and Communication"* (as mentioned above, at p. 34), *with its discussion of the impact of interpretations by therapists on their interactions with their patients, is thus considered by some as an early venture into theorizing about therapy applying second-degree cybernetics (cybernetics of cybernetics).*

3. Nietzschean Psychiatry Revisited
Preliminary Remarks

This is a corrected, updated, and extended version of an earlier essay that appeared as the chapter "Nietzschean Psychiatry" in *Nietzsche: A Collection of Critical Essays*, edited by Robert C. Solomon, 1973, pp. 293-315.

That essay was written at the invitation of the editor especially for the collection, which was published by Anchor Books/Doubleday (Garden City, NY), in its Modern Studies in Philosophy Series (Amelie Oksenberg Rorty, General Editor). The book was subsequently reprinted twice by Notre Dame University Press (in 1980 and again in 1990), without the biographical sketches of the various contributors found at the end of the first edition.

In the original book, the assumption made was that the collection would be used in graduate-level courses in universities where all of the original works of Nietzsche would be available nearby in the school's library system. The editorial principle proposed was to cite rather than quote passages, where possible, allowing the essays to be more concise. The works by Nietzsche were referred to by a standard system of abbreviations. *These standard abbreviations remain in the current version.* They refer to the works of Nietzsche, as follows:

A: *The Antichrist*
BGE: *Beyond Good and Evil*
CW: *The Case of Wagner*
Dawn: *The Dawn of Day*
EH: *Ecce Homo* [For citation purposes, this work consists of Nietzsche's Preface, a brief exuberantly reflective comment (An diesem vollkommnen Tage), then three sections, cited by a Roman numeral—and entitled (I) Why I Am So Wise, (II) Why I Am So Clever, (III) Why I Write Such Good Books, followed by discussions of various of his books—cited as EH-HAH, EH-GM, etc., and a fourth independent section, similarly cited by a Roman numeral (IV), entitled Why I Am A Destiny.]
GM: *The Genealogy of Morals*
GS: *The Gay Science*
HAH: *Human, All-too-human*
Twilight: *Twilight of the Idols* [For citation purposes, the chapters of this work are cited by Roman numerals, although the original German edition (1889) had only titles—*Sprüche und Pfeile, Das Problem des Sokrates,* etc.—for the various chapters.]
U_2: *Untimely Meditations II* [=*On the Advantage and Disadvantage of History for Life*]
U_3: *Untimely Meditations III* [=*Schopenhauer as Educator*]
WP: *The Will to Power*
W&S: *The Wanderer and his Shadow* [=last part of *Human, All-too-human*]
Z: *Zarathustra*

References to Freud's works by date and letter (e.g., 1915d) are in accordance with the conventional system as used in the bibliographies of the *Standard Edition of the Complete Psychological Works of Sigmund Freud*, J. Strachey ed., London: Hogarth Press, 1953. The primary collections of Freud's writings in German and English are cited in this paper using their accepted abbreviations, as follows:

CP: *Collected Papers* [5 volumes]

GW: *Gesammelte Werke* [18 volumes]

SE: *The Standard Edition of the Complete Psychological Works of Sigmund Freud* [24 volumes]

The 1973 Doubleday Anchor first edition gave a brief biographical sketch of the author, not included in the subsequent reprint editions, which read:

> Mitchell Ginsberg is presently doing psychotherapy work at the VA Hospital in West Haven, Connecticut. He has also been associated with the Connecticut Mental Health Center and the Connecticut Valley Hospital, and has taught philosophy at the University of Michigan and Yale University.

I make use here of this earlier essay from 1973 with prior permission from Robert Solomon, the editor of the work in question, and more recently from Kathleen Higgins, as present holder of the copyrights to the book in which this essay originally appeared.

3. Nietzschean Psychiatry Revisited

When we do call a child happy [εὐδαίμων *eudaimōn*], we do so by reason of the hopes we have for his future.

Aristotle, *Nichomachean Ethics*, 1100a3

I want, once and for all, *not* to know many things. Wisdom sets limits to knowledge, too.

Nietzsche, *Twilight* I 5

Even the delusional ideas of the insane would certainly be found to have a sense if only we understood how to translate them.

François Leuret (1797-1851), *Fragmens psychologiques sur la folie* (1834), in the summary by Sigmund Freud, SE 16: 257 [=GW 11: 264][1]

---

[1] Freud's résumé, at SE 16: 257 [=GW 11: 264] in *Introductory Lectures on Psycho-Analysis* (1916-1917) [SE 15-16 = GW 11], Lecture XVII, citing Leuret, *Fragmens psychologiques sur la folie*, p. 131; cf. mention of Leuret at SE 5: 529 [= GW 3: 534], in *The Interpretation of Dreams* (1900) [SE 4-5 = GW 2-3].

Leuret begins *Fragmens psychologiques sur la folie* (1834) describing the integrated harmony of thought, speech, emotion found in *l'homme sain d'esprit* (the man healthy in his mind), a norm then contrasted with the pattern he finds in *les aliénés* (cf. *asile des aliénés*, parallel to 'insane asylums'), "of whom the aberration is that their ideas, lacking a regular association, join together randomly and give birth to the most disparate groupings" (pp. 3-4).

An *aliéné* is an outsider, literally, one who is estranged, or alienated, one who is separated from property, from Latin *aliēnus*, belonging to another, out of place, and the verb *aliēnō*, *aliēnāre*, to make strange, to sell or transfer (property), to alienate, to separate. More on alienation and integration, below.

Leuret remarks that he cannot determine simply by considering it in isolation whether a given idea was or was not from delirium (*du délire*) or was or was not crazy (*folle*) or reasonable (*raisonnable*), and admits (with all due respect) that even some of the greatest philosophers have had some strange ideas themselves, suggesting further that we will not accept the ideas of a mad woman (but *will* accept those of philosophers and saints and savants) because she, unlike them, cannot arrange her ideas in an organized, logical fashion that shows the thinking that leads from the starting points to the conclusions (pp. 41-44). He describes the return to reason (*le retour à la raison*) for these *aliénés* as *the same process as occurs for us* (who are presumably not considered as being in such dire psychological distress) when we change our opinion (p. 131)—consider Freud's résumé, above, and T. Szasz, *Antipsychiatry: Quackery Squared*, p. 130. Further, Leuret writes (pp. 115, 203) of his intention of conversing with *aliénés*,

Historical Preface

Nietzsche is typically viewed—with the hindsight and horse blinders[2] of the "historical perspective"—as a precursor of Freud. As having a precocious, instinctively accurate but not fully articulated, unsystematic grasp on key Freudian concepts.

To add definition to the usual impressionistic image, I will draw attention here to (1) the unconscious and its relation to *Unlust*-bearing [unpleasant and stronger] material, (2) repression, (3) internalization, (4) sublimation, (5-6) projection and splitting, (7) the ego, and (8) overdetermination, as well as to (9) the notion of society as in conflict with and domesticator of the individual, (10) the contrast between a quantum of (psychic) energy and the particular manner of its discharge, (11) dreams as manifestations of the person, and (12) the paradoxical idea of action as driven, powerless reactivity, conceptualized in Freud as acting (or acting out), where there is no verbal or conscious recognition (or control) on the part of the person so acting.

To compare Nietzsche and Freud concretely at this point, along these twelve dimensions, consider these paired passages from Nietzsche[3] and Freud:

(1) the unconscious and its relation to *Unlust*-bearing [unpleasant and stronger] material: "Up, abysmal thought, out of my depth! . . . You are coming,

---

as an integral part of his working with them (cf. pp. 34, 302, 346, 376, 422). His works contain transcriptions of many of these conversations, *an interpersonal process some will later call psychotherapy.*

His *Des indications à suivre dans le traitement moral de la folie* (1845/1846) proposes that significant distinctions be made between states grouped together under the name of madness or mental alienation (p. 7). His method considers the behavior and demeanor of each person (symptoms), and also the history, *to see the origin of the problem* (etiology), e.g., if from a physical disease or psychological processes (pp. 9-29). He invites the doctor to recognize the individual traits of each patient as well his own particular abilities, inventiveness, and inspiration, and relatedly, writes of psychological medicine (*la médecine mentale*) as involving everything in the mind (*l'esprit*) of one man that can act upon the mind of another, not through physical means but in interpersonal interaction and communication. One can only give what is within, Leuret explains, but the inspired physician can offer a great deal, depending on his "psychological pharmacy"—what is in his head and his heart (pp. 111-112).

[2] Contrast esp. K. Jaspers, *General Psychopathology*, "Excursis into Psychoanalysis" (in Sect. 85 of Chap. 5), where psychoanalysis is seen as having *blocked* the direct influence on psychopathology of such greats as Nietzsche and Kierkegaard. Cf. below, p. 91, n. 71.

[3] **Nietzsche's works by title** are printed **in bold font** to have them stand out.

I hear you . . . Come here! Give me your hand! Huh! Let go! Huhhuh! Nausea, nausea, nausea—woe unto me!" (**Z** III 13) and the essay "The Unconscious."[4]

(2) repression: " 'I have done that,' says my memory. 'I cannot have done that,' says my pride, and remains inexorable. Eventually—memory yields" (**BGE** 68) and the essay "Repression."[5]

(3) internalization: "All instincts that do not discharge themselves outwardly turn inward—this is what I call the internalization of man" (**GM** II 16) and "we assume that, in the course of the development of human beings from their primitive state to civilization a considerable part of their aggressiveness is internalized or turned inwards."[6]

(4) sublimation: "and those innumerably many who miss love from their parents or children or lovers, particularly people of sublimated sexuality [*namentlich aber die Menschen der sublimierten Geschlechtlichkeit*], have struck gold in Christianity [*haben in Christentum ihren Fund gemacht*]" (**HAH** II 95) and "Sublimation is a process that concerns the object-libido and consists in the instinct's directing itself towards an aim other than, and remote from, that of sexual gratification; in this process the accent falls upon the deflection from the sexual aim."[7]

(5-6) projection and splitting: "People deal differently with their higher self ... Many live in awe and humility before their ideal and would like to deny it; they are afraid of their higher self ... frequently called a gift of the gods, ... this highest in man . . . is more appropriately recognized as belonging to man himself" (**HAH** I 624, fuller excerpt below, pp. 82-83; compare **A** 16) and splitting and projection in Freud: "To be thus able not only to recognize, but at the same time to rid himself of, reality is of great value to the individual, and he would thus wish to be equipped with a similar weapon against the often merciless claims of his instincts. That is why he takes such pains to project, i.e. to transfer outwards, all that becomes troublesome to him from within."[8]

(7) the ego: the passage entitled The so-called "ego" (**Dawn** 115) and the extended discussion in *The Ego and the Id.*[9]

(8) overdetermination: "The list [in **GM** II 13] is certainly not complete; it is clear that punishment is overdetermined [*überladen*] by utilities of all kinds

[4] (1915e) [in SE 14 = GW 10 = CP 4].
[5] (1915d) [in SE 14 = GW 10 = CP 4].
[6] "Analysis Terminable and Interminable" (1937c) [at SE 23: 244 = GW 16: 90 = CP 5: 348].
[7] "On Narcissism: An Introduction" (1914c) [at SE 14: 94 = GW 10: 161 = CP 4: 51].
[8] "A Metapsychological Supplement to the Theory of Dreams" (1917d) [at SE 14: 232-233 = GW 10: 423-424 = CP 4: 148]. Cf. below, p. 80, on **HAH** I 137.
[9] (1923b) [in SE 19 = GW 13].

[including important psychosocial ones]" (**GM** II 14) and *Studies on Hysteria*,[10] where Freud uses both the term *überdeterminiert*[11] and *überbestimmt*.[12]

(9) the notion of society as in conflict with and domesticator of the individual: "in menageries . . . beasts . . . are weakened, they are made less harmful, and through the depressive effect of fear, through pain, through wounds, and through hunger they become sickly beasts. It is no different with the tamed man whom the priest has 'improved'" (**Twilight** VII 2) and "The process is perhaps comparable to the domestication of certain species of animals and it is undoubtedly accompanied by physical alterations . . . The psychical modifications that go along with the cultural process are striking and unambiguous. They consist in a progressive displacement of instinctual aims and a restriction of instinctual impulses."[13]

(10) the contrast between a quantum of (psychic) energy and the particular manner of its discharge: "The first kind of cause is a quantum of dammed-up energy [*ein Quantum von aufgestauter Kraft*] that is waiting to be used up somehow, for something, while the second kind is, compared to this energy, something quite insignificant, for the most part a little accident in accordance with which this quantum 'discharges' [in quotation marks in the German: *„auslöst"*] itself in one particular way—a match versus a ton of powder" (**GS** 360) and "among the psychic functions there is something which should be differentiated (an amount of affect, a sum of excitation) . . .—a something which is capable of increase, decrease, displacement and discharge . . . We can apply this hypothesis, which by the way already underlies our theory of 'abreaction,' in the same sense as the physicist employs the conception of a fluid electric current."[14]

(11) dreams as manifestations of the person: "Our dreams . . . transcribe our experiences or expectations or circumstances with poetic boldness and definiteness" (**W&S** 194) and *The Interpretation of Dreams*.[15]

And (12) the idea of action as driven, powerless reactivity, contrasted with *refraining* from acting, with its related flexibility and greater power, in Nietzsche (e.g., **Twilight** V 2,[16] **EH** I 4-6[17]), echoed in Freud, with his concept of a person's acting without any verbal or conscious recognition (in English

---

[10]   (1895d) [in SE 2 = GW 1].

[11]   At SE 2: 263 = GW 1: 261.

[12]   At SE 2: 290 = GW 1: 294.

[13]   "Why War?" (1933b) [at SE 22: 214 = GW 16: 26 = CP 5: 286].

[14]   Emphases added; cf. the notions of libido and catharsis. Quotation from "The Neuropsychoses of Defence" (1894a) [at SE 3: 60 = GW 1: 74 = CP 1: 75].

[15]   (1900a) [SE 4/5 = GW 2/3].

[16]   **Twilight** V is the section entitled "Morality As Anti-Nature." I would like to thank Kathleen Higgins for bringing my attention to this passage in this context.

[17]   **EH** I is entitled "Why I Am So Wise."

often rendered as "acting out"), in contrast with the situation where there is full consciousness of our process, which permits easy verbalization and related flexibility, in *Fragments of an Analysis of a Case of Hysteria* (1905),[18] known as the Case of Dora; this is a concept further discussed in "Remembering, Repeating, and Working-Through" (1914),[19] this short essay being the second of the set of three essays entitled *Further Recommendations on the Technique of Psycho-Analysis, I-III* (1913-1915)—and again, in *Moses and Monotheism* (1939).[20]

Looking back at the preceding twelve topics (and others we can cite or will discuss below), it may be suggested that Nietzsche deserves some of the credit and glory now wrongly granted as originating with Freud.[21]

This is not a matter of reducing Nietzsche to the narrow-visioned status of a pre-Freudian, nor Freud to the simplistic status of a Nietzschean.

Relatedly, in this context, I have seen that in a 1997 journal article, Richard Chessick cited the original (1973) version of this essay, and then continued immediately—the juxtaposition is ambiguous—to state that it is misleading to approach Nietzsche primarily as a proto-Freudian,[22] a point that is, of course,

---

[18] (1905e) [at SE 7: 119 = GW 5: 283 = CP 3: 142].

[19] (1914g) [SE 12: 147-156 = GW 10: 126-136 = CP 2: 266-276]. Freud writes, "the patient does not *remember* anything of what he has forgotten and repressed, but *acts* it out. He reproduced it not as a memory but as an action; he *repeats* it, without, of course, knowing that he is repeating it." [at SE 12: 150 = GW 10: 129 = CP 2: 369]. Italics in original. The term 'working through' in this title renders *durcharbeiten* while the verb *agieren* and the related noun *das Agieren* are the terms regularly glossed 'acting' or 'acting out' and 'to act' or 'to act out' (both are transitive, so that something is acted, or acted out). To act something (out) here is to manifest it in action, rather than to describe it. An example would be a patient's being defiant or hostile, in current therapy, toward the analyst, rather than describing his earlier hostility, when a boy, toward his own parents. For discussion of this example, see SE 12: 150, cited above in this note.

[20] (1939a) [at SE 23: 89 = GW 16: 195]. In addition to these twelve we might also consider others cited by Paul Federn in the discussion about Nietzsche held by the Vienna Psychoanalytic Society on April 1, 1908: see the first volume of the *Minutes*, edited by H. Nunberg and E. Federn. And cf. below.

[21] *To regain a greater sense of the overall flow of the essay, I find it helpful to read this Historical Preface a second time, skipping over these notes. The twelve dimensions presented here add specificity (at the request of the editor, in 1973) to the summary claim of Nietzsche's influence on Freud's thinking.*

[22] R.D. Chessick, "Perspectivism, Constructivism, and Empathy in Psychoanalysis: Nietzsche and Kohut," *Journal of the American Academy of Psychoanalysis*, vol. 25, no. 3 (1997), p. 376; at p. 396, in the References listings, the 1973 essay is miscited (with three misspellings: Nietzschian, Soloman, *Neitzsche*).

well taken. I would like to be explicit on this and to agree with the position expressed by him there. I am in full accord with Chessick; let me add that I do not believe that there is anything in the original 1973 essay on which this current chapter is based, or in this chapter itself, that implies otherwise.

In any case here, I think the above suggestion—that Nietzsche might well deserve some of the credit often assigned to Freud—would actually have pleased Freud, first, because Freud was a great admirer of Nietzsche's writings,[23] and second, because Freud had elsewhere written about *another* precedent to his thinking, that of Empedocles, "I am very ready to give up the prestige of originality for the sake of such a confirmation, especially as I can never be certain, in view of the wide extent of my reading in early years, whether what I took for a new creation might not be an effect of cryptomnesia."[24] At another time, Freud did say of Nietzsche, "He makes a number of brilliant discoveries in himself ... The degree of introspection achieved by Nietzsche had never been achieved by anyone, nor is it likely to be reached again."[25]

Given this as background, the juxtaposing of Freud's and Nietzsche's somewhat parallel thoughts here also suggests that Freud might be seen (in part) as developing ideas nascent in Nietzsche. History as riverine self-development.

All of this is quite tidy and thus suspect, following **Twilight** I 26.

What is some of the history of these notions? To *start* small, we may first note that while the notion of the ego (mentioned above) is *not* something Freud claims to have gotten from Nietzsche, in discussing the related notion of the id, Freud does refer to Nietzsche's use of the German *das Es*, mentioning Georg Groddeck (1866-1934), passingly, in *New Introductory Lectures on Psycho-Analysis*[26] and elsewhere, with a brief explanation of the notion.[27] (Cp. the

---

[23] Cp. "An autobiographical Study" (1925d) [at SE 20: 60 = GW 14: 86] and *Psychopathology of Everyday Life* (1901b) (at SE 6: 146 note = GW 4: 162 note]. Freud earlier (1908) had claimed that he had never been able to study Nietzsche. See *Minutes of the Vienna Psychoanalytic Society, vol. 2 (1908-10)*, New York 1967, p. 33. Freud's explanation of why this was so is perhaps worthy of its own study! Of course, this hinges in part on just how detailed and thorough a reading counted here as "studying an author" for Freud himself.

[24] "Analysis Terminable and Interminable" (1937c) [at SE 23: 245 = GW 16: 90-91 = CP 5: 348]. The German term, at GW 16: 91, is Kryptomnesie, and the philosopher in question, Empedokles (English, Empedocles).

[25] *Minutes of the Vienna Psychoanalytic Society, vol. 2 (1908-10)*, pp. 32-33. The meeting, with notes entitled Minutes 56, was devoted to a discussion of Nietzsche. It took place on Oct. 28, 1908. An earlier meeting also on Nietzsche is recorded in volume 1 (Minutes 45).

[26] (1933a) [at SE 22: 72 = GW 15: 79].

[27] *The Ego and the Id* (1923b) [at SE 19: 23 = GW 13: 251].

term in **BGE** 17 with the notion already expressed in **Dawn** 120.) As for the term "ego," there are superficial complications in that it is the usual English rendering of German *Ich* ("I"), using the Latin pronoun 'ego' instead of the parallel English 'I'). This special use of the usual first person singular pronoun in German did *not* originate with Nietzsche, but was in use earlier, as in Schilling's *Vom Ich als Prinzip der Philosophie* (1795), or mid-1800s authors J.F. Herbart[28] and W. Griesinger.[29] Nietzsche used not only this by-then-common term *das Ich* (**Dawn** 281, **BGE** 16, **Twilight** III 5) but also *das Selbst* (**HAH** I 274, **GS** 60), the Self, and even (**Dawn** 516, **GS** 23) the Latin *das ego*—with the first letter *e* not capitalized, to indicate the noun's being foreign: cp. *ein décadent* (**Twilight** II 3), *eine contradictio in adjecto* (**Twilight** I 23); Freud regularly used *das Ich*, in parallel with the equally mundane *das Es*, literally, the "it"[30] (while English Freudian texts regularly use the Latin pronouns 'ego' and 'id').

The status of the notion of the unconscious is *slightly* more complicated in that, to begin with, there are now several notions going by this same term, involving different contrasts. Overlooking, e.g., the term "unconscious" in a "topological" or "systematic" sense, let me lay aside the contrast of (a) unconscious as not in fact in consciousness at the moment—this includes what Freud calls the preconscious—with (b) unconscious as not possibly in consciousness at the moment—which *excludes* the preconscious. I will not get into the significance of this "possibly" here. Still another contrast, which is relevant here, is that of unconscious as a descriptive notion with that of unconscious as a dynamic one.[31]

Historians who attempt to trace the notion (as if there were one notion) of the unconscious—some back to Plato,[32] but others back at least to the use by

---

[28] See, for example, *"das Ich"* in Herbart's *Lehrbuch zur Psychologie*, Third Part (*Theil*), Second Section (*Abschnitt*), Third Chapter (*Kapitel*), Section 202. At p. 162 in the second edition of 1834, and at p. 141 in Herbart's *Sämmtliche Werke*, Volume V (*Schriften zur Psychologie*), First Part (*Theil*), in the Leipzig edition of 1850.

[29] See, for example, *"das Ich"* in Griesinger's *Die Pathologie und Therapie der psychischen Krankheiten*, Book I, Part 3, Sect. 21 and 26 (in 1867 edition, at pp. 34, 44, respectively).

[30] On "IT" and Mary Barnes, see n. 45, below, at pp. 71-72.

[31] *New Introductory Lectures on Psychoanalysis* (1933a) [at SE 22: 70-72 = GW 15: 76-78].

[32] For example, O. Pfister, "Plato: A Fore-Runner of Psycho-Analysis," *International Journal of Psycho-Analysis*, vol. 3 (1922), pp. 169-174, esp. pp. 171-172, with reference to Otto Wichmann, *Platos Lehre vom Instinkt und Genie*, p. 78. (This is a casual, informal reference to the scholar Ottomar Wichmann.) The idea there of the Unconscious (*Unbewußtsein*) is linked both to instinct and also to genius (in the Greek perspective, divine inspiration).

Theophrastus Bombastus von Hohenheim,[33] known as Paracelsus (1493-1541), of the term *unwüssende* in *Von den Kranckheiten, so den Menschen der Vernunfft natürlich berauben*[34] (written in 1525 or 1526; published posthumously in 1567)—can be seen as pointing out that it has long been realized (by *some*, at *various* earlier ages) that consciousness is not a necessary attribute of an idea: as Nietzsche notes about Leibniz. (**GS** 357: his term rendered here as "idea" is *Vorstellung*—idea, presentation, representation, etc.) Such attempts see unconsciousness as a descriptive equivalent variant of something mental that is not in consciousness.

There remains, however, the notion of the *dynamic* unconscious: that what is *not* in consciousness is not always so by virtue of mere happenstance, but rather as a function of an *active* mental (but not phenomenological) process. *This* notion can also be traced from Freud to Nietzsche, but it too has a larger history. The German thinker Johann Friedrich Herbart, e.g., theorized in the first half of the nineteenth century that ideas *compete* for entry into consciousness, that some are not strong enough to defeat their opponents and consequently remain out of consciousness. He felt that they nevertheless continued to exist, and influenced the consciousness in various ways. (See Herbart's *Lehrbuch zur Psychologie* or the 1895 study *Die Urtheilsfunction. Eine psychologische und erkenntniskritische Untersuchung*, by Wilhelm Jerusalem.[35])

---

[33] This name in its fuller form is Philippus Aureolus Theophrastus Bombastus von Hohenheim.

[34] The term *unwüssende* (or, more precisely, in the sixteenth-century German of Paracelsus, *onwissende:* 𝖔𝖓𝖜𝖎𝖘𝖘𝖊𝖓𝖉𝖊) is found in this work—variously entitled (1) *Von den Kranckheiten, so den Menschen der Vernunfft natürlich berauben*, (2) *Von den Krankheiten, die der Vernunft berauben* (briefer version, in modern spelling), and, alternatively, (3) *Das siebente Buch in der Arznei*, or (4) *De morbis amentium*—in discussing Saint Vitus' Dance, in Chap. III. Paracelsus attributes this pathology not to the Saint but to other causes, with the suggestion of another name, Chorea lasciva (more recently named Rheumatic chorea or Sydenham's chorea). See, e.g., p. 407 in the Gothic-script 1930 reprint edition, *Sämtliche Werke, 1. Abteilung: Medizinische, naturwissenschaftliche und philosophische Schriften, 2. Band*, K. Sudhoff, ed.; for English, H.E. Sigerist, ed., *Four Treatises of Theophrastus von Hohenheim called Paracelsus*, pp. 127-212, esp. pp. 132, 158; cmp. H.M. Pachter, *Magic Into Science: The Story of Paracelsus*, pp. 227-238. For more on Sydenham and these phenomena, see e.g., P. Janet, *The Major Symptoms of Hysteria: Fifteen Lectures Given in the Medical School of Harvard University* (1907), pp. 14, 18, 121-123, 151, 271, etc.

[35] For example, Section 36 (in Part I, Chap. IV of the text; in 1834 ed., at p. 29). Cf. editor's notes, at SE 14: 143, with mention of Herbart's use of the term *Verdrängung* (Repression), well before Freud. At SE 14: 162 it is stated (editor's

Nietzsche and Freud both refer to Herbart in their writings, and Nietzsche takes a Herbartian view in suggesting that at present we are only conscious of the outcome of the battle between instincts [*Trieben*], in **GS** 111.

And Wilhelm Griesinger, in a work once used as a textbook for doctors and students, *Die Pathologie und Therapie der psychischen Krankheiten* (1845), talks of *Vorstellungsmasse* (idea complexes—cf. Hume's "bundles of ideas") that are overpowered by opposing processes, perhaps showing themselves as half-benumbed emotions [*halb erstorbene Regungen*], half-obliterated images and memories from better times [*halb erloschene Bilder und Erinnerungen aus besseren Zeiten*].[36] In this context I might also mention the work of Carl Gustav Carus, Eduard von Hartmann, Gustav Theodor Fechner, Hermann Ludwig von Helmholtz, Wilhelm Jerusalem, etc.

Again, if we look at the idea that an idea that is expressed outwardly in action somehow eludes consciousness and awareness, and yet has power, we may notice this interesting comment from an 1887 French text by Alexandre Herzen, of Lausanne: "When all of the energy of an idea is discharged immediately toward the exterior, we are not at all conscious of it; for us to have consciousness of an idea, it is necessary not only that it have a certain intensity, but that it also not be entirely poured out onto the organs of movement. An idea that disappears from consciousness does not therefore cease to exist; it can continue to act in a latent state, and to be, so to speak, below the horizon of consciousness."[37] (Herzen, in turn, was drawing his comments here from inspiration in the work in physiology and psychology of Henry Maudsley.[38] And so on, backwards through various generations of interconnected theorizing.)

---

comment, as well), "A recognition of the existence of unconscious mental processes played an essential part in Herbart's system."

Viennese author Wilhelm Jerusalem similarly argues for the theoretical (conceptual) acceptability of these unconscious psychological phenomena [*unbewusster psychischer Phänomene*], in *Die Urtheilsfunction* (1895), p. 10. Incidentally, the book's name index (pp. 268-269) mentions Charcot, Comte, Herbart, Hume, Kant, Mach, John Stuart Mill, Ribot, and Wilhelm Wundt, among others—*but not Freud*. This suggests that Freud, also centered in Vienna, would presumably become famous only later for his work on the unconscious.

[36] See Sections 25-31, in Book I, Part 3 (in 1867 ed., at pp. 41-55). Quoted phrases from Sect. 26 (in the same ed., at p. 45).

[37] Alexandre Herzen (Aleksandr Aleksandrovich Gersten, 1839-1906), *Le cerveau et l'acitivité cérébrale au point de vue psycho-physiologique*, p. 201; cf. pp. 242-244. The author was son of the similarly-named Russian philosopher Alexandre Herzen (Aleksandr Ivanovich Gersten, 1812-1870).

[38] This is Henry Maudsley, 1835-1918. See his *The Physiology of the Mind* (1877) and *The Physiology and Pathology of the Mind* (1867).

All of this, however, merely suggests that a cursory glance at Freud and Nietzsche will show little of the larger intellectual history of which they form a part: onflowing history as a river and not a stream.

II

With this apparent neatness still an unswallowed lump, I have been listening to Nietzsche (not at all solely) with an ear to issues about psychotherapy. This has opened up a new aspect of the Nietzsche-Freud (intellectual) relationship. And so, after an initial period (cf. **HAH** I 554) of starry-eyedness over Nietzsche's heritage to Freud, I began noticing such un-Freudian-sounding remarks as **W&S** 297: *"Not to wish to see prematurely.* As long as one is experiencing something, he must surrender himself to the experience and close his eyes, thus not to become *therein* an observer. *That* would disturb the good digestion of the experience: instead of wisdom one would obtain indigestion."

We may ponder here the ideas of *not* seeing too soon, not swallowing, the ability *not* to react, Russian fatalism, the growth of wisdom, and becoming less bilious, on the one hand, and, on the other, decadence, weakness of will, resentment (*ressentiment*), and a Rousseau-like "back to nature" or "letting go" or "flowing with it"—all as the *inability* to refrain from reacting: **EH** I 4-6,[39] **W&S** 348, **WP** 734, 1017, **BGE** 245, **Twilight** V 2, IX 48-50,[40] **U₂** 10, **GS** 225, 290.

The passage quoted just above (**W&S** 297) turns out not to be an isolated reference to the possible desirability of *ignorance*. Although Nietzsche associates the fear or anxiety of realizing something too soon with an incurable pessimism (**BGE** 59), he acknowledges the possibly great mistake in listening *too* carefully to the Delphic command: "where *nosce te ipsum* would be the recipe for ruin; forgetting oneself,[41] *misunderstanding* oneself, making oneself smaller, narrower, mediocre, become reason itself (**EH** II 9[42])."

---

[39] **EH** I is entitled "Why I Am So Wise."

[40] **Twilight** V is entitled "Morality As Anti-Nature"; **Twilight** IX is entitled "Reconnaissance Raids of an Untimely Man."

[41] Besides Nietzsche, the recognition that knowing closes us off to new realizations is appreciated elsewhere, as in the Sōtō Zen honoring of beginner's mind, characterized by curiosity and a lack of any dogmatic certainty called "knowing," as more valuable than a mind filled with knowledge and rigid reassurance, closed off to what is new and what remains to be learned (e.g., S. Suzuki, *Zen Mind, Beginner's Mind: Informal Talks of Zen Meditation and Practice*), and, quite distinctly, in the psychotherapeutic concept of mentalization, as in discussing the value of "sharing and provoking curiosity" (J.G. Allen and P. Fonagy, eds., *Handbook of Mentalization-Based Treatment*, p. 216).

[42] **EH** II is entitled "Why I Am So Clever." Cf. below, p. 75, n. 51, and p. 163.

What was Nietzsche suggesting? To answer this, I would like to relate his thoughts on self-ignorance to his view about bad conscience, or cruelty directed backward, i.e., against oneself (**GM** III 20).

Nietzsche, in what he considered to be "a first, provisional statement" of his own hypothesis concerning the origin of bad conscience (**GM** II 16), suggested that bad conscience results from man's being in a situation (viz., Society) in which his instincts cannot be expressed. Here there is internalization (cf. supra) with its resultant self-attacking. Here we have the repressing of, in particular, the instinct for freedom (**GM** II 17), which Nietzsche identifies with the will to power [*especially* over oneself] (**GM** II 18, cp. **WP** 720, 871, 933). Here we have man estranged from the animal, i.e., instinctual, in himself; humans at this stage must rely upon, in fact are "reduced to their 'consciousness,' their weakest and most fallible organ" (**GM** II 16). What does man with a bad conscience have? An "illness, there is no doubt about that, but an illness as pregnancy is an illness" (**GM** II 19).

Leaving the relation to the issue of self-ignorance aside here for the moment, we have what at first seems to be a rather Freudian view (to put it contra-historically)—Man is in conflict with Society. Socialization results in or involves repression and this manifests itself at later times in neurotic—cf. incidentally Nietzsche's use of this notion in **HAH** I 244—or psychotic behavior. (*Civilization and Its Discontents* [43] takes off from this.)

But although there is this resemblance, I want to focus here on two dissimilarities.

First, (a repressed individual's[44]) bad conscience is likened to pregnancy rather than to, say, cancer or lobar pneumonia (which are at first blush more of what I take to be pathologies). Having a bad conscience, to understand this pregnancy simile a little, is seen by Nietzsche as a process, something which *eo ipso* involves changing, and changing in a structured fashion.

Here a psychic attribute is not understood as a state or condition. Much more recently, such psychiatrists as David Copper and Kazimierz Dąbrowski have suggested that the natural *process* medically taken to be a psychotic *state* is basically hindered or totally inhibited from its natural course (rather than aided, or "cured" to put it medically) by typical hospitalization.[45]

---

[43] (1930a) [SE 21: 64-145 = GW 14: 421-506].

[44] This suggests that "treating mental illness" would be unrepressing the person (ending all blocks, repressions, screen memories), to whom all past experience is available to consciousness. Thus, a "clear" and the halfway house of a "release" found in the perspective of L.R. Hubbard, *Dianetics* (1950).

[45] For accounts of one process allowed and encouraged to flow its natural course, see M. Schatzman, "Madness and Morals," in *Counter Culture*, J. Berke, ed. (1969); and *Mary Barnes: Two Accounts of a Journey Through Madness* by

It was in intuitive pre-agreement with this view that Nietzsche's point was made. And, to continue, a bad conscience is not simply any process, but one with a result. By involving a deep dissatisfaction with oneself—the inward-turned man's "I am sick of myself!" (**GM** III 14)—a type of self-inflicted wound occurs that *brings about life*, through the individual's struggle against this wound (cf. **GM** III 13 and **Twilight** I 8's "What does not destroy me, makes me stronger"). Bad conscience is "pregnant with a future" (**GM** II 16).

Second, Nietzsche relates the development of a bad conscience with increased reliance on consciousness. Unlike Freud, however, Nietzsche does not at all see this reliance on consciousness as a desirable state of affairs. To repeat, for Nietzsche consciousness is man's "weakest and most fallible organ" (**GM** II 16). It is basically in this kind of consideration that I see the connection between the issues of bad conscience and self-ignorance for Nietzsche (read on), and because of which I sense a rather *anti*-Freudian perspective in his psychiatric theorizing.

Whereas in traditional or classical psychoanalytic theory the aim is to bring repressed material to consciousness in spite of the individual's, the patient's, strong resistance, Nietzschean psychiatry would reject such a view's underpinnings. This psychiatry (to free this term from its recent medical impaction)[46] is of course not committed to the position that the force or power of any-

---

M. Barnes and J. Berke (1972). Note her use, esp. at p. 348, of "IT" rather than the Latin name "id" as reflecting Nietzsche's and Freud's use of German *das Es*. Cf. discussion above, p. 67 (and notes 28-30); cp. R.D. Laing's *Knots*, p. 84. See also the film memorial to Mary (Feb. 9, 1923 – Jun. 29, 2001), "Going Down and Coming Up: Mary Barnes at Kingsley Hall" (2001), via mary-barnes.net or jhberke.com. (Schatzman and Berke are American psychiatrists living in London.) For Cooper's views, see *Psychiatry and Anti-Psychiatry*, pp. 79-81, 88-95. For a critique of this group in practice, see T. Szasz, "Debunking Antipsychiatry: Laing, Law, and Largactil," *Current Psychology*, vol. 27, no. 2 (Jun. 2008), pp. 79-101. On Szasz, cf. above, p. 61, n. 1, and below, p. 101, n. 129, p. 149, n 3.

See further, Dąbrowski, *Positive Disintegration* (1964); *Personnalité, psychonévroses et santé mentale d'après la théorie de la désintégration positive* (1965); *Psychoneurosis Is Not An Illness: Neuroses and Psychoneuroses From the Perspective of Positive Disintegration* (1972), etc. And compare these with the earlier writings of Janet on regression as a temporary, partial dealing with a situation in order to develop the means of addressing it in a deeply resolving, satisfying way, as discussed, e.g., in C.M. Prévost, *La psycho-philosophie de Pierre Janet: Économies mentales et progrès humain*, pp. 191-204.

[46] Psychiatry, in its contemporary sense, is typically defined as "the branch of medicine which deals with diagnosis, treatment, and prevention of mental disorders" (*Tauber's Cyclopedic Medical Dictionary*, 13th ed., page P-158). The lit-

thing unconscious is dissipated upon the switch to its being fully conscious. Taking such a position seems to have been a basic mistake on Freud's part. Compare the comments of Fritz Perls, in *Gestalt Therapy Verbatim*, "Talk," end of Sect. II. And, looking back earlier in the literature (the theorizing) about this topic, we may note further the contrast with what we might see as a Freudian optimism here about the power of having something become conscious (despite the pessimism we can often sense in Freud), much earlier, in *État mental des hystériques* (1892), the French philosopher and psychiatrist Pierre Janet[47] wrote, "I do not think that cure is that easy and that it suffices to bring about the expression of the fixed idea to eliminate it; treatment is unfortunately much more delicate."[48] And in *Les médications psychologiques* (1919), Janet had similarly

---

eral, that is, etymological, meaning of the word 'psychiatry' can be seen by considering the Classical Greek, from which the term is derived.

So, the OED, while defining 'psychiatry' as the study and treatment of mental disease, give the roots here as *psychē* (breath [yes?], life, soul) plus *iatreia*, healing, and *iatros*, healer, physician. So: from a healing of the soul, the meaning has moved to a medical—in more recent times, more specifically, a pharmaceutically-centered—curing of mental disease. (The basis of the shift is in this pathologized and medicalized interpretation of processes of the psyche.)

We may note that Liddell and Scott, *Greek-English Lexicon*, pp. 2026b-2027b, gloss ψυχή (*psychḗ*) as life, departed spirit (Homer), the immaterial soul (Pindar), the conscious self or personality, the source of life, etc. They question—*pace* the OED entry mentioned just above—interpreting *psychē* as breath.

[47] If the name is unfamiliar, this is not surprising. Even at the French web site psychiatriinfirmiere.free.fr/infirmiere/formation.htm, we do not find Pierre Janet cited among the therapists listed. Similarly, even the page linked there that is dedicated to hysteria (visited as recently as July 5, 2010), we find discussion of Jean-Martin Charcot, Joseph Babinski, and Sigmund Freud, but no mention at all of Janet. It is perhaps relevant that the site has a strong Freudian focus.

This is despite the decades that Janet dedicated, and the volumes that he contributed, to the domains of psychology and psychopathology. Janet is certainly not stressed in the English-speaking psychiatric community, at least until quite recently (thanks perhaps to some francophonic Dutch psychiatrists).

[48] See *L'État mental des hystériques*, 2nd ed. (1911), p. 352. The French reads, "Je ne crois pas que la guérison soit aussi facile et qu'il suffise de faire exprimer l'idée fixe pour l'enlever, le traitement est malheureusement bien plus délicat." Cf. C.M. Prévost, *Janet, Freud et la psychologie clinique*, p. 62. Also, Janet, in "Histoire d'une idée fixe," *Revue philosophique de la France et de l'étranger*, vol. 37 (Jan.-Jun. 1894), pp. 121-168, writes of Breuer and Freud, and the importance of "carrying out an investigation into the deep layers of consciousness, and bringing to the light of day these fixed ideas before trying to cure them. But that

written, "All nervous disorders do not cease when they become conscious."[49] (That is, some do not cease when they become conscious.) We might stress this observation and the issues that it raises about the Freudian view it is questioning.

The general principle here is that traumas are somehow removed from awareness but remain powerful; for Freud this removal is their becoming unconscious (going into repressed forgetting), while for Janet, they become subconscious (go into an isolated status unreachable in ordinary consciousness). For Freud, these are resolved when brought to consciousness. Janet, as the above quotations suggest, disagrees with this.

Relatedly, we might note that recent work with traumatic experience has brought to light, among other things, the possibility that these memories are not in fact forgotten, at least not in all cases. (More on this immediately below.)

This, though, is perhaps not really news, since, for example, the French physician Jacques-Henri-Désiré Pététin reported more than two hundred years ago (!) that a woman patient of his would sing incessantly, even when put into the most unusual postures in which breathing was rather difficult for her. Pététin mentions (in this incident from the late 1700s) that the woman explained that the singing was her attempt to distract herself from a visual memory that was terrifying for her and that would not leave her in peace.[50]

---

is unfortunately only the first part of the work, and the easiest, since a fixed idea is not cured when it is expressed, quite the contrary!" (p. 127).

[49] The French (*Les médications psychologiques*, vol. II, p. 283) reads, "Tous les désordres nerveux ne cessent pas quand ils deviennent conscients." The 1925 translation, *Psychological Healing: A Historical and Clinical Study*, p. 674, discussing the dissociation of consciousness, in the section, Treatment by Mental Liquidation) has, "It could not be said that in every case of nervous disorder the trouble ceased as soon as it had been brought back into consciousness."

[50] This follows A. Bertrand, "Un précurseur de l'hypnotisme," *Revue philoso-phique de la France et de l'étranger*, vol. 32 (Jul.-Dec. 1891), pp. 192-206, at p. 194: "elle déclara plus tard que ces chants avaient pour but de la distraire d'un spectacle qui la terrifiait." The work discussed by Bertrand, Pététin's *Électricité animale* (1808), provides information about the then-standard use of leeches for blood-letting and about his attentiveness to the young patient, his straight-forward speech to her, and his simply asking her what her singing was about. Her quoted reply (p. 11) was, "Il m'est très-facile de vous en apprendre la cause. Je chante, monsieur le Docteur, pour me distraire d'un spectacle qui m'épou-vante..." ("It is quite easy for me to let you know what the cause is. I sing, Doc-tor, to distract myself from a vision that is frightening to me...") There is good reason (the principle that the simplest explanation for a given set of data being preferable, called Occam's Razor) simply to accept her word rather than to pro-pose the otherwise perhaps gratuitous hypothesis that she was hallucinating.

Or again, as contemporary French psychiatrist Boris Cyrulnik writes,

It is not correct to speak of repression in children who had been hidden [during the Nazi occupation in France in the early 1940s] since, quite the contrary, they have traumatic hyper-memories that are precise, clear, and always present deep inside them. These representations [experienced recollections, images of particular memories, etc.] are difficult to put into words ...[51]

That does not at all mean that they are not being experienced with great intensity. (Quite the opposite!)

These traumatic memories are typically presented to consciousness as isolated scenes that have no contextualization and are often experienced with such an intensity that they cannot be verbalized or put into words at all; this is something that is familiar both to those who have had such experiences and to those who are have come to know about this dimension of people who have lived through such shocks. The ability of the conscious mind to deal with this material is quite limited, above all when the individual is feeling overwhelmed. More on these interconnected issues elsewhere in this book.

This means, in any case, that we can appreciate Nietzschean psychiatry with its suggestion that the above Freudian position embodies an unlikely if not foolish tack: either consciousness will merely be unable to help, or it will succumb (due to its relative weakness; cf. above) to the reverberations of the patient's new awareness.

For Freud is in this sense more of a rationalist, more convinced of the ability of the (conscious) mind to handle matters than is Nietzsche. Good contrasts to Freud's suggestion[52] of removing amnesias (repressions) to let consciousness take over are both the post-psychoanalytic course of events concerning awareness and amnesia in the case of little Hans,[53] as reported in the 1922

---

[51] B. Cyrulnik, *Parler d'amour au bord du gouffre*, p. 212, "Il n'est pas juste de parler du refoulement des enfants cachés puisque au contraire ils ont une hyper-mémoire traumatique, précise, claire, toujours présente au fond d'eux-mêmes. Cette représentation est difficile à mettre en mots ..." Compare 'représentation' in this context with the German *Vorstellung* (as for Immanuel Kant). Traumatic memories that are quite vivid but cannot be articulated in language are recognized in recent times as leaving the person feeling overwhelmed, literally at a loss for words (alexithemia). See, e.g., J.G. Allen, *Traumatic Relationships and Serious Mental Disorders*, pp. 156, 227. Cf. above, p. 70, n. 42; below, p. 163.

[52] "Freud's Psychoanalytic Method" (1904a) (at SE 7: 252-253 = GW 5: 8-9 = CP 1: 269-270].

[53] "Analysis of a Phobia in a Five-year-old Boy" (1909b) [SE 10: 5 = GW 7: 243 = CP 3: 149].

postscript (*Nachschrift*) to the case,[54] and also Nietzsche's suggestion of "an entirely new lesson just dawning on the human eye, and hardly yet plainly recognizable: to incorporate knowledge in ourselves and make it instinctive—a problem which is only seen by those who have grasped the fact that until saw only our errors have been incorporated in us, and that all our consciousness bases itself on errors!" (**GS** 11). The fact that Nietzsche's contrast here is between knowledge and error should not overpower the background view expressed in this passage—that the object is to incorporate (*einverleiben:* cf. **GM** II 1, where incorporation and "inpsychation" are related) knowledge and to make it instinctive.[55] It is not to make it conscious. (See **GS** 354, quoted just below.)

The Nietzschean view in **GS** 11 that I am concerned with *here*, however, stresses man as a living organism, an animal, a being originally instinctual, and one most able to fulfill itself when it so functions. The contrast with the Freudian model with its belief in consciousness as powerful—in the ways referred to above—is highlighted by these comments of Nietzsche's, and by his views that the "problem of consciousness (more correctly, of *becoming* conscious of *oneself*) confronts us for the first time when we begin to conceive—how much we could do without it" (**GS** 354), the notion that consciousness develops out of a constraining of natural processes, "The entire inner world, originally thin as if stretched between two membranes, separated and fermented, acquired depth, width, and height, as man's discharge outwards was hindered" (**GM** II 16),[56] that "the chamber of human consciousness is *small*" (**GM** III 18).

If, then, Nietzschean psychiatry would not suggest a Freudian working-through of unconscious material (whether by means of free associating and dream analysis as the central technique or of considering the transference relation and resistance as the central issues, as psychoanalysis variously viewed its defining characteristic[57]), and would place little confidence in the powers of consciousness, where does it lead? For Nietzsche, would there even be psychotherapy? What suggestions does he offer for an individual who would otherwise go to the nearest analyst? He would of course *not* offer himself as a replacement for

---

[54] At SE 10: 148-149 = GW 13: 431-432 = CP 3: 288-289.

[55] For those interested in an explanation of taking "Instinct" (rather than another term, especially "drive") as the translation of *Trieb*, I suggest the translator's comments in the section "Notes on Some Technical Terms whose Translation Calls for Comment," SE 1: xxiii-xxvi, under the entry *Trieb* (pp. xxiv-xxvi).

[56] In the original German of **GM** II 16, "*Die ganze innere Welt, ursprünglich dünn wie zwischen zwei Häute eingespannt, ist in dem Masse auseinander- und aufgegangen, hat Tiefe, Breite, Höhe bekommen, als die Entladung des Menschen nach aussen gehemmt worden ist.*" Cf. below, p. 79, for more on this.

[57] "On the History of the Psycho-Analytic Movement" (1914d) [at SE 14: 16 = GW 10: 55 = CP 1: 298].

the analyst, at least on one rather plausible reading of "I am a railing by the torrent: let those who can, grasp me! Your crutch, however, I am not" (**Z** I 6).

If the would-be patient *has* heard, *has* grasped Nietzsche, however, he can see that he has an involving experience ("task" just isn't adequate here) ahead of him. This needn't be at all be depressing, and definitely not shameful. (Taste for delicious inspiration: *"What we do. What we do is never understood, but always merely praised or criticized"* **GS** 264.) It is the presentation of a situation in which the person involved can ripen: "In the end there may still remain open the question of whether we could dispense with our illness in the development of our virtue" (**GS** 120). There are, however, no Nietzschean commands, no Nietzschean proscriptions. Quoting Wagner in **GS** 99, Nietzsche presents the thought that "each one who wishes to become free must become so through himself." There is much to look forward to: "What does not destroy me, makes me stronger" (**Twilight** I 8; cf. supra).[58]

But there is no rush; Nietzsche warns his fellow man in some hapless state (*Unglück*) against one called by the "religion of pity" or by "the heart" to help, thinking "to have helped best when he has helped the fastest" (**GS** 338). (Eager—or is that perhaps impatient?—administrators, friends, and therapists, *please* take note!) Nietzsche's belief here—that the person, viewed as a total organism, will evolve to health (freedom) to the extent that he/she reverses the social training of self-sacrifice (consider **GS** 21, **GM** II 6, **BGE** 33, **EH** IV 7,[59] etc. here)—starts from the notion that man has been crippled by what is now approvingly called "socialization." Morality, the key to society (any custom or moré rather than none taken as society's first principle: **Dawn** 16), crushes self-reliance (**Dawn** 163).

It is for this reason and others that Nietzsche realizes that one cannot *simply*—at *our* stage of societal ("political" as in Greek *polis*) structuring, of consciousness, and of introjected decadence (this being an over-all attitude concerned with death and decay rather than with life and growth: **Twilight** II 1-3, **CW** Preface, **WP** 7, etc., for example; cf. below)—trust one's feelings (cf. **A** 59): "To trust one's feelings—that means to obey one's grandfather and one's

---

[58] A basically Nietzschean view on the issues of great depression (of what used to be called melancholia: cf. "My Melancholy Baby") and solitude can be seen in the letter Rilke wrote on Aug. 4, 1904, at Borgeby gård, Flädie, Sweden, to Franz Kappus (Letter Eight in Rainer Maria Rilke's *Letters to a Young Poet*).

I will not enter here into the issue of the possible link between Nietzsche and Rilke—and also Freud!—via Lou Andreas-Salomé. See here esp. her *Lebensrückblick. Grundriß einiger Lebenserinnerungen* (1951), in translation as *Looking Back: Memoirs* (1991), as well as *Lou Andreas-Salomé*, title of biographies of her by A. Livingstone (London, 1984) and by Y. Simon (Paris, 2004).

[59] On pity, cf. pp. xix-xx, 96-98. **EH** IV is entitled "Why I Am A Destiny."

grandmother and their grandparents more than the gods which are in us: our reason and our experience" (**Dawn** 35). If this becomes expressed in the notion of
following oneself—cf. **GS** Overture/*Vorspiel* 7 (*"Vademecum—Vadetecum"*),
GS 255 and 338, etc.—the issue here is, what is one's path, one's direction,
one's way? And by this do *not* read: job, occupation, life's calling (**Twilight**
VIII 50); nor: role (**GS** 356). Further, why is it so difficult for anyone to answer
this question? (A philosopher's interlude: Just what does answering this question
amount to?)

III

  Non-philosophers may well reply to this parenthetical question with
either an "It's obvious" or a questioning "What problem does *that* try to create?"
Well, it's not obvious to me, and to answer this question, what *is* problematic
here is that an understanding of this question of what our path, direction, or way
is, depends on which concept of the person and his/her life or history we use.
This is the focus of this section.
  Should this concept be understood, then, in a very ordinary way?—that
a person *has* certain characteristics, traits, abilities, faults (lackings), etc., so that
the problem of self-awareness is therefore to be taken to be simply a matter of
learning the personal facts (about oneself)? Or is it a development of this basic
view into one considering both actual properties and also potentialities? Is Nietzsche suggesting an Aristotelian model here?
  This latter interpretation, for example, makes sense of the Pindarian
message Nietzsche repeats at different times in slightly different forms: *"What
does your conscience say? You shall become who you are."* (**GS** 270, cp. **GS**
335, **EH** subtitle, etc.), which on the former view is a rather silly command.
  This Aristotle-inspired model may well allow for such a popular view as
is manifest in "Just be yourself!" "Do your own thing!" etc.—against which a
good dose of *"Said once more. Public opinions, private lazinesses."* (**HAH** I
482) and of recalling Nietzsche's lamenting that "the time in which we live
throws its most 'timely' into us" (**GS** 378) are both helpful prescriptions. It does
not at all account, however, for the emphasis which Nietzsche places elsewhere
on total reversals of direction, in contrast to an Aristotelian model of developing
one's potentials (the "straight line" of **Twilight** I 44 and **A** 1 notwithstanding).
  The changes which can be best illuminated in a capacity/actuality model
are only *one* sort of change. Nietzsche *does* see change as integral to life (cf. **GS**
26, **Dawn** 573, **W&S** 333) but this change does not limit itself either to a mere
self-preserving (cf. esp. *Anti-Darwin*, at **Twilight** IX 14) or to a straightforward
"development" (cf. **Dawn** 560, **GS** 371, and below).
  Each individual is a mixture of different *types* of culture, at least so far
as each learns something from the political (again, as in *polis*) or societal environment. Part of this motley condition is having mixed instincts; *"each of us*

still has the bad instincts" (**A** 59, emphasis added), for example, in addition to other instincts. The "bad instincts" here are the Christian ones. Nietzsche ties *his* "discovery" of what a Christian viewpoint does to the individual with the start of psychology (see esp. **EH** IV 6[60]): before searching out, digging under and behind the *possibly* attractive veneer of Christianity—to find it an indoctrination into self-hatred, self-laceration, self-mistrust, into a praising of everything that is life-denying (**A** 15-18, 49, 51, etc., **EH** IV 7-8, etc.)—all putative psychology hid central political/sociological realities from its own eyes, Nietzsche proposes.

This addition of decadent (life-combating) instincts involves coming to mistrust one's own prior instincts ("to make mistrust of the instincts second nature": **EH** IV 8). *This Nietzsche sees as a main function of the concept of sin, which is a moralistic conceptualization of displeasure.* Instincts here are put into question, and moralizing (see the definition in **EH** IV 7) is then feasible.

Nietzsche feels the relationship between morality and instincts that are not smooth-functioning to be quite tight: both in fact are themselves manifestations (not causes: cf. **Twilight** VI I-2) of some sort of malfunctioning. The need to deliberate about the correctness of one's actions, whether performed or contemplated, the hesitating *against* what one is intuitively about to do, etc., are clear indications that one's nature is not ascendant, natural, unproblematic, smooth. *With* these characteristics, there is action and then one is done with it, whatever it was. To repeat the teaching cited above at p. 76, "The entire inner world [was] originally as thin as if it were stretched between two membranes"—between the let-go past and the not-contemplated future?—**GM** II 16.

The notion here of unconsciousness (lack of reflective consciousness) of instinct and of instinctive action fits well with Eduard von Hartmann's understanding of instinct: "Instinct is purposive action without consciousness of purpose" (*Philosophy of the Unconscious*, Book 1, Sect B, Part 3).

Nietzsche is *not* suggesting a dogmatic approach to life with this model of actions freed from prior or subsequent deliberation and scrutiny—cf. his critique of faith.

Rather, he is indicating some of the ways in which instinctive action has been hampered by the presence of decadence. This would be one in which the high value placed on deliberation and intentionality in modern morality (contrast, e.g., the Aristotelian concept of action flowing freely from a self-harmonious agent of practical wisdom with the Kantian one of a totally moral-minded agent determining moral law by use of a mechanical formula) might be questioned or revaluated. *This is, further, one in which it might be possible to demystify one's bad conscience, in the Laingian sense of demystifying.*[61]

---

[60] **EH** IV is entitled "Why I Am A Destiny."

[61] R.D. Laing, "Mystification, Confusion, and Conflict," in I. Boszormenyi-Nagy and J. Framo, eds., *Intensive Family Therapy* (1965), pp. 343-363.

IV

If this is something of what answering this question of what one's path is and is not, then the *outlines of an answer* to why it is so difficult to answer this question become clearer. For, first, this question is only asked in midstream (*in medias res*, as they said in Rome), when one has been drawn away from one's instincts. Second, the question calls for *decisions* possibly much more than for *discovering* the "facts." These decisions concern which directions to *direct* oneself in, which aspects of oneself to help to flourish, and which to cut short (cf. the passage on self-gardening, **Dawn** 560).

Then, one continually has the option of reevaluating directions set out upon, of deciding if one has obtained everything desired out of a given way of understanding things: Nietzsche talks of *using* convictions, "Convictions as a *means"* (**A** 54), and of modifying one's viewpoint *and* direction (**Dawn** 573, **W&S** 333, **GS** 371, **Twilight** IX 18).

These are some issues related to the answering this question of what one's path is and is not; how, though, is this answering to be accomplished?

Since an individual comes to have a great self-dissatisfaction due to a biting conscience (which can become a virtue, a tool) only after society's forces have de-instinctualized him/her, the first task becomes one of unlearning this aspect of what one has been taught. Man, for example, has been made prejudiced against himself (**W&S** 262). Self-love, like all love (**GS** 334), must be learned: "One must learn to love oneself—thus I teach—with a wholesome and healthy love, so that one can bear to be with oneself and need not roam" (**Z** III 11 Part 2). And for this, "free time," time not "filled" with busy work such as one's time-*occupying* occupation, walks, uncovering our own treasures by being with ourselves, by following our thoughts where (and wherever) they lead us ARE ALL EXTREMELY IMPORTANT (**GS** 329, **Dawn** 173, 178, 491, 500, **Twilight** I 1, 34, **HAH** I 284, **Z** III 11 Part 2).

The task of unlearning involves both rejecting values passively accepted, breaking old tablets—for "whoever heeds commands does not lead *himself"* (**Z** III 12 Part 7)— and also reversing the negative evaluations smuggled in with any (ascetic) ideal, which most strongly results in a self-dissatisfaction, a self-loathing. As Nietzsche puts this: "In every ascetic morality man prays to one part of himself as God and must consequently diabolize the remaining part" (**HAH** I 137). This source of self-hatred will be removed in pivotal moments of our life: "The great epochs of our life come when we gain the courage to re-christen our evil as what is best in us" (**BGE** 116).

Obviously this creativity ("To will liberates, for to will is to create: thus I teach," **Z** III 12 Part 16) will not be encouraged by some, if not most, of the people in one's environment, those closest *least* likely of all in many instances. ("The more anyone lets himself go, the less the others let him go," **HAH** II 83— can we see here a vision of the therapist as counterweight to others?)

But Nietzsche, as I think is clear, is not suggesting a simple policy of fulfilling one's virtues. He has much more to suggest than that we "become who we are." (Cf. Charles Andler, who, considering **GS** and **EH**, claims[62] that this is the only moral precept that these two works would recognize.) I take many of Nietzsche's comments about virtues (virtue—*Tugend*—ἀρετή *aretḗ*) to contrast with this, seeing virtues not as capabilities to be actualized, period (*tout court*); but, rather, as characteristics to be transcended or overcome (e.g., **GS** Overture/*Vorspiel* 5 [*"An die Tugendsamen"*], **Z** I Preface 4, **Z** I 5, **EH**-Dawn 2). And there are some virtues to be sacrificed to others, as I interpret **GS** 266: *"Where cruelty is necessary.* Whoever has greatness is cruel to his virtues and deliberations of the second order."

The notion that one has a given personality and character is a societal fiction whose purpose it is to fix the person into a pattern that is societally/politically desirable: "Man himself must first of all have become *calculable, regular, necessary*, even in his own image of himself, if he is to be able to stand security *for his own future*, which is what one who promises does!" (**GM** III; cf. the following sections in **GM** for the elaboration of this view).

If a person is convinced, that is, that he can only act a certain way, or totally accepts that he should only so act, he will be much less likely to try to act differently. (It is here, as elsewhere, that a mistaken *understanding* of reality makes an effective difference while that reality itself basically doesn't.) The positive aspect of a moral version of this is stated by Pierre-Joseph Proudhon, that we are obligated only to keep our word (in, for example, the Sixth Study of his *Idée générale de la révolution au XIXe siècle*). A Nietzschean response to this Proudhonian position is the claim of Max Stirner that to feel and accept this obligation is to abdicate one's freedom (*The Ego and His Own*, Part 2, Sect 2, Subsection 1). Others who have frozen themselves into stability (to refocus an image of Stirner's) might well find those persevering in their freedom to be unfathomable.

As Nietzsche puts it in **GS** 371, "we are mistaken by others, always growing, changing, shedding our bark each spring, becoming younger, higher, stronger. We grow like trees—that is hard to understand, like all life!—not in one place, but all over, not in one direction, but equally upwards and outwards as inwards and downwards."[63]

---

[62] From C. Andler, *Nietzsche: sa vie et sa pensée*, Chap. II: L'Université—L'influence de Ritschl, Part II: Leipzig (1865-1969). In vol. 2 of the original 1921 edition (*La jeunesse de Nietzsche, jusqu'à la rupture avec Bayreuth*), p. 80. Andler cites **GS** 270 in a linked footnote, also p. 80. The passage is in vol. 1 of the 1958 3rd edition of *Nietzsche: sa vie et sa pensée* (6 vol. in 3), at p. 306.

[63] Small omissions not marked. The section is entitled "We Unintelligible Ones." Cp. Aristotle, *De anima* [Περὶ ψυχῆς *Perì psychḗs*], 413a25-30.

Whereas Stirner is more interested here in man as a societal being (*zōon politikon*), Nietzsche has taken a new tack. He is looking at man as a being. Not a nothing which has nothing until a society puts something into him, and not something that would become nothing if these societal aspects were totally transcended. (*Pace* Robert Paul Wolff's "Beyond Tolerance" in the small collection *A Critique of Pure Tolerance*.[64]) There is an extra-societal ("non-null") aspect to the human being, and all theorizing which disavows this aspect is merely expressing its prejudice *for* total justification of any so-called "socialization." Here Nietzsche agrees with Indian metaphysics, Christian and social libertarian views which support a critique of traditional psychoanalysis as a means of changing the individual to accommodate to his/her society. What these perspectives agree on is that there is something beyond the societally inculcated, and something, therefore, that—to give a premature notice to the next generations— is being disregarded in certain conservative (re the society, *not* re the individual members thereof) philosophies, both rightist and leftist (to group a supposedly basically worlds-apart pair together).

Where this odd grouping of Nietzsche and cohorts will split up over is the issue of what this something else amounts to. Whereas, for example, in Hindu and Christian thought (to speak broadly) it is the universal within or without (God, the Lord, the Divine, etc.), for Nietzsche it is just the opposite of the universal—it is the most individual.

(A satisfying comparison of Nietzschean and even just some contemporary radical psychiatry would take us too deep into just this one issue, but briefly, the Radical Therapist suggestion. for example, of getting the individual, i.e., the "patient," into political activity of one sort or another—anti-police, anti-landlord, anti-war, anti-male, etc. actions—is clearly contra-Nietzschean. One form this sort of thinking has taken at various times, as in the early 1970s, was the idea that to break away from the sub-society one is a member of, it is necessary to form a caucus/tribe/"family"—*another subsociety!* Still no notion of the individual as an individual.)

As *Nietzsche* identified this extra-societal aspect of man: *"Dealing with one's higher self.* Everyone has his good day, when he finds his higher self [*Selbst*]; and true humanity demands each to be appraised only according to this state and not according to the workdays of dependence and servitude ... But men themselves deal differently with their higher self ... Many live in awe and humility before their ideal and would like to deny it; they are afraid of their higher self ... [I]t is frequently called a gift of the gods, while in fact everything

---

[64]   This chapter by Wolff is at pp. 3-52 of the book (which was published in 1965). Cf. Nathan Glazer, "Review of *A Critique of Pure Tolerance*, by Robert Paul Wolff, Barrington Moore, Jr., and Herbert Marcuse," *American Sociological Review*, vol. 31, no. 3 (Jun. 1966), pp. 419-420.

else is a gift of the gods (of chance); this highest in man, however, is more appropriately recognized as belonging to man himself (**HAH** I 624; cf. Kantian moral "knowledge" as *self*-ignorance, **GS** 335).

Nietzsche is suggesting that the individual find within ("intrapersonally")[65] what he or she is looking for. To look for what one desires to have, to see, to feel, to be—*outside* of oneself (whether in another person, a group, political party, nation, important cause, material objects)—is to deny one's own fecundity and ability. To direct one's admiration outward is often (perhaps usually) to disregard and disvalue oneself—something well taught by society. (Self-acceptance and self-assurance are felt to be narcissistic, referred to in another vocabulary as "ego-tripping." *Why is there such joy at seeing misery fall on someone who has been self-content?*)

Nietzsche likewise associated piety with an under-estimation and hence under-respect, if not disrespect, for oneself (**Dawn** 36). And so I find "perhaps man will climb even higher, when he no longer *flows out* into a god" (**GS** 285) a not-at-all-strange thought.

Following this, Nietzsche suggests that we learn the art of appreciating ourselves. This goes against typical socialization and education (compare German *Bildung*, French *formation*, etc.)—*then and now*—where "no one learns, no one strives after, no one teaches—*to bear solitude*" (**Dawn** 443). And so, this must be learned, despite the fear of "doing nothing" and the initial inertia that incline people to avoid being with themselves. (Thus diversions—games, hobbies, television, movies, much socializing, much writing,[66] etc.)

Relatedly, Nietzsche describes a person who realizes that the fountain of his self (*Selbst*) has not yet gushed forth water, and who adds with firm resolve, "Therefore I go into solitude—in order not to drink out of everyone's cistern" (**Dawn** 491, entitled *Auch deshalb Einsamkeit!* or "Solitude for That Reason, Too"). This echoes the image of water to be drawn from one's well in **HAH** I 286—an image also in Proverbs 5: 15 (although there the image is traditionally interpreted in another sense). Continuing this inner focus, Nietzsche later writes of what to expect when going in solitude: "In solitude, whatever one has brought into it grows—also the inner beast" (**Z** IV 13 Part 13).

What is Nietzsche suggesting? That the self-dissatisfied person reject all morality, as a kind of revenge against society for bringing out this dissatisfac-

---

[65] In this light, consider the "inner" of M. Ginsberg, *The Inner Palace*. For those interested in an in-depth examination of some of the world's most articulate mappings of the path inwards, this work may be quite relevant and helpful.

[66] Contrast Nietzsche's finding his own middle books, Dawn and GS, the "*sympathetischsten*" (most *simpático*, most likable) ones, since they were his most personal ones, as mentioned in Nietzsche's letter of Jun. 21, 1888, to Karl Knortz. I find them to be fine picnic grounds.

tion? That he stop admiring *all* figures—gods, heroes, friends, etc.? Or become isolated from as many people as possible, striving for total hermitism? That the inner beast be released to flourish? To this last question, No. The quotation just above continues, "Therefore solitude is inadvisable for many" (**Z** IV 13 Part 13). It is (*not* paradoxically) wise of those who are not wise to keep from going through experiences helpful only to the wise (cf. **W&S** 298); every organism can instinctively have its own wisdom.

Nietzsche is not proposing, then, the doctrine that everyone would benefit from the difficulties of these heights. Not everyone is a mountain climber. Nor does Nietzsche see, as all there is to aspire to, being a free spirit, one fully self-determining, unbound by the desire for knowledge and certainty (**GS** 347, cf. **EH**-HAH 1); one no longer a convict of his/her convictions (cf. **HAH** I 636-637); "who thinks other than one expects of him on the basis of his origin, environment, his position and job or on the basis of the dominant views of the day [*Zeitansichten*]" (**HAH** I 225; we may note, though, that this type of individual *is* taken to be possible in this passage!).

Recall that the "History of an Error" has as the end of its penultimate stage the *Teufelslärm*, devilish racket, of all free spirits (**Twilight** IV 5; cf. **GS** 290, **WP** 904). Nietzsche is not envisioning a world either of Brethren of the Free Spirit—seen as Heretics of the Free Spirit by Albertus Magnus (cf. Paul Zweig's *The Heresy of Self-Love*)—or of assassins/*hashshashin*.[67] Nietzsche is hardly ever to be understood coarsely. In short, the independent and cautious (epistemic) attitude of the free spirit (**HAH** I 282) is to be supplemented by a *self*-critical teasing-out process.

And, although the question may strike some as quaintly Greek, if not Ionian, let me ask how a self-pruning is possible, given that there is just *one* individual involved. How can *one* entity be in any conflict with itself? (Cp. "How is a plurality, differentiation, etc. possible, given a unity, homogeneity, etc.?") *If* such a question should be answered here, then let me say merely that an individual is not a psychologically homogeneous entity, nor even one whose interests, desires, needs, instincts, etc. are well integrated. The desire to fulfill or satisfy any of these is not automatically compatible with other personal desires. *The original desire for freedom or will to power is a many-vectored thing.*

---

[67] The assassins—from *assassin* (French), itself from *assassino* (Italian), in turn said to derive from *ḥaššāšīn* حشاشين or *ḥaššāšūn* حشاشون (Arabic, sellers/smokers of hashish)—were, to take the Christian Crusaders' perspective here rather than that of the Muslims being named, "Muslim fanatics sent on murder missions in the time of the Crusades" (*Concise Oxford Dictionary*, p. 64). Cf. *Larousse Lexis*, p. 118, and H. Wehr, *A Dictionary of Modern Written Arabic* (Arabic-Eng. sect.), p. 209. On "other-named" epithets as questionable on theoretical grounds, see M. Ginsberg, *The Inner Palace*, esp. pp. 325, 434, 447, 464, 491.

That is, as Nietzsche realized, in contrast to Goethe's *Faust*, one may contain many souls: **BGE** 244. Cf. Hesse's *Steppenwolf* and the Classical Greek image of the soul as a many-colored (ποικίλος *poikílos*) and many-headed (πολυκέφαλος *polyképhalos*) beast (θηρίον *thēríon*),[68] in Plato's *Republic*.[69]

The work of revaluing, selecting, developing, cultivating, or eliminating various aspects of our person (**BGE** 44, 203, 244, 258, etc.) amounts to the formation of a one-cultured individual, in Nietzsche's terms. In other concepts, this amounts to the self-integrating of a person, and in still another vocabulary, to the overcoming of alienation.[70]

V.1

What is the larger context of this topic of self-integration that has been of great importance to a variety of psychotherapeutic perspectives? To appreciate the scope of this issue, let us go beyond a concern only with Nietzsche and Freud, viewed with the narrow perspective of our times.[71] *This wider orientation is the lens of this section, to be divided into three sub-sections.* Perhaps a sampling of perspectives on this question of self-integration, although limited and selective, will bring into light some of the overall importance and significance of the proposals and perspective of Nietzsche here.

This issue of self-integration is one that we can see addressed even in ancient times and around the world, in various world cultures. In the *Republic* by Plato (428-348 BCE), for example, the ψυχή *psyché* (soul, mind, life-force, etc.), a many-colored and many-faced creature (as mentioned just above), was under-

---

[68] Liddell and Scott, *Greek-English Lexicon*, pp. 1430a, 1439a, 800a, respectively; *thēríon* is a wild animal, especially a hunted one (prey), or is used as a term of reproach. Greek terms given in citation form.

[69] In *Republic*, at 9.588b-c (that is, *Republic*, 588b-c, in Book IX).

[70] Alienation corresponds (in German philosophy) to *Entäusserung*, *Entfremdung*, or *Veräusserung*. In Marxism, in particular, alienation (or estrangement) is understood to involve expropriation (of property), following another feature of the Latin root (*aliēnus*), as in Russian отчуждение *otchuzhdenie*. See R.C. Solomon, *History and Human Nature: A Philosophical Review of European History and Culture, 1750-1850*, p. 399, n. 44; cf. p. 333.

And, on the overcoming of alienation as the central theme of the entire Hegelian *Phänomenologie* as a precursor to the Nietzschean issue we address here, that of how to achieve personal integration, see R.C. Solomon, *In the Spirit of Hegel*, pp. 546-552, esp. p. 549. More on integration, below, Chaps. 5 and 6.

[71] This would extend the point made in the early footnote on Karl Jaspers and his comment that psychoanalysis *blocked* the direct influence on psychopathology of other theoreticians. See above, p. 62, n. 2.

stood to need guidance (as does the State, the society) from a higher (third) part, distinct from both the rational (λογιστικόν *logitikón*) and the appetitive (ἐπθυμητικόν *epithymētikón*)[72] parts, this latter being the part of the psyche in which there are desires and affections.[73] Similarly, in Aristotle (384-322 BCE).[74] We might also think of the Stoic concept, as in the work of Zeno (of Citium)[75] of the ἡγεμονικόν *hēgemonikón*, the authoritative principle of the soul (which integrates all of the various aspects of the soul).[76]

We find this same sort of concern and interest in the process of coming to an integrated presence in the world, even earlier than this, and on the other side of the globe; for example, in the *Analects* (*Lúnyǔ* 論語) of Kǒngzǐ[77] 孔子 or Kǒngfūzǐ 孔夫子 (Confucius, 551-479 BCE), we find the Confucian idea of the exemplary person (*jūnzǐ* 君子), an individual who has achieved the delicate balance between basic disposition (*zhí* 質) and refinement (*wén* 文), each with its own tendency to overwhelm or become overgrown relative to other features of what remains in balance and proportion in the more respectable human being.[78]

And in such texts as the *Dàodéjīng* 道德經[79] (attributed to Lǎozǐ 老子, traditionally a contemporary of Confucius[80]), we find the stress in Daoism (or Taoism)[81] on the interplay between the parts of the whole, especially between opposing parts. In this process, a strong meeting or confrontation of these brings about a harmonized totality, a synergistic integration of opposites (rather than a homogenized blend): in particular, *yīn* 陰 and *yáng* 陽, complementary opposites

---

[72] Liddell and Scott, *Greek-English Lexicon*, pp. 1056b, 634b, resp.

[73] *Republic*, 4.440e-441a. *Symposium*, 189b-193d, describes yearning for reintegration (for a rejoining of our split halves), a familiar theme in Jungian theory.

[74] Aristotle, *Nichomachean Ethics*, 1102b22-30 (with the appetitive soul one of the parts of the non-rational part of the soul), Aristotle, *De anima*, 413b16, 414a29-32, 433a17.

[75] Not Zeno of the paradoxes, Zeno of Elea, died circa 430 BCE, but Zeno Ζήνων ὁ Κιτιεύς *Zénōn ho Kitieús* (d. ca. 264 BCE). Kitieús in Latin is Citium.

[76] Liddell and Scott, *Greek-English Lexicon*, p. 763a.

[77] I will not italicize Chinese personal names in this section.

[78] As in *The Analects*, 6.18. See R.T. Ames and H. Rosemont, Jr., *The Analects of Confucius: A Philosophical Translation*, pp. 107-108, with discussion of *jūnzǐ* 君子, at p. 60 of Introduction: Historical and Textual Background.

[79] In Wade-Giles transcription, *Tào Té Chīng*. Also, *Té Tào Chīng* 德道經.

[80] See R.G. Henricks, *Lao-tzu, Te-Tao Ching*, p. xiii of Introduction.

[81] For extended discussion, see A.C. Graham, *Disputers of the Tao: Philosophical Argument in Ancient China*, including Appendix 2 (The Relation of Chinese Thought to the Chinese Language), pp. 389-428. Cf. B.I. Schwartz, *The World of Thought in Ancient China*, esp. Chap. 6 (The Ways of Taoism), pp. 186-254.

interact in a continually balancing integration or synergy, a process of ongoingly creating harmony (hé)[82] that represents the ideal manifestation of the Dao, the Way (dào). The Dàodéjīng speaks of this dynamic balance, a vigorous confrontation (chōng) of vital energies (qì, perhaps more familiar in Wade-Giles transliteration, as ch'i) that produces harmony (hé).[83] This is the ideal of integrating our most elemental life energies as the path to a synergistic harmony.

In a more general way, in Daoist teachings is the idea of being and acting in the world in a way that is not based on small-minded consciousness—in other words, is not based on the limited and overly focused concentration on certain features of our life situation to the disregard of others, as is often the case when we are intent on some particular goal.

This is sometimes spoken of as acting from the axis of the Dao, the dào shū,[84] *the state of consciousness of someone who is aware of the processes and flow of the moment, and who can respond with the consciousness of the sage, with fully awakened consciousness, to the features of the situation with full relevance and appropriateness, without being frozen or rigidified by earlier doctrines or beliefs that make for a more selective (and so distorting) bias or perspective on the situation.*[85]

Similarly, the Buddhist tradition has as its starting point the recognition of our full life span and its changing circumstances, including the aging process, sickness, and death. And Buddhism clearly acknowledges the conflict between the natural human desire for happiness and the frustrations that we encounter ongoingly through life. It teaches that our overriding desire for happiness is in conflict with certain desires we mistakenly suppose will make us happy.

This situation with its consequent frustrations, discontent, lack of deep fulfillment, and inner tension, if not resolved or transcended, is seen as keeping us (as "worldlings") in a state of ongoing madness (craziness, not anger). As is said in Sinhalese Buddhism, "All worldlings are mad."[86]

---

[82] See R.T. Ames and D.L. Hall, *Dao De Jing, A Philosophical Translation*, on hé 和, pp. 61-62; on the interplay and potential harmonization between particular and context (or particular and totality: "the focus and its field"), pp. 11-54.

[83] The Dàodéjīng, Chap. 42. The statement reads in Chinese: chōng qì yǐ wéi hé 沖氣以為和 — as at J.C.H. Wu, *Lao Tzu / Tao Te Ching*, p. 60; the first character, chōng 沖, clash, dash against, pour or cascade over, rinse, blend, in some editions reads 中 zhōng, center, to balance, focus, attain. Cf. hé 和; dào 道; qì or ch'i 氣. See next note.

[84] Cf. Appendix, below, for the Chinese used in this book. Here, dào shū 道樞.

[85] Discussed in greater detail in the chapter on the pivot of the dao, below.

[86] In Pāli: *Sabbe puthujjanā ummattakā*, echoing the passage from 5th cent. CE Buddhaghosa, *Visuddhimagga*, XVII.261, mad like a worldling; in Pāli, *ummat-*

The Buddhist alternative here is to cultivate a consciousness that is clearly seeing and warmly compassionate to all living beings, including to ourselves, one in inner and outer harmony and integrity; in this sense, one of full integration.[87] This giving compassion a central role in our human situation is, of course, not unique to Buddhism, nor to the East.

We find it clearly expressed, to give one among many examples, in the Hawaiian wisdom teachings, where it is declared, *O ke aloha ka mea i ho'ola 'ai* (in English, compassion is the healer).[88]

Further, looking here into the Indocentric tantric traditions,[89] a basic idea is that we do not resist what we are presented with in life, but integrate everything that is present, including our longings and frustrations and inner conflicts, the encouraging and discouraging life situations we find ourselves facing in ease or with difficulty.

Life as a feast rather than a restricted diet.[90] Thus, in speaking of the personal transformation that brings about full and deep awakening (coming to

---

tako viya hi puthujjano. A worldling (Pāli, *puthujjano*; Sanskrit, *pṛthagjana*) is one not yet a "stream-entrant" or "stream-winner" (*sotāpanna*), one who has not even *begun* the psychospiritual transformation whose completion is called awakening; stream-entrance is *sotāpatti*. See Pāli Canon: *Sotāpatti-saṃyutta* in *Saṃyutta Nikāya* (esp. S.v.356-360) and *Mahāparinibbāna-sutta* in *Dīgha Nikāya* (esp. D.ii.92-93); cf. discussion in M. Ginsberg, *The Inner Palace,* p. 403, n. 2.

[87] Appreciating this active, directive function of consciousness, Pierre Janet discussed the power of consciousness, reporting that an investigation (into the ways consciousness influences, structures, and directs desire) has allowed returning to the earlier psychological understandings of consciousness and coming to appreciate it as one in the group of regulatory patterns of the individual. His more scholarly way of putting this—to render this part of his lecture more literally—was, "*The intervention of consciousness* in the desires has permitted returning to the psychological conceptions of consciousness and linking it to the set of the regulatory tendencies." The French text (italics as in original text) reads: "*L'intervention de la conscience* dans les envies a permis de revenir sur les conceptions psychologiques de la conscience et de la rattacher au groupe des tendences régulatrices." From P. Janet, "Les degrés d'activation des tendences," *Annuaire du Collège de France*, vol. 17 (1917), pp. 64-70, at p. 66.

[88] Title of a healers' conference, "O Ke Aloha Ka Mea I Hoʻola ʻAi—Compassion Is the Healer: An Indigenous Peoples Healing Conference, October 2000, Hawaiʻi" (a proverb, quoted in a song by Kawaikapuokalani (Frank) Hewett, *E 'akahai e na Hawaiʻi*). Thanks to K.L. Majersky for teaching me this proverb.

[89] For further discussion, see M. Ginsberg, *The Inner Palace*, pp. 87, 89, 171, 212, 228, 234, 237-238, 332, 400-401, 403, 446, 470, 478, 488, 559, 573-574.

[90] See M. Ginsberg, *The Far Shore: Vipassanā, The Practice of Insight*, p. 95.

absolute *bodhicitta*, the fulfilled or actualized thought of awakening, or enlightenment), a Tibetan Buddhist text states that what is particular about the tantric approach or path is that with it, "the basic energy involved in this profound process of tantric transformation is the energy of our own desires."[91] As Thai Theravada Buddhist Master V.R. Dhiravamsa has written, "If we maintain a realistic view of life and all the situations it presents to us, we can take the drama and the dilemma that we encounter as a challenge for bringing out and making use of our inner resources, our human capacities and potentialities ..."[92]

Similarly, a Hindu text explains that "the *sādhana* [or practice] for the Śākta [the practitioner of Śakti or Shakti Tantra] consists in a life of ceaseless activity and meditation. *He does not avoid the world, but embraces it in order to overcome it.* He sees the workings of the Divine everywhere, even in things and functions that are ordinarily held to be despicable and low."[93]

In one Buddhist teaching, this is said to be the identity of samsāra and nirvāna, depending on one's experiencing. This idea is found in the Sanskrit verse composition by the well-known second-century Buddhist philosopher Nāgārjuna,[94] *Mūlamadhyamakārikā*,[95] as well as in Tibetan texts, as by the nineteenth-century Nyingma Buddhist teacher, Lama Mi-pham,[96] in Korean Sŏn 禪 [the character read as Chán in Chinese, Zen in Japanese] Tradition,[97] etc.

All of these ideas are pointing to the extreme integration and unification of consciousness on a grand scheme. *The word 'integration' is obviously central here.* This is a matter of embracing the difficult, not avoiding it, of course. (How many times do we have to try to avoid some little problem, only to create a much

---

[91] T. Yeshe, *Introduction to Tantra: A Vision of Totality*, p. 17.

[92] V.R. Dhiravamsa, *The Dynamic Way of Meditation: The Release and Cure of Pain and Suffering*, p. 12.

[93] T.M.P. Mahadevan, *Outlines of Hinduism*, p. 208. Spelling, punctuation, italics, parenthetical glosses, as in original; italicization of the full sentence and glosses in brackets added.

[94] Dates uncertain; sometimes given as second half of the second century CE.

[95] K. Inada, *Nāgārjuna: A Translation of his Mūlamadhyamakārikā with an Introductory Essay*, p. 158 (*Mūlamadhyamakārikā*, ch. XXV, verses 19-20), or S. Batchelor, *Verses from the Center: A Buddhist Vision of the Sublime*, p. 129.

[96] Mi-pham (1846-1912): full name, Mi-pham 'Jam-dbyangs rnam-rgyal rgyamtsho. See his commentary to *A Letter to a Friend* by Nāgārjuna, entitled *The Garland of White Lotus Flowers*, in L. Kawamura (tr.), *Golden Zephyr*, p. 85.

[97] *Kyunyŏ-jŏn: The Life, Times and Songs of a Tenth Century Korean Monk*, e.g., p. 45; cf. A. Hirakawa, *A History of Indian Buddhism From Śākyamuni to Early Mahāyāna*, pp. 277-278, A.K. Warder, *Indian Buddhism*, p. 149, M. Ginsberg, *The Inner Palace*, pp. 168, 239, 468, M. Ginsberg, *The Far Shore*, pp. 18-20 (the chapter "The Far Shore's Under Your Feet"). Chán is also written 禪.

more complicated and difficult resultant situation, in order to see that such "wisdom" is quite myopic?) It is a matter of allowing ourselves to face whatever is given to us—to face it, to appreciate it, to see how to respond most wisely to it. This is looking and appreciating before reacting and making things worse. This is seeing what is difficult as being of great potential value in our development, allowing us to integrate it rather than fighting or disregarding it. (It is simpler if we are freed from trying to squirm out of some situation we take to be unattractive to us.)

On a larger scale, this would be our being ready to take into account whatever is going on in our lives in a way that allows us to take it in, digest it (to transform it and to be transformed by it), and to go forward, as the overall situation calls for. These various traditions can be seen in these ways as pointing in the same direction, or at least as indicating a similarity of interest and concern with the issue of self-integration in our lives, in ways that I have addressed in detail elsewhere.[98]

Furthermore, this issue of self-integration (beyond the interest that Nietzsche expressed in it) has its counterpoint in the related issue of non-integration (or that of disintegration).

Freud, among others, expressed a specific interest in this topic—we ourselves will continue this discussion in later sections of this present chapter, incidentally—as in a letter he wrote to Lou Andreas-Salomé, where he stated, "What interests me is the separation and breaking up into its component parts what would otherwise flow together into a primeval pulp."[99]

V.2

What is the larger context of this topic of self-integration? Here we can complement the preceding worldwide considerations about integration with those that address disintegration or non-integration.

*For a sampling and overview of some conceptualizations of this sort of process, this **non**-integration, and the transformation toward self-**integration**,* we may consider that this self-integrating would be, of course, an integration of that which is not yet integrated, or of that which has been separated out, that is, has disintegrated—as in Freud's image just above (more below). Or of that which has been reorganized into schematic segregations (as psychiatrist Mardi Horowitz described this process, using the term 'segregations' to refer to distinct, non-overlapping, sub-sets of some totality).[100]

---

[98] For more, see M. Ginsberg, *The Inner Palace.*

[99] Letter 170, of July 30, 1915, in E.L. Freud, ed., *Letters of Sigmund Freud 1973-1939*, pp. 316-317.

[100] See *Treatment of Stress Response Syndromes* (2003), p. 65, on dissociation.

Going back in time, we may notice that through the ages this separation or compartmentalizing or splitting apart into isolated parts has been understood in very different ways, not exactly equivalent to one another. The Greeks spoke, for example, of mania (μᾰνία *mănía*, madness, inspired frenzy[101]) and of possession (in which the usual personality was overcome and important changes made in the person's demeanor, thinking, speaking, and so forth) by the gods, a divine or daemonic—*not* demonic—possession.[102] This term is used (in a related form), at *The Gospel of Matthew*, 4: 24, which is taken to mean possessed by a demon (with this same δαίμον *daímon*, interpreted in this Gospel context as cognate to the more modern concept of a demon, quite *un*-divine, we might say). Subsequently, European medieval understanding took there to be possession, not by the gods (or by God), but by the devil (sometimes referred to as Satan or Lucifer).[103] Medieval and post-medieval theorizing has occasionally made use of this demonic understanding of some human thinking and activity, among other conceptualizations of this kind of phenomenon (or kinds of phenomena, perhaps). So, there has been talk of being a lunatic (from the influence of the luna, the moon).[104] Alternatively, this new way of acting and speaking has been described

---

[101] Liddell and Scott, *Greek-English Lexicon*, p. 1079a. Note that the cognate to μᾰνία *mănía*, in the Indic languages (for example, in Sanskrit and in Pāli) is the confused and torment-creating concern called māna, a comparing of oneself and others, resulting in some sense of ego, either superior to, equal to, or inferior to others: a way to mental torment, from the Indic (and Buddhist) perspective.

[102] The key term here is δαιμονίζομαι *daimonízomai*, to be under the power of a δαίμον *daímon*, to suffer by a divine visitation, to be possessed, to be mad (Liddell and Scott, *Greek-English Lexicon*, p. 365b); δαίμον *daímon* means a god or goddess, said of individual gods or goddesses, but more frequently refers to the Divine power. J.M. Rist, in *Stoic Philosophy*, speaking of *daimones*, in the plural, writes of "associating surviving souls with *daimones*, being more than mortal and less than divine." (p. 261, italics in original). Cf. below, p. 192.

[103] See preceding note, plus N. Caciola, *Discerning Spirits: Divine and Demonic Possession in the Middle Ages* (cf. C.T. Lewis and C. Short, *A Latin Dictionary*, pp. 510a, 646a, 1243a, 1403b, 1983c; *Oxford Latin Dictionary*, pp. 483, 607, 1223, 1410, 2052); S. Ferber, *Demonic Possession and Exorcism in Early Modern France;* P. Almond, *Demonic Possession and Exorcism in Early Modern England: Contemporary Texts and their Cultural Contexts*, with *The Story of the Lancashire Seven* (1600), in facsimile reproduction (pp. 219-220).

[104] In Classical Greek and its variant, New Testament Greek, to be σεληνιάζεται *selēniázetai*, influenced by the moon (as in being moon-struck or a lunatic), was to be epileptic, to have seizures! See Liddell and Scott, *Greek-English Lexicon*, pp. 1589b-1590a, at both σεληνιάζεται *selēniázetai* and σεληνιάζομαι *selēniázomai*, and *The Gospel of Matthew*, 4: 24, 27: 15.

in terms of the individual's being hysterical (from ὑστέρα *hystéra*, womb; Latin and English, uterus).[105]

Or, again, as still another possibility here, there may be theorizing about talk of having lost one's (usual) mind and so being demented, from de, without, + *mens/mentis*, mind. With this came a variant, a premature dementia (or *dementia praecox*; *praecox:* premature, hasty), later called schizophrenia (from σχίζων *skhízōn*, to separate, divide, cut out, branch off, curdle or separate into curds and whey—*an striking image of dis-integration!*—, etc. + φρήν *phrēn* or φρενός *phrenós*, the midriff, the heart as seat of passions, fear, joy, grief, or courage, the mind as seat of faculties, perception, and thought, the will, purpose, said of persons in their senses, etc.). *Note well: **not** a "split mind"!*[106]

And so on, to more recent descriptions of dissociating, disintegration (including positive disintegration, mentioned above), multiple personalities, depersonalization,[107] and so forth.

---

[105] Liddell and Scott, *Greek-English Lexicon*, p. 1906a, have the further entry, ὑστερικός *hysterikós*, suffering in the womb, hysterical, with ὑστέρα *hystéra*, womb, at p. 1905b.

[106] Liddell and Scott, *Greek-English Lexicon*, pp. 1746a-b, 1954b, respectively. We may note that *the Greek was disregarded* when this concept of a dissociating in the emotional life of the individual was reduced to the interpretation of this term, schizophrenia, to mean nothing more than split consciousness. Historian E. Shorter writes (*A History of Psychiatry: From the Era of the Asylum to the Age of Prozac*, p. 108), "The term schizophrenia was probably an unfortunate choice, for subsequent generations of physicians and nonphysicians alike would associate it with some kind of splitting or divided consciousness."

[107] This term was perhaps first used in the psychological literature by Ludovic Dugas, apparently in several articles published in 1898, such as "Observations et documents: Un cas de dépersonnalisation," *Revue philosophique de la France et de l'étranger*, vol. 45 (1898), pp. 500-507, and in more extended discourse, in L. Dugas and F. Moutier, *La dépersonnalisation* (1911). An earlier use of the word cited by the authors is that of Amiel (Henri-Frédéric Amiel) in his *Journal intime* or *Fragments d'un journal intime*, first ed., 1882, in fifth ed., 1887, vol. 1, pp. 141-142, vol. 2, pp. 292, 300, etc. The passages in question address a consciousness which is becoming more ethereal as it approaches death, and speak, more particularly, of the Buddhist *voluptuousness* of the Sufis (la volupté bouddhique des Soufis)!!—a cultural goulash, inviting distinctions as given in M. Ginsberg, *The Inner Palace*—, the kef of the Turks, the ecstasy of the Easterners, and with use of verbal forms, speak of one who becomes "*depersonalized*, detached, flown away" (*dépersonnalisé*, détaché, envolé) and who "*depersonalizes*" (*se dépersonnalise*), resp. "Easterners" here would range from those in the Proche-Orient (Near East) to those from the Extrême Orient (Far East). Quotes

This has been for a sampling and schematic overview; I am not trying to judge between these various conceptualizations at this point, nor suggesting that they are equivalent to one another.

V.3

Viewed developmentally (in this third part), we may, in one such understanding, see this lack of self-integration as a natural process in which integration is not a given at birth, not automatically present, and as something that may never be achieved. In this way, it would be something that we may bring about in our lives, but are not born with nor destined to achieve.

Or, from a second theoretical viewpoint, we may see it as a process in which integration is taken to be natural and normal. In this second understanding, we would then consider that it has been blocked or has broken down in cases of non-integration. In either case, at some important point in time, we have individuals for whom the idea (and the process!) of self-integration—or, of the elimination of disharmonies—will be of interest and of potential value.

The appreciating of the disharmonies in a person, and the ways in which these are dealt with, are quite important from a Nietzschean perspective. Part of these disharmonies may come from the family environment in which a child grew up, as **HAH** 379, "The unresolved disharmonies [*Dissonanzen*] in the relationship[108] between the parents' characters [*Charakter*] and ways of thinking[109] resonate on in the demeanor of the child and structure its inner story of suffering."

This issue of disharmonies that Nietzsche drew the reader's attention to in this passage operates on both a subtle level and in less elegant ways, as when

---

are from entries dated 9 Aug. 1859, 8 Jul. 1880, and 9 Sep. 1880, resp.; italics here as in original text. The verb here (se dépersonnalise) could also be glossed "depersonalizes himself." For much more recent discussions of depersonalization, derealization, and dissociation, see O. van der Hart, E. Nijenhuis, and K. Steele, *The Haunted Self: Structural Dissociation and the Treatment of Chronic Traumatization* (2006), pp. 28-29, 66-71, 90-91, 104-108, 115-121, 126, 190; V. Şar and E. Öztürk, "Functional Dissociation of the Self: A Sociocognitive Approach to Trauma and Dissociation," *Journal of Trauma and Dissociation*, vol. 8, no. 4 (2007), pp. 69-89; and V. Şar, and C. Ross, "Dissociative Disorders as a Confounding Factor in Psychiatric Research," *Psychiatric Clinics of North America*, vol. 29 (2006), pp. 129-144; etc.

[108] For more, see below, Chap. 5, pp. 108-116, a commentary on **HAH** 379.

[109] Relationship: *das Verhältnis*, which is also glossed: proportion, ratio, liaison, love affair. Way of thinking: *die Gesinnung*, which is also glossed: conviction, principle of action, intension, disposition, sentiment.

the disharmonies are so intense that they result in ongoing physical, emotional, and sexual violence against the child.[110] To appreciate *"Dissonanzen"* (dissonances, disharmonies, incongruities, or non-integrated features) of our consciousness, we need to have a deep honesty, making our experience the subject of our observations and our objectivity, as Nietzsche put it (**GS** 319).

We may have to recognize something clearly first, before we can act on it, or deal with it in an effective way, and, one's theory may make it difficult to recognize certain phenomena.

As contemporary French psychoanalyst, neuropsychiatrist, and trauma-survival specialist Boris Cyrulnik has noted[111]—and as has been obvious to those in the field of systemic family therapy, who take a Systems Theory perspective (in which the members of a family are seen as parts of a larger interconnected, inter-active, and integrated whole),[112] *long before it could be conceptualized and only then integrated into psychoanalytic theorizing*—there is an intimate link between non-integrated, unresolved, and otherwise disharmonious tendencies within and between parents, on the one hand, and, on the other, the subsequent problematic ways of dealing with life's situations for the child.

Nietzsche's formulation (in **HAH** 379, quoted just above) of the unresolved disharmonies of the parents as the source of torment for the child, raises the question of whether these disharmonies will define the life of the child, in other words, whether, the child is doomed to suffer its entire life as a result of these disharmonies (as the passage might be interpreted as suggesting) or—if we do not read too much fatalism into his original observation—whether there is a way for the child to become free of such consequent torment.

And, as we can sometimes understand the usual by paying attention to the unusual, or noticing the subtle by examining the exaggerated, or understand what we consider to be normal by investigating what we consider to be abnormal, there are those who have dealt with the extremes of the human condition, focusing on extremes of agitation or torment, extremes of the mundane reality in which what is happening has a strong unpleasant aspect to it, called Unlust (Unpleasure) by Breuer and Freud,[113] and in Buddhism called *duḥkha*.[114]

---

[110] The literature on this is growing. More on this, elsewhere in this book.

[111] *Parler d'amour au bord du gouffre*, pp. 173-174; in English, at p. 114 of *Talking of Love on the Edge of a Precipice*. Cf. below, p. 110, n. 5.

[112] For more, see the next chapter, pp. 103-107, on family therapy in France.

[113] See J. Breuer and S. Freud, *Studies on Hysteria* (1895d) [at SE 2: 116, 269-270 = GW 1: 174, 268-269]. Cf. the part of that text with Breuer as sole author, and also SE 2: xxi, and SE 2: 197, 210, which are from the Editor's Introduction to the English, neither of which appears in GW (since it contains only writings by Freud). See also S. Freud, "The Instincts and their Vicissitudes" (1915c) [esp. SE 14: 138-139 = GW 10: 230-231 = CP 4: 81-82].

From this Buddhist-meditation-inspired perspective, this unusual, specifically-focused attention has made it clearer than was possible by keeping our attention solely on the more usual variations. In a more general way, we can recognize that understanding can be cultivated by examining with clarity these unresolved incongruities, these troubling experiences and their intrusive memories that would not leave the person in peace, those examples in which it was quite obvious that there was the painful absence of a flowing and happily vibrant life experience.

And in a broader way here, we may look to understand the historical significance of this issue of self-integration, from the interest in France in the last quarter of the 1800s (and even well before then) and Freud's work in Vienna through the first half of the twentieth century, to more recent work in the field of psychotherapy in the late 1900s and moving into the early twenty-first century: an interest, that also has a long history from the time of Nietzsche on, in this self-integrating, or harmonizing and setting into order (including articulating or recognizing the hierarchy of importance) of our various, mutually conflicting interests and beliefs. In this light we may consider the studies on dissociation by the French, as Jean-Martin Charcot (1887) and his student-associate Pierre Janet (1880s on), who spoke of shocks, or traumas, that would bring about fixed ideas (*idées fixes*), emotionally-charged rigid ideas that were isolated from the rest of the individual's thinking, operating in a narrowed field of consciousness, perhaps as a response to feeling overwhelmed.[115]

This feeling overwhelmed, of being in what Heinz Kohut has called "psychological overburdenedness ... the essence of a traumatic state"[116] can be appreciated in these ways as quite central to understanding trauma and its aftermath.

We may notice in this context the line of thinking that extends from variations within Freudian psychoanalysis, where the unconscious is to be made conscious,[117] in Jungian analysis, where the shadow is to be investigated and brought into contact with the light,[118] in the Gestalt psychotherapy of Fritz

---

[114] This is the Sanskrit form; in Pāli (the related language of Theravāda Buddhism), the word is *dukkha*. For extended discussion of this and related issues, see M. Ginsberg, *The Inner Palace.*

[115] More on this issue of integration in its many facets and related meta-theoretical issues, in the chapter on Pierre Janet, misleading concepts, and integration.

[116] See *The Restoration of the Self* (1977), p. 162.

[117] See "Further Recommendations on the Technique of Psycho-Analysis II: Remembering, Repeating and Working-Through" (1914g) [esp. SE 12: 155-156 = GW 10: 135-136 = CP 2: 375-376]; *Inhibitions, Symptoms and Anxiety* (1926d) [at SE 20: 159-160 = GW 14: 191-192].

[118] See *The Development of Personality*, pp. 196-198; "The Philosophical Tree"

Perls[119] and of Claudio Naranjo,[120] where our conflicting goals, desires, beliefs, and so forth, define an inner tension or disharmony, and where these various elements are to be put into actual conversation with one another in order to reach harmonization and non-conflictual integration.

It may also be recognized in still other psychotherapies that formulate these same dynamics in alternative conceptual frameworks, such as that of the transmutation of the personality found in the writings of Roberto Assagioli, founder of Psychosynthesis,[121] to give one further example among many.

This process of transformation or transmutation, this search toward the goal of a deep integration and harmonization of our various needs, wants, yearnings, dreams to be realized, and so forth, in short, this self-integrating of a person, is something we thus find articulated in a number of different theoretical frameworks.

Yet, as was said above, this search needn't result in a one-track individual. And, as Nietzsche feels that solitude is not for everyone, others of his thoughts should be considered with similar provisos.

There is not only a pervasive feeling that solitude can be of great importance to a person's reaching the self that societal/political involvement keeps him or her from. (*Not* that this self, this higher, most individual self, is the same as at birth, or in childhood, or at any earlier period in one's life: one *deepens* through experience to new heights.)

Complementing this honoring of solitude, there is in Nietzsche's writings a counterpoising admiration of friendship. This will most likely make excellent sense to anyone who has been able to enjoy even just a modicum of solitude: it results in an extension of antennae into the worlds of others; then encounter with another is not so practiced, so hackneyed, that it jams the picking-up of the other's perhaps subtle differentness, individuality, personality.

As a reading of Nietzsche's comments on friendship show—e.g., **HAH** I 499, **GS** 61 (entitled "In Honor of Friendship"), etc.—he was not suggesting a hermitic life as desirable. His understanding of friendship (*not* equal to mutual pity) required spiritual—this is better than "psychological"—equals; "Are you a slave? Then you cannot be a friend" (**Z** I 14; the entire section is relevant here).

(1954), *Alchemical Studies*, pp. 251-349 [=*Collected Works*, vol. 13, 1967], pp. 265-266; *The Practice of Psychotherapy: Essays on the Psychology of the Transference and Other Subjects* [=*Collected Works*, vol. 16, 1966], pp. 101-103, 131-137, 168-171, 261-266. And see further, above, p. 86, n. 73.

[119] See F. Perls, *Gestalt Therapy Verbatim* (1969).

[120] See C. Naranjo, *The Way of Silence and the Talking Cure: On Meditation and Psychotherapy* (2006), pp. 17-22, 52-56, 64-69.

[121] See, R. Assagioli, *Psychosynthesis: A Manual of Principles and Techniques* (1965), pp. 49-52, 105, 187, 269-276.

VI

Does this view of friendship suggest a complement to Nietzsche's "I am a railing ... Your crutch, however, I am not" (**Z** I 6)? And is there a philosophy/theory of psychotherapy wrapped up in that fuller view? Note that some contemporary psychiatrists, psychologists, and other psychotherapists (Carl Rogers, Hellmuth Kaiser, Louis Fierman, Allen Enelow, etc.) suggest that in addition to actually seeing the patient or client often, all that is required is "that the therapist engage his patient in as open, direct, spontaneous, and genuine [a] communicative relationship as he can"[122] for successful psychotherapy to occur. Which sounds like being a good friend to someone (one, however, hard to find).

Given this, is Nietzsche perhaps accepting the possibility of psychotherapy that is *not directive* (i.e., with a therapist who does not direct)? Yet even for *this* type of therapy (related subspecies being called Rogerian, Kaiserian, etc.), can't one suggest that psychotherapy still essentially involves a specific type of asymmetrical relationship between two or more people which Nietzsche only criticizes? Namely, that type in which at least one of the people is accepted by those concerned as "healthy," "well," "strong," or at least the "helper," "facilitator," "doctor," "therapist," etc. And of the other or others involved, at least one as the "patient," the "mentally ill (or 'disturbed') one," the "client" or "guest" or "seeker"? If so, aren't Nietzsche's critiques of pity—with the contrast-complement of **Z** II 3—at **Dawn** 16 and 134-135, **GS** 99 and 338, **Z** III 5, **BGE** 225, **EH** I 8,[123] all directly opposed to any such relationship? And what of his non-respect for the weak, or the self-denying, or those who wallow in unhappiness while making no attempt at improving their state of affairs (**GS** 312)?

A first reply to this set of questions might be seen in the idea of certain London psychiatrists—most specifically R.D. Laing, David Cooper, Joseph Berke, Morton Schatzman, and associates—that there is nothing *defining* in an interpersonal relationship about one's accepting the function of helper at various moments. Part of the theoretical position of the Arbours Housing Association, Ltd,[124] for example, was that *any* member of the group at any given time may serve as a "host" while it is totally explicitly understood by all that this in no way places any stricture on future possibilities, such as this same individuals later wanting and receiving help him or herself. This view suggests the non-fac-

---

[122] L.B. Fierman, M.D., "Myths in the Practice of Psychotherapy," *Archives of General Psychiatry*, vol. 12 (Apr. 1965), pp. 408-14, at p. 412. Cf. L.B. Fierman, ed., *Effective Psychotherapy: The Contribution of Hellmuth Kaiser*, and L. B. Fierman, *The Therapist Is the Therapy: Effective Psychotherapy II.*

[123] On pity (Mitleid), see comments presented above in the Foreword by Claudio Naranjo, pp. xix-xx; cf. p. 77. **EH** I is entitled "Why I Am So Wise."

[124] A U.K. registered charity since 1970 (50 Courthope Rd., London, NW3).

ticity of people (as Jean-Paul Sartre might have said), the variability of their psychological and phenomenological states and the plurality of forms the interrelating of the same given people may take. Nietzsche's critique of psychotherapy, however, would seem more radical (i.e., more to the root of things) than that of Laing *et al.* if the preceding comments about his views are on the right track. For Nietzsche, the question does not focus on whether there is permanence—or anything that defines or sets in concrete (constricts, in Sartrean terms, into "facticity")—to these particular ways of acting and responding between various individuals (their "roles," to put this uglily); it focuses, rather, on whether these ways come about at all, even if evenly distributed in all ways possible.

Yet there is incorporated into this line of thinking a particular view of what psychotherapeutic relationships amount to which I want to question, and that is the aspect suggesting the personal (*qua* person) superiority of the therapist. The German-trained psychoanalyst Frieda Fromm-Reichmann once gave an orienting declaration in the Introduction to a textbook she wrote (which was dedicated to her four renowned teachers, Sigmund Freud, Kurt Goldstein, Georg Groddeck, and Harry Stack Sullivan): "It is my belief that the problems and emotional difficulties of mental patients, neurotics or psychotics, are, in principle, rather similar to one another and also to the emotional difficulties in living *from which we all suffer at times.*"[125] Of course, this touches on what has been called the delicate narcissism of the psychiatrist. *And would be something of potential value for such concerned individuals to be attentive to, particularly in professional work.* But this is quite distinct an issue, we might say in passing.

Here, dealing with another with compassion (especially if more accurately seen as pity) may be an instance of disrespecting the other under a self-disguised smugness (or felt to be that by the recipient, or both), and is barely harmonious with the nobility of either the "patient" or "guest," or the therapist.

Thus, even earnest, truthful, and true lauding ("stroking"), if given when a felt *need* for it is there, may well amount to a self-defeating act. Nietzsche does talk of treating the "mentally ill" [*Geisteskranken*]: "above all not with haughty mercy, but with medical sagacity, medical good will" (**Dawn** 202), and of physicians of the soul [*Ärzte der Seele*] (**Dawn** 52; cf. **Dawn** 322, **HAH** I 243, **Z** I 22 Part 2, etc.). In **GM** III 15 he talks of "the necessity of doctors and nurses who are themselves sick" (he takes these to include the ascetic priest).

This GM passage suggests that individuals who have gone through, or are in the process of going through, the kinds of experience the "patient" or "guest" is enveloped in (whether taken to be insanity, anxiety, psychological difficulty, self-questioning, self-hatred, or something else), can be of great help (not involving the haughty mercy mentioned above).

---

[125] F. Fromm-Reichmann, *Principles of Intensive Psychotherapy*, Introduction (1950), pp. xi-xii. Italics added.

As Laing suggests (*The Politics of Experience*, pp. 105-106), a respect-ful initiation may replace a degradation ceremonial, with the person being "guided with full social encouragement and sanction into inner space and time, by people who have been there and back again. Psychiatrically, this would ap-pear as ex-patients helping future patients to go mad."

Nietzsche, though, is not suggesting that therapists guide the other to go mad, even if some therapists will be comfortable in the other going mad *or not*. More generally, such therapists, having gone through the psychology of a bad conscience, of being sick of oneself, to a new location of self-acceptance (cf. **BGE** 287: "The noble soul has reverence for itself"), of self-love, beyond at-tacking themselves and their actions (the bite of conscience as the perpetration of cowardice against one's own acts: **Twilight** I 10), *illustrate* the possibility of each person transcending a current state. (Taking God as *Deus sive Natura*, as nature, as surroundings, I disagree with the determinism of Spinoza, *Ethics*, Book 1, Axiom 3 and Proposition 27.[126])

This Nietzschean understanding in no way denies that each person may be at a specific place along an individual path, each—as just above—self-trans-cending a particular self toward a unique result.

What some require to send their dog away (in the image of **GS** 312), to begin their *own* self-pruning, to feel their self-hatred and dissatisfaction and to nourish it to death—*this* suggestion being an intensified version of Montaigne's "I have allowed colds, migraines, and other ailments to grow old and die a natu-ral death within me; 1 lost them when I had half trained myself to harbor them. They are conjured better by courtesy than by defiance," *Essays* III: 13; cf. the third of six means mentioned by Nietzsche in **Dawn** 109)—what some require for this "sending away of their dog" is realizing the possibility of doing so. Real-izing that there is another "who had the courage to be himself, who knew how to stand alone without first waiting for heralds and signs from above" (**GM** III 5, in talking of Schopenhauer), who is "not only a great thinker, but also a real per-son" (**U₃** 7, also about Schopenhauer), in short, a philosopher. This does not mean an academic philosopher, nor a "philosophical laborer," but *one who cre-ates values* (**BGE** 211). And it means being noble, in Nietzsche's concept of no-bility. "The noble type of man experiences itself as determining values, it does not need approval; . . . it is value-creating" (**BGE** 260). There is something para-doxical, difficult about this, but *not* impossible. If one *does* need to see another as self-determining, self-pruning, etc., before beginning the same process him-self, won't his or her future actions, changes, etc., although seeming to be *self-*

---

[126] Recogizing only "determined" processes, more subtle ones are not acknow-ledged. To have broader scope, a shift is called for, as from Newtonian to Ein-steinian physics. See the transformational perspectives discussed in Chapter 13, on our third nature, below, and in *The Inner Palace* and *The Far Shore*.

governed, actually be *therapist*-governed? This *is* highly likely, but *not* necessary. The therapist *can* avoid directing the direction *or* the rate, the pace, of any
changes, and this is the attitude suggested by Nietzsche's "Vademecum—Vadetecum" (**GS** Overture/Vorspiel 7), "Imitators" (**GS** 255), **Z** I 6, etc.

(Of course those disagreeing basically with Nietzschean psychiatry will
not especially see this as something to avoid, and so we can see "behavior therapists"[127] giving patients "homework," i.e., exercises of certain sorts of activity to
practice between visits, *defined and directed by the therapist.*)

In fact, there is no reason for the therapist to have to indicate *that* the
patient change, or that it is desirable that the patient change. The whole situation
itself is an expression of the need or desire for change, and the patient's realization of this is already *incorporated* in his/her seeing the therapist, except in unusual cases. And if the patient is seeing the therapist but does not at all *feel* the
desire *or* need to change, this is as acceptable as any other attitude on change the

---

[127] Originally, behaviorism denied the use of any mental concepts or theoretical
constructs, leading to some heated discussions in the intellectual world, as the
famous exchanges between B.F. Skinner and Noam Chomsky)—as in Chomsky's 1959 "A Review of B.F. Skinner's *Verbal Behavior*" (1957), in *Language*,
vol. 35, no. 1 (1959), pp. 26-58—behaviorists are more accurately practologists
(formed from *praktikos/praxis* + *logos*) than psychologists (from *psychē* +
logos). On this issue, Chomsky wrote in 1968 (*Language and Mind*, p. 58),

> We live, after all, in the age of "behavioral science," not of
> "the science of the mind." I do not want to read too much
> into a terminological innovation, but I think that there is
> some significance in the ease and willingness with which
> modern thinking about man and society accepts the
> designation "behavioral science." No sane person has ever
> doubted that behavior provides much of the evidence for
> this study—all of the evidence, if we interpret "behavior" in
> a sufficiently loose sense. But the term "behavioral science"
> suggests a not-so-subtle shift of emphasis toward the evi-
> dence itself and away from the deeper underlying principles
> and abstract mental structures that might be illuminated by
> the evidence of behavior. It is as if natural science were to
> be designated "the science of meter readings."

On the other hand, much more recent developments in what is still called behavioral therapy now make use of undeniably mentalistic concepts, as in the early
twenty-first century mindfulness-based "behavioral" therapies. This is quite an
expansion or turn-about from earlier behaviorism, of course. There is perhaps a
touch of gentle humor and, clearly, significant irony in the theoretical "evolution" that we can notice here with our current half-century of perspective.

patient might have. Here we see the therapist as offerer, not as commander, not as leader (cf. **Twilight** I 14). A Nietzschean therapist is not attempting to derive self-satisfaction from the patient (having realized him or herself as an independent source of self-evaluation), and so is not needful of the patient's "success" or "cure." Cp. the Zen archer/samurai with no goal. He or she does not *rely* on the patient, does not *need* any particular outcome or change in the patient to establish his or her own orientation of sense of self-worth, and so is free to let the patient see, *however* the latter does or wishes to[128] (the therapist's *amor fati*). The patient is thus in a situation in which only his or her own view is of concern, and only his or her evaluation of it is relevant. *This is learning to evaluate for oneself by the absence (or removal) of external commands about how and what to evaluate.* (This relationship stands in contrast with involuntary psychotherapy not initiated by the patient: see here the writings of Thomas Szasz.[129])

VII

Now, all of this has been articulated as if there *is* a person, but one of Nietzsche's contributions (if not *the* contribution) to philosophical psychology has been the suggestion that there is no such thing (**BGE** 54, **Twilight** III 5, etc.). Perhaps some concerned with the issue of psychotherapy will say to this that they reject it as ridiculous, yet want to use these other components of Nietzsche's psychiatric views (following **HAH** II 201), but let me first take a more articulated version of this general no-ego position: consider **Twilight** VI 8, where critiques of the concepts of self and of causality are combined, and we find Nietzsche proposing that as for man, the "fatality of his essence is not to be disentangled from the fatality of all that has been and will be . . . One is necessary, one is a bit of fatefulness, one belongs to the whole, one is in the whole."

Nietzsche's point might be challenged in this context by questioning what it has to do with something like psychotherapy. This may allow us to recognize that it has a *lot* to do with it. For example, Nietzsche's perspective here is in harmony with the shift to family therapy suggested by the theorizing of such differently oriented psychiatrists as Freud, Ted Lidz, and R.D. Laing.[130]

---

[128] And thus I disagree with the view in A. Artaud's *Van Gogh, le suicidé de la société* (1947) that psychiatrists must see enemies in every artist, every genius. On the issue of the psychiatrist's self-esteem, see esp. F. Fromm-Reichmann, *Principles of Intensive Psychotherapy*, 1950, pp. 13-18, 23-25, 41, 198-199.

[129] From "The Myth of Mental Illness," *The American Psychologist*, vol. 15, pp. 113-118 (1960) and same-named book (1961/2010) to *Coercion as Cure: A Critical History of Psychiatry* (2009). Cf. above, p. 72, n. 45, and below, p. 145, n. 1.

[130] For something more specifically meta-familial, cp. Laing's *Politics of the Family*, esp. the notion of mapping images, with **HAH** I 379; **Dawn** 35, etc.

We can appreciate their analysis of the individual as being inextricably involved with and so best understood in terms of family[131] as the first defocusing of a vision of people as monads—totally separate substances in the world—into a vision of an ongoing, ever-evolving, inter-connected process.

This Nietzschean vision of a totally interrelated single universe (Z IV 19, Parts 10-11[132]) echoes a Buddhist understanding of the ultimate non-separateness of the person, taking the person as a convenient fiction but having no ultimate distinct reality—the emptiness of the person, as Buddhist texts put it.[133]

And given this vision, all of one's situations and states can be seen as part of this larger something. This does not at all imply that one has no role in the future, in one's own future, for one is, after all, a part of this larger world (cf. **HAH** II 363, **W&S** 61, etc.). This sense or recognition of interconnectedness is quite powerful. (Is to talk of the interconnectedness of *everything* with *everything* distorting this insight?) Here we may see depressions as experiences to ingest and thrive on and so to grow and change into joy; joy as a state dependent for its being on depression and as yet another stone tossed into one's soul to allow experience, feeling, questioning and resolving, changing, and a chance for acceptance or rejection. Change and repetition blend together on this level. There *is*, then, an alternative to anxiety's leading to the desire to seek allies, to disguise this drivenness into something positive such as sheer sexual attraction, and the failure of this itself to remove the initial anxiety, in turn leading to the confused desire for reproduction. (Consider here Hellmuth Kaiser on the universal symptom, the "attempt to create illusionary fusion relationships with others,"[134] or W.R. Bion on "pairing," for example in his *Experiences in Groups*.) A new perspective on the *original* situation is called for, that of *amor fati* (the love of fate): "Joy, however, does not want heirs, or children—joy wants itself, wants eternity, wants recurrence, wants everything eternally the same" (Z IV 19, Part 9).[135]

---

[131] Relevant to this topic is the next chapter, an English-language version of an article of mine published in French in 1983.

[132] **Z** IV 19 is called "The Drunken Song."

[133] For a much more extended discussion of emptiness (termed *śūnyatā* in Sanskrit and *suññatā* in Pāli) in Buddhist theoretical psychology (or *abhidharma/abhidhamma*), and its phenomenology, see M. Ginsberg, *The Inner Palace*, e.g., Chap. XVII (The Space of Emptiness) and Chap. XVIII (Sacred Emptiness).

[134] Quoted from L.B. Fierman, *The Therapist Is the Therapy: Effective Psychotherapy II*, p. 4; cf. L.B. Fierman, ed., *Effective Psychotherapy: The Contribution of Hellmuth Kaiser*, esp. the chapter discussing this symptom (pp. 14-171).

[135] On *amor fati*, cf. B. Babich, "Nietzsche's Imperative as a Friend's Encomium: On Becoming the One You Are, Ethics, and Blessing," *Nietzsche-Studien*, vol. 33 (2003), pp. 29-58.

4. Individual Therapy and Family Therapy *(à la française)*[1]
Preliminary Remarks

This article was written as a response to an interview reported in "Les thérapies familiales vont-elles vaincre l'individualisme français? Entretien avec le psychiatre Dr Bertolus" ("Are Family Therapies Going to Conquer French Individualism? An interview with psychiatrist Dr. Bertolus") in the Parisian physicians' journal *Quotidien du médecin*, number 2671 (dated Wednesday, April 21, 1982), p. 16. That interview took place at the time of the opening of the Centre de thérapie familiale, Center of Family Therapy, of the Association Jean-Coxtet (52 rue du Four, Paris 4e). Psychiatrist and family therapist Dr. Jean-Raymond Bertolus, interviewed by Dr. Aline Donsimoni, explained that family therapies were still only of limited presence in France, because, in particular, physicians consider exclusively the somatic or the psychological aspect of an ailment, in terms of the individual himself (and nothing else such as interpersonal or other features of the larger context of the situation). The editors of the journal prefaced my reply article with some introductory comments, basically as above, to put the article itself into context. The editors continued, mentioning that they later received this communication from me that underlined the need to consider the family as an "organism of several individuals" and not as the coincidental context in which the pathology of an isolated individual happens to occur.

In retrospect, this may be compared to several statements made in an important collection of essays published in 1965. For example, in one essay, this idea that the "family is the focus" of the psychotherapeutic endeavor is presented in these terms:

> We treat the family as a unit and insist that unless the entire unit is present, we have no "patient." We sometimes dramatize this structure by calling our patient the interlocked group or, graphically, a "people salad." ... They [the family] are a self-contained group ... [and here] *the patient, in this case an entire family*, is very much in balance ...[2]

In another essay, the point is made that what appears to be an individual phenomenon is as much a manifestation of what is going on in the various members of the family; Harold F. Searles (then a supervising and training analyst at the Washington Psychanalytic Institute) writes,

---

[1] I would like to thank Gérard Kouchner, Président du *Quotidien du Médecin*, for permission to make use of this article in the present context. The journal itself now has a website edition, www.quotimed.com.
[2] C.A. Whitaker, R.E. Felder, and J. Warkentin, "Countertransference in the Family Treatment of Schizophrenia," in I. Boszormenyi-Nagy and J. Framo, eds., *Intensive Family Therapy*, at pp. 325, 328. Italics added.

The emergency of psychosis in the patient represents, therefore, not only his own heretofore-thwarted striving toward individuality, but also the vicariously expressed strivings of a similar nature on the part of the other family members. It is probably more adequate to conceptualize this advent of psychosis as a shift in the total family's mode of dealing with their unresolved, conflicting needs for symbiosis and individuation.[3]

And James L. Framo, in the same collection, writes,

The essential thesis behind the transpersonal view of psychopathology is that people really do have an effect upon one another when they are in close relationship, a telling effect which is more than the resultant of two interacting intrapsychic systems. It has become a commonplace to find among Freud's germinal writings the foreshadowing of almost every development in psychiatric thinking ... One such notion that Freud anticipated but whose momentous implications he did not pursue is associated with the idea of cross-communication between the unconscious of one person and another.[4]

These various perspectives may give a somewhat fuller context to this idea of family as the unit of interest.

In any case, the article itself that we are presenting here followed the editors' introductory comments, described above, and appeared in French in *Le quotidien du médecin*, a Parisian daily directed to the concerns of physicians. It was entitled "La thérapie familiale reste en France trop centrée sur le «Malade»" (literally, "Family Therapy in France Remains Overly Focused on the 'I.P.' "); I translate "le malade" as "the I.P." (a common abbreviation in psychotherapeutic contexts for "the Identified Patient"). At about that time, I gave the article's title the gloss, "French Individualism & Family Therapy").

Written and submitted to the journal in the Spring of 1982, the article appeared in the issue of Thursday, March 3, 1983. The following is an English rendering, with minor revisions, rather than a rigorously literal translation.

---

[3] H.F. Searles, "The Contributions of Family Treatment to the Psychotherapy of Schizophrenia," in I. Boszormenyi-Nagy and J. Framo, eds., *Intensive Family Therapy*, at p. 480; cf. pp. 480-482, 487-488.

[4] J.L. Framo, "Systematic Research in Family Dynamics," in I. Boszormenyi-Nagy and J. Framo, eds., *Intensive Family Therapy*, at p. 451; cf. pp. 418-419, 450-452.

4. Individual Therapy and Family Therapy *(à la française)*

It would be of great value for the French professionals who have the responsibilities of providing therapy (physicians, and above all psychiatrists, with the help of psychologists, couples therapists, and social workers) to rethink completely their understanding of "systemic family therapy." If, as Dr. Bertolus says, French therapists are individualists and, consequently, resist a change in their psychoanalytically-based theoretical perspective, then it is interesting for us to notice what is then presented as an alternative to an individualistic, psychoanalytical, medico-pathological model, both in theory and in practice.

The individualism of French therapists that Dr. Bertolus speaks of is based on a theory. We may question the applicability of that individualistic theory to the field of family therapy, to see more clearly what distortions may be built into that theory and its application.

The remarks that I wish to make here concern this individualism in relationship to systemic family therapy theorizing. The danger in considering a new theoretical domain (that of family therapy) from the perspective of earlier experiences, whether good or bad—and I am considering here most centrally the fields and perspectives of personal psychoanalysis and of an individualistic conception of psychopathology—rests in the fact that one then bases one's thinking on familiar but inadequate concepts. *This is the danger of historical distortion.*

The implicit definition of family therapy that I understand to be operant in the interview with Dr. Bertolus is the following: family therapy is a complementary therapy or treatment (undertaken by the generalist or the psychiatrist) of a "sick member of the family," "the one who suffers some given psychiatric pathology." Furthermore, to act following this definition, is precisely to be in danger of being guided by this historical distortion. This danger is avoidable and this problem is one that can be overcome. Addressing this perspective, I would like to explain family therapy in the USA and the ways in which it is different from the viewpoint of individualism in the French context.

Historical Distortion

It is quite correct, as Dr. Bertolus says, that family therapy is appropriate in the case of family where one member is taken to be suffering from psychological difficulties, or where the diagnosis has been declared of psychosis, of schizophrenia, of neurosis, etc. From an historical point of view, it is starting from such cases (resistant to any individual psychoanalysis) that family therapy came to be developed. Historically, then, the domain of application of family therapy has limits, founded on clinical data, themselves in relation to preconceived ideas concerning the efficacy of individual therapy.

The principal difference between an individualistic point of view and one of systemic family perspective is that between a theory that wishes to give priority to the concept of the family as a unit and one that focuses its interest on each individual making up that group (that unit). When we speak of systemic family therapy, we are making it explicit that our interest is in the family considered as an organism in itself (or as the theoretician Arthur Koestler might say, as a holon, an entirety with sub-parts that may also be entireties)—with its rules, its own dynamic organization, constantly in interaction with the environmental context, and containing its own positive and negatives forces—a living unity that is, in fact, an "organism of several persons" (in a concept that will hopefully not create any misunderstandings or over-applications).

It is not easy to go from a perspective that takes into account the family as a collection of separate individuals to one that contains this same family considered as a unique organism with its own specific characteristics and its own behaviors.

Following these perspectives, one can, for example, with an individualistic focus, consider the anger expressed by one person as interesting to take into account in the context of an individual therapy. But this anger is not necessarily as interesting from the perspective of family therapy. What can be quite interesting from the perspective of systemic family therapy, by way of contrast, would be how this anger is tied to everything that happens in this family, how this family deals with this anger, with anger in various other contexts, who in the family takes on the role of expressing this anger and who might be consistently acting as calm, etc.

As Dr. Branko Gačić (a therapist in Beograd)* has said, "at that moment, family therapy is essentially a new approach, a new style of work, a new manner of considering human behavior." This apparently cannot be over-emphasized here, given the present *Zeitgeist* of French psychiatry.

Whether certain complementary technologies (cameras, cassettes, or other recording devices) are used or not, is not what is essential. What is important is the starting point here, which can be biased—as is the training and education of the therapist, which can also create biases in the thinking of the therapist. Whatever the training of the therapist, the key point in systemic family therapy is that central familial processes are the focus of observations and investigation (and not that of intra-psychic or intra-individual processes).

Furthermore, in defining systemic family therapy as the ancillary domain of supportive (secondary) psychotherapy of a sick individual (to whom one adds this secondary interest in the familial context), one reinforces the confusion brought on by this individualistic-oriented sort of bias (whether specifically psychoanalytic or not).

---

* This name appeared in the journal article as Bacia, a misprinted rendering of Gacic (Gačić, in more precise Serbian orthography). Beograd, in Serbia (formerly Yugoslavia), is alternatively called Belgrade.

First, because in considering the sick person as the source of the problem, one predefines the problem as identified purely in terms of the location (within the system) of where the process most obviously manifests itself. That would be an error as gross as that of considering chicken pox to be a dermatological pathology.

And second, because in defining the field of family therapy as that of a family with "a pathological member" one excludes by that definition all families that do not have "a pathological member" but who, nonetheless, suffer serious dissatisfactions, frustrations, ongoing disappointments, frictions, superficial relationships, or a whole array of complaints of this same type. And yet, it is precisely these families that are among the first candidates for a family therapy.

All of us, therapists as well as physicians, are concerned with the well-being and with the improvement of those who see us professionally. We can focus our interest in an organ, in a metabolic system, in a person subject to anxiety, or in the family fighting to create contact with others, fighting to create human warmth, mutual understanding, and respect, fighting to create the possibility of experiencing the joys of life more easily and fully.

In all of these cases, we can appreciate our common interest and we can come together to care for and help each and all to the best of our personal and professional qualities. This article is meant as an invitation to precisely such a joint endeavor.

5. Commentary on Nietzsche's HAH 379: Survival of the Parents[1]

The brief passage (Nietzsche, *Human, All-too-human*, Section 379) reads in Nietzsche's original German text:

> *Fortleben der Eltern.* — Die unaufgelösten Dissonanzen im Verhältnis von Charakter und Gesinnung der Eltern klingen in dem Wesen des Kindes fort und machen seine innere Leidensgeschichte aus.[2]

One rendering into English of this statement would be:

> *Survival of the Parents.* — The unresolved disharmonies in the relationship between the parents' characters and ways of thinking resonate on in the demeanor of the child and structure its inner story of suffering.

There are subtleties in the German that perhaps any single English translation will not make fully explicit. So, it may be helpful to go through this statement more slowly, as an introduction to this discussion. To repeat this passage, then, linking the German original, with a slight rephrasing of the English for clarity:

> *Survival [Fortleben] of the Parents [Eltern].* — The unresolved [unaufgelösten] disharmonies [Dissonanzen] in the relationship [Verhältnis] between the character [Charakter] and way of thinking [Gesinnung] of the parents [Eltern] resonate on [klingen fort][3] in the demeanor [Wesen] of the child and structure [machen aus] its inner [innere] suffering [Leiden] story [Geschichte].

These "Dissonanzen" (dissonances, disharmonies, incongruities, or non-integrated features) are those in the "Verhältnis" (relationship, proportion, ratio, liaison, or love affair) between features of the parents. *I find no one word in English that captures all of these senses.*

Specifically, these dissonances are in a relationship (in these various senses) between the "Charakter" and the "Gesinnung" (way of thinking, conviction, principle of action, intension, disposition, sentiment) of each of the parents.

---

[1] In this chapter, I italicize foreign words only as is done for English words: for emphasis, in titles, if in italics in the original text being quoted, etc.

[2] Quoted from F. Nietzsche, *Werke in Drei Bänden, Erster Band [Works in Three Volumes, First Volume]* (1966), p. 647. The text of *Menschliches, Allzumenschliches: Ein Buch für freie Geister [Human, All-too-human: A Book for Free Spirits]* is at pp. 435-1008. At pp. 871-1008 is the last part of this text, with its traditional separate title *Der Wanderer und sein Schatten [The Wanderer and His Shadow*.

[3] The 'fort' in 'Fortleben' and 'klingen fort' corresponds to 'forth' (living forth, i.e., through time, survival, and resonate forth, respectively).

These disharmonious relationships or contrasts between the parents' characters and dispositions ring on (klingen fort) in the "Wesen" (essence, being, demeanor) of the child and structure (machen aus) its inner "Geschichte" (story, history) of "Leiden" (pain, suffering).

This issue of disharmonies to which Nietzsche drew the reader's attention in this passage operates on both a subtle level *and also in less elegant or more violent ways*, as when the disharmonies between the parents—and also, disharmonies within each parent, since the parents themselves are children of still other parents—result in a child's not feeling appreciated or respected or encouraged, or, continuing on here with more disturbed and disturbing processes of the parents, when they result in ongoing physical, emotional, or sexual violence against the child.[4]

To appreciate these and other "Dissonanzen" (dissonances, disharmonies, incongruities, or non-integrated features) of our consciousness, we need to have a deep honesty, making our experience the subject of our observations and our objectivity, as Nietzsche put it (**GS** 319). That is, we may have to recognize

---

[4] The literature on such early-life violence is growing. We have, to begin with here, the well-known *but later repudiated* statements (**from 1895**) in J. Breuer and S. Freud, *Studies on Hysteria* (1895d) [in SE 2 = GW 1]; on this repudiation, this about-face, see the discussion in J.L. Herman, *Father-Daughter Incest*, pp. 9-12, and the extended presentation in J.M. Masson, *The Assault on Truth: Freud's Suppression of the Seduction Theory.*

We also see a recognition of sexual traumas *in non-Freudian (non-psychoanalytic) literature*, such as in the mention of a seduction and clandestine birth, of the memory of a rape or of sexual relations with a husband become odious, and of Ky., a woman who, at 18, became the mistress of her father, in P. Janet, *Les médications psychologiques*, vol. II, p. 207 (English in P. Janet, *Psychological Healing*, pp. 592-593); and, in the same work, *a much broader understanding, in which the etiology of neurotic problems—neurosis being understood as a condition that brings about repeated intense or even overwhelming anxieties, without psychotic manifestations—may be from any of a wide range of traumas, not only sexual*, as in the statement (quoting the English at p. 593, in the original French, at Vol. II, p. 208), "My studies in this field [**Janet writes in 1919**] have been confirmed by those of many other writers, and it may be regarded as proved that the memory of some particular happening can cause neuropathic symptoms. The traumatic memory must be regarded as an important factor of neurosis." Cf. also P. Janet, *Les névroses* (1909), p. 109; P. Janet, *État mental des hystériques. Les stigmates mentaux des hystériques* (1892), p. 100, in second ed. (1911), p. 275; J.L. Herman, J.C. Perry, and B.A. van der Kolk, "Childhood Trauma in Borderline Personality Disorder," *American Journal of Psychiatry*, vol. 146, no. 4 (Apr. 1989), pp. 490-495.

this phenomenon (described in **HAH** 379) with full clarity before we can act on it or deal with it in an effective way.

It is important to realize in this context that one's theory may make it difficult to recognize certain phenomena: as contemporary French ethologist, psychoanalyst, neuropsychiatrist, and trauma-survival specialist Boris Cyrulnik has written,[5] it has long been obvious to those in the field of family therapy that there is this intimate link pointed to by Nietzsche in this passage between—on the one hand—non-integrated, unresolved, and otherwise disharmonious tendencies within and between parents, and—on the other hand—the subsequent problematic ways of dealing with life's situations for the child.

In contrast, it was only long after that that these could first be conceptualized in psychoanalytic theorizing and thus capable of then being integrated into that theorizing.

Nietzsche's formulation (in **HAH** 379, quoted just above) of the unresolved disharmonies of the parents as the source of torment for the child, raises the question of whether these disharmonies will define the life of the child, whether, in other words, the child is doomed to suffer its entire life as a result of these disharmonies (as the passage might be interpreted as suggesting) or—if we do not read too much fatalism into his original observation—whether there is a way for the child to become free of such consequent torment. This is, of course, not just a theoretical question but one of great practical importance.

In a passage made all the more remarkable and significant when juxtaposed with this formulation of Nietzsche's that describes the child's suffering as a consequence of its parents' disharmonies (in which formulation, it is not obvious that there is a solution for the child at all), Cyrulnik goes on to articulate a way to go beyond the torments we experience in incorporating the unresolved disharmonies between our parents (and other "gifts" we carry with us from our early life with our parents).

Cyrulnik presents in a concrete form (as the thinking of such a child) the powerful thought that "il faut que je répare d'abord le mal-être[6] de mes pa-

---

[5] B. Cyrulnik, *Parler d'amour au bord du gouffre*, pp. 173-174; in English tr., *Talking of Love on the Edge of a Precipice*, p. 114. Cf. above, p. 94, n. 111.

[6] Mal eſtre (=mal estre, modern mal-être): first seen in Montaigne, *Essais* (ed. of 1588). Replaced centuries later by 'malaise'—uneasiness, discomfort, vague restlessness, being ill at ease—'mal-être' reappeared by the late 1980s, referring to something more profound or pervasive than a passing malaise. The contrast of 'mal-être' in this Cyrulnik passage is with 'bien-être' (well-being)—feeling well with all of one's needs satisfied (*Larousse Lexis*, 1979, p. 189). Cf. J. Lacomte, *La résilience. Se reconstruire après un traumatisme*, 2010, p. 26. Mal-être, or *being fundamentally ill at ease with needs unmet*, involves *adapting poorly to some larger context*, in part, *not finding one's place in society in a comfortable*

rents"[7]—in English, "what I must do first is to repair the ill-being, the unhappy life state, of my parents!" And, to repair this, it is important that we first come to appreciate it, to see it clearly.

For orientation here, let us recall that we can sometimes see the usual more clearly by paying attention to the unusual, or can notice the subtle by examining the exaggerated, or can understand better the usual or the normal by investigating the unusual or the abnormal. There are those who have dealt thoroughly with the extremes of the human condition, focusing on extremes of agitation or torment, extremes of mundane reality in which what is happening has various unpleasant features. What they have learned is relevant here.

Breuer and Freud gave these features the name in German of Unlust. The opposite of German Lust (pleasure, joy, delight, fancy, inclination), Unlust is dislike, aversion, or, in their theorizing, Unpleasure—unpleasantness, displeasure, torment, suffering, and so forth[8] (in Buddhism, termed duḥkha).[9]

That said, for context and orientation, and assuming that we are willing to begin by looking at what is not so pleasant, what is it to repair the ill-being of one's parents? That is a key next question in this line of contemplation, if we are to take this topic beyond Nietzsche's observation in this above-quoted passage.

Expressed this way, it may seem that we have to deal with our parents' ill-being, or with our parents themselves, in some direct way here. But given that these unresolved disharmonies are resonating out (or are resonating forth) in us, we perhaps have no further to look than at our own psychological-emotional processes, as an alternative starting point; in other words, we may begin by considering what in us is coming out of this earlier unresolved material (using the word 'material' in a non-material sense, to mean some subject matter or other).

This is not to suggest or to assume that what was going on for our parents will be reproduced with no transformations in us. We are in any case at one remove not only on a generational tree, but also in being separate individuals who are responding to the tensions within and between our parents as two other

---

way, if at all. Glosses: "dis-ease" (with hyphen) or illfare. Suggestively, illfare is the gloss for 'dukkha' given in N. Smart, "Action and Suffering in Theravadin Buddhism," *Philosophy East and West*, vol. 34, no. 4 (Oct. 1984), p. 371.

[7] B. Cyrulnik, *Parler d'amour au bord du gouffre*, p. 200. My gloss follows.

[8] See J. Breuer and S. Freud, *Studies on Hysteria* (1895d) [at SE 2: 116, 269-270 = GW 1: 174, 268-269]. Cf. SE 2: xxi, and SE 2: 197, 210, which are from the Editor's Introduction to the English, and in text by Breuer alone, resp., neither of which appears in GW. See also S. Freud, "The Instincts and their Vicissitudes" (1915c) [esp. SE 14: 138-139 = GW 10: 230-231 = CP 4: 81-82].

[9] This is the Sanskrit form; in Pāli (the related language of Theravāda Buddhism), the word is dukkha. For extended discussion of this and related issues, see M. Ginsberg, *The Inner Palace*. Cf. just above, note 6, on dukkha and illfare.

individuals, tensions that manifested in ways that partially involved us directly or indirectly.

How those tensions or disharmonies remain "resonating forth" in the child is more complex and variable a process, this suggests, than we might at first conclude from reading the passage by Nietzsche here.

This line of contemplation gives, perhaps, some ideas about where to put our attention that may not be obvious given the earlier phrasing of the issue, but does not answer the important question at this point of what repair amounts to in this sort of situation.

So if we are to look perhaps without (that is, outside of ourselves rather than within ourselves), to our parents, in order to appreciate the tensions or disharmonies or cacophonies in *their* ways of being, or within (that is, within ourselves, to ourselves), in order to see directly how these disharmonies are manifesting themselves *in us*, "resonating" in us, what might we see? And how might that give us at least a clue if not a clear indication of what is needed for the repair here?

We of course may keep ourselves from unhelpfully limiting our scope of vision here as we would be in taking the metaphor in Nietzsche too seriously. (In other words, the metaphor of resonating may have its limitations that do not have to be our limitations.) That is, we do not have to treat as real (to reify) the parental conflict here that Nietzsche highlights as some entity within us that is eating away at us and causing us grief. I have written on the problems of reification and the value of avoiding such thinking in other contexts, and will simply mention this concern here.[10]

While a metaphor may be a helpful tool at times to aid in our noticing certain processes, acting as a heuristic, we may be sidetracked in our self-investigation and our coming to self-awareness if we take these metaphors too seriously. Nor do we have to limit our scope of vision unhelpfully in other ways, by reading into Nietzsche's point here more than it is saying: it is not saying that *all* of our suffering is a function simply and solely of the dissonances between our parents, for example.

That is, while we can think of the conflicts and pains (Leiden) that we as children suffer that arise out of the conflicts between our parents as a couple, and within our parents as two individuals, children of *their* parents,[11] we are able,

---

[10] On reificiation in this sense, see M. Ginsberg, *The Inner Palace*, pp. 137-144, 162-163, 182, 217, 443, 451-452, 465-466, 505, 573.

[11] This question has lead to a field of inquiry into the relationship between the psychological, emotional, and interpersonal issues in earlier generations and our present realities. There are conventions of laying this out visually, on the model of family trees (our genealogy), called genograms in English. The field is known in French literature as psychogénéalogie, as, for example, in A.A. Schützenberg-

quite separately, to see our own conflicts and pains, even if we do not know the specifics of the tensions within and between our parents. (This includes all of our suffering based on *other* things going on in our world—our own bodily sicknesses, injuries, problems with others, and on and on.)

If, then, we are looking at our own consciousness, our own experience, in order to come to see the ways in which we are in inner conflict (wherever the ingredients making up or leading to these conflicts are from), we are putting ourselves in a position to deal directly with these unresolved issues.

And, if we take a clue from the French term (the verb 'réparer')[12] in the passage of Cyrulnik's here, the repairing here may be understood as a matter of bringing back into good condition something that has deteriorated, has gone into disrepair, of eliminating a fault that has come into being (as a hole in the cloth of some article of clothing), of compensating for some loss (as in war reparations, etc.), and so forth.

If we are to be a seamstress or tailor of our soul, so to speak, it may be helpful to have a good eye, a steady hand, and a calm foundation, in order to facilitate our task. But, again, what is our task here? And how do we approach it? Are we interested in putting a patch over the rent or holey material? in re-weaving the cloth with a fine thread? in not being ashamed to wear this garment? in passing unnoticed in our daily life when in this garment? in feeling quite well attired for any and all contexts? (These are all asked metaphorically.)

Whatever the specifics, and these we will surely vary not only from person to person, but also for any given person at different times in life, there are still the frames of mind that are helpful, and the frames of mind that are counterproductive here.

We might think of the skillful frame of mind here (a set or class or category of particular frames of mind) as one that is patient and attentive and good-willed, a frame of mind that is capable of seeing the conflict, the rent in the material, the hole in the cloth, so to speak, not pretending that everything is perfect when it is not, but also a frame of mind that maintains its interest in seeing how to improve the material, *that is,* **outside this metaphor,** *in seeing how to bring the conflict into integrated harmony.*

This integration is a slightly complicated process.[13]

---

er, *Psychogénéalogie. Guérir les tristesses familiales et se retrouver soi* (2007) [title in English, *Psychogenealogy: To Heal Familial Sadnesses and Find Oneself Again*]. Cp. such recent works in English as E. Walkenstein, *The Imprinters: Surviving the Unlived Life of Our Parents* (2008).

[12] *Larousse Lexis* (1979), p. 1616.

[13] For extended discussions on the issues of integration and non-integration, see above, Chapter 3, on Nietzschean psychiatry and, below, Chapter 6, on Pierre Janet, esp. pp. 140-141, notes 73-74.

We may nonetheless continue here, with our present focus. The process is complicated, that is, because it involves several sorts of understanding, of awareness, along with a caring, encouraging perspective on the whole situation.

The first sort of understanding or awareness is of the particular tensions or conflicting vectors of interest that are in play. With this sort of awareness, we can see whether there are ways to come to a win-win solution, that is, one in which all of the interests that are vying for satisfaction can in fact be satisfied.

In this, there is no compromise, which tends to prolong the conflict, in that the typical experience in compromising is that we are not getting what we want. Of course, the other party is also feeling this lack of satisfaction, or this renouncing on an interest. It has been pointed out that compromises tend to fester and develop into perhaps more violent activities, rather than be pathways to happiness and harmony among the contesting positions.

As an aside, the most striking example of the disaster of a compromise that I can think of here is that of what in United States history was called the Missouri Compromise. This was part of the long history of states debating whether slavery should be allowed, and in which states, and then in which territories of the country, slavery would be recognized. The compromise did not answer this question, in fact, but kept it alive.

There was a period of some forty-five years between the passage of that compromise, as a bit of legislation in the U.S. Congress (in the years 1820-1821)—with a modified extension brought about by the Kansas-Nebraska Act of 1854 (inspiring a massive immigration into Kansas and lots of bloodshed, where each side tried to establish a population majority either for or against slavery, depending on one's position on that issue)—and the American Civil War (1861-1865), also called The War Between the States and the War of the Rebellion. *During these forty-five years, several key bits of history came to pass.*

First, there was the development of an early version of the Gatling gun,[14] a piece of weaponry that allowed a number of shots in quick succession.[15] This made killing much more efficient. The Civil War involved, in fact, over half a million recorded deaths in battle or in death caused by wounds in battle, and over six hundred thousand in related deaths (including from battle-related infections and disease), a total of over one million military deaths, greater than the Americans killed in all other wars involving U.S. military.

---

[14] This was named for its inventor, Richard Jordan Gatling (1818-1903).

[15] This mechanism, in its early form consisting of a number of gun barrels on a rotating drum, driven by a hand-held crank, could fire as many as 200 rounds per minute. Later models, used in wars later in the nineteenth and early twentieth century were capable of firing 1,000 rounds per minute, with a comparably higher kill rate. It has been seen as the precursor of the modern machine gun. In any case, it was an effective machine.

It has been argued that the Gatling gun did not actually play that significant a role in the Civil War, given the low number of guns actually deployed in combat. Rather, it is suggested, other advances in the accuracy of the weaponry were quite significant, with rifling,[16] for example, available in large numbers of muskets such as the American Springfield rifle musket and the British Enfield rifle musket, with some 900,000 such British muskets imported for the war. In particular, in 1855 the U.S. Army adopted a .58-caliber rifled musket to replace the .69-caliber smoothbore, several years before the War actually broke out.[17] This greater accuracy made for a more deadly encounter in context: military commanders were still using Napoleonic tactics, with rows of foot soldiers lined up neatly from a time when 100 meters was the maximum distance for shooting. But many more would be wounded or killed at this distance than in the Napoleonic Wars, given this improved weaponry accurate to 500 meters.[18] *However we give relative weight to these various new features of the military situation, overall the improved weaponry here was critical in the higher number of casualties.*

The point of this gruesome example of compromise is that the compromise in focus here led to changes in other parts of the historical reality that was the context of the compromise. And that, furthermore, these superficially independent and superficially unrelated changes resulted in a more violent outcome than if the tensions had been dealt with in a definitive way earlier on in the story. *And to point out the difference between a compromise and a resolution.*

Let us return with this perspective to the issue of our own inner conflicts, or non-integration, and the question of how to come not to compromise but to resolution (given this historic caveat).

In order to come to resolution, the significant desires and needs of the given concerns must be recognized.

Some of these desires and needs are in many cases not at all presented explicitly. We may say that diplomatic negotiations can deal with these, even if they are left unspoken, but that this is not an easy or obvious task. In the case of dealing with ourselves, the first step is a parallel sort of awareness and recognition, even if these things are not verbalized.

I will not attempt to address the question here of whether it is always helpful to verbalize these features of the situation, or whether, in contrast, sometimes it is better to take these into account without making them explicit. There is a cultural bias (in Eurocentric cultures, especially America) to make every-

---

[16] Rifling was a spiral groove cut into the barrel of a weapon, resulting in a spinning of the ball or bullet that was shot out, which in turn resulted in a much more predictable and therefore accurate shot.

[17] Among many texts, see, G. Smith, *Warman's Civil War Weapons*, and J.G. Bilby, *Civil War Firearms: Their Historical Background and Tactical Use.*

[18] Meters/yards: 1 m.=1.09 yards; 100 m.=109.36 yards; 500 m.=546.81 yards.

thing explicit, and another cultural bias, such as in traditional Japanese culture, for example, in which such explicitness is considered to be harsh and insulting. And more specifically here, how we ourselves deal with such issues may depend not only on such general biases but also on the particulars we are addressing at the time. Whichever approach we find most appropriate, most effective, in dealing with our own inner tensions, the key is an openness to noticing and to recognizing and to dealing with whatever is clamoring for satisfaction. *This leads to a second dimension of this process.*

Not only is it important and helpful for us to be aware of what is going on for us, which concerns are at play, which needs are in danger of not being satisfied, and so forth, but it is of key importance in our coming to an integrated, self-harmonious state of mind (or state of being) that we have a perspective on our own urges that allows us to discriminate, to distinguish between those that are best left as wishes, and those that are best addressed as yearnings to be fulfilled. *This takes some sort of managerial skills over ourselves, we might say. And it takes a critical mind, as well,* one able to do a careful critique or evaluation of the topic at hand. (This is not 'critical' in the sense of criticizing and belittling or dismissing, but, rather, as made explicit here, is related to 'critique' or sizing up and carefully analyzing the issues at hand).

How we appease what is best left as a wish may seem a tricky business, but it relies on making clear that the realization of the wish in question is simply impossible (I wish I were living in fifteenth century Renaissance Florence as a nobleman) or would be a disaster if realized (I wish I would never die, no matter how ill, or sick, or poor, or outcast by society I would be). *And it relies most essentially on seeing in the wish what is of value, and to see how that particular consideration could be realized with **other** particular features present (**realized in another context or contexts**).*

That is, sometimes our wishing is too specific in unskillful, pain-producing or self-frustrating ways, even if there is truly something of value and importance in the wish.

This suggests, once again, that the work of coming to a self-integration can be a very demanding, labor-intensive, but very rewarding activity. It may call on us to cultivate and to practice patience, as well as determination and good-willed self-encouragement. There are many paths to this, including some traditional self-awareness and compassion-cultivating meditations.[19]

---

[19] More has been said on this elsewhere, e.g., in M. Ginsberg, *The Far Shore*, and M. Ginsberg, *The Inner Palace.*

6. Pierre Janet: Misleading Concepts and Integration[1]

Alternative, more precisely descriptive, title: Discussion recognizing an underlying historical interest not only in understanding but also in helping those in personal stress in their lives, this desire to be of help not being an abstract exercise in mere understanding, but one with a practical, originally-compassion-based interest as its root; this discussion arising out of an interest in appreciating the nature of integration, our understanding honed by consideration of theoretical constructs through the ages and the ways in which we may misunderstand earlier terms in virtue of the changes in meaning that those terms have undergone through time, having us interpret earlier writings as if they were using those more recent understandings of those same terms (and therefore using them inappropriately), so that we take earlier theoreticians as simple-minded, wildly ignorant, or just plain stupid, having us miss the point of earlier theories, teachings, or texts; with examples, some from the history of psychology (the term taken in a wide sense), to illustrate this, including the concepts rendered into English as causes, humors, electricity, and somnambulism, and returning to a concentration on the understanding of integration, with a focus on some of the writings and theorizing (including the additional concepts of idées fixes and the subconscious) of French philosopher-psychiatrist Pierre Janet (1859-1947) and of others; these are duly introduced, defined, and discussed in this work.

Historical Background as Orientation

We may look to understand the historical significance of the issue of self-integration addressed and discussed in the chapter above on Nietzschean psychiatry. The interest behind this is both theoretical and philosophical, on the one hand, and also, on the other, rather practical and moral, in the sense of being concerned with the well-being of people in society, of their individual experience, and of their harmony with the group.

In particular there is a background concern we may focus in on here, giving importance to an interest not only in understanding but also in helping those in personal stress in their lives. *This desire to be of help is no abstract exercise in mere understanding, but is rooted in a very practical interest in being of help to bring relief where there is torment, that is, in a caring compassion.*

---

[1] In this chapter, I italicize foreign words only as is done for English words: for emphasis, in titles, if in italics in the original text being quoted, etc.

This chapter took initial form while I was revising the article "Nietzschean Psychiatry" in preparing the above "Nietzschean Psychiatry Revisited."

Part of the interest of this chapter is to present an investigation that will help highlight the fact that our own language and assumptions can distort our understanding of the writings of others, especially others from different cultures and times, even if the language we are using is what we take to be common to us and them, or in which the particular teachings seem transparent and obvious to us. More on this as we go. Our main initial focus is the issue of non-integration and its relation to what was called hysteria—more on this below, to clarify the senses of this term as understood in these investigations that spanned at least a couple of centuries—as a psychological phenomenon, and a concern for those interested in the fulfillment and happiness of human beings.

To get a sense of the concerns of those investigating and dealing with ("treating") people with various intense degrees of torment in their lives, in the period mentioned above (Eurocentric late 1700s to early 2000s), to take one out of many possible examples, we may consider the 1891 discussion by philosopher-psychologist Alexis Bertrand (1850-1923)[2] about the much earlier work of Jacques-Henri-Désiré Pététin (1744-1808), as described in Pététin's two published books, *Mémoire* (1787) and *Électricité animale* (1808). What Pététin, President of the Medical Society of Lyon, noted in the strange behavior of a woman—as an example here of an early description of how people may attempt to deal with horrifying memories or life situations—was her incessant singing, which continued even when the doctor (Pététin himself) had her go into an uncomfortable bent-over position, her arms lifted, and her head on her knees.[3] Pé-

---

[2] "Un précurseur de l'hypnotisme," *Revue philosophique de la France et de l'étranger*, vol. 32 (Jul.-Dec. 1891), pp. 192-206.

[3] The original descriptions may be found at J.-H.-D. Pététin, *Électricité animale* (1808), pp. 6-7. An earlier rendering that gave more specifics of the life context of the young woman is in his *Mémoire sur la découverte des phénomènes que présentent la catalepsie et le somnambulisme. Symptômes de l'affection hystérique essentielle, avec des recherches sur la cause physique de ces phénomènes* [subsequently, *Mémoire*], pp. 6-8: She was married at 15 and a mother at 16, with—at the time of the doctor's treating her—a 3-year-old son who was severely, worrisomely sick, with "teigne" (tinea or ringworm on his thighs), "cepalalgie" (sic: céphalalgie, an alternative name for migraine), who was seeing frightening animals and yelling in fear, with swollen legs, little urination, no sound sleep, and fever recurring daily for two months. The physician-author adds that "il femble [=semble] menacé d'une mort inevitable" (he is apparently menaced by an inevitable death). In short, more than enough to worry and to frighten a young mother deeply!

Her bent-over position may, incidentally, remind us of some bioenergetic practices, such as the bioenergetic stress positions of Alexander Lowen (see *Bioenergetics*, pp. 73-81) as well as the Core Energetics work of John Pier-

tétin mentions (in this clearly-described incident from the late 1700s) that the woman explained to him, when asked, that her singing was an attempt to distract herself from a visual memory that was terrifying for her.[4]

What is quite striking about the doctor's writings is that he finds it quite appropriate to have a straight-forward, direct, and explicit conversation with the person he is treating, his patient, about what is going on for her, a conversation of interest to him as a key means of finding out more about her. And that she, once asked, was quite immediately capable of giving a clear, articulate, and cogent explanation of her own behavior. She was clearly not confused about herself, even if others were.

While this point may seem obvious to the casual reader, there is in some individuals learned, educated, and highly trained in these fields, a tendency to assume that they the professionals know more than the persons involved and have a clearer perspective on those individuals' worlds, and how they are in them, than those individuals themselves do, an attitude that leads all-too-easily to a dismissing of these other persons' perception and understanding. There is a subtle balance that can be reached and maintained, of course, in which training and education and experience are used not to become dogmatic but to be able to appreciate those who could most benefit from such sources of potential knowledge and wisdom. We will return to this general issue, below.

I would like to continue by reflecting on the concerns various theoreticians have had in coming to the concepts of personal integration and of hysteria (again, a term whose various, rather distinct, interpretations will be presented below, in context). Let me repeat that I take this to be a predominantly concern-driven interest, a compassion-inspired theorizing.

At this point, though, we may note that the issue of integration, to highlight the main thread of this chapter, has arisen because of what appears to be a breakdown in integration, in what has been called disintegration. In other words,

---

rakos (*Core Energetics*, pp. 210-226, and *Eros, Love & Sexuality*, pp. 81-112, esp. pp. 85, 101, 111).

[4] The original reads, as recounted in A. Bertrand, "Un précurseur de l'hypnotisme," *Revue philosophique de la France et de l'étranger*, vol. 32 (Jul.-Dec. 1891), pp. 192-206, at p. 194: "elle déclara plus tard que ces chants avaient pour but de la distraire d'un spectacle qui la terrifiait." The physician's own report, given in his *Électricité animale* (1808), p. 11, contains clear information about the use of leeches for blood-letting, and his attention to the young patient, his straight-forward speech to her, included his simply asking her what her singing was about. Her reply reads: "Il m'est très-facile de vous en apprendre la cause. Je chante, monsieur le Docteur, pour me distraire d'un spectacle qui m'épouvante…" (It is very easy for me to let you know what the cause is. I sing, Doctor, to distract myself from a vision that is frightening to me.)

the issue of integration is of interest because of the problems seen when its absence is felt in the specific contexts of particular individuals being considered.

Briefly, to set the context here, in considering the lack of personal integration—one way of conceptualizing conflicts we notice in actual life situations—we might begin by suggesting what integration amounts to. We may first understand that for each individual there are dynamic components—interests, concerns, desires, beliefs, values, etc.—that are variously active. There is a complexity here, given all of these components, and when their complete functioning occurs in internally coherent ways, we have personal integration. When they are not, they may well be mutually frustrating, working at cross-purposes to one another, with tensions, turmoil, and an inner disharmony.

Further, it is a major task to come to personal integration, to an overall self-harmonious attitude toward one's life that gives us a perspective and an all-inclusive sense of what our life is about. This integration provides a defining of our place in the world, a giving form (a gestalt[5]) to our life. The lack of integration calls for an integration, or for a reintegration, if this is post-disintegration. Correspondingly, when there is a lack of integration within the person, a lack of personal integration, we have these various components acting at cross-purposes to one another (not interacting in an open, fully harmonious way). When this is the case, we might ask how these various components are mutually conflictive or are isolated or separated out from one another, and how they are working in smaller units at cross-purposes with other such smaller units.

To put this into a larger historical context, a first step in our understanding the long-term cultural history of the interest in personal integration—both theoretical and practical—is to begin seeing the ways in which *its lack, its absence, has been noticed*, described, understood, and addressed in recent (and not so recent) times. *In general, to repeat, something is noticed in its absence.*[6] The

---

[5] A gestalt here (form, unified perception) follows its sense in German, in the related psychology of perception, Gestalt Psychology, and in the psychotherapeutic practice called Gestalt Psychotherapy. On gestalt therapy as making use of a playful, fuller vision allowing a self-regulative shifting toward "a deeper coherence and wisdom of the mind," in a parallel to the Dao, see C. Naranjo, *The Way of Silence and the Talking Cure: On Meditation and Psychotherapy*, pp. 17-18. On Gestalt therapy and Gestalt psychology, see M. Joslyn, "Figure/Ground: Gestalt/Zen," in J.O. Stevens, ed., *Gestalt Is*, pp. 229-246.

[6] This idea that we achieve great awareness of something when its absence is felt in our lives in a significant way is the psychological parallel of the more general conceptual principle that all attribution (any description of something) is negation (or a description of what is missing in that something). This principle can be traced back to Spinoza, if not beyond that. For more on this, see M. Ginsberg, *Mind and Belief: Psychological Ascription and the Concept of Belief* (esp.

arising of the concern here in integration, when its absence is painfully felt, has a parallel at those times when a society is felt to be going painfully off-course (Shakespeare's Marcellus remarked, "Something is rotten in the state of Denmark"), when there are many people who are recognized as *not* being moral anymore. As suggested long ago in *Dàodéjīng* (or *Tào Té Chīng*) 道德經,[7] an ancient Chinese Daoist text, people talk of how wonderful and important it is to be moral, to act morally, precisely at such sad and tormented times.

Noticing changes in the theoretical contexts and meanings of key terms
What these intense versions of non-integrated consciousness, of disharmonies within the person would be called, and how these features of consciousness would be described, is an important question here, in large part because some of these names and descriptions would be read in later times in ways that quite misunderstood the observations being noted, the points being made. This is a perennial issue, as we will see below.

In general in this discussion (as well as elsewhere), we might thus remind ourselves here, warn ourselves here, not to be misled by what terms seem to suggest to us, or what dead-end associations we have with the words used. In a Zen-inspired metaphor, when we see a finger pointing to the moon, let us not be like the cat that approaches the finger to sniff it, as if that were the point of the finger's being extended! The name is not the thing named; that which points is not what is being pointed to![8]

In other words (we will have occasion to notice), the terms to describe these important internal processes and their manifestations have changed, and meanings of terms used have been modified as well, depending on the author, or the school of psychology or of psychotherapy in focus. Since this is so, we will help to keep ourselves from becoming quite misled and confused if we apply an attentiveness to these changes and ambiguities, in our general considerations and in our reading of old and new texts (as in applying, for example, Nietzsche's nuanced critique of names vs. misnomers vs. reality vs. interpretations[9]).

We may be reminded as well of what Pierre Janet wrote (in 1929), "One changes the word in order to change something, in order to have the right to

---

Chap. 3) and *The Inner Palace* (esp. Chap. XX).
[7] Shakespeare, *Hamlet*, Act 1, Scene 4; R.T. Ames and D.L. Hall, *Dao De Jing* [道德經]—*"Making This Life Significant"—A Philosophical Translation*, Chap. 38, pp. 135-136; Red Pine, tr., *Lao Tzu's Taoteching*, Chap. 38, pp. 76-77.
[8] I owe this cat image to Paul Ziff, from a class with him in Spring 1964 in the Philosophy Department at the University of Pennsylvania.
[9] For example, at **GS** 14, 34, 58, 261, 298, 333-334, 353, 355. This follows the system of abbreviations given in the introductory comments to "Nietzschean Psychiatry Revisited" (above). Here, **GS** = *The Gay Science*.

come back to what one had neglected."[10] That is, our ways of describing any given phenomenon may not help us notice something important about it, and describing it differently (with different words, *or with the same words understood in a new way, with a new meaning*) may allow us to become refocused and more nuanced in our perception and understanding, in new, illuminating ways. Hence, the function and justification of redefining key terms in ongoing theorizing.

This calls on us to be aware of any such changes, to see into what is inspiring that shift, and into what of importance is actually modified there. This awareness is prior to being able to return to the earlier usage and then to consider the shifts, to reevaluate and reconsider *them*. And, doubly important is a correlate of this, that we are in ongoing need of noticing the way in which we distort an earlier teaching in light of our more recent understanding of the terms that are being employed. (This is stating the point generally; specific examples may be helpful to make this idea clearer.)

Redefinition, frequently appealing to theoreticians, typically creates a set of evolving concepts all associated with the same term (word or phrase) with several if not many meanings, in need of differentiation each from the others[11] *and can be contrasted with the use of different terms to talk about one basic topic.*

This latter is illustrated by the shift from what was once described as Pneumatologie (Pneumatology, literally, the science or description of the pneuma, the breath of life[12]) and as Geister-Lehre (Spirit-study or Spiritology),[13]—for example, by the German philosopher, Christian Wolff (1679-1654),[14]—was later

---

[10] In *L'évolution psychologique de la personnalité*, Lecture XXI (Les somnambulismes), given Feb. 28, 1929 (passage at p. 465; in electronic edition, p. 259): "On change le mot pour changer quelque chose, pour avoir le droit de revenir en arrière et de s'occuper de ce qu'on avait negligé."

[11] See the problem of homonyms in Aristotle, *Categories*, 1a1-6; *De interpretatione*, 17a35, 23a7.

[12] Liddell and Scott, *Greek-English Lexicon*, p. 1424a, glosses πνεῦμα pneûma (cf. Eng. pneumonia), as wind, breathed air, breath of life, spirit (of man), etc.

[13] On the second day of the Robert C. Solomon Memorial Conference held at the University of Texas, in Austin (Feb. 15-16, 2008), Richard Schacht gave a talk simply titled "Spirit," in which he suggested that second best to leaving the term in its German form (as 'Geist'), to avoid the impression that we understand what it means, is rendering 'Geist' by 'Spirit,' rather than by such familiar alternatives as 'Ghost,' 'Soul,' 'Mind,' etc. (My paraphrase of his point here.)

[14] Christian Freyherrn von Wolff, the early mentor of Immanuel Kant, was the philosopher from whom Kant developed a strong respect for thorough, methodical philosophizing; Kant is thus seen—in his "pre-Critique period" (the period before Kant wrote the *Critique of Pure Reason*) only—as a Wolffian.

replaced by a term that is now much more familiar than these, the Greek-rooted term, Psychologie (the German cognate of Psychology).[15]

Of course, to think of old theoreticians as quaint or simple-minded and ignorant louts, believing in something like the pneuma (since they spoke of pneumatology), is to be overly constrained in our understanding, lost in words.

This has been going on for a long time, at least since we misunderstood the Ancient Greek concept of explanation and understanding, when we refer to that idea by the English term 'cause' or its equivalents in other modern languages, with a modern understanding of scientific explanation, taking the term 'cause' in the modern scientific sense of a pre-existing reality (some condition or process) that brings about, that is, causes, in this modern sense, some consequence (its "effect").[16]

Similar systematic confusions may arise in taking the term 'element' in its modern sense, when what was being highlighted was perhaps much more what we would term qualities rather than substances. Of course, if in the original texts and contexts the focus is on qualities or features that can be found repeated in our world, rather than as a thesis or theory that the entire universe is composed of elements, and we take the list (a traditional one consists four items) to be referring to those particular things, not interpreting these as representative, and then go into the question of what sort of a theory of elements these texts (or

---

[15] See C. Wolff, *Vorbericht von der Welt-Weisheit*, Sect. 12 (Dritter Theil); in *Gesammelte Werke, 1. Abteilung (Deutsche Schriften, Band 1), Vernünftige Gedanken (1) (Deutsche Logik)*, also referred to as more succinctly as *Vernünftige Gedanken* (1713), in 1965 reprint ed., pp. 115-120, at p. 118.

[16] On "cause" in Classical Greek, αἰτία aitía and αἴτιος aítios (cf. Eng. aetiology or etiology), Liddell and Scott, *Greek-English Lexicon*, pp. 441a-b; see esp. discussion in J.M.E. Moravcsik, "Aristotle on Adequate Explanations," *Synthese*, vol. 28 (1974), pp. 3-17, where the idea that Aristotle was talking about four "causes" (in a very expanded and strange sense of 'cause') is replaced by interpreting him as addressing the question of what consistituted adequate explanations in various contexts; cf. Plato, *Phaedo*, 96a-102a; Aristotle, *Metaphysics*, 33b26-29, 41a14-29, 43b4-13, 44a15-b14, 45a7-b23, 52b7-15; Aristotle, *De anima*, 415b8-20, 430a10-15; Aristotle, *Physics*, 195a18; Aristotle, *Posterior Analytics*, II.10 (93b29-94a19). Cf. D. Ross, *Aristotle*, pp. 51-52, 71-75, 155; M. Furth, tr., *Aristotle Metaphysics: Books Zeta, Eta, Theta, Iota (VII-X)*, pp. 17-19 (Zeta 8, 33a31-34a1), 42 (Zeta 17, 41a14-31), 51 (Eta 3, 43b13), 53-58 (Eta 4-6, 44a32-45b23), 82 (Iota 1, 52b7-14), 141, 149; *Aristotle's De Anima Books II and III*, D.W. Hamlyn, tr., pp. 18, 60, 90, 95-96, 159; and G. Lloyd, "Ancient Greek concepts of causation in comparativist perspective," in D. Sperber, D. Premack, A.J. Premack, eds., *Causal Cognition: A Multidisciplinary Debate*, pp. 536-556. (Page citations for *Metaphysics* are shortened: 34a2 for 1034a2, etc.)

cultures) had, we are quite tangential to the original orientation and interests, and to what was actually being proposed and understood in those contexts.

This can occur, for example, when we interpret talk of the "four elements" to be earth (rather than hardness), air or wind (rather than movement), water (rather than wetness), fire (rather than heat).[17]

Further, *to consider concepts used to understand the human being*, we have a similar systematic confusion arising if we think of the humors as literally the substances that are named (as above, earth, air, water, and fire), namely, black bile, yellow bile, phlegm, and blood, rather than explanatory principles to illuminate the presence or absence of various mood patterns.[18]

In the present context, we may notice a number of terms that, in another age, were used in an attempt to bring attention to some interesting phenomenon, but now sound silly. (It may be we who are silly in our literalist interpretation of more subtle thought, although we may well see the simplicity as elsewhere.)

Staying with concepts used to understand humans, we may nonetheless notice a similarity between talk of energy and of vital force and of cakras (or chakras) and of kuṇḍalinī energy and of animal electricity, and on and on, as the-

---

[17] The Indic Buddhist theory of the four elements is a non-Western theory that we could consider here. See, e.g., A. Hirakawa, *A History of Indian Buddhism: From Śākyamuni to Early Mahāyāna*, p. 151. Another model that is also Indic links these "elements" with consciousness, in quite a second way—*earth:* smell, fragrance; *water:* tasting, taste; *fire:* vision, light; *ether/wind:* hearing, sound). See H. Zimmer, *Myths and Symbols in Indian Art and Civilization*, J. Campbell, ed., p. 204, note (unnumbered).

[18] We could evaluate the literal claims about these substances and what differences they actually make, if any, from a modern medical/biochemical perspective, or, alternatively, could investigate the theory as an attempt, in part, to explain in these humoral terms, various psychological moods or states of mind that we humans go through, in which an over-abundance of each humor was linked with a particular mood (melanchole or black bile with being melancholic, pensively sad; chole or yellow bile with being choleric, easily irritable or excitable; flegma or phlegm with being phlegmatic, emotionlessly calm, unexcitable, unemotional; and sanguis or blood with being sanguine, optimistic, confident). See, e.g., Galen, *On the Natural Faculties*, R.J. Brock, tr.; R.M. Stelmack and C. Doucet, "A Dialogue with Galen on Zuckerman's *The Psychobiology of Personality*," *Psychological Inquiry*, vol. 4, no. 2 (1993), pp. 142-146—note the root 'chole' (bile) in 'melancholic' and 'choleric' (with related discussion in article, p. 143); and R.M. Stelmack and A. Stalikas, "Galen and the humour theory of temperament," *Personality and Individual Differences*, vol. 12, no. 3 (1991), pp. 255-263, esp. pp. 255, 258-260.

oretical constructs (terms within some theory) attempting to highlight the sense of change and power felt in the body or mind. Of course, that does not mean that all such terms are in any sense fully equivalent to one another, or are synonymous with one another. There will be additional assumptions that make for perhaps important (or perhaps quite secondary) additional differences.

If we consider the issue from another perspective while remaining with this question of changing meanings for various *seemingly* stable terms, we may turn our attention to Jacques-Henri-Désiré Pététin (we have discussed him above), who, harking back to the theories of Descartes, Newton, and Leibniz, wrote about a "fluide électrique" (electric fluid) to explain some of the breathing difficulties he noted, as well as other symptoms in his patients.[19]

This was described earlier as fluide, électricité, and as magnétisme animal (fluid, electricity, animal magnetism), which were explained as *ways of speaking succinctly about movement within the body rather than as a literal movement of fluid through the body.*[20] (At least these authors were explicitly clear about their terms being nonliteral, even if in reading them, we are not.)

In scientific discourse, with terms that are evolving through time, there is an ongoing *tension* between, on the one hand, *a desire to put into words* what so far has eluded articulation, in which case, we are always looking for something close enough to make sense of what we are trying to verbalize, and, on the other hand, *the distortions that will arise out of this extension* or metaphoric application of a term from one domain into that of another.[21]

We may apply this consideration, *with its recognition of this tension*, to the often hot-and-heavy debate around the role of sexuality in human development and maturity, especially concerning the *Freudian* concept of sexuality, a discussion often more like wind, dust, and smoke than composed of the clear light of understanding. And it may prove interesting and enlightening to consider early and later considerations about the Freudian conceptualization from the perspective of the philosopher-psychiatrist Pierre Janet.

---

[19] J.-H.-D. Pététin (1787), *Mémoire*, pp. 34-39. A. Bertrand (in 1891) remarked that Pététin (*from a century before*) made the "unpardonable error of being right too soon." Quoted from "Un précurseur de l'hypnotisme," *Revue philosophique de la France et de l'étranger*, vol. 32 (Jul.-Dec. 1891), pp. 192-206, at p. 192.

[20] Marquis de Puységur (1786), *Mémoires pour servir à l'histoire et à l'établissement du magnétisme animal*, pp. 6-8.

[21] The theoretical interest in the status of metaphor, of non-literal use of terms, and of their application to new realities can be traced back through the Encyclopédistes—as Du Marsais, *Traité des Tropes* (1730), subtitled *Or on the different senses in which one can take a single word in a single language* (*Ou des différents sens dans lesquels on peut prendre un même mot dans une même langue*)—back to Aristotle, *On Rhetoric* (also cited as *The Art of Rhetoric*).

Janet offered an understanding for us when doing a critique of the Freudian concept of sexuality, holding that the concept had been extended in Freudian contexts quite beyond its usual sense. In that context, Janet pointed out that at a conference he had attended in London in 1913, Ernest Jones—an important English Freudian and author of *The Life and Work of Sigmund Freud* (a monumental work in three volumes)—had explained that the sense that Freud took for the term 'sexual instinct' is the same as that of the term 'will to power' in Schopenhauer or that of the term 'élan vital' in the philosophy of Henri Bergson.[22] Janet goes on to mention that he had for a long time fought against such abuses of language (including the extension of what counts, for Freudians, as sexual, sexual instinct, and genital desire).[23]

Janet, of course, is not alone in wanting some clarity and clear understanding when trying to communicate in language to others, and not the only one aware of problems in language, in particular, in metaphoric, extended, or otherwise unusual and possibly misleading use of language. (More on Janet's longtime position on this topic, below.)

In a similar vein, Nietzsche, warning about our unrecognized confusions, wrote in an 1873 essay about the human use of language in general, and about metaphors in particular, "we believe that we know something about the things themselves[24] when we speak of trees, colors, snow, and flowers; and yet we possess nothing but metaphors for things—metaphors which correspond in no way to the original entities."[25]

We can begin to look here at some concepts that were introduced to explain unusual psychological processes, unexpected behavior, activities, or what was said, which caught people's attention and concern.

*In this discussion on theorizing about unusual human behavior and states of mind, we might first of all notice that **several key terms do not mean** what we might think they mean from ordinary language.* For example, *somnam-*

---

[22] *La psychanalyse de Freud* (2004), pp. 9-11, 105, which book reproduces the journal article, "La psycho-analyse," *Journal de psychologie normale et pathologique*, vol. 11 (1914), pp. 1-36, 97-130, a partial record of discussions held at the 17th International Congress of Medicine, Aug. 1913, London.

[23] *La psychanalyse de Freud*, pp. 105-106.

[24] As in the Kantian Dinge-an-sich (singular, das Ding-an-sich).

[25] Nietzsche, *Truth and Lies in an Extra-Moral Sense* (*Über Wahrheit und Lüge im aussermoralischen Sinne*), in Nietzsche, *Philosophy and Truth: Selections from Nietzsche's Notebooks of the Early 1870s*, D. Breazeale, ed., tr., pp. 79-97, at pp. 82-83. My thanks to Kathleen Higgins for referring me to this text. The abridged version of the essay in *The Portable Nietzsche*, W. Kaufmann, ed., tr., pp. 42-47, does not contain the passage quoted here, whose deletion in the Kaufmann edition is indicated by the ellipses at the top of p. 46, line 4.

bulism (literally and ordinarily understood as sleepwalking, from Latin somnus, sleep, and ambūlāre, walk) *in this context (especially in French and German writings we will be discussing here) is a state of consciousness, **not** a way of walking.* More precisely, the individual in this state of consciousness *is not sleeping at all*, but is in a particularly sensitive state of mind.

This is rather similar to what we now speak of as a trance state, an altered state of consciousness. This is the understanding we find already in the late 1700s, in which artificial somnambulism (i.e., an artificial trance) was induced in June of 1784 by Amand-Marc-Jacques de Chastenet, Marquis de Puységur (1752-1825),[26] who described somnambulism as a new state of sensitivity for man that, lifting him above the ordinary sphere, erases in him all the motley mixes (toutes les bigarrures) of our errors and puts him in a state of receiving the impressions of which he is capable, in a manner more or less fresh and innocent (vièrge, virgin).[27] Puységur was inspired by the teachings (especially from the 1770s and 1780s) of the Viennese-transplant-in-Paris physician Franz Anton Mesmer (1734-1815),[28] whose name is echoed in describing someone or something as being mesmerizing, meaning hypnotizing, captivating, enchanting.[29]

Similarly (concerning again the idea of somnambulism now), there are the related statements by Jean-Martin Charcot and Janet (then a disciple of Charcot's),[30] both psychiatrists at the Salpêtrière Hospital in Paris (which Freud

---

[26] See, e.g., *Mémoires pour servir à l'histoire et à l'établissement du magnétisme animal* (1784). A reprint with two new essays appeared in 1986, and in 2003, in an edition entitled *Aux sources de l'hypnose*, with the earlier title kept as a new subtitle. In *L'évolution psychologique de la personnalité*, pp. 464-465 (in electronic ed., pp. 258-259), Janet comments on this research by Puységur.

[27] *Mémoires pour servir à l'histoire et à l'établissement du magnétisme animal*, p. 194.

[28] See, e.g., *Mémoire sur la découverte du magnétisme animal* (1779). We may understand the attempt by Puységur and others to describe some sorts of change or movement using some scientific concepts of the period and its own historical context, from those of Newton, Boyle, Dalton, Benjamin Franklin, and earlier, Paracelsus and Jean-Baptiste Van Helemont (Bruxelles, 1577-1644) about energy, mass, chemistry, electricity, and so on, applied to living organisms. Talk of animal magnetism or of a universal fluid or of electricity were attempts to articulate this vision of Man, as at pp. 6-7; on the cultural or intellectual context of this conceptual scheme, see the appended essay by P. Pédalahore ("Une vie, une passion: Puységur et le magnétisme animal"), pp. XIV-XX; Newton and Mesmer are discussed in J. Ochorowicz, *De la suggestion mentale* (1887), pp. 480-481.

[29] This is discussed in J. Ochorowicz, *De la suggestion mentale* (1887), p. 165.

[30] The long history of differences and animosity between Freud and Janet (not parallel to that between Freud and Carl Gustav Jung, who began his analyst's

visited, before beginning his own independent work in Vienna; there is a question of whether Freud actually met or encountered Janet at that time).[31]

In any case, Charcot wrote in 1887, "during this *somnambulatory* period, all of the senses [of these patients or subjects] are open and one can even say that even if the mind is constricted, sensibility to what is communicated to their senses is intensified. It consequently becomes easy to enter by various means into relationship with the *hypnotized* person" (here, explicitly, somnambulism is likewise understood as being in a hypnotized state).[32]

And Janet, being equally explicit, wrote that for years he had often proposed that "these abnormal psychological states—the first characteristic of which is to be strange, extraordinary, very different from the normal psychological state of the subject,"—that these *"should not be understood in a literal fashion,"*[33] *that the sleep here is not "sommeil véritable" (true sleep).*[34]

---

career as a Freudian) is the material for some serious study. In the meantime, we may consider the two-volume work by E. Roudinesco, *La bataille de cent ans: histoire de la psychanalyse en France* [=*The One-hundred-year Battle: History of Psychoanalysis in France*], where Janet is grouped with the individualist psychology of Adler and the analytic psychology of Jung, all distinguished from the Freudian perspective in terms of the issue of the primacy of sexuality in psychological processes (p. 118), and Henri Frédéric Ellenberger's *The Discovery of the Unconscious: The History and Evolution of Dynamic Psychiatry*, esp. the long Chap. 6-9, on Pierre Janet and Psychological Analysis (pp. 331-417), Sigmund Freud and Psychoanalysis (pp. 418-570), Alfred Adler and Individual Psychology (pp. 571-656), and Carl Gustav Jung and Analytical Psychology (pp. 657-748), respectively.

[31] Freud studied and lived in Paris from Oct. 13, 1885 through Feb. 28, 1886 (with a week at Christmas, 1885, in Wandsbek, near Hamburg, Germany), less than four and a half months in all, at the Salpêtrière studying under Charcot: Freud's letters to his fiancée suggest that Freud first met Charcot on Oct. 20, 1885 and last saw him on Feb. 23, 1886 (4 months and 3 days). See E. Jones, *The Life and Work of Sigmund Freud*, vol. 1, p. 207; A. de Mijolla, *"Les letters de Jean-Martin Charcot à Sigmund Freud (1886-1893). Le crépuscule d'un dieu,"* *Revue française de psychanalyse*, vol. 52 (May-Jun. 1988), pp. 702-725, esp. pp. 704, 709 (re Oct. 20, 1885, and Feb. 23, 1886, respectively); and also Letters 81 (of Oct. 19, 1885) and 82 (of Oct. 21, 1885) in E.L. Freud, ed., *Letters of Sigmund Freud 1873-1939*, pp. 182-188, esp. pp. 182-183, 186-187.

[32] J.-M. Charcot, *Oeuvres completes, vol. III: Leçons sur les maladies du système nerveux*, p. 339. Italics highlight the connection between somnambulism, in this relevant sense, with hypnotized consciousness.

[33] P. Janet, *L'État mental des hystériques* (1911), p. 353.

[34] P. Janet, *Névroses et idées fixes* (1898), p. 53, note 1. In this note he refers

Janet was quite aware of the possible literal misinterpretations to avoid and advised against such readings quite explicitly. This is perhaps a philosopher's respect for language; relatedly, and looking back more than two millennia, we may recall that Aristotle had already made some distinctions about consciousness in waking life and consciousness during dreams, noting that what appears to us during a dream is not perception in the sense of perceiving any external object.[35] As Janet and fellow observers understood somnambulism (which we might well take at first sight—incorrectly—in its literal or etymological sense of sleepwalking, as discussed above), it was not a matter of being awake in one's usual state of mind and not a matter of being asleep in the usual way. This was made clear in a discussion of a number of names that might be used for this, such as "somno-vigil" (sleeping vigil), "veille somnambulique" (somnambulistic wakefulness), "hémi-somnambulisme" (partial somnambulism), "sommeil hypnotique" (hypnotic sleep), and so forth: *all trying to put this into words.*

Freud writes, equally explicitly, in an 1890 paper, "Psychical Therapy" (also cited as "Mental Therapy"): "In its lightest degree the hypnotic subject is aware only of something like a slight insensibility, while the most extreme degree, which is marked by special peculiarities, is known as 'somnambulism', on account of its resemblance to the natural phenomenon of sleepwalking. But hypnosis is in no sense a sleep like our nocturnal sleep or like the sleep produced by drugs. Changes occur in it and mental functions are retained during it which are absent in normal sleep."[36] And, in a more general way, given the tendency to interpret somnambulism as just that (as literally simply sleepwalking), the fact that this is meant in the present context, *and all related contexts*, as a modified state of consciousness, can perhaps not be overly stressed.

Given this, if we read these discussions of somnambulism, interpreting them (incorrectly) to be talking about sleepwalking, we will find ourselves once again quite misled in our understanding.

With these various considerations as orienting background, let us return in a more focused way here to the question that we were addressing in the essay

---

back to a published discussion of this issue from 1891, cited as: *Revue philosophique*, 1891, I, p. 394. The Roman numeral "I" here identifies the first volume (of two) for the given year. The essay in which that discussion is found is "Étude sur un cas d'aboulie et d'idées fixes," *Revue philosophique de la France et de l'étranger*, vol. 31 (Jan.-Jun. 1891), pp. 258-287, 382-407.

[35] For his original ponderings about dreams and the issue of perception, see Aristotle, Περὶ ἐνύπνιον *Perì enúpnion*, in Latin, *De Insomniis*, 458a33-463b11, subsequently taken as part of the collection *Parva Naturalia*. Greek text and English trans. in D. Gallop, *Aristotle on Sleep and Dreams: A Text and Translation*, pp. 84-104, with extensive notes and discussion, pp. 135-155.

[36] "Psychical (or Mental) Treatment" (1890a) [at SE 7: 295 = GW 5: 305].

on Nietzschean psychiatry, that of self-integration, to consider now more specifically the terms used to describe self-integration.

What is striking here is the way in which this issue of self-integration (and the contrasts of non-self-integration or internal conflict and such) has had an important if not central position in the world of psychotherapy and its interest in the workings of the mind and of human development, and this, across a variety of psychotherapeutic theoretical orientations and practices. We touched on this in the relevant sections of the chapter on Nietzschean psychiatry, above.

One area of interest in which particular forms of non-integration could be seen has been the concern with what has been called hysteria. *With the appearance of this strong word ('hysteria'), some preliminary remarks to orient the discussion might be very helpful at this point, to minimize misunderstanding and to reorient the reader to considerations of central relevance here.*

For now we will try to develop a clearer sense of how hysteria has been (variously) understood in the history of psychiatry, in particular, and in psychological theorizing, in general. First, in thinking of the term here, hysteria (derived etymologically from the Greek word for uterus or womb),[37] we may recognize a lay sense of what hysteria amounts to—in which hysteria is an exaggerated, overly dramatic, highly emotional reaction to the situation at hand.

By way of contrast, though, we are interested here in *technical* senses of hysteria *as used to understand non-integration*, that is, in theorizing that makes use of particular technical concepts of hysteria, in order to explain certain oddities in behavior that were noticed. (More on this below.) Let us at this point consider various concepts of hysteria that were formulated in the interest of coming to an understanding of what struck some people as remarkable or noteworthy.

Historically, then (to look especially at the 1800s and the era of Nietzsche), talk of hysteria became newly significant in considering patients in whom there was the presence of physical symptoms that did not have any physical basis, which led to the questioning of what might be going on in the minds of these patients that was manifesting itself in these unusual ways.[38]

---

[37] Freud, in "Hysteria" (1888b) [at SE 1: 41], cites the underlying Greek root as ὑστέρα (hystéra), womb. More on this throughout this chapter.

[38] See "Report on My Studies in Paris and Berlin" (1956a [1886]) [at SE 1: 10-11]. For more recent concerns with psychosomatic medicine (as it is sometimes called), cf. research of the Paris School of Psychosomatics, e.g., in Pierre Marty, Michel de M'Uzan, and Christian David, *L'investigation psychosomatique: Sept observations cliniques*, 1963; 2nd updated ed., 1994, with essay (Sep. 1993), "Préliminaires critiques à la recherché psychosomatique" by M. de M'Uzan and C. David (Marty having died earlier in 1993), such works as V.S. Ramachandran, *The Emerging Mind: The Reith Lectures 2003*, pp. 99-101, etc. On Marty, cf. below, p. 163, n. 15.

Charcot, who was an accomplished neurologist, showed that some paralyses—that is, unusual limitations on movements—at first thought to be neurological in nature (due, for example, to a lesion on a nerve making innervation beyond that point impossible) could in some cases *not* be explained in terms of known neurological pathways of the body.

He used, in one instance, the example of a paralyzed hand whose movement stopped abruptly at the wrist, rather than in accordance with possible injury or pathology of the nerves going to the muscles controlling the hand. This of course suggested that the basis of the problem was not neurological, but, rather, in this classic example, followed the common names for various parts of the anatomy: hand vs. wrist.[39] And in general, was governed by the language—and thus by the thinking and conceptualizing—of the person in question. *For further features to be explained, see below.*

We may take a moment to consider some of the major definitions of hysteria that were developed, based on such observations by physicians of the time. Before that, we may take a moment to point out that Janet noted the text by physician-author Jean-Louis Brachet, *Traité de l'hystérie* (1847), with its fifty-some definitions of hysteria in use at that time—the relevant chapter begins in the *Traité* at p. 202[40]—and (Janet added) Charcot had done much to hone down the psychiatric understanding of what hysteria was.

Relatedly, and jumping ahead in time in this brief aside to a quite contemporary perspective for a moment, we may note that in the most recent version of the DSM (*Diagnostic and Statistical Manual*), the American psychiatric community's diagnostic bible—to cite the DSM-IV-TR, the most recent version of this ongoingly modified collection of particularly American diagnostic categories, published in 2000—there is no longer any such diagnosis at all (speaking of hysteria here, of course)! We should perhaps *not* conclude from the elimination

---

[39] Cf. P. Janet, *The Major Symptoms of Hysteria: Fifteen Lectures Given in the Medical School of Harvard University*, Lecture VII: Paralyses—Diagnosis, pp. 138-158. Diagrams on pp. 156-157 show what Janet describes as a paralysis corresponding "to the popular conception of the organ rather than to its anatomic conception." On Charcot's contribution, see pp. 16-17, 20-21, 153, 161-162; on Brachet's approximately 50 definitions, p. 320. Cf. p. 145 for Janet's non-hostile mention of Freud. Freud wrote on this topic in one of his early papers (written in French, several years after attending the conferences of Charcot in Paris, 1885-86), "Quelques considérations pour une étude comparative des paralysies motrices organiques et hystériques)" (1893c) [SE 1: 157 = GW 1: 39 = CP 1: 42].
[40] Brachet (*Traité de l'hystérie*, Chap. II, pp. 202-204), lists a number of these in the chapter Janet refers to (cf. note 39), and continues with a large variety of features, theorizing about causes, discussing the course, duration, prognoses, and so forth, for much of the rest of the treatise (of more than 500 pages).

of this diagnostic category in 2000 that this is one quick way to "cure" many earlier-diagnosed patients, all in the stroke of a pen, as we used to say.

In any case—noting that Charcot and Janet later come to another perspective on these issues—we may review some statements made in the late 1800s concerning the nature of hysteria. As an overview, we can note a variety of understandings of the term: (i) as a woman with a wandering uterus (rejected explicitly by Freud, as discussed below), [41] (ii) as histrionic overreacting to some situation, a lay sense of the term 'hysterical' mentioned above, (iii) as psychological tensions being expressed physically (sometimes called conversion reactions, as in the circles of Freud and others from his epoch), or (iv) as some concepts of hysteria still to be presented and described later in this chapter.

Let us consider here the ways in which a given term (here, 'hysteria') may be embedded or situated in a series of quite distinct theoretical models and understandings, and appreciate more fully the ways in which it may be easily misunderstood when read as defined in one context and theory but interpreted as if *defined from another theoretical understanding.*

Freud discussed the topic of hysteria early in his writing. In a "more accurate" and "more modern" statement of the issue, as Freud put it, he explains (in 1886) that the "name 'hysteria' originates from the earliest times of medicine and is a precipitate of the prejudice, overcome only in our own days, which links neuroses with diseases of the female sexual apparatus..."[42] The explanation of hysteria as coming from the female uterus is, then, something that Freud is suggesting be dismissed as not only ancient but also as a distorted prejudice without merit: a shift again in theoretical model, in theoretical presuppositions, in theoretical implications, in basic understanding of the concept, we may note.

Adding to what has been sketched above concerning views by Freud and others of what hysteria amounts to, we may consider these perspectives:

(1) In talking of hysteria (in the late 1700s) in the form of a "hysterical catalepsy," Pététin (mentioned above), in a posthumous text from 1808, *Électricité animale*, states that the "médecins modernes" (modern physicians, modern, that is, relative to 1800) have only an incomplete sense of "catalepsie hystérique" (hysterical catalepsy) and that the term is in need of a new (improved) definition, taking into account new clinical observations newly made by the author himself.[43] There, he defines hysteria as one of "les maladies convulfives [convulsives]" (sicknesses that involve convulsions).

---

[41] The issues of more modern theories of hysteria, such as those that preoccupied Freud, Janet, and others in more recent Western traditions interested in psychopathology, are not those of the Ancient Greeks. I include an addendum to this chapter on Greek theorizing for those who might be interested in that area.

[42] "Report on My Studies in Paris and Berlin" (1956a [1886]) [at SE 1: 10-11].

[43] *Électricité animale*, p. 112. Cf. above, pp. 118-119, notes 3-4.

Pététin draws attention to various epileptic or hypertonic postures (positions based on extreme tension in the larger musculature of the body), as well as other "fymptômes [symptômes] bizarres" as the paralysis of an arm, of the tongue, or of the organ of sight or of hearing, and so on. That is, succinctly, hysteria (in this case, more specifically, hysterical catalepsy) as convulsive.

(2) Freud (as above, 1886) notes, "hysteria *can scarcely be regarded as a name with any well-defined meaning...* it has been studied little and unwillingly; and it labours under the odium of some very wide-spread prejudices. Among these are the supposed dependence of hysterical illness upon genital irrigation [a woman's period, that is, her menses or monthly period of bleeding]."[44]

(3) Breuer and Freud in their seminal work, *Studies on Hysteria*, write, "Hysterics suffer mainly from reminiscences."[45] We will return to the issue of what these memories (reminiscences) are, below.

(4) Freud remarks, "It was his [Charcot's] pupil, Janet, who first attempted a deeper approach to the peculiar psychical processes present in hysteria, and we followed his example when we took the splitting of the mind and dissociation of the personality as the centre of our position"[46] ... along with the further concept from Janet, that of the feature of "the narrowness of the 'field of consciousness (*champ de la conscience*)'..."[47]

(5) Presenting a contrast to this last item, Freud also writes, "In contradistinction to Janet's view, ... there is the view put forward by Breuer in our joint communication (Breuer and Freud, 1893).[48] According to him [to Breuer, that is, Freud writes here], 'the basis and *sine quâ non* of hysteria' is the occurrence of peculiar dream-like states of consciousness with a restricted capacity of association for which he [Breuer, again] proposes the name 'hypnoid states.' In that case, the splitting of consciousness is secondary and acquired; it comes about because the ideas which emerge in hypnoid states are cut off from associative communication with the rest of the content of consciousness."[49]

---

[44] "Hysteria" (1888b) [at SE 1: 41]. Italics added for emphasis.

[45] *Studies on Hysteria* (1895d) [at SE 2: 7 = GW 1: 86].

[46] "Five Lectures on Psycho-Analysis" (1910a) [at SE 11: 21 = GW 8: 17].

[47] "The Neuro-psychoses of Defense" (1894a) [at SE 3: 46 = GW 1: 60 = CP 1:60].

[48] This is a reference to Breuer and Freud, "On the Psychical Mechanism of Hysterical Phenomena: Preliminary Communication" (1893a) [SE 2: 3 = GW 1: 81 = CP 1: 24], in *Studies on Hysteria* (1895d) [in SE: 2 = GW 1].

[49] "The Neuro-psychoses of Defense" (1894a) [at SE 3: 46 = GW 1: 60 = CP 1: 60]. Freud's paraphrase of Breuer can be compared with the original comments (at SE 2: 12 = GW 1: 91; cf. SE 2: 215-222). The "secondary and acquired" part, which gives extra weight to the "contra-distinction" Freud mentions, is Freud's added emphasis in this paraphrase. The Latin *sine quâ non* renders "Bedingung"

In this description of ideas "cut off from associative communication with the rest of the content of consciousness" we have clear reference to the issue of *dissociation, or of a lack of integration*, that we have been interested in here as our underlying focus. Given Freud's comment here, we have the question of whether this distinction of his, as part of a presentation of the Viennese position (of Breuer and Freud) versus that of the Parisian perspective (of Janet), is ultimately significant and basic, or minor, and itself an example of what Freud elsewhere spoke of as the narcissism of minor differences.[50]

In any case, there was apparently an important difference for Freud (for these or other reasons), given that he replied to a letter from Ernest Jones telling of the defeat (by Jones) of Janet's position at the 1913 conference (referred to in various discussions in this chapter): Freud's congratulatory reply to Jones that he sent with his expression of full confidence in Jones to carry on, on behalf of Freudian teachings in England, was all warmth and encouragement, after all. Freud apparently found joy in this putative victory by Jones over Janet.[51]

Such personal issues aside, these are some of the senses of hysteria that were being offered and considered. The inspiration for this theorizing included, as mentioned, behavior that looked like neurological damage but could not be explained by the current information available at the time about neurological innervation and its pathways (and remain inexplicable even now, in those terms!)

And, if we follow the observations being made in those years, as in the reports from some 200 years ago[52] concerning his medical practice by Pététin, to appreciate better some of what these theoreticians were interested in explaining (in addition to the just-mentioned bodily paralyses and other problems that could not be explained neurologically, for example), we find reports of recurring perceptual memories (recalling some visual, auditory, olfactory, gustatory, or kinesthetic experience) that were at times considered as hallucinations, as having an "aspect anormale" (an unusual or abnormal[53] feature).

(condition, stipulation) in the original text. Other differences may be noted.

[50] Is the incidental comment "further to demolish" a Janet myth, in the editors' prefatory comments to "Hysteria" (1888b)—see notes at SE 1: 40—a "narcissism of minor differences"? Cf. M. Ginsberg, *The Inner Palace*, pp. xv, 324. The term ('narcissism of minor differences') was introduced by Freud in "Contributions to the Psychology of Love III: The Taboo of Virginity" (1918a) [at SE 11: 199 = GW 12: 169 = CP 4: 224]; cf. his later works, *Group Psychology and the Analysis of the Ego* (1921c) [at SE 18: 101, n. 4; cf. GW 13: 111], *Civilization and its Discontents* (1930a) [at SE 21: 114 = GW 14: 473-474], *Moses and Monotheism: Three Essays* (1939a) [SE 23: 91, n. 1; cf. GW 16: 197].

[51] See P. Janet, *La psychanalyse de Freud*, pp. 9-11, 105; Freud quoted at p. 10.

[52] *Électricité animale*, op. cit. (cf. above, n. 3), pp. 194, 197.

[53] The term 'anormal' (fem., 'anormale') means etymologically that which is

It may be of interest to see how these perceptual memories were understood, described, and explained. For example, we may start with the earlier observations by Pététin that speak to the same (subsequent) concern of Breuer and Freud in the reminiscences, or disturbing memories, of the hysteric, as quoted above.[54] Typically, these memories were not pleasant.

To understand them as recollections of earlier traumas makes this unpleasantness not especially surprising, of course. To understand them as workings of a mind that was going off in strange directions not related to the actual personal and interpersonal context of the person in question, of course makes such things seem (ex hypothesi, simply based on the hypothesis that is being accepted for the moment) out of any "touch" with reality, and thus, almost by way of definition of craziness or psychosis, quite strange if not absolutely crazy (if not definitively "psychotic").

For which the paraphrastic résumé by Freud of the French psychiatrist François Leuret (1797-1851) is relevant: "Even the delusional ideas of the insane would certainly be found to have a sense if only we understood how to translate them."[55]

Furthermore, in ways that Janet described with great clarity, the focus on these recurring perceptual memories is part of the limited consciousness that kept these memories in the center of awareness. More on this, below.

We might consider such images or thoughts, recognized as not related to the present situation of the individual, as reflecting some sort of preoccupation with ideas having to do with this person's past, and so already in place (present rather than absent, even if from the past rather than from the present) and having a very specific, quite unpleasant nature, as noted just above.

This is an alternative to ascribing hallucinations to the individual, which remain rather unexplained and inexplicable. Of course, if these are hallucinations at all, they are rather specific, emotionally significant hallucinations. They are what in these past few decades have been called "flash-backs" and understood to be memories revived because of some association in the mind of the individual, in ways that would make sense if we knew the specifics.

We will address the issue of describing individuals in distress as having no rationality, and the way this invites incomprehension, which is itself the foundation for dismissing another person as beyond the pale of sanity, suffering from "delusions" and "hallucinations" and such, and being labeled as "mentally ill."

---

not (a-) normal. It is that which is away from the norm, the unusual or irregular, and also from (ab-) the norm, the abnormal. The English sense (in the word 'abnormal') has the suggestion of pathology rather than simply being unusual.

[54] See note 41, citing *Studies on Hysteria* (1895d) [at SE 2: 7 = GW 1: 86].

[55] See beginning of chapter on Nietzschean Psychiatry Revisited for citation of this résumé by Freud of Leuret, with further discussion (esp. pp. 61-62).

It may be helpful to point out, however, that this dismissive attitude toward those in distress has not always been predominant. Of course, there were violent times when people in obvious psychological distress were chained down, or burned at the stake, or (in a less immediately violent way) sent off onto Narrenschiffe (ships of fools), and so forth, but there have also been times and places of a more compassionate and gentle attitude toward those in distress.

And to point out, as well, that the dismissing of what are now often called the "mentally ill" or the "psychotic" as irrational and so forth, has also not always been the attitude of professional caretakers. Here, if we look again at the writings of Pététin, it is perhaps surprising that this physician from the late 1700s goes on to remark that the soul of an hysterical woman demonstrates as much good judgment, as much wisdom, as the soul of Socrates and of Cato.[56] This, we might note, is in marked distinction from the tendency of some more current psychopathological understandings to attribute little or no understanding or wisdom to people being described in psychopathological terms.

We will consider this unhappy recurrence of these upsetting images, sensations, or thoughts, just below, in the context of discussing "idées fixes subconscientes" (subconscious fixed ideas) from some "délire" (delirium, in the etymological image of getting out of the ploughed furrow, the regular path, going off track), actively occupied in organizing and integrating a group of perceptual memories, to the exclusion of all other thoughts, as in an essay by Janet.[57]

As with other significant terms in this domain, we might think (in an unhelpful way) of this "idée fixe" from this title in a commonly-held understanding of the term, as a fixed or rigid idea, as in a dogmatic frame of mind or as in the repetitive thinking of a monomaniac (someone who just keep thinking incessantly about some particular consideration or issue).[58] This is in any case a lay sense of the term: *Webster's* and the *Oxford English Dictionary* both define it as "an idea that dominates the mind; an obsession."[59]

Janet in some contexts speaks in a similar way, as where he explains the term 'idées fixes' (here in the plural) simply as "erroneous but fixed beliefs, developed by a psychological mechanism analogous to that of suggestion."[60]

---

[56] J.-H.-D. Pététin (1787), *Mémoire*, pp. 3, 28, 33-34. This Cato whom Pététin mentions is presumably Cato the Elder (or Cato the Censor), 234-149 BCE, or his great-grandson, Cato the Younger (or Cato of Utica), 95-46 BCE, both Roman statesmen and moralists highly respected for their honoring Roman ideals.

[57] "Histoire d'une idée fixe," *Revue philosophique de la France et de l'étranger*, vol. 37 (Jan.-Jun. 1894), pp. 121-168, at pp. 126-127.

[58] See J. Breuer and S. Freud, *Studies on Hysteria* (1895d) [in SE 2 = GW 1].

[59] *Webster's New World Dictionary* (1957), p. 720; *The Concise Oxford Dictionary* (1992), p. 585.

[60] P. Janet, *La médecine psychologique*, at the beginning of Part III (Les résul-

It is helpful to appreciate the more nuanced understanding that Janet laid out in other contexts, however, if we are to appreciate the elegance of his explanations using this concept of the idée fixe. *Here the same term is used in more or less subtle ways, and interpreting the more subtle by applying the less subtle throughout is missing out on some nuanced, elegant thinking.*

Elsewhere,[61] then, we should note that Janet has a more precise conceptualization in mind, as where he points out that this "idée obsédante" (obsessing idea) is never abstract or cold, but is an "émotion fixe" (a fixed emotion), a complex *emotion* that is recreated always the same.

Significantly, this idée fixe is not a simple matter of psychotic dogmatism (insisting that I am Napoleon Bonaparte or Jesus of Nazareth the Christ, for example, despite evidence to show the absurdity of my claim[62])—which is one common interpretation of what having an idée fixe amounts to.

Rather, Janet remarks, as Charcot had put it, the idée fixe is a preoccupation, an emotion, an anguish ("préoccupation, émotion, angoisse"), and that, in the simplest cases, *"the idée fixe and the clinical symptom thereby determined are the reproduction of an event in the life of the patient, are in tight rapport with a very precise accident."* An example of a man being hit by a carriage is given at this point in the text.[63]

This linking of the emotional aspect of the idée fixe and a specific trauma in the person's life represents a great understanding of what might otherwise seem to be the irrational workings of a deranged mind, beyond understanding, explanation, or basis. *It is in some important ways tragic* (to state my personal opinion here) that this insight was disregarded in the history of psychiatry for so long, when an interest in the inner fantasy life of the individual was accepted as the focus of investigation for understanding these processes.

Janet points out that this idée fixe, in general, is a combination of thoughts or cognitions plus emotionally powerful memories of associated experiences. *The idée fixe is understood,* in this 1894 paper by Janet being discussed here, *not as an abstract concept but as a combination of thoughts, ideas, and often-intense emotions, such as fear, in addition to having a phenomenological dimension, including images, sounds, smells, etc.*[64]

---

tats des psychotherapies), Chap. I (Les applications), Sect. 2 (Les traitements des déviations fonctionnelles), p. 235; Fr. electronic ed., p. 130; 2005 Fr. reprint ed., p. 133: "croyances erronées mais fixes, développées par un mécanisme psychologue analogue à celui de la suggestion." In Eng. tr., *Principles of Psychotherapy*, p. 257.

[61] P. Janet, *L'état mental des hystériques.* See citations in the following notes.

[62] Cf. M. Rokeach, *The Three Christs of Ypsilanti: A Psychological Study.*

[63] P. Janet, *L'état mental des hystériques*, 2nd ed., p. 625. Italics added.

[64] Cf. introductory comments to the chapter on the concept of love and its logic,

Furthermore, this entire complex is subconscious: Janet explains in one text what *subconscious* ideas amount to (in contradistinction to the concept of *unconscious* ideas, found in the writings of Breuer and Freud):

> This word should not raise any philosophical argument. It is not a matter of seeking to determine if the mind is or is not divisible, whether these ideas maintain a particular form of consciousness; such questions are quite useless for a healer. The term 'subconscious' simply expresses one fact and one unquestionable fact, that the subject *can express his fixed idea at certain moments* and in certain conditions and that he *can absolutely not do so in others.*[65]

Also in hysteria, Janet continues, there is a narrowing of the field of consciousness, a disassembling of the mind (désagrégation de l'esprit), and a difficulty in the mind to synthesize, to integrate, all of the relevant considerations of the given context.[66]

Here we can see the link between the issue of non-integration that began this chapter and this issue of hysteria and idées fixes (fixed ideas).

These passages highlight the separation between various groups of thoughts and mind-states and others, in ways that do not suggest an open flow of information and perspectives between them. We see here one pattern of non-integration that is of special interest in this context.

Relatedly, the Alexis Bertrand article describes the compartmentalization of memories and the ability to shift from one group of memories to another, only to return much later to the first, depending on the changed context. *This compartmentalization is often described as a feature of non-integration,* a major underlying focus of this present chapter. The first was seen as an unusual (or, in more recent terms, an altered) state of consciousness, and described, in an attempt at articulating and organizing observations about this remarkable behavior (and for lack of a better comparison?), as a sleep state.[67]

In some circles, such as in the writings of Janet, two groups of ideas came from this.

---

on the emotions as involving thinking, judging, reasoning (as in the 1923 article by Dugas, cited above, p. 5, n. 18). Cf. discussion in G. Heim and K.-E. Bühler, "Les idées fixes et la psychologie de l'action de Pierre Janet," *Annales médico-psychologiques, revue psychiatrique,* vol. 161, no. 8 (Oct. 2003), pp. 579-586. The 1894 Janet article here is "Histoire d'une idée fixe," *Revue philosophique de la France et de l'étranger,* vol. 37 (Jan.-Jun. 1894), pp. 121-168.

[65] P. Janet, *L'état mental des hystériques,* 2nd ed., p. 630. Emphasis added.

[66] Idem, 2nd ed., pp. 628-637. My résumé.

[67] A. Bertrand, "Un précurseur de l'hypnotisme," *Revue philosophique de la France et de l'étranger,* vol. 32 (Jul.-Dec. 1891), p. 197. Cf. above, pp. 118-119.

The first of these is somnambulism, discussed above. The second of these is the idea of the non-perception of something that might ordinarily be perceived. This too had various names offered up, with similar lack of unanimity of agreement: "hallucination négative" (negative hallucination), "anesthésie systematisée" (systematized anesthesia), "perception inconsciente" (unconscious perception), or it was described as a conscious experience that is separated or in a state of dissociation from the remainder of the organized consciousness that gives a sense of self ("sensation ... consciente ... séparée de l'ensemble des phénomènes psychiques dont la synthèse forme l'idée du moi").[68]

The significance of these different names (here, in these just-discussed two groups) for the same process can be used to highlight, again, the important fact that names come to us in one or another theoretical context, which orients us to questions that can be asked, issues that can be addressed, as well as assumptions of how these sorts of phenomena behave in the world.

All of these considerations can differ radically from name to name (depending on the theoretical context). If, for example here, we are dealing with hallucinations, we have one sort of concern; if we are dealing, instead, with limited perception, we have another sort of concern.

Here again we may remind ourselves that we should not jump to conclusions (interpretations) based on what terms have come to mean, when seeing them in a much earlier and theoretically (conceptually) differently-dressed appearance. *This means that our descriptions are not innocuous!*[69]

In a partial overview, looking at these various descriptions, there is, first, the Nietzschean concern with self-integration, and also a general interest in this self-integrating, or harmonizing and setting into order what is structuring us (beliefs, preferences, yearnings, fears, in short, those vectors having impact on what we think, feel, desire, plan, and carry out in action), including recognizing and articulating the hierarchy of these mutually interacting vectors.

---

[68] For discussion and these particular passages, see P. Janet, "L'anesthésie systématisée et la dissociation des phénomènes psychologiques" (1887), *Revue philosophique de la France et de l'étranger*, vol. 23 (Jan.-Jun. 1887), pp. 449-472, at pp. 450-455, 471. Cf. the idea of the "marks" (stigmata)—not the stigmata of Jesus on the Cross, but—the noticeable psychological features ("stigmates mentaux" or mental stigmata) of hysteria, in P. Janet, *L'État mental des hystériques. Les stigmates mentaux des hystériques* (1892/1911), with discussion at pp. 8, 305-307, 390, 422. (The first edition of this text is cited by the shorter title, *Stigmates mentaux des hystériques*, in P. Janet, *Névroses et idées fixes*, p. 55, n. 1.)

[69] There may be interesting and important features of this issue to be highlighted by investigating Chinese philosophy and the concept of right naming, esp. the Confucian concept of rectifying names (zhèng míng 正名), as at *Analects*, 13.3, etc., but I will not extend this discussion in that direction here.

This interest has been shown from Europe in the 1700s, through to contemporary times (passing through the various physician-healers at Salpêtrière in
Paris to Breuer and Freud in Vienna, through to more recent work in the field of
psychotherapy in the late 1900s and early twenty-first century: in this light we
may consider the studies on dissociation[70] by the French, as Charcot (1887)[71]
and Janet (1880s on),[72] who spoke of shocks, or traumas, that would bring about

---

[70] Not to mention ancient Greek interest in the issues of disintegration and reintegration (cf. above, p. 86, n. 73, along with further discussions there and in this
present context). Dissociation renders the French dissociation, as in P. Janet,
"L'anesthésie systématisée et la dissociation des phénomènes psychologiques,"
Revue philosophique de la France et de l'étranger, vol. 23 (Jan.-Jun. 1887), pp.
449-472, at pp. 471-472, and also désagrégation (=dés+agrégation), as in P.
Janet, "Histoire d'une idée fixe," *Revue philosophique de la France et de
l'étranger*, vol. 37 (Jan.-Jun. 1894), pp. 121-168, at p. 168. We might more
clearly understand it to be dis-association, in parallel to de-construction (as dis-
tinguished from destruction): the undoing of what was grouped together, the
isolating of parts from the larger context. Cf. O. van der Hart and B. Friedman,
"A Reader's Guide to Pierre Janet on Dissociation: A Neglected Intellectual
Heritage," *Dissociation*, vol. 2 (1989), pp. 3-16; D. Meichenbaum, *A Clinical
Handbook/Practical Therapist Manual for Assessing and Treating Adults with
Post Traumatic Stress Disorder (PTSD)* (1995), pp. 35, 205, 354; J. Herman,
Trauma and Recovery (1997), pp. 87-89, 99-103, 186; J. Allen, *Traumatic Relationships and Serious Mental Disorders* (2001), esp. dissociative compartmentalization, pp. 181-186; J. Briere, *Psychological Assessment of Adult Posttraumatic States: Phenomenology, Diagnosis, and Measurement*, 2nd ed. (2004), pp.
49-60; D. Spiegel, "Recognizing Traumatic Dissociation," *American Journal of
Psychiatry*, vol. 163, no. 4 (Apr. 2006), pp. 566-568, with brief communication
to the editor, by O. van der Hart and M. Dorahy, "Pierre Janet and the Concept
of Dissociation," *American Journal of Psychiatry*, vol. 163, no. 9 (Sep. 2006), p.
1646; cf. cross-cultural studies by E. Somer, "Advances in Dissociation
Research and Practice in Israel," *Journal of Trauma Practice*, vol. 4, no. 1/2
(2005), pp. 157-178, and "Culture-Bound Dissociation: A Comparative Study,"
Psychiatric Hospitals of North America, vol. 29, no. 1 (2006), pp. 213-226.
[71] See *Leçons sur les maladies du système nerveux faites à la Salpêtrière*, vol. 3.
[72] See "L'anesthésie systématizée et la dissociation des phénomènes psychologiques," *Revue philosophique de la France et de l'étranger*, vol. 23 (Jan.-Jun.
1887), pp. 449-472; "Étude sur un cas d'aboulie et d'idées fixes," *Revue philosophique de la France et de l'étranger*, vol. 31 (Jan.-Jun. 1891), pp. 258-287 and
pp. 382-407; "Histoire d'une idée fixe," *Revue philosophique de la France et de
l'étranger*, vol. 37 (Jan.-Jun. 1894), pp. 121-168; *Névroses et idées fixes* (1898),
where an idée fixe or "fixed idea" is described (pp. 216-217) more in terms of a

idées fixes (fixed ideas)—again, not in the often-used interpretation taking this term to mean simply a rigid or dogmatic belief that is not subject to change, a matter of stubbornness, but, rather, as a more subtle and sophisticated, nuanced concept—in which fixed ideas are emotionally-charged rigid ideas that were isolated from the rest of the individual's thinking, operating in a narrowed field of consciousness,[73] perhaps from having felt overwhelmed.

There is a background to these ideas of the narrowing of consciousness and in the theorizing that was interested here in understanding something about the ways in which non-integration operates in the human being.

There was, for example, the theorizing of an influential psychology professor of Janet's, Théodule Ribot (1839-1916), founder and editor-in-chief of *La revue philosophique de la France et de l'étranger*, with this narrowing as part of the phenomenon of the weakening of the will, with research into how this general process worked in particular situations.[74]

---

perceptually-based system of psychological and physiological phenomena that are mutually associated, as in an emotional state such as having great fear or being terrified (une terreur); "L'amnésie et la dissociation des souvenirs par l'emotion," *Journal de psychologie normale et pathologique*, vol. 1 (1904), pp. 417-453, with the concept of idées fixes associées (emotionally-charged, attention-captivating, isolated or dissociated ideas: that is, ideas that are emotionally charged through association with some traumatic experiences, that contain strong perceptual components related to that time, and that are powerful and attention-defining to the exclusion of other features of the present situation, in this way, isolated as ideas from the rest of the person's experience and consciousness, pp. 125-126); *État mental des hystériques* (1892, 2nd ed. as *L'État mental des hystériques*, 1911); *The Major Symptoms of Hysteria* (1907; with updated Introduction, 2nd ed., 1920), p. 332, where Janet considers hysteria to be a malady of "personal synthesis" [=integration] with a "retraction of the field of personal consciousness and a tendency to the dissociation and emancipation [=non-integration, split-off separate operating] of the system of ideas and functions that constitute personality." This narrowing down of the "field of personal consciousness" is "an absence of every sensation and every memory that is not connected with that delirium" or emotional focus of the individual (p. 36).

[73] In his intriguing reviews of two of Pierre Janet's books, found in "Hysteria" (signed W.J.), *Psychological Review*, vol. 1 (1894), pp. 195-200, William James speaks of "physical and moral shocks and strains" (read: physical and psychological traumas) and of subconscious fixed ideas or split-off fixed ideas, as well as of the narrowing of the individual's principal consciousness. In the same article collecting several of his book reviews, James notes the idea (1893) by Breuer and Freud that hysteria always starts from a shock (read: trauma).

[74] See T. Ribot, "Les affaiblissements de la volonté," *Revue philosophique de la*

Janet expounded on this idea, formulating a framework in which this narrowing and limiting of our mental capacities could be understood in a three-dimensional matrix or system of theorizing (a theory in which there were three groups of independent considerations, each defining a "dimension").

First, there are the tendencies (les tendances), that is, various patterns of thinking and activity, from very simple ones of bodily function to more complex or sophisticated ones of more intricate plans and actions that carry out these plans.

Second are the degrees of activation of these tendencies (les degrés d'activation), the degree to which these various tendencies are active.

And third, are the degrees of psychological tension (les degrés de tension psychologique),[75] where tension is understood in the sense of high tension wires of electricity: not tension as stress or anxiety, etc., but tension as potential of charge to be put into action, the amount of organizational energy to deal with a variety of complex demands on our presence, on our thinking about issues, on our organizing our perspective, on our integrating various considerations that are relevant to the concern at hand, and so forth. When we are tired, for example, our ability to deal with complex issues diminishes, at times significantly. (We want to "zone out.")

These three—tendencies and degrees of activation and of tension—in other words, are the patterns of bodily and thinking activities of varying degrees of complexity and difficulty of being carried out, either physically or psychologically (or, as could be said in French, moralement[76])—the tendencies. There is the degree to which we are involved in, committed to, or desirous of, carrying out any given tendency—the degree of activation. And there is the energy available to us at any given time, the amount of psychological force that is available to act as the motor for carrying out the given tendency, the given activity involving thought and action—the degree of psychological tension.

This model, with its three distinct features or dimensions in which to analyze human psychological process from this perspective,[77] suggests a way to

---

France et de l'étranger, vol. 14 (Jul.-Dec. 1882), pp. 391-423, and *La logique des sentiments* (1905/1907). On integration of information and energy as maximizing complexity (distinctions in the mind) with resonance (mutual influence), coherence, and flexibility, leading to a more complex, functionally linked system, see D.J. Siegel, *The Developing Mind*, pp. 320-322, and M. Ginsberg, *The Inner Palace*, Chap. XX (Polysociative Vision), pp. 280-318, 537-593.

[75] Cf. B. Sjövall, *Psychology of Tension: An analysis of Pierre Janet's concept of «tension psychologique» together with an historical aspect* (1967).

[76] Compare the idea of having the morale to do something.

[77] See P. Janet, "La tension psychologique et ses oscillations," in G. Dumas *et al.*, *Traité de Psychologie* (1922), pp. 919-952, and *La médecine psychologique*

understand which processes remain isolated or non-integrated, in terms of the energy required for the individual to deal with what is at times quite a draining process, emotionally speaking. This was one of the interests of Janet, as part of the larger history of this interest in conceptualizing, in understanding, and in appreciating the breakdown of our actions in the world (as well as our own "inner" or "interior" thinking processes).

In considering the history of this interest—born out of a caring concern—in non-self-integration, and its torments, we quickly come to the questions of how integration might be blocked in its initial formation, and of what might block (shatter, or otherwise destroy) our otherwise integrated, unified beings. These processes (such as psychic traumas) and related issues are further addressed in other chapters of this collection.

ADDENDUM ON ANCIENT GREEK THEORIZING

Above, note 41 on p. 132 made reference to Greek theorizing about hysteria in various senses of the term. This addendum addresses this further.

The issues of more modern theories of hysteria—such as those that preoccupied Freud, Janet, and others in the Western traditions interested in psychopathology—are not identical with those of the Greeks, who were attempting to understand a number of conditions in terms of changes in the uterus, in which that individual was hysterical, that is, suffering in the womb.[78]

We may speculate that if the Greeks had only had access to current theories about hormones—products of the endocrine organs that as signaling molecules "wander" via the blood—they might well have described certain processes that occur in humans as involving interactions between the hormones, the body, and consciousness, rather than in terms of the uterus and its changes.

One theory we hear about had the uterus wandering about in the body, a theory sometimes attributed to Plato and Hippocrates.

Looking more carefully, we may come to understand the sophistication of Plato, Hippocrates, and other Greeks, rather than take them to be at best silly and quaint. One reading of Plato, for example, suggests that he considered the issue not as physical, but as psychological. The so-called wandering is based on an interpretation of πλανάω planáō, a root glossed as wander, do irregularly or

---

(1923), e.g., in Part II (Les principes), Chap. IV (Les acquisitions psychologiques), Sect. 3 (Les trois principes de l'excitation), pp. 207-219; in Fr. electronic ed., pp. 115-121; in 2005 Fr. reprint ed., pp. 118-124; in Eng. tr., *Principles of Psychotherapy*, pp. 226-239. See further, P. Janet, *La force et la faiblesse psychologiques* (1932), pp. 309-324.

[78] Or ὑστερικός hysterikós; from the noun ὑστέρα hystéra, womb; Latin and English, uterus: Liddell and Scott, *Greek-English Lexicon*, pp. 1905b, 1906a.

with variation, be misled, etc.[79] Something was wandering or perhaps irregular, then, for Plato,[80] and that was the ὑστέρα hystéra or the ζῷον zōon, living being: "Plato surpassed the older animistic theory and even the newer Hippocratic one. These theories, physiologically absurd, Plato insightfully and tactfully revised into a plausible psychological explanation. Hysterical misery, which others attributed to a wandering womb, Plato attributed to a moving psychological force which arises from the womb: sexual desire perverted by frustration."[81]

And in understanding the position of *Hippocrates*, one issue is the interpretation of τραπῶσιν trapōsin (citation form of this verb, τρέπω trépō), which is glossed as turn (towards, around, in a certain direction), alter, change, etc.,[82] *and not as* wandering *or as* traveling![83]

See especially Plato, *Republic*,[84] and Aristotle, *De anima* and *Nichomachean Ethics*, on the psychological dimension[85] and on parts of the soul in Greek thinking here—where the appetitive soul is understood to be one part of the non-rational part of the soul,[86] where desire is found—all of these features understood in those texts as belonging to the soul, not to a body or bodily structure or organ (such as the uterus),[87] parts calling out for integration. That much is clear.

---

[79] Liddell and Scott, *Greek-English Lexicon*, p. 1411a-b.

[80] See πλανώμενον planōmenon, in *Republic* 8.556e, *Timaeus* 91c-d.

[81] M.J. Adair, "Plato's View of the 'Wandering Uterus'," *The Classical Journal*, vol. 91, no. 2 (1996), pp. 153-154, discussing the role of the psyche (mind, soul) of an individual representing desire, the part called the ζῷον ἐπιθυμητικόν zōon epithymētikón (desirous animal, desiring soul, sexual appetitive impulse, etc.), which when frustrated generates yearnings and perhaps physical manifestations (including "symptoms"), pp. 161-163; on wandering, esp. pp. 155-161.

[82] Liddell and Scott, *Greek-English Lexicon*, p. 1813a-b.

[83] Hippocrates, in E. Littré, *Oeuvres complètes d'Hippocrate*, vol. 7-8, on the uterus in transformation, from rotation upwards to retroflexion; vol. 8, p. 266, the first line of Sect. 123 contains this significant verb (τραπῶσιν trapōsin).

[84] *Republic*, 4.439c-e, 9.588b-590a.

[85] Liddell and Scott, *Greek-English Lexicon*, pp. 760a (zōon: living being, animal, image, figure; and zōos, zōon, living), 634b (epithymētikón: desiring, lusting after; also, the part of the soul which is the seat of desires and affections).

[86] *Nicomachean Ethics*, 1102b22-30; *De anima*, 413b16, 414a29-32, 433a17; in D.W. Hamlyn ed., with notes at pp. 89, 92, 152.

[87] Cf. the 1271 CE commentary by Aquinas on Aristotle: *Aristotle's De anima, in the [1267 Latin] version of William of Moerbeke [Guillaume de Moerbeke, Willem van Moerbeke, Flemish Dominican, 1215-1286] and Commentary [1271] of St. Thomas Aquinas [1225-1274]*, pp. 187-203, 468-476.

7. Pathologizing Distress

What is the function of a psychiatric diagnosis? What makes diagnosis interestingly powerful? What are its benefits and its possible limitations? What are possible problems built into diagnosis, given its application in the context of one's society, whose values and defining beliefs are operating within powerful political structures? Without getting ahead of ourselves, let us start in a simple way. *Let me first note that many skillful and sensitive psychiatrists are not at all constricted by diagnostic thinking, using it, instead, for its help, but remaining significantly more aware than diagnostic categories alone would allow.*

That stated, and looking now directly at the practice of diagnosing people (first the process itself and then its political context), what is often left implicit is that it *can be*—and often, if not usually, *is*—a matter of turning human suffering into sickness. In this, what is part of the human condition (*"la condition humaine"*), perhaps an uneasy or troubled time, is transformed into an illness, a psychopathology, a mental sickness. This pathologizing of human distress may seem to be a subtle matter, but it is certainly not a minor one!

Before addressing the value, functions, and politics of diagnosis, let us ask what a diagnosis provides ("She is suffering from Major Depressive Disorder") versus what a description of a person in distress provides ("She is not melancholy, she is hopeless"[1])—*to me, the latter draws attention to the experienced human realities of how we deal with the stress in our lives.*

As psychoanalyst Frieda Fromm-Reichmann wrote, "It is my belief that the problems and emotional difficulties of mental patients, neurotics or psychotics, are, in principle, rather similar to one another and also to the emotional difficulties in living *from which we all suffer at times.*"[2] This approach, which breaks down the sharp distinction between the "sick" and us (presumably the "healthy" or "normal") will perhaps not be comfortable for some to contemplate, since it raises questions about ourselves we may wish urgently to dismiss.

When I was focused on learning about what is called psychopathology, the study of people in distress that analyses various forms of the human condition that are more torment-filled than most, or at least more torment-filled in ways that people can recognize, it was, in part, through a Clinical Psychology In-

---

[1] X. Guo [郭小櫓], *A Concise Chinese-English Dictionary for Lovers*, p. 147, in speaking of Billie Holiday. Cf. W. James, *The Varieties of Religious Experience* (1902/1929/1961), esp. Lectures 1, 6-7, 16-17, e.g., pp. 13/14/29, 145/142/127, 413/404/324, resp.; J. Rubin, "William James and the Pathologizing of Human Experience," *Journal of Humanistic Psychology*, vol. 40 (2000), no. 2, pp. 176-226. Cf. on T. Szasz, above, p. 72, n. 45, p. 101, n. 129, and below, p. 149, n. 3.

[2] F. Fromm-Reichmann, *Principles of Intensive Psychotherapy*, Introduction (1950), pp. xi-xii. Italics added.

ternship through the Yale Clinical Psychology Program, in one of Yale Psychiatry's teaching hospitals, the West Haven VA Hospital. Yale Psychiatry in those years was strongly Freudian in its orientation, and especially so in its training facilities, including YPI (Yale Psychiatric Institute), where, the year before (1971-72), I sat in on rounds—a weekly seminar for therapeutic staff only—with Ted Lidz as moderator and members including Ruth Lidz, Rebecca Z. Solomon, and Cynthia Wild. The textbooks I consulted in learning this way of thinking not only gave descriptions of patterns that were found and named, but also provided *a theoretical explanation of what would have been going on to make sense of each given pattern.* This involved seeing the pattern as the outcome of life experiences, giving an organic sense to what was being described. It also gave a sense of *how people with such difficulties in life might be helped.*

Since then, as the psychiatric community (in the USA) moved on, there have been repeated revisions or "up-dates" of a key text used, called the *DSM,* short for *Diagnostic and Statistical Manual.* Given its title, we might note that *this manual has never cited any statistics for any condition.* More, below.

In these revisions, there was the elimination of some diagnoses and the addition of others. While it is almost silly to wonder if this meant that some "mental diseases" went out of existence and others appeared, we may think back here to the statement made in 1930 by Pierre Janet, "Hysteria patients seemed to disappear because they were now designated by other names."[3] More recently, with ongoing changes in criteria for given diagnoses and changes in the diagnostic categories recognized, we find in the *DSM* such statements as, "Some cases previously diagnosed as Borderline, Latent, or Simple Schizophrenia are likely to be classified in this manual as Schizotypal Personality Disorder," and, as is made explicit, this matter of defining a system (or integrated set) of psychopathologies is an ongoing process of theory construction and revision: "this final version of *DSM-III* is only one still frame in the ongoing process of attempting to better understand mental disorders."[4]

While this may be clear to those who are actually putting together these manuals, as this quotation illustrates, we often find people simplistically taking each new version as definitive of reality, with very important consequences.

Now, with these ever-growing categories of diagnosis—the *DSM* began as a booklet and is now a small encyclopedic text[5]—we may wonder if there are

---

[3] J. Janet, "Autobiography of Pierre Janet," in C. Murchison, ed., *History of Psychology in Autobiography,* vol. 1, pp. 123-133, at p. 127.
[4] American Psychiatric Association, *Diagnostic and Statistical Manual of Mental Disorders, Third Edition* (1980)—also *DSM-III*—p. 310, 12, resp.
[5] The first edition was *Diagnostic and Statistical Manual: Mental Disorders* (1952)—in which *the "statistical" part consisted of **instructions on how to keep records*** in hospitals or clinics for epidemiological purposes, strictly a matter of

ever more forms of mental disease that are being discovered (or invented), but we can definitely notice there has come to be a great interest in determining which diagnosis is correct. *In part, this simply follows appropriate medical procedure, in which it is considered paramount to analyze correctly symptoms in order to come to understand which disease was present.* And the people involved (those identified as "patients") are also interested in these categories, and in this way, also follow the medical model. What we see now is people worried about whether they are "normal" or whether they "have" some sort of "mental condition" and people with whom they might become involved emotionally or romantically, wondering if it would be better simply to stay away from them!

Not to mention another powerful practical feature of diagnosis: ***diagnosis as insult!*** Specifically, there is a powerful societal context in place when there is a history of some psychological problem or "psychiatric condition," or of any psychotherapy to deal with such personal concerns ("problems" or "mental illnesses"). The impact of such a history can be quite significant: those who have been fired because someone learned of a history of psychotherapeutic interventions for personal psychological issues know this. As do those who refuse to let their family or insurance company learn that they are involved in a psychotherapeutic endeavor, for fear of social complications. As did Senator Thomas Eagleton (Missouri), Democratic Party Vice-Presidential candidate from July 14, 1972, until his resignation a fortnight later on August 1, triggered by reports that he had been treated earlier for Depression, receiving ECT (Electro-Convulsive Therapy, less formally called electroshock). His story suggests that recognizing and wanting to do something about being depressed—seeking out therapy—is seen as a good reason for that person *not* to hold office. We like our heroes hard as nails, with no "personal" issues! ("Voters prefer politicians to be strong and wrong than weak and right," to modify President Clinton's idea.) *This is just a social or political commentary, but there is more to see here than such matters, which, although perhaps of interest, do not cut to the core here.*

---

providing methodological instructions for keeping hospital records—***not citations of statistics for any conditions***. The title then became *Diagnostic and Statistical Manual of Mental Disorders* (keeping the "Statistical" part, *even while deleting the statistics-keeping instructions*). Each edition (*DSM-I, -II, -III, -III-R, -IV*, and *-IV-TR*: 1968, 1980, 1987, 1994, and 2000, resp.) contained an ever-growing number of pages—with page size growing—from *DSM-I* (23 cm.) at xii+130 pp. to *DSM-IV-TR* (26 cm.) at xxxvii+943 pp. The multiple-axis approach began with *DSM-III* (1980). Revisions, in an ongoing process, keep appearing: www.dsm5.org reports that *DSM-V* is to be published in May, 2013. *For all those interested in this multidimensional process, with significant power struggles between various factions, here is a fascinating study of the interface between science, politics, and economics, one that I will not undertake.*

So, back to diagnostic manuals: it seems that the professional (psychiatric) community cannot agree about what brings on which "conditions" (patterns of thought and behavior), about the etiology of disease, that is, about what causes which pathologies. (The question of etiology arises from the assumption that mental distress is pathological.) What this lack of agreement has meant, in a practical way, is that recent revisions of this text, the *DSM*, offer no statements about how each given "condition" comes about. This is just a practical consequence of the fact that the different current theoretical orientations held within the hierarchy of the psychiatric professional community cannot come to a consensus opinion. One implication of this is that the issue of what brings these forms of distress on is left unanswered—and in the *DSM* itself, is unasked.

This, in turn, puts on the back burner—or "off the chart" (not even considered)—the issue of what to do to prevent the stress factors and other features of life histories regularly found in various sorts of patterns of distress.

As these categories are essential in at least five critical areas, all of this is rather important. The first of these is in psychiatric hospitalization and its record-keeping: a psychiatric admission, treatment, and discharge (this in particular, except when a person demands to leave, despite medical-staff opinion to the contrary), must all be justified in diagnostic terms. In short, the person's hospital stay is understood and operates largely in terms of the diagnoses chosen.

The second area of significance here is that of medications, whose use is guided in terms of the psychopathological diagnosis chosen. Different diagnoses are linked with different drugs, and drugs are defined for use relative to specific diagnostic categories. For some, the first action of relevance in helping a patient suffering from some psychopathology—to use this medicalized vocabulary—is to prescribe the best drug for that condition, and so, diagnoses find their value in part when used to suggest treatment using particular drugs.

The third area is insurance, as insurance companies (in the USA) define the diagnoses whose psychotherapy costs they will or will not partially cover.

The fourth concerns psychiatric diagnostic thinking: what we notice is often guided—if not limited—by our theoretical perspective. Given this, if we take the diagnosis we are to use in describing someone ("labeling" as some say) as the most significant thing we can say about that person, what is *not* captured by recognized diagnoses will *not* be seen, *not* recognized, at least not in any defined way. *It is hard to see a pattern if we are using diagnoses to hone our perception, and what is going on is not yet defined in a diagnostic way! If we look only through such a grid, we will recognize only that which is already identified.* Relatedly, diagnoses also define research topics, so there may be no funding money for research into a condition not yet already a recognized diagnosis.

Fifth, this focus on diagnosis *tends to dismiss as irrelevant (since not treating pathology)* all positive urges to feel more satisfied, fulfilled, peaceful, and appreciative of life, any idea of being healthier and happier, and any pro-active (and preventative) use of therapy to facilitate a more satisfying life.

8. From Psychotherapy to Psychospirituality

There are many forms of human interaction that are termed psycho-therapy. To start with, we might understand psychotherapy as a process in which the central interest is in making for a less tormented, more happy, more fulfilled individual, psychologically speaking.

One description or definition of psychotherapy that stated the idea more precisely is this one, from an article back in 1965:

> Psychotherapy is a nonorganic, nonphysical, nonphar-macological treatment aimed at influencing, modifying, or re-moving undesirable aspects of the patient's personality, reactions, and behavior patterns.[1]

A recent book has spoken of the model of psychotherapy as "transformation through relationship."[2] This opens up questions about which transformations are relevant here, and what might be the means of bringing these about.

I make no assumption here that all schools of psychotherapy will agree with both or even one of these statements.

In general, we might consider psychotherapy to be an organized system of activities whose aim is to help an individual (the person "in" psychotherapy) to change in certain specific ways. This might include the person's coming to feel less anxious, less confused, less worried, less sad, less lacking in energy, or less frustrated.

By way of contrast, some understand psychotherapy to be grounded in the analysis of symptoms permitting a recognized diagnosis of some mental disorder (or psychopathology), and from this, to interventions (including the use of psychotropic drugs) designed to remove all noted symptoms.[3]

---

[1] L.B. Fierman, "Myths in the Practice of Psychotherapy," *Archives of General Psychiatry*, vol. 12 (Apr. 1965), pp. 408-414, at p. 409. Reprinted in L.B. Fierman, *The Therapist Is the Therapy: Effective Psychotherapy II*, pp. 107-126, quote at p. 111.

[2] D.J. Wallin, *Attachment in Psychotherapy* (2007), p. 2.

[3] Psychoanalyst Thomas Szasz has criticized "writing prescriptions for psycho-active drugs and pretending that they are therapeutically effective against mental illnesses." "Psychiatric relations are either concentual-contractual or coercive-carceral [involving incarceration]," proposes Szasz, who practices "concentual psychiatry" (or psychotherapy) with "voluntary" clients. He has long held that "mental illnesses do not exist, and coercions justified by them are wrong" ("the fiction of mental illness and the fact of coercion-therapy")—all making him "persona non grata among psychiatrists and psychoanalysts." Quoted, respectively, from T. Szasz, *Antipsychiatry: Quackery Squared* (2009), pp. viii, 143, 26 (two quotations), ix-x, 22, 30. Cf. above, pp. 61, 72, 101, 145.

Now, psychospirituality is a perspective on our life condition that recognizes and honors the deeper, more subtle, less obvious aspects of our experience, that goes beyond features of body, personality, personal history, interpersonal context including family, culture, societal values, and so forth.

In more contemporary terms, a psychospiritual orientation takes us beyond the personal, the familial, the interpersonal, and even the transpersonal, to the aspects of our mind, our psyche, that are transcultural.

We might emphasize that psychospirituality typically involves a yearning for a greater sense of a personally vibrant and fulfilling interconnection with the universe, and as such is perhaps the core foundation of all spiritual yearning and all spiritual traditions. These were investigated in detail in some of my earlier writings.[4]

Psychospirituality in this way is a search for the dimension of our mind that is not defined or limited by this complex conditioning, our mind that is a radiant and vital consciousness, called by some the soul (*psyche*): let's recall that the 'psycho-' of various words—psychology, psychospirituality, psychotherapy, and so forth—has the Greek root ψυχή *psyché*. This term was rendered in Latin as *anima* (as the principle that animates, that gives life, that creates activity).[5]

To interpret *psyche* as mind—and psychology as the study of the mind—is to deprive the concept of its intensity and power. Reference to mind may sound more scientific, but speaking of the soul reminds us that we are interested in the very deep and powerful driving vitality of human beings.

There have been books written on this very topic, hoping to remind us of the non-trivial nature of the interest here in the *psyche*, one that is quite different from any concern with maintaining people in their familial, social, and work responsibilities.

This latter may suggest a vision of the psychiatrist as agent of the sociopolitical status quo, as some have unhappily experienced through imposed psychiatric interventions in some contexts, in countries around the world.[6]

---

[4] Esp. M. Ginsberg, *The Inner Palace: Mirrors of Psychospirituality in Divine and Sacred Wisdom-Traditions*. Note the term 'psychospirituality' in the subtitle.

[5] Cf. Aristotle, Περὶ ψυχῆς *Perì psychēs*, usually cited as *De anima*.

[6] *This is not to imply that such a political stance or function is that of all, most, or any particular psychiatrist.* The work of Bruno Bettelheim, *Freud and Man's Soul*, for example, is one extended presentation of this just-mentioned more passionate interest. He begins this work quoting from a letter to Jung from Freud (Dec. 6, 1906), "Psychoanalysis is in essence a cure through love."

In this light, we may note that Freud had written explicitly and emphatically (in 1905) of "the omnipotence of love" in "Three Essays on the Theory of Sex" (1905d) [at SE 7: 192 = GW 5: 61]. This suggests an image rather different

One individual told me, relatedly, that he once went to see a psychiatrist and spoke of being anxious and feeling low.

The psychiatrist prescribed two drugs, one to control the anxiety and the other for depression. "You'll need these to be able to go back to work next week," the psychiatrist said.

The man himself did not want to take drugs at all. He wanted to learn how to deal on his own with feeling anxious, jittery, blue, down in the dumps.

Here we see two quite distinct perspectives on the situation. Basically, the man felt that the psychiatrist's focus on getting him back to work quickly did not respect his own interest in addressing the troubles and difficulties in his life.

On the significance of *psyche* (soul), Bettelheim, for example, noted in *Freud and Man's Soul* that the English version of Freud in the *Standard Edition* gives many distortions—in particular, he highlighted the corruption in rendering Freud's original title *Psychische Behandlung (Seelenbehandlung)*[7] as "Psychical (or Mental) Treatment." For Bettelheim, *Seelenbehandlung* (the part of the title in parentheses) is more accurately translated as "Treatment of the Soul."

Glossing Freud's remark *"Die Psychoanalyse ist ein Stück der Seelen-kunde der Psychologie"* as "Psychoanalysis is a part of psychology dedicated to the science of the soul," Bettelheim further points out the distortion in the *Standard Edition*, which renders this as "Psychoanalysis is a part of the mental science of psychology."[8]

Bettelheim remarks, "There really was no reason—apart from a wish to interpret psychoanalysis as a medical specialty—for this corruption of Freud's references to the soul. There was no reason for the English translators [of the *Standard Edition*] to misunderstand these references."[9]

Bettelheim emphasizes that the soul here is the spiritual part of man in contrast with the purely physical and the emotional part of man's nature. *This is the sense we have in English when we speak of Mankind's most soulful yearnings*. The importance of this should not be overlooked.

We may sense, accordingly, that presentations of spiritual teachings that hold them to be a way to remove symptoms, or a means of stress-management, or a set of "wellness" techniques, *all trivialize psychospirituality*, as if to suggest

---

from that of a cold and distant professional treating a patient as a dysfunctional object, as some people being "treated" for psychological distress (especially when understood as a "psychopathological condition") sometimes report feeling.

[7] "Psychical (or Mental) Treatment" (1890a [1905b]) [SE 7: 283 = GW 5: 289].

[8] B. Bettelheim, *Freud and Man's Soul*, p. 76. Freud's German and Bettelheim's own gloss in English are found there at idem, p. 75.

[9] Idem, p. 76, within fuller discussion, pp. 70-78. The translation that Bettelheim cites is found in Freud's "Some Elementary Lessons in Psycho-Analysis" (1940b) [at SE 23: 282 = CP 5: 377, with German at GW 17: 142].

that we would best appreciate Beethoven symphonies by understanding them to be pleasant elevator music and nothing more significant. More below on this.[10]

If we look at the evolution of the world of psychotherapy this past century (or a tad more), there are some basic movements or changes that we might note. Let me present something about these here, in very broad terms.

To start with, and put into very large categories, we can say that the first large movement was based on the work of Freud, which set up psychoanalytic practice and theory (also called psychodynamic theory), with variations in that theme. Among the most significant variations came out of the work of the Swiss psychiatrist Carl Gustav Jung and the French analyst, Jacques Lacan.[11]

A second approach, quite different from this first, was called behaviorism, in which the behavior (observable actions) of a given individual were taken as the basic data to be considered and understood. In its most strict form, there was in this approach absolutely no reference at all to any mentalistic concepts (mind, beliefs, desires, yearnings, and so forth). The orienting concern for behavioristic therapy became the question of how to change a person's behavior.

Out of this duality came what some called the third stream or wave of psychotherapy, which was specifically known as humanistic psychology. There were various particular forms that this basic orientation took. In general, it opposed traditional behavioristic presuppositions, in that it recognized mentalistic concepts.

In contrast with the psychoanalytic perspective, it tended to de-emphasize the issues of the unconscious, transference, the id, the ego, and the superego, and the various stages of development posited in psychoanalytic theory. It also eliminated various psychoanalytic practices such as free association, and especially took issue with the idea that the therapist should be a blank screen, remaining totally neutral and undefined to the patient in order to allow in part for a more transparent "transference" relationship. Instead, the importance of the interpersonal relationship between the therapist and the patient was held to be of utmost significance and power in the therapeutic relationship.

More recently, some of these distinctions have been blurred, and new theories put forth that made use of mentalistic as well as behavioral concepts, and added an interest in various bodily processes, especially a focus on the brain and its physiology and functional evolution. This works especially well with an

---

[10] See also the poem on this same topic, "The Yearnings of Psychospirituality" (below, pp. 262-263), where some of the basic orienting questions that delineate a psychospiritual approach are presented.

[11] E.g., C.G. Jung, *The Practice of Psychotherapy: Essays on the Psychology of the Transference and Other Subjects* (and cf. above, p. 150, n. 5), and J. Lacan, *The Four Fundamental Concepts of Psycho-Analysis* (where these four concepts are the unconscious, repetition, transference, and drive; see, e.g., p. 263).

approach that makes use of various substances that impact states of mind, as in the drugs that can be offered and prescribed to the patient.

There are also approaches that variously define the process and focus of psychotherapy, with relatedly different definitions of what the goal of psychotherapy would be. For example, if psychotherapy is viewed as a form of professional intervention into someone's specific life-context difficulties, with a focus on how to get people back into the interpersonal, social, or work contexts they have been in, then the goal of psychotherapy can be understood to be the resolution of those specific difficulties. This has been termed problem-solving therapy; in some applications, there is the program of defining some very specific issue at the start of therapy, with the therapy thereby delineated and limited.

This in turn often works well with what is called brief therapy. In the early days of "brief" psychotherapy, this would be a series of 20 sessions. This was back in the 1970s. In this first decade of the twenty-first century, a brief therapy might be limited to some 5 sessions in all.

These evolving concepts are all variations on the theme of psychotherapy, which is being contrasted here with psychospirituality. And in that context, these comments are just meant as a sketch, to indicate briefly and schematically some of the approaches that we can find within the field of psychotherapy.

We may return now to the idea that in our human condition, there are some very powerful soulful yearnings, and these are not always satisfied, or even recognized, in many instances. This does not mean that the yearnings are at peace, simply because they are not clearly recognized.

It will be important to know that in some situations what is being offered as psychotherapy will address some of these yearnings but not others.

Depending on what the individual's interests, concerns, and needs are, and the orientation or scope of the specific psychotherapy being offered—or the particular psychospiritual path being contemplated—the match between the two may be meager or splendid. And it will presumably help if we know what we want in this context, even if we do not know how to get it. We may have to discover whether it is a psychospiritual path or a psychotherapeutic one that will better address our yearnings that call out for attention.

9. Before the First Step[1]

The psychiatrist John Pierrakos (a disciple of Wilhelm Reich, and co-founder of bioenergetics, along with Alexander Lowen), writes that the first step in personal development toward a full and vibrant life is to recognize and to acknowledge one's negative emotions (meaning those emotions that incorporate ill-will or anger or resentment, or that block us off from vibrant, relaxed, open experience, and such) *without* blaming oneself.[2]

What happens, though, if this "first" step is not taken? We can say that we keep ourselves at zero, at the starting point. But what does that amount to?

We can fail to take the first step, or can avoid taking it, in several ways. We may not recognize these negative emotions at all, for example. Or, we may recognize them but dismiss them or disown them in various ways: "Oh, I didn't really feel that way, or think those thoughts seriously, etc." Or, we may blame ourselves, or criticize ourselves, or attack ourselves in various ways (mentally, in thoughts, or physically, in bodily actions against ourselves).

In these and other ways, we may find that we are not taking this first step that Pierrakos describes (nor any further steps, either, of course). We will consider in this chapter the situation in which we do not (yet) achieve the recognition and blame-free accepting that together make up this first step.

Taking a wide view of this process, we may want to see *how to make use of our wisdom—our intelligence balanced by an open, caring (good-willed) heart.* This calls for a broad concept of intelligence, in which it is recognized to be in part a matter of being insightful, of taking in information and drawing various conclusions, making explicit various implications, becoming more aware of and alert to the presuppositions, the entailments, the implications, and the new issues[3] that this information may provide us with, when we actively consider it.[4]

We may ask whether we deal with our specific life context here (and in general), with our feelings and our sense of what is going on, etc., making use of this sort of insightful intelligence? When do we? When don't we? What conditions allow us to use our intelligence effectively, and allow us to avoid going through life so painfully? How it is that we sometimes feel that we ourselves are uncomfortably slow in our learning. In other words, *how do we manage to be so good at being so bad at sizing up our situation? How is our wisdom blocked from arising and operating?* We address these questions in this chapter.

---

[1]   In this chapter, I italicize foreign words only as is done for English words.
[2]   J.C. Pierrakos, *Eros, Love & Sexuality: The Forces That Unify Man and Woman*, pp. 19-26.
[3]   M. Ginsberg, "The Entailment-Presupposition Relationship," *Notre Dame Journal of Formal Logic*, vol. XIII, no. 4 (Oct. 1972), pp. 511-515.
[4]   These and related activities are sometimes termed information processing.

In looking at these not-yet-developed abilities, at our currently limited intelligence, what can help us to look without criticizing ourselves?

We might do well to respect this idea of being aware of ourselves and how we are, of what we are experiencing, what we are feeling, etc., *without going into critical self-judgment or attacking ourselves in thought, word, or bodily harm*, as this is quite an important and powerful idea.

We may stress the importance here of *not* criticizing ourselves: that self-criticism blinds us to what there is to investigate, and diverts our attention and emotions into feeling bad about ourselves, feeling that we need to justify or to protect ourselves, etc. All of this redirection of our consciousness takes away from our ability to deal with the root issues at hand, whatever they are.

Perhaps we can sense that our criticizing mind closes off the urge to investigate, pushes us to look elsewhere, to distract ourselves.[5] This constrained intelligence keeping us stuck may be felt whenever we see a situation repeating, as if on a revolving turntable. Here we might feel an urge to accomplish something in a satisfying way or to come to a sense of resolution, but find ourselves experiencing instead one more hurt or frustration after another. We may feel the confines of our perspective on reality, the confines of our limited understanding. This is a frame of mind that can feel cramped, like a constraining mind-set.

French philosopher-psychiatrist Pierre Janet (1859-1947) wrote about this limited mind-set, one sort of mental structure, which he called a constitution (meaning that which constitutes or structures). This constitution was a mental framework (a particular "second nature") that might have developed during periods of great unhappiness, fear, violence, or other trauma, and became the structure of one's consciousness or perspective on reality. It was aimed at protecting us from feeling overwhelmed, of being attacked by intense anxiety of one form or another. Underlying this structure, this understanding, was *a psychological interweaving of thinking and feeling*, as Janet emphasized. (More, below.)

With fresh disturbances, such a protective framework could come to show its limitations and inabilities to deal with the fresh, new demands these disturbances entail. The very inadequacy of this earlier constitution leads to the need for a more sophisticated, complex, distinction-making, subtle, and skillful understanding of one's world (a new constitution or structure, in Janet's term).[6]

Janet's perspective concerns the *resultant transformations*, at a stage when they have already helped the individual to integrate and adapt to the turbulent experiences of his past. (More, below.)

---

[5] M. Ginsberg, "Making War on Ego," in *The Far Shore*, pp. 31-32.

[6] Much of the closing chapter ("Polysociative Vision") of M. Ginsberg, *The Inner Palace*, addresses this beneficial complexity. The process described here may remind us here of the work by Kazimierz Dąbrowski (*Positive Disintgration*, etc.) discussed in the above chapter on Nietzschean psychiatry.

The related focus in this chapter will be on these *thinking-and-feeling processes* that are established by individuals who have undergone such traumas, and especially on how these, in turn, are overcome, thus allowing us to take "the first step" that is honored by Pierrakos, above. (More on these, below, as well.)

We may recognize the very powerful human urge to overcome what was not working well, to use our intelligence, to allow the arising of some insight into what is going on and wisdom about how to deal with it better, to "get it right" or to "do it right for once." It is as if we need to conquer what was too much for us, either in the original context, or in some new contexts, in order to have the whole process come to resolution. It is as if we want to learn a lesson, to learn how to do something, to learn how to satisfy our desire in the given context, and to continue to want to learn this lesson despite our failures.

Going beyond these failures, we call upon our wisdom and in particular our intelligence, which is in part a matter of elegantly processing information. Here, it is important to be open to and attentive to new information, if we are to use our intelligence helpfully.

But the most important information may be quite unpleasant and, as Carl Gustav Jung once pointed out, such unpleasant experience is not very popular, is not something that most people are ready to undertake if it can be circumvented or bypassed. As he wrote, "Filling the conscious mind with ideal conceptions is a characteristic feature of Western theosophy, but not the confrontation with the shadow and the world of darkness. *One does not become enlightened by imagining figures of light, but by making the darkness conscious. The latter procedure, however, is disagreeable and therefore not popular.*"[7]

Which in turn leads to the question, What helps overcome this natural inclination to avoid, to look away from, such unpleasantness? How, in other terms, can we break out of the positive feedback loop (this being a pattern that becomes ongoingly more intensive—a sense of 'positive' other than that meaning "approving of")? Especially breaking out of the one here that has us look away from, disregard (dis-regard) what is important but unpleasant information?

So far this is speaking in general terms. A specific example may be helpful, in order to consider one given context where this first step of Pierrakos is not being taken. What is said in addressing this example will have relevance for other instances of this same general "before the first step" situation.

I would like to present one imaginary, repeating scenario, to describe and thereby encourage some important shifts open to us in such situations. Before presenting that imagined scenario, I would like first to make a few prefatory comments to orient this discussion, so that the reader's attention is not misdirected.

---

[7] "The Philosophical Tree" (1954), *Alchemical Studies*, pp. 251-349 [=*Collected Works*, vol. 13, 1967], at pp. 265-266. Italics added for emphasis.

There is one situation that has been known to repeat itself (one out of many, we can say) and that is one in which there is violence. This is pertinent as it may be of interest to a number of readers, and as it highlights some powerfully significant features of recurring torment. We could take an example in which there are ongoing arguments or fights within a family, arguments that seem to repeat incessantly. I would like to consider the example, in particular, of another form of repeated violence, that of sexual violence.

Before presenting a theoretical (hypothetical, imaginary) example of repeating sexual violence, I want to make it explicit that I do *not* draw the conclusion that someone who undergoes sexualized violence (rape) is "inviting" it or is "encouraging" it or "deserves" it in any way. I am *not* supporting in any way the idea that we should "blame the victim" (using this important term that appeared in the psychological theorizing of the late 1940s). Nor am I suggesting that those who commit violence are free of responsibility or guilt, simply because of something about the target of that violence. Furthermore, even if someone is totally oblivious to such impending violence, this does not in the least justify, excuse, mitigate, or exonerate the unwelcome actions of a rapist! I hope this is clear.

That said emphatically, I would like to take an example, to illustrate something important here, something presumably of potential value to some people, if not everyone. As an example to illustrate the issues being considered here, it is not meant to include or to represent all instances of sexualized violence, nor to report on any particular actual instance of repeated rapes.

I would like to consider here some hypothetical (imagined) instances where someone is experiencing an unpleasant situation that feels like an unwelcome but familiar repetition, in order to appreciate the processes operating there. In particular, these hypothetical situations involve repeated rapes, where the person in question recognizes at one time or another in each instance that what is happening is very unpleasantly familiar, and where *these instances of violence are not quite foreseen* **in a way** *that allows the person being raped repeatedly to avoid impending subsequent violence.*

Once again, let us recognize that it is **not** always possible to avoid being treated violently: consider imprisoned torture, or someone captured and then forced to submit to harsh, even life-threatening, mistreatment!

Now, when there is a series of rapes, each one may theoretically be preceded by signs of danger. When there are, in fact, signs of danger, is something blocking these signs from being clearly seen and this repeated violence avoided?

And in a more general way, when we find ourselves involved repeatedly in situations that are undesired, unpleasant, pain-filled—or (in Buddhist terms) dukkha-filled—could we possibly avoid these repetitions if only our attentiveness were operating in some different way (in **some** *cases, at least)?*

Specifically in instances of sexual violence where something is obvious to others (that we are in danger, for example) but remains something not seen clearly by us, who are about to suffer one more rape, *we may look to see what we are in fact primarily focusing our attention on.* Are we distracting ourselves, drawing our attention away from something that may be important for us to notice and appreciate?

We may remember in the magic show, the performer—the magician, the prestidigitator, the entertainer—draws out attention to something *other* than what is key, central, to notice if we are to see what he is doing that is meant to appear to be magic. We can certainly distract ourselves from what will be, or would be, important for us to notice.

We may pay a great deal of attention to someone who seems so pleasant to us, or is saying such nice things to us, in such gentle and pleasant ways. Or to the way he (or she) is touching our face or our neck which is so pleasantly exciting, and on and on. Or we may start to feel "spacey" (defocused) or in "mind clouds" (having a cloudy consciousness). And why should we distract ourselves in a way that will not protect us from harm? One important short-term benefit is that it *keeps away from us any anxiety that we might feel if we were to sense ourselves in danger. Pleasantness is more pleasant than anxiety*, we might say. Of course, this is not helping us to come to new realizations or insights about what is going on other than the pleasantness, in this instance.

So, to shift consciousness, we might begin to appreciate that our focused attention in this context is being fully present to *one* set of features of the situation but at the same time we are distracting ourselves from some *other* set of features that are also of importance. To spell out one imaginary scenario, other people may be slowly leaving the room, or, in another sort of case, we are now one of the few females in the group, and, a little later, are the only female. And so on. (Not that only females are raped. This is just a specific imagined context to illustrate the more general points being made.)

While such evolving situations are not always followed by a rape, when there *is* such a pattern, and we are not considering such a possibility, how do we manage to do this? or not do this? (with a different "this" in mind in each of these questions). And at other times, by way of contrast, we may be anxious and terrified, sensing an impending rape when that is not in the cards at all. It is as if our danger-sensing system is miscalibrated. It reads "No problem" when there is a real threat, and reads "Panic time!" when there is no threat.

If we do not see clearly enough to distinguish between when there is a problem here and when there is no problem here, we are not in the most effective state (somewhere along the continuum from being highly aware to being highly oblivious) to deal effectively and efficiently with the issue at hand.

How do we end up at such times with such a distorted calibration that misinterprets the situations in both of these ways?

That is, at the same time, on the one hand, we avoid seeing clearly and precisely what is going on, do not "face" it directly, do not put ourselves in a position (epistemologically speaking, that is, in terms of what we know and can be aware of) that would allow us to begin to draw *more distinctions of value* in helping us to differentiate when there is actually something that we should deal with, to act in ways that will keep us safe and unharmed.[8]

And we simultaneously, on the other hand, do not face it clearly enough to notice when there is actually no problem. Or, to express this second half differently, we do notice peripherally, do glimpse, that there is something that might be problematic. With such a perhaps-subliminal awareness, we may react with an intuitive sense of danger, and act out of such a fear, although actually not in a dangerous situation. Notice that if we begin to pay more careful attention, if we begin to take more care to attend to the situation, to face or accept that we *may* be entering dangerous waters—but may not be!—we could determine this issue by continued attentiveness to the situation.

To have the option of evaluating carefully, of determining that this situation may in fact be safe, not dangerous, we must first allow the realization that it may be unsafe, may actually be dangerous. This may make us uncomfortable: will this prevent us from thinking about and observing and evaluating our situation?

If we do not look carefully in a way that is allowing us to evaluate the actual degree of danger in our situation, we may end up having *many dangerous experiences but being very ignorant about how to recognize them!* This is no laughing matter, of course!

This does not at all mean that we are doomed to a lifetime of more of the same. As soon as we begin to pay attention to the sorts of situations that we have been repeatedly experiencing, we can begin to become knowledgeable, more familiar with, these situations.

Furthermore, and also importantly, we do not have to experience additional, potentially dangerous situations to learn here! We may, instead, begin reviewing earlier situations, to learn more of what was going on that we did not at the time pay clear attention to, that *could have helped us notice danger signs, when danger was forthcoming, and lack of danger, when there was none.*

In these ways, for our own well-being in the present moment, and for future times, we can use our memories to learn now what we did not learn well at the time.

Historical Context

We may place these preceding reflections, observations, and comments into the context of the broad theorizing about mind that has taken center stage for over a full century now. There was an earlier focus on traumas that is returning in recent years with renewed interest, in the context of trying to understand

---

[8] On making key distinctions in the process of psychotherapy, and in various spiritual traditions and practices, with the Buddha being known as the King of the Distinction-makers, see M. Ginsberg, *The Inner Palace*, pp. 314, 354, 572.

the impact of trauma (war, single-incident traumas, and also repeated childhood physical, emotional, and sexual abuse).

Let us consider some comments of Pierre Janet (introduced above) at the occasion of the Harvard Tercentenary (in 1937). In this context, he speaks of *liquidation*, in the French-based meaning of dissolution, ending of a business, especially with the sale of all stock and supplies, complete resolution, etc., and speaks of *constitution*, also in the French-based meaning, in the sense of the organizing elements of a structure, person, or body politic, and, in this case, more particularly, temperament, or system of patterns—that is, structure—of thought and behavior and such.

The text I quote here uses Janet's terms in English, but in the French sense. For a more flowing reading of the passage, I will replace the term 'liquidation' with 'complete resolution' and 'constitution' with 'structure' (both in brackets to indicate substitution from the quoted text). Keeping clear about this rephrasing of the text in this way, we may read his comments:

> The emotionally disturbing event and the prolonged absence of [complete resolution] have transformed the mind and have left behind a new [structure], partly analogous to the first hereditary [structure] ...
>
> The emotion which diminished and disorganized the psychological forces [=available organized energy] has placed the patient in an entirely new situation, requiring the establishment of a completely new balance of forces, whatever the past circumstance may have been which caused this modification. One must live in the present, and it is not always useful to begin the past all over again in order to live in the present.[9]

In other words, an appreciation of the role in earlier traumas in the development of the psychological complexities of what Janet is describing (most usually, with the now-obsolete diagnostic label of hysteria[10]) is important in the appreciation of the etiology (the arising) of the problem. This focus on early traumas—"external" and possibly interpersonal—is an idea that became eclipsed by a now-long-term interest in the "inner workings" of the troubled mind.

---

[9] Parts in brackets not in original. P. Janet, "Psychological Strength and Weakness," pp. 64-106, in *Factors Determining Human Behavior* (1937), at p. 102. An endnote to the English-language text (on p. 106) cites Janet, *De l'angoisse à l'exstase*, II, 488 (that is, vol. 2, p. 488). The middle chapters of Part II (Les régulations de l'action/The Regulations of Action) of volume 2 are esp. of interest in this context (Chap. II: Les états d'inaction morose et les fatigues, and Chap. III: Les états mélancoliques et les tristesses).

[10] More on hysteria elsewhere, esp. in the chapter on Janet. The technical term in its various senses is quite different from the popular meaning, let me mention.

This interest, in contrast, assumed that mental problems arose not out of a stifling life situation but out of problematic or retarded or inhibited development of the thinking processes of the maturing individual (more on this, below).

One set of issues here concerns the sorts of experiences that are considered to be significant in the etiology of, the arising of, great anxiety and tension in later life. Another set of issues concerns the ways out of that tendency or mind-set: the two together raise the questions of which problems bring on these mind-sets and how are people freed from those same tendencies.

These two groups of issues may be placed into the long evolving disagreement between Janet and Freud on the status of traumas: whether always sexual, as Freud suggested, or sometimes but not always, as Janet proposed; whether bringing these histories to clear, verbalized consciousness takes away all of their power and influence on our thinking and acting, as Freud proposed,[11] or in many cases are at best a first step with more difficult parts to address still remaining, as Janet suggested; whether the treatment is defined by this process of bringing to consciousness and working through, as Freud, or not necessarily so, as Janet in this passage quoted just above.

Notwithstanding these differences, the two are in agreement that psychological pain in a repeated, patterned way can be understood better by looking at the personal history of the person involved. Even though the early finding of sexual abuse as children was later put into question by Freud (and his society, which began ostracizing him completely for his claims felt to be outlandish and insulting), Janet readily acknowledged such abuse, sometimes incestuous, as being involved, in *some* histories.

At the same time, keeping that finding in context, Janet contrasted it with other instances of trauma that were clearly non-sexual in nature (only being sexual in an extremely wide sense—for Janet, a distorted one—of the term 'sexual'). It is important not to forget that this entire issue played itself out in a

---

[11] The issue is perhaps more subtle than we might realize on a quick reading here. Breuer and Freud had written, more carefully, that to their surprise (initially), *"each individual hysterical symptom immediately and permanently disappeared when we had succeeded in bringing clearly to light the memory of the event by which it was provoked and in arousing its accompanying affect, and when the patient had described that event in the greatest possible detail and had put the affect into words.* Recollection without affect almost invariably produces no results." Italics in original, quoting "On the Psychical Mechanism of Hysterical Phenomena: Preliminary Communication" (1893a) [at SE 2: 6 = GW 1: 85 = CP 1: 28]. One issue is what describing an event "in the greatest possible detail" amounts to and, relatedly, whether that can be kept from being a vacuous escape clause or theoretical defense ("Well, it wasn't described in *enough* detail!").

society that found abhorrent and repulsive the idea that bourgeois and noble families would have incestuous activities.[12]

   We may say that those healers of the soul (some of whom are psychiatrists)[13] who are looking at these issues one century later are finding—and publishing findings that indicate that early violence against the child, physical, emotional, and sexual, brings about many a tormented adult. (This strongly suggests that society is now more able to recognize these sad and perhaps disturbing facts about the violence in early family life for many children—a first step toward society's concern and readiness to do something to protect these children.)

   These findings are not especially real news, and clearly not welcome news, of course, as it raises, touched on just above, the question of what society is going to do about such unhappy happenings. What societies around the world are doing about such a phenomenon is not especially in synch with the import and importance of this sort of observation. That is a matter with another focus, quite significant in its own right. Personally, I do not find much to be

---

[12] This was even the case in the mid-twentieth century, as has often been reported. One powerful and poignant documentation of this is in the autobiographical letter to her daughter by the French-American artist Niki de Saint Phalle, née Cathérine Marie-Agnès Fal de Saint Phalle (b., 1930, Neuilly-sur-Seine, near Paris, d. 2003, San Diego) in her published, hand-written text *Mon Secret*, describing her father's physical advances beginning when she was 11 years old. Her father was an important banker, and believed to be above such vulgar (that is, belonging to the masses, to the lower classes; Latin, vulgāris, belonging to the common masses, crowd, rabble, etc.) sorts of misdeeds.

[13] The traditional role of the healer whose dedication is admirable, sometimes seen in the modern physician, is still at the core of the concept, as in the French "médecin" (doctor-healer); the word has been defined as a person with a doctorate in medicine who exercises the profession of caring for and healing others, as in *Larousse Lexis* (e.g., 1979 ed., p. 1129): "personne qui est titulaire du diplôme de docteur en médecine et exerce la profession de soigner et de guérir." Thus, Albert Camus, on the closing page (p. 247) of *La Peste* (*The Plague*), his novel inspired by the plague in Algiers in 1944, writes of those who came forth as médecins (healers, physicians) at that time, confronting the plague taken literally and also metaphorically. The French speaks of "tous les hommes qui, ne pouvant être des saints et refusant d'admettre les fléaux, s'efforcent cependant d'être des médecins." The R. Buss tr., *The Plague* (at p. 237, the penultimate page of the text) has "all men who, while not being saints but refusing to give way to the pestilence, do their best to be doctors." The S. Gilbert tr., *The Plague*, p. 278, speaks of "all who, while unable to be saints but refusing to bow down to pestilences, strive their utmost to be healers." (Each translation highlights one part or other of the doctor-healer concept.)

proud of as a human being here, given the lack of interest in protecting those who are so terribly treated in our very midst.

In any case, Janet—in the present context in which this passage of his is being quoted—is here noting that there are changes to the structure of one's consciousness, one's thinking-and-feeling reality (the two being one interwoven reality) through the disturbance in earlier frameworks (structures or *constitutions*, in other terms), the result being a more sophisticated, complex, distinction-making, adaptable, and subtle understanding of one's world.

Also focusing on these mind-redefining transformations is the work of Polish psychiatrist Kazimierz Dąbrowski, including his *Positive Disintegration*, discussed in the above chapter on Nietzschean psychiatry. Or, from another perspective, the writings of French psychiatrist Boris Cyrulnik on resilience and the construction of memory out of particular recollections—a combination of crystal-clear experiential moments and creative additions, typically assembled as a chimera, a non-existent totality.[14] Cyrulnik focuses on the ways this representation ("re-presentation") of the past becomes the basis for establishing a coherent understanding of our own lives and a redefining of our current and future possibilities.[15] *Mind is recognized here as a liberating force.*

These last perspectives consider the resultant transformations, at a stage at which they have already helped the individual to integrate and adapt to the turbulent experiences of one trauma or another. To complement this focus, the major interest in this chapter has been on the thinking and feeling processes that are predominant in some individuals who have undergone various traumas, with some suggestions about a shift in consciousness that could be cultivated, all preparatory to the taking of the first step, in the phrase of Pierrakos.

---

[14] The chimera (or chimaera), a whimsical creation of the imagination, was understood in ancient Greek mythology to be a non-existent or fantasy creature; one description portrayed the chimera as a fire-breathing monster having a lion's head, a she-goat's body, and a dragon's serpent-like tail.

[15] In *Je me souviens...* (2009/2010), B. Cyrulnik discusses his childhood and the nature of memory (and the chimera, pp. 46-49). Recognizing the power of avoidance—he shied away from discussing his late father, Aaron Cyrulnik, with psychoanalyst Pierre Marty (cf. above, p. 130, n. 38), who had known Aaron earlier (p. 47/p. 48)—he credits his hiding when others were herded off to Auschwitz *in part* to having had the psychological distance to consider the situation for himself, an active presence of mind not taken in or confused by what others say or do (p. 65)—and *in part* to chance (luck) smiling on him that day (p. 85/p. 84). This taking distance from what is going on—perhaps with a sense of humor—to appraise features of the situation otherwise overlooked, this fresh "beginner's mind" ready to see what is problematic or even dangerous, is *a valuable asset in our appreciating and responding appropriately to changing life contexts.*

10. The Liberating Power of Mindfulness[1]
Preliminary Remarks

The mindfulness that is the subject of this chapter is part of a practice designed for the development of a sense of calm, clarity of perception, and full-hearted compassion, for "the development of non-judgmental, choiceless and insightful awareness which leads to the complete evolution of consciousness."[2]

This practice operates within a comprehensive path having three parts or aspects: first is what is called pariyatti (accomplishment, especially in the teachings)—coming to understand what this path is and how it is to be applied. This involves studying and learning, as in reflecting on relevant teachings.[3] In that way, pariyatti is an intellectual activity. (More, just below.) Second is paṭipatti (practice)—a personal investigation into our own consciousness, called meditation, which is the focus of this chapter. And third is paṭivedha (penetration, understanding, realization)—the realization of understanding and transformation of mind (citta), achieved through the application and integration of the first two aspects (pariyatti and paṭipatti, learning and meditation).

The practice of mindfulness (of compassionate and clearly understanding attentiveness[4]), in this light, is something to learn about and something to practice. This chapter and traditional texts invite this double application!

This practice is presented in Pāli Buddhism within a particular understanding of the nature of mind and experience, whose most relevant features for this discussion are:

(I) There are six senses: the body's five, and the mind, *considered as a sixth sense*, (II) Experience occurs when consciousness, a sense organ, and its object meet or come together, (III) Experience is a complex process which—when not interrupted—includes an awakening of sense consciousness, stimulation (contact) by some sense object, a feeling or sense of something pleasant or unpleasant or neutral, and ultimately full perception (cognition).[5] Any such experience itself will *often* be followed in actual ("real-life") situations by thinking, reflecting, and perhaps ruminating; by desire, craving, action, etc.[6]

---

[1]   In this chapter, I italicize foreign words only as is done for English words: for emphasis, in titles, if in italics in the original text being quoted, etc.

[2]   V.R. Dhiravamsa, Vipassanā Meditation Master, review of M. Ginsberg, *The Far Shore: Vipassanā, The Practice of Insight* (back cover). Cf. below, p. 262.

[3]   Literacy is not required: Chan/Zen Patriarch Hui Neng awakened upon hearing and being lectured on the *Diamond Sutra*. P.B. Yampolsky, *The Platform Sutra of the Sixth Patriarch*, pp. 127, 133 (Sects. 2, 9). Cf. below, p. 215, n. 2.

[4]   The two wings of acceptance (see T. Brach, *Radical Acceptance*, pp. 27, 45).

[5]   Pāli, viññāṇa, phassa, vedanā, and saññā.

[6]   Pāli, vitakka, vicāra, papañca; chanda, taṇhā, kamma.

Relatedly, since the perception of any given sense object may lead to psychological agitation (anger, anxiety, fear, etc.), clouding our consciousness and our understanding, any such object of perception is sometimes thought of as a "dust" (Pāli, raja; Chinese, chén 塵); they are known collectively in Chinese Buddhism as the liù chén 六塵 (six dusts). Any of these can be made the focus of our attention in a variety of ways. We will return to this idea, below.

Basically, the five bodily sense organs and their "objects" are the eye and sights, the ear and sounds, the nose and smells, the tongue and tastes, and the body and bodily (proprioceptive or interoceptive) sensations.

These five bodily forms of consciousness are not themselves thinking—smelling is not thinking, etc.—but they can be followed by thinking about them (for example, thinking about a smell). Importantly, *thoughts about bodily perceptions are thoughts (mental), and are not themselves bodily perceptions.*

Considering the mind as the sixth sense organ stresses its parallels with the other five. In particular, it is the organ whose "objects" (or, as just above, "dusts") are our ideas, thoughts, evaluations, etc. These include recollections of and reflections on experience, *which include thoughts about bodily perception.*

The mind, then, is the organ of our reflections, thoughts, mental images and (in sleep) our dreaming, of each state of consciousness, each phenomenon,[7] of contemplating (with good-will or mettā, or without) and planning, of patterns of thinking and psychological tendencies. The very general term for all of these "objects" of the mind is dhammā (singular, dhamma, in Pāli, a "thing"[8]).

These relevant features of this Buddhist understanding of mind and experience provide the context for us now to introduce the practice of satipaṭṭhāna, which in Pāli means foundations (paṭṭhāna) on which to build attentiveness (sati), or ways of establishing (paṭṭhāna) mindfulness (sati). The study of the *Satipaṭṭhāna Sutta* and other texts (as pariyatti, a term introduced above) can give us an orientation to the path being proposed, a first appreciation of the teaching, and some sense of how to begin. In this way, such study is itself part of creating a foundation on which to establish mindfulness.

The practice is traditionally described as having four specific parts.

The **first** focus of mindfulness is the body (kāya). This includes awareness of body and a following of the breath (both widely discussed), but it also

---

[7] C.A.F. Rhys Davids gives the last two as exact equivalents of 'dhamma' in her Introductory Essay, p. xxxv, *A Buddhist Manual of Psychological Ethics* (1900); it is also glossed as a mind (mental) object/datum/content/event/process/pattern. Cf. below, p. 173, n. 23; V.R. Dhiravamsa, *The Way of Non-attachment*, p. 152, Soma Thera, *The Way of Mindfulness: The Satipaṭṭhāna Sutta and Commentary*, p. 26, Nyanaponika Thera, *The Heart of Buddhist Meditation*, pp. 73, 214.
[8] *The Pali Text Society Pali-English Dictionary*, pp. 335b-339b: "thing" (the term 'thing' in a very broad, inclusive sense here). Cf. below, p. 166, n. 9.

involves meditations on the mortality of the body, investigating this impermanence in our own imagination: thus, pariyatti and paṭipatti combined (as above).

Second is vedanā. This is precisely defined as a physical or mental
experience that is pleasant, unpleasant, or neither-pleasant-nor-unpleasant. This
term is sometimes translated as "feeling" (despite the many irrelevant senses of
the word 'feeling'), and even as "sensation" (although the term 'sensation' does
not usually apply to *mental* moments of consciousness).

Third is citta, which often means thought. Examples of citta given in
the sutta refer to consciousness and its various states, such as a mind filled with
hate, or with lovingkindness (mettā), or a mind that has grown calm.

Fourth is dhamma (as discussed briefly above). The *Satipaṭṭhāna
Sutta*, which precisely defines the third satipaṭṭhāna by examples, does so again
here. The dhammā (plural form) to observe are our own forms of thinking. These
are to be understood in a spiritual or psychospiritual way (***concerned with the
evolution of personality and mind leading to their radical, liberating transformation***), in terms of processes hindering or aiding our progress that are discussed in detail in the *Satipaṭṭhāna Sutta* and elsewhere: as hindrances to clarity
and wisdom, as bases of clinging, as sense perception and fetters that arise in relation to them, and also as factors of enlightenment, or as illuminating the Four
Noble Truths—all these being among the most fundamental of all ideas or concepts in Buddha Dhamma.[9] This fourth satipaṭṭhāna meditation returns us to our
own experience (including perception, as above), to our observing and investigating mind consciousness.

And, pointing out another parallel, as the second satipaṭṭhāna is seeing a
moment of experience insofar as it is pleasant or unpleasant (or neither), the
fourth is seeing an idea or thought insofar as it is (or is not) one of the mental
phenomena defined by these Buddhist concepts, which requires us to know what
they are (in part, by study of texts).

The dhammā as the fourth satipaṭṭhāna, then, form the basis of our own
investigation into the mind. This is, first of all, a matter of being mindful of our
thoughts *as thoughts*, to appreciate them as being *merely thoughts*—not as accurate news reports, wise utterances, or divine revelations. Thoughts may reflect
either insight *or* habitual, conditioned reactivity: seeing thoughts *as (merely)
thoughts* allows us to investigate them directly, using when helpful the roadmap
of the Buddhist understanding of the mind and the dhammā it defines.

---

[9] Pāli, dhamma/Sanskrit, dharma: the root dhṛ means carry, support, maintain,
be firm, survive, etc. Dharma means that which is firm or supports (the world),
truth, (natural or moral) law, decree, practice, duty, virtue, morality, or justice.
(See further, above, p. 165, note 8.) Buddha-dharma is Dharma (the processes of
reality, morality, truth) as presented by the Buddha; his understanding of what
Dharma/Dhamma is. Some render Buddha-dharma as Teachings of the Buddha.

In the intellectual investigation of these dhammā defining this roadmap, we prepare ourselves to appreciate our own dhammā, that is, our own specific thinking/emotional processes, understanding how to address them in ways allowing our own transformation toward greater freedom and ease in life.

This transformation (as discussed in part, above) has been termed spiritual, psychospiritual, or (in an older vocabulary) moral, especially in the sense of being related to our mind (citta; Chinese, xīn 心) and (heartfelt) thinking, in general, and to our character make-up and personal psychology, in particular.[10]

Mindfulness of the dhammā encourages understanding, wisdom, and transformation; it allows for study, mindful observation, and realization. In these ways, the dhammā themselves are "intellectual and spiritual subjects"[11]—basically, a psychospiritual focus for our understanding, growth of wisdom, and personal transformation. *This fourth satipaṭṭhāna is thus a matter of considering these Buddhist concepts as ideas in their own right, and of seeing how our own thinking processes illustrate and exemplify these concepts.*

This seeing our dhammā in the light of the Buddha Dhamma ("one who sees the dhammā, sees the Dhamma") is called the investigation of dhamma (in these intertwined senses of dhamma). Its importance is reflected in its being considered a Factor of Awakening, explicitly recognized in this way as central to **psychospiritual** transformation (as defined above). This invites an integration of pariyatti, paṭipatti, and paṭivedha (in these terms introduced above, at p. 164).

In mindfulness practice centered on the fourth satipaṭṭhāna, that is, on the dhammā, then, our focus is on applying these concepts and teachings, leading us to a powerful appreciation of our processes of perception, and of our psychological make-up and tendencies, to further our own transformation. We will discuss this application in detail, just below.

---

[10] The older sense here—*still found in French*—interprets the adjective 'moral' as concerning "the intellectual powers of man, as distinct from his physical powers" or "of, pertaining to, or acting on the mind, feelings, will, or character" (quoting relevant senses of the term here, from the 1828 edition of *Webster's* and from *Random House Unabridged Dictionary*, respectively). Cf. *Larousse Lexis* (in second entry for 'moral'), where the adjective 'morale' as in "la force morale" is contrasted with physical strength; cf. next note. On citta or, in Chinese, xīn (heart-mind), see above, pp. i, vi-viii.

[11] To use Dhiravamsa's phrase. The Sinhalese scholar-monk who worked many years in France, W. Rahula, *What the Buddha Taught*, p. 69, described the dhammā as "moral and intellectual subjects"—as related to the mind, especially one's character and personal psychology, and as involving reasoning or learning—*taking the adjectives more in their French senses*, reflecting here the older English sense of the term mentioned above, in the preceding note.

10. The Liberating Power of Mindfulness

When life presents us with a difficult moment, we seek relief, some reassurance, and perhaps a sense of safety. In moments of stress (when we are worried, frightened, agitated, confused, angry, or frustrated), we want things to be better somehow, whether in resolution or by finding a place of quiet in our mind—and, if the moment is sufficiently disagreeable, in any way whatsoever! This is sometimes the function of a strong drink, some drugs, or some intense physical—possibly sexual—activity.

What might be of great value to us, as an alternative here, if we could make use of it, could be the transformative practice of mindfulness.

This practice of mindfulness is special in that it is available to us no matter what the physical environment. We can cultivate mindfulness even if we are in prison, even if we are poor, no matter what our health, social status, or age.[1] So, what is this mindfulness and how do we cultivate it?

Mindfulness is a practice that begins with our paying attention[2] *at each moment to what is most obvious in our experience at that moment.* To begin with, that is, we are being attentive in order to notice what is happening right now (for each "right now"). This is sometimes described as minimally noticing, or bare mindfulness. We then go on to the next moment of consciousness, with the same interest. *This ongoing awareness leads gradually to insight into our own processes, to peaceful groundedness, and to an evolution of consciousness.*

Traditionally, it is said that this activity or practice involves one of four positions, defined by the body's posture: we are sitting, or standing, or walking (moving, including running), or lying down. When we talk of a "formal meditation" as a sitting, standing, walking, or lying meditation, we are identifying it simply in terms of the "form" or posture of the body during the meditation.

Of these four postures of "formal" meditation, the best known is perhaps a sitting meditation. This is where we sit upright yet comfortably, without being stiff in our posture. We allow our eyes to close (Thai Theravāda Buddhist style) or to remain slightly open (Japanese Rinzai Zen practice). Some teachings suggest that we have no major movement during the period of sitting, or that we move *mindfully* if we do move. Length of sittings varies, depending on the tradition. People sometimes start with sitting for very short periods of time.

Let us shift from the body's posture to what is going on *in our consciousness* during this period of time, looking at the way in which this mindfulness operates, its specific features, its impact on us, and what about mindfulness is so powerful about practicing the cultivation of mindfulness and insight.

---

[1] I do not address here the case of being in a coma, in a deteriorated mental condition such as Alzheimer's Disease, having serious brain injuries, etc.

[2] Cf. Pāli, samannāhāro (Buddh. Skt. samanvāhāro), manasikāra, or āvajjana.

While practicing mindfulness meditation, we are to notice whatever comes up in our minds. We have, then, the very simple rule—*initially*—of noticing what is going on in our consciousness, that is, in our experience. This is a meditation practice that can stabilize our consciousness ongoingly or repeatedly. We may also do this as a "formal" meditation (as defined just above), of varying lengths of time, once or twice day, or randomly throughout the day.

In any posture (any of the four described above), we may put our attention on any of the four foundations of mindfulness (the four satipaṭṭhānas): kāya (body), vedanā (feeling), citta (consciousness and its states), and dhammā (the particulars of mind consciousness, or the intellectual and spiritual subjects, to use Dhiravamsa's phrase from above, in the preliminary remarks). These "forms" of meditation posture and "foundations" briefly delineate this practice.

In this practice of mindfulness, we employ the attitude of a fresh mind or beginner's mind[3]—a calm attentiveness that floats relaxedly from moment to moment of conciousness, *evenly hovering over experience*. This is the mind that observes with no preconceptions or conclusions closing off curiosity.[4] This is a mind ready to notice *whatever* arises in our body and mind—in contrast with our mundane way of pushing away what we don't like, which in more severe forms involves repressing, blocking, and shutting down totally. (Relatedly, in the central chapters of *The Inner Palace*, I question whether eliminating all thoughts is actually part of the shift toward an awakened mind.)

There is a balance here. While we do not push away any given state of mind—the wandering mind, for example—we do not encourage it, either. That is, we do not feed that mind state. The only energy, attention, or interest we give it, is in simply noticing it. (We do not invite it to tell us its full life history.) *As Dhiravamsa would say, we welcome it, and let it leave when it is ready to go.*

As Dhiravamsa has described it, mindfulness in satipaṭṭhāna practice—by its nature open (to every experience)—allows attention to be placed on each new object (bodily-sense or mental), as rapidly as needed, with no distractions.

Likewise, but expressed differently, there is an elegant teaching that is attributed to the Third Chinese Patriarch, Sēngcàn, in Chan Buddhism. Sēngcàn 僧璨,[5] proposes an attitude toward thinking (mind objects) that is not hostile

---

[3] M. Ginsberg, *The Inner Palace: Mirrors of Psychospirituality in Divine and Sacred Wisdom-Traditions*, pp. 34, 129, 211, 233, 246, 497, 508, on V.R. Dhiravamsa, J. Krishnamurti, S. Batchelor, etc.; cf. S. Suzuki, *Zen Mind, Beginner's Mind*. See, further, preceding note, and below, p. 209, n. 81.

[4] Cf. Freud's "evenly-suspended attention" in "Recommendations to Physicians Practicing Psycho-Analysis" (1912e) [at SE 12: 111 = GW 8: 376 = CP 2: 323].

[5] Full name, Jiànzhì Sēngcàn 鑑智僧璨; Japanese, Kanchi Sōsan. He is traditionally recognized as the author of the *Xìnxīnmíng* 信心銘; Japanese, *Shinjin-*

toward them, either. In the background is the idea of there being six senses, six kinds of sense experience, and six dusts (liù chén 六塵), as mentioned above. With this as context, we may consider the teaching of Sēngcàn: liù chén bù wù, hái tóng zhèng jué 六塵不惡、還同正覺.[6]

Various renderings of this phrase[7]—offered here for the reader's consideration and use, some more literal, and some more focused on expressing the "spirit" of the text—may give a sense of its significance: (1) If you wish to move in the One Way do not dislike even the world of senses and ideas. Indeed, to accept them fully is identical with true enlightenment,[8] (2) Not disliking the six sense-objects turns out equal to perfect awakenness,[9] (3) For when the senses are not maligned, that itself is perfect awakening,[10] and (4a) Les six souillures non détestées, retournez vous unir au pur Eveil,[11] that is, (4b) The six dusts not detested, return to unite yourself with pure awakening.

As the First Chinese Buddhist Patriarch (Bodhidharma; in Chinese, Pútídámó 菩提達磨[12]—who brought Buddhism to China from India) is quoted by tradition as teaching, "If you seek direct understanding, don't hold on to any appearance whatsoever, and you'll succeed. I have no other advice."[13]

This readiness to experience everything, this open mindfulness, is also taught in Sōtō Zen 曹洞禪, a tradition linked with Dōgen 道元 (died 1253 CE), who is credited with bringing Zen teachings back to his native Japan from his sojourn (1223-1227 CE) in China.[14] This is the practice of shikantaza 只管打坐,

---

mei. Older texts give his name as Chièn-chìh Sēng-ts'àn (in Wade-Giles transliteration). The character 鑑 (Jiàn) of his full name is alternatively written 鑒.

[6] Seng-ts'an, *Hsin Hsin Ming. Ecrit d'un cœur confiant*, D. Giraud, tr., p. 30.

[7] Variations are in part based how the translator understands the fifth character, 還 (hái, also read huán): it can be interpreted (first reading) *as an adverb:* still, yet, also, even, at the same time, rather, in addition, quite, etc., or (second reading) *as a verb:* restore, repay, return, go back, come back home.

[8] Richard Clarke, *Hsin Hsin Ming: Verses on the Faith Mind*, 1973 ed., p. 5 of the translation section. Cf. below, p. 171, n. 16.

[9] Gloss by Dušan Pajin, in Mu Soeng, *Trust in Mind: the Rebellion of Chinese Zen*, p. 154; his alternative, in email (June 2009): "… awakenedness …"

[10] Capitalization normalized for prose, from Andy Ferguson, *Zen's Chinese Heritage: The Masters and their Teachings*, p. 463.

[11] Tr. at Seng-ts'an, *Hsin Hsin Ming. Ecrit d'un cœur confiant*, Daniel Giraud, tr., p. 31. The French reads as slightly Sinocized, with a bit of a Chinese feel.

[12] Shorter version of name: Dámó 達磨; Japanese, Bodaidaruma, Daruma, resp.

[13] Bodhidharma, *The Zen Teaching of Bodhidharma*, p. 27 (tr. by Red Pine).

[14] Lectures and essays (1231-1253) by Dōgen in Japanese are collected in his major work, the *Shōbōgenzō* 正法眼藏 *(The Eye and Treasury of the True Law)*.

literally "just sitting" (or, character by character—cf. Chinese reading, zhǐ guǎn dǎ zuò—"merely, be in charge of/manage, doing, sitting"). This "merely sitting" is a matter of not becoming attached to, *nor rejecting of*, any of the "dusts" or "appearances"—the various perceptions of the six senses, which are the five senses (recognized in the West) and of the thoughts and images of the mind, as the sixth (as discussed above in the preliminary remarks).[15]

In Theravāda Buddhism (where the *Satipaṭṭhāna Sutta* is found), this "not disliking the six dusts" (the liù chén 六塵) is taught as the importance of watching out for and not being controlled by our cravings.[16] This craving (or thirst)—in both its attraction and repulsion versions—is taught as a chief root of suffering, throughout Buddhist theorizing. Not being reactive to the six sense experiences is easier when we can notice in our tendencies to be reactive here: to encourage them and to try to keep them going, when experiences that come to us through our senses, including our mind,[17] are pleasant, or to discourage them and to try to change them, when they are unpleasant.

Experiences that are pleasant (or not) are the bedrock of our emotions and emotional states, rich in the excitement—if not the turmoil—of pleasure or displeasure, satisfaction or frustration.

An emotion as understood in Western thinking is a complex phenomenon, composed of emotional states (in Buddhist terms, mental states), bodily sensations, thinking, evaluating, various attitudes, plans, intentions, and so forth. In this way, an emotion is a rather complex reality, consisting of *various* moments of experience, thoughts, ideas, bodily sensations, attitudes, etc.[18]

---

[15] This shikantaza 只管打坐 is task-free, and contrasts with the problem-solving mental contortions inspired by working with kōans (more from the tradition of Rinzai Zen 臨濟禪). The za 坐 here is the za 坐 in zazen 坐禪, sitting zen.

Shikantaza is described as "a sitting meditation in which one does not try to solve questions or attain realization" (hence, "just sitting"—vs. solving kōans). See Dōgen, *Moon in a Dewdrop: Writings of Zen Master Dōgen*, p. 6.

[16] See, e.g., the source of pain as "sensual craving, craving for existence, and craving for non-existence." (*Mahāsatipaṭṭhāna Sutta, Dīgha Nikāya* Sutta 22, at D.ii.308.) The alternative to setting up this pain is the omnipresent "being at ease" that Sēngcàn 僧璨 taught (in tr. by R. Clarke, above, p. 170, n. 8), which is brought about by *not following either the yearning* (taṇhā, literally, thirst) for action, for creating some new situations (bhava-taṇhā) *or the yearning* (taṇhā) for eliminating or annihilating that which is already there (vibhava-taṇhā).

[17] The mind is discussed as the sixth sense, above, esp. pp. 164-165, 170.

[18] The features of this complexity are addressed and analyzed in abhidhamma (the theoretical psychology of Buddhism) and in philosophy of mind or philoso-

With this understanding (or "translation" into Buddhist terms), we can appreciate the importance of watching each facet of this overall complex reality that in Western terms we call the emotion. Here, we can begin to distinguish between a given perception, its feeling (pleasant or not), judgments, bodily sensations, related thoughts, consciousness states (fear, anger, etc.), ideas, desires, cravings, plans, intentions, etc. This allows a clear perception of each moment of our experiential life[19]—most effectively, when carried out ongoingly, with calm and mindfulness in balance, as in Buddhist samatha-vipassanā practice.[20]

This awareness is available to us, whether we are at a rigorous meditation workshop or retreat with "formal" meditation periods, or not.[21]

Outside of the context of a formal meditation retreat, we may think of our mindfulness without regard to our bodily posture (or "form") at any given moment. This application of mindfulness where "form" has no central importance is often described as a "formless" meditation. In this sense of the term, *a formless meditation is an awareness that can be cultivated ongoingly through time*, a very calm and discerning awareness of our own body, feelings, state of mind, and mental landscape—to refer to concepts discussed above: kāya, vedanā, citta, and dhamma (or dhammā).

In general, this practice of mindfulness is the middle path between blocking or repressing or trying to shift away from something, on the one hand, and, on the other, diving into that something, encouraging it to play itself out in full intensity. This is neither a traditional "Keep a stiff upper lip" (to quote the British expression suggesting that we not let our lip quiver or tremble, as when we are on the verge of crying) nor "Let your emotion come out! Express yourself! Don't hold back!"

We let it (or its various components) arise, not encouraging it/them to arise; we let it/them end, not building it/them up into something dramatic. (I talk about some of this meditative attitude in *The Far Shore*.[22] Examples given in that book and in this one, as well, illustrate the understanding and insight into our own consciousness derived from remaining mindful, or "calm and clear.") *This avoids suppressing and forcing emotionality, neither being suggested here.*

As the reader may imagine simply from these descriptions—in ways that will be more obvious if these practices are actually tried out for a while and

---

phy of the emotions. There is much more on this topic, above, in the first chapter of this book, which discusses the concept of love (pp. 1-25).

[19] Cf. above, pp. 164-165, for specifics about components of consciousness.

[20] This is a practice that develops both tranquility (samatha) and insight (vipassanā), sometimes seen as building insight on a foundation of tranquility.

[21] This refers back to the comments about "formal" meditation being meditation described simply in terms of bodily posture or ("form"), above, at p. 168.

[22] See, e.g., its chapters "Anger and Ill-will" (p. 68) and "The Past" (p. 84).

in a consistent way—the mindfulness described here, an openness to experiencing life as it actually is, may be very relaxing while being interesting, informative, energizing, and, quite satisfying—a vibrant calm and clear state of mind.

When we experience this calm and clear state of mind, we are free of the intense, indecisive thinking that hesitates to see what is there to see—we are free of indecision and hesitation about perceiving clearly; we are open, relaxed, and available to notice what there is to notice.[23]

Mindfulness here is stable in the midst of one after the other of life's moments, placing full attention flowingly on each experience. This practice, perhaps guided helpfully by the rich Buddhist mapping of the mind's powerful patterns, is to bring us to deep understanding—to insights into ourselves and our interactions with others, to enlightened wisdom, a full-hearted, discerning understanding—and to allow us to achieve the fullest of our human potential, free of torment, pain, and anguish. This practice and the related evolution are much more than a salve to lessen our pain; this practice is no mere sedative, no mere "stress-reduction" technique, and no cutely spiritual way to "grin and bear it." In short, the path of mindfulness is not a palliative.

Rather, it is a path to a radical transformation of the mind in its widest sense. This path involves becoming free from earlier unhelpful patterns of thinking and acting. Here we feel relaxed, alert, curious, and open to life's possibilities. We can see things afresh, being clear, flexible, and creative. With this, we can appreciate the fullness of gently-caring, non-constricted consciousness and life energy.[24] Here—to refer back to this chapter's Preliminary Remarks[25]—is a powerful way to the "complete evolution of consciousness."[26]

---

[23] Cf. above, p. 165, n. 7; below, p. 204. The mind here is one free of vicikicchā (sceptical doubt, suspiciousness, perplexity, lack of a wish to learn or—in a Buddhist context—to cure oneself). See 5th cent. CE Buddhaghosa, *Visuddhimagga*, XIV.177; cf. the partial analysis as evasion or hesitation, in Book III, Part I, Chap. I, Par. 1004, p. 260, of C.A.F. Rhys Davids, tr., *A Buddhist Manual of Psychological Ethics* (1900), which translates the mid-300s BCE *Dhamma-sangaṇi*, first book of *Abhidhamma-piṭaka*, itself one part of the three-fold *Tipiṭaka* (Pāli, ti + piṭaka, "Three Baskets"), or Pāli Buddhist Canon.

[24] These were illustrated in M. Ginsberg, *The Far Shore: Vipassanā, The Practice of Insight* (e.g., "Spiritual Development," "The passionate Buddhist," or "Heart-felt Thinking," with its idea of loving caring—mettā: cf. above, p. 166), and discussed in detail in M. Ginsberg, *The Inner Palace: Mirrors of Psycho-spirituality in Divine and Sacred Wisdom-Traditions*. On this complete evolution or radical transformation, see also Introduction, above, esp. p. vi.

[25] See above, p. 164.

[26] My thanks to V.R. Dhiravamsa for helpful communications on these topics through the decades, including our most recent discussions in 2008-2010.

11. Inter-Personal Mindfulness Practice (IPMP)[1]

Mindfulness practice, presented in the preceding chapter, guides us to awareness of sensation, perception, and thinking, all based on contact. This contact-dependent arising of experience also extends to contact with others, where our responses may resonate more powerfully, intensifying, into emotional agitation, unclarity, and reactivity. Here, mindfulness can provide a steadying influence leading to greater calm, clarity, deep listening, empathy, and compassion.

Generally, meditation practices (including mindfulness) are seen as being quite personal, individual, and even isolated endeavors. We can easily bring to mind images of the lone sage on a mountaintop, in a cave, or in the desert, and may even hold the belief that wisdom only arises through intense personal devotion and practice. Relatedly, instructions regularly include information on body position and posture while meditating, and direct our attention to breath or to bodily sensations, or to sounds, smells, tastes, and such, or to thoughts, mental images, and patterns of conditioned reactivity in our thinking and feeling.

In Inter-Personal Mindfulness Practice (IPMP), by way of initial contrast, we are looking at our own experience and behavior, and also at how others are with us, considering *their* experience and behavior.[2]

---

[1] In this chapter, I italicize foreign words only as is done for English words: for emphasis, in titles, if in italics in the original text being quoted, etc.

[2] An aside here is called for to mention the ground-breaking work of Claudio Naranjo in this area of interpersonal extensions of meditation, interpersonal meditation, meditation-in-relation, or intersubjective meditation (as it is variously called) that should not be overlooked, nor its impact on other theoreticians of the mind and the cultivation of awareness. See, e.g., C. Naranjo, *The Way of Silence and the Talking Cure: On Meditation and Psychotherapy*. The entire book is filled with discussions of various meditative traditions, with Naranjo's in-depth discussions and understanding placing them into a very integrated vision of mind, and here, of the interpersonal dimension of consciousness. See esp. pp. 67-68, 95-113, 134-135, 157, 194, 227. Chap. 5, Meditation-in-Relation, pp. 95-112, is a good starting point. In particular, there is the transcript of a workshop in which Naranjo presented work totally focused on interpersonal mindfulness, from 1991 (in a session of the Symposium of Man held in Toledo, Ohio), "A Demonstration Workshop of Meditation-in-Relation" (pp. 96-112). The original passage here deserves the reader's careful attention. Equally relevant is the extended discussion of Chap. 6, Self-Knowledge Through Free Association in a Meditative Context: A Therapeutic and Educational Proposal (pp. 113-142). The specific information conveyed in those passages can aid in the focus of any meditator, that is, of *anyone interested in cultivating this sort of awareness and sensitivity*—both sympathetic (having concern for the difficulties

While I do not want to deny the importance in a meditation practice of our being aware of our own experience, feelings, states of mind, and thoughts, here I would like to bring attention, and give emphasis, to a complementary set of considerations raised by various specific teachings I want to mention here.

These teachings speak of the spiritual life and good[3] companionship, of spiritually valuable interactions, and of the locations for the application of mindfulness. To clarify what these teachings are concerned with, let me present these teachings more specifically and fully with some quotations now, each followed by some comments to bring a context and a greater focus:

(1) "Truly, the entire spiritual life, Ananda, is this: encouraging[4] friendship, encouraging companionship, encouraging intimacy."[5] The question of our connections with one another is presented in this teaching as quite important and valuable, cutting against the idea that our spiritual path requires isolation and turning inward to the exclusion of relationship with others.

(2) "Conversation is for this purpose, consultation is for this purpose, getting close is for this purpose, listening is for this purpose—for the clinging-

---

of another person) and empathetic (appreciating the troubles or torments, the dukkha, that another individual is experiencing). The overall scope of this work is quite significant, as I suggested in a review written when the book was being prepared for publication: "Claudio Naranjo, M.D., a major disciple of Gestalt psychotherapist Fritz Perls and leading theoretician of the psychology of meditation, has distilled in this book work of over four decades as a psychiatrist, innovator in the contemporary application of the practices of various of the world's great wisdom traditions as part of the great twentieth-century Human Potential Movement, and professor of comparative religion, music, psychiatry and humanistic psychology. This book, *The Way of Silence and the Talking Cure,* will make fascinating and stimulating not-to-be-missed reading for all those interested in the worlds of religious-spiritual teachings and the most creative innovations in psychotherapy of the past half century." (This quotation is found in the first pages of the book, at an unnumbered p. ii.)

Also historically significant here is R.D. Laing, H. Phillipson, and A.R. Lee, *Interpersonal Perception: A Theory and a Method of Research* (1966).

[3] The term 'kalyāna' is rendered here as "good."

[4] The term 'kalyāna' is rendered here as "encouraging." This Pāli word means beautiful, agreeable, good, noble, generous, excellent, beneficial, virtuous, auspicious, that which encourages, that which inspires; a kalyāna mitta (mitta means friend)—in the Theravāda Buddhist Tradition, a meditation teacher—is a good friend, a virtuous friend, a friend (in this Buddhist context) who inspires and encourages us in our process of coming to awakening and freedom.

[5] *Samyutta Nikāya*, S.i.87-88. The Pāli reads: Sakalameva hidam ānanda brahmacariyam, yadidam kalyānamittatā kalyānasahāyatā kalyānasampavankatā.

free liberation of consciousness."[6] Here in particular, we are given the link between our interactions with one another and the psychospiritual path of self-transformation that was described in the preceding chapter in various terms, as spiritual realization, as our psychospiritual progress, as the complete evolution of consciousness, and as a radical, liberating transformation.[7] In particular, our attention is drawn here to the idea of a consciousness that has been liberated, and this is defined specifically in terms of its being free of clinging.

And (3) The teaching in the *Satipaṭṭhāna Sutta* (a sutta or discourse that was discussed in greater detail in the preceding chapter), that mindfulness can be applied "ajjhattaṃ"[8] (internally, in other words, being attentive to ourselves) or "bahiddhā"[9] (externally, that is, being attentive to others).[10] *The brief mention in the sutta of this dual focus has great implications for all mindfulness practices,* because it indicates the relevance of our being aware of those around us and directs us to come to wisdom through this inclusion of others to the otherwise more restricted domain of attention "inwards" only.

The paying attention to our life situation, moment by moment, will *in part* lead us to notice our own bodily experience and our own thought processes. Here, the task of coming to appreciate what and how each of us is feeling, thinking, acting, and reacting, is not easy. It is part of what has recently been called "mentalizing," attempting to understand ourselves (and others) in terms of beliefs, desires or motivations, and other psychological or mentalistic concepts that help us to understand people, including ourselves.[11]

We may begin by considering only our own experience and interpretations of each situation and interaction with others. Even here, we still have the significant task of coming to understand ourselves.[12]

---

[6] *Vinaya-Piṭaka*, Vinaya.v.164. The Pāli reads: Etadatthā kathā, etadatthā mantaṇa, etadatthā upanisā, etadatthā sotāvadhānaṃ yad idaṃ anupādā cittassa vimokkho 'ti.

[7] See also psychotherapy vs. psychospirituality, discussed above (Chap. 8), as well as the comments by François Lauret (1846), cited above, p. 61, n. 1 (esp. last two lines of the note on that page, continuing onto p. 62).

[8] Cp. Sanskrit, adhyātma (adhi+ātma: own, belonging to self).

[9] Cp. Sanskrit, bahirdhā (bahir+dhā: out, outward, outside of).

[10] *Satipaṭṭhāna Sutta, Majjhima Nikāya*, Sutta 10, at M.i.57, etc.

[11] More on "mentalizing" (or "mentalization") in other chapters.

[12] At one time, Bob Solomon was interested in unconscious motivation and how our interests and desires come to be recognized and understood, and I was coming to an understanding of unconscious beliefs (what we think is true, even if we are not aware of these opinions, beliefs, thoughts). Our work culminated in our dissertations (Bob's *Unconscious Motivation* and my *Belief: Its Conceptual and Phenomenological Structure*), both, University of Michigan, 1967.

That is, we are not transparent to ourselves. We do not already know ourselves. Understanding ourselves is not automatic, not something to take for granted. At times, our appreciation of our own experience, understanding, and yearnings, can be quite a challenge. Beyond this, there is even more to consider!

And that "more" is everything going on around us, the rest of reality in its great variety. Most centrally, what there is also to be attentive to is our real-life, inter-personal situation, which involves other people and what is going on between us and those we interact with, and how both we and these other people are experiencing and dealing with each situation we are sharing.[13] For this reason, life in society may be richer, more challenging, and more vital a domain for practice than the isolated life of a hermit. As is said in Classical Chinese,

小隱隱於山、 大隱隱於市。

xiǎo yǐn yǐn yú shān; dà yǐn yǐn yú shì.

> Petty seclusion is seclusion in mountains,
> Great seclusion is seclusion in town.[14]

These specific teachings all point in various ways to the significance of our interactions with one another, to the value of such interactions in terms of our mutual psychospiritual evolution, and to the ways in which mindfulness practice may be carried out, given these considerations.

In IPMP, as mentioned above, we are looking at our own experience and behavior, and at how others are with us, considering as well *their* experience and behavior. *This investigation is like looking lovingly at a child we are taking care of. It is wanting to see the interests, concerns, dreams, fears, and irritations of the child, seeking to be of benefit to this child, encouraging it along its way, giving it security and love when it especially needs them, or guidance when it is a bit lost, letting it know where its home of safety is (psychologically speaking), so that it can venture forth on its own, with a sense of security and hopefulness. Here, our attention is directed to ourselves and to others we have contact with.*

So when we are having a discussion, or seeing the other person upset, or happy, or agitated, or confused, or notice that we ourselves are this way, we may use this sort of open mindfulness to investigate further. The basic idea that we are to be mindful both internally and externally[15] contains the implication that our consciousness, our experience, covers everything that we can experience and become aware of, both the internal and the external (as above).

---

[13] Cf. recent discussions in Western theorizing, such as D.J. Siegel, *The Mindful Brain: Reflection and Attunement in the Cultivation of Well-Being*.

[14] Or: Small hermits live in mountains; great hermits live in town. An alternative reading replaces shān 山 (mountain/mountains) with yě 野 (wilderness). Yú 於 = yú 于. My thanks to Chén Zhìmíng 陳志明 (Anatole Ginsberg) for the Classical Chinese text and for the precise rendering into English.

[15] On "internal" and "external" observation, see above, p. 176.

This relatively simple-sounding implication means in part that we have information within our consciousness about our own "internal" processes and about the "outside" world, as well. It is a question of being attentive. And while awareness is not automatic, simply because we are alive, and knowledge is certainly not automatic, either, the implicit suggestion here is that we are capable of coming to see, know about, and understand others, as we can understand ourselves. This takes our being open to noticing, to experiencing without blocking off our awareness, as a practical matter. It also suggests the similarity of processes involved in our coming to have awareness, whether of another human being or of ourselves.

This may not be surprising to the reader, stated so simply.

Still, if we start from the idea that we are separate entities, we may wonder how we can become aware of anything at all outside of ourselves! How, that is, can we come to know anything about anyone else, other than ourselves? (What seems difficult here depends in part on which theoretical starting point we adopt in thinking about such processes.)

Now, whatever we want to say and whatever we want to think, somehow we do manage to notice that someone (ourselves, or, just as well, some other individual) is happy, or sad, or annoyed, or sick, or being playful, and so on.

An aside for those interested in the question of the neurological basis of this awareness of—as well as empathy for—others: a linking of these forms of interpersonal perception and sensitivity with brain cells (neurons) called mirror neurons is one facet of investigations guided by a deep interest in integrating findings of neurological development, neuroplasticity, and psycho-emotional development, the inter-disciplinary field of interpersonal neurobiology (IPNB).[16]

Here, however—leaving aside the neurobiological context and returning to the processes of IPMP themselves—it is perhaps enough to know that one

---

[16] See discussions in J.M. Schwartz and S. Begley, *The Mind and the Brain: Neuroplasticity and the Power of Mental Force* (2002) and in D. Siegel, *Mindsight: The New Science of Personal Transformation* (2010). Cf. L. Fadiga, L. Fogassi, G. Pavesi, G. Rizzolatti, "Motor facilitation during action observation: a magnetic stimulation study," *Journal of Neurophysiology*, vol. 73 (1995), pp. 2608-2611; G. Rizzolatti, M.A. Arbib, "Language within our grasp," *Trends in Neurosciences*, vol. 21 (1998), pp. 188-194; M.A. Umiltà, E. Kohler, V. Gallese, L. Fogassi, L. Fadiga, C. Keysers, G. Rizzolatti, "I know what you are doing: a neurophysiological study," *Neuron*, vol. 32 (2001), pp. 91-101; B. Wicker, C. Keysers, J. Plailly, J.-P. Royet, V. Gallese, G. Rizzolatti, "Both of us disgusted in *my* insula: The common neural basis of seeing and feeling disgust," *Neuron*, vol. 40 (2003), pp. 655-664; J.H. Pfeifer, M. Iacoboni, J.C. Mazziotta, M. Dapretto, "Mirroring others' emotions relates to empathy and interpersonal competence in children," *NeuroImage*, vol. 39 (2008), pp. 2076–2085.

way or another, this consciousness of others is indeed not only possible, but readily within our grasp, if we are simply attentive, internally *and* externally.

This starting point here has the meditator—any of us—looking at particulars of any situation both of these ways, with an eye to understanding what is going on, to noticing processes that are described, as a guideline. This is an opportunity for us to notice physical or bodily states (including bodily positions and movements) as well as any of a large group of psychological states (from irritation to calm to good-will and lovingkindness, from confusion to clarity, from fear to confidence, and so on). Information about these concerns is available to us—once again—whether we are focusing on ourselves or on others as we perceive them.

We may hear a story, as in the *Fables* of Aesop or any other piece of fiction, see a play or a film, and notice what is portrayed in the given situation in the story, play, or film. We can sense here the ideas, thoughts, concerns, hopes, fears, or irritations that *may arise* for someone in that situation. This gives us some options to evaluate further.

With this as a starting point, we can become more definite if we then notice how given individuals *in fact* appear (facial expressions, bodily postures and movements), notice what is *actually* said and done, and come in this way to have a very clear sense of what these individuals are actually going through.

Furthermore, this can be not only a matter of what we might call intellectual knowledge (recognizing or noticing that something is the case), a matter of coming to have a belief (or good guess) about such things, but, rather, a fully resonating appreciation of what another person (perhaps imaginary, in the case of a fictional tale) is going through, concerned with, including what that person's state of mind is. This is a strongly felt experience on our part, a rather intense awareness (which is "located" in what is called the heart-mind in some cultures).[17] It is what is happening when we sense that someone toward whom we are directing our attention (our heart-mind) is enraged, insulted, exuberant, satisfied, worried, pining away, and so on.

This ability, which has been present since very early in our lives—we may remember this or may notice it in seeing babies interacting with those around them—does not require great intellectual sophistication (beyond the normal). And we can appreciate what someone is experiencing, whether this someone is ourselves, someone we are interacting with, or even someone in an imaginary story.

That is, we may notice that this situation stirs up fear, or love, and so forth, and we may appreciate deeply—*intellectually and also emotionally*—what is there to experience in such a situation. We may come to this experientially felt realization, whether what we are contemplating is a story, the events unfolding

---

[17] This idea of the heart-mind was touched upon in the Preface (pp. i-iv).

in real life to someone else, or what we ourselves are facing. *All of this suggests a universal human ability to empathize with others, to experience what they might be experiencing, one that we can close down, as when such experiences are too uncomfortable or disagreeable in some ways.* (More on this last, below.)

This turns an old question on its head (upside-down): we do not have to wonder here how we can empathize with another person, but would ask instead what makes it difficult or practically impossible to do so. To use a very old image of awakened mind and our sometimes *not* having access to it, we do not wonder about how it is that when we look up in broad daylight, we can easily see the sun in the sky (*unless* clouds block that sunlight from us).[18]

This process by which certain information (realizations or knowledge) does not operate in an active way is addressed in some of the other chapters in this book, especially the chapters on Nietzsche and Janet, which consider the processes of splitting or dissociation, among various facets of this general phenomenon (with the suggestion by such terms of some pathology).

Actually, this sort of process can be seen in what would be deemed the most "normal" and even "healthy" individuals: this is a very common function of selective information processing, one that allows us to be efficient in taking into consideration what is relevant and leaving aside what is not. The background question is whether the selection of what is relevant is actually that.

One brief example of the way in which we disregard information as a service to our emotional peace of mind or to our belief system (with its core values) can be seen in current contexts by considering news reports of violence in various areas of the world, where we can see people wounded and bleeding, or dying or dead.

We may feel touched and saddened (or disgusted) by such scenes, but when we learn who the people are (for example, people who belong to a group we feel allied or associated with, or, in contrast, to a group we feel hostile toward), what we then feel and think about the scenes we are seeing portrayed may differ greatly. (Compare the thought "They deserve it!" with its possible contrast here, "What horrible people they are who did this to them!")

In any case, the ways in which this judgmental process can create problems rather than be helpful is a large topic. I will not go into a discussion of that here, but will simply point out its existence. In any case, this biased attitude is *a rigid, constricted consciousness*, and we are sadly all-too-familiar in our lives with this sort of narrow-mindedness.

There is an ability we have, to notice what given situations are about, and bring into play our own knowledge of what this implies (from our own experience and ability to think about such matters). *When this is all operating without being blocked or shut down, simple feelings will be able to arise: a sense of*

---

[18] Cf. B. Cyrulnik, *Autobiographie d'un épouvantail*, on desensitized empathy.

happiness in a happy situation, or sadness when there is something sad. This in turn leads to a number of states of consciousness that are very special, from a Buddhist meditative point of view. There are in particular four such states. First of these is lovingkindness or wishing another well (often in a very generalized form, of having good-will toward all living beings). This is called mettā. Second is noticing something sad or unfortunate, and having the related wish for that situation to be ended or resolved or transformed into a problem-free one. This is called karuṇā (sympathy, not to be confused with condescending pity). Third is joy felt when being aware of a joyous situation, in which the person in question is another person. This is called muditā (sympathetic joy). This joy is the opposite of envy in the same situation (where we then sense our own lack of joy and wish that *we* were the other person with joy). And fourth is the looking at the situation with calm, called upekkhā (equanimity).

These four states are called the divine[19] abodes (one rendering of the term here, brahma-vihāra). These are considered to be of unlimited scope, and so are called appamaññā (the immeasurables, that is, immeasurable states of consciousness). We have access to these various states, which are expansive, flowing, and energizing, through our deeply felt and realized appreciation of any situation, in terms of how we or others are experiencing it, and feeling about it.

We might notice that three of these four are explicitly a matter of deep connection with other individuals, with other beings (that is, not necessarily only with other humans). The fourth, equanimity, is a spacious consciousness in which we are able to consider in a state of calm whatever there is for us to face, including any imbalance that might arise in the other three.[20]

With mindfulness being directed in the above ways to particular situations, we are in a position to come to understanding, to comprehension, to empathy with, and to sympathy for, whoever it is that is going through the situations we are being attentive to. This attentiveness is basically a matter simply of noticing what is going on and how the people here (ourselves included) are feel-

---

[19] Called the four "radiant" abodes in J. Kornfield, *The Wise Heart: A Guide to the Universal Teachings of Buddhist Psychology*, p. 385. In M. Ginsberg, *The Inner Palace*, I discussed the root metaphors of the divine and the sacred.

[20] For example, our sympathy with another may lead us to a pressured urge to "fix things," even when it is not possible for us to do anything on a practical level. This could lead to an uncomfortable sense of our impotence (which is sometimes almost as intense a source of anxiety as our sense of mortality), which in turn may lead us to shut off any sympathy about the given situation *in order to lessen our sense of stress or discomfort.* Or, sympathetic joy may lead us to an exuberance or mania that can be quite stressful to the body and mind. *Equanimity, then, can aid in allowing us to experience these other states intensely, in a grounded way.*

ing, *and to use this as the orienting basis* of what we then pay attention to, discuss, bring up for consideration, and so forth. And part of our coming to appreciate what is going on within us, or between us and others, is defining (or describing) this experience. Words can be quite helpful here.

After all, whatever their limit, words have the power of transforming our thinking and feeling (and then acting). So to put into words the conflicts that we are feeling can be a powerful step. Description can aid in observation and memory, giving form to otherwise perhaps vague awareness or memory. Instead of feeling chaotic turmoil, we can formulate this. (For instance: "I feel in conflict. The conflict is between a desire to push that person away and to come closer.") Similarly, emotions might be identified as pleasant, powerful, confusing, etc. (or not)—a step leading us to see the concerns alive in that emotional context. Just to think it, to describe it, to say it, brings a degree of clarity about what the turmoil is that we are going through. Not that such clarity is the end-point, but it can be useful, redirecting what then happens in our body-mind processes.

As an example, if another person is angry, we may start by noticing that (perhaps also describing it in words). With this, we may notice how this anger in this other person is impacting us, having us feel or think, and what in particular it has us feel inclined to say or do. In this, we are already seeing a great deal about ourselves as well as about the other. *If we can stay grounded and focused on these basics, we will not be distracted* into other issues or pseudo-issues, but can help the other appreciate this anger (in this imagined example), how it is being expressed, how that expression influences what is then happening, including how we are feeling and what we are doing in response to that angry expression.

Or—a second example—when there is jealousy, we may notice the frustration or unhappiness that is driving this jealousy, recognizing if these current features are echoing some earlier jealousy. And to see what is being valued. This helps us to appreciate how what is going on now may be influenced by what preceded it. *This is not to justify or to excuse anything at all, but simply to put it into its own context,* helping us to appreciate this state of mind (ours, another's) and its history. All of this, in turn, is to allow us to appreciate the stress and torment that we and others are dealing with, just trying to get through life.

Or—a third example—if we are experiencing sadness or loss, as when we are separated from someone we find dear and precious, whether that person has moved far away, or, in a more definitive way, has died, we may appreciate the sense of loss, and can also recognize our appreciation of how special and wonderful that relationship has been to us, or what a gift it is to have shared something with that person. This is honoring that person and that relationship.

Or—a fourth example—if we are noticing fear, we may come to notice a yearning for security or for acceptance now sensed as threatened; we may see the value of developing a sense of reassurance or safety in such a context.

In general, we can dig deeper, go to the roots or the underlying issues at play, to see what may be quite important for us to recognize in the situation—all of this with our sympathy and compassion for the life difficulties that we each have occasion to experience ourselves and to recognize in others. We should "carry on digging," as is said in a Buddhist discourse.[21]

In the context of our experienced life, whether we are children growing up, or monks in some secluded residence, are living in a couple, or in a family raising children (as the traditional "householder"), following a career or a profession, watching the seasons go by, or are considering situations we may read or hear of, in whatever the situation, we have all of the information we need, to learn about ourselves, and about others living in perhaps quite different circumstances. *Each of these situations will allow us to become understanding and caring companions to friends (to others), and to ourselves, as well—to develop our awareness, insight, caring, compassion, and wisdom.*

In fact, these various capacities are quite intimately interconnected: each is strengthened in the process of developing any of the others. We tend *not* to notice[22] such interconnectedness when we think in traditional concepts used to distinguish between, and disconnect from one another, the various features of our heart-mind (or *xīn* 心),[23] our wise and understanding heart.

In seeing beyond those conceptualizations, however, we can come to appreciate these features of our deepest understanding—and the ways they mutually influence one another—to give honor to the integrated nature of this full-hearted wisdom[24] that is part of our human potential and promise.

---

[21] In the *Vammīka Sutta (The Discourse on the Ant-hill)*, *Majjhima Nikāya*, Sutta 23 (M.i.142-145). The title is alternatively rendered *Vammika Sutta*. Using a tool to dig is a symbol for using wisdom to investigate in depth: as Dhiravamsa has written (in an unpublished paper, *Understanding the Buddha Nature*, which he sent to me by email, early 2009), "it is the process of the symbolic digging into our psychophysical systems deeply and thoroughly that will help us encounter our enlightened state of being or our Buddha Nature awaiting us at the completion of our digging process." There is further (earlier) discussion by Dhiravamsa on this sutta, in *The Dynamic Way of Meditation: The Release and Cure of Pain and Suffering* (1982), Chap. 12, Digging an Ant-hill, pp. 111-118.

[22] As discussed above, esp. in the introductory sections and in Chaps. 1 and 6.

[23] Cf. "heart-and-mind" (pp. 77, 210), "hearts-and-minds" (p. 226), or "thoughts and feelings" (p. 105), as alternative glosses for xīn 心 (or 心), in R.T. Ames and H. Rosemont, Jr., *The Analects of Confucius: A Philosophical Translation* (*The Analects*, variously, at 2.4, 17.22, 20.1, 6.7). Cf. above, n. 22, and Preface, p. i.

[24] This wise heart, caring, seeing, non-needy, non-clinging, continually flowing, agile, is the mind that rests nowhere, xīn wú suǒ zhù 心無所住 (Japanese, shin mu shojū), in an image inspired by the *Diamond Sutra*, Sect. 10: Let mind function dwelling nowhere, yīng wú suǒ zhù ér shēng qí xīn 應無所住而生其心 (J., ōmushojū jijōgoshin). Cf. M. Ginsberg, *The Inner Palace*, pp. 81-83, 397-398.

12. The Pivot of the Dao[1]
Preliminary Remarks

The considerations raised in the preceding two chapters—on the liberating, transformative power of the practice of mindfulness and on Inter-Personal
Mindfulness Practice (IPMP)[2]—rest within the Buddhist tradition, an immense
collection of teachings, texts, concepts, images and stories, specific practices,
and so on, all embodying principles and values for living life (as are many of the
world's great spiritual and religious traditions).[3] Relative to that greater context,
these considerations, addressing a core meditative practice found throughout
Buddhism, were quite focused and reflected a specific interest in our experience
and the ways we shift to calmer and wiser states of mind.

We may now refine our sense of what this transformation involves. We
want to understand more deeply this shift toward a refreshing, vibrant, secure,
calm, and clear[4] state of consciousness—and to experience this state, in which
we are curious about our evolving life and are good-willed toward others and toward ourselves. In this, our experience is looked at directly, clearly, as it presents itself, in a way that is free of judgmental self-lauding or self-denigrating.[5]

As a path to our appreciating mind cultivation or meditation more fully,
let us now consider a further perspective, that of the Chinese Daoist tradition,
beginning with a glimpse at its literature and cultural context in these next pages,
which will especially help orient those who are not Chinese scholars.

This will set the stage for a rather focused discussion of some of the
teachings from within this tradition. In particular, a group of concepts found in
Daoist texts, and elsewhere in the cultural history of China, will be introduced
below that will have direct application to an understanding of the meditative
process and of the workings and the potential of the mind, making use of several
rather vibrant and fresh images or metaphors.

---

[1]   In these preliminary remarks, I italicize foreign words except for names or
words now incorporated into English, e.g. Hui Neng, kung fu, pinyin, Dao, etc.

[2]   The practice is also known as insight or *vipassanā* (Pāli; Sanskrit, *vipaśyanā*)
meditation. See M. Ginsberg, *The Inner Palace*, esp. p. xlii; cf. pp. lxiv, lxviii,
31, 90, 116, 129, 292, 334, 368, 402, 423, 444-445, 451, 453, 496, 533.

[3]   I address some of these traditions in *The Inner Palace*, as the sub-title suggests: *Mirrors of Psychospirituality in Divine and Sacred Wisdom-Traditions*.

[4]   As in the Tibetan Buddhist text by Lama Mi-pham (d. 1912), *Calm and Clear:
The Wheel of Analytic Meditation and Instructions on Vision in the Middle Way*.

[5]   The direct application of this non-judgmental approach has been illustrated in
M. Ginsberg, *The Far Shore: Vipassanā, The Practice of Insight*. See chapters
describing, e.g., mind clouds, love and respect, fear, anger and ill-will, memories
in the present, self-criticism, and troubles in relationship.

Following the Preliminary Remarks here, these inter-connected teachings will be explained in the core of this chapter. They will make much more sense *if considered by applying them in actual life sitiuations*, including our dealing with the aftermath of life difficulties that we might have lived through.

After all, we may debate and theorize indefinitely. *When, however, we pay full attention to the particulars of real life, to deeply felt, clearly appreciated experiences, we do not need to speculate; we know.*

As the old expression has it, concerning the actual taste of Chinese tea whose taste was being debated theoretically with no tea being poured or tasted, "He who tastes knows, he who tastes not, knows not."[6]

Some orienting information

For those who wish to move immediately to the body of this chapter, below, with its meditative focus and discussion of forms of consciousness that can be appreciated even more so when considered in relation to the preceding two chapters: please note that the comments here, accompanied by explanatory notes, will give a synoptic context to that discussion. This context is historical and theoretical, especially in terms of textual traditions of thought. These comments may also be referred to later, after having read the discussion in the body of this chapter, which begins on p. 191.

The tradition that is the focus of this chapter is a rich and complex one, with many facets and concerns. As with the preceding two chapters that took a rather specific focus within the much broader tradition of Buddhism, the central concern here is with one strand within the teachings and practices of Daoism.

To place the comments of this chapter into their larger context, this orienting information will briefly introduce several background considerations: the Chinese origin of this tradition, the richness and vastness of its teachings, and the broad range of concerns it addresses (its numerous topics and texts).

This will bring us to the focus of this chapter and its application to self-awareness and self-transformation, including the relationship between these considerations coming out of Daoist teachings and the more Buddhist-formulated interests of the preceding chapters.

These discussions in the body of this chapter will be followed by a list of references for reading in general areas considered here, including source material for some of the specific discussions in this chapter, and beyond, in the broad domain of Daoist studies.

---

[6] From a teaching story called The Story of Tea, from Yūsuf Hamadhānī, died 1140 CE. On Hamadhānī as precursor to the Naqshbandi Sufis, see A. Schimmel, *Mystical Dimensions of Islam*, pp. 364, 496. The story is retold in I. Shah, *Tales of the Dervishes*, pp. 88-90 (with an anglicized, simplified spelling, Hamadani). More on Yūsuf Hamadhānī in M. Ginsberg, *The Inner Palace*, pp. 19, 352-353.

On this tradition originating in ancient China

The tradition that is the focus of this chapter has its origins in China. Its first teachings go back to ancient China, and as a living tradition, there are teachers, teachings, texts, and practices that are still to be found and discovered. The key term that gives this tradition its name is the word 'dao' (also written, 'tao'),[7] the way.

In this chapter, we will have occasion to cite the Chinese for certain ideas and concepts in this tradition.[8] I will do this using the written form of Chinese, making use of Chinese characters (in Chinese,[9] called *hanzi*,[10] and in Japanese, *kanji*, denoting especially the use of these in writing Japanese).

Names, words, phrases, and titles will also be given in transliteration, a rendering that attempts to approximate pronunciation, here into the Latin alphabet (this form of transliteration being known as romanization).

Several systems of transliteration have been developed over the centuries since Chinese culture became known to the West. One of the earliest, developed by Jesuit missionaries (we might specifically mention Matteo Ricci, working in the late sixteenth century), rendered the names of some famous ancient Chinese philosophers, especially Kongfuzi and Mengzi,[11] by giving their Chinese names the Latin ending *–us* (a declension form for the nominative case), going in this way through "Kongfuzi-us" and "Mengzi-us" to names that have been recognized through the centuries: Confucius and Mencius.

Mostly, however, the transliteration systems presently in use are the more modern Wade-Giles and pinyin systems. This latter was first presented in China in February 1958 and is slowly replacing Wade-Giles worldwide.

An appendix of characters for reference (with pinyin, Wade-Giles, and Japanese *kanji* readings) precedes the bibliography at the back of the book.

We may note that Chinese is a tonal language (where the meaning of words is in part determined by which tone is used, and distinguished from other words solely in virtue of the difference in tone). Given this, tones are indicated in these transliterations, as given in notes here and in the appendix.

One initial example of this would be the character 道, which in pinyin is dao (or dào) and in Wade-Giles, tao (or tào). Relatedly we have the terms Daoism and Taoism. Citations in this chapter may go from one system of translitera-

---

[7] These words are not italicized, except when cited in fuller Chinese passages.

[8] For more on Chinese, see esp. Y. R. Chao, *A Grammar of Spoken Chinese*, J. DeFrancis, *The Chinese Language*, J. Norman, *Chinese*, and E.G. Pulleyblank, *An Outline of Classical Chinese Grammar*.

[9] I will indicate tones and Chinese characters, primarily in footnotes. I will use mostly pinyin spellings except for some terms more familiar in another spelling.

[10] P: *hànzì* 漢字 (WG: *hàn-tzù*). Japanese pronunciation of 漢字: *kanji*.

[11] P: Kǒngfūzǐ 孔夫子 (WG: K'ǔng-fū-tzǔ) and Mèngzǐ 孟子 (WG: Mèng-tzǔ).

tion to the other, depending on what is being discussed. As a general plan, I will tend to use pinyin transliteration here as the primary system of rendering the Chinese, unless directly quoting another text that uses Wade-Giles spelling.

Most relevantly, two early texts that we refer to here are perhaps more familiar in Wade-Giles spelling: the *Tao Te Ching* (also called the *Lao Tzu*) and the *Chuang Tzu*. The first is traditionally ascribed to Lao Tzu and the second to Chuang Tzu. These are more recently given, in pinyin, as the *Daodejing* (less commonly, *Dao De Jing*), or the *Laozi*, and the *Zhuangzi*.[12] These last two titles follow a tradition in the Chinese culture of naming a work after the author.

On topics, texts, and differences within the tradition

Depending on which Daoist texts we consider, we may be addressing a philosophy, a cosmology or vision of the universe, a psychology, a sociopolitical-governmental model, descriptions of rituals for invoking the powers of charms or talismans (*shen fu*),[13] or alchemical studies including meditative and other psychospiritual practices. We may find a vision of our place in the world, as well as systems of symbolism concerning the internal organs, an analysis of the human body, its processes and energies, of our physical, sexual, mental, and spiritual well-being, and of our fitness, longevity, and health, including exercise manuals and medical texts. Among Daoist teachings there are, as well, great resources and inspirations for Chinese poetry.

This is obviously an impressively wide range of contemplations and teachings. Although these are all topics discusssed in various Daoist texts, *we will not attempt to address all or even most of these here*.

Placing these teachings in time, it has traditionally been held—perhaps beginning in the Han Dynasty (206 BCE-8 CE) and its formulation of the concept of Daoism (*daojia* or *daojiao*)[14]—that the earliest Daoist texts date from about the period of Confucius (551-479 BCE). The exact dates and definition of specific layers or parts of these texts that had been modified and added to through the centuries is an issue still being debated by scholars.

To give a general idea, though, the earliest authors *now widely recognized as Daoist* (especially Laozi and Zhuangzi—each perhaps actually a composite of several authors) are generally held to have been active before 300 BCE.

This is to place the beginnings of this tradition into a larger historical timeline. As with other living traditions, new perspectives and interpretations of basic ideas, teachings, and practices of the tradition can be found.

---

[12] P: *Dàodéjīng* 道德經 (WG: *Tào Té Chīng*), Lǎozǐ 老子 (WG: Lǎo-tzǔ or Lǎo Tzǔ), Zhuāngzǐ 莊子 (WG: Chuāng-tzǔ or Chuāng Tzǔ).

[13] P: *shén fú* 神符 (WG: *shén fú*).

[14] P: *dào jiā* 道家 (WG: *tào chiā*), *dàojiào* 道教 (WG: *tào chiào*). Cf. next note.

Since that is the case, it may be helpful to state explicitly that in talking of the Daoist tradition in the singular (as one tradition), I do not mean to imply that there is one single set of teachings universally acknowledged and given the same relative importance by all those later identified as Daoist.

We may appreciate that even an individual philosopher may present very different understandings and orientations in works written through a long intellectual career. In fact, any of us with some age may notice that through the years, we regularly have ongoingly different interests, values, understandings of ourselves and of the world, different beliefs, plans, projects, and concerns.

It is even more so that those joined together as a "school" will present perhaps great variation and disagreements among themselves. In fact, the concept of a Daoist tradition has been seen as an *ex post facto* grouping of works of varying natures, as just mentioned, suggesting a reconstruction of the past creating a school *retrospectively* taken to be a tradition.[15] In any case, I do not mean to imply any homogeneity or unanimity of opinion and perspective for those who are identified as Daoists, or for Daoism overall, by anything that I write here. Still, I intend to discuss particular concepts as they are variously presented in texts that address these concepts, to see the application to our understanding of consciousness, its processes, and its transformations, without suggesting that these define some hypothetical core teaching of Daoism.

Considerations about the dating of texts

The issue of dating some early Daoist texts is unsettled, due in part to recent findings of important versions of several of these texts that had been placed in burial caves in China.

These are primarily texts on silk from the Mawangdui caves in Hunan Province, China, excavated in the 1970s, with Western Han Dynasty artifacts (earlier half of the second century BCE), and texts on bamboo slips or *jian* among the tomb findings at Guodian in the ancient state of Chu,[16] Hubei Province, China, discovered in 1993, which are dated from the Warring States Period (mid-fourth to early third century BCE).

Documents among these findings raise interesting questions of textual traditions and have renewed discussion and speculation about which specific Daoist texts were the earliest, and their dates, as well as questions about the relationship between Daoist texts and discussions, and those of the Buddhist tradition. This issue of the relationships between various traditions that evolved in the

---

[15] Scholars differ on interpreting the terms *dàojiào* and *dàojiā* (*jiào*: teaching, religion; *jiā*: family, school) and on what they each refer to. Cf. preceding note and extended discussion in Li Yangzheng (Y. Li), *History of Chinese Taoism*.

[16] P: Mǎwángduī 馬王堆 (WG: Mǎ-wáng-tuī), *jiǎn* 簡 (WG: chiěn), Guōdiàn 郭店 (WG: Kuō-tièn), Chǔ 楚 (WG: Ch'ǔ).

same area of the world during a given span of time is, of course, a general historical question, and, not surprisingly, a similar question arises in the Indic context,
where texts from what is now called Hinduism have been in dialogue for many
centuries with those of a series of Buddhist discourses and theorizing: neighbor-
ing traditions often address overlapping issues (theories, principles, practices,
etc.) in parallel and in interaction with one another through time.

This is to acknowledge that these great traditions are alive and have
evolved in time, with later discussions of earlier topics that have broadened and
given greater subtlety, nuance, and complexity to the tradition. In some traditions these are considered to be commentaries or paraphrasings or re-organized
presentations of the core (or "original") teachings; in others, these are taken to be
further, equally significant, reflections on the issues that have evolved out of
those earlier (or earliest) presentations. While these questions are central to historians of ideas, our interest will not focus on these issues.

We, on the other hand, will be primarily concerned with appreciating
the nature of *experience, consciousness, understanding, and the development of
wisdom as seen from within the large Daoist tradition.*

We will in this way be focusing on a rather specific topic within this
larger tradition, as we did above with Buddhist awareness practices in relation to
Buddhism overall.

The Canon(s) and Beyond

This section presents a general overview of various texts from the Daoist tradition. We may speak of the Daoist Canon (in the singular), but this has not
actually been a constant collection of texts: the literature of the tradition has
been collected several times (perhaps first by Lu Xiujing,[17] 406-477 CE), growing through the centuries, as Daoism came to be a recognized tradition. Here, the
Daoist Canon (the *Daozang*) is understood to refer to a collection (of over 1,400
texts), also known as the *Zhengtong dazang*[18] (the *Zhengtong Daoist Canon*). In
scholarly contexts, the *Dazang* is abbreviated DZ.

This version of the Canon is from the Ming Dynasty (1368-1644 CE). It
was printed in 1444-1445, during the period referred to in Chinese history as the
Zhengtong reign, 1436-1449, for which this Canon is named. Relatedly, the personal name of the emperor during this reign was Ming Yingzong (Ming Ying-
tsung),[19] who is also referred to in relationship to this reign as the Zhengtong
(the Cheng-t'ung) Emperor.

The almost 1,500 texts found in this Canon are formally divided into
Three Grottoes—or *Caves*—(*Sandong*) and *Four Supplements* (*Sifu*). In a simi-

---

[17] P: Lù Xiūjìng 陸修靜 (WG: Lù Hsiū-chìng).

[18] P: Zhèngtǒng dàozàng 正統道藏 (WG: *Chèng-t'ǔng tào-tsàng*).

[19] P: Míng Yīngzōng 明英宗 (WG: Míng Yīng-tsūng).

lar way, the *Buddhist Canon*, in Pāli, *Tipiṭaka* (Sanskrit, *Tripiṭaka*), *Three Baskets*, is also in three parts. Its Chinese names—*Sanzang* or *Three Depositories*, and *Dazang* or *Great Depository*—mirror the above *Sandong* or *Three Grottos*, and the earlier-mentioned *Daozang* or Daoist Grotto.[20]

This parallel between these canons is somewhat limited, however, since the organization of material is not at all the same within this three-part structure, nor in the twelve chapters according to category—in Chinese, *lei*—into which each of the three parts of the Daoist Canon are broken down.[21]

In terms of this particular Daoist Canon, only a very small number of the almost 1,500 texts collected in it will be referred to in context when relevant, or will be cited in the bibliographic references at the end of this chapter.

This perspective may put into context the best-known texts that represent Daoism to many of us, the two early works mentioned above, the *Laozi* (the *Daodejing*) and the *Zhuangzi* (with its specific system of citation),[22] as two out of hundreds of texts. This is not meant to decide how representative these two works are of all Daoist teachings of all periods. Historians of Chinese culture may disagree about their status relative to the much larger corpus of writings in this tradition, in terms of dating, direction of influence, and so forth.

I leave aside the question of the relationship between all of these texts, their relative importance, and their precise dating, in part because what I am interested in here does not rest on any particular position about such matters.

And with this providing some orienting background, let us now enter into the teachings of Daoism as they are of special interest here.

---

[20] P: *Sānzàng* 三藏 (WG: *Sān-tsàng*), *Dàzàng* 大藏 (WG: *Tà-tsàng*), *Sāndòng* 三洞 (WG: *Sān-tùng*), *Dàozàng* 道藏. Here, note *sān* 三 (three) as well as the contrasting pairs *zàng* 藏 (depository, storehouse, texts, canon) vs. *dòng* 洞 (grotto); *dà* 大 (great) vs. *dào* 道 (Way).

[21] P: *lèi* 類 (WG: *lèi*): kind, type, class, category, etc.

[22] See above, p. 187, note 12. The *Zhuangzi* is often cited with reference to the edition of the text found in the *Concordance* ed.—the *Zhuāngzǐ yǐndé* 莊子引得, *Zhuangzi Concordance*. The *Zhuāngzǐ yǐndé* is referred to as HY (for Harvard-Yenching Institute, publisher of the first edition of this text, in 1947). I follow that text's convention: a citation of "*Zhuangzi* 12/4/90" would indicate that the passage cited is at page 12 of the *Zhuangzi* text, from its Chap. 4, and at line 90 of the text of that chapter. A two-part citation would indicate chapter and line in the chapter (as "*Zhuangzi* 4/90" for the same passage). The *Zhuangzi* found in that edition runs 94 pages. Not all editions have the same pagination and line formatting as the HY edition—e.g. the *Zhuāngzǐ zhú zì suǒ yǐn* 莊子逐字索引, *Verbatim Index/Concordance to the Zhuangzi* (where the *Zhuangzi* text runs 101 pages, with modern punctuation and line numbering for each page, not chapter).

12. The Pivot of the Dao

Given the overview and background information just provided in the Preliminary Remarks, which serve as an introduction to this section, the body of this chapter, let us now look into the teachings I wish to focus on at this time. *The body of this chapter may be read without reference to footnotes.*[1]

A cautionary note: This, as any discussion of Classical Chinese texts (held to be notoriously difficult to interpret), will necessarily be tentative and open to scholarly challenge. The translations I offer, while plausible, reflect my own perspective and understanding of the issues I discuss here. I claim no more.

It has been said: the way that can be walked is not the constant way; those who know don't talk and those who talk don't know; when there is disharmony in the family, there is talk of filial piety and familial love; soft water can wear away the hardest of substances (we may imagine mountain streams wearing grooves in rock). Or, there is the story of Zhuangzi who dreams he is a butterfly but then wonders if he is not a butterfly dreaming of being Zhuangzi!

These snippets paraphrase ideas expressed in the *Laozi* (the *Lao Tzu*), in the *Zhuangzi* (the *Chuang Tzu*),[2] and elsewhere. Let us go beyond these snippets to our present specific interest in applying teachings from the large Daoist tradition to the issues of consciousness that are the focus of this chapter.

If our interest were in considering models of experienced states of consciousness from Daoism alongside those from a wide range of other psychospiritual traditions, to notice their similarities of interest here as well as possible differences in understanding, interpretation, and emphasis, we might begin with a broad overview of these traditions in comparison with one another.[3]

Here, though, our primary interest is in the relationship between Daoist and Buddhist teachings on consciousness and practices for overcoming torment. For this, we will be focusing more on the experiential and transformational—or, in another vocabulary, the *phenomenological* and *psychospiritual*—features of some Daoist concepts and some of their Buddhist correlates.

We will begin with a basic orientation, which will then be used to consider particular Daoist teachings, and the relationship between the ideas we will

---

[1] *Footnotes here are primarily for secondary consultation,* to cite sources of quotations, to offer further reading, and to give more precise information about the Chinese—in particular, showing the Chinese characters and transliteration, with tones, both pinyin (and in parentheses, Wade-Giles). Except for proper names, foreign terms will generally be italicized unless considered as incorporated into English.

[2] See above, p. 187, n. 12, and p. 190, n. 22.

[3] As was done, e.g., in M. Ginsberg, *The Inner Palace: Mirrors of Psychospirituality in Divine and Sacred Wisdom-Traditions*, esp. in its Chap. XIX: The Tao.

soon present and discuss, and Buddhist concepts and practice. One entrance into this rich domain is by considering some of the specific ideas and ideals, concepts, stories, images, metaphors, and paradoxes we find in the texts of Daoism, as teachings on consciousness, presented in the literature in a variety of ways.

There are descriptions and definitions of certain idealized individuals, and suggestions about their awareness, understanding, thinking, and ways of dealing with the world. There are stories and metaphors that hint at what is within our human potential, and images to give a concrete sense of what is beyond our ordinary awareness. There are paradoxes that leave us perplexed and perhaps curious about what they imply for us.

All of these offer us a fresh vision of life's options in a broad perspective. These teachings invite us to consider a number of unusual but intriguing topics, encouraging us to question our understanding of the mind, of knowledge, and of our potential as humans in the fullest (or highest) sense of that term.

The idea of an ideal

To consider a concept or idea as an ideal is to contemplate the particular value that it defines. By comparing ourselves with this ideal, we may become clearer about how close or distant to this ideal we are. There will almost always be a difference to be noticed between our ideal and how we actually are in our own eyes. How we experience and understand this comparison may have a powerful impact on how we feel about ourselves (or about others).

We may simply notice the difference. We may reassuringly conclude that we are in fact already wonderful human beings. We may be inspired to change in order to become closer to this ideal. We may judge ourselves as inferior, or failures, or simply bad, in relation to this ideal.

If we are inspired by the values that this ideal defines, we may come to appreciate the impact of this ideal, and the related transformation that we find, or hope to find, in our lives. Such a transformation can be very dynamic and satisfying, occurring in a systematically integrated and naturally evolving way.

The idea of an ideal in Daoism and in Buddhism

In both Daoism and in Buddhism, we read of certain idealized individuals: these provide us with descriptions of what we have as our human promise or potential, especially in terms of ways of experiencing and dealing with life's varieties of more-often-than-desired troublesome situations.

Beginning with the idea of the idealized individual will allow us to consider specific features of the possibilities of human consciousness as highlighted in Daoist texts where we find presentations of such idealized individuals.

In addition to the *sheng*, translated here as sage, there are several further concepts expressed in Chinese making use of the word *ren*—which means man, men, person, people (Chinese nouns being both singular and plural). These further names (keeping *ren* as "man" here) include the *sheng ren:* a man who is sagely; the *shen ren:* a man who is spiritual (or numinous, daemonic, holy, or saintly); the *zhen ren:* a true (or authentic) man; the *zhi ren:* a perfect (or realized) man; the *tian ren:* a heavenly man; the *dao ren:* a man of the Way (Dao), and so on.[4] How are these described in Daoist texts?

As the *Zhuangzi* puts it in one passage, describing three key concepts here, "Consequently, it is said: the perfect man (*zhi ren*) has no self (*ji*), the man of spirit (*shen ren*) has no achievements (*gong*), the man who is sagely (*sheng ren*) has no name-fame (*ming*)."[5]

Or, to put these values into other words, we may say that in becoming perfect or accomplished, we are attuned to the Dao, the Way, and are not operating from the mind that is concerned with self; that when we have become spiritual—as conceived of in the texts—we do not hold to a sense of accomplishment; and, when wise (as a sage), we have no concern with reputation or fame, and relatedly, as the *Zhuangzi* says in another passage, we are not bound by the viewpoint of all of those, the multitude, around us.[6]

Without going into an investigation of how these terms might be used differently in other Daoist texts, we can sense that here they are pointing us to the appreciation of individuals guided by the powers of a special awareness or consciousness, as in the paraphrased descriptions of features of consciousness.

What is perhaps clear, in the *Zhuangzi* above—however we might understand the differences between the sagely person, the perfect one, and the man of spirit—is that there is an admiring and a proposing as an ideal the having of no self, no achievements, and no name or fame.

This is information about how we might experience, think about, and deal with our situation and our sense of ourselves. For now, it is not information about how to cultivate these traits, or how to become one of these individuals.

We may compare the concept of the group here that includes the sage, the spiritual person, and the others, from the *Zhuangzi* just above, with the fami-

---

[4] P: *shèng* 聖 (WG: *shèng*), *shèng rén* 聖人 (WG: *shèng jén*), *shén rén* 神人 (WG: *shén jén*), *zhēn rén* 真人 or 眞人 (WG: *chēn jén*), *zhì rén* 至人 (WG: *chìh jén*), *tiān rén* 天人 (WG: *t'iēn jén*), *dào rén* 道人 (WG: *tào jén*) On the numinous, the divine, and the sacred, see M. Ginsberg, *The Inner Palace.*

[5] The Chinese text in *Zhuangzi* 2/1/21-22 (on this form of textual citation, see above, p. 190, n. 22) reads, in P: *gù yuē: zhì rén wú jǐ, shén rén wú gōng, shèng rén wú míng* 故曰: 至人無己, 神人無功, 聖人無名 (WG: *kù yüēh: chìh jén wú chǐ, shén jén wú kūng, shèng jén wú mìng*). The perfect man, *zhì rén* (see preceding note), is discussed at length in the *Zhuangzi*, Chap. 6; *tiān rén* and *dào rén* are also found in the *Zhuangzi*, in Chap. 12 (at 32/12/86,88).

[6] This further passage reads in the Chinese: *yǐ guān zhòng rén zhī ěr mù zāi* 以觀眾人之耳目哉 (*Zhuangzi* 18/6/70-71). Again, see above, p. 190, n. 22.

ly of noble persons that is defined in the Buddhist tradition. Thus, in Buddhism there is not only the ideal (or idea) of an awakened being (a buddha, taking this term literally), but also of a noble person.[7] A noble person is one *who has at least begun the transformation* referred to as crossing the stream (to the far shore,[8] to nirvana), and one who has begun this crossing is thus called a stream-entrant.[9] Not all noble ones are awakened, of course.

The minimal shifts in consciousness in this transformation for one to move from being what we may call a worldling (an ordinary human) to a noble individual, is the elimination of three features of consciousness. In Buddhism, these are called the first three fetters (*saṃyojana*), which are bindings to or connections with what are immediately or ultimately painful realities.

These three fetters are traditionally cited as personality belief, *sakkāya-diṭṭhi* (or self-illusion: a speculative view about an enduring individuality), skeptical doubt (or hesitant perplexity), *vicikicchā*, and clinging to mere rules and rituals (or seizing on practices and rituals), *sīlabbata-parāmāsa*.[10]

Paraphrasing, the elimination here is a matter of *becoming free* of (1) a distorted understanding of personal identity, of (2) crippling doubt and a refusal to investigate our reality, and of (3) an over-evaluation of the power of rites and rituals. The next two steps, incidentally, are our *becoming less controlled* by (4) desires for pleasurable sense experiences and sensuality and by (5) ill-will.

As noted just above, these parts may be the first steps but knowing this will not especially have us take these first steps, or even indicate to us how those first steps are to be taken. We have a significant part of the story, if we know all of these sorts of information, but this is just the start, not the story in its entirety.

Still, the first step here is to appreciate what the process is, and then to observe, and in particular, to notice what is true of us in relevant contexts, in other words, to notice where we ourselves are on the path being described to us.

So, without going into further details now about the psychospiritual transformations that are defined in Daoist and Buddhist discussions, the basic idea *for this context* is that we now have a glimpse of how we can experience and respond to our experiences other than in our usual, all-too-frequently not-en-

---

[7]   Glossing the terms *ārya pudgala* and *ariya puggala* in Sanskrit and Pāli, respectively. This is a matter of some interest and I have discussed such a gradual but nonetheless deeply transformative process elsewhere in much detail, as in Chap. 10, above, as well as in *The Inner Palace*.

[8]   Thus, the title of my book, *The Far Shore*.

[9]   In Sanskrit and Pāli, respectively: *srotāpanna* and *sotāpanna*. For more on stream-entrants, noble ones, and related concepts, see M. Ginsberg, *The Inner Palace*, esp. pp. 43, 403, 422, 454, 483-484, 486. These are related to the further concepts of the once-returner and non-returner.

[10] In Sanskrit: *satkāyadṛṣṭi, vicikitsā, śīlavrata-parāmarśa.*

tirely-happy ways. The practical value of considering these concepts or ideals is that we are presenting ourselves with a new understanding of life's options.

And what is next? What might the next steps be?

One quick path is to turn away from these considerations since they provide no clear instructions on how to get from here to there, so to speak, and certainly no cookbook recipe for this transformation. Without such information, we may feel like people invited to look at sumptuous meals being served at a fine restaurant but who are turned away like scrounging dogs, hungry and salivating.

An alternative is for us to persist a little before giving up and turning away. After all, if there is an appeal in the ideals we are learning about, at least in the way of our admiring them, why not stay with that appreciation for now?

Of course, the few phrases and basic ideas that have been offered in the preceding pages are surely not all there is to consider before drawing any significant conclusions. Perhaps we may take our initial enthusiasm (here and elsewhere) and have it guide us to seek further.

So, what are some of the other basic ideas in Daoism (and perhaps related ideas in Buddhism) that we might consider at this time in this context?

To return to the inspiration of the sage (and related idealizations), and to look further in Daoist teachings, there we find a brief expression that captures some of the importance of being a sage, as a next step forward here. Elsewhere in the *Zhuangzi* is a related teaching about being inwardly a sage, outwardly a king, *nei sheng wai wang*. This is seen as an illustration of being in the Dao, the Way; in the original, *nei sheng wai wang zhi dao*.[11] This points to the possibility of developing or recognizing a wisdom (the "inwardly a sage" part) that will be shown by actions arising out of this consciousness (the "outwardly a king" part).

This idea that our actions follow from our mind and our understanding is something that is similarly expressed in the Buddhist tradition, as in the opening to the collection of teachings in verse, the *Dhammapada*, that with poetic imagery speaks of the suffering or happiness following us unfailingly, depending on the state of the mind that guides us in doing what we do.[12]

Such considerations may point us in the most helpful general direction to focus on in our appreciating what is involved in the shift toward being sage-like or noble (in Daoist and Buddhist metaphors, respectively): inwardly.[13]

And what exactly is this "inwardly" part? There are of course many ways to describe this feature or set of features, but one way we find is when "one regulates the external from the core of his person," *yi zhong zhi wai*, as one Dao-

---

[11] P: *nèi shèng wài wáng zhī dào* 內聖外王之道 (WG: *nèi shèng wài wáng chīh tào*). At *Zhuangzi* 91/33/13-14 (p. 91, in Chap. 33, chapter lines 13-14; cf. above, p. 190, n. 22).

[12] *The Dhammapada*, verses 1-2.

[13] This is the orientation, as its title indicates, of M. Ginsberg, *The Inner Palace*.

ist text, the *Yuan Dao*[14] (late second century BCE), puts it.[15] Whatever this core of a person is, it is basic and fundamental, in some sense.

Another early text, the *Neiye* (late fourth century BCE), which is found as Chapter 49 of a collection called the *Guanzi*, describes this process as one of grasping within or inner grasping, *zhong de*,[16] a matter of not having external things disrupt the senses and not having the senses disrupt the mind.[17] Inner grasping involves being settled within, clear within, whatever is going on in our experience and in our life situation.

Here we may catch a glimpse of the states of mind that are being encouraged in these writings, and their link to the consciousness of the idealized individuals of the tradition: a consciousness that is very centered, one that can notice what is going on in the environment without having the senses become agitated, and one that has the heart (the *xin*, the heart-mind)[18] stable throughout.

This is a basic form of consciousness that is smooth and at peace, even in the midst of turbulence in the environment or in our sensory perceptions. It is a state of mind that has a center, or core, with a peaceful cohesion, a harmonious integrity about it. This allows the regulating what is outside of us, the external, from our center, our core, to echo the terms from the *Yuan Dao*, above.

This may sound appealing. If so, a question presents itself: *which paths actually lead us to such an integrated core?*

One description of this centered form of experienced reality is found in the *Zhuangzi*: "Where 'this' and 'that' cease to be opposites, there lies *the pivot of the Way*.[19] Only when the pivot is located in the center of the circle of things can we respond to their infinite transformations."[20] In other words, in such a

---

[14] The *Yuán Dào* is the first treatise in a collection, the *Huáinánzǐ*, which Lau and Ames, p. 3, date at about 139 BCE. P: *Yuán Dào* 原道 (WG: *Yüán Tào*), *Huáinánzǐ* 淮南子 (WG: *Huái-nán-tzǔ*).

[15] P: *yǐ zhōng zhì wài* 以中制外 (WG: *ǐ chūng chìh wài*). From Sect. 16, passage 160, at pp. 112-113 in D.C. Lau and R.T. Ames, *Yuan Dao*.

[16] This reflects contemporary Mandarin: P: *zhōng dé* 中得 (WG: *chūng té*).

[17] P: *Nèiyè* 內業 (WG: *Nèi-yèh*), *Guǎnzi* 管子 (WG: *Kuǎn Tzǔ*). Chinese and English, at H.D. Roth, *Original Tao*, pp. 68-69.

[18] P: *xīn* 心 (WG: *hsīn*). This concept is discussed in this chapter, in the Preface, and in Chaps. 10, 11, 14; see above, esp. p. i and notes 23-24 on p. 183.

[19] P: *bǐ shì mò dé qí ǒu wèi zhī dào shū* 彼是莫得其偶, 謂之道樞 (WG: *pǐ shìh mò té ch'ǐ ǒu wèi chīh tào shū*). At *Zhuangzi* 4/2/30-31 (cf. above, p. 190, n. 22).

[20] P: *shū shǐ dé qí huán zhōng yǐ yìng wú qióng* 樞始得其環中, 以應無窮 (WG: *shū shìh té ch'ǐ huán chūng ǐ yìng wú ch'iúng*). English of this full quotation in V. Mair, *Wandering on the Way: Early Taoist Tales and Parables of Chuang Tzu*, p. 15. Chinese text continuing here at *Zhuangzi* 4/2/31 (see preceding note).

place, or rather, in such a way of experience, there is no setting up of contrasting opposites. Here we are the center of a circle, to use one metaphor here, and so can respond fully to all, without moving.[21] This passage introduces, of course, the concept of the pivot of the Way, the *dao shu*, as in the title of this chapter.

To stay within the metaphor of the pivot or hub for a moment, we may think of an image in the *Daodejing*, Chapter 11: "Thirty spokes converge at a single hub (*gu*): it is the vacancy (*wu*) that begets the vehicle's usefulness."[22] So, to speak concretely, where there is nothing (*wu*), that empty space inside the hub (or nave) allows a place for the axle to fit and to operate.

Or, less concretely but more specifically, when we allow ourselves the space (the option) to appreciate the situation, from a variety of perspectives, in a centered, grounded way, we are beginning to be able to see clearly.

To continue following this metaphor or image closely for a moment, a vision from the center allows us to appreciate a wide range of features of the situation, not closing ourselves in with preconceptions or a very focused, limited interest in seeing only what we are specifically wanting to see (tunnel vision, an "agenda" or interest only in some given outcome). Here we can act in a way that is in touch with all features of the situation (idea of the pivot of the Way).

A start of wisdom is not having our understanding placed into some small, biased, preconceived set of ideas that allow no recognition of the niceties of the situation, of what is actually present and what is actually going on that is of importance; *wisdom involves some encompassing vision and an inclusive appreciation of reality*. This is a start; Daoist teachings say more, we will see here.

So, what is it to be beyond thinking in contrastive terms? Isn't our consciousness a matter of one thought after the other, and each one, a making of distinctions and contrasts? How would we go beyond that, except by becoming unconscious? This travel to the place or state of mind in which 'this' and 'that' have no opposites may seem a Herculean task, as when we are given the negative instruction, "Do NOT think about a pink elephant!"

Still, what seems very puzzling or difficult may be rather simple and easy, though, if approached with a different perspective. That is what I will continue with here, hopefully in a usable way.

One alternative to understanding is to stand in confused awe at what does not quite make sense and admire those who *can* understand. (This is an old way in some mystical teachings,[23] which were intentionally couched in less than transparent ways, given the danger in some societies of others becoming hostile when hearing of esoteric teachings without especially understanding them.)

---

[21] Cf. V.H. Mair, *Wandering on the Way*, p. 15.

[22] P: *wú* 無 (WG: *wú*); *gǔ* 穀 (WG: *kǔ*). M. Cheng, *Lao-tzu: "My Words Are Very Easy To Understand,"* Chap. 11, Chinese text at p. 50, English at p. 51.

[23] This was discussed in M. Ginsberg, *The Inner Palace*.

Here, again, we are considering the idea from the *Zhuangzi* about being at the pivot of the Way, where there are no contrasting opposites in our thinking, where particulars we are aware of are not considered to have opposites.

One context in which we are in a state of mind that does not see contrasts and opposites, or dualities—and does not create them, either—was identified by Derk Bodde in a discussion of the idealized personages of Daoism introduced above (the sage and relatives), when he proposed that we understand their names (*sheng, sheng ren,* etc.) as "designations for those who have reached the state of pure experience."[24] Pure here means not mixed with anything else at all (in the way we can talk of pure gold or pure silliness).

The "pure" experience Bodde is highlighting is one free of any intellectual knowledge, one that is intense in its experiencing the immediate sense impression of the moment. This "pure experience" is experience *not mixed in any way with our understanding or interpreting of those experiences,* through the intellectual mind. *This is consciousness without interpretation.*

To acknowledge that there might be such a thing as perception without interpretation (as Bodde offers above, following the philosopher and psychologist of religion and spirituality, William James[25]), we might begin by appreciating the distinction between the two (these being perception and interpretation).

Briefly, for example, hearing a bird chirping is an instance of auditory perception (of a sound); smelling the aroma of brewed coffee is an instance of olfactory perception (of a smell), and so forth. These are moments of sensorial perception, or of perception through the senses.

And these are different from our thinking about one topic or another, even if the topic is that of a bird chirping or of the smell of coffee. The general point here is that there is a difference between these two different happenings in consciousness (a moment of sense perception versus a moment of thinking).

For those with a mindfulness (or awareness) meditation practice of simply sitting (or standing) and paying attention to what there is to notice, there may be familiarity with the sheer intensity of sense perception on its own. We may also notice little children experiencing such intensity, and perhaps even joy or bliss, at least at certain moments (or, in other instances, intense discomfort).

There may also be a familiarity with the way in which our perceptions are quickly shifted into thoughts about whatever it is that we have just been experiencing, and almost as quickly, a shift into judgments, of liking or disliking, of approving or disapproving of something we are perceiving. These latter are, of course, all various functions of thinking, or cognition.

---

[24] Fung Yu-lan (Y.-L. Fung), *A History of Chinese Philosophy*, vol. 1, D. Bodde, tr., pp. 239, 243 (n. 2, Translator's Note, 1937).

[25] See esp. W. James, *The Varieties of Religious Experience* (based on lectures given in Edinburgh in 1901-1902).

In order to experience the difference between the two, it may help to slow down our activity, stilling for a moment our tendency to react to whatever it is that we are noticing in our perception. This has an immediate impact on our demeanor, in that we will tend to become less reactive. (Such an impact may be quite impressive, but it does not typically remain for very long![26])

If we are slowing down, so that what we are perceiving is allowed to be, we may appreciate the experience fully, before we begin a train of thought about what it amounts to, and even more so, before we begin to act on our thinking; here we are developing a more grounded way of being in our world.

This point was certainly not missed in many of the spiritual (or psycho-spiritual) traditions of the world, a topic of interest to some here, perhaps.[27]

If we experience what enters consciousness through any of the senses, and simply notice these moments arising and ending, one after the other, we may already have an experience of great clarity, simplicity, and ease, and perhaps even of peace, joy, and profound well-being. For some, this "pure" experience, as Bodde suggested just above, is being one with the universe.

Still, this is most likely not an ongoing experience for most of us.

And yet, even a glimpse gives us a sense of what is possible that we might otherwise not have imagined at all. So far, so good—so now, how can we get more than just a glimpse? Let us look further into this teaching.

What is being proposed is the idea of perceptual (or sense) experiences with no distinction-making interpretations coloring them. These are "pure" or complete moments of consciousness, described in one vocabulary as non-dual.

The term 'non-dual' has a few meanings. Here, what is non-dual is consciousness itself. This means that in the experience, there is no split within consciousness into self and non-self (no awareness of oneself versus others), no perceiver-perceived dichotomy (not someone noticing something).

Various traditions talk of non-dualistic consciousness with a special sense of wonder, suggesting the possibility of our having this unusual and yet simple form of perception ourselves.

Some conclude that dualistic consciousness is somehow intrinsically inferior, and that anyone with such experience is spiritually inferior because of that! But in Daoism, the world of dualities is viewed in a more subtle way.

One of the most basic distinctions in some Daoist texts speaks of the interplay between the parts of the whole of reality, especially between the opposing parts. In this process, a strong meeting or confrontation of these brings about

---

[26] The joy at such moments, a mere glimpse—in Japanese, *kenshō* 見性, Chinese, *jiàn-xìng*, literally, to see nature or essence—of enlightened consciousness (*satori* 悟), may be misidentified as definitively achieving this *satori*. On seeing our nature, and its also being called original face, cf. p. 207, n. 68.

[27] These topics are discussed at length in M. Ginsberg, *The Inner Palace.*

a harmonized totality, a synergistic integration of opposites (rather than a homogenized blend). In particular, *yin* and *yang*,[28] complementary opposites, interact in a continually balancing integration or synergy, a process of ongoingly creating harmony, *he*,[29] that represents the ideal manifestation of the way, *dao*. This state is represented by the well-known design or symbol ☯, called *Taiji*, the Great Ultimate, or *Taiping*, the Great Peace or Balance, or Celestial Peace.[30]

The *Daodejing* speaks of this dynamic balance as a vigorous process of vital energies, *qi*, that confront, *chong*, one another, bringing about continually refreshed harmony, *he*. The text reads: *chong qi yi wei he*.[31]

This is the ideal of integrating our most fundamental life energies as a path to a flowing harmony. This dynamic movement involves looking at process, in which each moment is seen within the larger transformations we are experiencing, rather than looking only at static states or goal-defined outcomes.

To contrast "the power of now" with the power of process, when we are completely in some quite miserable present, we are still not at all free of torment, and yet as movement, this torment becomes our next focus to address, as part of the ongoing changes in consciousness we experience in life. Let me illustrate the power of this concept of process by considering one relevant practice.

If we start with simply being miserable, as above, and focus attention on the experience and our resistance to it, this is a dualistic consciousness in a first sense. We now intensify the dualism by observing each thought and judgment that arises, creating a strong split between our noticing and what is noticed; this is a second sense of dualism. This doubly dualistic experience gives us distance from, and a perspective on, our own patterns of thinking and reacting.

This practice encourages our noticing these patterns with more familiarity and less agitation, allowing calm and clarity to develop ongoingly, returning us to a simplicity that is more compassionate and caring, less attacking and critical, while we remain quite aware of, and present to, what is going on for us.

A dualistic consciousness is thus seen as dynamically valuable in our coming to peace and harmony within ourselves, in both Buddhist and Daoist tra-

---

[28] P: *yīn* 陰 (WG: *yīn*), *yáng* 陽 (WG: *yáng*). Cf. below, p. 207, n. 68.

[29] See R.T. Ames and D.L. Hall, *Dao De Jing, A Philosophical Translation*, on *hé* 和 (WG: *hó*), pp. 61-62; on the interplay and potential harmonization between particular and context (or totality): "the focus and its field," pp. 11-54.

[30] P: *taìji* 太極 or 太极 (WG: *t'ai chí*), *taìping* 太平 (WG: *t'aì p'íng*).

[31] Cf. above, notes 26 and 28, and below, p. 207, n. 68. *Dàodéjīng*, Chap. 42. Chinese at J.C.H. Wu, *Lao Tzu / Tao Te Ching*, p. 60; the first character, *chōng* 沖, clash, dash against, pour over, rinse, blend, in some editions is 中 *zhōng*, center, to balance, focus, attain. P: *hé* 和 (WG: *hó*), *chōng* 沖 (WG: *ch'ūng*), *qì* 氣 (WG: *ch'ì*), *chōng qì yǐ wéi hé* 沖氣以為和 (WG: *ch'ūng ch'ì ǐ wéi hó*).

ditions. This harmony within ourselves is a way of thinking about personal integration, an important issue that I have addressed earlier in this book in a more
focused way.[32] Interestingly here, one scholar interprets in just this way, as a
personal integration, the *de* that is part of the title—spelled here to emphasize the
de part—the *Dao-de-jing* (or *De-dao-jing*, its alternative title[33]).[34]

What we do with that fresh and perhaps not-self-conflicted perception is
another story. We may just enjoy it, or may use it to feel spiritually superior (a
practice which Chögyam Trungpa called "spiritual materialism"[35]). We may use
its freshness to come to a deeper and more insightful appreciation of what we are
noticing. In particular, a potential benefit is that we are freed here from our
habitual understanding that is limited to our past experience and conditioning.

We can perhaps appreciate the double-edged sword that our intellect is,
in that it provides us with a sometimes exquisite and elegant appreciation of our
world that we could not otherwise attain, and yet at times offers us interpretations of our world from our past, defining what we can expect from others, from
ourselves, from situations, and so on.

In such cases, we may sense that we are confined by our ideas of how
things simply must be (in some sense of "must" or another)! With this perspective, we can appreciate the emphasis in a number of world teaching traditions
encouraging us not to be limited, even if our understanding is.[36]

This appreciation can free us from a blind reactivity to what we are experiencing, a freedom to let the situation show itself to us before we come to any
conclusive sense of its features. This means that we give ourselves the time and
attentiveness to the situation to appreciate it fully, to come to understand it more
deeply than when we relied only on our reactive thinking.

The idea in Zen of being without mind is a specific idea, amounting to
being free of our narrow, conditioned mind with its limited understanding. Relatedly in Daoism, with this conditioned mind as our usual mind, it can be said that
sages are constantly free of an ordinary or usual mind; they are not limited by
what has been claimed to be so, and has been accepted by others because they
have heard these claims so often for so long.

---

[32] See Chaps. 3, 5, and 6, above.

[33] Cf. above, p. 188, n. 16.

[34] V. Mair, *Tao Te Ching*, esp. p. xix: "I spent two full months ... to arrive at a
satisfactory translation of *te* [pinyin: *dé* 德]... based on a thorough etymological
study of the word, together with a careful consideration of each of its forty-four
occurrences in the text ... 'integrity' is the only word that seems plausible
throughout. By 'integrity,' I mean the totality of an individual including his or
her moral stance, whether good or bad."

[35] C. Trungpa, *Cutting Through Spiritual Materialism*.

[36] This is the focus of many discussions in M. Ginsberg, *The Inner Palace*.

In this process, we are coming to realizations that are beyond our conditioned mind, beyond the beliefs we have come to hold dear, beyond our intellect. In this context, the alternative is a different kind of awareness or mind that presumably is in some important ways wiser, fresher, and more perceptive than is our ordinary, limited consciousness.

If we can get beyond this limited awareness and understanding, we may have access to another kind of *shen* (spirit) that we find recognized and discussed in some Daoist texts. This wise spirit (*shen*) is called Primal or Original Spirit, *yuan shen*, in contrast with the rational mind, called Conscious Spirit or Recognition Spirit, *shi shen*.[37] Thomas Cleary writes of these, "The distinction between the original spirit and the conscious spirit is one of the most important ideas in Taoist psychology."[38]

The contrast between these two has been presented using the traditional Chinese respect for what is ancient (even to the China of Confucius), in speaking of Earlier Heaven (*xian tian*) and Later Heaven (*hou tian*).[39] Parallel to this is a contrast between a simpler spirit, earlier in that it involves no distinctions in consciousness, and a more complex spirit that builds on distinctions based on our particular life experiences, creating our practical understanding of life.

So, there is a mind built upon our experience and beliefs and there is another form of mind that is beyond such limitations. In gaining access to this second, called here original spirit, we would come to the wisdom and awareness of a sage. The idea behind the image of the sage is that it is possible to act in ways not derived from our personal, conditioned, knowledge, but with an understanding in harmony with the wisdom of the dao.

This distinction highlights the possibility of a deeper appreciation and comprehension of our world. This is discussed in a variety of vocabularies and contexts within the Daoist tradition.

For example, in Chapter 49 of the *Daodejing*, we find: *sheng ren heng wu xin*, the sage constantly has no fixed mind.[40] Or, in a variant reading of that same passage, *sheng ren wu chang xin*, the Sage is without a set mind.[41]

This means that there is a readiness to consider what is outside of our usual personal understanding in order to take into account whatever we are capa-

---

[37] P: *yuán shén* 元神 (WG: *yüán shén*).

[38] T. Cleary, *The Taoist Classics*, vol. 3, p. 325, n. 1; cf. pp. 365-375.

[39] P: *xiān tiān* 先天 (WG: *hsiēn t'iēn*), *hòu tiān* 後天 (WG: *hòu t'iēn*).

[40] R.G. Henricks, *Lao-tzu: Te-Tao Ching*, pp. 125-126. This passage as quoted follows the Mǎwángduī (or Mǎ-wáng-tuī) texts. P: *shèng rén héng wú xīn* 聖人恒无心 (WG: *shèng jén héng wú hsīn*).

[41] M. Cheng, *Lao-tzu: "My Words Are Very Easy To Understand,"* pp. 160-161. P: *shèng rén wú cháng xīn* 聖人無常心 (WG: *shèng jén wú ch'áng hsīn*).

ble of noticing *beyond* this mind-set, both in terms of our own fuller perception and the perspectives we can gather by noticing others and by interacting with them. In other words, we are not relying on our background assumptions and other conclusions drawn from our past experience to give us the full story of what is going on now. This idea is expressed in the paradoxical expression in some Daoist texts as knowing without knowing.

As with paradoxical statements in general, which seem self-contradictory or otherwise incomprehensible, often they are a way of stimulating our minds into reconsidering some stale ideas, implicitly suggesting how to revise our understanding of certain key terms.

We find such suggestions for redefinition, called persuasive definitions in philosophical circles,[42] in a wide range of contexts, such as in the Buddhist tradition, with its persuasive redefinition of what a Brahman is, in the chapter by that name in the Buddhist text, the *Dhammapada*, where a Brahman is not someone born of Brahman parents, but someone who is beyond attachment, who is free of anger, and who comes to know the end of sorrow.[43]

In several Daoist texts spreading over several centuries beginning with the *Xisheng Jing* (*The Scripture of Western Ascension*),[44] from the fifth century CE,[45] we read, to be able to know something without knowledge is the pivot of the Tao.[46] The Chinese reads: *Neng zhi wu zhi dao zhi shu ji.*[47]

This is possible, if this perspective has validity, since by coming to the pivot of the Dao, by coming to the state of mind that does not make comparisons, by experiencing each moment with a great intensity, we may be open to the full freshness of the moment, with a deep presence of mind. Here, the paradoxical statement about knowledge without knowledge is meant in part to offer a persuasive redefinition of the concept of knowledge. Chinese philosopher and

---

[42] C.L. Stevenson, "Persuasive Definitions," *Mind*, New Series, vol. 47, no. 187 (July 1938), esp. pp. 331, 336-337, 349.

[43] See the *Dhammapada*, esp. verses 393, 396-397, 400, 402.

[44] P: *Xīshēng Jīng* 西昇經 (WG: *Hsīshēng Chīng*). There are also the *Wushang biyao*, from the sixth century CE, and the *Daode zhenjing guangsheng yi* by Du Guangting, from the ninth century CE. See L. Kohn, *Taoist Mystical Philosophy*, pp. 259, 269, on the *Wúshàng bìyào* 無上祕要 and the *Dàodé zhēnjīng guǎng-shèng yì* 道德真經廣聖義 (by Dù Guāngtíng 杜光庭).

[45] Foreword by Donald Munro to L. Kohn, *Taoist Mystical Philosophy*, p. ix.

[46] L. Kohn, idem. For the *Xīshēng Jīng* 西昇經, 13.10 (Chap. 13, Passage 10): Chinese at pp. 323, 329; English at p. 244; cf. this same statement (English), at p. 259, in the *Wúshàng bìyào* 無上祕要, 65.11a.

[47] P: *néng zhī wú zhì dào zhī shū jī* 能知無知道之樞機 (WG: *néng chīh wú chìh tào chīh shū chī*).

historian Fung Yu-lan suggested that there is a second "higher kind of knowledge" and that this is "knowledge which is not knowledge."[48] This is most definitely not the mundane opinionatedness that usually passes for knowledge!

These various concepts can be understood to be one way to conceptualize or to think about the difference between our usual understanding—as our rational mind—and a more subtle, more attuned consciousness, as a different kind of mind or spirit.

Whether we see this distinction as arising through time or simply as a distinction to make use of at any given moment, we are talking here of a more subtle wisdom that goes beyond knowledge. *This wisdom is a manifestation of the liberating power of the consciousness that is beyond the conditioned mind.*

This is the vision, perception, and understanding, of what in Buddhism is called the unconditioned (or "unborn") consciousness of the arahat or Buddha; again, expressed in Daoist terms, it is called original spirit, *yuan shen*, in contrast with recognition spirit, *shi shen*.

The implication that we can be freed from our past understanding—one that we may very well feel to be a constraint on our mind and experience—is a special invitation to our looking reality in the eye, with a freshness that is quite alive, deeply aware, and wonderfully invigorating.

In this context, as A.C. Graham put it, the "spontaneity of Taoism and its successor Zen is not a disruption of self-control, but an unthinking control won, like the skill of an angler or charioteer, by a long discipline."[49] *This is an "unthinking" control that is not at all absent-minded, unconscious, or passive!*

This "unthinking" control is acting from the axis of the Dao, the *dao shu. This is being aware—from a central position—of the processes and flow of the moment, responding with the deeply awakened consciousness of a sage to all of the major features of the situation with relevance and appropriateness, while not being frozen or rigidified by earlier doctrines or beliefs that make for a more selective (and distorting) bias or perspective on the situation.*

It is, then, in understanding the significance of the image of the pivot of the dao in this way that we may consider passages that speak of operating from no knowledge, from non-knowing.[50]

If in this light we consider one who is attuned to the dao, a saint as some call such a person, this awareness is not limited to that of a conditioned mind, even if an intelligent one, but is a consciousness not limited or defined by the

---

[48] In Chap. X (Chuang Tzu) of *A Shorter History of Chinese Philosophy*, D. Bodde, ed., at pp. 113-114; this work is also in *Selected Philosophical Writings of Fung Yu-lan*, where the same passage is found at p. 318.

[49] A.C. Graham, tr., *The Book of Lieh-tzǔ*, p. 9.

[50] A number of such concepts are discussed in R.T. Ames and D.L. Hall, *Dao De Jing*, pp. 40-48, 67-68.

concepts, contrasts, and dualities that we have previously come to use to make sense of whatever we are experiencing.

The underlying ability here, to respond with awareness, is grounded and oriented in alertness to the particulars of the situation, in part in a pre-verbal appreciation of a situation—it is a question of our sense of the situation rather than of our making moral judgments. As Bryan Van Norden wrote, "the highest sage does *not* make evaluative judgments at all."[51]

This reference to a consciousness that does not involve intellect, judgments, considered evaluations, and so forth, is not an excuse for taking random opinions as absolute undebatable truths in a kind of blind dogmatism, and is most especially not an excuse for non-debatable ethical declarations, and not a form of ethical intuitionism implying an infallibility of one's moral judgments.

It is, rather, quite importantly, a way of becoming aware of and responding to our real-life situation that takes into account what is there to be noticed in the situation. Rather than being a blind and rigid dogmatism, it is elegantly available to everything that is going on, because it is not constrained by our beliefs and hopes and prejudices about what should be the case.

It is in these ways an awareness grounded in the full reality that we are facing—or at least in a much fuller appreciation of that reality; it is an awareness that leads to action not by rigidly following some predefined and predetermined rule or idea of action, or by attempting to coerce reality, but by dealing with it openly, fully, harmoniously, and effectively, with deeply grounded stability.

This is our aligning with the way of the Dao, which has us child-like, spontaneously free from the constraints of conditioned experience and its reactive tendencies that Zhuangzi alludes to here; in Buddhist terms, this being beyond conditioned mind is named No Mind (discussed in *The Inner Palace*[52]).

How we come to this stability (termed in some Indic texts as the unshakable consciousness) is a question we have discussed in other contexts, in terms of practices that establish grounded, stable states of mind; in general, these are focusing and calming practices that bring our mind into one-pointedness, to use one common description of this state of mind.[53]

This difference between acting in rather comprehensive harmony with, and appreciation of, the situation is contrasted in some Daoist writings with actions dictated by some pre-judged idea about what should be and what is.

This is the distinction expressed in a contrast between *yin* and *wei*. The *yin* here means: a reason, because, therefore, for this reason, on the basis of, in

---

[51] B.W. Van Norden, "Competing Interpretations of the Inner Chapters of the *Zhuangzi*," *Philosophy East and West*, vol. 46, no. 2 (Apr. 1996), p. 259.

[52] See *The Inner Palace* (esp. Chaps. XV and XVI, pp. 123-173).

[53] As, for example, above, Chap. 10, on grounding in mindfulness practice; cf. *Bhagavadgītā (or Bhagavad Gītā)* II.70.

the light of, etc., [54] while its contrast, *wei*, means: to do, act, be, signify. This is the *wei*, we might point out, of terms for action and non-action.

With these two words explained here, we may render the statement "*yin er bu wei*" partly in English, with the two key terms remaining in Chinese, as "*yin is not wei*."[55] Incidentally, this is not the *yin* of *yin-and-yang*.[56] To render this now totally in English, "responsiveness or adaptation[57] is not acting."[58]

Obviously this is a special sense of the idea of action. Here we have the context of the idea of *wu wei* ("non-doing")[59] that is made rather explicit.

This we see with the concept of *wu wei*, which is usually rendered as non-action. Alternatively, the idea is referred to by the phrase *wei wu wei* (the action of non-action, or the doing of non-doing).[60]

The question arises of what this non-action is. At times, it implies being loose, relaxed, not fighting things, as in the Taiji[61] concept of *song*,[62] understood as a relaxing even of the sinews attaching muscle to bone, and refraining from acting blindly out of an urge to alleviate a sense of confusion or frustration. This non-doing avoids making things worse or more complicated and difficult to resolve. This is presumably important even if there is more being suggested in the idea than this simple and direct interpretation and application.

Whatever it is, the idea of *wu wei* is not a matter of becoming catatonic or being rigidly immobile in body and mind. We might say, as a first approximation, that *wu wei* is a refraining from action or effort. What it is precisely remains to be explicated. We have still to explain what a "Daoist" wisdom is, or what the relationship is between it and the idea of *wu wei*, above. Our questions

---

[54] P: *yīn* 因 (WG: *yīn*).

[55] P: *yīn ér bù wéi* 因而不爲 (WG: *yīn érh pù wéi*).

[56] P: *yīn* 陰 (WG: *yīn*), *yáng* 陽 (WG: *yáng*).

[57] H.D. Roth, "Redaction Criticism and the Early History of Taoism," *Early China*, vol. 19 (1994), p. 6, and *Original Tao*, p. 28.

[58] The *Lǚ shì chūn qiū* 呂氏春秋 (239 BCE), *The Spring and Autumn of Master Lü* or *The Annals of Lü Buwei*, Book 17, Chap. 5. P: *Lǚ shì chūn qiū* 呂氏春秋 (WG: *Lǚ shìh ch'ūn ch'iū*); *yīn ér bù wéi* 因而不爲 (*yīn érh pù wéi*); *Lü Bùwéi* 呂不韋 (WG: *Lü Pùwéi*); *chūn qiū* 春秋 (WG: ch'ūn ch'iū): spring and autumn, year, years, annals.

[59] P: *wú wéi* 無爲 (WG: *wú wéi*). Cf. next note.

[60] P: *wéi wú wéi* 爲無爲 (WG: *wéi wú wéi*). Cf. preceding note.

[61] P: *tàijí* (WG: *t'ài-chí*); the full name is (in pinyin) *taìjíquán* 太極拳 (WG: *t'ài-chí ch'üán*).

[62] P: *sōng* 松 or 鬆 (WG: *sūng*). See esp. M. Cheng and R.W. Smith, *T'ai-chi: The "Supreme Ultimate" Exercise for Health, Sport, and Self-Defense*, p. 99.

are: what is this special wisdom, how does it relate to the concept of *wu wei*, and what does all of this tell us about our own states of consciousness, awareness, and self-transformation toward greater calm, clarity, and awakened kindness?

Let us look here into the idea of *wu wei, bu wei*[63] (as the *Daodejing* puts it in its Chapter 48, *wu wei er wu bu wei*[64]). Henricks glosses this, "They do nothing and yet there's nothing left undone."[65] There is an elegant efficiency and efficacy about this non-action! And in the *Zhuangzi*, we find *wu wei* in "I take inaction to be true happiness"[66] (*wu yi wu wei cheng li yi*).[67]

This "inaction" (*wu wei*) is a matter of not (*wu*) acting (*wei*), or, more specifically, of refraining from acting coercively, from trying to force things on a situation in ways that do not quite fit, that are not in total harmony with it. Non-doing is acting non-coercively.

This is going beyond our conditioned preferences, a returning to our mind before it took on various agendas or demands on reality. This brings us back to the idea of original spirit, *yuan shen*, discussed earlier in the chapter.[68] This non-action (*wu wei*) is a return to *wu* (nothing).

This inner-focused returning to nothing may remind us of the idea in Chinese Buddhism[69] of original (or fundamental) face, as in the story of the Sixth Chinese Chan (Zen) Patriarch, Huineng (638-713 CE), perhaps first found in a text dating back to 1153 CE.[70] He enlightens the former military general, Hui-ming,[71] with the instruction: "Not thinking of good, not thinking of evil, just at this moment, what is your original face before your mother and father were born?"[72]—or, "at that moment, what is your fundamental face?"[73]

---

[63] P: *wú wéi, bù wéi* 無爲, 不爲 (WG: *wú wéi, pù wéi*). Cf. p. 208.

[64] P: *wú wéi ér wú bù wéi* 無爲而無不爲 (WG: *wú wéi érh wú pù wéi*).

[65] R.G. Henricks, *Lao-tzu: Te-Tao Ching*, Chap. 48, p. 123; cf. p. 270.

[66] B. Watson, *The Complete Works of Chuang Tzu*, p. 191 (from Chap. 18).

[67] P: *wú yǐ wú wéi chéng lè yǐ* 吾以无爲誠樂矣 (WG: *wú ǐ wú wéi ch'éng lè ǐ*). At *Zhuangzi* 46/18/11; wú 无 and wú 無 both mean "not" or "without."

[68] Being beyond the duality of yin and yang allows seeing xìng 性, nature or essence—this is called original face: see *The Secret of the Golden Flower*, in T. Cleary, *The Taoist Classics*, vol. 3, p. 281, p. 325, n. 3; cf. above, p. 199, n. 26.

[69] A.C. Graham, tr., *The Book of Lieh-tzǔ*, pp. 8-10, and Preface to its Morningside Edition (Columbia Univ. Press), pp. xii-xiii.

[70] P: Huì-néng 慧能 (WG: Huì-neng). On this late dating of the story, see P.B. Yampolsky, *The Platform Sutra of the Sixth Patriarch*, pp. xi, 26, 60, 90, 99.

[71] P: Huì-míng 慧明 (WG: Huì-míng).

[72] P.B. Yampolsky, idem (at n. 70, just above), pp. 73, 110.

[73] The rendering "fundamental face" is found in the translation by Lu K'uan Yü (C. Luk), *Ch'an and Zen Teaching*, vol. 3, p. 27.

We find this same story in Japanese literature, where this key question has been rendered, "When you do not think good and when you do not think not-good, what is your true self?" (true self: *honrai menmoku*[74]).[75]

This fundamental face or true face—both renderings of *benlai mianmu* 本來面目 original or natural face, etc.[76]—is a state of consciousness that is phenomenological (experiential), pre-verbal (before this experience is described in words and concepts), and elusive. It is not one's conditioned mind with its verbal understanding, not conscious spirit or recognition spirit, *shi shen*.

This is not a dogmatic frame of mind (*bu wei*, above, p. 207), but one open to noticing even what is quite unexpected and unpleasant, without expectations or hopes interfering with perception and awareness. This is the responsiveness or adaptation we discussed when introducing the term *yin* (above, p. 205).

It is, furthermore, as has been pointed out in various contexts here and elsewhere, *a state of consciousness that has the potential of great transformation*, especially and most specifically, the transformation known as awakening (coming to *bodhi*, to awakening, or enlightenment, as the Buddhist idea is alternatively rendered into English). This is a much more dynamic and vibrant sense of what our "nature" is than we might otherwise suspect.

This awareness allows for a flexibility and adaptability that in Daoist writings is referred to as *ruo*.[77] This term is generally considered to mean weak or yielding; in Daoism, it is a virtue, not a deficiency.

As one statement in the *Daodejing* remarks, *rou ruo sheng gang qiang*,[78] rendered into English as "The soft (or submissive) and weak vanquish (or overcome) the hard and strong."[79]

---

[74]   Or *honrai memboku*, same characters and meaning as Chinese *běnlái miànmù* 本來面目. The concept is discussed above, p. 207. Cf. below, note 76.

[75]   P. Reps, *Zen Flesh, Zen Bones: A Collection of Zen and Pre-Zen Writings*. Quote from Story 23 (pp. 108-109); from *The Gateless Gate* by Ekai, called Mumon; dated as 1228 CE (p. xiii); the *Wúménguān* 無門關, Japanese, *Mumonkan* (p. 87). Ekai is the Japanese of Huìkāi 慧開, died 1260 CE. His full name was Wúmén Huìkāi 無門慧開 (Japanese, Mumon Ekai). See *Japanese-English Buddhist Dictionary, Revised Edition*, pp. 57, 226. Cf. below, p. 216, n. 3.

[76]   P: *běnlái miànmù* 本來面目 (WG: *pĕn lái miènmù*). This "face" (Japanese, *menboku* or *memmoku*) is also the term for honor, prestige (as in "losing face"). See J. Halpern, ed., *New Japanese-English Character Dictionary*, at char. 2087 (1b), p. 940, and char. 3043 (6), p. 1390. Cf. above, note 74; below, p. 241.

[77]   P: *ruò* 弱 (WG: jò).

[78]   P: *róu ruò shèng gāng qiáng* 柔弱勝剛強 (WG: *jóu jò shèng kāng ch'iáng*).

[79]   Compare the glosses from the *Daodejing*, Chap. 36, in R.T. Ames and D.L. Hall, *Dao De Jing*, p. 133, R.G. Henricks, *Lao-tzu: Te-Tao Ching*, p. 91, J.C.H.

The similarity is striking between this Daoist perspective and Buddhist mindfulness practice, even if the descriptions used in each tradition are rather different from one another—both in terms of the grounded presence and open awareness that are encouraged, and also in the value given to the cultivation of a consciousness not directed by our past conditioning and the reactivity that follows that conditioning.

We may compare the Chinese concept of *wu wei* here and that of acting without creating, or, in Buddhist terms, acting without creating any more karmic processes (arising out of confused and limited awareness). Interestingly and relatedly, Wing-tsit Chan writes that "*wu-wei* is not simply 'inaction' but 'taking no unnatural action,' or in Buddhist usage, 'not produced from cause.'"[80]

This presumably makes sense here on its own and especially in the context of the discussions earlier in this chapter, and brings into parallel some of the Daoist and Buddhist understanding of this domain of consciousness.

Daoist and Buddhist visions have overlapping features, some of which we have noted above. For example, the gentle accepting of consciousness, with an eye to guiding it from wisdom, can be found in such contemporary teachers as Dhiravamsa (also known by his title and name when Abbot of the Thai Buddhist Mission to Great Britain, as Chao Khun Sobhana Dhammasudhi), who has encouraged *the gentle acceptance of all states of consciousness*, not trying to fight with our inner reality but to appreciate it in its fullness.[81] Jiddu Krishnamurti, from a related Indic-based tradition, made a similar point.

Parallel to this honoring of the soft, malleable mind in Buddhist meditation is the Daoist teaching—captured in the modern proverb, "Mind like parachute, only function when open" (from the film *Charlie Chan at the Circus*, 1936)—of the power of keeping the mind open and relaxed (*xu*),[82] and the Daoist ideas discussed above of *being like soft water that does not resist but triumphs through its adaptability*, of *ruo*, and of *wu wei*. Understood this way, the Buddhist mindfulness practice we have described can be appreciated as a "soft" vipassanā (insight) meditation, a Daoist-like mindfulness.

Wu, *Lao Tzu / Tao Te Ching*, pp. 52-53, D.C. Lau, *Lao Tzu Tao Te Ching*, p. 95.

[80] *A Sourcebook in Chinese Philosophy*, p. 791; italics in original. On "naiṣkarmya" (literally, abstention from action/karma, inactivity), cf. *Bhagavadgītā*, XVIII.49 (Chap. XVIII, verse 49); on acting non-coercively, cf. R.T. Ames and D.L. Hall, *Dao De Jing*, Chap. 48, p. 151.

[81] On open mindfulness, fresh mind, and beginner's mind, cf. above, p. 169 (including its n. 3). On the soft, malleable, and open mind, see above.

[82] See *Daodejing*, Chap. 3, in M. Cheng, *Lao-tzu: "My Words Are Very Easy To Understand*," pp. 28, 31. P: *xū* 虛 (WG: *hsū*), empty, open, relaxed; compare the expression "*xū huái ruò gǔ*" 虛懷若谷 (WG: *hsū huái jò kǔ*), "receptive as an echoing canyon" (modest and open-minded, a mind open to learning).

With these teachings and metaphors guiding us, we may recognize that even if these visions are radically different from our usual understanding of the mind, and even if they are suggestive of the capacity of the human to undergo vast transformations to a consciousness of great understanding and appreciation of each context of life that is even hard to imagine, the actual processes involved may have a subtlety and naturalness to them that is also hard to imagine.

In a Buddhist metaphor, it may be as subtle as the clouds easily moving away from blocking the sun's light, having us basking comfortably in the clear light of deep perception and understanding of an open heart-mind (*xin*[83]).[84]

Additional Readings on Daoism and Chinese Thought

The interested reader is referred here to the bibliography at the end of this book, where texts listed under the following authors—*or titles*—will be of relevance to topics addressed in this chapter. In these listings, family names are given in SMALL CAPS. Chinese names, normally cited in traditional form with family name first, do not appear with a comma after the family name (as FUNG Yu-lan), unless westernized (as CHAN, Wing-tsit). Some authors cited here appear in the bibliography as the first author of jointly-written texts:

AMES, Robert T.; BLOOM, Irene; BODDE, Derk; CHAN, Alan K.L.; CHAN, Wing-tsit; CHAO, Yuen Ren; CHENG Man-ch'ing; CHONG, Kim-chong; CLEARY, Thomas; COOK, Scott; CSIKSZENTMIHALYI, Mark; DEFRANCIS, John; DE REU, Wim; DUYVENDAK, Jan Julius Lodewijk; FENG, Gia-fu; FOX, Alan; FUNG Yu-lan; GRAHAM, Angus; HANSEN, Chad; HENRICKS, Robert; HUEBNER, Jon; IVANHOE, Philip; KJELLBERG, Paul; KNOBLOCK, John; KOHN, Livia; KOMJATHY, Louis; LAU, Dim Cheuk; LEE, Jung H.; LEGGE, James; LI Yangzheng; LIN, Shuen-fu; LOY, David; LU, David C.; LU K'uan Yü (Charles LUK); LUSTHAUS, Dan; MAIR, Victor H.; MITCHELL, Stephen; MORAN, Patrick Edwin; MUNRO, Donald J.; NORMAN, Jerry; PALMER, Martin; PULLEYBLANK, Edwin G.; RAPHALS, Lisa; RED PINE; ROBINET, Isabelle; ROSEMONT, Henry, Jr.; ROTH, Harold D.; SHEN, Helen H., SIMONIS, Fabien; SLINGERLAND, Edward; STIMSON, Hugh M.; TORCHINOV, Yevgeny; VAN NORDEN, Bryan W.; WATSON, Burton; WU, John Ching-hsiung; WU, Kuang-ming; YU, David C.; ZHAO Bichen; ZHU, Rui; ZHUANGZI; *Zhuāngzǐ yǐn dé*; *Zhuāngzǐ zhú zì suǒ yǐn*.

---

[83] This metaphor was discussed in M. Ginsberg, *The Inner Palace*, pp. 222, 228, 262, 317-318, 503, 590. For more on the heart-mind (*xīn* 心), see above, p. 196, n. 18, and references there to further discussions in this and other works.
[84] My thanks to a number of scholars and acutely attentive readers of earlier drafts of this chapter for their perspectives and recommendations, taken to heart even if not always fully adopted in this text. I have thanked these individuals more explicitly and at greater length in the Acknowledgments Page of this book.

13. The Second Transformation: Our Third Nature & Recalibration[1]

We are born with various human characteristics, such as our basic form of body (being a particular variation of mammalian primates), our requiring a long period of being cared for (unlike some species where the new-born is fully functioning), our ability to learn and to use language, and on and on. We might call all of these our *first* nature. These are characteristics that we share with all others of our species, the human race. We may refer to this *first* nature as *our nature*, as in saying, for example, "It is *our nature* to need oxygen."

Furthermore, the very particular circumstances of our individual lives have left their impact on us, on what we enjoy, avoid, what makes us relaxed or nervous, and so on. This is our conditioning, with its individual patterns of how we deal with old *and* new situations. These patterns we call our *second* nature.

This second nature is a combination of rather basic repetitive actions (including habits), such as our ability to write without thinking about each step of the process, and other actions that we take "automatically" with no thinking involved. Our second nature is also shown in some rather deeply entrenched patterns of thinking and acting. If we were made to feel ashamed at a part of our body (our feet, our hips, our nose, etc.), or at our way of responding to certain situations (crying at the sight of someone in pain, laughing at someone else's misery, etc.), we have here examples of what seems quite natural to us, but *which have been learned, often through much anguish or pain.*

Our own, individual second nature may be quite different from the second nature of others in our species, and in this way, there is a basic distinction between first and second natures. This transformation from a baby with basic human anatomy, biology, organic needs, and so forth, into a person with a specific history of conditioning, is *the first major transformation.* In this, we go from human nature (what we have in common with all other people) to the conditioned style of thinking and acting in our own particular lives.

Our learned habits, tastes, beliefs, hesitations, fears, and urges to react in specific ways to given situations (our second nature) direct us to think, feel, and act in ways that seem to be quite natural. This suggests that if we let things run their "natural" course, our second nature (our conditioning) will be defining the ways in which we deal with our life and the situations we are faced with. As we realize, we may not always be happy with how we handle ourselves in this "natural" or "second nature" way.

There *are* other options. When we are no longer constrained or determined by our *second* nature, we go beyond the reactivities we have come to see over and over again in the course of our life. That is, beyond our reactivity (or second nature) there is a much more open and relaxed experience for us. This is

---

[1] In this chapter, I italicize foreign words only as is done for English words.

an experience of being in the current situation with an ability to reflect, consider, and respond in ways that are fully appropriate to this situation as it is. In this, we have a sense of a great freedom of spirit, sometimes described in various psychotherapeutic and psychospiritual (psychologically spiritual) teachings.

We may speak of this usual state of affairs—where our entire being is defined by our first and second natures taken together—as the "mundane" world. This invites a contrast with the "supra-mundane" world, a way of dealing with life that is beyond, or an improvement on, the mundane world. Or we can talk of going beyond or transcending this world and its limitations, and so talk of the "transcendent" world.[2] There is a variety of terminology available here.

In all cases, this involves a shift that is the second major transformation we humans are capable of. This does not mean going to another world or denying this world in any way. It is a matter of attitude (a change of consciousness, not of the "external" world, the world around us).[3]

This transformation—which can be described as involving the complete evolution of consciousness,[4] to underscore the powerful nature of this process of shifting beyond *second* nature—brings us to what I call our *third* nature.

Our third nature involves our ability to refrain from being controlled by our second nature. This does not require the annihilation of our second nature,[5] but is more a matter of bringing it under control, so that *it* does not drive *us* (either blindly or irresistibly).

---

[2] In Buddhism, there is the mundane (lokiya) world and the supra-mundane (lokuttara) or transcendent world. More on this distinction in *The Inner Palace.*

[3] This answers the question posed by Robert C. Solomon in his Foreword to my book, *The Inner Palace*, at p. iv. Bob wrote, "Perhaps Mitchell and I disagree on the meaning of 'transcendental.' For me it does not refer to any other realm or world but to a richer conception and *per*ception [the first syllable here, *per*-, is intentionally italicized, following Bob's orthography in his Foreword] of this one. I think that this is what he means by 'experience,' and if so the difference may be one of semantics rather than metaphysics..." Quite so: Bob and I were in agreement, and he correctly understood 'experience' as I used the term.

[4] The entire book, *The Inner Palace*, addresses the teachings of a variety of world spiritual traditions that investigate, describe, and explain the ways in which the individual can come to this sort of transcendent consciousness.

The smaller book, *The Far Shore*, was described by V.R. Dhiravamsa, International Vipassanā Meditation Master, and former Chao Khun (Abbot) of the Thai Buddhist Mission to Great Britain, as "a precise, simple and clear practical book on the development of non-judgmental, choiceless and insightful awareness which leads to the *complete evolution of consciousness.*" (Italics added; quotation from the back cover of the book in its Indian editions.)

[5] This was discussed in "Making War on Ego" (in *The Far Shore*, pp. 31-32).

One important part of our second nature is our sense of how others treat us and how we are to treat others. Our experience teaches us about our interactions with others, the workings of our interpersonal or social world.

A central issue here is what is acceptable behavior from others and toward others, and what is intolerable, not to be tolerated. What is clear is that people disagree about what counts as unacceptable behavior from others.

An example might make this clearer: John is being insulted and spoken to in very denigrating, critical terms by Jim while at a dinner in a restaurant with friends Mary, Harry, Beatrice, and Felix. John does not even notice the harsh treatment he is receiving, except to have the thought that it was a bad day for Jim, and that he himself would be able to improve Jim's mood by trying to cheer him up. Harry feels, by way of contrast, that if *he* had been treated that way, he would leave not only the table but also the restaurant, and never make contact with this "friend" again.

How are we to explain such a difference?

I find this to be a question of calibration, a concept that may shed light on these individual differences and also be used to make clearer the transformation that takes us beyond our second nature.

Calibration is the marking of, or determining, a system of measurement for a given range of phenomena. *More generally, it is a set of criteria for classification in a particular area of interest.* In the interpersonal realm, Shirley *perceives* violence only if she is sent injured to the hospital; Anne "sets the bar" lower, *perceiving* a threat (a raised fist, even a raised voice) as already violent.

We each have a sense of what we will count as nastiness or violence, what we will find acceptance in how we are treated and in how we treat others, depending on how we calibrate such issues. *Importantly, we have bodily and mental experiences that go along with our situation.* If there is a discrepancy between our experiences and (calibrated) sense of what we deserve, for example, we may recognize the appropriateness of our rethinking this calibration.

To make the practical significance of this more obvious, let us consider an example of spousal abuse: *when* our second nature involves calibrations of interpersonal processes in which we give very little importance to our own well-being, *where* we see nothing wrong with our being insulted, or beaten and sent to the hospital when our partner is frustrated, enraged, or drunk (or several of these), *where* we quickly accept the idea that this is just the way he happens to act in those contexts, *where* we are willing to take him back if he sheepishly mumbles something about feeling sorry that he injured us or broke just a few of our bones, and so forth, *and we do this repeatedly*, only to be subjected to further incidents in which we again require hospitalization, *here* we have *calibrations it would presumably benefit us to review and revise.*

This review and revision are a recalibrating of acceptable social interaction. This involves re-evaluations that lead us to see clearly how we now feel that we deserve to be treated (and how to treat others) and what the limits are of how we will let ourselves be treated, without distorting these interests with other issues we face. The value of this review and revision of our calibrating may not occur to us, however, in the course of ordinary preoccupied life, unless we interrupt that automatic flow and raise this question for serious consideration!

We may see here the beneficial value of having friends or others we can reflect on the situation with—in this case, we may find it easier to reconsider what is happening between us and others in our interpersonal, social world.

The recalibration just described can cover any of a variety of considerations about our personal life, from the above examples to further issues concerning what we can (or "deserve to") accomplish in our life, what our social status (or "position") is, and so forth. These judgments or calibrations set the limits of what we are to expect, as well as of what we should not even dare to consider, in any planning or dreaming about our life possibilities, and so forth. Their power is therefore significant.

This points to the value for us to reflect upon the perspectives of our second nature and perhaps to reevaluate (and recalibrate) these at various times in our lives. A first step here is for us to appreciate the promising possibility of such shifts away from the particular second nature that was established earlier in our life[6]. These recalibrations are one way of bringing about the further transformation introduced here that takes us quite beyond this second nature.[7]

---

[6] On this anti-fatalistic attitude *in which we do* not *deem people to be doomed* by their early life, compare R.A. Spitz, "La perte de la mère par le nourrisson. Troubles du développement psycho-somatique," *Enfance*, vol. 1, no. 5 (Nov.-Dec. 1948), pp. 373-391, J. Bowlby and M.D.S. Ainsworth, *Child Care and the Growth of Love* (2nd ed., 1965), E.E. Werner, J.M. Bierman, and F.E. French, *The Children of Kauai: A Longitudinal Study from the Prenatal Period to Age Ten* (1971), E.E. Werner and R.S. Smith, *Vulnerable but Invincible: A Longitudinal Study of Resilient Children and Youth* (1982), J. Bowlby, *A Secure Base: Parent-Child Attachment and Healthy Human Development* (1988), J.M. Lewis and J.T. Gossett, *Disarming the Past: How an Intimate Relationship Can Heal Old Wounds* (1999), S. Vanistendael and J. Lecomte, *Le bonheur est toujours possible. Construire la résilience* (2000), B. Cyrulnik and M. Elkaïm, *Entre résilience et résonance. À l'écoute des émotions*, with chapters by Guy Ausloos, on resonance, resilience, and competence, and by Edith Goldbeter-Merinfeld, on resilience and resonance in families (2009), Boris Cyrulnik discussing his understanding of resilience, in N. Martin, A. Spire, and F. Vincent, *La résilience. Entretien avec Boris Cyrulnik* (2009), J. Lecomte, *La résilience. Se reconstruire après un traumatisme* (2010), and D. Siegel, *The Mindful Therapist: A Clinician's Guide to Mindsight and Neural Integration* (2010).

[7] See above, p. 212, n. 4, and extensive discussion in *The Inner Palace*. And cf. above, p. 79, on the concerns about second nature in Nietzsche's **EH** IV 8.

14. The Transmission of Mind[1]

Consider the Zen story of an intimate, solitary meeting between a great teacher and a most advanced disciple. In a very intense and brief period of time, it is said, the student becomes awakened, enlightened. This process is traditionally called the transmission of mind, and this mysterious term seems to beg for answers to a number of perhaps-obvious questions.

What is the transmission in this Zen story? What is the mind that is being transmitted? Is the mind of the teacher really passed on to the student and reproduced there, in some wondrous sort of psychospiritual process? Could this teacher "transmit mind" to anyone who happens to meet him at this important moment? And if not, what is different about the disciple that makes this transmission possible to him but not in general?

Furthermore, what does this story have to do with the rest of us? Is there something of value here that will be of personal relevance to us, beyond that of our humbled admiration of these special beings with their impressive minds?

If we look at Chinese Chan (Zen) Buddhism, we can see the brief description of this process in the *Platform Sutra*, the discourse of the Sixth Chinese Patriarch, Huì Néng 慧能 (638-713 CE). He is recorded as having said that the Fifth Patriarch met him at night, explained the *Diamond Sutra* to him (briefly), that he became enlightened at that time, and received the dharma (the teaching). He reports then that the Fifth Patriarch spoke of this teaching (dharma; Chinese, *fǎ* 法) as something "to be handed down mind to mind"[2] and that awakening is what people are to do themselves (*dāng lìng zì wù* 當令自悟).

This with its textual explanations by the Fifth Patriarch might be remembered here, since there are some teachings that offer a different model or paradigm of what this transmitting of mind is about, or how it works.

In this Chan tradition, the Buddha is said to have held up a flower that he showed to the audience in one context, and of all those present, one monk experienced this deeply and in the process, it is told, became enlightened, or in other terms, awakened, then and there. This monk, considered in some Buddhist lineages as the First Indian Patriarch, was named Kāśyapa (or in Pāli, Kassapa).

This example might suggest to some that a transmission that is totally absent of words (and in this way, completely nonverbal) is the essence of the transmission of mind. Now, given these stories, not limiting our examples to the

---

[1] In this chapter, I italicize foreign terms, except for words adopted into English (found in recent English-language dictionaries—e.g., 'dharma') and for names.

[2] In the Yampolsky tr. (*The Platform Sutra of the Sixth Patriarch: The Text of the Tun-huang Manuscript*), Sect. 9, p. 133; the Chinese reads: *fǎ yǐ xīn chuán xīn* 法以心傳心 (Chinese text, p. 五/p. 5). More on these terms, below, p. 217.

flower-transmission tale alone,[3] if we try to understand the actual process here, it may be helpful to orient ourselves with some basic observations.

First of all, this transference or transmission is presented in the tradition as something wonderful. It is considered to be very special. It involves in some way or another the very deep, subtle, and powerful connection between two individuals, in a deeply transformative and mind-liberating way.

In some texts that discuss this psychospiritual transformation (whatever its ultimate specifics),[4] we can see that the mind being transmitted is not simply

---

[3] **Some details:** Kāśyapa (or Mahākāśyapa) was central in the first recitation of the teachings after the death of the Buddha. *In the early teachings, this flower-transmission story of his awakening does not at all appear.* The earliest traced source of the flower-transmission story is the *Tiansheng Expanded Lamp Record, Tiān shèng guǎng dēng lù* 天聖廣燈錄, compiled by Lǐ Xūnzù 李遵勗 in **1036** CE (I. Miura and R.F. Sasaki, *Zen Dust: The History of the Koan and Koan Study in Rinzai (Lin-chi) Zen*, pp. 151-152), with retelling by Báiyún Shǒuduān 白雲守端, 1025-1072 CE (A. Ferguson, *Zen's Chinese Heritage: The Masters and their Teachings*, p. 396). Two (thirteenth-cent.) sources of the story are a lecture by Japanese Sōtō Zen Master Dōgen 道元 in the *Shōbōgenzō* 正法眼藏 (Chap. 64: Udonge 優曇華, Udumbara-tree Flower) and in a Zen collection, the *Wúménguān* 無門關 (Japanese, *Mumonkan*), Story 6 (*The Gateless Gate—Mumonkan*, in P. Reps, *Zen Flesh, Zen Bones*, p. 95). The flower-transmission story joins the idea of a sudden, non-textually-based awakening and a self-serving lineage—cf. Hézé Shénhuì 荷澤神會, 670-762 CE (I. Miura and R.F. Sasaki, *Zen Dust*, p. 192; A. Ferguson, *Zen's Chinese Heritage*, p. 58; B. Faure, *The Rhetoric of Immediacy: A Cultural Critique of Chan/Zen Buddhism*, pp. 12, 36-38)—in "an effort to substantiate a unique identity" (A. Welter, "Mahākāśyapa's Smile: Silent Transmission and the Kung-an (Kōan) Tradition," in S. Heine and D.S. Wright, eds., *The Kōan: Texts and Contexts in Zen Buddhism*, p. 100). **Kāśyapa, *but not the flower transmission*, is mentioned earlier**, in the *Xuèmàilùn* 血脉論 *Bloodvessel Discourse/Bloodstream Sermon* (*The Zen Teaching of Bodhidharma*, Red Pine, tr., p. 25), attributed to fifth-cent. Bodhidharma (Dámódàshī 達磨 大師, Great Master Dámó), First Chinese Chan Patriarch—and in the *Jingde Records of the Transmission of the Lamp, Jǐngdé chuándēng lù* 景德傳燈錄 (Japanese, *Keitoku Dentō-roku*), compiled by Dàoyuán 道原 (Shì Dàoyuán 釋道原) in **1004** CE, a "transmission of the lamp" compilation, one with *many transmission-of-mind stories using dialogues (not flowers)!* **All of this suggests a Chinese origin of the story, from between 1004 CE and 1036 CE.**

[4] The processes comprising this transformation of consciousness are a major focus of discussion of M. Ginsberg, *The Inner Palace.*

any mind, but is, rather, a quite special mind, an unusual mind. If we are inspired by some of the Zen texts on this sort of process, we may easily come away with the sense that this transformation is quite rare, almost beyond what is humanly possible, and that the individuals involved in this transmission are worthy of our very highest admiration and respect.[5]

Back to the present context, looking at this teaching here and now, we can see that indeed the original texts are talking of just this. Specifically, in Chinese texts, the key term is *chuán* 傳, which does carry the idea of transmitting, conveying, handing down, expressing, or propagating.[6] This process is termed *chuán xīn* 傳心, transmission of heart-mind (*xīn* 心),[7] or *yǐ xīn chuán xīn* 以心傳心, transmission from mind to mind, or is termed *chuán xīn fǎ yào* 傳心法要, the essential teaching (dharma: *fǎ* 法) on the transmission of mind.[8]

Being so direct, it is described as a special transmission outside the teaching (*jiāo wài bié chuán* 教外別傳; in Japanese, *kyōge betsuden*), which joins with Chan's proposal—ideas also in the daughters of Chinese Chan (禪), Japanese Zen (禪) and Korean Sŏn/Soen (禪): Do not rely on written words (*bù lì wén zì* 不立文字; in Japanese, *furyūmonji*).

Still, there may be two misleading features to the name. First is the idea of transmitting, as if we were sending forth one mind (that of the teacher) and having it be received by and planted into the second mind (that of the student), thereby transforming this second mind in some mysterious way that mirrors or recreates the mind of the teacher. And second is the idea of the "mind," which is perhaps not the most precise or accurate word here for talking about what is transmitted, even if the idea of transmission were unproblematic.[9]

---

[5] Or at least this was my own impression upon first reading of this idea in what was the first book I ever read from the Buddhist tradition, when I was 17, in my last year of high school. I was dumbfounded and confusedly impressed by the idea that some individual was taking the essence or key features of his own mind and somehow implanting that into the consciousness of another individual. This book (*On the Transmission of Mind*, by Huang Po, in the Blofeld tr.) is still in print, a reflection of its being widely appreciated.

[6] Glosses of *chuán* 傳 (from *Mathews Chinese-English Dictionary* and *Concise English-Chinese Chinese-English Dictionary*) include: propagate, preach; summon, transmit verbally, convey, express; conduct (heat, electricity); spread (disease, rumor), pass on, hand down. Note above gloss as a noun ('transmission').

[7] Cf. discussion of the heart-mind (*citta* or *xīn*), above, p. i.

[8] In Japanese, e.g., these same three terms (傳心, 以心傳心, and 傳心法要) are read *denshin*, *ishin denshin*, and *denshin hōyō*, resp. Cf. above, p. 215, n. 2.

[9] We might note that there are some concepts in Tibetan Buddhism that might be

This "transmission" is, after all, not a matter of transmitting or activating certain bits of information. It is not a matter of teaching facts to the student! (I take this to be one key feature of the point of the Mahākāśyapa enlightenment-by-seeing-a-flower story.) *As we have probably noticed, we cannot think ourselves into enlightenment (awakened consciousness).*

And this "mind" is quite specific; it is not just any mind. In particular, it is a heart-mind that is clear, calm, and loving. That is, it is *an enlightened state of consciousness, one that balances and integrates wisdom and gentle good-will.*

This is a consciousness with active deep compassion, respect, gentleness, one with a humane attitude toward all beings (ourselves included). This is a caring about what is going on between all those in our environment, a seeing clearly, one that includes seeing through the partial truths or other forms of ultimately distorting ideas we have come to accept. (More on this, below.)

This awakened mind is not a matter of having any particular beliefs or thoughts. It is a way of perceiving and tuning into what is going on, of experiencing reality.[10] The question at this point is, when we have an interaction with another individual, what are the processes that bring us to experience this awakened consciousness and have it be ongoingly alive and active in us?

The mind that has been changed (or transformed) in this process is not simply or especially a mind that now has certain facts that it did not have before. It is more a change of the pervading state of consciousness than a gathering of information or facts. This is not a matter of certain information, for which language is quite helpful if not requisite. *And, again, this may be the element of insight in the Kāśyapa paradigm of the transmission of mind, mentioned above.*

And yet, taking the Kāśyapa flower-transmission story as the defining, most typical model of transmission of mind misses something. Missing is the way in which communication of these frames of mind or states of consciousness (calm, caring, seeing, appreciating, wishing happiness and peace to all beings,

---

taken as equivalents to these Chinese Buddhist ideas. We might respect the precaution not to interpret dogmatically a given term as having the same significance in two different theories, which was offered in the chapter on Pierre Janet, above (Chap. 6, pp. 117-144). Here, for example, Tibetan *'pho-ba* (Sanskrit, *saṅkrānti*), the transference of consciousness, is the transference of consciousness at death into a next realm of existence, in other words, from one lifetime to the next. Tibetan Buddhism also has *lung* (Skt., *āgama*), transmission, but this refers to the transmission of *bshad* (Skt., *ākhyā*), texts, commentaries, and teachings, or the transmission of *bka'* (Skt., *subhāṣita, pravacana*), precepts. On these concepts, see *The Nyingma School of Tibetan Buddhism: Its Fundamentals and History*, vol. 1, pp. 674, 682, 737, 872, 890; vol. 2, pp. 351, 380-381.

[10] Many traditions have spoken to this form of consciousness, whose nature is the core issue and major focus of my two-volume work, *The Inner Palace.*

and so on) can in fact be communicated by *something* about our words, rather than our words themselves: if we think of the tone of voice and the smoothness of speech of someone we feel to be calm and friendly, for example, these special states of consciousness can be communicated by those words (or the way they are spoken) or by further actions that do not involve any words at all.

So when we are communicating with one another by talking with one another (or by non-verbal actions, as just mentioned), there is much more going on interpersonally than simply the transmission of various ideas that could be written down on a page. As said above, communication is much richer than simply the offering up of certain facts, bits of information, or beliefs.[11]

In even the simplest interaction, what is communicated[12] is extremely complex and rich. For example, even with a simple greeting, we may sense how a person is feeling (happy, sad, irritable, frightened, and so forth). Simply by noticing someone walk into a room, or approach us, for example, what we are sensing or learning about this person may be very important. In general, after all, *people* (and animals of other species) *are communicating in every aspect of what they say or do,*[13] *and we are perceiving in similarly complex ways.*

Even the context itself of an interaction has great significance and may be very powerful for those involved, whether the context is acknowledged explicitly or not. For example, the Master-Disciple interview (meeting) is in the context of a shared search for enlightenment, a shared appreciation of an entire cultural or spiritual understanding that the meeting makes use of (and presupposes), and with *the mutual interpersonal respect* that those shared features create.

The transmission of mind being focused on here makes use of our general ability to be nourished by our relationships and to understand, appreciate, and sympathize with one another in many interpersonal contexts. *When linked, then, to these more general features of our human inter-connectedness, this "transmission" process may seem much more familiar.*[14]

In the above stories of the transmission of mind, the specific form of mind that is being transmitted, as already noted, is the awakened consciousness, a mind (consciousness) that is grand, visionary, calm, seeing clearly and distinctly what is of importance—of importance to the discussion, to the well-being of those present, to the interaction, and so on. What, then, allows a shift into this state of consciousness for someone who is perhaps close to but not quite fully in that state, as suggested by these texts and by other considerations?

---

[11] For more, see Chap. 2, on action and communication, above (pp. 26-58).

[12] See preceding note.

[13] Cf. Freud on people communicating "from every pore": see the case of Dora, "Fragments of an Analysis of a Case of Hysteria" (1905e) [at SE 7: 77-78 = GW 5: 240 = CP 3: 94]. On these forms of citation, see above, p. 60.

[14] For more on interpersonal awareness, see Chap. 11, above (pp. 174-183).

When we are in the presence of certain other individuals, we may have the context for certain realizations or experiences. This is not a matter of their reciting certain facts to us, or reminding us of some bit of information we had forgotten. It involves, rather, a deep calm and a full acceptance of what is going on and of how we are, of what we are like, of who we are (related to different degrees of completeness of our sense of ourselves in our world).[15]

What is "transmitted" in this context is this non-judgmental but deeply seeing mind (or consciousness), one free of judgment, hate, irritation, or anger. We can sense here that we are not being judged or criticized, that we are being deeply heard, understood, appreciated, and respected. There is a sense of a compassionate attitude toward what we may recall as moments of great pain, fear, worry, agitation, hurt, shame, remorse, confusion, and so on.

In such a context, when we feel this full acceptance, understanding, and caring for everything that we are and have been (or so conceive as defining who and what we are), we may well begin to sense the reality of compassion, wisdom, calmness, joy, and deep acceptance. Such a sense of connection, with its communication of our reality that is being validated in this situation, gives a basis on which to feel a grounding problem-free connection with the world, to feel our safety, our well-being, our aliveness, and our capacity to deal with life.

If so, with this sense, we may be in the first stages of this transformation. This touches on the question posed at the beginning of this chapter of what might have been in place before that critical moment of transmission between teacher and disciple.[16] What is making the present "transmission" possible may be in large part what we experienced in our lives before this moment.

We are, after all, repeatedly given the opportunity of experiencing someone's caring, concern, gentleness, compassion, and many nourishing and beneficial features of the human condition very early in life, even before words became significant to us. And in unpredictable ways, with a variety of individuals that we have contact with—a calm grandfather, a loving aunt, an enthusiastic uncle, a playful cousin, a protective brother, an appreciative friend. (We may notice that this sense may have come from our parents, although it may not.)

These rather pivotal aspects of life are, in fact, communicated, and sensed, and appreciated, without fanfare, in all societies, in all segments of society, and involving a large variety of people in our personal world.

These are, sadly, also missing in many people's lives.

More than a matter of someone trying to install his mind into ours, this is a matter of our waking up to what is there to behold, once we have stopped judging ourselves, defending ourselves, defining ourselves in ways that place future demands on us and worries for us to be driven by.

---

[15] In this sense, this mind is not intellectual. Cf. above, pp. 199-201, etc.
[16] See p. 215, above.

Relatedly, in some traditions, rather than speaking in this perhaps mis-leading way of a transmission of mind, this process is described as the direct introduction to one's own nature, to one's own awakened mind, to one's own potential for wisdom. This would suggest more of an activating of the wisdom that is dormant or clouded over by more mundane agitation, worry, and confusion, than a transmission. This may be a much clearer, a much less confusing way of thinking about these processes than as a transmission of mind.

Adding a fuller picture of this understanding of what goes on in this psychospiritual transformation that is the "complete evolution of consciousness," to quote the words of V.R. Dhiravamsa,[17] are various additional key ideas in Tibetan Buddhism. As we read at the beginning of *The Three Statements that Strike the Essential Points*, a respected text attributed to ancient teacher, Garab Dorje,[18] there is the important process by which "one is introduced directly to one's own nature" (*ngo rang thog tu sprad*).[19] The contemporary Tibetan monk-scholar Dudjom Rinpoche writes of this process, "As for the direct introduction to one's own nature: This fresh immediate awareness of the present moment, transcending all thoughts related to the three times, is itself that primordial awareness or knowledge (*ye-shes*) that is self-originated intrinsic Awareness (*rig-pa*). This is the direct introduction to one's own nature."[20]

We may also understand it as the transmission of the Dharma or the teachings or the Buddhist understanding and vision transmitted mind to mind.

In any case, we are here in a realm where what is important is not facts or bits of information but a particular sense of ease, expansive awareness, immeasurable compassion and good-will, and deep peace. *Given this, we may well ask what is keeping us from this mind*, what is keeping this state of conscious-

---

[17] See above, p. 164, n. 2.

[18] Birth date of Garab Dorje, recognized as the first Dzogchen teacher, uncertain: traditionally, 521 BCE or 337 BCE. Cf. *The Nyingma School of Tibetan Buddhism: Its Fundamentals and History*, vol. 1, p. 491; vol. 2, p. 404. See further, J.M. Reynolds, *The Golden Letters: The Three Statements of Garab Dorje, The First Teacher of Dzogchen*, op. cit., p. 349.

[19] Touching on this are Tibetan *ngo sprod pa* (direct instruction), *ngo sprod kyi gdams pa* (pointing-out instruction, that is, the direct introduction to the nature of mind), *sems* (mind, *citta*, or, more specifically, the highest spiritual consciousness or Mind: *sems kyi gno-bo*, the essence of mind), and *sems ngo sprod* (introduction to the nature of mind). Cf. Chökyi Nyima Rinpoche, *The Union of Mahamudra and Dzogchen*, p. 233; L.A. Govinda, *Foundations of Tibetan Mysticism*, p. 19; J.M. Reynolds, *The Golden Letters*, op. cit., pp. 39, 41, 141; G. Tucci, *The Religions of Tibet*, pp. 31-33, 59-61, 63-73, 80-83, 106-109.

[20] J.M. Reynolds, *The Golden Letters*, op. cit., p. 41. Italics in original. Cf. G. Tucci, *The Religions of Tibet*, op. cit., pp. 44-46, on the role of the teacher here.

ness from being our basic mode of experiencing the world. In part here, we do not see what is actually happening because of distorting ideas or beliefs—*these are called ignorance, but are more precisely instances of **disinformation (false assumptions parading as if importantly true)***. These typically are thoughts about who we are or what our "worth" as a human being is. In this situation, *part of the shift* that is the awakening of mind, which has great power and liberating force, is when we experience being seen by a compassionate, caring, attentive consciousness. Our being calmly seen offers us the opportunity of experiencing (by feeling the reality of this caring vision), without the judgments that close down our capacity to have wisdom operating freely within us.

Perhaps this calls for a glance, for a gentle hand on one's shoulder in support and to give tactile proof that we are not isolated and alone—something that has us sense that we are seen and accepted, something that allows us to have a bit of distance on some worry, instead of our being tormented by it. In short, whatever is needed here would be conveyed in this transmission of liberated heart-mind. It is perhaps clear that *this is typically not a matter of information or facts that we could state as a news bulletin, but a new way of experiencing and appreciating the life we are living, an experienced new reality.*

We may focus on this special transmission of mind, and consider what has already given us particular features of this consciousness. What, for example, has already given us a sense of calm, of curiosity about the world, of being acceptable as we are, of the presence of compassion, caring good-will, and understanding of what we are experiencing? What has allowed us to make peace with our conditioned mind,[21] as part of this? What has helped us experience seeing everything with peace in our heart, with ease, wonder, and awe?

We perhaps all have had those in our lives who have offered us such a freedom and a calming and vitalizing perspective. This may be from a presence we have felt rather than statements that that person has uttered to us. It is perhaps not the words but what is conveyed by the words, what is communicated by a look, a touch, a smile, a whistled song, and even by the holding up of a flower, however powerfully symbolic that image might be.

We do not have to wait to be in the Zen-like Master-Disciple relationship lauded by Shénhuì and others. We already have the opportunity of appreciating and benefiting from what is happening in our own lives, of seeing that our experiences and interactions with others allow the blossoming of our most vibrant heart-mind.

---

[21] Some call this small self or ego (or, more precisely, the processes directed by conditioning). On going beyond this fighting, see M. Ginsberg, *The Far Shore*, "Making War on Ego" (pp. 31-32). When we are not controlled by this conditioned mind, or ego, this is who we were "before we were born" (to use a phrase found in Chan/Zen). This is *freedom **from** the ego.*

15. After the Death of Mahāmāyā[1]

The texts of Buddhism (especially of Theravāda Buddhism)—which preserve many detailed interactions between the Buddha and others, and recount his birth and, in informative detail, the last months of his life—have great value to those engaged in Buddhism, and also to those studying various psychological and interpersonal issues, some of which I will address in this chapter.

A Thai physician who became a Theravāda Buddhist monk (a bhikkhu), known by his monk's name as the Venerable Dr. Mettānanda, recently reviewed the symptomatology that is described in passages reporting on the last *months* of the Buddha's life, and came up with an altogether new understanding of that death. The Buddha's death had been discussed for many centuries, even in fairly recent academic, scholarly journals, with the two main proposed hypotheses both proposing that he had food poisoning and died in the following *days*.

The debate focused on the food that he had eaten, identified (in the Pāli language) as sūkara-maddava—or to give the English parallel—pig-delicacy or pig-softness. The compound could be understood as softness or tenderness (maddava[2]) that *consisted of* boar or pig (sūkara[3]), that is, a delicacy *of* boar or pig. The alternative takes the term to mean something soft or delicate *for* a boar or pig. The compound has been interpreted in this second way to mean mushrooms that had grown where pigs had stomped and left the ground soft, and has been postulated to be a kind of poisonous mushroom.[4] Walshe offers "pig's de-

---

[1] In this chapter, I italicize foreign words only as is done for English words: for emphasis, in titles, if in italics in the original text being quoted, etc.

[2] For grammatically possible options for interpreting the compound here, see A.A. Macdonell, *A Sanskrit Grammar for Students*, 3rd ed., Sect. 185-189, pp. 168-178, esp. 173; L. Renou, *Grammaire sanscrite*, Chap. IV, Sect. 74-96, pp. 82-122; M. Mayrhofer, *A Sanskrit Grammar*, Sect. 141-147, pp. 104-107.

[3] Cp. Skt. cognates to the Pāli 'sūkaramaddava' here: MONIER-WILLIAMS, *A Sanskrit-English Dictionary*, p. 1240b, glosses 'sūkara' as boar, hog, pig, swine (also: a kind of deer, white rice, etc.); p. 813b, 'mārdava' as softness, pliancy; cf. p. 830b, where the related term 'mṛdu' is glossed as soft, tender, pliant, etc.

[4] G.G. Wasson, "The Last Meal of the Buddha, with Memorandum by Walpola Rahūla and Epilogue by Wendy Doniger O'Flaherty," *Journal of the American Oriental Society*, vol. 102, no. 4 (Oct.-Dec. 1982), pp. 591-603. Wasson suggests that the food was a mushroom called pūtika, and that 'sūkara-maddava' in the *Canon* was a neologism, to disguise reference to the mushroom—*given the hostility against mushrooms in the Brahmanic world, as Wasson elaborates in detail*. This 'sūkara-maddava' occurs in the Pāli Canon only in *Dīgha Nikāya*, at D.ii.127, and in the same story as told at *Udāna* 81, in *Cunda Sutta* (*Udāna*, Chap. 8, Sutta 5). Cf. *The Pali Text Society Pali-English Dictionary*, p. 721a.

light,"[5] Malandra, "delicacy of boar"[6] (keeping the ambiguity of the Indic term), and Cleary, "mushroom soup" (in the context of a Chinese text).[7]

From textual information he reviewed, including mention of an acute episode months earlier, "with sharp pains as if he [i.e., the Buddha] were about to die,"[8] Mettānanda Bhikkhu concluded that the cause of death was not a poison but a physical condition of the Buddha, exacerbated by a rich meal that stressed his body. In short, the cause of death was understood not to be food poisoning by bad pork or poisonous mushrooms. The death was attributed, rather, to a mesenteric infarction due to occlusion of the superior mesenteric artery.[9]

This analysis by the physician-monk Mettānanda, not at all universally accepted, concerns the last months of the life of the Buddha. I turn now to certain earlier times in that lifetime that will be the central focus of this chapter.

The man who came to be awakened (or as it is often termed, "enlightened") and was thenceforth known as The Buddha (literally, the awakened one, from the root budh, to wake up), was known through his earlier years (his pre-enlightenment years) as Siddhārtha (to use the better-known Sanskrit form of the name). More fully, he was called Siddhārtha Gautama Shākyamuni (Siddhārtha, of the Gautama clan, the muni or sage of the Shākya tribe).

Sometimes there is a merging of this man and what he did or said *prior* to going forth into the wandering ascetic's life and then coming to awakening, with this man from the point in time onwards *after* becoming the Buddha, an awakened monk, "wandering in complete freedom" (to use the phrase from Daoist philosopher, Zhuangzi 莊子: xiāo yáo yóu 消遙游).[10] *The early texts clearly present Siddhārtha* **before awakening** *as an unawakened individual, without the vision, perspective, consciousness, and compassion of an enlightened being.*

---

[5] *The Long Discourses of the Buddha: A Translation of the Dīgha Nikāya*, M. Walshe, tr., p. 256, i.e., *Mahāparinibbāna Sutta*, Sect. 4.17-4.19 (D.ii.127).
[6] W.W. Malandra, "Atharvaveda 2.27: Evidence for a Soma-Amulet," *Journal of the American Oriental Society*, vol. 99, no. 2 (Apr.-Jun. 1979), pp. 222.
[7] T. Cleary, *Sayings and Doings of Pai-chang*, p. 75. Pai-chang in pinyin is Băi Zhàng 百丈; he lived 720-814 CE. This is obviously from a later text.
[8] On this episode, see *Mahāparinibbāna Sutta*, Sect. 2.23 (DN.ii.99); on its occurring more than 3 months before the death of the Buddha, notice esp. *Mahāparinibbāna Sutta*, Sect. 3.37 (DN.ii.114).
[9] Cf. M. Ginsberg, *The Inner Palace*, p. 333; Ven. Dr. Mettānanda Bhikkhu, "Did [the] Buddha die of mesenteric infarction?" *Bangkok Post*, 17 May 2000.
[10] This is from the title of Chap. I of *Zhuangzi* (Wandering in Absolute Freedom: 消遙游. Xiāo yáo yóu/Hsiāo yáo yú. See Zhuangzi, *Library of Chinese Classics: Zhuangzi* 庄子, vol. 1, Table of Contents (before text with translation).

In any case, this *not-yet*-awakened person—the bodhisatta (satta, being, bound for bodhi, awakening), as this pre-buddha individual is referred to in Pāli texts—the Sanskrit cognate ('bodhisattva') has quite a distinct meaning—lived his first 35 years *unawakened*. At that age, he is held to have come to the fruition of a long process: he woke up (came to awakening). Importantly, some things that happened to him and that he did in those first 35 years may be misunderstood if one assumes that he was already awakened during that earlier period of time. This would be a mistake: *whatever went on before that shift does not reflect the subsequent mind-set of the one who was thenceforth the Awakened One.*

The following discussion is based on sections in the Pāli Canon (or *Tipiṭaka*) and its later commentaries and sub-commentaries. There is some question of the accuracy of the story. What is said here proposes a perspective to give understanding of some of the family dynamics that may be proposed—*admittedly in a quite speculative way*—as a pattern for us to contemplate.

Siddhārtha, it is taught, was born of a father, Suddhodana (Sanskrit, Śuddhodana), said to be "chief ruler of Kapilavatthu"[11]—in some popular retellings, the king, with Siddhartha thus a prince—and of a mother, Suddhodana's mahesī (wife or consort), his aggamahesī (main wife or chief consort), named Mahāmāyā or Māyā—māyā being literally the delusionary face of reality, its magical and often confusing façade. Whatever her name, she died, reportedly in her forties, when the baby was about one week old. The younger sister of Mahāmāyā, Pajāpatī (or Mahāpajāpatī), another wife of his father—therefore Siddhārtha's maternal aunt and also his step-mother—was second consort of Suddhodana. At Māyā's death, Pajāpatī became Suddhodana's new chief consort (aggamahesī), and took over breast-feeding baby Siddhārtha, the Buddha-to-be.

It is interesting to note that Mahāpajāpatī had herself a new-born boy, Nanda, also a son of Suddhodana—who was thus Siddhārtha's half brother (same father) and parallel cousin (first cousin with mothers as sisters). Nanda—not Ānanda, another family member who will figure importantly in the life of the Buddha, in *other* ways—is given to some other woman to breast-feed. So Nanda is taken from his mother's breast and touch, and Siddhārtha replaces him.

Returning to Mahāpajāpatī, the replacement mother and wet nurse of the Buddha-to-be, we may wonder what relationship developed between her and little Siddhārtha: after all, another woman was taking care of her own birth son, and here she was, nursing her dead sister's little boy. It was perhaps quite intense and complex a situation to live through, with sadness and grief, with mourning, perhaps frustration at not feeding her own baby, joy at feeding Siddhārtha, and perhaps annoyance that she needed (in some sense) to feed him as part of her familial duties. Was she feeling a new love being created? Was she distracted? Was she longing for her own son? *These are all quite speculative questions.*

---

[11] References to the Pāli Canon sources here will be given in a note, just below.

And what was the story, the dynamics, between Siddhārtha's father and this mother-substitute that was part of her giving her own son to another in favor of Siddhārtha? Presumably she was not capable of feeding both, or it was felt better for her not to feed both, or that her taking over the role of chief consort to Suddhodana required her to care for her late sister's baby, and consequently, had her give her own birth son, Nanda, to be fed by wet nurses. (*More speculation.*)

Many of these issues are merely being raised here, as the information of what was going on specifically is simply not available at this time. There are also questions of how these sorts of familial complications were understood or evaluated at the time and in that society. *These questions are of value to those who contemplate family dynamics, to allow reflection on these processes.*

Given all of those considerations, we now move forward in time to when Siddhārtha was a young adult, married to a woman later referred to as Rāhulamātā (the mother of Rāhula), and most commonly called Yasodharā or, in Sanskrit texts, Yaśodharā (Yashodharā). After being married to Siddhārtha since the age of 16, she conceives, and when the couple are both 29 years old, she gives birth to a first child, a boy (Rāhula, as her name Rāhulamātā suggests).[12]

It is well known that Siddhārtha leaves home *not* when he learns that she is pregnant and that he is going to become a father (with a father's mundane responsibilities), *but, rather,* on the first night of the birth of his son, whom he describes as a burden (rāhu), declaring, as the scholar-monk Nārada renders it, "An impediment (rāhu) has been born; a fetter has arisen." Texts suggest that this was interpreted as a statement naming the boy ("To me Rāhula is born"), who is consequently so named.[13]

What was it about the actual birth of this baby that made this the precise moment for Siddhārtha to go forth out of his mundane status as new-father, to that of a śramaṇa, a shramaṇa, an ascetic wanderer? Siddhārtha is reported to have gone forth despite his own father's desperate and impossible desire to spare

---

[12] For these personages and their stories, see collected information from the Pāli Canon, in G.P. Malalasekera, *Dictionary of Pali Proper Names*, vol. 1, pp. 249 (Ānanda), 788 (Gotama, whose personal name was Siddhattha or Siddhārtha), and vol. 2, pp. 10-11 (Nanda), 522-523 (Mahāpajāpatī), 608-610 (Māyā), 737-739 (Rāhula), 741-742 (Rāhulamātā), 1200-1201 (Suddhodana). Cf. extended presentations in Nārada Māha Thera, *The Buddha and His Teachings*, and in Bhikkhu Ñāṇamoli, *The Life of the Buddha, According to the Pali Canon*. (A bhikkhu is an ordained monk; a māhathera, a monk for 20 consecutive years.)

[13] Nārada, *The Buddha and His Teachings*, p. 10: "bound or seized (la) by a fetter (rāhu)." Italics removed. Or—cf. G.P. Malalasekera, *Dictionary of Pali Proper Names*, vol. 2, p. 739, on *Udāna* Commentary—as Rāhu swallowed the moon (ending moonlight: an eclipse), so might this child block Siddhārtha's renunciation ("going forth" to gain enlightenment). On Pāli la, cf. Sanskrit lā.

his son, Siddhārtha, from any awareness of impermanence, aging, sickness, death, and other representations of the unhappinesses and torments (the duḥkhas or dukkhas) of this world. And at the birth of a new-born son, was Siddhārtha thinking that perhaps his own wife would die in one more week, as his birth mother had after his own birth? that his own son was about to be motherless, the way he was? Did he in fact know of his babyhood? *Presumably Siddhārtha did know, since this was later fully described and recorded in the Buddhist Canon.*

So, if we imagine this man, 29 years old and a father for the first time, returning to the memories of his own birth situation, something that quite regularly happens when we become parents (remembering what it was like for us to be a new-born baby, in the very specific family life situation that we were born into), he will be thinking about his mother who died after giving birth (was he feeling guilt at causing her death?), about his abandonment through her dying, about his being rescued by his step-mother and maternal aunt, his replacing his cousin and half-brother (retrospective guilt at separating this innocent baby from its mother?). These lead to the question of which of these features would be repeated in the present. Will the mother (this time, Rāhulamātā!) die again? Will Siddhārtha lose twice? In short, this birth of his son, his Rāhula, was perhaps an intense re-awakening of his own birth issues. This is not discussed in the Canon, which talked, rather, of how Siddhārtha felt not only his own personal situation, but rose above that, to realize that the entire world is drowning in its own torment, and that he could do best from this more global or universal perspective, by finding a way out of this torment for all beings. *(More speculation.)*

Often—to make a general point—when we become aware of a pattern in our family that was unfortunate (or miserable), we are inspired to do something different. And, ironically, what we end up doing is indeed different, and yet, somehow may create parallel dynamics in a new format. As when a person grows up in a family of intense arguments and fighting, then becomes someone who is focused on the horrors of arguing or fighting, to be avoided at all costs. In this way, arguing and fighting—even in their absence—may remain the focus for this later family: the more something changes (one way), the more it remains the same (on a deeper level of process). If we imagine Siddhārtha not wishing on his baby, Rāhula, what he himself lived through—being orphaned by his mother's sudden death—then by leaving, Siddhārtha certainly did not recreate *that* particular painful situation. Instead, Rāhula would experience *his father's absence*, and Siddhārtha himself, the absence of his beloved wife, Mother-of-Rāhula.

Still, we know that Siddhārtha did *not* grow up in a nuclear family (consisting of parents and children in isolation), but in a large familial and social network, with many mothers, aunts, caretakers. Given that more populated familial context, perhaps his mother's death had a relatively minimal impact on him.

Such considerations suggest that some of these speculations may ultimately be of greater significance to us than to Siddhārtha! Further, these reflections may help us appreciate the impact on us of the family we each grew up in.

16. Shame
Preliminary Remarks

We may look at shame in this context (considering the range of issues addressed in this book) as an example of one of the more powerful states of mind in which we may find ourselves. On a theoretical level, the topic of shame raises a number of issues concerning the process, its roots, its experienced reality (or phenomenology), and its resolution or, perhaps more precisely, its being transcended through one means or another. We are not required to assume that all instances of shame or feeling shame or being ashamed are all identical with one another. There may be some general features, however, that it may be of value to recognize, if we are to appreciate this state of mind and come to a vision of how these periods of shame might be transformed into less tormented, more grounded and satisfying frames of mind.

16. Shame[1]

Shame is a very early state of mind, or emotion (if we want to consider it an emotion[2]). By very early, I mean that it can be experienced by a young child,[3] much earlier in life than when we can first feel pride or guilt, for example. Or that it can be experienced much earlier in life than when we can first answer the question of what we would like to be when we grow up. And so on, in terms of the sophistication required to have certain awareness come to be.

Shame, unlike pride, is an outer-oriented or an outer-focused state of mind. It has to do with our sense of how we are being perceived or judged by others. In this way it differs from pride or guilt, which are both much more inner-focused realities, much more based on how we think of or judge ourselves, from our own values and personal orientation to the world.

Considering pride for a moment here, we take pride, for example, in having done something successfully, or in being someone in particular. As a child, we are proud, for example, to be voted to the Student Council, or to be a Brit (or an American or a Dane or a citizen of whatever country we are growing up in), or proud to have been given a special gift by a special relative because it

---

[1] In this chapter, I italicize foreign words only as is done for English words.

[2] Breuer and Freud classified shame as a disturbing affect, in "On the Psychical Mechanism of Hysterical Phenomena: Preliminary Communication" (1893a) [at SE 2: 6 = GW 1: 85 = CP 1: 28]. The term 'affect' ('Affekt') suggests viewing shame as an emotional state, or state of mind with specific agitated (or energized) features, tending toward action (respecting the root here in the Latin 'affectus'). For an extended discussion of affect, see E.K. Sedgwick and A. Frank, eds., *Shame and its Sisters: A Silvan Tomkins Reader*.

[3] Freud grouped "shame, disgust, pity and the structures of morality and authority erected by society" as "forces restricting the direction taken by the sexual instinct" (presenting some of their functional commonality, we might say, despite their differences from other perspectives). This joined his observation earlier in this same work suggesting that shame is a later phenomenon, that children "at some periods of their earliest years show an unmistakable satisfaction in exposing their bodies, with special emphasis on the sexual parts." From "Three Essays on the Theory of Sex" (1905d) [at SE 7: 231, 192 = GW 5: 133, 92, respectively]. He complemented this idea later, suggesting that during puberty, "the *reaction-formations* of morality, shame and disgust are built up." From "An autobiographical Study" (1925d) [at SE 20: 37 = GW 14: 62]. Italics in original. We might wonder if shame is not present much earlier, despite these observations; psychiatrist Donald Nathanson held, e.g., that there was clear evidence of shame in infants aged 6-to-8 months: D.L. Nathanson, "A Timetable for Shame," in D. Nathanson, ed., *The Many Faces of Shame* (1987), at p. 7.

shows how special we are. Pride has to do with a positive judgment of who we are, and of our own actions and decisions. All of these are reflections of our own values and judgments, in a positive way, about ourselves.

The direct opposite of pride is guilt. Guilt is the sense that our active role in some situation, in which we acted from our own understanding and motivation, was a mistake, went against some of our moral principles, or was in some other way judged to be bad. This feeling of guilt requires a sense of our own agency (source of action) and a value scheme to judge what we have done out of that agency, that perspective and decision-making.

Guilt depends on activity (rather than passivity): we are not guilty for what was done to us. It is only if we think that we brought on or invited or instigated or caused another person to act some way that we can feel guilt for what is done to us. This is sadly the situation with many people who were abused as children. The primary options in understanding here are to realize that our caretakers, typically, our parents, are not sources of safety and consolation in the world, but the source of our needing safety and consolation (from them, not by them), or to conclude that the problem is not with dangerous unloving parents but with how we ourselves are, bringing them to act in ways blocking their (assumed) loving natures to be active. The first option may be unrealistic but of great survival value for a child in such a situation to select!

But both pride and guilt are in these described ways a matter of our own judgments and understanding about who we are, in our own sense of that, and what we have done or accomplished.

Shame, on the other hand—in contradistinction to both pride and guilt—is something that we feel when being seen or noticed by others (and not in positive appreciation, either). We are ashamed that our clothes are hand-me-downs, that we are from some family that is not respected in the community. Or, we are ashamed that when we are sick in a hospital bed and our body is trying to rid itself of some infection, that we create feces that disgust our caretaker who is cleaning us up after a bowel movement. Or we are ashamed because we like something that other people laugh at us about. *Shame in this way is our uncomfortable sense of how we are being seen by unfriendly eyes, in which we sense what we experience as the hostile or loveless attitudes of others toward us.*

This, incidentally, is not[4] shame in the sense, similar to that of modesty—and in contrast to being shameless—of what we believe goes is the limit of acceptable behavior, beliefs that bring us to change our actions, as in "Have you no shame?" (compare: "Have you no modesty? no self-respect?").[5]

---

[4] Cf. the Grk. distinction between αἰσχύνη aiskhúnē (shame, as sense of dishonor) and αἰδώς aidós (shame, as respect for one's own or others' moral opinion): Liddell and Scott, *Greek-English Lexicon*, pp. 43b, 36b, resp.

[5] This latter sense of shame is defined as "a mind that abandons misconduct for

Nor is it shame in the sense of a mildly unfortunate event, as in "It's a shame that we have rain now, forcing this little tea party from outside in the garden to inside in the parlor."

The shame being addressed here, rather, is the shame of feeling horrible inside, of wishing to disappear, of wishing not to be seen at all. This relates to one postulated etymology of the word, having to do with covering something up so that it is not seen—in some analyses held to be the same root as in the French word 'chemise' (a shirt as that which covers the chest and back).[6]

Shame is something that we feel when sensing ourselves seen and judged negatively by others, or ridiculed by others[7] by what we are saying, doing, or not saying, not doing. And so forth. We perhaps feel shame that we are so uncoordinated in gym class, or so bad in spelling, or so slow to understand some idea being presented to us in class. We may feel shame simply because our parents look at us with disgust, annoyance, or frustration. We can feel shame if we are accused of being bad, of deliberately making trouble (when we knocked something over accidentally, for example). The examples can be multiplied.

When we feel ashamed, we want not to be seen, not to be noticed. (That makes this the opposite of pride, in this particular way.) We may actually turn our face away, as if this would prevent others from seeing us. We may leave the place where we are, or hide in a corner, or behind some large object. (But the fact that our action is unlikely to succeed in keeping us from being seen is not the first thing I want to point out here.)

Rather, what is of importance here is the fact that we feel an urge to do some such thing, showing its power, its automatic power, in that it is something we do without having to think or to decide what to do. It is our second nature, something natural to us, but something that we have actually learned to do (a topic addressed in the preceding chapter.) These matters of second nature are very difficult to shift, as they are quite practiced, having perhaps been repeated many times, are often quite deeply entrenched patterns of thinking or acting.

---

reasons that concern oneself," described as one of 33 "conceptions indicative of the mind of white appearance" (as Geshe Kelsang Gyatso put it, in *Clear Light of Bliss: A Commentary to the practice of Mahamudra in Vajrayana Buddhism*, p. 90). This is the sense in Indic Buddhism where lack of this sort of shame is termed anottappa or anapatrāpya (Pāli and Sanskrit, resp.): a lack of shame, shamelessness; see M. Ginsberg, *The Inner Palace*, p. 484.

[6] Cf. *The Oxford English Dictionary*, 2nd ed. (1989), vol. XV, p. 162: "many scholars assume a pre-Teut. [=pre-Teutonic] *skem-, variant of *kem-, to cover ... 'covering oneself' being the natural expression of shame." (All postulations, Pre-Teutonic forms are sometimes cited along with Proto-Indo-European forms.)

[7] Freud wrote explicitly of feelings of shame in front of others, in *Mourning and Melancholia* (1917e [1915]) [at SE 14: 247 = GW 10: 433 = CP 4: 157].

Still, *what is difficult to shift is not necessarily impossible to shift.* Feeling shame is a very uncomfortable thing. We can feel fidgety or want to scratch or hit or cut ourselves, or turn into a little ball, or become invisible, or jump off a cliff. We may feel numb. We may have no sense that there are unmet needs operating here. Or if we do, we may feel quite incapable of putting into words or telling anyone what those needs are. It is as if we had no place to go where we could be safe. And as if we had no right to expect any safe haven, as if we deserved this shame that we are feeling. *We feel so bad, down to our core.* This can lead to a sense of desperation, a sense of sheer panic.

While speaking in general terms, this issue may not seem very difficult (or may in other instances seem incredibly difficult, depending in part on our life experiences to date, of course).

For those for whom this seems particularly inconsequential, easy, a cakewalk, let me introduce a consideration that may lend importance and weight to this issue, and a clue about why it might be quite daunting for some to contemplate. In a passage to be quoted just below, mentalization is discussed, mentalization being basically the describing of what is going on in the mind.

More precisely, in one text mentalization is defined as "the mental process by which an individual implicitly and explicitly interprets the actions of himself and others as meaningful on the basis of intentional mental states such as personal desires, needs, feelings, beliefs, and reasons. It is a function of the prefrontal cortex and is in effect a 'folk psychology'[8] which every individual uses to interact with and to make sense of others as well as themselves."[9] It is suggested later in this same text:

> The weakness of the capacity for mentalization and the re-emergence of more primitive modes of experiencing psychic reality make individuals with a history of psychological neglect exceptionally vulnerable to brutalization in attachment contexts ... a person in whom this capacity [for mentalization] is weak or absent will experience the subjective experience of humiliation evoked by helplessness as tantamount to the destruction of the self ... The humiliation can be so intense that all things felt to be internal (subjectivity) become experiences to be resisted. In describing their experiences of brutalization, maltreated prisoners frequently report finding the very act of thinking unbearable. Explicit

---

[8] What is called folk psychology is the intuitive, usually not made explicit, and informal theories we each have about why people do what they do.

[9] A. Bateman and P. Fonagy, *Psychotherapy for Borderline Personality Disorder: Mentalization-based Treatment*, p. xxi; relatedly, at p. 377, the index entry for 'mentalization' should perhaps begin "xxi-xxii" (rather than "xvii-xviii").

phrases such as " 'I stopped thinking' or 'I went numb', 'I could not bear to think' are quite common ...[10]

The text continues, presenting this powerful consideration:

Unbearable shame is generated through the incongruency of having one's humanity negated, exactly when one is legitimately expecting to be cherished. *Violence or the threat of violence to the body is literally soul-destroying because it is the ultimate way of communicating the absence of love by the person inflicting the violence, from whom understanding is expected.*[11]

These passages may give a clearer sense of the underlying anguish that may be felt when a given person is feeling shame. So when considering this issue of shame here, we might keep in mind not only the mild discomfort that we might feel at some given time, but this much more frightening and agitating experience.

We might ask: *What shame in this intense form and the related presence of panic both beg for, from one vantage point, is relief, some calm, some safety, some sense of self-worth, and perhaps more deeply, some sense of being lovable. How can we bring this to ourselves? Or how can we have others help us to feel lovable in this way? How can we begin to feel some relief, calm, safety, self-worth, when we are feeling shame? How do we get from here to there?*

This may not be a matter of convincing ourselves of anything. That is, *we may not be able to talk our way out of shame.* It may *not* be a matter of being reasonable and getting a hold on ourselves, of convincing ourselves that we are really all right after all, that we are respect-worthy and honorable human beings. The path *may require something to happen*—beyond the domain of some train of thinking and coming to some conclusion—*something other than convincing ourselves* about who we are or what we are like.

What makes us have a sense of self-worth, what makes us feel loveable, is not especially something that we feel in virtue of having gone through a certain line of thinking or having considered certain features of our life with calm and clarity. *Thinking, whatever its powers and virtues, does not especially work here in a powerful, efficient way.* Being loveable, or, rather, feeling loveable, develops in a different way, it would seem. Relatedly, the calming of this driven sense of shame, replaced by our feeling that we are at our core quite acceptable, that we are really honorable human beings, and so forth, may come about

---

[10] A. Bateman and P. Fonagy, *Psychotherapy for Borderline Personality Disorder: Mentalization-based Treatment*, p. 96. The ellipsis at the end here (...) indicates the omission of the final part of the last sentence quoted.

[11] A. Bateman and P. Fonagy, *Psychotherapy for Borderline Personality Disorder: Mentalization-based Treatment*, p. 97. Italics added.

indirectly, through *other* things happening for us, or our doing other things (perhaps not at all directly related to the shame we are feeling), rather than through our *thinking* our way out of the situation.

There may be an extremely important, although not especially initially pleasant, nor especially easy, self-investigation that can be undertaken here, especially in the search for feeling lovable, and this is perhaps something best undertaken in moments of calm or of relative groundedness. And that is the questioning of *when it is in our life that we have felt worthwhile or lovable.* The reason that such a self-investigation is important and required is that *different people feel that they are loved because of different features of the situation.*

(And, incidentally, having certain thoughts about oneself is apparently *rarely* the royal road to feeling lovable, which suggests that "self-affirmations" or repeating declarations to ourselves of how lovable we are is perhaps not the most powerful way to come to feel lovable.)

So, then, to return to the question here, what has made us feel lovable and worthwhile at different points in our life? If we allow our mind to roam at such a moment of investigation, we may come to be reminded of various incidents. Even if these are perhaps rather minor and seemingly unimportant at the time, they can give us a clearer sense of what really touches us, makes us feel a bit of the wonderfulness of life and our presence here in this world, *and come to see what makes us—us in particular (in ways that do not apply to all people)—feel profoundly safe and dearly loved.*

If we are starving for love, taking care of this need clearly takes precedence over other concerns. The issue, we might say, is how to do this without hurting ourselves. This requires a perspective on ourselves and on our lives that we may benefit by cultivating, by applying, in order to help guide ourselves into fulfillment here rather than continued frustration and torment.

If this short chapter were an entire book personalized to each reader, at this point might come the bulk of the text, describing in great detail the very individual facts—very specific to the person—about what the situations are in which there has been (and is) the actual experience of being appreciated, respected, protected, and loved.

This might have a number of sub-topics that could be entire chapters, each on its own, that would go into detail about what is going on in the situation, who is there, what the discussion or talking is about, what the smells are in the air, the sounds, the music, the temperature, and on and on, in very specific, precise ways that all add to the overall feeling—when it is felt—of security, protection, and loving care.

This sort of information could then be used in other contexts as guidelines of the sorts of situations to encourage, to nurture, to practice, that could strengthen the somewhat tenuous sense of security and lovability that we might be dealing with. This would be part of the story of our personal emotional well-being and its evolution.

Now, if we look at the issue of our momentary state of mind, when we are in agitation or anguish, in fear or feeling abandonment, in feeling danger all around or in feeling the need to seek out safety, we may notice what has brought on these concerns. Even seeing these, though, how do move to safety and calm?

In an interest in understanding the overcoming or transforming such states of mind into groundedness, we may look at the *Analects* (*Lúnyǔ* 論語) of Confucius (Kǒngzǐ 孔子, 551-479 BCE), at *Analects* 2.1, where it is said that governing with excellence is like the North Star, which dwells in its place while other stars pay it tribute (and move about it).[12]

Focusing here on this image of the orienting North Star in the *Analects*, we may ask, what has shifted us from the innocence of mind that we once knew and that gave us orientation and grounding, to a state of agitation in which we are driven by a desire to hide? And what can allow us to reestablish this orientation and grounding?

In Tibetan Buddhist terminology, we may ask what the antidote is for our shame.[13] To paraphrase this while keeping the metaphor, what can be used to neutralize and to eliminate shame as a frame of mind that will otherwise, quite sadly, like a poison, bring on still further pain or anguish?

We actually have more than one question here: there is the issue of having some frame of mind that we can cultivate, practice, encourage, strengthen, that will replace shame, and there is the issue of what we can do when we are in the throws of shame, when shame has taken over and is controlling our awareness, our thinking, our feeling, our actions. The second—freeing ourselves from shame—is a short-termed handling of the immediate issue; the first—cultivating a grounded shame-free frame of mind—is a more thorough and definitive concern. *(This is not to say that either can be brought about instantaneously, or definitively, in one single concentrated period of time.)*

Let us address the second issue (freeing ourselves from shame) first.

So, what is to be done when we are under the control of an intense feeling of shame, when the first thing we have is the urge to do is to hide (as in trying to become invisible)? How we deal with this depends on what is happening moment by moment. This freeing ourselves from shame may be a gradual process, in that what we can notice at first may be just one or two instants of the process, but not the rest. We may come to be able to recognize and to appreciate

---

[12] See R.T. Ames and H. Rosemont, Jr., *The Analects of Confucius: A Philosophical Translation*, p. 76. The Chinese rendered "excellence" here is dé 德, which is the same dé in the title *Dàodéjīng* 道德經. The term is glossed as virtue or power, and also as integrity (for which, see above, p. 201, n. 33).

[13] The metaphor of the antidote suggests that there are ways to counter-balance any tendency that has unhappy outcomes (and is therefore called unskillful, in Buddhist terms).

more of what is going on, moment by moment, if we have the opportunity of noticing these waves of shame on numerous occasions. But with whatever we can
notice at any given time in our learning how shame operates for us, there is a
basic underlying principle that indicates that there is not one way out, but many.

The principle is that this process of shame is a group of particular states
of consciousness that occur in a given order (one after the other). The way out of
a given pattern at any point in the pattern is for the next moment to be different
from what it has been in the past. That is, we have the opportunity at each
moment in a sequence that makes up a wave of shame to refrain from doing the
next step. In Chinese philosophy, this is the way of not acting (wú wéi 無爲).

In Daoism in particular, in *Zhuangzi* (the writings of Zhuangzi), we can
find wú wéi 無爲 in the statement, "I take inaction to be true happiness"[14] or "In
my opinion, genuine happiness lies in the refrainment from action,"[15] to give two
glosses of wú yǐ wú wéi chéng lè yǐ 吾以无爲誠樂矣.[16]

In practice, the way of non-action is not very far from what is going on
for us, if under the influence of a tidal wave of shame. That is, when in this tidal
wave of shame, we are in a way frozen in space, like the proverbial deer caught
in the headlights of an oncoming automobile. *But there is a subtle and yet important difference:* Non-action here is a matter of attentive and quite conscious
refraining from doing: it gives us the space to pay attention to what is happening,
without acting (yet) on our awareness. It is, for example, *not* getting up and running, but just watching the feeling in the body or the images, thoughts, or judgments in the mind. And *doing nothing* about them at this point *except noticing*
them as carefully as we can. This is presumably easier to describe than to carry
out when in crisis mode, when the feeling of shame is so overpowering that we
feel driven to run away or to hide.

Which leads to the question of what makes it more likely, more doable,
for us to refrain from reacting as we would otherwise do automatically? Perhaps
some possible influences on us are "inside" us and others are in our context, perhaps some within our control and some not. Specifics may be helpful here. So,
for example, if we have on soothing music, what difference does that make? Or,
if we are in the middle of walking rhythmically around, what difference does

---

[14] B. Watson, *The Complete Works of Chuang Tzu*, p. 191 (from Chap. 18).

[15] Zhuangzi, *Library of Chinese Classics: Zhuangzi* 庄子, vol. 2, p. 287 (tr. into
English by Wāng Róngpéi); Chinese text (in simplified characters), p. 286; from
Chap. 18.

[16] Zhuangzi, in Chap. 18, in W. Hung, ed., 莊子引得 *[Zhuangzi yin de: A Concordance to Chuang Tzu]*, p. 46, line 11. In wú wéi as 無爲 and as 无爲, 無 wú
and 无 wú, both are negative particles meaning not, without, to lack, not to have.
The latter, 无 wú, now serves as the simplified character for the former, 無 wú.

that make? Or, if we have someone holding us gently and lovingly, perhaps singing soft lullabies in our ear, or kissing our hand with reverence, how does that change things for us? Or, if we are taken for a little walk, hand in hand, with someone we trust, what does that do for us? Or, if instead of running away, we sit down in a seated meditation (whether in a comfortable chair, in a full lotus posture, or in some other position), or even lie down, what does that do? Or, what difference does it make if we are lying down on our stomach, on our back, on our left side, or on our right side? If we jump up and down, what does that do? And what if we recite a verse that is reassuring to us (not especially the Twenty-third Psalm,[17] but that could be considered here as one option)? We may use our imagination and inspiration here to consider possible courses of action and mental focus might be of benefit to us, in context.

All of these possibilities are merely examples of our refraining from doing some specific action by doing something else. They are our *not* carrying out actions that would continue and perhaps intensify the shame. At this moment we are considering doing this (refraining from acting automatically, out of shame) by substituting something else. This would perhaps be a "non-action by alternative-action" (if it needed a name).

These are all examples of attempting to adapt to the situation rather than remain with actions that are undertaken while guided by some sort of automatic pilot (a "second-nature" sort of response), principally because these actions tend to bring on more pain and torment (in Buddhism, that which brings on less torment or dukkha is termed skillful; more torment or dukkha, unskillful[18]).

Experimentation (and so many "failures" or attempts that did not lead us beyond shame into freedom and relaxation and contentment) is perhaps the most direct way to self-knowledge here. This cultivation of various forms of non-action would perhaps involve a gradual lessening of the intensity of the shame and the power it has over us. The particulars may be worked out best individually, as we gradually come to see what is going on, and how our thinking and reacting are operating to drive us into oblivion, into a lost, agitated state.

Our own particular situation is always quite specific. It helps to be able to think out of the box, to think in creative ways especially in harmony with, in synch with, the particulars that are important in our own situation.

(Textbook cases tend to present themselves only in textbooks! Generalities are necessarily generalized. And what is specific may be the most important and powerful part of what is going on for us. This is perhaps clear if we have tried "cookbook" solutions and found how wanting, how inadequate, how ineffective they have been for us.)

---

[17] This is the well-known psalm that begins, "The Lord is my shepherd, I shall not want," and so on.

[18] Skillful (unskillful): in Pāli, kusala (akusala); in Sanskrit, kuśala (akuśala).

Which leaves the long-term issue, one of becoming like the iron ox in the Chinese poem:

蚊子叮鐵牛，無渠下嘴處。

wénzi dīng tiě niú, wú qú xià zuǐ chǔ.

A mosquito that stings an iron ox, finds nowhere to sink its
    proboscis.[19]

This "mosquito stinging an iron ox" (蚊子叮鐵牛 wénzi dīng tiě niú) presents here—from the point of view of the iron ox, that is—the image of being some- one who is untouched in the context of some problem that could torment us (and typically has done so in the past). This image suggests a path when in such con- texts inviting shame: to become like this ox whose skin a mosquito cannot pene- trate. This suggests becoming, in other terms, a person of unshakable stability.[20]

Until we come to be impervious to the mosquito bites of our world, until we come to be unshakable no matter what the personal earthquake we are being subjected to, we have a situation in which we can do our best but in which we will presumably not come through untouched, will not come through with no im- pact being felt, will not come through without having to deal with the disturbing situation as a situation that really is disturbing us (even if not driving us to dis- traction or to madness).

Here, in mid-stream—rather than being on the far shore of existence,[21] where none of life's trials and tribulations are agitating for us in the least—we are called upon to help cultivate our own sense of balance in the waves of the storm, and to help nurture our own sense of self-worth and of being lovable.

---

[19] This is a poem by Hán Shān 寒山 (Hán Shān is also known as Cold Moun- tain, which translates the name, this being in line with the ancient Chinese prac- tice of using the name of the relevant location or monastery for giving a new family name to a recluse or monk). See Red Pine (Bill Potter), tr., *The Collected Songs of Cold Mountain* [寒山詩 *Hán Shān Shī*], revised ed., pp. 80-81. Other examples of this practice of naming include poet Sīkōng Tú 司空圖 (Wade- Giles, Ssū-K'ūng T'ú) and Buddhist monks Huáng Bò 黃檗 (Wade-Giles, Huáng Pò) and his own teacher Bǎi Zhàng 百丈 (Wade-Giles, Pǎi Chàng), named for the mountains in China where they each resided. Huáng Bò is also known as Xī Yùn of Huáng Bò (Huáng Bò Xī Yùn or Huáng Pò Hsī Yün 黃檗希 運; Japanese, Ōbaku Kiun or, more briefly, Kiun). See *Japanese-English Bud- dhist Dictionary, Revised Edition—Nichi-Ei Bukkyō Jiden* 日英佛教辞, at en- tries for 'Kiun' (p. 194) and 'Ōbaku-san' (Ōbaku Mountain; p. 252). Cf. M. Ginsberg, *The Inner Palace*, pp. 421-422, 477, 534-535.

[20] This is from *Bhagavadgītā*, II: 70 (rendering the Sanskrit 'acala-pratiṣṭam').

[21] This metaphor inspired the title for M. Ginsberg, *The Far Shore*.

These various facets of a self-awareness practice, in which we begin seeing more clearly how we operate, or what makes us feel one way or another, begin seeing what agitates us, or frightens us, or makes us feel insecure or in danger, what makes us feel shame, and so forth, are part of the self-reflective or *intra-personal* (within the person)—the "inner"—dimension of any transformative process here.[22] Complementing (completing), this dimension is the *interpersonal* (between persons, between people) dimension of a presumably more thorough transformative process.[23] This interpersonal dimension can be overlooked or denied in some meditative approaches, which might be interpreted in an exaggerated way as suggesting the rather questionable principle that we should focus our attention only on our own consciousness, look to guide and modify our world by dealing solely with this intrapsychic (within the psyche or mind) complex, and not distract ourselves with anything outside ourselves.

This principle begins with the observation that we do not control much of what is happening in our life context, and certainly do not have much control over the opinions and actions of others around us, especially not in any sure, regular, reliable way. And perhaps pushes this idea to the extreme, unsupported, and not especially wise, conclusion that we and others have no mutual influence on one another, cannot have any such influence, or should not have any such influence. Each of these questionable conclusions has powerful implications.

In short, the idea that we are isolated creatures with no mutual interactive influence on one another, keeps us blind to the ways in which others have had a powerful influence on how earlier, or how we now feel, and in the context of the present focus, on the shame that we might feel in various contexts.

On this interpersonal dimension in the cultivation of shame, psychiatrist James Gilligan, at the time Director of the Center for the Study of Violence, Harvard Medical School, wrote,

> The two possible sources of love for the self are love from others, and one's own love for oneself. Children who fail to receive sufficient love from others fail to build those reserves of self-love, and the capacity for self-love, which enable them to survive the inevitable rejections and humiliations which even the most fortunate of people cannot avoid. Without feelings of love, the self feels numb, empty, and dead.
>
> The word I use in this book to refer to the absence or deficiency of self-love is *shame;* its opposite is pride, by which

---

[22] On inner practice or training, see extended discussion in H.D. Roth, *Original Tao: Inward Training (Nei-yeh 內業) and the Foundations of Taoist Mysticism*, esp. pp. 62-71, 134-142, etc.

[23] For more on this, consider the chapter in this book on Inter-Personal Mindfulness Practice (IPMP), above.

I mean a healthy sense of self-esteem, self-respect, and self-love. When self-love is sufficiently diminished, one feels shame. But it may be somewhat paradoxical to refer to shame as a "feeling," for while shame is initially painful, constant shaming leads to a deadening of feeling, an absence of feeling. An analogous image comes to mind if we think of our experience of cold. If we say we are "cold," we experience cold as a feeling, as something that exists and is painful. But we know from physics that cold is really the absence of heat, or warmth. Shame is also experienced as a feeling, and an intensely painful one; but like cold, it is, in essence, the absence of warmth, emotional warmth, or love for the self. And when it reaches overwhelming intensity, shame is experienced, like cold, as a feeling of numbness and physical death.[24]

It may be helpful here to keep these observations in balance if we remain aware both that (i) the way others have treated us has made a huge difference in how we have come to feel about ourselves and about life in a general way, and that (ii) changes in our consciousness are possible through future (different) interactions—a forward-looking possibility; this balances our reflecting on the past here, which if done without this balance might be rather discouraging an endeavor.

In addition, it is also especially relevant, I would suggest here, to keep in mind that immense shame has been "taught" and in this way is part of our conditioning. In this perspective, it is at most our second nature, a "nature" that we have come to have because of important life experiences, but not our "first" nature, not anything that we must have as a human being—it is a bit of conditioning that *can be modified* by further conditioning, most relevantly here, *by further life experiences of a different and more heart-filled nature.*

Given that how others have treated us (or mistreated us) is so important for this sense of shame, we might find that some radically different interpersonal experiences may be restorative or healing, aiding the transcending of our second nature, our no longer being limited to and directed and controlled by our second nature (this transformed reality is our "third nature").[25]

In other words, if the way in (into great shame) was through interpersonal experiences (of one harsh, unloving pattern or another), then the way out (beyond great shame into a freer and vibrant "third nature") may essentially in-

---

[24] J. Gilligan, *Violence: Reflections on a National Epidemic*, pp. 47-48. Cf. earlier in this chapter for ways in which shame and pride are not exactly opposites.
[25] On third nature, cf. the preceding chapter. That new *interrelational experiences* can bring about deep changes is one theme of psychiatrist-psychoanalyst S.C. Vaughan's *The Talking Cure: The Science Behind Psychotherapy.*

volve new interpersonal experiences (of one gentle, loving pattern or another).[26]
If here our past has taught us to feel shame, to want to hide our face and not be
seen, in other words for us to lose face, then the task here could be described as
one of saving face,[27] a matter of some sort of corrective activity that allows the
regaining of respect, of regaining face, in Zen terms, to return to original face.

   *I am in the process of proposing here what might be **life-saving and
life-honoring ways of regaining face**, ways that do not call on anyone to commit
hara-kiri! (Onwards in gentleness, please!)*

   This is returning to what has been termed běnlái miànmù, 本來面目;
original or natural face, etc. This "face" (in Japanese, menboku or menmoku) is
also the term for honor, prestige (as in "losing face").[28] These same characters,
in Japanese, 本來面目 honrai menmoku (or menboku), have also been rendered
as true self.[29] Given such considerations, we may see that the sense of shame is
clearly not specifically Western (or Eurocentric) and not specifically Oriental. It
is more universally human than that!

   Our path is a human path here, beyond such root conditioning, and beyond our "second nature" that produces so much torment for us. This second facet of a path suggested here, this interpersonal facet, if nourishing, would com-
pensate in its own little way, for the harsh and cruel treatment we received earlier in our lives. It is a way that can encourage us (can give us courage) to take

---

[26] We might be reminded that Freud spoke explicitly and emphatically of "the
omnipotence of love" in "Three Essays on the Theory of Sex" (1905d) [at SE 7:
192 = GW 5: 61].

[27] These two idioms in English that echo the Japanese—and in a broader way,
Oriental—sense of regaining respect, regaining face. We may remember that
losing face would lead in some important contexts to the individual's commit-
ting hara-kiri 腹切 (literally cutting the hara, or the life force in the mid-abdo-
men). Hara-kiri 腹切 (Chin. fùqiè) is more formally termed seppuku 切腹 (Chin.
qièfù), using the same kanji but in opposite order and pronounced quite differently. Kanji 漢字 (Chin., hànzì 漢字—in simplified Chinese, 汉字—lit., characters of the Hàn, i.e., Chinese characters) are Chinese characters used in written
Japanese.

[28] See J. Halpern, ed., *New Japanese-English Character Dictionary*, at character
2087 (1b), p. 940, and character 3043 (6), p. 1390. Cf. above, p. 208.

[29] This version from P. Reps, *Zen Flesh, Zen Bones: A Collection of Zen and
Pre-Zen Writings*, Story 23 from *The Gateless Gate* (by Ekai, called Mumon);
cf. p. 87, p. 108. Ekai is the Japanese version of Huìkāi 慧開 (fuller name, Wúmén Huìkāi 無門慧開; Jap., Mumon Ekai). He died in 1260 CE. The text has the
Chin. name, *Wúménguān* 無門關 (Jap., *Mumonkan*). See *Japanese-English Buddhist Dictionary, Revised Edition*, pp. 57, 226.

little (doable) steps toward facing the present situations we go through, without the controlling constraints of our past-developed second nature with its high concentration of shame and feelings of being unlovable. *It is a way of love and respect derived from caring and supportive interactions.* This is part of the role of what in Buddhism has been called encouraging companionship.[30]

May we feel encouraged and also hopeful in our task here. With this interest, and as an offering to ourselves, we may consider such a formulation as this Buddhist-influenced expression of caring that is appropriate in this context (inspired by the Theravāda text in Pāli here, from the Pāli Canon or Three Baskets, the Tipiṭaka-pāli): "May all beings be happy. May all beings be secure. May all beings be healthy. May all beings be fulfilled. May all beings be content. May all beings have good, caring, encouraging companionship. May all beings develop clear awareness and the lovingkindness of unlimited compassion."[31]

---

[30] For example, in the Pāli Canon, it says in *Saṃyutta Nikāya* (at S.i.87-88), "Truly, the entire spiritual life, Ananda, is this—encouraging friendship, encouraging companionship, encouraging intimacy." The Pāli text reads: "Sakalameva hidaṃ ānanda brahmacariyaṃ, yadidaṃ kalyāṇamittatā kalyāṇasahāyatā kalyāṇasampavaṅkatā." The key word that is repeated here, *kalyāṇa* (rendered immediately above succinctly as "encouraging") means beautiful, agreeable, good, noble, generous, excellent, beneficial, virtuous, auspicious, that which inspires, that which encourages. Relatedly, a *kalyāṇa mitta* (mitta means friend)—in the Theravāda Buddhist Tradition, this is one of the names for a meditation teacher—is a good friend, a virtuous friend, a friend (in this Buddhist context) who inspires and *encourages* us in our process of coming to awakening and freedom.

[31] These are among the sentiments found in *Mahāmaṅgala Sutta* (in *Sutta Nipāta*, Sn 2.4, at Sn 258-269) and in *Maṅgala Sutta* (in *Khuddaka Pātha*, Khp 5).

17. Remorse
Preliminary Remarks

We may look at various psychological realities in terms of what is actually experienced, including thoughts, states of mind, sensations, and other components of consciousness: moods, emotions, concerns, worries, trains of thought, musings, hopes, wishes, or daydreaming, for example. Any such approach is called phenomenological (experience-focused). This and the next chapters will be phenomenological in precisely this sense.

This chapter in particular looks into the experience of the tormented thinking of remorse. Let us start with what we understand remorse to be.

We can imagine what it feels like when there are nagging issues that keep disturbing us about what we have said or done, that do not leave us in peace, that trouble our morale, our spirits, that raise questions for us that may be quite uncomfortable to face, that trouble our sleep. This is remorse at work.

Buddhist psychology has described the criticizing mind that revisits earlier actions felt or judged to be bad or poorly done, a mind characterized by agitation, instability,[1] and unclear perception of our psychological processes and of our basic life situation. This mind is called *kukkucca* (in Pāli).[2] This is remorse,[3] being attacked by self-questioning. Imagine a pot of water agitated by a strong wind, with ripples and wavelets. As a mirror, it does not allow us to see our own face as it really is. So, too, remorse keeps us from seeing our own good, our own welfare (or to see another's good, another's welfare) as it really is.[4]

The numbered sections of this chapter, below, represent various moods, ways of thinking and feeling, or points of view, which someone in the throes of remorse might experience. This may represent an actual sequence, but the basic aim here is simply to illustrate various torments and other features of remorse.

---

[1] From Asaṅga (4th century CE): W. Rahula, tr., *Le Compendium de la Super-doctrine (Philosophie) (Abhidharmasamuccaya) d'Asaṅga*, pp. 14, 76, 214, 224.

[2] Sanskrit, *kaukṛtya*, derived from *kukṛta*, badly done, or *kukṛtya*, an evil deed, wickedness. See M. Monier-Williams, *A Sanskrit-English Dictionary*, p. 285c.

[3] We find *kukkucca* also glossed as anxiety or worry, neither of which makes explicit the concern with our own past misconduct (or what we take to be such). Soma Thera writes of "worry in the form of repentance or remorse" (*The Way of Mindfulness: The Satipaṭṭhāna Sutta and Commentary*, p. 165). Cp. the parallel "hate that which one has done" in W.E. Soothill and L. Hodous, *A Dictionary of Chinese Buddhist Terms*, p. 371b, of 惡作 è zuò (do or regard as wicked).

[4] In discussing the five hindrances, A.v.193 (*Aṅguttara Nikāya*, The Fives, Sect. 193) describes remorse with this image of turbulent water (in Par. 11: in the Pali Text Society ed., *citing vol. and pg.*, at A.iii.235). The term *attha* (above: good, welfare) is also glossed result, gain, advantage, wealth, meaning, matter, etc.

17. Remorse

Remorse (1)
"I have done that," says my memory. "I cannot have done that," says my pride, and remains inexorable. Eventually—memory yields. (Quote from Nietzsche, *Beyond Good and Evil*, Sect. 68.) This would be a model of how *not* to feel remorse: by distorting memory. If we avoid that, though, we can perhaps see what pride is not comfortable with seeing ...

Remorse (2)
What have I done? I couldn't have been in my right mind to have done that! Is anything that I can say after having done that, anything but just empty words? Can what I say undo the harm? Am I condemned to be unforgiven, eternally?

Forget about eternity. How can I face others *right now* that know what I have done? How will they not hate me, not despise me? How can I look myself in the mirror and not be disgusted by what I see, knowing what I have done? I feel that I have betrayed all that I have been taught to regard as holy, as pure, as good, and have sunk to the lowest depths of inhumanity. Have I massacred a thousand people? No, but could I feel worse than I do, even so? I do not even know how to answer such a theoretical or hypothetical question. Comparisons seem irrelevant; such questions do not come across as helpful.

Remorse (3)
But I, like a soldier returning from the war, like a concentration-camp survivor, have seen a hell realm here on earth. It's worse than that, though. I feel branded "Monster" on my soul, as if on my forehead. Woe is me!

Remorse (4)
If only I could forget. Forgive and forget. Or forget and forgive. This makes no sense! A wish: just to be able to go to sleep and be in peace. No rest for the weary, no rest for the scumbags of humanity (they deserve to rot in hell); no rest for me (I deserve to rot in hell).

Remorse (5)
I was acting for a just cause, for a just idea, for that, I should be lauded. Please laud me. (So far so good, assuming this might inspire applause and respect.) What doesn't feel right, though? What doesn't go along with this idea, this reasoning? What grates here is the experienced sense that what I did was horrible, that I was horrible, that I am horrible. I feel doomed to a living hell.

Remorse (6)
To hell with it all! I demand exoneration. Perhaps a medal! O.K., I'll settle for forgetting it all. What's their talk here about fairness and justice (punishment?)

What do they know of my punishment already? How many times do they want an apology, an acceptance (an acknowledgement) of responsibility, an expression of remorse? Do they just want more hurt, in the name of justice,[1] the harsh revenge of a cruel God! Who wants such a God! That's *their* problem. So, why do they want me to suffer for *their* problem? And I'm sure it's *not* their *only* problem.

Who do they think they are here? Pure water lilies? They're full of shit! They're deluded if they think they have angels' wings. I haven't seen any of them fly away flapping such gossamer appendages! These vampires are just sucking my life's blood! Can't they just get a life and leave me alone? Or maybe I can give them a life. But not one that sucks mine out of me. Why don't they leave me alone, leave me in peace? Let bygones be bygones. Wait! I've got it! Come, I'll buy us all a round of beer! OK? Yes? No? Won't you answer me? To hell with you, then! Boy, am I angry!

To feel remorse (7)

Who am I kidding here? Who I am trying to kid here? Me? You? Someone else? Someone no longer alive, who is cursing me from hell? Or from heaven? It won't work! I see through me. Oh, woe! Rot in hell, me!

Remorse (8)

I walk around with a stench I cannot cover up. Am I the only one who can smell my disgusting, poisoned soul? I feel faint! I will never be able to wash away the nauseating smell of my soul spreading its poison everywhere!

Remorse (9)

I disgust me. I am disgusting. I deserve whatever I get. Who am I to complain (after what I have done)? I have it coming to me, whatever it is!

Remorse (10)

Please forgive me. Please love me. I am unlovable, but please. OK: I understand how you, too, must feel disgust (at me). And why forgive such a low-life? Could

---

[1] The topic of justice—its proper domain as well as its misuse in the political sphere—has been discussed from Plato on (*Laws*, *Republic*, etc.), through the millennia, to contemporary writers as John Rawls (*A Theory of Justice*), Michael J. Sandel (*Justice: What's the Right Thing to Do?*), and others. We may join the issue of justice with that of forgiveness, in the great search for balance between, or integration of, these two. Cf. the next chapter, below, p. 256. The questions here comprise a huge topic that has been discussed in theory of law (jurisprudence) as well as in psychospiritual works of various traditions from around the world. For more on these last, see M. Ginsberg, *The Inner Palace*.

I do anything to deserve forgiveness or love? I can't image what that would be. I don't see it. I'm unredeemable material, lost to eternity.

Remorse (11)

I want to be an ostrich. I want not to see. And not to be seen. I play peek-a-boo but keep my eyes covered at all times. I am hidden. You cannot see me. I cannot see you. Hmm. Can I really make myself blind? Can I blind everyone who knows my horrible past? Or, rather, is my own death plus the death of those *who remind me of me* the only way beyond this? I hope not. I pray not. Is this the mechanism of the mass suicide of cult groups?

Remorse (12)

I am caught in a mind hell that has one door out, and it is locked from the outside. If someone can unlock the lock, filling me with gracious love (love coming out of grace, undeserved by me but given to me in spite of that worthlessness), I may be saved. I just want to live. Please forgive me and love me, unlovable me, love-seeking me, love-starved me, nonetheless. Bless this worthless one.

Remorse (13)

Just give me peace. A feeling of hope. A fresh start. A new mind. A healed mind. A mind that can love breathing again. Be gentle and loving to me, please. I am defenseless.

Remorse (14)

Getting an overview on all of this: All of this ruminating and clutching at straws is from a mind that is out of balance, a mind that has lost its grounding, a mind that does not see the way to resolve, to integrate, to make amends, to come to peace, to move on in life, accepting but not being crushed. It is coming from a frame of mind that needs first to find its plumb line, its clear sense of grounding, which is needed before we can even begin looking honestly at what we are feeling remorse about *in a way that will bring about these yearned-for shifts.*

It is not a matter of forgetting or erasing memories, but of facing them fully, appreciating what they are about, seeing what must be done and what must be changed for things to come to peace. This is not easy work. (Rewarding and fulfilling does not mean pleasant-along-the-path.) As is said in some spiritual practices, it is a time to go "back to the meditation cushion!"

18. Forgive and Remember[1]

When someone has hurt or betrayed us, how do we reconcile and come to peace with this, without distorting or denying our own experience?

Not all hurts or betrayals are of the same magnitude. If someone steps on our toe and says, "Excuse me," we may reply with a brief, "Sure." No big deal, right? In contrast, if someone screams at us nastily, a casual, "Sorry; I'm just letting off steam!" would perhaps seem inadequate.

Now, in real-life contexts, the question of forgiving arises when something serious has happened, where we are considering some harm already done to us, or at least assumed to have been done to us. In the clearest examples, this harm was done with an awareness that we would end up hurt. In such cases, these are actions done with someone willing to, or even wanting to, hurt us.

A natural impulse before forgiving anyone, is to figure out what actually happened and, relatedly, what specifically there might be to forgive, if anything. Our first search for clarity may be in trying to find fault: we may ask, why did they do this? Or, turning the focus back on ourselves, we may ask, what did I do to deserve or to instigate such treatment? We may generalize, asking, what kind of people are they? Or, what kind of a person am I, given this harsh treatment I have received? We will consider more helpful options, below.

In this context, we may feel confused, hurt, defenseless, or ashamed. Any lack of clarity or of appreciating just what happened will produce in us a blurry sense of reality and both doubtful questioning and anxiety.

Our confusion may have served a vital purpose at the time—that of keeping us alive. For example, mistreated children often are faced with concluding *either* that the adults hurting them are cruel or bad *or* that they themselves deserve such treatment and are therefore bad themselves.

It may be safer and more reassuring to believe that those in power are actually good-willed and kind, than to have them realize that we think they are mean, cruel, and frightening. They may not want to recognize how nasty, unmerciful, and restless they are. *They may not want to see their violence reflected in our eyes.* Their discomfort could lead to even more violence against us.

Here, being violent is an effective distraction from one's own torment, while giving a feeling of power, even if this feeling is paid for by a child being hurt. Focusing on this child, who is seen as deserving such violence, is also an effective distraction from one's own pain, fear, or agitation.

And so, when being harshly treated by these adults who are our guardians and perhaps our parents, we might literally stand a better chance of surviving if we focus on the thought that we children are the ones who are bad. Why

---

[1] In this chapter, I italicize foreign words only as is done for English words: for emphasis, in titles, if in italics in the original quoted text, etc.

else would such good and loving people hurt us so much? And how often have parents told their children, "This hurts me more than it hurts you; I'm only doing this for your own good" or offered strict, authoritarian parenting as "firm love"?

To revisit conclusions arrived at earlier in our lives, when we were instinctively managing to minimize the violence and were perhaps literally keeping ourselves alive, may be an important part of coming to true clarity about our past. In this, we now consider events that took place when we were young and when we did not understand the complexities of adult thinking and acting.

In a general way here, in this activity of reviewing and searching for forgiveness, if we are feeling even slightly confused, hurt, or defenseless, it will not be easy to forgive those we feel have wanted to hurt us—and perhaps have indeed done us great personal harm. After all, a primary task when vulnerable is to seek safety, and *in such situations, focusing on forgiveness typically intensifies our sense of vulnerability and our need for safety, rather than relieving them.* So, even if there is a time and place for everything, *before we try to forgive, there may be some important preliminaries to address first.*

Clarity is a first step. Then, having looked honestly into the situation of concern, we may arrive at least at a basic understanding of what actually has happened. And in this open investigation, we may recognize the sad fact that not all people are at all times and in all contexts kind, good-willed, considerate, and respectful of others, not all are even merely polite and civil to others. In our world, people have intentionally acted violently against others, and here, quite relevantly, have so acted against us, we can add.

What do we do with such realizations? If we are feeling hurt and vulnerable, we may want to see about protecting ourselves. If we are feeling anger and resentment, we may be considering the issue of what to do with those feelings, which are actually judgments or attitudes toward others.

We may act to make ourselves feel more secure (study a martial art, take self-defense classes, purchase weapons, hire someone as a body guard); we may imagine the responsible parties punished for misdeeds against us.

Still, these activities rarely give a deep sense of solace and security.

We may wonder if there isn't another, more skillful path here for us.

We may think about our forgiving the guilty party (person). In fact, we may feel in a rush to come to this forgiveness. We may be told by others that we need to forgive in order to "get on with our lives" or that we should simply "forgive and forget" or should "let bygones be bygones." That we should stop holding grudges and resentments, that we can't change the past, that we should come back to the present, that we should move on with our lives, that we should not let ourselves be stuck in resentment, and so on. (We may feel a somewhat-hidden judgmental attitude against us in this friendly advice.)

There can be pressure here from our friends and relatives—and from us ourselves! And, given teachings that may have touched us in our lives, we may be contemplating the thought from what is called the Lord's Prayer, from the

Roman Catholic Catechism, "And forgive us our trespasses, as we forgive those who trespass against us"—we return below to consider this prayer and its deeper vision—a thought implying that we should forgive these trespassers quickly, in order to benefit from the request we are making that we ourselves be forgiven.

What happens, though, if we are asked for forgiveness by these very people? We may be dealing with emotional turmoil so intense that although we can hear these requests, we cannot address them at the time. *What are we to do in such a situation?*

We are perhaps not in a calm enough state of mind to enter into the reflections involved in forgiving. If so, we are not yet ready to address this request. Rather, there are shifts in our frame of mind that will make our considering such requests a much more straightforward process. First things first.

While others may be impatient in wanting us to forgive them, we will perhaps all benefit by our dealing first in a more focused way with our own emotional agitation. This is a time for compassion and patience on their part and on our part. If we need soothing, considering the other person's apology is not the first concern for us to address.

We can simplify our concerns by dealing only with the most central of them at the time, lessening the demands about what to deal with now. In this, we are placing ourselves in a better position to take care of one issue after the other. This is an alternative to facing a set of demands that are quite beyond our capabilities at the time to satisfy. (Relevant here is the analysis of mental capacity by Pierre Janet, discussed above, especially at pages 142-143, that makes sense of this idea of simplifying at certain times what we are directly dealing with.)

In short, when we are in emotional turbulence and are asked to forgive, we can benefit from appreciating our own limits. On a practical level, to let the others know that we will talk to them later, but not now, may be sufficient as a response to them. But if we cannot talk now at all, patience and compassion are important for us, to recognize this.

And yet, we may feel a sense of urgency to forgive and to forgive *now*, with no delay! Assuming that we can, in fact, address this issue now, this still raises the question of what exactly we are asking in demanding of ourselves that we forgive. What exactly is this forgiving that we are contemplating?

There are two interconnected senses of forgiving in this context.

In the first sense, to forgive someone is to give up any claim to punish or to demand punishment of that person for any misdeed committed, to overlook and to disregard that action, and to cancel any indebtedness of the other for that action against us. To forgive in this sense is to pardon, to excuse, to absolve or release from obligation and responsibility, to let off, to hold exempt from any consequences, and so forth.

In any of these first ways, we can decide and then forgive, immediately. Here, forgiving is subject to our will and under our control, as in raising our hand if we decide to do so, assuming no neuromuscular problems.

In the second sense, to forgive is to stop holding any resentment or anger or desire to have the other punished or hurt in any way. This forgiveness is quite different from the first sense of forgiving. In this context, it is important to notice the principle in the background that we can change if we just decide to do so, from being resentful to not being resentful. And so, it is critical to recognize that there are several important states of mind we cannot in fact change simply by deciding that they should be different or not there at all.

Most centrally here, such states beyond our will and immediate control include our being angry, resentful, desiring something, feeling a particular way in certain contexts, and responding the way we do to the people we are interacting with. For example, we may decide that we will not feel angry or will not want to see the other punished, and yet feel anger or have such a desire.

So, if our forgiving is a matter of our making a public declaration giving up claim to recompense or punishment, that can be done by a decision to do so. On the other hand, if we are asking ourselves to stop resenting, feeling anger, or wanting to see revenge or at least justice done for the other's misdeeds against us, this shift cannot at all be accomplished simply by a decision to do so!

This realization may lead us to notice that we have perhaps no clear idea of what to do in order to forgive here—even if we are very eager to forgive in this second sense! *If we feel that we* should *somehow forgive, even if we have no idea of how to do so*, we may attack ourselves for being so rigid and bitter and angry and "stuck" in the stew of our hatred. This is not going in a good direction! We are back to attacking ourselves.

We may stir up hatred against ourselves, or begin to feel numb or confused about what is going on, which may give us a moment's pause, but if we continue, looking more deeply into what is going on, what do we notice? We may sense that there is something about the situation that is unresolved for us.

For example, perhaps we observe that those who attacked and hurt us, psychologically or physically or both, have not acknowledged their actions at all. Or that there is no expression of sympathy for our hurt. Or that we ourselves are not looking into the fear and anger that arise from having been treated violently. Something may be keeping us in our hearts and minds from making peace with this history of mistreatment.

What is there to appreciate further here, and how might this clearer understanding and new perspective on our history be significant for us?

If we ponder the idea that forgiveness for another's violence against us may be facilitated by our dealing first with our hurt and with our anger, we may conclude that *if somehow* we had no unresolved concerns about our being hurt and had no anger at all, we would have a simpler road to travel now.

But that "if somehow" talks of an unlikely and certainly atypical story. So, before forgiving another, let us look at the more usual situation, and begin by coming face to face with our own hurt and anger. This may be quite painful, and so going immediately into anger can be relieving, since it is a diversion from this pain. Or, going into believing that we have forgiven, when we have only mouthed the words in one context or another, may also put a veil over this pain, and have us believe at least superficially that everything is completed and finished about this part of our lives.

We may think and hope that we are finished with these issues. And yet we often find that things are not the way we would like to think they are. When we are surprised in this way, we typically recognize that we have no effective idea about how to get out of this torment that keeps coming back on us.

Let me suggest this. *Despite initial hesitation, there may be great value in going into hurt to come to peace about that hurt, and into anger to come to resolution about that anger. The question is how to bring about these transformations effectively.* We will naturally ask here how these take place. *They may not happen in the way we suppose.*

This suggests that we are starting without seeing a path from here to resolution. We may find ourselves stopped here by fear that if we start feeling this hurt, we may never come out of it. Or by fear that if we start feeling this anger, we may be unable to keep from being violent toward those who hurt us or perhaps toward others who happen to be nearby when we explode.

So what would be the alternative? Let us start with the first steps.

For the hurt, the alternative to feeling bad, depressed, and hopeless, starts with feeling the hurt, *leading us to acknowledge the sadness of the story and of what we went through.* For the anger, the alternative starts with feeling the anger, *leading us to appreciate our sense of life that was violated, the values that we held dear that were not respected, all allowing us to come to recognize ourselves on a very deep, emotionally rich level.*

Both of these activities begin by looking into the emotions we have gone through in the earlier situation. To come to resolution is a process that can be described relatively briefly but may represent many visits to the same issues, and months if not years of reviewing, rethinking, and revisiting our emotionally-charged past.

It is clearly not enough simply to label our emotions, even if that is a start. We have to uproot the emotions, as is said in some traditions. (This is quicker said than accomplished!) This uprooting requires going to the specifics that will show the power of the emotions.

This may involve very particular moments of awareness: awareness of sensations from different parts of the body (tightness in abdomen, sweating, constrictive chest pains, acidity in the stomach, burning in the eyes), sense-specific perceptions (particular smells, tastes), and mental particulars (memories, images, thoughts, fantasies), as well as their overall interactions and patterns.

This may involve putting words to the story, having us be clear about our emotions, feelings, and thoughts.

Let us start with this verbal description of the past situation. To this we add our recollections of key, emotionally-charged experiences of that situation.

With these two coupled together, we are in a position to address this part of our past. Here we review this past afresh, with our present awareness.

This is re-experiencing the basic defining features of the earlier experience, but with our present consciousness. So that, for example, our recollection of what we experienced one day when we were eight years old is perceived through our current perspective and appreciation that is not limited to the mind of that eight-year-old. We are reviewing, but with distance and clarity that was not possible back then.

Reviewing these particulars, integrated in this way with this fresh consciousness, is the mechanism involved in embracing the intensity of the felt reality, to have sympathy and compassion for ourselves, wishing we had not had such a history and hoping that we be free of such violence now and in the future.

Perhaps we will be able to discuss with those involved, the fact that they have not yet acknowledged their harsh actions. We may be offered apologies, declarations of remorse, and a firm commitment by them never to act in the same violent or harsh ways again. If so, all of that may be reassuring, but it may not: we may find that even these do not resolve our issues about this history. We may receive the sympathy of others, which can act as a salve to our wounds. On the other hand, we may never have an opportunity to have such a discussion, or those involved may deny and reply with counter-accusations.

What else, then, can we do to experience some relief in this situation?

Whether or not there is recognition by those involved or by others, our own thinking about the sad story we are remembering, *allows and encourages the development of compassion and respect for ourselves as having been put into a terribly difficult situation and yet somehow having survived.*

Here we will sense our vulnerability, separate from any anger we might feel by criticizing and judging either the situation, those who mistreated us, or ourselves. Furthermore, this same sympathy and compassion for ourselves can lead us to recognize that there have been many people in the world who have suffered severe violence or have been left defenseless, and can also lead us to feel compassion for that pain.

It is important to recognize here that this consideration is not meant to deny our own pain, to minimize it, to dismiss it as insignificant or as nothing special. It is certainly not meant to pretend that everything is fine.

In fact, its function is just the opposite. We begin here with our own pain, appreciated through what might be years of nightmares and remembering some frightening incidents in our lives all-too-well. We now open our consideration to different forms of pain and anguish that others have lived through. This is not to replace our pain, but to appreciate, in this larger context, how many have been mistreated around the world and through the centuries.

This leads to the somber realization that we are a blind species, that we act in ways that are all-too-often based on dissatisfaction, frustration, agitation, irritation, anger, rage, anxiety, a sense of being out of control, an urge to take some action, any action, in order to change things. All of these are acting out of a state of desperation.

We may read the prayer partially quoted earlier (at the top of page 249) as a reminder that there is an epidemic in our species of acting in ways that are hurtful if not fatal to others, often quite intentionally. These actions arise out of not seeing a more satisfying and fulfilling alternative, one that would leave us with a greater sense of self-respect for how well we have managed the situation.

If we imagine humans acting in calm and clear understanding of what is happening and with good-will toward others, or at least with a lack of hatred, vengefulness, envy, or jealousy, we are thinking about a world other than ours as it now shows itself to be operating.

But this is an inspiring thought, which invites a tender compassion that recognizes all of the waste of human energy in this sort of unseeing torment that brings on further torment. *The teachers of many spiritual traditions have talked to this point for thousands of years!*

Despite this inspiring thought, we may still feel irritation or anger. We may think that we no longer have such ill-will, but may notice how sensitive we are at certain moments: someone says something we think is meant sarcastically, someone does not return a smile, someone we do not even know cuts in front of us driving on the road, to which we respond strongly with feeling hurt or insulted, by screaming curses, by judging the other to be a selfish maniac. This may show us that our response is more severe and weighty than the action itself.

In this discrepancy, we may appreciate an idea from Buddhist theory of mind and consciousness, that our conditioning, or past experience, and the current tendencies that have been created by that past, contribute to the nature of our present thoughts, feelings, and reactions to whatever is happening. In seeing this discrepancy in this particular context, we may recognize annoyance, anger, or even a boiling pot of rage within us, and perhaps this pot is all-too-familiar. It may be relevant, then, for us to look more closely here at rage.

Rage is intense, dark, overpowering, controlling our thoughts and actions, making us feel bad, upset, out of control, shattering our peace. It undermines our sense of mastery over the situation and our emotions. It leads to feelings of shame or to fear of being rejected or judged negatively. These and other particular thoughts, feelings, and judgments, varying from context to context, form a constellation of features that is our very own particular rage.

What is there to do with all of this! Breathing is always helpful, especially a breathing that is slow and long and that allows us to settle down from this whirlwind of ideas and judgments.

A next step is to appreciate all of these thoughts, but not to follow them.

How do we do this? For example, how do we deal with agitating and upsetting and potentially violent thoughts without being taken over by them?

A traditional approach is to begin by cultivating calm using some practice of concentration such as focusing on the breathing or reciting some phrase.

Then, with calm at least somewhat established, we allow a thought to arise that we will notice and contemplate during its brief presence in our mind. The titration (here, the slow addition of one after the other) of such thoughts is by returning repeatedly to a simple breathing, to reinstall a calm presence. This will then allow a next thought to be considered and investigated.

A key part of this process is that *we are watching each thought, not taking it to be a report of reality*. This is recognizing the thought *as a manifestation* of our particular situation, attitude, interpretation, and so forth.

This involves refraining from assuming that the thought is a truth to base further thinking and planning on. This takes each thought as a thought and nothing more. Doing so allows us to appreciate its impact on our mind and sense of reality more clearly. We do this with some psychological distance, as we observe the thought as something to notice, become aware of, and understand.

This "dualistic" practice (being dualistic in that we are aware of our observing something as well as there being something going on in consciousness for us to observe) and its value in transforming consciousness may take us back to earlier relevant discussions of dualism, especially in the chapter on the pivot of the Dao.

In recognizing our angry thoughts as instances of our thinking, for example, we begin to appreciate that we do not have to act on those thoughts at all. Instead, we have the opportunity of noticing the frustration that we felt earlier.

Here we can understand anger and hurt as two manifestations or states of mind that come out of the same unhappy, unfortunate, or miserable situation.

Focusing on this sad situation, we may appreciate how common it is for people to feel frustration in their lives. We may wish for ourselves to be safe, healthy, satisfied, and fulfilled, and may recognize that others wish the same for themselves. In looking through and beyond the anger and hurt that may show themselves to us, we may begin to sense that our wishes for ourselves can apply equally to others just by being made more general.

This hints at the possibility of a great friendship among humans who are recognizing how much suffering has gone on, and continues, everywhere we look. This invites a sense of friendship with the world.

Taking this idea of friendship further, we may consider mettā, a word in the Pāli language of ancient India that means friendship. Let me say more to make clear what this friendship amounts to.

In Indic theory of mind and consciousness, mettā is one of four very special states of mind. These four are understood as having unlimited value, offering great potential benefit, and are described partly for these reasons as being endless or infinite in scope. These states are described as brahma-vihāras, that is, are vihāras or dwellings (a vihāra in one common meaning is an abode where Buddhist monks live together, a Buddhist monastery) that are brahma-like (divine, sublime, high, spiritual). This term brahma-vihāra is customarily rendered as divine abodes. The four are clearly highly respected in the tradition.

To consider mettā in context and to appreciate the complementarity of these states of mind or divine abodes, we might list and describe the other three as (1) compassion or kindness in being moved by the suffering of others, (2) sympathetic joy or non-envious happiness at another's success or well-being, and (3) equanimity or a serene impartiality free of resentment or approval, repulsion or greed, in which our attentiveness to each moment of experience does not lead to any reactivity in thought or judgment.[2] These four are taken as states to understand deeply, to experience fully, and to cultivate methodically.

The particular divine abode that we are focusing on here, mettā, is often rendered in English as lovingkindness. It is a special friendliness, not based on our own benefit, but focused on those toward whom we are friendly.

Thus, mettā has been translated as friendliness, kindness, or lovingkindness. In Theravāda Buddhist texts, it is explained as the wish that all beings "be happy and free from affliction" or that "all beings be free from enmity, affliction, and anxiety, and live happily."[3]

In this understanding, the cultivation of mettā is seen as a gradual path to the relinquishing of ill-will. Or, perhaps more clearly, ill-will is replaced at the center of our reflections by a respect for the yearning we have for happiness and by a more profound appreciation of the difficulty of realizing this yearning.

As ill-will becomes less dominant as an orienting frame of mind, we become more open to recognizing and appreciating more clearly this profound human desire for well-being. This alone does not eliminate ill-will, but *in a very powerful and liberating way puts ill-will into a larger context.*

A powerful feature of mettā, lovingkindness, is that it is a way to overcome hate (called an antidote to hate, in some texts). *How does this work?*

Suppose that there is someone who once bullied us. If we think of this person as violent, and base a judgment on that perception, we may easily experience ill-will (in addition, perhaps, to fear).

By way of contrast, we may imagine this individual as just one more person frustrated and distraught in a non-realized search for peace. In this, we are now thinking about a person who is unhappy and unpeaceful. This is a sad thought.

In cultivating mettā in this context, we may actually experience the relief of having our ill-will replaced by sympathy and compassion.[4]

---

[2] One extended discussion of these concepts can be found in the work of Buddhaghosa, *Visuddhimagga*, Chap. IX, Sect. 93-96 (in short, IX.93-96). Cf. Vsm.I.54, IV.112, 114, 165, IX.88, 96, 101, XXI.63, XXII.51. The other three terms here are (1) karuṇa, (2) muditā, and (3) upekkhā, respectively.

[3] See, for example, Vsm.III.58, IX.8-9.

[4] Cf. Vsm.III.58, 122, IV.160, IX.3, 9-10, 97-101, 105-110, 115-123, XIV, 154. (Citation abbreviations explained just above in note 2.)

This idea will perhaps have us wonder how to feel this sympathy at all while there may be something else heavy in our hearts.

After all, if in our own understanding of our life we are angry, hurt, or have suffered at the hands of another, don't we feel irritated, angry, resentful, or perhaps have a wish for justice?[5]

To give this last concern a context for reflection, it might be helpful to remark that one important question here is whether we need to resolve any of this before we can truly embrace such sympathy or compassion.

If we look at this in terms of what is going on for us in our own minds and in terms of what we are actually experiencing, we may notice that resentment and anger, which are turbulent states, *keep us unpeacefully focused on judgments* of having been wronged, hurt, or left with substantial problems that we now have to deal with.

More basically, these are keeping us in a judgmental stance, in which we are considering our history and drawing evaluative conclusions about it and about those who were involved in that history. It is important at such times for us to have compassion for ourselves by acknowledging the hurt that is still perhaps quite raw and demanding a healing salve.

It may be too soon for us to shift away from what we are experiencing as our wounds. Kindness and gentleness toward ourselves may be the next step for us at such moments. We may then return to the issue of re-evaluating and rethinking what was going on between us and these others, and take a fresh view of the entire situation we are still feeling tender about. We may feel that we are see-sawing back and forth here, at some times feeling an urge to forgive and move on, and at other times feeling a hesitancy to forgive the others and a desire, instead, to be comforted ourselves.

How do we go beyond such an unresolved situation?

Forgiveness and its opposite, unforgiveness, both involve the judgmental functions of the mind. Both keep us considering, reflecting, evaluating, and coming to evaluative conclusions. And here, limiting the focus to the story, the conclusion to reach is rather obvious: we were wronged and they were wrong.

What shift can expand our sense of the situation to get us out of this tiny loop that focuses on the story with this judgmental mind?

Our understanding of the situation may begin to shift when we recognize clearly that forgiveness and mettā *operate according to different considerations, each with its own focus.*

More explicitly, we may contrast the thinking involved in considering whether to forgive, with the reflections and meditations guided by teachings that explain the concept of mettā. In this latter, we are developing a deeper understanding and a greater appreciation of our situation. And we are coming to be

---

[5] On the issue of justice in a larger framework, cf. above, p. 245, n. 1.

more at peace with these events, not by erasing them from our memory, but in having them no longer be a haunting torment that invades our consciousness repeatedly and destroys our peace relentlessly.

We are asking ourselves to forgive these actions against us, but this does not require seeing them as tolerable, and certainly not as honorable. We may come to understand better those we see as having treated us so harshly. We may come to feel compassion for what they lived through in their own childhood. We may even feel that given their upbringing, they did the best they could in raising us. But this does not mean that we find how we were treated to be any less violent or hurtful. The principle that we must forgive both the person and the action in order to become free of this burden is perhaps a dogma rather than a truth.[6]

We may believe that forgiveness in one of these forms will bring us lightness of spirit and freedom from the past, with a consciousness in which these incidents are no longer persistently demanding, and in which we do not recall them in rage, agitation, or with a determined call for justice. If this is our interest, *the question becomes how to shift a focus that otherwise keeps us locked in a judgmental attitude*. The way we accomplish this shift *may be indirect*.

One indirect approach here is the practice of mettā we have described. This invites a more inclusive vision of our past and our present that allows us a glimpse of a new perspective, not limited or defined by the world's harshness. Without taking on the naïve belief that everyone in the world has now become wise, caring, and respectful, we can still appreciate what might be possible in a world where caring and compassion guide all of us. One indirect result of this practice is precisely such a powerful shift from this judgmental attitude.

We may experience this transformation as our declaring that our current thinking, remembering, hoping, and yearning *will not* be determined or defined by this past harshness or violence! Or, as a realization that we are committed to becoming a catalyst for well-being in the world, in our thoughts, words, and actions, despite the painful situations that were part of our past.

Our reconciling and coming to peace with our past, without distorting or denying our own experience, will come in cultivating a gentle appreciation for ourselves and in recognizing the core values that reflect our strongest yearnings and aspirations. Here there is full, clear memory and also a liberating expansiveness in our consciousness that provides the freedom to think afresh, breathing now deeply and with rich awareness of life.

---

[6] On this distinction between the person and the actions themselves, and a questioning of the idea that forgiveness is required for resilience, see, e.g., J. Lecomte, *La résilience. Se reconstruire après un traumatisme*, pp. 47-52.

19. Life, Death, and Survival

We are alive and, being mortal, one day we will die. We may contemplate death, but personally experiencing the death of someone important to us may be the beginning of a deeper search into the meaning of life and death in a conceptual way. It may also inspire a more immediate, very personal quest.

Perhaps one of the most powerful sources of religious reflection is this attempt to give sense to life, death, and survival. We need to survive, to have a way to deal with death and go on, when we must. These are part of the human condition, features of our lives that define boundaries on our existence, making life, death, and survival part of what some call our existential predicament.

Some of these features of undeniable limit are specific to us as individuals, given our own personal temperament and mind, bodily features, physical abilities, experience, family interactions, place in society and in history, and so forth. Some are universal to all humans. Death is certainly one of the latter.

It is significant that if we look at a text describing an ongoing attentiveness to our own lives designed to help us develop calm, awareness, insight, understanding, and compassion, from the Buddhist meditative tradition, we find more specific meditations or contemplations on death than on any other single topic. There, dead bodies in various stages of decomposition are understood as showing us what will happen, as well, to our very own body.

Rather than being morbid, the point of this reflection is to allow us to appreciate life while it is still here, and to know, at the same time, that change will happen, and that our life will not go on forever.[1]

We may meditate on the limited life span we all have, or we can be brought to face human mortality in specific situations. After all, death is difficult to avoid and can be quite upsetting. When, in particular, we are young at the time of death of someone important in our family, this loss can have an impact that lasts our entire life. Even if we are much older, the death of someone we have been close to and have interacted with for decades can be quite shocking. As in the death of a parent, grandparent, or other close relative.

In some cultures, families have deep respect for their now-deceased ancestors. This "ancestor worship" is a matter of honoring significant members of earlier generations in the family, their values, ways of life, understanding, and wisdom, in part for the inspiration and guidance through life that this provides.

For those who survive a death, there may be a very strong sense of loss: something very central to our daily life or to our sense of who we are may be shifted with this death. We may ask ourselves very basic and profound questions about who we are and what life is about, why our own life is continuing, what we are afraid of, what we want from life, what we still hope for, and so on.

---

[1] For more on this practice, see esp. Chap. 10, above.

This is all part of grieving or mourning. But these issues do not necessarily arise precisely when someone important to us dies. At first, there may simply be a deep sense of loss and hopelessness, no interest in being with others, with eating, with living. Memories may overwhelm us at times. We may have regrets about what we did or did not say or do with this person. There may be tears, crying, or sobbing, which we perhaps try to suppress. Or there are none of these at all, at least not at the time.

Anyone who has lost someone close will recognize in at least some these descriptions, experiences that came and were troubling, sooner or later, at *some* point after that loss. We each deal with this in a different way, at our own tempo for reflecting on and coming to terms with this change. What is also individual is which parts of this process happen before and which later.

If we let others tell us here what we should be experiencing or thinking about or feeling, or how soon we should be finished with this process, we are in danger of losing touch with our own needs and manner of integrating this possibly life-altering change. We may appropriately be wary of others who think "to have helped best when he has helped the fastest" (to quote Nietzsche).[2]

When we feel the loss of someone who has died, there is often the realization, new or perhaps familiar yet intensified, of how special this person was for us and for others.

This may be a source of torment, but can also be appreciated as a heartfelt reflection on who this person was and how special it was to share a world together, in specifics that are quite varied. In existentialist terminology, this is the *Mitwelt* (literally, from the German, a "With-world"), the interpersonal world created by our personal connection with one another, giving much of the flavor and value to our personal reality.

This loss may have us yearning to feel once again that life is *not* futile, *does* have meaning, *is* precious. For the time being, though, we may experience it more as a difficult and perplexing situation, as an empty, uncomfortable, disturbing existence. In short, as an existential predicament.

Taking this existential predicament and seeing in it existential value, its significance to us as human beings, may at times be more important than eating or drinking. Here, life and death are not mere facts, are not what some philosophers call neutral *Faktizitäten* or *facticités* ("facticities" or factualities).[3]

Death plummets us into our very core needs and values. It is among the most powerful of life's gifts to bring us back to what is significant and valuable. It can lead us to have a perspective on our life events that is illuminating, calm,

---

[2] Cf. discussion above, p. 77, and reference there to Nietzsche, **GS** 338.

[3] E.g., Martin Heidegger or Jean-Paul Sartre. See R.C. Solomon, *From Rationalism to Existentialism: The Existentialists and Their Nineteenth-Century Backgrounds*, p. 274; cf. pp. 209-210 and 272-279, respectively.

compassionate, and grounded. Because of this, death is recognized in one tradition as a divine messenger, a *deva-dūta*.

In this understanding, death, along with illness and old age, prods us to wake up to the reality of living, and to deal with life in a more enlightened way. By our sensing their closeness and yet imagining their absence, these three bring us the message that the alternative to being alive is not ever to have been born, inviting an appreciation of the life we have had with those we have known. How many in this way have come to understand the importance that another person has had in their lives only after that person is gone? There is a bittersweet flavor to this, but a strong, vibrant, and emotionally rich flavor, nonetheless.

We may feel that death marks the end of a life, but may also recognize a different form of connection in our memories and thoughts. The thread connecting us to someone who has been dear to us does not end at that person's death. The influence of someone, our appreciation of that person, our reflections, discussions, consultations, our memories, inspiration, and yes, even our annoyances, worries, or frustrations, all remain there for us to experience, savor, and deal with, if and when we are ever ready to engage in such an activity.

When a family is changed radically by the divorce of the parents, the relationship between the parents is often not at all ended, but simply transformed into something different. Similarly, with death, our connection is not severed. This is not to pretend that someone who has died is actually alive. It is simply to notice that we do not erase that person or that person's memory when the final rites have been performed. And as a divorce formally ends a marriage and shifts all familial relationships in a fundamental way, death demonstrates the finitude of each life while also inviting us to recognize in our lives *this universal human condition of being allotted a limited but potentially remarkably rich existence.*

For a character in Sartre's *Huis clos* (*No Exit*), other people offer us a rich existence that is an existential hell.[4] But let us consider this universal human condition in a specific situation, such as where we are mourning the death of someone special to us and are reflecting on these issues. Here we typically experience many imaginary conversations, hearing helpful advice that comes from the values of this individual, have memories, thoughts, or other interactions with this person in our thought processes or that are even felt in our bodies.

While we know that the dead are truly dead, they are undeniably with us *in memory*, available in this way for guidance, solace, warmth, confrontation, and other aspects of a relationship. This sense of contact is a deeply experienced form of human consciousness that can allow us a fulfilling existential survival, a creative path to a perspective on life and the human condition that is grounded, accepting, and deeply appreciative.

---

[4] For Sartre (distinguished from this character, Garcin), this statement applies only to *unhealthy relationships*. Cf. comments by Sartre in *Huis clos CD*.

20. Can't I Do Anything Right, Daddy?

I try so hard, but it seems I can't do anything right. My daddy seems to be angry at me for doing something wrong, or for not doing something I should have, almost all the time. Well, just about every day. But I can't figure it out. I don't know what he wants, I mean what I should do to be a good girl.

When I ask him what I've done wrong, or what he wants me to do, he gets even angrier. He calls me stupid and hits me. I feel that I am worthless.

I know that when he's at work, or out of the house, that I can just play with my dolls, but I'd better not get too relaxed or happy, because then I get surprised by his barging into my room when I'm not at all expecting him. That's very scary to me.

The only time when he seems to be a little nice to me is when he takes me on his lap and strokes my hair. That's the way it starts—usually, anyway. Then his breathing gets louder, but it is not his angry breathing. Sometimes he shuts his eyes and looks almost peaceful, or maybe it's daddy's way of looking happy. I can't tell. I've learned not to ask him, though, because then he gets mad at me again, and I certainly don't want that. So I just call it his nice breathing, to give it a name; I think it's not quite the right name for it, though.

When he rubs me, and I can hear his nice breathing, I close my eyes. I feel almost loved and I like that. Please love me, daddy! If I tell him how much I like him when he's like this, when he's making me feel good, then he gets very red in the face and says I'm just a dirty slut. I don't know what he's talking about, what these words mean, but I feel bad when he says that stuff. So I've learned not to talk to him at such times, and not to show him how much I like him to like me. Still, sometimes it's just too much for me to try to hide. So I find myself holding him tight to me, squeezing him with all of my might. I push against him to feel his love, and I yell out, "Yes, daddy. I love you so much! Please love me!" And sometimes he actually tells me just that, that he loves me. I feel wonderful.

21. The Yearnings of Psychospirituality

Psychospirituality:
the complete evolution of consciousness,[1]
its radical transformation,[2]
in accordance with inspired ideals.

What is actually happening to me here?

What is troubling me,
disturbing me?

How can I develop greater
clarity,
understanding,
security,
loving,
wisdom?

How can I be more at peace,
inspired,
creative,
fulfilled?

In this turmoil,
what can I
with tenderness
appreciate
about the longings and the values in my heart?

What do I see of my own humanity,
my honesty,
my desire for my best self,
my most honorable,
noble,
and wise self?

---

[1] Cf. above, p. 164, quoting V.R. Dhiravamsa, Vipassanā Meditation Master, in his review of M. Ginsberg, *The Far Shore: Vipassanā, The Practice of Insight* (on its back cover).
[2] Cf. above, p. vi, proposing as a defining issue of psychospirituality, "a personal transformation to a soulful, integrated completeness of heart-and-mind."

How can I develop my greatest potential?

Beyond my childhood,
beyond my family,
beyond my experiences, adventures, boredoms, and crises,
beyond my land, my society, my culture,
what is my deepest and highest nature?

May I,
may we all,
experience
and nurture
this great potential we each have,
in this very lifetime.

22. We Know the Path

We know the path
that is not a straight path;
we know
that approaching the heart
that opening the heart
goes slowly, then quickly, or not at all,
goes in its own tempos, in its own directions.

We know the yearning
that will not die
no matter what the pain, no matter what the tearful sobbing.

We know the tenderness
that is cautious; we know
the urge to hide, to stop,
the urge to close off, to close down.

We know the tenderness
the gentleness, the sense of caring,
the sense of touching another's soul
the sense of reaching out,
softly, gingerly, hesitatingly.

We know the path
that is a long one
the path back to our source, to our heart, to our drive for life.

We know the wordless
awe of human contact,
so rare, so fragile
so promising, so fleeting
so nourishing.
We know
at times very little of how we shall go
but onwards we go, refusing to settle
for less than we need, for less than we deserve.

This is our human
strength and power.

23. When You Yell At Me

Why are you yelling at me?
I'm not deaf.

When you yell something at me, whatever it is, it is hard for me to hear what it is that you are saying, because I hear mostly your yelling.

If you are frustrated, I want to hear about your frustration and want to know what you are frustrated about, and how I might help you in your frustration, but I do not want to be attacked in order to feel your frustrations and certainly do not want you to dump your frustration or me, or use me as your whipping boy.

When you insult me, I cannot feel or sense your respect for me, or your caring for me, or your love for me. I want your love and your respect. When you are condescending to me or act disgusted by me, I feel neither your love nor your respect. *And it is just about impossible for me to feel love and respect for you when you are acting that way.* So neither of us wins in that situation, so far as I can tell.

Do you think that I enjoy being the target of your frustration, even if I am not the reason you are frustrated? Do you think you are attractive when you act this way? Do you think I deserve such a harsh treatment? Do you want my love in this? Do you at least want my presence? Is this the most effective way to get these from another person?

If you are yelling at me in the hopes of inspiring me to act in a more mature or grounded or calm or clear-minded way, that is a painfully inefficient means to achieve such a goal. Your yelling only leads me to be uncomfortable and frightened. And then I want no contact with you at all. This is a lose-lose situation. How might it be changed into a win-win interaction, in which we both win, rather than where at least one of us loses?

24. I Walk Around

I walk around
(that is, go through my life)
and, without knowing it, I am
hoping that people will
not become angry at me,
and, without knowing it, I
am trying to avoid experiencing
what then happens, in my
imagined fear, when they
are angry at me.

What happened that I want
not to repeat, not to
experience one more time?

Can I put this thought, this
memory, this belief, down?
What is it that I want to put down?

This is, I feel, the next question
to look into.[1]

---

[1] On acting or hoping or fearing without knowing it (without knowing that we
are hoping or fearing or expecting some undesirable outcome), see discussions
on unconscious processes in writings from the 1960s touching on these issues, in
the doctoral dissertations by M. Ginsberg, *Belief: Its Conceptual and Phenomenological Structure* and by R.C. Solomon, *Unconscious Motivation*, as well as in
the slightly more recent work, M. Ginsberg, *Mind and Belief* (1972).

25. Being Hopeful, Being Fearful

Being hopeful that others will not become angry at me,
being fearful that others will become angry at me,
I can, in an image, turn away and move toward them,
backwards.

This not only in an image;
eyes closed (so to speak)
trembling inside and perhaps outside,
waiting for the trouble to start.

But what are they doing and
how are they feeling?
If I can look, I will see better.
Yes, but do I want to see better?
(What can I do about how they feel?
What can I do about what they will then do?)

I see I feel myself powerless here.
Better not to look perhaps.

Still, I see some thoughts and thinking called for here.

What do *I* want to *happen* here and *not* to happen here?

If they begin acting on their anger,
what would I like *my* responses to be here?
And what can *I* do to change what *next* happens now,
in ways that I couldn't before?

The beginning of seeing,
the beginning of understanding,
the beginning of a sense of power and new possibility,
the beginning of power itself,
the beginning of reassurance,
the beginning of wisdom.

26. If Only I Could, I Would

If only I could ´
give you bliss
fulfill your every yearning
satisfy your every need
soothe your every ache
heal your every wound
hold you in total safety
in total security
in total peace
kiss your every hurt
change each bitter tear
of sadness
into a honeyed tear of joy
of love
of beauty
give you fulfillment
give you a grounding in security
warmed by my heart
and by my caring presence
give you completeness, contentment,
give you a safe haven
give you shelter from every tempest
give you peace.
(Oh, for a fairy godmother's wand!)

If only I could
(and here, a deeper wish)
take you beyond
even these joys
to the wonder
of the radiant
seeing feeling
caring accepting
complete
marriage of insight and lovingkindness,[1]
in a heartbeat
I would.

---

[1] On the marriage of such psychospiritual couples, see M. Ginsberg, *The Inner Palace*, pp. 85, 129, 308, 580, 591-592.

27. Options When Overwhelmed

Orienting Considerations
When acutely overwhelmed, we are not able to think clearly, if at all, are unable to deal well with what is occurring, and are *not* experiencing things in a calm, clear, and loving way. So, *now, when we are able to think,* is a perfect time to ask what we can do to shift things for ourselves when overwhelmed.

One thing is probably evident to us here by this point in our lives: there is no one-size-fits-all solution to our situation, and no quick fix. What will bring about this change, this shift, varies in important ways from person to person, and even varies for one person from situation to situation. We are not round pegs in search of a square hole. We need our own personalized recipes or menus.

There is great benefit here in our being attentive to ourselves and in becoming familiar with what actually works for us individually. That is, *we tend to see more about our own path by looking at how we deal with our own lives, I feel, than by anything that could be said in a general way applicable to all life histories. Some* things, nonetheless, can be said that may be helpful.

When overwhelmed, we may be trying to handle overly difficult tasks, too many tasks, or trying to satisfy too many demands from people. *Further, there is also a more acute form of being overwhelmed, when our mind is spinning or numb*—and both variations here are very immediate and pervasive. Typically, this is feeling quite agitated, anxious, or like a raging fire. Or it is, quite differently, not feeling anything at all, numbed, absent, in an eerie limbo of blank, frozen emptiness, feeling "out to lunch" and out of touch (with ourselves and with others).[1] Whichever of these two is the form we are facing, *it is important for us to discover here our own path beyond feeling acutely overwhelmed.*

The Work
When overwhelmed, our first priority is to seek relief and to be kind to ourselves in some very basic, simple ways: *to become calm, clear, and loving.* With lovingkindness or compassion operating with insight and understanding, we can define our own personal, individualized remedy for ourselves. The goal here: feeling centered, grounded, feeling at peace with room to breathe, experi-

---

[1] When in acute trauma or panic, thinking and verbalizing are partially if not completely closed off, while we feel frozen, disoriented, confused, and such. These processes are linked to less higher brain functioning, especially of the cerebral cortex, and greater activity in the right limbic system, the amygdala, etc. Perhaps this suggests we calm these hyperactive centers and reactivate this deactivated higher brain functioning. When in an actual situation of panic, though, we still have an immediate question to answer directly. *The urgent initial focus when we are overwhelmed is to bring calm into a world of panic.*

encing the situation with a rich presence and clear sense of our viewpoint, our personal worth, a feeling of well-being. *What works here for us will vary.*

So, we seek a shift from a spinning mind or having "mind-freeze" and from having no sense of grounding, center, or worth. The means available for us in this context are *our coming back to our senses* and *our positive connecting with our world.* There is great value in seeing how we each do these best, for our own evolving use through time in our own particular lives. Let me explain what I mean by these two ideas to make them clearer and usable.

First: coming back to our senses is making use of the five senses (sight, hearing, smelling, tasting, and body-sensation). *So, which experiences involving these senses enhance our lives?* These allow us to refocus our mind and calm ourselves. *Noticing these allows us to create our own recipes, to build our own menus, for becoming calm, clear, and loving.* This can be done in gentle, caring ways, *appreciating the value of being kind to and taking care of ourselves.*

Examples: we take a nice bath, have a refreshing cup of tea, sing or listen to music, take a walk, breathe in fresh air, taste appetizing foods, smell mild incense, feel an expansion in our chest or belly as we breathe, sense power in our body as we stretch, or enjoy the peace of sitting still. The good news from science: these sense-based activities involve lower portions of the brain still functioning when the frontal cortex is on temporary vacation. *(And your ways?)*

Second: a positive connection with our world (people, pets, nature) here is a soothing connection: having someone with whom we feel safe hold us gently, hearing a friend sing to us, being with calm people, playing with a pet, hiking in the woods. Do we recall times when we felt calm and at peace? Good news: We may also enjoy any of these in our imagination. *(And your ways?)*

Discussions (on shame, remorse, love, anger, fear, etc.) here—and in *The Far Shore*—are relevant to our understanding *the ways of our own mind and heart*, which can guide our self-transformation in more elegant, efficient ways.

It may be of great value to keep in mind that when looking for progress, *the first signs of a positive shift may be* the same unhappy pattern we have been experiencing—now taking less time from beginning to end, or now going to less extreme forms. Rather than thinking, "Same old, same old," noticing these very first signs of a positive shift may help us recognize and appreciate progress in its earliest subtle forms. It would be similarly valuable to acknowledge our actions explicitly ("I am taking care of myself" and "This is important and valuable, and I receive my own caring interest with appreciation"). *This can provide us with a strong sense of our own capacity to guide our lives and let us begin to feel calm and clear, to feel respect, love, and caring for ourselves.*[2]

---

[2] On love, compassion, and insight-guided lovingkindness, see M. Ginsberg, *The Far Shore*, pp. 24-29, 51-67; and M. Ginsberg, *The Inner Palace*, pp. 84-85, 249, 254, 256-257, 305, 312, 333, 478, 499, 523-525, 592-593.

28. An Enigma No More

Our restless soul
longs to feel itself
belovèd

striking out in one direction
or another

seeking to recognize
to accept
to love
itself and to be
loved

even, and especially, in its harshness
or ugliness

until
finally, almost hopeless,
it glimpses
and honors
the heartfelt longing
the guiltless struggling

for a welcome home.

With this, it unveils itself, free to taste
calm and love,
ultimately fulfilled
in radiant clarity
unashamedly complete.

29. We are Creatures

We are creatures
of clarity and confusion
of soaring imagination and sleepy boredom
of fresh perception and stale prejudice
of passion and peace in their many forms
of love and hate in their many forms
of longing and of fulfillment
of fear and of courage
of pride and shame
of adventure and security
of reassuring habit and exciting spontaneity
of doubt and of certainty
We are difficult and we are easy
We want it all and we can let it all go
We are this and much more
We are this and much less
We are creatures of life and of death
We are here and we are gone.
We are complex and we are simple.

29. Love

Love
is caring, good-will, warmth, gentleness.

Love
is active, not passive. It is what we do, not what happens to us.

Love
is coming to know the other, and it
is respecting the other's yearnings and needs and personality.

Love
is attentive, appreciative, and caring.

Love
looks outward to the other and sees
another individual,
not a mirror image of ourselves.

Love
looks inward and sees
the delicate intimacy of our connection with the other,
a combination of separateness and closeness.

Love
calls us
to reach out, to seek understanding,
to seek being understood, to find harmony and respect.

Love
is patient, enduring, persevering.

Love
is deeply engaged with heart-felt commitment
when disharmonies reign,
and it flows gently and effortlessly,
when relationships are relaxed and easy,
letting closeness blossom.

Love
is soulful intensity, and, as well, passionate appreciation.

30. Full Circle Transformation

When we have done all of our reading and reflecting and meditating on the topic of our mind and our experience and our relationships to others, we have the opportunity of returning full circle to ourselves.

There is, then, the question of what all of this reflecting on our lives means to us, and how it makes a difference in our experience, states of mind, calm, understanding, relationships with others, and the degree to which there is easy flowing, grounded experience of whatever there is presented to us.

We may know first-hand, or may have heard, that life takes turns that we could never predict—with times of joy and of turbulence in unforeseen patterns—that what is here today will not be what will be the case for us for the rest of our existence.

If these reflections and the coming to a clear understanding of the workings of our mind have any impact on us, we will see a difference in how we experience repeating situations from the way they were to us earlier on in our lives, and we will also see a difference in how we experience others, how we relate to them, on many dimensions.

Full Circle

When we come full circle
having reflected, analyzed, contemplated
the nature of consciousness,
having looked into our
innermost chambers,
and seen the workings and pathways
of our mind,
when we have taken this trip
and have returned home,
come back
full circle

we may sense, tasting the newness of the moment, that
it is not as it was.
We are not as we were.

Same context,
new awareness, mind, thoughts, response,

moving to new clarity,
the circle opening into
liberating transformation.

Has it been a pointless voyage
that we soon forget?
Or, do we find ourselves different, transformed?
What in fact have we seen, discovered, appreciated?
Perhaps we have seen what centers us,
have seen what replaces needy hungry loneliness
with vibrant, satisfied fullness, rich solitude,
have seen what brings us agitation and so what brings us calm,
have seen what brings us confusion and so what brings us clarity,
have seen what brings us fright or anger or envy and so what allows
us to feel sympathy, compassion, good-will, lovingkindness.
Perhaps we have seen
what we value and
appreciate, what makes us
feel at peace and
fully alive.

Appendix: Pinyin/Wade-Giles Transcriptions and Kanji

The Wade-Giles equivalents of the terms given in pīnyīn (or, more fully, especially in Chinese contexts, hànyǔ pīnyīn) transcription of Chinese terms in this book are as follows, with order determined by Romanized alphabetical order, following the pīnyīn spellings. The fonts used in this appendix have been chosen for their clarity in reading. There is a separate section giving Japanese kanji that follows below as the second part of this appendix.

Pīnyīn	Wade-Giles	Chinese characters
Báiyún Shǒuduān	Pái-yǔn Shǒu-tuān	白雲守端
Bǎi Zhàng	Pǎi Chàng	百丈
běnlái miànmù	pěnlái mièmù	本來面目
bǐ shì mò de qí ǒu,	pǐ shìh mò te ch'í ǒu,	彼是莫得其偶、
wèi zhī dào shū	wèi chīh tào shū	謂之道樞 [謂 = 谓;
		樞 = 枢]
bù lì wén zì	bù lì wén zì	不立文字
chán	ch'án (shán)	禪 = 禪
chén	ch'én	塵
chōng	ch'ūng	沖
chōng qì yǐ wéi hé	ch'ūng ch'ì ǐ wéi hó	沖氣以為和
Chǔ	Ch'ǔ	楚
chuán	ch'uán	傳
chuán xīn	ch'uán hsīn	傳心
chuán xīn fǎ yào	ch'uán hsīn fǎ yào	傳心法要
chūn qiū	ch'ūn ch'iū	春秋
dà	tà	大
Dámó	Támó	達磨
(= dharma, for Bodhidharma)		
Dámódàshī	Támótàshīh	達磨大師
(= dharma great teacher, for Bodhidharma)		
dāng lìng zì wù	tāng lìng tzù wù	當令自悟 [令 = 令]
dào	tào	道
Dàodéjīng	Tào Té Chīng	道德經 [經 = 經]
Dàodé zhēnjīng	Tào té chēn-chīng	道德真經
guǎngshèng yì	kuǎng-shèng ì	廣聖義 [經 = 經]
dào jiā	tào chiā	道家
dào jiào	tào chiào	道教
dào rén	tào jén	道人

dào shū	tào shū	道樞
Dàoyuán	Tào-yuán	道原
Dàozàng	*Tào-tsàng*	道藏
Dàzàng	*Tà-tsàng*	大藏
dé	té	德
dòng	tùng	洞
Dédàojīng	*Té Tào Chīng*	德道經 [經 = 経]
Dù Guāngtíng	Tù Kuāng-t'íng	杜光庭
è zuò	ò tsò	惡作
fǎ	fǎ	法
fǎ yǐ xīn chuán xīn	fǎ ǐ hsīn ch'uán hsīn	法以心傳心
Féng Mènglóng	Féng Mènglúng	馮夢龍
Guǎnzǐ	*Kuǎn Tzǔ*	管子
Guōdiàn	Kuō-tièn	郭店
gǔ	kǔ	轂
hái (or huán)	hái (or huán)	還
Hán Shān	Hán Shān	寒山
Hán Shān Shì	*Hán Shān Shì*	寒山詩
hànyǔ	hànyǔ	漢語 [漢 = 汉; 語 = 语]
hànyǔ pīnyīn	hànyǔ p'īnyīn	漢語拼音 [漢 = 汉; 語 = 语]
hànzì	hàn-tzù	漢字 [漢 = 汉]
hé	hó	和
Hézé Shénhuì	Hó-tsé Shén-huì	荷澤神會
Huáinánzǐ	*Huái-nán-tzǔ*	淮南子
huán (or hái)	huán (or hái)	還
Huángbò	Huáng Pò	黃檗
Huángbò Xīyùn	Huáng Pò Hsī Yùn	黃檗希運
Huìkāi	Huì-k'āi	慧開
Huì-míng	Huì-míng	慧明
Huì-néng	Huì-néng	慧能
jī	chī	機
jiǎn	chiěn	簡
jiàn-xìng	chièn hsìng	見性
Jiànzhì Sēngcàn	Chièn-chìh Sēng-ts'àn	鑑智僧璨 [鑑 = 鉴]
jiāo wài bié chuán	chiāo-wài piéh-ch'uán	敎外別傳
Jǐngdé chuándēng lù	*Chǐng-té Ch'uán tēng lù*	景德傳燈錄
jūnzǐ	chǔn tzǔ	君子

Kǒngfūzǐ (= Confucius)	K'ǔng-fū-tzǔ	孔夫子
Kǒngzǐ (= Confucius)	K'ǔng-tzǔ	孔子
Lǎozǐ	Lǎo-tzǔ	老子
lèi	lèi	類
liù chén	liù ch'én	六塵
liù chén bù wù,	liù ch'én pù wù,	六塵不惡、
hái tóng zhèng	hái t'úng chèng	還同正
jué	ch'üéh	覺
Lǐ Xūnzù	Lǐ Hsūn-tsù	李遵勗
Lǚ Bùwéi	Lǚ Pùwéi	呂不韋
Lù Xiūjìng	Lù Hsiū-chìng	陸修靜 = 陆修静
lùn	lùn	論
Lúnyǔ (= *The Analects*)	*Lúnyǔ*	論語
Lǚ shì chūn qiū	*Lǚ shìh ch'ūn ch'iū*	呂氏春秋
Mǎwángduī	Mǎwángtuī	馬王堆
Mèngzǐ	Mèng-tzǔ	孟子
míng	míng	名
míng	míng	明
Míng Yīngzōng	Míng Yīng-tsūng	明英宗
nèi shèng wài wáng	nèi shèng wài wáng chīh	內聖外王
zhī dào	chīh tào	之道 [內 = 内 = 内 = 內]
Nèiyè	*Nèi-yèh*	內業 [內 = 内 = 内 = 內]
néng zhī wú zhī	néng chīh wú chīh	能知無知
dào zhī shū jī	tào chīh shū chī	道之樞機
pīnyīn	p'īnyīn	拼音
Pútídámó	P'út'ítámó	菩提達磨
(= Bodhidharma)		
qì	ch'ì	氣 = 气 = 炁
Qīng	Ch'īng	清
qíng	ch'íng	情
Qí wù lùn	*Ch'í wù lùn*	齊物論
rén xìng	jén hsìng	人性
róu ruò shèng	jóu jò shèng	柔弱勝
gāng qiáng	kāng ch'iáng	剛強
ruò	jò	弱
sān	sān	三
Sānzàng	*Sān-tsàng*	三藏
Sāndòng	*Sān-tùng*	三洞

Sēngcàn	Sēng-ts'àn	僧璨
shān	shān	山
shén	shén	神
shén fú	shén fú	神符
shèng rén	shèng jén	聖人
shèng rén héng wú xīn	shèng jén héng wú hsīn	聖人恒无心
shèng rén wú cháng xīn	shèng jén wú ch'áng hsīn	聖人無常心
shéng shéng bù kě míng, fù guī yú wú wù	shéng shéng pù k'ě míng, fù kuēi yǘ wú wù	繩繩不可名、復歸於無物
Shénhuì	Shén-huì	神會
shén míng	shén míng	神明
shén rén	shén jén	神人
Shì Dàoyuán	Shìh Tào-yüán	釋道原
shí shén	shih shén	識神
shū	shū	樞
shū jī	shū chī	樞機
shū shǐ de qǐ huán zhōng, yǐ yìng wú qióng	shū shǐh te ch'ǐ huán chūng, ǐ yìng wú ch'iúng	樞始得其環中、以應無窮
Sīkōng Tú	Ssū-k'ūng T'ú	司空圖
Taìjí	T'aì chí	太極 [極 = 极]
Taìpíng	T'aì p'íng	太平
Tài yǐ jīn huá zōng zhǐ	*T'ài ǐ chīn huá tsūng chǐh*	太乙金華宗旨
Táng Jūnyì	T'áng Chūn-ì	唐君毅
tiān rén	t'iēn jén	天人
Tiān shèng guǎng dēng lù	*T'iēn shèng kuǎng tēng lù*	天聖廣燈錄
Tú Sīkōng	T'ú Ssū-k'ūng	圖司空
Wáng Bì	Wáng Pì	王弼
wéi	wéi	爲 = 爲
wén	wén	文
wénzi dīng tiě niú, wú qú xià zuǐ chù	wén-tzu tīng t'iěh niú, wú ch'ǘ hsià tsuǐ ch'ù	蚊子叮鐵牛、無渠下嘴處
wú	wú	無 = 无 = 无
Wúménguān	*Wú-mén-kuān*	無門關
Wúmén Huìkāi	Wú-mén Huì-k'āi	無門慧開
wú míng	wú míng	無名

wú qíng	wú ch'íng	無情
wú qíng rén	wú ch'íng jén	無情人
Wúshàng bìyào	*Wúshàng pìyào*	無上祕要
wú shì	wú shìh	無事
wú wéi	wú wéi	無爲
wú wéi, bù wéi	wú wéi, pù wéi	無爲、不爲
wú wéi ér wú bù wéi	wú wéi érh wú pù wéi	無爲而無不爲
wú xīn	wú hsīn	無心 [心 = 心]
wú yǐ wú wéi	wú ǐ wú wéi	吾以無爲
chéng lè yǐ	ch'éng lè ǐ	誠樂矣
wú yù	wú yù	無欲
wú zhēng	wú chēng	無爭
wú zhī	wú chīh	無知
xiāo yáo yóu	hsiāo yáo yú	消遙游
xiǎo yǐn yǐn yú shān	hsiǎo yǐn yǐn yǔ shān	小隐隐於山 [於 = 于]
dà yǐn yǐn yú shì	tà yǐn yǐn yǔ shìh	大隐隐於市 [於 = 于]
xiǎo yǐn yǐn yú yě	hsiǎo yǐn yǐn yǔ yěh	小隐隐於野 [於 = 于]
dà yǐn yǐn yú shì	tà yǐn yǐn yǔ shìh	大隐隐於市 [於 = 于]
xīn	hsīn	心 = 心
xìng	hsìng	性
xīn wú suǒ zhù	hsīn wú sǒ chù	心無所住
Xìnxīnmíng	*Hsìn hsīn míng*	信心銘
Xīshēngjīng	*Hsīshēng chīng*	西昇經 [經 = 經]
Xī Yùn	Hsī Yùn	希運
xū	hsū	虛
Xuèmàilùn	*Hsüèhmàilùn*	血脉論
xū huái ruò gǔ	hsū huái jò kǔ	虛懷若谷 [虛 = 懷;
		虛 = 怀]
Xúnzǐ	Hsún-tzǔ	荀子
yáng	yáng	陽 = 阳
Yán Zūn	Yén Tsūn	嚴遵
yīn	yīn	陰 = 阴
yīn	yīn	因
yīn ér bù wéi	yīn érh pù wéi	因而不爲
Yǐn Xǐ	Yǐn Hsǐ	尹喜
yīng wú suǒ zhù ér	yīng wú sǒ chù érh	應無所住而
shēng qí xīn	shēng ch'í hsīn	生其心
yǐ xīn chuán xīn	ǐ hsīn ch'uán hsīn	以心傳心

yǐ zhōng zhì wài	ǐ chūng chìh wài	以中制外
yǒu qíng rén	yǔ qíng rén	有情人
yú	yǔ	于 = 於
Yuán Dào	*Yüán Tào*	原道
yuán shén	yüán shén	元神
zàng	tsàng	藏
Zhāng Zhàn	Chāng Chàn	張湛 [張 = 张]
zhèng míng	chèng míng	正名
Zhèngtǒng dàozàng	*Chèng-t'ǔng tào-tsàng*	正統道藏
zhēn rén	chēn jén	真人 [真 = 眞]
zhí	chíh	質
Zhī dù	*Chīh tù*	知度
zhì rén	chìh jén	至人
zhī wú zhī	chīh wú chīh	知無知
zhōng	chūng	中
zhōng dé	chūng té	中得
zhōng qì yǐ wéi hé	chūng ch'ì ǐ wéi hó	中氣以為和
Zhuāngzǐ	Chuāng-tzǔ	莊子 [莊 = 庄]
Zhuāngzǐ yǐndé	*Chuāng-tzǔ yǐn-té*	莊子引得 [莊 = 庄]
Zhuāngzǐ zhú zì suǒ yǐn	*Chuāng-tzǔ chú tzù sǒ yǐn*	莊子逐字索引

As the second part of this appendix, following here are Japanese terms in standard transliteration, along with the kanji 漢字 (Chinese, hànzì), the Chinese characters used in Japanese texts, where they read, of course, in their Japanese pronunciation. This chart also includes the pīnyīn transliteration of these characters when read using Mandarin Chinese pronunciation.

Japanese	Kanji	Pīnyīn
Bodaidaruma	菩提達磨	Pútídámó
Daruma	達磨	Dámó
denshin	傳心	chuán xīn
denshin hōyō	傳心法要	chuán xīn fǎ yào
Dōgen	道元	Dàoyuán
Ekai	慧開	Huìkāi
furyūmonji	不立文字	bù lì wén zì
hara-kiri	腹切	fùqiě

honrai menmoku	本來面目	běnlái miànmù
(= honrai menboku)		
ishin denshin	以心傳心	yǐ xīn chuán xīn
Kanchi Sōsan	鑑智僧璨 [鑑 = 鑒]	Jiànzhì Sēngcàn
kanji	漢字 [漢 = 汉]	hànzì
kanjō ronri	感情論理	gǎn qíng lún lǐ
kenshō	見性	jiàn xìng
Keitoku Dentō-roku	景德傳燈錄	*Jǐngdé chuándēng lù*
Kiun	希運	Xī Yùn
kyōge betsuden	敎外別傳	jiāo wài bié chuán
menboku = memboku	面目	miànmù
menmoku = memmoku	面目	miànmù
Mumon Ekai	無門慧開	Wúmén Huìkāi
Mumonkan	無門關	*Wúménguān*
Ōbaku Kiun	黃檗希運	Huáng Bò Xī Yùn
Ōbaku-san	黃檗山	Huáng Bò Shān
ōmushojū	應無所住	yīng wú suǒ zhù
jijōgoshin	而生其心	ér shēng qí xīn
Rinzai Zen	臨濟禪 [禪 = 禅]	Línjìchán
satori	悟	wù
Seishin shinkeigaku	精神神経学雑誌	*Jīng shén shén jīng xué*
zasshi	雑誌	*zá zhì*
seppuku	切腹	qiěfù
shikantaza	只管打坐	zhǐguǎndǎzuò
shin	心 = 心	xīn
Shinjin-mei	信心銘	*Xìnxīnmíng*
shin mu shojū	心無所住	xīn wú suǒ zhù
Shōbōgenzō	正法眼藏	*Zhèngfǎyǎnzàng*
Sōsan	僧璨	Sēngcàn
Sōtō Zen	曹洞禪 [禪 = 禅]	Cáodòngchán
Udonge	優曇華	Yōutánhuá
za	坐	dǎ
Zazen	坐禪 [禪 = 禅]	dǎ-chán
Zen	禪 = 禅	chán

BIBLIOGRAPHY

Citations to the works of Freud (and Breuer) follow the style used in the *Standard Edition of the Complete Psychological Works of Sigmund Freud* (which gives the year of publication and a lower-case letter to distinguish various works from the same year, followed by the *Standard Edition* volume and the first page of the text). The order disregards titles beginning with an article (definite or indefinite), as *The* ..., *A* ..., etc., or foreign equivalents. Family names are given in this bibliography in SMALL CAPS; names with du, van, von, le, la, der, de, etc. are listed accordingly (e.g., at DE REU, DU MARAIS, LA FONTAINE, VON HARTMANN, rather than at REU, MARAIS, FONTAINE, HARTMANN), unless there is a different established usage for the individual. Chinese, Japanese, and Korean names traditionally give the family name before the personal name, with no comma called for (as FUNG Yu-lan), unless westernized by the individual (as CHAN, Wing-tsit).

ADAIR, Mark J. "Plato's View of the 'Wandering Uterus'," *The Classical Journal*, vol. 91, no. 2 (1996), pp. 153-163.

AINSWORTH, Mary D. Salter: see as second author with BOWLBY, John.

ALLEN, Jon. *Coping With Trauma: A Guide to Self-Understanding*. 1995: Washington (American Psychiatric Press).

ALLEN, Jon. *Traumatic Relationships and Serious Mental Disorders*. 2001, Chichester, West Sussex, England (John Wiley & Sons Ltd).

ALLEN, Jon, and FONAGY, Peter, editors. *Handbook of Mentalization-Based Treatment*. 2006, Chichester, West Sussex, England (John Wiley & Sons Ltd).

ALMOND, Philip. *Demonic Possession and Exorcism in Early Modern England: Contemporary Texts and their Cultural Contexts*. 2004, Cambridge (Cambridge University Press).

ALSTON, William. "Emotion and Feeling" (1967), in Paul EDWARDS, editor, *The Encyclopedia of Philosophy*, vol. 2, pp. 479-86.

AMERICAN PSYCHIATRIC ASSOCIATION. *Diagnostic and Statistical Manual: Mental Disorders.* ["DSM-I"]. 1952, Washington (American Psychiatric Association).

AMERICAN PSYCHIATRIC ASSOCIATION. *Diagnostic and Statistical Manual of Mental Disorders, Fourth Edition*. ["DSM-IV"]. 1994, Washington (American Psychiatric Association).

AMERICAN PSYCHIATRIC ASSOCIATION. *Diagnostic and Statistical Manual of Mental Disorders, Fourth Edition, Text Revision.* ["DSM-IV-TR"]. 2000, Washington (American Psychiatric Association).

AMERICAN PSYCHIATRIC ASSOCIATION. *Diagnostic and Statistical Manual of Mental Disorders, Second Ediion.* ["DSM-II"]. 1968, Washington (American Psychiatric Association).

AMERICAN PSYCHIATRIC ASSOCIATION. *Diagnostic and Statistical Manual of Mental Disorders, Third Edition.* ["DSM-III"]. 1980, Washington (American Psychiatric Association).

AMERICAN PSYCHIATRIC ASSOCIATION. *Diagnostic and Statistical Manual of Mental Disorders, Third Edition, Revised.* ["DSM-III-R"]. 1987, Washington (American Psychiatric Association).

AMES, Roger T. "The Mencian Conception of *Ren xing* 人性: Does it Mean 'Human Nature'?" in Henry ROSEMONT, Jr., editor, *Chinese Texts and Philosophical Contexts: Essays Dedicated to Angus C. Graham*, pp. 143-175.

AMES, Roger T., and HALL, David L. *Dao De Jing* [道德經]—*"Making This Life Signifi-cant"—A Philosophical Translation.* 2003, New York (Ballantine/Random House).
AMES, Robert T., and ROSEMONT, Henry, Jr. *The Analects of Confucius: A Philosophical Translation* (1998). 1999, New York (Ballantine Publishing Group/Random House).
AMIEL, Henri-Frédéric. *Fragments d'un journal intime.* [Also cited as *Journal intime.*] Pre-ceded by a study by Edmond Henri Adolphe SCHERER (1882). In 2 volumes. Fifth edition with modified pagination, 1887, Geneva (H. Georg, Libraire-Éditeur).
ANDLER, Charles. *La jeunesse de Nietzsche, jusqu'à la rupture avec Bayreuth.* Identical with *Nietzsche: sa vie et sa pensée.* Volume 2. 1921, Paris (Éditions Bossard). Identical with the second half of Volume 1 of *Nietzsche: sa vie et sa pensée.* 1958 (6-vol-umes-in-3 edition), Paris (Gallimard).
ANDLER, Charles. *Nietzsche: sa vie et sa pensée.* In 6 volumes. 1920-31, Paris (Éditions Bos-sard). 1938 [6-volume edition] and 1958 [in an edition combining each two volumes in one tome, resulting in a 6-volumes-in-3 edition], Paris (Gallimard).
ANDREAS-SALOMÉ, Lou. *Lebensrückblick. Grundriß einiger Lebenserinnerungen.* Ernst PFEIF-FER, editor. 1951, Zurich (M. Niehan, Publisher). Translated by Breon MITCHELL as *Looking Back: Memoirs.* 1991, New York (Paragon House).
Aṅguttara Nikāya: see also *Numerical Discourses of the Buddha.*
Aṅguttara-Nikāya. Volume III (Pañca-Nipāta and Chakka-Nipāta) [The Fives and the Sixes]. Edited by Edmond Hardy (1897). Reprint edition, 1958, London (Luzac & Co. Ltd, for The Pali Text Society).
An Anthology of French Poetry from Nerval to Valéry in English Translation. Angel FLORES, editor. 1958, Garden City (Doubleday).
ARISTOTLE: see also FURTH, Montgomery; GALLOP, David.
ARISTOTLE. *Aristotle's De anima* [=Περὶ ψυχῆς *Perì psychēs*]. Books II and III. Translated by David W. HAMLYN. 1968, Oxford (Oxford University Press).
ARISTOTLE. *Aristotle's De anima, in the [1267 Latin] version of William of Moerbeke [Guil-laume de Moerbeke, Willem van Moerbeke, Flemish-born Dominican, 1215-1286] and the [1271] Commentary of St. Thomas Aquinas [1225-1274].* Translated from the Latin texts by Kenelm FOSTER and Silvester HUMPHRIES. 1951, New Haven (Yale University Press).
ARISTOTLE. *Aristotle's Categories and De interpretatione.* Translated by John L. ACKRILL. 1963, Oxford (Oxford University Press).
ARISTOTLE. *The Art of Rhetoric.* Greek text, Περὶ ῥητορικῆς *Perì rhētorikēs*, with translation by John Henry FREESE. 1926. London (Heinemann) and New York (Putnam).
ARISTOTLE. *Metaphysics.* Greek, with translation by Hugh TREDENNICK. *Loeb Classical Lib-rary.* 1961-1962, London (Heinemann) and Cambridge (Harvard University Press).
ARISTOTLE. *Nichomachean Ethics.* Translated by Martin OSTWALD. 1962, Indianapolis (Bobbs-Merrill).
ARISTOTLE. *On Rhetoric: A Theory of Civic Discourse.* Translation, with Commentary, by George A. KENNEDY. Revised edition, 2006, New York (Oxford University Press).
ARISTOTLE. *Posterior Analytics.* Greek, with translation by Hugh TREDENNICK. *Loeb Classical Library.* 1960, London (Heinemann) and Cambridge (Harvard University Press).
ARISTOTLE. *Physics.* Greek, with translation by Philip Henry WICKSTEED and Francis Mac-donald CORNFORD. In *Loeb Classical Library.* 1934-1957, Cambridge (Harvard University Press) and London (Heinemann).
ARTAUD, Antonin. *Van Gogh, le suicidé de la société.* 1947, Paris (K éditeur).
ASSAGIOLI, Roberto. *Psychosynthesis: A Manual of Principles and Techniques.* 1965/1971, New York (Viking Press).
AYER, Alfred Jules, editor. *Logical Positivism.* 1966, New York (The Free Press).

BABICH, Babette. "Nietzsche's Imperative as a Friend's Encomium: On Becoming the One You Are, Ethics, and Blessing," *Nietzsche-Studien*, vol. 33 (2003), pp. 29-58.

BARNES, Mary, and BERKE, Joseph. *Mary Barnes: Two Accounts of a Journey Through Madness*. 1972, New York (Harcourt Brace Jovanovich).

BATCHELOR, Stephen. *Verses from the Center: A Buddhist Vision of the Sublime*. 2000, New York (Riverhead Books).

BATEMAN, Anthony, and FONAGY, Peter. *Psychotherapy for Borderline Personality Disorder: Mentalization-based Treatment*. 2004, New York (Oxford University Press).

BATESON, Gregory, JACKSON, Don, HALEY, Jay, and WEAKLAND, John. "Toward a Theory of Schizophrenia," *Behavioral Science*, vol. 1, no. 4 (October 1956), pp. 251-64.

BEDFORD, Errol. "Emotions," *Aristotelian Society Proceedings*, vol. 57 (1956-57), pp. 281-304.

BERKE, Joseph, editor. *Counter Culture*. 1969, London (Peter Owen Ltd/Fire Books. Ltd).

BERTRAND, Alexis. "Un précurseur de l'hypnotisme," *Revue philosophique de la France et de l'étranger*, vol. 32 (July-December 1891), pp. 192-206.

BEYLE, Marie Henri (STENDHAL). *Stendhal: On Love*. Translated by H.B.V. [coded reversal of initials VBH, for Vyvyan Beresford HOLLAND]. 1947, Garden City (Doubleday).

Bhagavad-gītā. Translation (ca. 1902-1904) by Sylvain LÉVI and Joseph Trumbull STICKNEY (first published, 1935). 1976, Paris (Librairie Adrien Maisonneuve).

La Bhagavad-gîtâ. Sanskrit text with translation by Émile SENART. 1922, Paris (Bossard); third printing, 1967, Paris (Société d'Édition « Les Belles Lettres »).

The Bhagavad Gita. Sanskrit text in devanāgarī script with translation by Annie BESANT (1904). Thirteenth edition, 1973, Adyar, Madras (The Theosophical Society).

The Bhagavadgītā. Sanskrit text with translation by Sarvepalli RADHAKRISHNAN. 1948, London (George Allen and Unwin, Ltd); 1973, New York (Harper & Row).

BILBY, Joseph G.. *Civil War Firearms: Their Historical Background and Tactical Use*. 2005, New York (Da Capo Press).

BION, Wilfred R. *Experiences in Groups*. 1961, London (Tavistock Publications).

BLOOM, Irene. "Mencian Arguments on Human Nature (Jen-hsing)," *Philosophy East and West*, vol. 44, no. 1 (January 1994), pp. 19-53.

BODDE, Derk. "Two New Translations of Lao Tzu [Review article of J.J.L. Duyvendak, *Tao tö king, le livre de la voie et de la vertu*]," *Journal of the American Oriental Society*, vol. 74, no. 4 (October-December 1954), pp. 211-217.

BODHIDHARMA. *The Zen Teaching of Bodhidharma*. Translated by RED PINE. 1987, Port Townsend, WA (Empty Bowl); 1989, New York (North Point Press/Farrar, Strauss and Giroux).

BOSZORMENYI-NAGY, Ivan, and FRAMO, James, editors. *Intensive Family Therapy*. 1965, New York (Hoeber Medical Division of Harper and Row).

BOWLBY, John. *A Secure Base: Parent-Child Attachment and Healthy Human Development*. [Collected essays, 1979-1988.] 1988, London (Routledge).

BOWLBY, John, and AINSWORTH, Mary D. Salter. *Child Care and the Growth of Love*. Second edition. 1965/1973/1977, Harmondsworth, Middlesex, UK (Penguin Books).

BRACH, Tara. *Radical Acceptance: Embracing Your Life with the Heart of a Buddha*. Foreword by Jack KORNFIELD. 2003, New York (Bantam Dell/Random House).

BRACHET, Jean Louis. *Traité de l'hystérie*. 1847, Paris (J.-B. Baillière, libraire, and Germer-Baillière, libraire) and Lyon (Charles Savy, Jeune, libraire).

BRENNER, Hans Dieter, BÖKER, Wolfgang, and GENNER, Ruth, editors. *Towards a Comprehensive Therapy of Schizophrenia* (translation of the German text, *Therapie der Schizophrenie*). 1997. Seattle (Hogrefe & Huber).

BREUER, Joseph, and FREUD, Sigmund. *Studies on Hysteria* (1895d) SE 2/GW 1: 77.

BREUER, Joseph, and FREUD, Sigmund. "On the Psychical Mechanism of Hysterical Phenomena: Preliminary Communication" (1893a) SE 2: 3/GW 1: 81/CP 1: 24. [Introductory section of BREUER, Joseph, and FREUD, Sigmund, *Studies on Hysteria* (1895d).]

BRIERE, John. *Psychological Assessment of Adult Posttraumatic States: Phenomenology, Diagnosis, and Measurement* (1997). 2nd edition, 2004, Washington (American Psychological Association).

BROWN, G.W., MONCK, Elizabeth M., CARSTAIRS, G.M., and WING, J.K., "Influence of Family Life on the Course of Schizophrenic Illness," *British Journal of Preventive and Social Medicine*, vol. 16 (1962), pp. 55-68.

BUDDHAGHOSA. *Visuddhimagga*. English edition: *The Path of Purification (Visuddhimagga)*, by Bhadantācariya Buddhaghosa. Translated by Bhikkhu ÑĀNAMOLI (1956). Second edition, 1964: Colombo, Ceylon (A. Semage/M.D. Gunasena & Co. Ltd).

BURTON, Robert (pseudonym, Democritus Junior). *THE ANATOMY OF MELANCHOLY, VVHAT IT IS. VVITH ALL THE KINDES, CAVSES, SYMPTOMES, PROGNOSTICKES, and SEVERALL CVRES OF IT. IN THREE MAINE PARTITIONS with their feuerall SECTIONS, MEMBERS, AND SVBSECTIONS. PHILOSOPHICALLY, MEDICINALLY, HISTORICALLY, opened and cut vp. BY DEMOCRITVS Iunior. With a Satyricall PREFACE, conducing to the following Difcourfe.* 1621/1624/1628/1632/etc., Oxford (John Lichfield and James Short, for Henry Cripps). Reprint edition in 3 volumes, 1903, London (George Bell and Sons) and New York (Macmillan).

BUSHNELL, Rebecca. "Dean's Column: Transformations," *Penn Arts and Sciences Magazine, Spring/Summer 2008*, p. 3. 2008, Philadelphia (University of Pennsylvania, The School of Arts and Sciences, Office of External Affairs).

CACIOLA, Nancy. *Discerning Spirits: Divine and Demonic Possession in the Middle Ages.* 2003, Ithaca (Cornell University Press).

CAMUS, Albert. *Le mythe de Sisyphe. Essai sur l'absurde.* 1942, Paris (Gallimard). Translated by Justin O'BRIAN, as *The Myth of Sisyphus and other essays* (1955). 1959, New York (Vintage Books).

CAMUS, Albert. *La Peste.* 1947, Paris (Gallimard). Translated by Gilbert STUART, as *The Plague.* 1948, New York (Modern Library). Translated by Robin BUSS, as *The Plague.* 2001, London (Allen Lane/The Penguin Group).

CARNAP, Rudolf. "The Old and the New Logic," in A.J. AYER, editor, *Logical Positivism* (1966), pp. 133-46.

CARNAP, Rudolf. "Psychology in Physical Language," in A.J. AYER, editor, *Logical Positivism* (1966), pp. 165-98.

CASANOVA, Giacomo. *Mémoires* [1700s]. In 3 volumes. 1958-1960, Paris (Gallimard). Unabridged translation by Arthur MACHEN as *Memoirs*. 1959-1961, New York (Putnam).

CHAN, Alan K.L. "[Review of] *Taoist Mystical Philosophy: The Scripture of Western Ascension* by Livia Kohn," *Philosophy East and West*, vol. 43, no. 2 (April 1993), pp. 313-321.

CHAN, Wing-tsit [陈荣捷]. *A Sourcebook in Chinese Philosophy.* 1963, Princeton (Princeton University Press).

CHAO, Yuen Ren. *A Grammar of Spoken Chinese.* 1965, Berkeley (University of California Press).

CHARCOT, Jean-Martin. *Leçons sur les maladies du système nerveux faites à la Salpêtrière.* Identical with *Oeuvres complètes. Volume III: Leçons sur les maladies du système nerveux.* Collected by Joseph BABINSKI, Claude BERNARD, Marie FÉRÉ, and Gilles DE LA TOURETTE. 1887, Paris (Bureaux du Progrès médical + A. Delahaye & E. Lecrosnier, Libraires).

CHENG Man-ch'ing [ZHENG Manqing]. *Lao-tzu: "My Words Are Very Easy To Understand."* Chinese text with translation by Tam C. Gibbs. 1971, Richmond, CA (North Atlantic Books).

CHENG, Man Ch'ing [ZHENG Manqing], and SMITH, Robert W. *T'ai-chi: The "Supreme Ultimate" Exercise for Health, Sport, and Self-Defense* (1967). Second printing with corrections, 1967, Tokyo (John Weatherhill) and Rutland, VT (Tuttle).

CHESSICK, Richard D. "Perspectivism, Constructivism, and Empathy in Psychoanalysis: Nietzsche and Kohut," *Journal of the American Academy of Psychoanalysis*, vol. 25, no. 3 (1997), pp. 373-398.

CHISHOLM, Roderick M. "Marvin Farber, 1901-1980," *Proceedings and Addresses of the American Philosophical Association*, vol. 55, no. 5 (June 1982), pp. 578-579.

CHOMSKY, Noam. *Language and Mind*. 1968, New York (Harcourt, Brace & World).

CHOMSKY, Noam. "A Review of B.F. Skinner's *Verbal Behavior*," *Language*, vol. 35, no. 1 (1959), pp. 26-58. Reprinted in Jerry A. FODOR and Jerrold J. KATZ, editors, *The Structure of Language: Readings in the Philosophy of Language*, pp. 547-578.

CHONG, Kim-chong. "Zhuangzi and the Nature of Metaphor," *Philosophy East and West*, vol. 56, no. 3 (July 2006), pp. 370-391.

CHUANG TZU 莊子: see ZHUĀNGZĬ 莊子.

CIOMPI, Luc. "Is Schizophrenia an Affective Disease? The Hypothesis of Affect-Logic and Its Implications for Psychopathology," in William F. FLACK, Jr., and James D. LAIRD, editors, *Emotions in Psychopathology: Theory and Research* (1998), pp. 283-297.

CIOMPI, Luc. "Non-linear dynamics of complex systems: The chaos theoretical approach to schizophrenia," in Hans Dieter BRENNER, Wolfgang BÖKER, and Ruth GENNER, editors, *Towards a Comprehensive Therapy of Schizophrenia* (1997), pp. 18-31.

CIOMPI, Luc. *The Psyche and Schizophrenia: The Bond between Affect and Logic*. 1988, Cambridge (Harvard University Press). Translated by Deborah Lucas SCHNEIDER from *Affektlogik. Über die Struktur der Psyche und ihre Entwicklung. Ein Beitrag zur Schizophrenieforschung*. 1982/1998, Stuttgart (Klett-Cotta).

CIOMPI, Luc. "The Soteria Concept. Theoretical Bases and Practical 13-Year Experience with a Milieu-Therapeutic Approach of Acute Schizophrenia," *Psychiatria et Neurologia Japonica [Seishin shinkeigaku zasshi* 精神神経学雑誌 *]*, vol. 99 (1997), pp. 634-650.

CLAY, John. *Laing: A Divided Self*. 1996: London (Hodder and Stoughton).

CLEARY, Thomas. *The Essential Tao: An Initiation into the Heart of Taoism Through the Authentic Tao Te Ching & Inner Teachings of Chuang-tzu*. 1991: San Francisco (Harper Collins).

CLEARY, Thomas. *Sayings and Doings of Pai-chang: Ch'an Master of Great Wisdom*. Translation of 洪州百丈山大智禪師語錄 *Hóngzhōu Bǎizhàng shān dàzhìchánshī yǔlù/ Hung-chou pai-chang shan ta-chih ch'an shih yu lu* by 百丈懷海 Bǎizhàng Huáihǎi/ Pǎi-chàng Huái-hǎi. 1978, Los Angeles (Zen Center of Los Angeles/Institute for Transcultural Studies).

CLEARY, Thomas. *The Taoist Classics, Volume 3: Vitality, Energy, Spirit; The Secrets of the Golden Flower; Immortal Sisters; Awakening to the Tao*. 2000, Boston (Shambhala).

CLEARY, Thomas. *Taoist Meditation: Methods for Cultivating a Healthy Mind and Body*. Texts compiled and translated by Thomas CLEARY. 2000, Boston (Shambhala).

The Connected Discourses of the Buddha. A Translation of the Samyutta Nikaya. Bhikkhu BODHI, translator. 2000, Boston (Wisdom Publications).

Concise English-Chinese Chinese-English Dictionary. Second edition, 1999, Hong Kong (Oxford University Press).

The Concise Oxford Dictionary. Eighth edition. 1990, New York (Oxford University Press).

COOK, Scott, editor. *Hiding the World in the World: Uneven Discourses on the Zhuangzi.* 2003, Albany (State University of New York Press).

COOPER, David. *Psychiatry and Anti-Psychiatry.* 1967, London (Tavistock Publications).

CYRULNIK, Boris: see also MARTIN, Nicolas.

CYRULNIK, Boris. *Autobiographie d'un épouvantail.* 2008/2010, Paris (Odile Jacob).

CYRULNIK, Boris. *Je me souviens....* 2009, Le Bouscat, France (L'Esprit du Temps). Preface/ Présentation (« Présentation L'exil de l'enfance ») by Philippe BRENOT. Complete reprint edition, with distinct pagination, 2010, Paris (Odile Jacob).

CYRULNIK, Boris. *Parler d'amour au bord du gouffre.* 2004/2007, Paris, (Odile Jacob); translated by David MACEY as *Talking of Love on the Edge of a Precipice.* 2007, London (Allen Lane/Penguin).

CYRULNIK, Boris, and ELKAÏM, Mony. *Entre résilience et résonance. À l'écoute des émotions.* Under the direction of Michel MAESTRE. 2009, Paris (Éditions Fabert).

CSIKSZENTMIHALYI, Mark, translator and editor. *Readings in Han Chinese Thought.* 2006, Indianapolis (Hackett Publishing Company).

DĄBROWSKI, Kazimierz. *Personnalité, psychonévroses et santé mentale d'après la théorie de la désintégration positive.* 1965, Warsaw (Państwowe Wydawnictwo Naukowe).

DĄBROWSKI, Kazimierz. *Positive Disintegration.* J. ARONSON, editor. 1964, Boston (Little, Brown).

DĄBROWSKI, Kazimierz. *Psychoneurosis Is Not An Illness: Neuroses and Psychoneuroses From the Perspective of Positive Disintegration.* 1972, London (Gryf Publications).

DANNEBERG, Lutz, and MÜLLER, Hans-Harald. ",Der intentionale Fehlschluß'—ein Dogma? Systematischer Forschungsbericht zur Kontroverse um eine intentionalistische Konzeption in den Textwissenschaft. Teil II," *Zeitschrift für allgemeine Wissenschaftstheorie [Journal for General Philosophy of Science],* vol. XIV, no. 2 (1983), pp. 376-411.

DEFRANCIS, John. *The Chinese Language.* 1984, Honolulu (University of Hawaii Press).

DELANEY, Shelagh. *A Taste of Honey.* 1959, New York (Grove Press).

DE REU, Wim. "Right Words Seem Wrong: Neglected Paradoxes in Early Chinese Philosophical Texts," *Philosophy East and West,* vol. 56, no. 2 (April 2006), pp. 281-300.

DE SILVA, Padmasiri. *An Introduction to Buddhist Psychology* (1977). Fourth edition, 2005. New York (Palgrave Macmillan/St. Martin's Press).

Dhammapada: see also RADHAKRISHNAN, Sarvepalli; *The Text of the Minor Sayings.*

Dhammapada. Bilingual edition. With translation by Buddhadatta Māhathera. N.d. (1954), Colombo, Ceylon/Sri Lanka (The Colombo Apothecaries' Company).

Dhammapada. Translated by Nārada Thera. 1954, London (John Murray, Publishers).

DHIRAVAMSA, V.R. *Understanding the Buddha Nature.* Part of the unpublished manuscript, *Nirvana Upside Down* (2009), currently in review by publishers.

DHIRAVAMSA, V.R. *The Way of Non-attachment: The Practice of Insight Meditation.* 1975, London (Turnstone Books). Dutch translation as *De ongedwongen weg: Meditatie voor innerlijke vrijheid.* 1990, Utrecht and Antwerp (Uitgeverij Kosmos b.v.) French translation by Marie-Béatrice Jehl as *La voie du non-attachement: pratique de la méditation profonde selon la tradition bouddhique.* 1979/2010, St. Jean de Braye, Loiret, France (Editions Dangles). Spanish translation as *La vía del no apogo: La práctica de la vision profunda.* 1991, Barcelona (Editorial La Liebre del Marzo).

DHIRAVAMSA, V.R. *The Dynamic Way of Meditation: The Release and Cure of Pain and Suffering.* Foreword by Claudio NARANJO (1982). 1983, Wellingborough, Northamptonshire, G.B. (Turnstone Press Limited/Forson Publishing Group). French translation by Ghislaine Berger as *L'attention, source de la plénitude. Pratique de la médi-tation Vipassana*. 1983/2010, St. Jean de Braye, Loiret, France (Editions Dangles).

DĪGHA NIKĀYA: see *The Long Discourses of the Buddha*.

DŌGEN. *Moon in a Dewdrop: Writings of Zen Master Dōgen*. Edited by Kazuaki TANAHASHI. 1985/1997, New York (North Point Press/Farrar, Straus and Giroux).

DŌGEN. *Shōbōgenzō* 正法眼藏 *The Eye and Treasury of the True Law*. Translated by Kōsen NISHIYAMA. 1988, Tokyo (Nakayama Shobō and Japan Publications Trading Company Ltd).

DONSIMONI, Aline. "Les therapies familiales vont-elles vaincre l'individualisme français? Entretien avec le psychiatre Dr Bertolus" ["Are Family Therapies Going to Conquer French Individualism? An interview with psychiatrist Dr. Bertolus"], *Le quotidien du médecin* (Paris), Number 2671 (Wednesday, April 21, 1982), p. 16.

DUGAS, Ludovic. "Observations et documents: Un cas de dépersonnalisation," *Revue philosophique de la France et de l'étranger*, vol. 45 (1898), pp. 500-507.

DUGAS, Ludovic. "Les passions," in Georges DUMAS *et alia, Traité de Psychologie*, Vol. I (1923), pp. 480-501.

DUGAS, Ludovic, and MOUTIER, François. *La dépersonnalisation*. 1911, Paris (Librairie Félix Alcan).

DU MARSAIS, César Chesneau. *Traité des Tropes, ou des différents sens dans lesquels on peut prendre un même mot dans une même langue* (1730). Reprint edition, with *Traité des Figures* by Jean PAULHAN, *Postface* by Claude MOUCHARD. 1977, Paris (Nouveau Commerce).

DUMAS, Georges, *et alia. Traité de Psychologie*. Volume I. 1923, Paris (Librairie Félix Alcan).

DUYVENDAK, Jan Julius Lodewijk. *Tao tö king, le livre de la voie et de la vertu. Texte chinois establi et traduit avec des notes critiques et une introduction*. 1953, Paris (Librairie d'Amérique et d'Orient).

EBN-E MONAVVAR, Moḥammad. *The Secrets of God's Mystical Oneness, or The Spiritual Stations of Shaikh Abu Saʿid*. Translation of *Asrār al-Towḥid, fi Maqāmāt al Šeyḵ Abu Saʿid* (late 1100s) by John O'KANE. 1992, New York (Mazda Publishers and The Bibliotheca Persica).

EDWARDS, Paul, editor. *The Encyclopedia of Philosophy*. Volume 2. 1967, New York (Macmillan).

ELLENBERGER, Henri Frédéric. *The Discovery of the Unconscious: The History and Evolution of Dynamic Psychiatry*. 1970, New York (Basic Books).

ESTERSON, Aaron, COOPER, David, and LAING, Ronald D. "Results of Family-oriented Therapy with Hospitalized Schizophrenics," *British Medical Journal*, vol. 2 (December 18, 1965), pp. 1462-1465.

EWING, Alfred Cyril. "The Justification of Emotions," *Aristotelian Society Supplementary Volume* 31 (1957), pp. 59-74.

Factors Determining Human Behavior [Papers by Edgart Douglas ADRIAN, James Bertram COLLIP, Jean PIAGET, Charles (Carl) Gustav JUNG, Pierre JANET, Rudolf CARNAP, Abbott Lawrence LOWELL, and Bronislaw MALINOWSKI, in honor of the Harvard Tercentenary Conference, 1637-1937]. 1937, Cambridge (Harvard University Press). Reprint, 1974, New York (Arno Press).

FADIGA, Luciano, FOGASSI, Leonardo, PAVESI, Giovanni, and RIZZOLATTI, Giacomo. "Motor facilitation during action observation: a magnetic stimulation study," *Journal of Neurophysiology*, vol. 73 (1995), pp. 2608-2611.

FAURE, Bernard. *The Rhetoric of Immediacy: A Cultural Critique of Chan/Zen Buddhism* (1991). Corrected reprint edition, 1994, Princeton (Princeton University Press).

FENG, Gia-fu, and ENGLISH, Jane, translators. *The Inner Chapters: Chuang-tzu.* 1974, New York (Vintage Books/Random House).

FERBER, Sarah. *Demonic Possession and Exorcism in Early Modern France.* 2004, London (Routledge).

FERGUSON, Andy. *Zen's Chinese Heritage: The Masters and their Teachings.* 2000, Boston (Wisdom Publications).

FIERMAN, Louis B., editor. *Effective Psychotherapy: The Contribution of Hellmuth Kaiser.* Foreword by Allen J. ENELOW and Leta McKinney ADLER. 1965: New York (Free Press).

FIERMAN, Louis B. "Myths in the Practice of Psychotherapy," *Archives of General Psychiatry,* vol. 12 (April 1965), pp. 408-414.

FIERMAN, Louis B. *The Therapist Is the Therapy: Effective Psychotherapy II.* Foreword by Peter D. KRAMER. 1997, Northvale, NJ (Jason Aaronson).

FLACK, William F., Jr. and LAIRD, James D., editors. *Emotions in Psychopathology: Theory and Research,* 1998, New York (Oxford University Press).

FODOR, Jerry A., and KATZ, Jerrold J., editors. *The Structure of Language: Readings in the Philosophy of Language.* 1964, Englewood Cliffs, NJ (Prentice-Hall).

FOX, Alan. "Reflex and Reflectivity: *Wuwei* 無爲 in the *Zhuangzi,*" in Scott COOK, editor, *Hiding the World in the World,* Chapter 7, pp. 207-225.

FRAMO, James L. "Systematic Research in Family Dynamics," in Ivan BOSZORMENYI-NAGY and James L. FRAMO, editors, *Intensive Family Therapy* (1965), pp. 407-462.

FREUD, Ernst L., editor. *Letters of Sigmund Freud 1873-1939.* Translated by Tania and James STERN. 1961, London (Hogarth Press).

FREUD, Sigmund: see also BREUER, Joseph (with Freud as second author).

FREUD, Sigmund. "Analysis of a Phobia in a Five-year-old Boy" (1909b) SE 10: 3/GW 7: 243/ CP 3: 149.

FREUD, Sigmund. "Analysis Terminable and Interminable" (1937c) SE 23: 211/GW 16: 59/CP 5: 316.

FREUD, Sigmund. "An autobiographical Study" (1925d) SE 20: 3/GW 14: 33.

FREUD, Sigmund. *Civilization and Its Discontents* (1930a) SE 21: 59/GW 14: 421.

FREUD, Sigmund. *The Collected Papers of Sigmund Freud* [citation: CP or *Collected Papers*]. In 5 volumes. Authorized translation under supervision of Joan RIVIERE. 1924-1925, London (International Psycho-analytical Press); 1959, New York (Basic Books).

FREUD, Sigmund. "Contributions to the Psychology of Love III: The Taboo of Virginity" (1918a) SE 11: 193/GW 12: 161/CP 4: 217.

FREUD, Sigmund. *The Ego and the Id.* (1923b) SE 19: 3/GW 13: 237.

FREUD, Sigmund. "Five Lectures on Psycho-Analysis" (1910a) SE 11: 3/GW 8: 3.

FREUD, Sigmund. "Fragments of an Analysis of a Case of Hysteria" (1905e) SE 7: 3/GW 5: 163/CP 3: 13.

FREUD, Sigmund. "Freud's Psychoanalytic Method" (1904a) SE 7: 249/GW 5: 3/CP 1: 264.

FREUD, Sigmund. "Further Recommendations on the Technique of Psycho-Analysis II: Re-membering, Repeating and Working-Through" or (with briefer title) "Remember-ing, Repeating, and Working Through" (1914g) SE 12: 147/GW 10: 126/CP 2: 366.

FREUD, Sigmund. *Gesammelte Werke* [citation: GW]. In 18 volumes. Edited by Anna FREUD *et alia.* 1940-1952, London (Imago Publishing); 1964-1968, Frankfurt am Main (Fischer).

FREUD, Sigmund. *Group Psychology and the Analysis of the Ego* (1921c) SE 18: 69/GW 13: 73.

FREUD, Sigmund. "Hysteria" (1888b) SE 1: 39.

FREUD, Sigmund. *Inhibitions, Symptoms and Anxiety* (1926d) SE 20: 77/GW 14: 113.

FREUD, Sigmund. "The Instincts and their Vicissitudes" (1915c) SE 14: 111/GW 10: 210/CP 4: 60.

FREUD, Sigmund. *The Interpretation of Dreams* (1900a) SE 4-5/GW 2-3.

FREUD, Sigmund. *Introductory Lectures on Psycho-Analysis* (1916-1917) SE 15-16/GW 11.

FREUD, Sigmund. "A Metapsychological Supplement to the Theory of Dreams" (1917d) SE 14: 219/ GW 10: 412/CP 4: 137.

FREUD, Sigmund. *Moses and Monotheism* (1939a) SE 23: 3/GW 16: 103.

FREUD, Sigmund. *Mourning and Melancholia* (1917e [1915]) SE 14: 239/GW 10: 428/CP 4:152.

FREUD, Sigmund. "The Neuro-psychoses of Defense" (1894a) SE 3: 43/GW 1: 59/CP 1: 59.

FREUD, Sigmund. *New Introductory Lectures on Psycho-Analysis* (1933a) SE 22: 3/GW 15.

FREUD, Sigmund. "On the History of the Psycho-Analytic Movement" (1914d) SE 14: 3/GW 10: 44/CP 1: 287.

FREUD, Sigmund. "On Narcissism: An Introduction" (1914c) SE 14: 69/GW 10: 138/CP 4: 30.

FREUD, Sigmund. "Postscript [Nachschrift] to the 'Analysis of a Phobia in a Five-Year-Old Boy' " (1922c) SE 10: 148/GW 13: 431/CP 3: 288.

FREUD, Sigmund. "Psychical (or Mental) Treatment" (1890a) SE 7: 283/GW 5: 289.

FREUD, Sigmund. *Psychopathology of Everyday Life* (1901b) SE 6/GW 4.

FREUD, Sigmund. "Quelques considérations pour une étude comparative des paralysies motrices organiques et hystériques" (1893c) SE 1: 157/GW 1: 39/CP 1: 42.

FREUD, Sigmund. "Recommendations to Physicians Practicing Psycho-Analysis" (1912e) SE 12: 111/GW 8: 376/CP 2: 323.

FREUD, Sigmund. "Remembering, Repeating, and Working Through" or (with fuller title) "Further Recommendations on the Technique of Psycho-Analysis II: Remembering, Repeating and Working-Through" (1914g) SE 12: 147/GW 10: 126/CP 2: 366.

FREUD, Sigmund. "Report on My Studies in Paris and Berlin [1886]" (1956a) SE 1: 3.

FREUD, Sigmund. "Repression" (1915d) SE 14: 143/GW 10: 248/CP 4: 84.

FREUD, Sigmund. "Some Elementary Lessons in Psycho-Analysis" (1940b) SE 23: 281/GW 17: 141/CP 5: 376].

FREUD, Sigmund. *The Standard Edition of the Complete Psychological Writings of Sigmund Freud* [standard citation: SE or *Standard Edition*]. In 24 volumes. Translated from the German under the general editorship of James STRACHEY, in collaboration with Anna FREUD, assisted by Alix STRACHEY and Alan TYSON; editorial assistant, Angela RICHARDS. 1953-1974, London (Hogarth Press and Institute of Psycho-Analysis).

FREUD, Sigmund. *Three Essays on the Theory of Sex* (1905d) SE 7: 125/GW 5: 29.

FREUD, Sigmund. "The Unconscious" (1915e) SE 14: 161/GW 10: 264/CP 4: 98.

FREUD, Sigmund. "Why War?" (1933b) SE 22: 197/GW 16: 13/CP 5: 273.

FREUND, Wilhelm. *Wörterbuch der lateinischen Sprache. Nach historisch-genetischen Principien, mit steter Berücksichtigung der Grammatik, Synonymik und Alterthumskunde*. In 4 volumes. 1834-1845, Leipzig (In der Hahn'schen Verlags-Buchhandlung).

FROMM-REICHMANN, Frieda. "Notes on the Development of Treatment of Schizophrenics by Psychoanalytic Psychotherapy," *Psychiatry*, vol. 11 (1948), pp. 263-273.

FROMM-REICHMANN, Frieda. *Principles of Intensive Psychotherapy*. 1950, Chicago (University of Chicago Press).

FUNG Yu-lan. *Chuang-tzŭ: A New Selected Translation with an Exposition of the Philosophy of Kuo Hsiang* (1933, Shanghai). Reprint, 1964, New York (Paragon Book Reprint Corporation).

FUNG Yu-lan. *A History of Chinese Philosophy, Vol. 1: The Period of the Philosophers (from the Beginnings to circa 100 B.C.)* Translation of *Chūng-kuó Ché-hsüéh Shĭh* 中國哲學史 (1931, Shanghai), with introduction, notes, bibliography, and index, by Derk

BODDE. 1937, Peping/Beijing (Henri Vetch, Publisher). Reprint, 1952, Princeton (Princeton University Press).

FUNG Yu-lan. *Selected Philosophical Writings of Fung Yu-lan* (1991). 1998, Beijing (Foreign Languages Press).

FUNG Yu-lan. *A Short History of Chinese Philosophy*. Edited by Derk BODDE (1948). 1966, New York (The Free Press/The Macmillan Company).

FURTH, Montgomery, translator. *Aristotle Metaphysics: Books Zeta, Eta, Theta, Iota (VII-X)*. 1985, Indianapolis (Hackett Publishing).

GALEN. *On the Natural Faculties*. Robert John BROCK, translator. 1916, Cambridge (Harvard University Press). Reprint edition, 1979, London (W. Heinemann).

GALLOP, David. *Aristotle on Sleep and Dreams: A Text and Translation*. With Introduction, Notes, and Glossary. 1996, Warminster, Wiltshire, England (Aris & Phillips Ltd).

GARCÍA LORCA, Federico. *Antología Poética*. 1960, Buenos Aires (Editorial Losada).

Gateless Gate: see SEKIDA Katsuki; YAMADA Kōan; REPS, Paul.

GIDE, André. *Les faux-monnayeurs*. 1925, Paris (Gallimard). Translated by Dorothy BUSSY as *The Counterfeiters*. 1927, New York (Alfred A. Knopf).

GIDE, André. *La porte étroite*. 1917/1951, Paris (Mercure de France). Translated by Dorothy BUSSY as *Strait is the Gate*. 1924, London (Jarrolds). Reprint editions, 1949, New York (Alfred A. Knopf); 1952, London (Secker & Warburg); 2004, New York (Overlook Press).

GILLIGAN, James. *Violence: Reflections on a National Epidemic*. 1997: New York (Vintage).

GILLIGAN, Stephen. *Therapeutic Trances: The Cooperation Principle in Ericksonian Hypno-therapy*. 1987, New York (Brunner/Mazel).

GINSBERG, Mitchell. "Action and Communication," *The Human Context [London]*, vol. 6, no. 1 (1974), pp. 81-102.

GINSBERG, Mitchell. *Belief: Its Conceptual and Phenemenological Structure*. Doctoral Dissertation, Philosophy Dept., Univ. of Michigan, 1967. UMI Microfilm #68-7607 (Ann Arbor, MI).

GINSBERG, Mitchell. "Concern and Topic," *Nous*, vol. 5, no. 2 (May 1971), pp. 107-138.

GINSBERG, Mitchell. *The Far Shore: Vipassanā, The Practice of Insight*. 1980, London (Regency Press Ltd); 1996/2001/2009, New Delhi (Motilal Banarsidass Publishers).

GINSBERG, Mitchell, "How To Say It And Mean It," *Philosophical Studies*, vol. 22 (April 1971), pp. 43-48.

GINSBERG, Mitchell. *The Inner Palace: Mirrors of Psychospirituality in Divine and Sacred Wisdom-Traditions* (2 volumes). Foreword by Robert C. SOLOMON (2002). 6th edition, 2010, Nevada City, CA (Blue Dolphin Publishing).

GINSBERG, Mitchell. "Katz on Semantic Theory and 'Good,'" *The Journal of Philosophy*, vol. LXIII, no. 18 (September 29, 1966), pp. 517-521.

GINSBERG, Mitchell. *Mind and Belief: Psychological Ascription and the Concept of Belief*. 1972, New York (Humanities Press) and London (George Allen and Unwin Ltd).

GINSBERG, Mitchell. "Nietzschean Psychiatry" in Robert C. SOLOMON, editor, *Nietzsche: A Collection of Critical Essays* (1973), pp. 293-315.

GINSBERG, Mitchell. "La thérapie familiale reste en France trop centrée sur le «Malade»" ["Family Therapy in France Remains Overly Focused on the 'I.P.' "], *Le quotidien du médecin* (Paris), number 2890 (Thursday, March 3, 1983), p. 16.

GINSBERG, Mitchell. "Towards Statement Identity," *Crítica* (*Revista hispano-americana de Filosofia*, México, D.F.), vol. 4, no. 11-12 (May-September 1970), pp. 13-41.

GLAZER, Nathan. "Review of *A Critique of Pure Tolerance*, by Robert Paul Wolff, Barrington Moore, Jr., and Herbert Marcuse," *American Sociological Review*, vol. 31, no. 3 (1966), pp. 419-420.

GOODMAN, Nelson. *Fact, Fiction, and Forecast* (1955). 4th edition, 1983, Cambridge (Harvard University Press).

GOLDMAN, Alvin. *Action.* 1965, Doctoral thesis. Department of Philosophy, Princeton University.

GOVINDA, Lama Anagarika. *Foundations of Tibetan Mysticism.* 1969, York Beach, ME (Weiser).

GRAHAM, Angus C. "The Background of the Mencian Theory of Human Nature," *Tsing Hua Journal of Chinese Studies,* vol. 6, no. 1/2 (1967). Reprinted in *Studies in Chinese Philosophy and Philosophical Literature.* 1986, Singapore (Institute of East Asian Philosophies) and 1990, Albany (State University of New York Press).

GRAHAM, Angus C. *The Book of Lieh-tzŭ: A Classic of the Tao* (1960). Updated with new Preface by the translator-author, 1990, New York (Columbia University Press).

GRAHAM, Angus C. "Chuang-tzu's Essay on Seeing Things As Equal," *History of Religions,* vol. 9, no. 2/3 (November 1969/February 1970), pp. 137-159.

GRAHAM, Angus C. *Chuang-tzŭ: The Seven Inner Chapters and Other Writings from the Book Chuang-tzŭ.* 1981, London (George Allen & Unwin). Reprinted as *Chuang-tzŭ: The Inner Chapters,* with Introduction by Henry ROSEMONT, Jr. 2001, Indianapolis (Hackett).

GRAHAM, Angus C. *Chuang-tzŭ: Textual Notes to a Partial Translation.* 1982: London (School of Oriental and African Studies/University of London).

GRAHAM, Angus C. *Disputers of the Tao: Philosophical Argument in Ancient China.* 1989, La Salle, IL (Open Court Press).

GRAHAM, Angus C. "How Much of *Chuang Tzu* Did Chuang Tzu Write?" *Journal of the American Academy of Religion Thematic Issue: Studies in Classical Chinese Thought* (1979; also cited as 1980), Supplement to *JAAR,* vol. 47, no. 3 (September 1979), or no. 3S ["Supplement"]—Henry ROSEMONT, Jr. and Benjamin I. SCHWARTZ, Guest Editors, pp. 459-501. Reorganized text in Harold D. ROTH, editor, *A Companion to Angus C. Graham's Chuang Tzu,* pp. 58-103, and in A.C. GRAHAM, *Studies in Chinese Philosophy and Philosophical Literature,* 1983, Ithaca (Scholars Press), 1986, Singapore (Institute of East Asian Philosophies), 1990, Albany (State University of New York Press), pp. 283-321.

GRAHAM, Angus C. "Reflections and Replies," in Henry ROSEMONT, Jr., editor, *Chinese Texts and Philosophical Contexts: Essays Dedicated to Angus C. Graham,* pp. 267-322.

GREEN, Hannah [Joanne GREENBERG]. *I Never Promised You A Rose Garden.* 1964, New York (Holt, Rinehart and Winston/New American Library).

GRIESINGER, Wilhelm. *Pathologie und therapie der psychischen Krankheiten.* 1845; enlarged edition 1861/1867, Stuttgart (A. Krabbe); 1867 reprint, 1964, Amsterdam (E.J. Bonset).

The Group of Discourses (Sutta Nipāta). Volume I. Kenneth Roy NORMAN, translator; alternative translations by I.B. HORNER and Walpola RAHULA. 1984, London (Pali Text Society).

GUO Xiaolu [郭小橹]. *A Concise Chinese-English Dictionary for Lovers.* 2007, London (Chatto &Windus/Random House Group Ltd).

GYATSO, Geshe Kelsang. *Clear Light of Bliss: A Commentary to the practice of Mahamudra in Vajrayana Buddhism* (1982). Second revised edition, 1992, London (Tharpa Publications). Reprint edition, 2002, Glen Spey, NY (Tharpa Publications).

HAKEN, Hermann. *Synergetics: Introduction and Advanced Topics* [=1983 texts, *Synergetics,* 3rd edition, and *Advanced Synergetics,* 1st edition]. 2004: Berlin (Springer-Verlag).

HAKEN, Hermann, and MIKHAILOV, Alexander S., editors. *Interdisciplinary Approaches to Nonlinear Complex Systems.* 1993: Berlin and Heidelberg (Springer-Verlag).

HALEY, Jay, editor. *Advanced Techniques of Hypnosis and Therapy: Selected Papers of Milton H. Erickson, M.D.* 1967, New York (Grune & Stratton).

HALPERN, Jack, Editor-in-Chief. *New Japanese-English Character Dictionary*—新漢英字典 *Shin Kan-Ei jiten*. 1990, Tokyo (Kenkyusha Ltd) and 1993, Chicago (NTC).

HANSEN, Chad. *A Daoist Theory of Chinese Thought: A Philosophical Interpretation*. 1992, New York (Oxford University Press).

HARVARD-YENCHING INSTITUTE: see *Zhuāngzǐ yǐn dé* 莊子引得/*A Concordance to Chuang Tzu*.

HAWTHORNE, Charles. "Chance, Love, and Incompatibility," *Philosophical Review*, vol. 58 (1949), pp. 429-450.

HEIM, Gerhard, and BÜHLER, Karl-Ernst. "Les idées fixes et la psychologie de l'action de Pierre Janet," *Annales médico-psychologiques, revue psychiatrique*, vol. 161, no. 8 (October 2003), pp. 579-586.

HEINE, Steven, and WRIGHT, Dale S., editors. *The Kōan: Texts and Contets in Zen Buddhism.* 2000, New York (Oxford University Press).

HENRICKS, Robert G. *Lao-tzu: Te-Tao Ching [*德道經 *Dedaojing]: Translated from the Ma-wang-tui [Mǎwángduī* 馬王堆 *Mǎ-wáng-tuī] Texts, with an Introduction and Commentary.* 1993, New York (Modern Library/Random House).

HERBART, Johann Friedrich. *Lehrbuch zur Psychologie.* Second edition. 1834, Königsberg (A. W. Unzer); reprint, 1964, Amsterdam (E.J. Bonset).

HERBART, Johann Friedrich. *Sämmtliche Werke*, Volume V (Schriften zur Psychologie), First Part (Theil). 1850, Leipzig (Verlag von Leopold Voss). [Includes *Lehrbuch zur Psychologie*, at pp. 1-174.]

HERMAN, Judith. *Father-Daughter Incest.* 1981 and 2000 (with a new Afterword), Cambridge (Harvard University Press).

HERMAN, Judith. *Trauma and Recovery: The Aftermath of Violence.* 1997, New York (Basic Books).

HERMAN, Judith, PERRY, J. Christopher, and VAN DER KOLK, Bessel A., "Childhood Trauma in Borderline Personality Disorder," *American Journal of Psychiatry*, vol. 146, no. 4 (April 1989), pp. 490-495.

HERZEN, Alexandre [=Aleksandr Aleksandrovich GERSTEN]. *Le cerveau et l'activité cérébrale au point de vue psycho-physiologique.* 1887, Paris (Librairie J.-B. Baillière et fils).

HESSE, Hermann. *Der Steppenwolf.* 1927, Berlin (S. Fischer). Translated by Basil CREIGHTON as *Steppenwolf.* 1929, New York (Henry Holt).

HEWETT, Kawaikapuokalani [Frank], ALAILIMA, Cecelia, KAMAKEA-'OHELO, Kawahine, and MANN, Kawena. "O Ke Aloha Ka Mea I Ho'ola 'Ai—Compassion Is the Healer: An Indigenous Peoples Healing Conference. October 2000, Hawai'i," *Pacific Health Dialog: Journal of Community Health and Clinical Medicine for the Pacific*, vol. 8, no. 2 (September 2001)," pp. 417-422.

HIRAKAWA Akira. *A History of Indian Buddhism From Śākyamuni to Early Mahāyāna.* Translation by Paul GRONER of Volume I of インド仏教史 [仏 = 佛] *Indo bukkyō shi [Indic Buddhism History].* 1990, Honolulu (University of Hawaii Press).

HORNSTEIN, Gail A. *To Redeem One Person Is to Redeem the World: The Life of Frieda Fromm-Reichmann.* 2000, New York (The Free Press/Simon & Schuster).

HOROWITZ, Mardi. *Treatment of Stress Response Syndromes.* 2003, Washington (American Psychiatric Publishing).

HUANG, Martin W. "Sentiments of Desire: Thoughts on the Cult of *Qing* [qíng 情] in Ming-Qing [Míng 明-Qīng 清] Literature," *Chinese Literature: Essays, Articles, Reviews*, vol. 20 (December 1998), pp. 153-184.

HUANG PO. *The Zen Teaching of Huang Po on the Transmission of Mind*. Translated by John Blofeld. 1958, 1994, 2006 New York (Grove Press).

HUBBARD, L. Ron. *Dianetics*. 1950, New York (Hermitage House).

HUEBNER, Jon. "[Review of] *A Latterday Confucian: Reminiscences of William Hung (1893-1980)* by Susan Egan," *The Australian Journal of Chinese Affairs*, No. 24 (July 1990), pp. 415-417.

HUME, David. *A Treatise of Human Nature* (1740). Many editions, including Edition, with index, by Sir Lewis Amherst Selby-Bigge, 1888. Oxford (Clarendon Press). Reprint edition, 1975, Oxford (Clarendon Press). Critical edition, 2007, New York (Oxford University Press).

HUNG, William, editor. *Zhuāngzǐ yǐn dé* 莊子引得: see *Zhuāngzǐ yǐn dé; Zhuāngzǐ zhú zì suǒ yǐn*.

INADA, Kenneth K. *Nāgārjuna: A Translation of his Mūlamadhyamakārikā with an Introductory Essay*. 1970, Tokyo (The Hokuseido Press).

IVANHOE, Philip J., and VAN NORDEN, Bryan W., editors. *Readings in Classical Chinese Philosophy* (2001). 2003, Indianapolis (Hackett Publishing Company).

JAMES, William [W.J.]. "Hysteria" [book reviews, signed W.J.], *Psychological Review*, vol. 1 (1894), pp. 195-200.

JAMES, William. *The Varieties of Religious Experience: A Study in Human Nature. Being the Gifford Lectures on Natural Religion delivered at Edinburgh in 1901-1902*. 1902/1906, New York (Longmans, Green, and Company); 1929, New York (Modern Library); 1961, New York (Collier Books); 2002, London (Routledge).

JANET, Pierre. "L'amnésie et la dissociation des souvenirs par l'emotion," *Journal de psychologie normale et pathologique*, vol. 1 (1904), pp. 417-453.

JANET, Pierre. "L'anesthésie systématizée et la dissociation des phénomènes psychologiques," *Revue philosophique de la France et de l'étranger*, vol. 23 (January-June 1887), pp. 449-472.

JANET, Pierre. *De l'angoisse à l'extase: Études sur les croyances et les sentiments*. In 2 volumes. Volume 1 (*Un délire religieux. La croyance*), 1926; Volume 2 (*Les sentiments fondamentaux*), 1928, Paris (F. Alcan). New edition with new pagination, in 2 volumes, 1975, Paris (Société Pierre Janet). Electronic edition of both volumes, at http://classiques.uqac.ca/classiques/janet_pierre/janet_pierre.html, consisting of several files (with distinct pagination).

JANET, Pierre. "Autobiography of Pierre Janet" (article translated by Dorothy OLSON), in Carl MURCHISON, editor, *History of Psychology in Autobiography*, vol. 1, pp. 123-133. Available online at http://psychclassics.yorku.ca/Janet/murchison.htm.

JANET, Pierre. "Les degrés d'activation des tendences," *Annuaire du Collège de France*, vol. 17 (1917), pp. 64-70. [Part of a series of articles comprising a course during 1916-1917, at the Collège de France, *Les degrés d'activation*, published serially in the *Annuaire*.]

JANET, Pierre. *L'État mental des hystériques*: see *État mental des hystériques*.

JANET, Pierre. *État mental des hystériques. Les stigmates mentaux des hystériques*. 1892, Paris (Rueff et Compagnie). Second edition, as *L'État mental des hystériques. Les stigmates mentaux des hystériques*. 1911, Paris (Félix Alcan, Ancienne Librarie Germer Ballière).

JANET, Pierre. "Étude sur un cas d'aboulie et d'idées fixes," *Revue philosophique de la France et de l'étranger*, vol. 31 (January-June 1891), pp. 258-287, 382-407.

JANET, Pierre. *L'évolution psychologique de la personnalité*. 1929, Paris (Edition Chahine). See http://classiques.uqac.ca/classiques/janet_pierre/janet_pierre.html for electronic edition (with distinct pagination).

JANET, Pierre. *La force et la faiblesse psychologiques.* Lecture notes edited by Miron EPSTEIN. Paris, 1932, Paris (N. Maloine, Editeur).

JANET, Pierre. *The Major Symptoms of Hysteria: Fifteen Lectures Given in the Medical School of Harvard University.* First edition, 1907; Second edition (unchanged text but with Introduction to the Second Edition, pp. xi-xxiii), 1920/1929, both New York (Macmillan). Reprint of 1920/1929 edition, 1965, New York (Hafner Publishing). Reprint of 1907 edition, 2007, Whitefish, MT (Kessinger Publishing).

JANET, Pierre. *La médecine psychologique* (1923). 1924/1928, Paris (Flammarion). New edition with new pagination, 1980, Paris (Société Pierre Janet); reprint of 1980 edition, 2005, Paris (L'Harmattan). Electronic edition (with distinct pagination) at http://classiques.uqac.ca/classiques/janet_pierre/janet_pierre.html. Translation by H. M. and E.R. GUTHRIE, as *Principles of Psychotherapy.* 1924, New York (Macmillan). Reprint of 1924 edition, 1971, Freeport, NY (Books for Libraries Press).

JANET, Pierre. *Les médications psychologiques.* In 3 volumes. 1919, Paris (Librairie Félix Alcan). Translation by Eden and Cedar PAUL, in 2 volumes, as *Psychological Healing: A Historical and Clinical Study.* 1925, London (George Allen and Unwin Ltd). Reprint of 1925 edition, in 2 volumes, 1976, New York (Arno Press).

JANET, Pierre. *Névroses et idées fixes.* 1898, Paris (Félix Alcan). Electronic edition (distinct pagination) at http://classiques.uqac.ca/classiques/janet_pierre/janet_pierre.html.

JANET, Pierre. *Principles of Psychotherapy:* see under *La médecine psychologique.*

JANET, Pierre. *La psychanalyse de Freud.* Introduction by Serge NICOLAS. 2004, Paris (L'Harmattan). Reprint of "La psycho-analyse," *Journal de psychologie normale et pathologique,* vol. 11 (1914), pp. 1-36, 97-130. [Journal gave Janet's paper presented in London at 17th International Congress of Medicine, August 1913, but not the subsequent discussion.]

JANET, Pierre. *Psychological Healing:* see under *Les médications psychologiques.*

JANET, Pierre. "Psychological strength and weakness in mental diseases," in *Factors Determining Human Behavior* (1937), pp. 64-106.

JANET, Pierre. "La tension psychologique et ses oscillations," in Georges DUMAS *et alia, Traité de Psychologie,* pp. 919-952. 1923, Paris (Librairie Félix Alcan).

Japanese-English Buddhist Dictionary, Revised Edition—Nichi-Ei Bukkyō Jiden 日英佛教辭典. 1991, Tokyo (Daitō Shuppansha 大東出版社/Daitō Publishing Company).

JASPERS, Karl. *General Psychopathology.* 1963, Chicago (University of Chicago Press). Translation of *Allgemeine Psychopathologie,* 1913, Berlin (J. Springer Verlag).

JERUSALEM, Wilhelm. *Die Urtheilsfunction. Eine psychologische und erkenntniskritische Untersuchung.* 1895, Wien/Vienna and Leipzig (Wilhelm Braumüller).

Jingde Records of the Transmission of the Lamp: see *Records of the Transmission of the Lamp.*

JONES, Ernest. *The Life and Work of Sigmund Freud. In three volumes. Volume 1: The Formative Years and the Great Discoveries, 1856-1900.* 1953, New York (Basic Books).

JOSLYN, Marc. "Figure/Ground: Gestalt/Zen," in J.O. STEVENS, editor, *Gestalt Is: A Collection of Articles about Gestalt Therapy and Living* (1975), pp. 229-246.

JUNG, Carl Gustav. *The Development of Personality.* 1964/1981, Princeton (Princeton University Press).

JUNG, Carl Gustav. "The Philosophical Tree" (earlier text, 1945; revised version, 1954), pp. 251-349 in *Alchemical Studies.* Identical with *The Collected Works of C.G. Jung,* Volume 13. 1967, Princeton (Princeton University Press).

JUNG, Carl Gustav. *The Practice of Psychotherapy: Essays on the Psychology of the Transference and Other Subjects.* Identical with *The Collected Works of C.G. Jung,* Volume 16. 1966/1970, Princeton (Princeton University Press).

KAWAMURA, Leslie (translator). *Golden Zephyr*. With NĀGĀRJUNA's *A Letter to a Friend* and commentary by MI-PHAM, *The Garland of White Lotus Flowers*. 1975, Berkeley (Dharma Publishing).

KENNY, Anthony. *Action, Emotion, and Will*. 1963, London (Routledge & Kegan Paul) and New York (Humanities Press).

Khuddaka-pātha: see *The Minor Readings (Khuddakapātha)* and *The Text of the Minor Sayings*.

KIERKEGAARD, Søren. *Works of Love: Some Christian Reflections in the Form of Discourses*. Translated from *Kærlighedens gerninger* (1847) by Howard and Edna HONG. 1962, New York (Harper and Brothers, Publishers).

KJELLBERG, Paul. "[Review of] *A Companion to Angus C. Graham's Chuang Tzu*," *China Review International*, vol. 12, no. 1 (Spring, 2005), pp. 222-225.

KJELLBERG, Paul, translator. Chapter 5 (Zhuangzi), in Philip J. IVANHOE and Bryan W. VAN NORDEN, editors, *Readings in Classical Chinese Philosophy*, pp. 203-245.

KNOBLOCK, John, and RIEGEL, Jeffrey. *The Annals of Lü Buwei [呂氏春秋 Lǚ shì chūn qiū]: A Complete Translation and Study*. 2000, Stanford (Stanford University Press).

KOESTLER, Arthur. *The Ghost in the Machine*. 1967, London (Arkana/Penguin).

KOHN, Livia. *Taoist Mystical Philosophy: The Scripture of Western Ascension*. With Foreword by Donald J. MUNRO. 1991, Albany (State University of New York Press).

KOHN, Livia. "Yin Xi: The Master at the Beginning of the Scripture," *Journal of Chinese Religions*, vol. 25 (Fall 1997), pp. 83-139.

KOHUT, Heinz. *The Restoration of the Self*. 1977, New York (International Universities Press).

KOMJATHY, Louis. "[Review of] *The Taoist Canon: A Historical Companion to the Daozang*, edited by Kristofer Schipper and Franciscus Verellen." Available only online at the URL/website daoiststudies.org/dao/?q=node/650.

KOMJATHY, Louis. *Daoist Texts in Translation* (2004). Available only online at the URL/website www.daoistcenter.org/bibliography.pdf.

KOMJATHY, Louis. *Title Index to Daoist Collections*. 2002, Cambridge (Three Pines Press).

KORNFIELD, Jack. *The Wise Heart: A Guide to the Universal Teachings of Buddhist Psychology*. 2008, New York (Bantam Dell/Random House).

KRUSE, Peter, and STADLER, Michael. "The Significance of Nonlinear Phenomena for the Investigation of Cognitive Systems," in Hermann HAKEN and Alexander S. MIKHAILOV, editors, *Interdisciplinary Approaches to Nonlinear Complex Systems*, pp. 138-160.

Kyunyŏ-jŏn: The Life, Times and Songs of a Tenth Century Korean Monk. Translation by Adrian BUZO and Tony PRINCE. 1993, Broadway, NSW, Australia (Wild Peony Publications/University of Sydney) and Honolulu (University of Hawaii Press).

LACAN, Jacques. *The Four Fundamental Concepts of Psycho-Analysis*. Translation by Alan SHERIDAN of *Le seminaire de Jacques Lacan, Livre XI, Les quatre concepts fondamentaux de la psychanalyse*, 1973, Paris (Seuil). 1978, New York (Norton).

LAING, Adrian. *R.D. Laing: A Life*. Second edition, 2006, London (Sutton Publishing Ltd).

LAING, Ronald David. *Knots*. 1970, New York (Pantheon Books/Random House).

LAING, Ronald David. "Mystification, Confusion, and Conflict," in Ivan BOSZORMENYI-NAGY and James FRAMO, editors, *Intensive Family Therapy* (1965), pp. 343-363.

LAING, Ronald David. *The Politics of Experience*. 1967, New York (Pantheon/Random House).

LAING, Ronald David. *The Politics of the Family*. Revised edition. 1971, New York (Pantheon). 1978, Harmondsworth, Middlesex, UK (Penguin Books).

LAING, Ronald David, PHILLIPSON, Herbert, and LEE, A. Russell. *Interpersonal Perception: A Theory and a Method of Research*. 1966, London (Tavistock Publications).

Larousse Lexis (or, *Larousse de la langue française, Lexis*). 1979, Paris (Librairie Larousse).
LAU, Dim Cheuk. *Lao Tzu Tao Te Ching*. 1963, Harmondsworth, Middlesex, UK (Penguin Books).
LAU, Dim Cheuk and AMES, Roger T. *Yuan Dao: Tracing Dao to Its Source*. 1998, New York (Ballantine Publishing Group/Random House).
LECOMTE, Jacques: see also as second author with VANISTENDAEL, Stefan.
LECOMTE, Jacques. *La résilience. Se reconstruire après un traumatisme*. 2010, Paris (Éditions Rue d'Ulm/Presses de l'École normale supérieure).
LEE, Jung H. "Finely Aware and Richly Responsible: The Daoist Imperative," *Journal of the American Academy of Religion*, vol. 68, no. 3 (September 2000), pp. 511-536.
LEGGE, James, translator. *The Sacred Books of East. Volume 39*. Identical with *The Sacred Books of China, The Texts of Taoism, Part I*. 1891, Oxford (Clarendon Press). Reprint edition, 1962, New York (Dover Publications).
LEURET, François. *Fragmens psychologiques sur la folie*. 1834, Paris (Crochard, libraire-éditeur).
LEURET, François. *Des indications à suivre dans le traitement moral de la folie: mémoire lu à l'Académie royale de Médecine, le 2 décembre 1845*. 1846, Paris (Librairie Veuve Le Normant). Reissue, with new Préface by Pierre MOREL. 1998, Paris (L'Harmattan).
LEURET, François. *Du traitement moral de la folie*. 1840, Paris (J.-B. Baillière, libraire).
LEWIS, Charlton Thomas, and SHORT, Charles. *A Latin Dictionary Founded on [Ethan Allen] Andrews' Edition of [Wilhelm] Freund's Latin Dictionary [Wörterbuch der lateinischen Sprache], revised, enlarged, and in great part rewritten* (1879). 2002, Oxford (Oxford University Press).
LEWIS, Clarence Irving. *Mind and the World-Order: Outline of a Theory of Knowledge*. 1929/1956: New York (Dover Publications).
LEWIS, Jerry M., and GOSSETT, John T. *Disarming the Past: How an Intimate Relationship Can Heal Old Wounds*. 1999: Phoenix (Zeig, Tucker & Theisen).
Lǐ Yǎngzhèng 李养正. *History of Chinese Taoism*. Compiled, systematically reorganized, and translated into English by YÁN Zhōnghù 颜钟祜. 2009, Beijing (Foreign Languages Press).
LIDDELL, Henry George, and SCOTT, Robert. *Greek-English Lexicon* (1843). Ninth edition with *Revised Supplement*. 1996, Oxford (Oxford University Press).
LIN, Shuen-fu. "Transforming the Dao: A Critique of A.C. Graham's Translation of the Inner Chapters of the *Zhuangzi*," in Scott COOK, editor, *Hiding the World in the World*, Chapter 10, pp. 263-290.
LITTRÉ, Émile. *Oeuvres complètes d'Hippocrate* (bilingual French-Greek edition, in 10 volumes). 1839-1861, Paris (J.B. Baillière); reprint edition, 1961-1962, Amsterdam (A. M. Hakkert). In vol. 7, Περὶ γυναικείης φύσιος *[Perì gynaikeíēs phýsios, De la nature de la femme]*, pp. 312-431; in vol. 8, Γυναικείων πρωτον καὶ δεύτερον *[Gynaikeíōn prōton kai deúteron, Maladies des femmes, Parts I and II]*, at pp. 10-233 & pp. 234-407, respectively.
LIVINGSTONE, Angela. *Lou Andreas-Salomé*. 1984, London (Gordon Fraser Gallery).
LLOYD, Geoffrey. "Ancient Greek concepts of causation in comparativist perspective," in Dan SPERBER, David PREMACK, Ann James PREMACK, editors, *Causal Cognition: A Multidisciplinary Debate*, pp. 536-556.
The Long Discourses of the Buddha: A Translation of the Dīgha Nikāya, Maurice WALSHE, translator (1987). 1995, Boston (Wisdom Publications).
LORCA, Federico García: see GARCÍA LORCA, Federico.
LOWEN, Alexander. *Bioenergetics* (1975). 1976, New York (Penguin Books).

LOY, David. *"Wei-wu-wei:* Nondual Action," *Philosophy East and West,* vol. 35, no. 1 (Jan. 1985), pp. 73-86.

LU, David C. *History of Chinese Daoism.* 2000, Lanham, MD (University Press of America).

LU K'uan Yü (LUK, Charles). *Ch'an and Zen Teaching,* Volume 3 (1962). 1993, York Beach, ME (Samuel Weiser).

LU K'uan Yü (LUK, Charles). *Taoist Yoga: Alchemy and Immortality. A translation, with introduction and notes, of The Secrets of Cultivating Essential Nature And Eternal Life (Hsin [sic, for 'Hsing'] Ming Fa Chueh Ming Chih) by the Taoist Master Chao Pi Ch'en, born 1860.* [Or, in pinyin: *Xìng mìng fǎ jué míng zhǐ* 性命法訣明指, by Zhào Bìchén 趙避塵, 1860-1942.] 1970, London (Rider & Company); 1973, York Beach, ME (Samuel Weiser).

LUSTHAUS, Dan: see also SHIH, Heng-ching.

LUSTHAUS, Dan. "Aporetics Ethics in the *Zhuangzi,*" in Scott COOK, editor, *Hiding the World in the World,* Chapter 6, pp. 163-206.

LUSTHAUS, Dan. *Buddhist Phenomenology: A Philosophical Investigation of Yogācāra Buddhism and the* Ch'eng wei-shih lun. 2002, London (RoutledgeCurzon).

LUSTHAUS, Dan. "Zhuangzi's ethics of deconstructing moralistic self-imprisonment: standards without standards," in Youru WANG, editor, *Deconstruction and the Ethical in Asian Thought,* Chapter 3, pp. 60-80.

MACDONELL, Arthur A. *A Sanskrit Grammar for Students* (1901). Third edition, 1927; reprint, 1971, Oxford (Oxford University Press).

MACE, Cecil Alec. "Emotions and the Category of Passivity," *Aristotelian Society Proceedings,* vol. 62 (1961-62), pp. 135-142.

MAHADEVAN, Telliyavaram Mahadevan Ponnambalam. *Outlines of Hinduism.* Foreword by Sarvepalli RADHAKRISHNAN. First edition, 1956; revised edition, 1960/1971: Bombay (Chetana).

MAIR, Victor H. *Tao Te Ching: The Classic Book of Integrity and the Way.* Translation based on the Ma-wang-tui Manuscripts. 1990, New York (Bantam Books).

MAIR, Victor H. *Wandering on the Way: Early Taoist Tales and Parables of Chuang Tzu.* 1994, New York (Bantam Books).

Majjhima Nikāya: see *The Middle Length Discourses of the Buddha.*

MALALASEKERA, George Peiris. *Dictionary of Pali Proper Names.* In two volumes. 1974, London (Pali Text Society).

MALANDRA, William W. "Atharvaveda 2.27: Evidence for a Soma-Amulet," *Journal of the American Oriental Society,* vol. 99, no. 2 (April-June 1979), pp. 220-224.

MANDELBROT, Benoit B. *The Fractal Geometry of Nature.* 1982, San Francisco (W.H. Freeman).

MANDELBROT, Benoit B. *Fractals and Chaos: The Mandelbrot Set and Beyond.* 2004, New York (Springer Verlag).

MANDELBROT, Benoit. *Les objets fractals. Forme, hasard et dimension.* 1975, Paris (Flammarion).

MANDLER, George. "Emotion," in *New Directions in Psychology* (1962), pp. 269-343.

MARSAIS, César Chesneau du: see DU MARSAIS, César Chesneau (1676-1756).

MARSH, Robert Charles, editor. *Logic and Knowledge.* 1966, London (Allen and Unwin).

MARTIN, Nicolas, SPIRE, Antoine, and VINCENT, François. *La résilience: Entretien avec Boris Cyrulnik.* Preface by François VINCENT. 2009, Lormont (Le Bord de l'eau éditions).

MARTY, Pierre, M'UZAN, Michel de, and DAVID, Christian. *L'investigation psychosomatique: Sept observations cliniques.* 1963, Paris (Presses Universitaires de France); Second updated edition, with a commemorative/memorial essay dated September 1993, written shortly after the death of Marty in June 1993, entitled "Préliminaires critiques à la recherché psychosomatique" by Michel de M'UZAN and Christian DAVID. 1994, Paris (Presses Universitaires de France).

MASSON, Jeffrey M. *The Assault on Truth: Freud's Suppression of the Seduction Theory.* 1984, New York (Farrar, Straus and Giroux). With new Afterword, 2003, New York (Ballantine).

MATHEWS, Robert Henry. *Mathews' Chinese-English Dictionary* (Revised American Edition, 1943). 1993, Cambridge (Harvard University Press).

MAUDSLEY, Henry. *The Physiology and Pathology of the Mind.* 1867, London (Macmillan). Re-edition, 1977, Washington, DC (University Publications of America).

MAUDSLEY, Henry. *The Physiology of the Mind.* 1877, London (Macmillan).

MAYRHOFER, Manfred. *A Sanskrit Grammar.* Translated by Gordon B. FORD, Jr. from the second edition of *Sanskrit-Grammatik mit sprachvergleichenden Erläuterungen* (Berlin, 1965). 1972, University, AL (University of Alabama Press).

McDOUGALL, William. "An Introduction to Social Psychology," in Thorne SHIPLEY, editor, *Classics in Psychology* (1961) pp.1290-1336.

McRAE, John R. *Seeing Through Zen: Encounter, Transformation, and Genealogy in Chinese Chan Buddhism.* 2003, Berkeley (University of California Press).

MEICHENBAUM, Donald. *A Clinical Handbook/Practical Therapist Manual for Assessing and Treating Adults with Post Traumatic Stress Disorder (PTSD).* 1994, Waterloo, ONT (Institute Press/Department of Psychology) and Clearwater, FL (Institute Press).

MENNINGER, Karl, M.D. *Love Against Hate.* 1942, New York (Harcourt, Brace).

MESMER, Franz Anton. *Mémoire sur la découverte du magnétisme animal.* 1779, Paris (Chez Pierre François Didot le jeune, libraire-imprimeur de Monsieur, quai des Augustins).

METTĀNANDA Bhikkhu, The Venerable Dr. "Did [the] Buddha die of mesenteric infarction?" *Bangkok Post,* 17 May 2000. At lankalibrary.com/Bud/buddha_death.htm (visited at site, July 7, 2010).

The Middle Length Discourses of the Buddha: A New Translation of the Majjhima Nikāya. Bhikkhu ÑĀṆAMOLI and Bhikkhu BODHI, translators. 1995, Boston (Wisdom).

The Minor Readings (Khuddakapātha): The First Book of the Minor Collection (Khuddakanikāya). Translated by Bhikkhu ÑĀṆAMOLI. 1978, London (Pali Text Society).

MIJOLLA, Alain de. "*Les letters de Jean-Martin Charcot à Sigmund Freud (1886-1893).* Le crépuscule d'un dieu," *Revue française de psychanalyse,* vol. 52 (May-June 1988), pp. 702-725.

MITCHELL, Stephen. *Tao Te Ching.* 1988, New York (Harper Collins).

MI-PHAM, Lama Jamgön: see also KAWAMURA, Leslie (translator); PETTIT, John Whitney.

MI-PHAM, Lama Jamgön. *Calm and Clear: The Wheel of Analytic Meditation [1891] and Instructions on Vision in the Middle Way [1892].* 1973: Emeryville, CA (Dharma Publishing).

MIURA Isshū, and SASAKI, Ruth Fuller. *Zen Dust: The History of the Koan and Koan Study in Rinzai (Lin-chi) Zen.* 1966, New York (Harcourt, Brace & World).

MONIER-WILLIAMS, Monier. *A Sanskrit-English Dictionary.* 1899, Oxford (Oxford University Press). Reprint edition, 1963/1993, Delhi (Motilal Banarsidass Publishers).

MONTAIGNE, Michel Eyquem de. *Essais* [1580/1976]. *Reproduction photographique de l'édition originale de 1580.* 1976, Geneva (Librairie Slatkine) and Paris (Librairie Champion).

MONTAIGNE, Michel Eyquem de. *Essais de Michel de Montaigne* [1587/1870]. *Texte original de 1580 avec les variantes des éditions de 1582 et 1587.* Edited by Reinhold DEZEIMERIS and Henri Auguste BARCKHAUSEN. 1870-1873, Bordeaux (Féret).

MONTAIGNE, Michel Eyquem de. *Les Essais de Michel de Montaigne* [1588/1906]. *Publiés d'après l'exemplaire de Bordeaux, avec les variantes manuscrites & les leçons des plus anciennes impresssions, des notes, des notices et un lexique, par Fortunat Strowski. Tome premier.* [This "Exemplaire de Bordeaux" is the 1588 edition with handwritten corrections by Montaigne. These were later consulted for some subsequent editions of the text, with varying degrees of correctness, as in some misreadings of these by the copyist then found in the edition of 1595. In this edition, the changes are printed in various fonts to maintain the levels of correction made by the author.] 1906, Bordeaux (Imprimerie Nouvelle F. Pech & Cie).

MONTAIGNE, Michel Eyquem de. *Les Essais de Montaigne* [1588/1873]. *Réimprimés sur l'édition originale de 1588 avec notes, glossaire et index.* Edited by Henri MO-THEAU and Damase JOUAUST. Notes by Silvestre de SACY. 1873, Paris (Librairie des Bibliophiles).

MONTAIGNE, Michel Eyquem de. *Les Essais. Édition conforme au texte de l'exemplaire de Bordeaux* [1588/1924/1965]. Edited by Pierre Villey (1924), then by Verdun-Louis Saulnier (1965). 1965/1978/2004, Paris (Presses Universitaires de France).

MONTAIGNE, Michel Eyquem de. *Essais.* 1962/2007, Paris (Gallimard/Collection Pléiade).

MONTAIGNE, Michel de. *The Complete Essays.* Translation by Michael Andrew SCREECH. 2003, London (Penguin).

MORAN, Patrick Edwin. *Explorations of Chinese Metaphysical Concepts: The History of Some Key Terms from the Beginnings to Chu Hsi (1130-1200).* Doctoral Dissertation, Department of Oriental Studies, University of Pennsylvania, Philadelphia, 1983.

MORAN, Patrick Edwin. *Three Smaller Wisdom Books: Lao Zi's Dao de jing, the Great Learning (Da xue), and the Doctrine of the Mean (Zhong yong).* Lanham, MD, 1993 (University Press of America).

MORAVCSIK, Julius M.E. "Aristotle on Adequate Explanations," *Synthese*, vol. 28 (September 1974), pp. 3-17.

MOREAU DE TOURS, Jacques-Joseph. *Du hachisch et de l'aliénation mentale. Etudes psychologiques.* 1845: Paris (Librairie de Fortin, Masson). Reprint, 1990, Geneva (Slatkine Reprints). Translation by Gordon J. BARNETT, *Hashish and Mental Illness.* Introduction by Bo HOLMSTEDT. 1973, New York (Raven Press).

Mumonkan: see REPS, Paul; SEKIDA Katsuki; YAMADA Kōan.

MURCHISON, Carl, editor. *History of Psychology in Autobiography.* Volume 1. 1930, Worcester MA (Clark University Press).

ÑĀṆAMOLI, Bhikkhu. *The Life of the Buddha, According to the Pali Canon.* 1972, Kandy, Sri Lanka (Buddhist Publication Society).

NĀRADA Māha Thera. *The Buddha and His Teachings* (1964). Revised and enlarged edition, 1973, Colombo, Ceylon [Sri Lanka] (The Author, at the monestary, Vajirārāma).

NARANJO, Claudio. *The Way of Silence and the Talking Cure: On Meditation and Psychotherapy.* 2006, Nevada City, CA (Blue Dolphin Publishing).

NATHANSON, Donald L., editor. *The Many Faces of Shame.* 1987, New York (Guilford Press).

NATHANSON, Donald L. "A Timetable for Shame," in Donald NATHANSON, editor, *The Many Faces of Shame* (1987), pp. 1-63.

New Directions in Psychology. 1962, New York (Holt, Rinehart & Winston).

NICHOLSON, Reynold A., editor. *The Mathnawí of Jalálu-ddin Rúmí.* In 6 volumes. 1926/1990, Cambridge (The E.J.W. Gibb Memorial Trust).

NIETZSCHE, Friedrich. *On the Advantage and Disadvantage of History for Life [=Untimely Meditations II].* Translation of *Vom Nutzen und Nachteil der Historie für das Leben* (1874) by Peter PREUSS. 1980, Indianapolis (Hackett Publishing Company).

NIETZSCHE, Friedrich. *The Antichrist.* Translation of *Der Antichrist* (1895), with an introduction, by H.L. MENCKEN. 1918, New York (A.A. Knopf); translation by Walter KAUFMANN, in Friedrich NIETZSCHE, *The Portable Nietzsche* (1954).

NIETZSCHE, Friedrich. *The Birth of Tragedy* and *The Case of Wagner*. Translated, with commentary, by Walter KAUFMANN. 1967, New York (Vintage).

NIETZSCHE, Friedrich. *Beyond Good and Evil: Prelude to a Philosophy of the Future*. Translation of *Jenseits von Gut und Böse: Vorspiel einer Philosophie der Zukunft* (1886), with commentary, by Walter KAUFMANN. 1966, New York (Vintage Books).

NIETZSCHE, Friedrich. *The Case of Wagner*. Translation of *Der Fall Wagner: Ein Musikanten-Problem* (1888), by Walter KAUFMANN, in *The Birth of Tragedy* & *The Case of Wagner* (1967).

NIETZSCHE, Friedrich. *The Dawn of Day*. Translation of *Die Morgenröte* (1881) by Johanna VOLZ. 1903, London (T.F. Unwin). Translation by John McFarland KENNEDY. 1964, New York (Russell & Russell).

NIETZSCHE, Friedrich. *Ecce Homo*. Translation of *Ecce homo* (1895), by Walter KAUFMANN, in Friedrich NIETZSCHE, *On the Genealogy of Morals* and *Ecce Homo* (1967).

NIETZSCHE, Friedrich. *The Gay Science*. Translation of *Die fröhliche Wissenschaft* (1882), with commentary, by Walter KAUFMANN. 1974, New York (Vintage Books). *Le gai savoir*. Translation by Henri ALBERT. 1911, Paris (Mercure de France).

NIETZSCHE, Friedrich. *On the Genealogy of Morals* and *Ecce Homo*. Translation of *Zur Genealogie der Moral* (1887), and of *Ecce Homo* (1895), with commentary, by Walter KAUFMANN. 1967, New York (Vintage Books).

NIETZSCHE, Friedrich. *Human, All-too-human: A Book for Free Spirits*. Translation of *Menschliches, allzumenschliches* (1878-79) by Reginald John HOLLINGDALE. With Introduction by Erich HELLER (1986); with Introduction by Richard SCHACHT (1996). 1986/1996, Cambridge (Cambridge University Press). [The German original consists of Volume 1 with a foreword, 9 chapters, and a poem, and Volume 2 with a foreword and two chapters, the second entitled *Der Wanderer und sein Schatten*, *The Wanderer and his Shadow*, often cited independently under its own title.]

NIETZSCHE, Friedrich. *Philosophy and Truth: Selections from Nietzsche's notebooks of the early 1870s*. Translated and edited, with an introduction and notes, by Daniel BREAZEALE. Foreword by Walter KAUFMANN. 1979, Atlantic Highlands NJ (Humanities Press).

NIETZSCHE, Friedrich. *The Portable Nietzsche*. With complete translations by Walter KAUFMANN of *Thus Spake Zarathustra*, *Twilight of the Idols*, *The Antichrist*, and *Nietzsche contra Wagner*. 1954, New York (Vintage Books).

NIETZSCHE, Friedrich. *Thus Spake Zarathustra*. Translation of *Also sprach Zarathustra* (1883-85) by Walter KAUFMANN. 1966, New York (Vingtage Books).

NIETZSCHE, Friedrich. *Truth and Lies in an Extra-Moral Sense*. Translation of *Über Wahrheit und Lüge im aussermoralischen Sinne* (1873), by David BREAZEALE in Friedrich NIETZSCHE, *Philosophy and Truth: Selections from Nietzsche's Notebooks of the Early 1870s* (1979). There is an abridged translation by Walter KAUFMANN, in *The Portable Nietzsche* (1954).

NIETZSCHE, Friedrich. *Twilight of the Idols*. Translation of *Die Götzen-Dämmerung* (1889) by Walter KAUFMANN, in *The Portable Nietzsche* (1954).

NIETZSCHE, Friedrich. *Schopenhauer as Educator [=Untimely Meditations III]*. Translation of *Schopenhauer als Erzieher* (1874) by Eliseo VIVAS. 1965, Chicago (Regenery).

NIETZSCHE, Friedrich. *The Wanderer and his Shadow*. Translation of *Der Wanderer und sein Schatten* (1880) [=Band/Volume 2, Hauptstück/Chapter 2, of *Menschliches, allzumenschliches/Human All-too-human*], by Reginald John HOLLINGDALE, in Friedrich NIETZSCHE, *Human, All-too-human: A Book for Free Spirits*.

NIETZSCHE, Friedrich. *Werke in Drei Bänden, Erster Band [Works in Three Volumes, First Volume]*. 1966, München/Munich (Carl Hanser Verlag).

NIETZSCHE, Friedrich. *The Will to Power.* Translation of *Der Wille zur Macht* (1895) by Walter KAUFMANN and Reginald John HOLLINGDALE, with commentary by Walter KAUFMANN. 1968: New York (Vintage Books).

NORMAN, Jerry. *Chinese.* 1988, Cambridge (Cambridge University Press).

Numerical Discourses of the Buddha: An Anthology of Suttas from the Aṅguttara Nikāya. Selected and translated from the Pali by NYANAPONIKA Thera and Bhikkhu BODHI. 1999, Walnut Creek, CA (AltaMira Press) and Boston (Rowman & Littlefield).

NUNBERG, Hermann, and FEDERN, Ernst, editors. *Minutes of the Vienna Psychoanalytic Society.* In 2 volumes. 1962-1975, New York (International Universities Press).

NYANAPONIKA Thera. *The Heart of Buddhist Meditation: A Handbook of Mental Training Based on the Buddha's Way of Mindfulness. With an Anthology of Relevant Texts translated from the Pali and Sanskrit* (1962, 1965). 1988, York Beach, ME (Samuel Weiser).

NYIMA, Chökyi, Rinpoche. *The Union of Mahamudra and Dzogchen.* With *A Commentary on The Quintessence of Spiritual Practice, The Direct Instructions of the Great Compassionate One* by Karma CHAGMEY Rinpoche. Translated from Tibetan by Erik Pema KUNSANG. 1994, Hong Kong, Kathmandu, Boudhanath, and Århus (Ranjung Yeshe Publications).

The Nyingma School of Tibetan Buddhism: Its Fundamentals and History. Volume I: The Translations. Text by H.H. DUDJOM Rinpoche. *Volume 2: Reference Material.* Translation and Materials by Gyurme DORJE and Matthew KAPSTEIN. 1991: Boston (Wisdom).

OCHOROWICZ, Julian. *De la suggestion mentale.* 1887, Paris (Octave Doin, éditeur).

The Oxford English Dictionary. Second edition (in 20 volumes). 1989, Oxford (Clarendon Press/Oxford Univeristy Press).

Oxford Latin Dictionary. 1996, Oxford (Oxford University Press).

PACHTER, Henry. *Magic Into Science: The Story of Paracelsus.* 1951, New York (Henry Schuman).

The Pali Text Society Pali-English Dictionary. Edited by T.W. RHYS DAVIDS and William STEDE (1921-1925). 1972, London (Pali Text Society/Routledge & Kegan Paul).

PALMER, Martin, translator, with Elizabeth Breuilly, Chang Wai Ming and Jay Ramsay. *The Book of Chuang Tzu.* 1996, London (Arkana/Penguin).

PARACELSUS [Philippus Aureolus Theophrastus Bombastus von Hohenheim]. *von den kranckheyten, so die vernunfft berauben.* 1567. Basel (Adamum von Bodenstein/Petreus Perna). Reprinted as *Von den Kranckheiten, so den Menschen der Vernunfft naturelich berauben.* 1576, Straßburg (Niclauss Wyriot). Modern reprint in *Sämtliche Werke. 1. Abteilung: Medizinische, naturwissenschaftliche, und philosophische Schriften. 2. Band.* Edited by Karl SUDHOFF. 1930, München/Munich and Berlin (Druck und Verlag von R. Oldenbourg). An electronic version of this text is available through http://www.digibib.tu-bs.de/?docid=00000703.

PERLS, Frederick [Fritz]. *Gestalt Therapy Verbatim.* 1969, Moab UT (Real People Press).

PETERS, Richard S. "Emotions and the Category of Passivity," *Aristotelian Society Proceedings,* vol. 62 (1961-62), pp.117-134.

PÉTÉTIN, Jacques-Henri-Désiré. *Électricité animale, prouvée par la découverte des phénomènes physiques et moraux de la Catalepsie hystérique, et de ses variétés.* 1808, Paris (Chez Brunot-Labbé, libraire, and Gautier et Bretin, libraires) and Lyon (Chez Reymann et compagnie, libraires).

PÉTÉTIN, Jacques-Henri-Désiré. *Mémoire ſur la découverte des phénomenes que préſentent la catalepſie et le ſomnambuliſme. Symptômes de l'affection hyſtérique eſſentielle, avec des recherches ſur la cauſe phyſique de ces phénomenes.* 1787, Lyon. Reprint edition, 1978, Nendeln, Lichtenstein (Kraus Reprint). [Note: f=s; phénomenes=phéno-mènes.]

PETTIT, John Whitney. *Mi-pham's Beacon of Certainty: Illuminating the View of Dzogchen, the Great Perfection.* 1999: Somerville, MA (Wisdom Publications).

PFEIFER, Jennifer H., IACOBONI, Marco, MAZZIOTTA, John C., DAPRETTO, Mirella. [On the role of the MSN, the Mirror Neuron System:] "Mirroring others' emotions relates to empathy and interpersonal competence in children," *NeuroImage,* vol. 39 (2008), pp. 2076–2085.

PFISTER, Oskar. "Plato: A Fore-Runner of Psycho-Analysis," *International Journal of Psycho-Analysis,* vol. 3 (1922), pp. 169-174.

PIAF, Edith. "C'est l'amour," n.d., Disques Assimil, No. ESRF-1898(M). Also in CD *The Best of Edith Piaf: C'est l'amour,* 1999, Delta Records, ASIN # B000021XWP.

PIERRAKOS, John. *Core Energetics: Developing the Capacity to Love and Heal.* 1990, Mendecino CA (LifeRhythm). English version of *Core Energetik.* 1986, Essen, Germany (Synthesis).

PIERRAKOS, John. *Eros, Love & Sexuality: The Forces that Unify Man and Woman.* 1997, Mendecino, CA (LifeRhythm Publication).

PLATO. *Plato: The Collected Dialogues.* Edited by Edith HAMILTON and Huntington CAIRNS. Second printing, with corrections. 1963, Princeton (Princeton University Press). Texts cited are (translator mentioned in parentheses): *Laws* (A.E. TAYLOR), pp. 1225-1513; *Phaedo* (Hugh TREDENNICK), pp. 40-98; *Republic* (F.M. CORNFORD), pp. 575-844; *Symposium* (Michael JOYCE), pp. 526-574; *Timaeus* (Benjamin JOWETT), pp. 1151-1211.

PORTER, Bill: see BODHIDHARMA; RED PINE.

PRÉVOST, Claude M. *Janet, Freud et la psychologie clinique.* 1973, Paris (Payot).

PRÉVOST, Claude M. *La psycho-philosophie de Pierre Janet: Économies mentales et progrès humain.* 1973, Paris (Payot).

PRIGOGINE, Ilya, et al. *Chaos: The New Science.* Nobel Conference XXVI, Gustavus Adolphus College, St. Peter, MN. John HOLTE, editor. 1993, Lanham, MD (University Press of America).

PRIGOGINE, Ilya, and STENGERS, Isabelle: *La nouvelle alliance: Métamorphose de la science.* 1979, Paris (Gallimard). Revised English edition, as *Order out of Chaos: Man's New Dialogue with Nature.* 1984, Boulder (New Science Library).

PROUDHON, Pierre-Joseph. *Idée générale de la révolution au XIXe siècle.* 1851, Paris (Librairie Garnier Frères).

PROUST, Marcel. *Sur la lecture.* Reprint of article in *La Renaissance latine* [Paris], June 1905, pp. 379-410, then used as Preface to his translation of John RUSKIN, *Sésame et les lys* (Paris, 1906, Mercure de France). 1988, Arles (Editions Actes Sud).

PULLEYBLANK, Edwin G. *An Outline of Classical Chinese Grammar.* 1995, Vancouver (University of British Columbia Press).

PUYSÉGUR, Amand-Marc-Jacques de Chastenet, Marquis de. *Mémoires pour servir à l'histoire et à l'établissement du magnétisme animal.* 1784. Reprint edition with "Les somnambules de Buzancy" by Georges LAPASSADE and "'Une vie, une passion: Puységur et le magnétisme animal" by Philippe PÉDELAHORE. 1986, Toulouse (Edition Privat). Same text, with new title before the earlier title, *Aux sources de l'hypnose: Mémoires pour servir à l'histoire et à l'établissement du magnétisme animal.* 2003, Toulouse (Privat).

RADHAKRISHNAN, Sarvepalli, translator. *The Dhammapada.* Bilingual edition: Pali text with English translation. 1950, London (Oxford University Press). Reprint edition, 1966/2003, New Delhi (Oxford India Paperbacks/Oxford University Press).

RAHULA, Walpola, translator-editor. *Le Compendium de la Super-doctrine (Philosophie) (Abhidharmasamuccaya) d'Asaṅga* (1971). Second edition, 1980, Paris (École française d'Extrême-Orient).

RAHULA, Walpola. *What the Buddha Taught* (1959). 1962, New York (Evergreen/Grove Press). Reprint editions, 1988/1990/2006, Bangkok (Haw Trai Foundation).

RAMACHANDRAN, Vilayanur S. *The Emerging Mind: The Reith Lectures 2003.* 2003, London (Profile Books Ltd).

RAND, David. "Getting a Mathematical Hold on Life" (downloaded July 7, 2010). Available online via a title search at www.epsrc.ac.uk, with link to this research article.

Random House Unabridged Dictionary. 1997, New York (Random House).

RAPHALS, Lisa. "Skeptical Strategies in the 'Zhuangzi' and 'Theaetetus,'" *Philosophy East and West,* vol. 44, no. 3 (July 1994), pp. 501-526.

RAWLS, John. *A Theory of Justice.* 1971/2005, Cambridge (Harvard University Press).

Records of the Transmission of the Lamp (Ching Tê Ch'uan Têng Lu). Compiled by TAO YUAN, a Zen monk of the Sung Dynasty. Translated by Sohaku OGATA. 1986, Albuquerque (The Asian Cultural Studies Project of the University of New Mexico/Hummingbird Press).

RED PINE (PORTER, Bill): see also BODHIDHARMA.

RED PINE (PORTER, Bill), translator. *The Collected Songs of Cold Mountain* [寒山詩 *Hán Shān Shī*]. Intro by John BLOFELD. 2000, Port Townsand, WA (Copper Canyon Press).

RED PINE (PORTER, Bill), translator. *Lao-tzu's Taoteching: With Selected Commentaries of the Past 2000 Years.* Second edition. 1996, San Francisco (Mercury House).

REICHENBACH, Hans. "Bertrand Russell's Logic," in P.A. SCHILPP, editor, *The Philosophy of Bertrand Russell,* volume 1, pp. 21-54.

RENOU, Louis. *Grammaire sanscrite.* 1975, Paris (Librairie Adrien Maisonneuve).

REPS, Paul. *Zen Flesh, Zen Bones: A Collection of Zen and Pre-Zen Writings.* 1961, Garden City, NY (Anchor Books/Doubleday).

REYNOLDS, John Myrdhin. *The Golden Letters: The Three Statements of Garab Dorje, the first teacher of Dzogchen.* With "The Special Teaching of the Wise and Glorious King" by Dza PATRUL Rinpoche, *Short Commentary on the Three Statements of Garab Dorje* by DUDJOM Rinpoche, Foreword by Namkhai NORBU Rinpoche. 1996, Ithaca (Snow Lion).

RHEES, Rush. "Can There Be a Private Language?," *Supplementary Volume of the Aristotelian Society,* 28 (1954), pp. 77-94.

RHYS DAVIDS, Caroline A.F., translator. *A Buddhist Manual of Psychological Ethics of the Fourth Century B.C., being A Translation, now made for the First Time, from the Original Pali, of the First Book of the Abhidhamma-piṭaka, entitled Dhamma-san-gaṇi.* 1900, London (Royal Asiatic Society). 1975, New Delhi (Oriental Books).

RIBOT, Théodule. "Les affaiblissements de la volonté," *Revue philosophique de la France et de l'étranger,* vol. 14 (July-December 1882), pp. 391-423.

RIBOT, Théodule. *La logique des sentiments.* 1905; second edition, 1907, Paris (Félix Alcan).

RILKE, Rainer Maria. *Letters to a Young Poet.* Translation of *Briefe an einen jungen Dichter* (1929) by Stephen MITCHELL. 2001, New York (Modern Library).

RIST, John M. *Stoic Philosophy.* 1969, Cambridge (Cambridge University Press).

RIZZOLATTI, Giacomo, and ARBIB, Michael A. "Language within our grasp," *Trends in Neurosciences,* vol. 21, no. 5 (May 1, 1998), pp. 188-194.

ROBINET, Isabelle. *Méditation taoïste.* 1979, Paris (Dervy Livres). Translated by Julian F. PAS and Norman J. GIRARDOT, as *Taoist Meditation: The Mao-shan Tradition of Great Purity.* With new afterword by Isabelle ROBINET. 1993, Albany (State University of New York Press).

ROKEACH, Milton. *The Three Christs of Ypsilanti: A Psychological Study.* 1964, New York (Borzoi Books/Knopf).

ROSENBERG, Marshall B. *Nonviolent Communication: A Language of Compassion.* 1999, Del Mar, CA (PuddleDancer Press). Second edition, with Foreword by Arun GANDHI. 2003, Encinitas, CA (PuddleDancer Press).

ROSS, David. *Aristotle* (1923/1949). 1964, London (Methuen & Co Ltd) and New York (Barnes & Noble).

ROTH, Harold D. "Bimodel Mystical Experience in the 'Qísùlún 齊物論' Chapter of the *Zhuangzi* 莊子," in Scott COOK, editor, *Hiding the World in the World,* Chapter 1, pp. 15-32.

ROTH, Harold D., editor. *A Companion to Angus C. Graham's Chuang Tzu.* 2003, Honolulu (University of Hawai'i Press).

ROTH, Harold D. *Original Tao: Inward Training (Nei-yeh 內業) and the Foundations of Taoist Mysticism.* 1999, New York (Columbia University Press).

ROTH, Harold D. "Redaction Criticism and the Early History of Taoism," *Early China,* vol. 19 (1994), pp. 1-46.

ROTH, Harold. "Who compiled the *Chuang Tzu*?" in Henry ROSEMONT, Jr., editor, *Chinese Texts and Philosophical Contexts: Essays Dedicated to Angus C. Graham,* pp. 79-128.

ROSEMONT, Jr., Henry, editor. *Chinese Texts and Philosophical Contexts: Essays Dedicated to Angus C. Graham.* 1991, La Salle IL (Open Court Publishing).

ROUDINESCO, Elisabeth. *La bataille de cent ans: histoire de la psychanalyse en France.* In 2 volumes. 1986, Paris (Seuil).

RUBIN, Jeffrey. "William James and the Pathologizing of Human Experience," *Journal of Humanistic Psychology,* vol. 40 (2000), no. 2, pp. 176-226.

RUBIN, Theodore, M.D. *Lisa and David.* 1963, New York (Ballantine Books).

RUSSELL, Bertrand. "Logical Atomism," in A.J. AYER, editor, *Logical Positivism,* pp. 31-50.

RUSSELL, Bertrand. "The Philosophy of Logical Atomism," in R.C. MARSH, editor, *Logic and Knowledge,* pp. 175-281.

SAINT PHALLE, Niki de [Catherine Marie-Agnès Fal de Saint Phalle]. *Mon secret.* 1994, Paris (Éditions La Différence).

Saṃyutta Nikāya: see The Connected Discourses of the Buddha.

SANDEL, Michael J. *Justice: What's the Right Thing to Do?* 2009, New York (Farrar, Straus and Giroux).

SANDS, Kathleen R. *Demon Possession in Elizabethan England.* 2004, London (Praeger).

ŞAR, Vedat, and ÖZTÜRK, Erdinç. "Functional Dissociation of the Self: A Sociocognitive Approach to Trauma and Dissociation," *Journal of Trauma and Dissociation,* vol. 8, no. 4 (2007), pp. 69-89.

ŞAR, Vedat, and ROSS, Colin. "Dissociative Disorders as a Confounding Factor in Psychiatric Research," *Psychiatric Clinics of North America,* vol. 29 (2006), pp. 129-144.

SARTRE, Jean-Paul. *L'être et le néant. Essai sur l'ontologie phénoménologique* (1943). 1980, Paris (Gallimard). Translated by Hazel E. BARNES as *Being and Nothingness: An Essay on Phenomenological Ontology.* 1956, New York (Philosophical Library). With a new Introduction by Mary WARNOCK (1969). 2003, London (Methuen).

SARTRE, Jean-Paul. *Huis clos CD* [*Huis clos* with comments by Sartre]. 2004, Paris (Gallimard).

SCHATZMAN, Morton. "Madness and Morals," in Joseph BERKE, editor, *Counter Culture* (1969), pp. 288-313.

SCHILLING, Friedrich Wilhelm Joseph von. *Vom Ich als Prinzip der Philosophie.* 1795, Tübingen (Heerbrandt). 1911, Leipzig (Meiner).

SCHILPP, Paul Arthur, editor. *The Philosophy of Bertrand Russell.* Volume 1. 1951, New York (Tudor Publishing Company); 1963, New York (Harper and Row).

SCHIMMEL, Annemarie. *Mystical Dimensions of Islam.* 1975, Chapel Hill (University of North Carolina Press).

SCHLESINGER, Izchak M. "A Note on the Relationship between Psychological and Linguistic Theories," *Foundations of Language,* vol. 3, no. 4 (November 1967), pp. 397-402.

SCHÜTZENBERGER, Anne Ancelin. *Psychogénéalogie. Guérir les tristesses familiales et se retrouver soi.* 2007, Paris (Editions Payot).

SCHWARTZ, Benjamin I. *The World of Thought in Ancient China.* 1985, Cambridge (Harvard University Press).

SCHWARTZ, Jeffrey M., and BEGLEY, Sharon. *The Mind and the Brain: Neuroplasticity and the Power of Mental Force.* 2002, New York (HarperCollins Publishers).

SEARLES, Harold F. "The Contributions of Family Treatment to the Psychotherapy of Schizophrenia," in Ivan BOSZORMENYI-NAGY and James L. FRAMO, editors, *Intensive Family Therapy* (1965), pp. 463-495.

The Secret of the Golden Flower. English translation of the Chinese text entitled *Tài yǐ jīn huá zōng zhǐ* 太乙金華宗旨, in Thomas CLEARY, translator, *The Taoist Classics, Volume Three,* pp. 273-376.

SEDGWICK, Eve Kosofsky, and FRANK, Adam, editors. *Shame and its Sisters: A Silvan Tomkins Reader.* 1995, Durham, NC (Duke University Press).

SEKIDA Katsuki. *Two Zen Classics: The Gateless Gate and the Blue Cliff Records.* Translation of *Mumonkan* and of *Hekiganroku,* with commentaries. 2005, Boston (Shambhala).

SENG-TS'AN [SENGCAN]. *Hsin Hsin Ming. Ecrit d'un cœur confiant [Traité de spiritualité Ch'an du VIe siècle].* Translated, with an introduction, by Daniel GIRAUD. 1992, Paris (Les Éditions Arfuyen).

SENG-TS'AN [SENGCAN]. *Hsin Hsin Ming. Verses on the Faith Mind.* Translated by Richard B. CLARKE. 1973, Toronto (The Coach House Press) and Sharon Springs NY (The Zen Center). Reprint, 1974, Boulder, CO and Virginia Beach, VA (Alan Clements). New translation; illustrations by Gyokusei Jikihara. 2001, Buffalo (White Pine Press).

SHAKESPEARE, William. *Hamlet.* Albert R. BRAUNMULLER, editor. 2001, New York (Penguin).

SHAH, Idries. *Tales of the Dervishes: Teaching-Stories of the Sufi Masters over the Past Thousand Years. Selected from the Sufi classics, from oral tradition, from unpublished manuscripts and schools of Sufi teaching in many countries.* 1967, London (Octagon Press Ltd and Jonathan Cape); 1969/1970, New York (E.P. Dutton); 1993, London (Arkana/Penguin).

SHEN, Helen H., TSAI, Chen-Hui, and ZHOU, Yunong. *Hànyǔpīnyīn rùmén* 汉语拼音入门 *Introduction to Standard Chinese Pinyin System.* 2007, Beijing (Beijing Language and Culture University Press).

SHIH, Heng-ching, translator, in collaboration with Dan Lusthaus. *A Comprehensive Commentary on the Heart Sutra (Prajñāpāramita-hṛdaya-sūtra). From the Chinese of K'ueichi.* 2001, Berkeley (Numata Center for Buddhist Translation and Research).

SHIPLEY, Thorne, editor. *Classics in Psychology.* 1961, New York (Philosophical Library).

SHORTER, Edward. *A History of Psychiatry: From the Era of the Asylum to the Age of Prozac.* 1997, New York (John Wiley & Sons).

SIEGEL, Daniel J. *The Developing Mind: How Relationships and the Brain Interact to Shape Who We Are.* 1999, New York (Guilford Press/Guilford Publication).

SIEGEL, Daniel J. *The Mindful Brain: Reflection and Attunement in the Cultivation of Well-Being.* 2007, New York (W.W. Norton).

SIEGEL, Daniel J. *The Mindful Therapist: A Clinician's Guide to Mindsight and Neural Integration.* 2010, New York (W.W. Norton).

SIEGEL, Daniel J. *Mindsight: The New Science of Personal Transformation*. 2010, New York (Bantam Books).

SIGERIST, Henry E., editor. *Four Treatises of Theophrastus von Hohenheim called Paracelsus*. Includes *The Diseases That Deprive Man of His Reason, Such as St. Vitus' Dance, Falling Sickness, Melancholy, and Insanity, and Their Correct Treatment*, translated by Gregory ZILBOORG, pp. 127-212. 1941, Baltimore (The Johns Hopkins Press).

SILK, Jonathan A. "Child Abandonment and Homes for Unwed Mothers in Ancient India: Buddhist Sources," *Journal of the American Oriental Society*, vol. 127, no. 3 (July-September 2007), pp. 297-314.

SIMON, Yves. *Lou Andreas-Salomé*. 2004, Paris (Éditions Mengès).

SIMONIS, Fabien. *A Chinese Model of Cognition: The Neiye, fourth century B.C.E.* 1998, Montreal (McGill University, History Department).

SINGH, Jaideva, translator. *Vijñānabhairava or Divine Consciousness*. 1979/1993, Delhi (Motilal Banarsidass).

SJÖVALL, Björn. *Psychology of Tension: An analysis of Pierre Janet's concept of «tension psychologique» together with an historical aspect*. Translated by Alan DIXON. 1967, Stockholm and Uppsala (Uppsala University/Scandinavian University Books/Svenska Bokförlaget).

SKINNER, Burrhus Frederic. *Verbal Behavior*. 1957, New York (Appleton-Century-Crofts).

SLINGERLAND, Edward. *Effortless Action: Wu-wei as Conceptual Metaphor and Spiritual Ideal in Early China*. 2003, New York (Oxford University Press).

SLUZKI, Carlos, BEAVIN, Janet, TARNOPOLSKY, Alejandro, and VERÓN, Eliseo. "Transactional Disqualification," *Archives of General Psychiatry*, vol. 16 (April 1967), pp. 494-504.

SMART, Ninian. "Action and Suffering in Theravadin Buddhism," *Philosophy East and West*, vol. 34, no. 4 (October 1984), p. 371.

SMITH, Graham. *Warman's Civil War Weapons*. 2005, Iola, WI (Krause Publications).

SOENG Mu. *Trust in Mind: the Rebellion of Chinese Zen*. Foreword by Jan Chozen BAYS. 2004, Boston (Wisdom Publications).

SOLOMON, Robert C. *From Rationalism to Existentialism: The Existentialists and Their Nineteenth-Century Backgrounds*. 1972, New York (Harper & Row).

SOLOMON, Robert C. *History and Human Nature: A Philosophical Review of European Philosophy and Culture, 1750-1850*. 1979, New York and London (Harcourt Brace Jovanovich). Reprinted as *The Bully Culture: Enlightenment, Romanticism, and the Transcendental Pretense*. 1992: Lanham, MD (Rowman & Littlefield).

SOLOMON, Robert C. *In the Spirit of Hegel*. 1983, New York (Oxford University Press).

SOLOMON, Robert C. "The Logic of Emotion," *Nous*, vol. 11, no. 1 (March 1977), pp. 41-49.

SOLOMON, Robert C. *Love: Emotion, Myth, and Metaphor*. 1981, Garden City, NY (Doubleday Anchor).

SOLOMON, Robert C. "A More Severe Morality: Nietzsche's Affirmative Ethics," in Yirmiyahu YOVEL, editor, *Nietzsche as Affirmative Thinker: Papers Presented at the Fifth Jerusalem Philosophical Encounter, April 1983*, pp. 69-89.

SOLOMON, Robert C., editor. *Nietzsche: A Collection of Critical Essays*. 1973, Garden City, NY (Doubleday Anchor Books). Reprint editions, 1980/1990, Notre Dame, IN (Notre Dame University Press).

SOLOMON, Robert C. *Not Passion's Slave: Emotions and Choice* [Selected Essays, 1973-2001]. 2003, New York (Oxford University Press).

SOLOMON, Robert C. *The Passions*. 1976, Garden City (Anchor Press/Doubleday); 1983, Notre Dame, IN (Notre Dame University Press); 1993, Indianapolis (Hackett Publishing), as *The Passions: Emotions and the Meaning of Life*.

SOLOMON, Robert C. *True to Our Feelings: What Our Emotions Are Really Telling Us.* 2006, New York (Oxford University Press).

SOLOMON, Robert. *Unconscious Motivation.* Doctoral Dissertation, Philosophy Dept., Univ. of Michigan, 1967. UMI Microfilm #68-7731 (Ann Arbor, MI).

SOLOMON, Robert C., and HIGGINS, Kathleen M., editors. *The Philosophy of (Erotic) Love.* Foreword by Arthur C. DANTO. 1991, Lawrence, KS (University of Kansas Press).

SOMA Thera. *The Way of Mindfulness: The Satipaṭṭhāna Sutta and Commentary* (1941). Third edition, 1967, Fourth edition, 1975; Fifth revised edition, 1981, Kandy, Sri Lanka (Buddhist Publication Society); Sixth revised edition, 1985/1998, Singapore (Singapore Buddhist Meditation Centre).

SOMER, Eli. "Advances in Dissociation Research and Practice in Israel," *Journal of Trauma Practice,* vol. 4, no. 1/2 (2005), pp. 157-178.

SOMER, Eli. "Culture-Bound Dissociation: A Comparative Study," *Psychiatric Hospitals of North America,* vol. 29, no. 1 (2006), pp. 213-226.

SOOTHILL, William Edward, and HODOUS, Lewis. *A Dictionary of Chinese Buddhist Terms* (1937). Reprint edition, 1994, Delhi (Motilal Banarsidass).

SPERBER, Dan, PREMACK, David, and PREMACK, Ann James, editors. *Causal Cognition: A Multidisciplinary Debate.* 1995, Oxford (Oxford University Press).

SPIEGEL, David. "Recognizing Traumatic Dissociation," *American Journal of Psychiatry,* vol. 163, no. 4 (April 2006), pp. 566-568.

SPITZ, René Árpád. "La perte de la mère par le nourrisson. Troubles du développement psycho-somatique," *Enfance,* vol. 1, no. 5 (November-December 1948), pp. 373-391.

STELMACK, Robert M., and DOUCET, Cynthia. "A Dialogue with Galen on Zuckerman's *The Psychobiology of Personality,*" *Psychological Inquiry,* vol. 4, no. 2 (1993), pp. 142-146.

STELMACK, Robert M., and STALIKAS, Anastasios. "Galen and the humour theory of temperament," *Personality and Individual Differences,* vol. 12, no. 3 (1991), pp. 255-263.

STENDHAL: see BEYLE, Marie Henri (STENDHAL).

STEVENS, John O., editor. *Gestalt Is.* 1975, Moab, UT (Real People Press); 1977, New York (Bantam Books).

STEVENSON, Charles Leslie. "Persuasive Definitions," *Mind,* New Series, vol. 47, no. 187 (July 1938), pp. 331-350.

STIMSON, Hugh M. *Introduction to Chinese Pronunciation and the Pinyin Romanization.* 1975, New Haven (Yale University, Far Eastern Publications).

STIRNER, Max. *The Ego and His Own.* 1907, New York (Benjamin R. Tucker). Introduction by James L. WALKER. Translation by Steven T. BYINGTON of *Der Einzige und sein Eigentum.* 1845, Leipzig (Otto Wigand). New edition, edited by David LEOPOLD. With introduction. 1995, Cambridge (Cambridge University Press).

STRONG, Dawsonne Melanchthon, translator. *The Udāna or Solemn Utterances of the Buddha.* 1902, London (Luzac & Co., Publishers, for the India Office).

SULLIVAN, Harry Stack. *The Interpersonal Theory of Psychiatry.* 1954, New York (W.W. Norton).

SUNDARARAJAN, Louise. "The Plot Thickens—or Not: Protonarratives of Emotions and the Chinese Principle of Savoring," *Journal of Humanistic Psychology,* vol. 48, no. 2 (April 2008), pp. 243-263.

Sutta Nipāta: see *The Group of Discourses (Sutta Nipāta).*

SUZUKI Shunru. *Zen Mind, Beginner's Mind: Informal Talks of Zen Meditation and Practice.* 1970, Tokyo (John Weatherhill).

SZASZ, Thomas. *Antipsychiatry: Quackery Squared.* 2009, Syracuse (Syracuse University Press).

SZASZ, Thomas. "Debunking Antipsychiatry: Laing, Law, and Largactil," *Current Psychology*, vol. 27, no. 2 (June 2008), pp. 79-101. [Largactil in Europe and Canada, and Thorazine in the USA, brand names for Chlorpromazine hydrochloride.]

SZASZ, Thomas. "The Myth of Mental Illness," *The American Psychologist*, vol. 15, no. 2 (1960), pp. 113-118.

SZASZ, Thomas. *The Myth of Mental Illness: Foundations of a Theory of Personal Conduct.* 1961, New York (Hoeber Medical Division of Harper and Row). Re-edition: Fiftieth Anniversary Edition with New Preface and Two Bonus Essays. 2010, New York (Harper).

SZASZ, Thomas. *Coercion as Cure: A Critical History of Psychiatry.* 2009, New Brunswick, NJ (Transaction Publishers).

TARSKI, Alfred. *Logic, Semantics, Metamathematics.* Translated by Joseph Henry WOODGER. 1956, Oxford (Oxford University Press).

The Text of the Minor Sayings. Volume 1 of *The Minor Anthologies of the Pali Canon.* Translation of *Dhammapada* and *Khuddaka-pātha* by Mrs. C.A.F. RHYS DAVIDS (1931). 1997, Oxford (Pali Text Society).

THOM, René. *Modèles mathématiques de la morphogenèse: Recueil de textes sur la théorie des catastrophes et ses applications.* 1974, Paris (Union général d'éditions). Translation by William M. BROOKES and David RAND as *Mathematical Models of Morphogenesis.* Foreword by René THOM. 1983, Chichester, GB (Ellis Horwood).

THOM, René. *Parabole e catastrofi: intervista su matematica, scienza e filosofia.* Edited by Giulo GIORELLO and Simona MORINI. 1980, Milan (Il Saggiatore). French edition with interview/introduction by René THOM, as *Paraboles et catastrophes: Entretiens sur les mathématiques, la science, et la philosophie.* 1983, Paris (Flammarion).

THOM, René. *Stabilité structurelle et morphogénèse: essai d'une théorie générale des modèles.* 1972, Reading, MA (W.A. Benjamin); 1977, Paris (InterÉditions). English translation by David H. FOWLER as *Structural Stability and Morphogenesis: An Outline of a General theory of models.* With a foreword by Conrad Hal WADDINGTON. 1975, Reading, MA (W.A. Benjamin).

TOMKINS, Silvan: see SEDGWICK, Eve Kosofsky, and FRANK, Adam, editors.

TORCHINOV, Yevgeny/Евгений ТОРЧИНОВ. Даосизм: опыт историко-религиозного описания/*Daosizm: Opyt istoriko-religioznogo opisaniya.* 1998, Санкт-Петербург/Saint Petersburg (Лань/Lan). Publication of English version, pending.

TRUNGPA, Chögyam, Rinpoche. *Cutting Through Spiritual Materialism.* 1973, Boston (Shambhala).

TUCCI, Giuseppe. *The Religions of Tibet.* Translated from the German and Italian by Geoffrey SAMUEL, from *Die Religionen Tibets* by Giuseppe TUCCI, in *Die Religionen Tibets und der Mongolei* by Giuseppe TUCCI and Walther HEISSIG, 1970, Stuttgart (W. Kohlhammer GmbH). English text, 1980, London (Routledge & Kegan Paul Ltd) and Berkeley (University of California Press).

UMILTÀ, M. Alessandra, KOHLER, Evelyne, GALLESE, Vittorio, FOGASSI, Leonardo, FADIGA, Luciano, KEYSERS, Christian, and RIZZOLATTI, Giacomo. "I know what you are doing: a neurophysiological study," *Neuron*, vol. 31 (2001), pp. 155-165.

VAN DER HART, Onno, and DORAHY, Martin. "Pierre Janet and the Concept of Dissociation," *American Journal of Psychiatry*, vol. 163, no. 9 (September 2006), p. 1646.

VAN DER HART, Onno, and FRIEDMAN, Barbara. "A Reader's Guide to Pierre Janet on Dissociation: A Neglected Intellectual Heritage," *Dissociation*, vol. 2 (1989), pp. 3-16.

VAN DER HART, Onno, NIJENHUIS, Ellert, and STEELE, Kathy. *The Haunted Self: Structural Dissociation and the Treatment of Chronic Traumatization.* 2006, New York (W.W. Norton).

VAN DER KOLK, Bessel A. "Developmental Trauma Disorder: Towards a Rational Diagnosis for Complex Trauma Histories," *Psychiatric Annals*, vol. 35 (2006), pp. 401-408.

VANISTENDAEL, Stefan, and LECOMTE, Jacques: see also LECOMTE, Jacques.

VANISTENDAEL, Stefan, and LECOMTE, Jacques. *Le bonheur est toujours possible. Construire la résilience.* Preface by Michel MANCIAUX. 2000, Paris (Bayard Éditions).

VAN NORDEN, Bryan W.: see also as second author with IVANHOE, Philip J.

VAN NORDEN, Bryan W. "Competing Interpretations of the Inner Chapters of the *Zhuangzi*," *Philosophy East and West*, vol. 46, no. 2 (April 1996), pp. 247-268.

VAN NORDEN, Bryan W. *Virtue Ethics and Consequentialism in Early Chinese Philosophy.* 2007, Cambridge and New York (Cambridge University Press).

VAUGHAN, Susan C. *The Talking Cure: The Science Behind Psychotherapy.* 1997, New York (Holt).

VON BERTALANFFY, Ludwig. *General System Theory: Foundations, Development, Applications.* 1968, New York (George Braziller).

VON FOERSTER, Heinz, editor. *Cybernetics of Cybernetics: Or, The Control of Control and the Communication of Communication.* With papers presented by Robert ABRAMOVITZ and others. Second edition, 1995, Minneapolis (Future Systems).

VON FOERSTER, Heinz, editor; with Margaret MEAD and Hans Lukas TEUBER, assistant editors. *Cybernetics: Circular Causal and Feedback Mechanisms in Biological and Social Systems: Transactions of the Eighth Conference, March 15-16, 1951, New York City.* 1952, New York (Josiah Macy, Jr. Foundation).

VON HARTMANN, Eduard. *Philosophy of the Unconscious.* 1884, London (Trübner). Translation by William Chatterton COUPLAND of *Philosophie des Unbewußten* (first edition, 1869, Berlin, Carl Duncker Verlag), the translation being based on the seventh edition (1876, with a foreword to that German edition by the author, dated 1875).

VON HOHENHEIM, Theophrastus Bombastus: see Paracelsus.

VYGOTSKY, Lev Semenovich. *Language and Thought* (1962). Revised edition, 1986, Cambridge (MIT Press).

WALKENSTEIN, Eileen. *The Imprinters: Surviving the Unlived Life of Our Parents.* 2008, Redding, CT, and Phoenix, AZ (Zeig, Tucker & Theisen, Inc., Publishers).

WALLIN, David J. *Attachment in Psychotherapy.* 2007, New York (Guilford Press).

WALSHE, Maurice, translator. *The Long Discourses of the Buddha: A Translation of the Dīgha Nikāya.* 1995, Boston (Wisdom Publications).

WANG, Youru, editor. *Deconstruction and the Ethical in Asian Thought.* 2007, Abingdon, Oxon [i.e., Oxfordshire], UK (Routledge).

WARDER, Anthony Kennedy. *Indian Buddhism.* 1970, Delhi (Motilal Banarsidass). Third revised edition, 2000, Delhi (Motilal Banarsidass).

WASSON, G. Gordon. "The Last Meal of the Buddha, with Memorandum by Walpola Rahula and Epilogue by Wendy Doniger O'Flaherty," *Journal of the American Oriental Society*, vol. 102, no. 4 (October-December 1982), pp. 591-603.

WATSON, Burton. *Chuang Tzu: Basic Writings.* 1964/2003, New York (Columbia University Press). Also cited as *Zhuangzi: Basic Writings.*

WATSON, Burton. *The Complete Chuang Tzu.* 1968/2002, New York (Columbia University Press). Also cited as *The Complete Zhuangzi.*

WEBSTER, Noah. *An American Dictionary of the English Language.* 1828, New York (Sherman Converse). Reprinted as *American Dictionary of the English Language: Noah Webster 1828 Original Facsimile Edition.* 1968/1989/2000, San Francisco (Foundation for American Christian Education).

Webster's New World Dictionary of the American Language, College Edition. 1957, Cleveland and New York (The World Publishing Company).

WEHR, Hans. *A Dictionary of Modern Written Arabic (Arabic-English)*. Edited by J. Milton COWAN. Fourth enlarged and amended Edition. 1979, Wiesbaden (Harrassowitz); compact reprint of this complete edition, 1994, Ithaca (Spoken Language Services).

WELTER, Albert. "Mahākāśyapa's Smile: Silent Transmission and the Kung-an (Kōan) Tradition," in Steven HEINE and Dale S. WRIGHT, editors, *The Kōan: Texts and Contexts in Zen Buddhism* (2000), pp. 75-109.

WERNER, Emmy E., BIERMAN, Jessie M., and FRENCH, Fern E. *The Children of Kauai: A Longitudinal Study from the Prenatal Period to Age Ten*. 1971, Honolulu (University of Hawaii Press).

WERNER, Emmy E., and SMITH, Ruth S. *Vulnerable but Invincible: A Longitudinal Study of Resilient Children and Youth*. 1982, New York (McGraw-Hill).

WHITAKER, Carl A., FELDER, Richard E., and WARKENTIN, John. "Countertransference in the Family Treatment of Schizophrenia," in Ivan BOSZORMENYI-NAGY and James FRAMO, editors, *Intensive Family Therapy* (1965), pp. 323-341.

WHITEHEAD, Alfred North, and RUSSELL, Bertrand. *Principia Mathematica To *56*. Abridged edition of three-volume work, 1910-1913; second edition of full text, also in three volumes, 1925-1927. 1962, New York (Cambridge University Press).

WICHMANN, Ottomar. *Platos Lehre vom Instinkt und Genie. [=Kantstudien, Ergänzungshefte im Auftrag der Kantgesellschaft*, No. 40]. 1917, Berlin (Reuter & Reichard).

WICKER, Bruno, KEYSERS, Christian, PLAILLY, Jane, ROYET, Jean-Pierre, GALLESE, Vittorio, and RIZZOLATTI, Giacomo. "Both of Us Disgusted in *My* Insula: The Common Neural Basis of Seeing and Feeling Disgust," *Neuron*, vol. 40, no. 3 (October 30, 2003), pp. 655-664.

WILLS, David, editor. *Jean-Luc Godard's Pierrot le fou*. 2000, Cambridge and New York (Cambridge University Press).

WITTGENSTEIN, Ludwig. *Philosophical Investigations*. Translated by G.E.M. [Gertrude Elizabeth Margaret] ANSCOMBE. 1963, Oxford (Blackwell) and New York (Macmillan). Third edition, 2003, Oxford (Blackwell).

WITTGENSTEIN, Ludwig. *Remarks on the Foundations of Mathematics*. Translated by G.E.M. [Gertrude Elizabeth Margaret] ANSCOMBE. 1956, London (Macmillan). Third edition, 1991, Oxford (Wiley-Blackwell).

WOLFF, Christian. *Gesammelte Werke, 1. Abteilung (Deutsche Schriften, Band 1). Vernünftige Gedanken (1) (Deutsche Logik)*. 1713, Halle. Reprint edition; Hans Werner ARNDT, editor. 1965, Hildesheim (Georg Olms Verlagsbuchhandlung).

WOLFF, Christian. *Vorbericht von der Welt-Weisheit*, in Christian WOLFF, *Gesammelte Werke, 1. Abteilung (Deutsche Schriften, Band 1), Vernünftige Gedanken (1) (Deutsche Logik)* (1713/1965), pp. 115-120.

WOLFF, Robert Paul. "Beyond Tolerance," in Robert Paul WOLFF, Barrington MOORE, Jr., and Herbert MARCUSE, *A Critique of Pure Tolerance* (1965), pp. 3-52.

WOLFF, Robert Paul, MOORE, Barrington, Jr., and MARCUSE, Herbert. *A Critique of Pure Tolerance*. 1965, Boston (Beacon Press).

WU, John Ching-hsiung. *The Golden Age of Zen*. With an Introduction by Thomas MERTON (1966). Second revised edition, 1975.

WU, John Ching-hsiung. *Lao Tzu / Tao Te Ching*. Edited by Paul Kwang Tsien SIH. 1961, New York (St. John's University Press).

WU, Kuang-ming. *The Butterfly as Companion: Meditations on the first Three Chapters of the Chuang Tzu* (1989). 1990, Albany (State University of New York Press).

WU, Kuang-ming. *Chuang Tzu: World Philosopher at Play*. 1982, New York (Crossroad Publishing) and Chico, CA (Scholars Press).

Wumen kuan [Wumenguan, Mumonkan]: see REPS, Paul; SEKIDA Katsuki; YAMADA Kōan.

YAMADA Kōan, Roshi [Zen Master]. *Gateless Gate* (1979). Translation of *Wumen kuan [Mumonkan]* with commentary. Second edition, 1990, Tucson (University of Arizona Press).

YAMPOLSKY, Philip B. *The Platform Sutra of the Sixth Patriarch: The Text of the Tun-huang Manuscript*. 1967, New York (Columbia University Press).

YÁN Zhōnghù: see Lǐ Yǎngzhèng.

YESHE, Lama Thubten. *Introduction to Tantra: A Vision of Totality*. Compiled and edited by Jonathan LANDAW. 1989, Boston (Wisdom).

YEVTUSHENKO, Yevgeny/Евгений ЕВТУШЕНКО. Стихи разных лет/*Stikhi raznykh let*. 1959, Москва/Moscow (Молодая гвардия/Molodaya gvardiya).

YOUNG, Paul Thomas. *Emotion in Man and Animal*. 1943, New York (J. Wiley & Sons).

YOVEL, Yirmiyahu, editor. *Nietzsche as Affirmative Thinker: Papers Presented at the Fifth Jerusalem Philosophical Encounter, April 1983*. 1986, Dordrecht (Martinus Nijhoff).

YU, David C., translator. *History of Chinese Daoism*. Translation of Volume 1 of *Zhōngguó daòjiào shǐ* 中國道教史 *(History of Chinese Daoism)*, a 4-volume work compiled by QĪNG Xītài 卿希泰 *et alia*. 2000, Lantham, MD (University Press of America).

ZHÀO Bìchén [=CHAO Pi Ch'en]: see also LU K'uan Yü (LUK, Charles), *Taoist Yoga*.

ZHÀO Bìchén [=CHAO Pi Ch'en] 趙避塵. *Xìng mìng fǎ jué míng zhǐ* 性命法訣明指. Reprint of 1933 edition, 1963, Taipei (Zhēnshànměi chūbǎnshè 真善美出版社).

ZHU, Rui. "*Wu-Wei: Lao-zi* and *Zhuang-zi* and the aesthetic judgement," *Asian Philosophy*, vol. 12, no. 1 (January 2002), pp. 53-63.

ZHUĀNGZǏ 莊子: see also *Zhuāngzǐ yǐn dé* 莊子引得; *Zhuāngzǐ zhú zì suǒ yǐn* 莊子逐字索引.

Zhuangzi: The Essential Writings with Selections from Traditional Commentaries. Translation and introduction by Brook ZIPORYN. 2009, Indianapolis (Hackett Publishing).

ZHUANGZI. *Library of Chinese Classics, Dà zhōng huá wén kù* 大中华文库: *Zhuāngzǐ* 庄子. Translated into English by WĀNG Róngpéi 汪榕培, and into Modern Chinese (and in Simplified Characters) by QÍN Xùqīng 秦旭卿 and SŪN Yōngcháng 孙雍长. In two volumes. 1999: Hunan (Hunan People's Publishing House) and Beijing (Foreign Languages Press).

Zhuāngzǐ yǐn dé 莊子引得: see also *Zhuāngzǐ zhú zì suǒ yǐn* 莊子逐字索引.

Zhuāngzǐ yǐn dé 莊子引得. *A Concordance to Chuang Tzu*. William HUNG, editor. HYSIS [Harvard-Yenching Sinological Index Series] Supplement, No. 20. 1947, Peiping/Beijing (Yenching University Press); second printing, 1956, Cambridge (Harvard University Press for 哈佛燕京學/Harvard-Yenching Institute—now Harvard-Yanjing Institute). Reprint editions, 1966, Taipei (Chinese Materials and Research Aids Service Center, a subsidiary of the Association for Asian Studies); 1971, Taipei (Hóng dào wénhuà shiyè gōngsī 洪道文化事業公司); 1986—in Volume 3 (*Lǎozǐ yǐn dé* 老子引得; *Zhuāngzǐ yǐn dé* 莊子引得) of the six-volume set *Zhūzǐ yǐn dé* 諸子引得 *Classical Schools of Thought in Ancient China Indices*, within the series *Hàn xué suǒ yǐn jí chéng* 漢學索引集成 *Chinese Studies Complete Index Series*— Taipei (Zōng qīng tú shū gōngsī 宗青圖書公司). **With full text** of the *Chuang Tzu/ Zhuāngzǐ* 莊子, pp. 1-94. [Line numbering indicates the line of the chapter, not of the page. This differs from the line numbering system of the *Zhuāngzǐ zhú zì suǒ yǐn* 莊子逐字索引, described below at that title's entry.]

Zhuāngzǐ zhú zì suǒ yǐn 莊子逐字索引: see also *Zhuāngzǐ yǐn dé* 莊子引得.

Zhuāngzǐ zhú zì suǒ yǐn 莊子逐字索引. *A Concordance to Zhuangzi*. Identical with *The ICS Ancient Chinese Texts Concordance Series, Philosophical Works, No. 43*. 2000,

Hong Kong (The Chinese University of Hong Kong, ICS/Institute of Chinese Studies). **With full text** of the *Zhuāngzǐ* 莊子, pp. 1-101. [With modern punctuation; line numbering indicates the line of the page, not of the chapter, empty lines being counted in this numeration. This differs from the line numbering system in the *Zhuāngzǐ yǐn dé* 莊子引得, described above at that title's entry.]

ZIMMER, Heinrich. *Myths and Symbols in Indian Art and Civilization.* Joseph CAMPBELL, editor (1946). 1972, Princeton (Princeton University Press).

ZIFF, Paul. *Semantic Analysis.* 1960, Ithaca (Cornell University Press).

ZWEIG, Paul. *The Heresy of Self-Love: A Study of Subversive Individualism.* 1968, New York (Basic Books).

Notes for an Index

To give a sampling of what a fuller index might be, here are some key topics and authors that are highlighted in this book. I have found in the past that an index has a life of its own, and that it given half a chance, it will keep growing, like an exuberant adolescent.

For example, the index in the first edition of *The Inner Palace* was 73 pages long. By the sixth edition, it had grown to cover some 99 pages. That's 26 additional pages of fine-print entries in 8 years! The growth was due primarily to people who would contact me to ask about whether a given topic was discussed in *The Inner Palace*, and my recognizing that I had, but that there was no reference to those passages in the index. And so it was repeatedly appropriate to add such further entries to the index. Hence the growth.

Here, I plan to add to this index as the occasion calls for, to make it easier to find passages of relevance to given topics of interest. I will make these changes and additions in a file to be placed online, as time permits and as people's inquiries suggest further entries here. The version of any such index can be determined by looking for the date of the file. To find it on the internet, I suggest doing a search for a term such as "CCAL" or "CCAL_Index" (perhaps refining the search by adding my name as a second search item).

Several of the entries in this simple listing (in place of an index) could cite relevant pages in the book by an entry such as "i *et passim*" (which would mean to look starting at page i, and continuing throughout to the very end of the book). The page citations here are more limited and explicit.

The eBook version of this text will presumably be read in a program that has its own search capabilities, which can supplement the entries given here.

Reviews and an Invitation

My intention is to develop a web page that contains comments, reviews, and recommendations of *Calm, Clear, and Loving*. Below, I begin with comments taken from the book's Forewords.

At this time, the reader may find a directory listing current web pages dedicated to this book at the URL Jinavamsa.com/books/CalmClearAndLoving. I have already set up a web page there, CCAL_Reviews.html. If not found when you read this, a web search for CCAL_Reviews (in precisely that orthography, with no spaces) will perhaps lead to the relevant site at that time.

I also invite people to contact me with comments, questions, or for other exchanges on the topics addressed in this book.

I would also like to put some of these exchanges up on the web for others to read. If you send me an email, I will try to respond, and if you would like to add to a web discussion about such material, please let me know. My most recent email address should be available at Jinavamsa.com, my home page as of the printing of this book.

If you receive no reply, perhaps your email has been filtered out and placed in some sort of junk mail or spam mail category, and was not seen by me. I suggest adding "On the book CCAL" in the subject line of any email to make it more likely that it will be successfully delivered to me and read.

Some first comments on the book

This book is heartening in the same way that some of Nietzsche's writings and the classics of Daoism are. All of these texts emphasize the on-going process and the potential for one to take matters in hand *right now*. One of the gifts this book offers to the reader is a sense of empowerment in the present, wherever in life one happens to be.

Excerpted from the Foreword by Kathleen Higgins, Ph.D.

An author who covers so much with comparable mastery is like a rare flower … his panoramic gaze is a beautiful thing to see; so I hope that, beyond its subject matter, the present volume may constitute to some extent a cultural influence remedial to our overspecialized and greedy times, when wonder has gone the way of extinct species, and when the love of knowledge is now only rarely free and disinterested.

Excerpted from the Foreword by Claudio Naranjo, M.D., Ed.D.

Calm, Clear, and Loving offers with gentle and heartfelt compassion, very pragmatic suggestions for alleviating torment in our lives. For anyone who has experienced violence, this book shows how to shift from automatic patterns of self-blame, shame, self-attacking, and fear, to a state of calm, clarity, and loving-kindness to ourselves and to others... This book teaches how to begin to live a full and vibrant life.

With an open heart, I gently invite you to embark on a journey of self-transformation through self-observation. I encourage you to take this first critical, necessary step. This book can change your life in profound ways; the time and energy of your courageous work can reap unlimited rewards. You are worth it. And now, I extend a sincere invitation to you, to read this book with your heart.

Excerpted from the Foreword by Audrey Rachel Stevenson

About the Author

The author received his doctorate in philosophy from the University of Michigan in 1967, and has taught there and also at Yale, the American Institute of Buddhist Studies, Antioch University, the University for Humanistic Studies, the International University of Professional Studies, and elsewhere, in departments of Philosophy, Buddhist Studies, Far East Studies, Transpersonal Psychology, Counseling Psychology, and Clinical Psychology.

He has held Post-doctoral or Visiting Scholar appointments in Psycholinguistics at the Massachusetts Institute of Technology (MIT), in Buddhist Studies at the University of Texas, Austin, in Indic Studies at Yale University, in Short-term Psychodynamic Psychotherapy for Complicated Grief, at the Langley-Porter Neuropsychiatric Institute of the School of Medicine, University of California, San Francisco (UCSF), and in the Judaic Studies Program, in the Middle East Studies Program, and also in the Psychiatry Department of the School of Medicine, all at the University of California, San Diego (UCSD).

After early experience in the Yale University administered Connecticut Mental Health Center, the country's first community mental health center, and research on schizophrenic family communication at Connecticut Valley Hospital, a state mental hospital, he completed a Clinical Psychology Internship through the Yale University Department of Clinical Psychology at the West Haven Veterans' Administration (VA) Hospital, and later, in 1982, Advanced Family Therapy training at the Istituto di Terapia Familiare, with Maurizio Andolfi, in Rome, Italy. In the late 1970s, the author worked in the Soteria Project of the National Institute of Mental Health (NIMH) with young adults diagnosed as schizophrenic, using the Kingsley Hall model. He has been a licensed psychotherapist in California since 1981. He has also served as an expert witness in US Immigration Court for cases of asylum, providing testimony and Psychological Evaluations for people with reported histories of torture, and has done psychotherapeutic work with this same group of individuals.

As the first Western disciple of V.R. Dhiravamsa—formerly Chao Khun, or Abbot, of the Thai Buddhist Mission to Great Britain—, the author has been a teacher in the Thai Theravāda Buddhist Insight (vipassanā) meditation tradition since 1975, leading workshops and retreats in England, the USA, France, and Norway, and has been Moderator of the on-line discussion group Insight Practice since 1996.

He is author of a number of scholarly articles published in four countries; his books include *Mind and Belief: Psychological Ascription and the Concept of Belief; The Far Shore: Vipassanā, The Practice of Insight;* and *The Inner Palace: Mirrors of Psychospirituality in Divine and Sacred Wisdom-Tradition.*